CLASS STRUCTURE

CLASS STRUCTURE

A Critical Perspective

Albert Szymanski

PRAEGER SPECIAL STUDIES • PRAEGER SCIENTIFIC

Library of Congress Cataloging in Publication Data

Szymanski, Albert, 1941-
   Class structure.
   Bibliography: p.
   Includes index.

   1. Social classes.   2. Social structure.
3. Social conflict.   4. Race discrimination.   I. Title.
HT675.S99   1983   305.5   82-18055
ISBN   0-03-061759-6
ISBN 0-03-061761-8 (pbk.)

Published in 1983 by Praeger Publishers
CBS Educational and Professional Publishing
a Division of CBS Inc.
521 Fifth Avenue, New York, New York 10175 U.S.A.

©1983 by Praeger Publishers

3456789 052 987654321

Printed in the United States of America
on acid-free paper

FOR SUE

Acknowledgments

The ideas contained in this book developed over the course of 20 years as a political activist and social scientist. Like all books dealing with social structures, it is very much a product of the contest among classes that occurred in the world system during its production.

The fundamental orientation of the book germinated in the U.S. student movement of the 1960s and matured through tempering by the mass of careful theoretical and empirical work produced in the 1970s (in good part by others, who like myself, were shaped during the earlier decade). Throughout the 1960s I was an activist in the "civil rights," student, peace, and antiimperialist movements of my generation. I was a member of the Students for a Democratic Society from 1961 when Al Haber "signed me up" in Madison, Wisconsin, until its demise in 1969.

Upon becoming a student activist in 1961 after attending the national convention of the National Student Association as a representative of the University of Rhode Island Student Senate, I changed my major from physics to sociology and began reading C. Wright Mills. Since it was only logical to assume that in spite of Mills' tragic early death his influence had to be considerable at Columbia, I began graduate school there in 1964. Finding that Mills had been a maverick who left no legacy other than rather bad feelings on the part of most faculty, I became involved in both the Congress of Racial Equality and the Columbia Committee to End the War in Vietnam, the two major political organizations on the Columbia campus in 1964 and 1965, while at the same time spending most of my time in Butler Library plunging into both the major works of academic sociology, such as the tomes of Talcott Parsons, and the volumes of *Das Kapital*.

In 1967 there was a renaissance of radical intellectual work among graduate students at Columbia, especially in sociology, history, political science, and English literature. The 1968 strike at Columbia was a decisive event. It made many of us realize the central importance of political confrontation as well as of the potential for the sudden and massive growth of revolutionary movements. Twenty-six graduate students in the Sociology Department were arrested, along with almost 800 others in April 1968 for occupying half of Columbia's buildings. The strike and its aftermath produced both a considerable widening of support for the radical perspective in the social sciences and an increase in the commitment to challenge the dominant institutions of American capitalism.

The energy from the Columbia strike spilled over to the American Sociological Association (ASA) meetings in Boston in the fall of 1968, in good part because of the initiative of Carol Brown (who thought up our name, the Sociology Liberation Movement) and Sherry Gorelick (who coined our slogan "Knowledge for Whom?"). Columbia's radical sociology students showed up in strength in Boston and, in conjunction with other radicals from around the country, took over the old liberal antiwar caucus, reorganizing it into the Sociology Liberation Movement, and organized a major demonstration at the address of the Secretary of Health, Education and Welfare, culminating in Martin Nicolaus' iconoclastic speech entitled "Fat Cat Sociologists." The ASA was shaken up and the "long march through the institutions" began.

In 1970 I was hired as an assistant professor at the University of Oregon. During the next half dozen years I wrote a number of articles on class, race, and sex. It was out of these articles that this present book grew (although the ideas expressed here underwent considerable transformation over the next six years). In the latter part of the 1970s and early 1980s, my view of class (and the related issues of race and sex) were fundamentally transformed both by my involvement with the women's and antiracist movements and through digesting the considerable quantity of good Marxist scholarship that appeared in English during these years. I was especially impacted (somewhat belatedly) by the works of Louis Althusser and Nicos Poulantzas, works which have only begun to have the impact on Marxist scholarship they deserve. Also important was the breakthrough work on race produced by Michael Reich, William J. Wilson, and Edna Bonacich and that produced on patriarchy by Karen Sacks and Eleanor Leacock. The work of Erik Wright, Michael Buraway, Marvin Harris, Richard Hamilton, and Eugene Genovese as well as the world-systems perspective of Immanuel Wallerstein also advanced my understanding of class in these latter years.

I would like to thank Ralph England, who first introduced me to sociology, as well as C. Wright Mills and my professors at Columbia, including Juan Linz and Terry Hopkins (who was so generous with his time and energy both with me and the other radical students during our years at Columbia). Terry, who suffered considerably for his support of the Columbia student radicals, was a most important influence on so many of us during the crucial years of the late 1960s.

I am especially indebted to Sue Jacobs, my lover and wife during the years in which many of the ideas expressed in this book germinated and the early drafts of parts of the manuscript were produced. From the fall of 1968 when we first met as graduate students at

Columbia, Sue and I worked closely together on the *Human Factor* and *Ripsaw*, in the Graduate Sociology Student Union, and in and around the Union of Radical Sociologists. She was one of the principal organizers of the radical caucus in sociology in 1971 and 1972, as well as of the first two West Coast socialist sociology camps, and one of the most committed workers on the *Insurgent Sociologist* from 1971 to 1974. Without her intellectual stimulation and support this book would be much weaker than otherwise.

I would like to thank those who were responsible for my being hired at the University of Oregon in 1970 in the face of considerable resistance by the Oregon administration and other conservative forces; especially Jerry Neilson, the head of the undergraduate Sociology Student Union (SSU), and other members of the SSU together with a few graduate students and faculty supporters who worked so hard to get me the job, and Ivar Berg, at the time a Columbia dean, whose timely phone call to the University of Oregon Administration convinced them to withdraw their pocket veto of my appointment.

I would also like to thank Vicki Van Nortwick, who typed and retyped the drafts of most of the original manuscript of this book. It was a heroic effort for which I will always be grateful. Doris Boylan and Linda Kelm, who typed parts of the manuscript, are also thanked. The research librarians at the University of Oregon, above all Robert Lockhard, must be thanked for their invaluable assistance in locating sources. I would also like to thank Lynda Sharp of Praeger for her cooperation and encouragement.

Those who have had an impact on this work through their reading of various draft chapters and discussions include Berch Berberoglu, Val Burris, Marv Dunn, David Elliott, John Evansohn, Paul Fitzgerald, Harry Humphries, Steve Johnson, Charles Kaften, Jerry Lembcke, Katherine Gorem, Jan Newton, Cheyney Ryan, Walt Shesby, Amy Wharton, and Erik Wright.

Thanks are extended to Joan Acker, Grieg Bustos, Sharon Claeyssens, Colleen Fong, Sandy Gill, Sara Goodman, Judith Green, Brenda Granquist, Aliza Keddem, Becky McGovern, Clay Newlin, Tyree Scott, and David Wellman for the challenge and stimulation they provided in forcing me to fundamentally rethink and work out the ideas on the relationships between class, race, and sex contained in Chapters 10, 11, 12. As I am sure they would agree, the ideas developed in this book, however, are solely my responsibility. I would also like to thank Madeleine Arnot, Donna Rae Crawford, Catherine Dureiz, Sandi Francisconi, Michael Francisconi, Michael Goldstein, Gail Lemberger, Hi and Julia Schwendinger, Evelyn Sparks, and Janice Zagorski for their friendship, support, and intellectual stimulation during the time of this volume's preparation.

Contents

ACKNOWLEDGMENTS   vii

LIST OF TABLES   xv

1 INTRODUCTION   1
Definitions   3
Marx's Concept of Class   5

2 THE HISTORICAL DEVELOPMENT OF CLASS INEQUALITY   8
Primitive Equalitarian Societies   8
The Development of Rank Societies and Chiefdoms   15
The Origin of Class Structures and the State   21
Slavery   29
Serfdom   47
Peasantry   52
The Triumph of Capitalist Relations of Production in Europe   58
Summary   65
Appendix: The Determinants of rural Relations of Production   65

3 THE CLASS STRUCTURE OF ADVANCED CAPITALISM   76
Classes as Relations of Production   76
The Class Structure of Contemporary Capitalist Societies   84
The Distribution of Wealth and Income in the United States   94
Comparisons among the Advanced Capitalist Countries   110
Social Class Formation   116

4 THE CAPITALIST CLASS   120
The Origin and Development of the Capitalist Class   120
The Specification of the Capitalist Class   123
The Economic Basis of the U.S. Capitalist Class   129
Capitalists as a Social Class   144
Summary   156

5 THE MIDDLE CLASS   157
The Specification of a Single Petty Bourgeoisie   157
The Decline of the Independent Petty Bourgeoisie   163
The Rise of the New Middle Class   177
The Petty Bourgeoisie as a Social Class   185

6 THE HISTORICAL DEVELOPMENT
    OF THE WORKING CLASS   194
The Shaping of the Modern Industrial Working Class   195
The Transformation in the Forms of Control
    of the Labor Process   203
The Making of the American Working Class   217

7 THE STRUCTURE OF THE
    CONTEMPORARY U.S. WORKING CLASS   229
The Specification of the Contemporary Working Class   229
Working Class Economic Position   256
The Working Class as a Social Class   261
Conclusion   278

8 THE REPRODUCTION OF CLASS POSITION   280
Social Mobility   280
Education and the Intergenerational Transmission
    of Class Position   289
Conclusion   296

9 THE PERSONAL EFFECTS OF CLASS POSITION   297
Life Expectancy and Health   298
Happiness and Mental Health   314
Marriage, Sexuality, Childbearing, and Friendship   319
Religion   327
Consumption, Leisure, and Mass Media   330
Crime   334
General Attitudes   342
Conclusion   354

10 THE STRUCTURE OF RACE AND CLASS   355
A Brief History of Races and Racialist Ideology   356
Race as a Structure   365
Relationships of Exclusion   373
Relationships of Mediation   377
Relationships of Special Exploitation/Disorganization   398
Non-European Racist Structures   409
Racist Structures and Class Differences   417
Conclusion   431

11 THE POSITION OF BLACKS AND LADINOS
    IN THE U.S. CLASS STRUCTURE   433
Blacks and U.S. Capitalism   433
Blacks as Defined by Their Working Class Position   441
Class Differentiation among Blacks   451

The Black Excluded Population   456
The Relative Size of the Different Classes among Blacks   471
Ladinos and U.S. Capitalism   476
Who Benefits from Economic Discrimination
    against Black and Ladino Workers?   491

12 THE STRUCTURE OF PATRIARCHY AND CLASS   497
Origins of Patriarchal Structures   499
Women's Position in the Capitalist Mode of Production   516
The Parallel between Racism and Sexism   536
Homemaking   541
Conclusion: Women and Class in Monopoly Capitalism   555

13 CONCLUSION: ALTERNATIVES TO CLASS SOCIETY   561
The Early History of Anticlass Movements   561
Utopian Socialism   564
The Socialist Working Class Movement   566
The Socialist Movement in the United States   576
The USSR   584
Chinese Socialism   592
Conclusion: Future Prospects   598

APPENDIX: A CRITIQUE OF ALTERNATIVE
    CONCEPTUALIZATIONS OF CLASS   602
Class as a Common Position in the Distribution of Power   602
Class as a Relation of Distribution or
    Common Market Position   612
Class as a Common Position within the Technical Division
    of Labor   619
Subjectivistic Conceptualizations of Class   624
Some Contemporary Marxist Variations   637
Conclusion   644

REFERENCES   646

INDEX   664

ABOUT THE AUTHOR   675

List of Tables

Table		Page
2.1	Frequency of Craft Specialization and Stratification by Societal Type	16
3.1	Estimate of the Class Structure of the United States in 1970	93
3.2	Personal Wealth; Value of Assets Held by All Persons in the United States	95
3.3	Share of Wealth Held by Richest 1 Percent of U.S. Adults	96
3.4	Percentage of Stock Value Owned by Families with the Highest Income	97
3.5	Mean Value of Assets of Specific Types as a Percentage of the Mean Value of Wealth of All Types, by Wealth Class of Consumer Units, 1962	98
3.6	Composition of Assets by Size of Net Worth, 1976	99
3.7	Aggregate Family Income	100
3.8	Types of Income by Income Size, 1978	102
3.9	The Class Structure of the Advanced Capitalist Countries, ca. 1979	112
3.10	Quintile Share Distribution of Total Pretax Income for Selected Countries and Years, 1966-73	114
3.11	Class Identification, 1977	117
4.1	Twenty Leading Industrial Corporations in the United States, 1980	130
4.2	Twenty Leading Financial Institutions in the United States, 1980	131
4.3	U.S. Billionaires, 1982	132
4.4	Percentage of Total Value Added by Manufacturing for the Largest Manufacturing Companies	133
4.5	The Role of Finance Capital in the U.S. Economy	135
4.6	The Ten Highest Paid Chief Corporate Executives in the United States in 1980	143

5.1   Trends in the Independent Petty Bourgeoisie in the
      United States   165

5.2   The Independent Petty Bourgeoisie in the Advanced
      Capitalist Countries, 1960 and 1978   166

5.3   Retail Businesses in the U.S., 1929 to 1977   169

5.4   Service Establishments in the United States,
      1933 to 1977   171

5.5   The Decline of the Family Farmer
      in the United States   173

5.6   The Increasing Size of U.S. Farms   174

5.7   Trends in the Major Components of the Middle
      Class for Employed Males   180-81

5.8   The Structure of the U.S. Middle Class in 1970   182

5.9   Income in 1978 of Different Sectors of the
      Petty Bourgeoisie   187

6.1   The Forms of Control of the Labor Process
      by Capital   208-9

6.2   Areas of Origin of Immigrants to the United States   221

7.1   The Occupational Composition of the U.S. Working
      Class, 1900-79   231

7.2   The Changing Structure of the U.S. Working Class,
      1900-79   232

7.3   The Structure of the U.S. Working Class in 1970   233

7.4   Changes in Number of Employees by Economic
      Sector in the U.S. Economy   248

7.5   Economic Sector of U.S. Men   249

7.6   Distribution of Nonsupervisory Employees in the
      U.S. Manufacturing Sector   250

7.7   Changes in the Service Sector of the Economy   251

7.8   Monopoly (Capital-Intensive) and Competitor (Labor-
      Intensive) U.S. Economic Sectors, 1970   252-53

7.9   Annual Median Earnings of Those with Earnings
      in the United States   260

7.10 U.S. Unemployment Rates: 1975-79 Average by
      Occupation and Industry   262

8.1 Occupations of Indianapolis White Males by Father's Occupation: 1910, 1940, and 1967   285

8.2 Percentage Distribution of the American Business Elite Born in Specified Years, by Father's Occupation   286

8.3 Social Origins of the Superrich, 1900-70   287

8.4 Rates of Intergenerational Mobility   288

8.5 Intergenerational Movement into the Upper Class from Various Other Classes   290

9.1 Annual Death Rates per 1,000 and Ratios: White Males, by Age and Major Occupation Group, United States, 1950   300

9.2 Mortality Ratios by Family Income Level for White Family Members Aged 25-64: United States, May-August 1960   301

9.3 Age-Adjusted Death Rates for Chicago by Socio-economic Status of Neighborhoods, 1960   302

9.4 Differential Expectations of Life at Birth: Chicago 1940 and 1960 by Socioeconomic Status of Neighborhoods   303

9.5 Mortality Ratios by Level of Education for Various Diseases: Chicago 1960   304

9.6 The Cumulative Impact of a 1.4 Percent Rise in Unemployment on Social Stress Indicators, 1970-75   305

9.7 Percentage of Respondents in Each Social Class Recognizing Specified Symptoms as Needing Medical Attention   311

9.8 Chronic Disease by Family Income for Ages 45-64, 1969-73   313

9.9 Class and the Rate of Different Types of Psychoses per 100,000 of Population   317

9.10 Distributions of Respondents on Mental Health by Parental SES Strata for Ages 20-59   318

9.11 Average Number of Children Ever Born to Wives Aged 35-44, by Spouse's Occupation   320

9.12 Sources of Orgasms for Single Males Aged 21-25, by Educational Level, 1948   322

9.13   Mothers' Socioeconomic Status and Choice of "Most
        Desirable" Characteristics in a Ten- or Eleven-
        Year-Old Child   326

9.14   Religious Denomination and Class   328

9.15   Households Owning Cars and Appliances, 1971:
        Percentage Distribution by Income Level   332

9.16   General Attitudes by Class and Class Strata, 1977   344-45

11.1   The Distribution of the Black Population of the
        United States   436

11.2   Net Migration of Blacks out of the South   437

11.3   The Occupational Structure of Whites, Blacks, and
        Ladinos in the United States, 1977   442

11.4   The Ratio of the Percentage of All Economically
        Active Blacks to the Percentage of All
        Economically Active Whites in Each Occupational
        Category   443

11.5   The Ratio of the Percentage of All Black Workers in
        Manufacturing in Each Industry to the Percentage
        of All White Workers in Manufacturing in Each
        Industry   444

11.6   Nonwhite/White Median Annual Income Ratios,
        1950-79   446

11.7   White and Black Median Annual Earnings by
        Occupation, 1969 and 1979   448-49

11.8   Ratio of the Income Received by the Top 20 Percent
        of Families to Income Received by the Bottom
        40 Percent   455

11.9   Percentage of Persons in the Civilian Labor Force   457

11.10   Male Unemployment Rates for Persons Aged 16
        and Over   459

11.11   Occupational Unemployment Rates by Race and Sex,
        1977   460

11.12   Differential Death Rates by Race   464

11.13 Percentage of Deaths in the Specified Group That Would Not Have Occurred as Compared with the Age-Specific Death Rate for Whites of the Same Sex in the Highest Socioeconomic Districts for Ages 25-64 in Chicago, 1960   465

11.14 Estimates of the Size and the Rate of Growth of the Basic Classes among Blacks in the United States, 1960 and 1977   473

11.15 The Relative Structural Position of Blacks and Ladinos in the United States, 1970 and 1977   486

11.16 Ratio of the Number of Ladinos to Blacks Employed by Industry, 1970   487

11.17 Median Annual Earnings of Full-Time, Year-Round U.S. Workers: Whites, Blacks, and Ladinos, 1969 and 1979   488

11.18 The Relationship between Black Male/White Male Earnings and Measures of White Gain, 1969   493

11.19 Relationship between Percentage of Population That Is Minority and Measures of White Gain, 1969-70   494

11.20 Relationship between the Measures of Racism and White Male Earnings, 1969-70   496

12.1 Equality between the Sexes by Societal Type   502

12.2 Women Workers as a Percentage of the Civilian Labor Force   520

12.3 Marital Status of Women in the Labor Force   521

12.4 Civilian Labor Force Participation Rates of Women, by Marital and Child Care Status   522

12.5 Part-Time/Full-Time Work   524

12.6 The Relation between Husband's and Wife's Occupations When Both Are Employed, 1978   525

12.7 The Percentage of Each Occupation That Is Female   527

12.8 The Female Occupational Structure   528

12.9 The Ratio of Female to Male Median Wage or Salary Income   530

12.10 Economic Discrimination against Women and Male Gain, 1969   537

12.11 The Effect of Economic Discrimination against Women and the Strength of the Working Class as Measured by the Percentage of the Nonagricultural Labor Force in Unions, ca. 1969   539

12.12 The Relation between Racial and Sexual Economic Discrimination, 1969, 1970   540

12.13 Political Attitudes by Sex and Women's Employment Status, 1975-76   547

12.14 Political Attitudes for Middle Class and Working Class by Sex and Women's Employment Status, 1975-76   548-49

12.15 Political Attitudes by Sex and Women's Employment Status for Persons Less Than 40 Years Old, 1975-76   550-51

12.16 Labor Force Participation of Wives in March 1969, by Earnings of Husbands in 1968   556

13.1 Changes in Average Wages in the USSR, 1965-73   586

CLASS STRUCTURE

Introduction

Class is the most important explanatory category in social science. Class structures virtually all aspects of society, social conflict, and historical development. Class position permeates not only economic life (both productive and consumption relationships), but also consciousness, culture, politics, and such ultimate and intimate things as life expectancy, sexual relations, marriage, religion, and the very possibilities of happiness and mental health. This volume explores the significance, depth, and breadth of the impact of class structures.

The book first traces the origin and historical development of class structures. After showing that class is a relatively recent development in the history of Homo sapiens, the causes of the breakdown of primitive equalitarianism are systematically treated. The concomitant origins of the state and the first class societies in the river valleys of the Middle East approximately 6,000 years ago are analyzed in depth, and the essential variety of developing class systems are then treated. Ancient slavery, modern slavery, serfdom, peasantry, and the origins of the distinctively capitalist form of class relations (which became dominant for the first time around the end of the eighteenth century) are examined in turn.

The remainder of the early chapters of the book systematically define class and each of the major classes in contemporary advanced capitalist society (capitalists, the petty bourgeoisie, and the working class), and then examine in considerable depth the recent historical development, economic basis, and tendencies toward social class formation of each. The basic distribution of wealth and income, the nature of the poor, the forms by which capital exercises economic power, the relationship between the old petty bourgeoisie and the new middle class are all treated at length. The trends in the size and composition of the basic classes, especially the petty bourgeoisie and the working class, are carefully examined. The fundamental transformations in both the forces of production and the forms of capital's control of the labor process, which have shaped the position of the working class, are treated, as is the particular historical development of the U.S. working class. In these chapters as well as in most of the rest of the book, the discussion focuses on the class structure of the United States, with some comparative evidence brought in to demonstrate the generality of the conclusions drawn from this, by far the largest and most important of all advanced capitalist societies, in the mid- and late twentieth century.

After a specification and examination of the basic classes of contemporary advanced capitalist society, the intergenerational linkage between one's class position and that of one's parents is examined to show that class position is in good part hereditary and that there is little difference among the advanced capitalist societies in this regard. To complete the demonstration of the centrality of class in affecting virtually all aspects of our lives, the impact of class on life expectancy, health, mental health, sexuality, friendship, leisure, crime, and general social and political attitudes is examined at length.

The final chapters of the book focus on the relationship between race and class, and between patriarchy and the sexual division of labor and class. A theory of "race" relations is developed that clarifies groups socially labeled as distinct "races" as essentially being in special class positions in society that generate a discourse of racialism as the legitimation of their position. The relations between people in such special class positions, and the various classes in the "majority" group are examined as well as the development of class differentiation within the "racial" groups. The chapters on patriarchy and class discuss the origins and development of patriarchal structures, showing that the degree of equality between the sexes is a product of women's relation to production. Thus, underlying both racist and patriarchal structures are shown to be relations of production.

The theoretical framework of this book has been heavily influenced by the Marxist structuralism of Louis Althusser and Nicos Poulantzas as well as by the work of Guglielmo Carchedi, Erik Wright, Eugene Genovese, Richard Hamilton, Michael Burawoy, Karen Sacks, Eleanor Leacock, Marvin Harris, and Edna Bonacich. Throughout, the volume stresses the salience of defining class in terms of relations of production and understanding class as a position in a social structure defined in the last instance by the logic of modes of production.

DEFINITIONS

There are many different ways to define "class." Some definitions focus on subjective factors (factors inside of the heads of people) while others focus on objective factors (which can be ascertained or measured without reference to what people think about themselves or other members of society). Some objective definitions focus on economic factors, others on generalized power, and still others on technical knowledge as the basis of social differentiation. Definitions that stress the economic in turn differ on whether it is "common market position," income, consumption patterns, economic function/contribution, or relation to the means of production that is central.

It is quite arbitrary how one defines "class." One can define a class any way one pleases. However, some definitions are more useful than others as tools in the analysis of social structures, processes, and historical development. Some ways of looking at social structure clarify, while looking at social structure in other ways obscure. Which definition of class is most "correct" must be judged solely on the basis of which conceptualization of class structure best accounts for observable social differentiation in other phenomena, such as consciousness, culture, life-style, and above all, in political behavior.

Just as there are many ways of conceptualizing classes, so too a wide variety of factors are seen as the cause of classes (or the dynamic of stratification). There are four principal materialist approaches: first, functionalism, which sees inequality as necessary for the survival and prospering of *all* societies; second, the force theory, which sees force, ultimately superior military strength, as the basis of class and stratification; third, the organization/ideology theory, which sees control over information, organization, and ideology as central; and fourth, Marxist theories, which see class as an outgrowth of the logic of the mode of production.

All of these approaches are essentially materialistic in their explanations because all trace the origin and reproduction of class/strata to their material basis in either universal societal needs, military supremacy, ideological structures/organization, or control of the means of production. In addition to these materialist explanations there are also two principal types of idealist accounts of class/stratification: first, objective idealism, which sees class as a result of the development of ideas, attitudes or consciousness beyond the control of the individual, e.g., Hegel; and second, subjective idealism, which sees class as a state of mind of the individual that can be changed through an act of conscious will or social redefinition. Researchers in the former idealist tradition tend to utilize objective measures of class consciousness to determine the layout of the classes (such as can be inferred from sample surveys), while those in the latter tradition utilize the opinions of "informants" about their class position (what is sometimes called the "emic" approach). Intermediate between the purely objective and purely subjective idealist approaches is the common approach of relying on others' opinions about an individual's class position, e.g., the so called "reputional method" (made famous by Lloyd Warner).*

There are those that take either a multidimensional or eclectic, and those that take essentially an unidimensional view of the problem of stratification within a society. The eclectic or multidimensional approach is common among those who define class in terms of market position/income/life-style. They often tend to construct composite indexes of class in terms of some combination of income, education, job status, value of house, and so forth. Alternatively, many also tend to see "class" as only one dimension of a broader "social stratification" that includes components of class (economically defined), prestige or status, and political power. The socioeconomic status index (composed equally of measures of family income, years of education, and occupational prestige) is the most widely employed eclectic measure.

Another aspect of the various modes of defining classes is whether or not they see an essential *continuity* in the class structure (or within social stratification), or whether or not they see classes as organic units fundamentally distinct from each other. This is especially reflected in those that define class in terms of obviously continuous factors such as status/prestige, income, and education, and those that talk of "social stratification" rather than class. In such approaches, classes (or strata), since they are not organic or real social entities, are not generally seen as actors in society or historical development. Others do see classes as organic and active units in society and historical development. Such an approach is most likely to be true of those theories that define class in terms of political power, economic function, market position, or relation to the means of production.

The Marxist conceptualization of class is employed in this book. This work can, thus, be considered as an attempt to demonstrate the power of the mode of class analysis that defines class as a relation of production.

---

*For a detailed examination and evaluation of these various approaches, see the Appendix at the end of this book.

MARX'S CONCEPT OF CLASS

Marx defined class as a relation of production:

> In the social production of their life, men enter into definite relations that are indispensable and independent of their will, relations of production which correspond to a definite stage of the development of their material productive forces. The sum total of these relations of production constitutes the economic structure of society, the real foundation, on which rises a legal and political superstructure and to which correspond definite forms of social consciousness. . . . At a certain stage of their development, the material productive forces of society come in conflict with the existing relations of production, or—what is but a legal expression for the same thing—with the property relations within which they have been at work hitherto (Marx 1859, pp. 362–63).*

Relations of production are relationships of economic power or property. Social positions with the same relation to production, or the same relationship to property or economic power, are in the same class. Relations of production implies first, a *quantitative* dimension, or differences in power within the production process (property), i.e., who makes the decisions about what is produced, how it is produced, and how the product is distributed, who allocates and directs labor in the production process, and consequently, who obtains the economic benefit from the labor process (i.e., the degree of exploitation of the producing class by the dominant or property-holding class); and second, the *quality* of productive (property) relationships, or what is the specific nature of productive relations, and thus what is the specific form of exploitation (is exploitation of the producers achieved through slavery, serfdom, wage labor, tenancy, or by some other means). Productive relationships are those of masters and slaves

---

*In 1846 Marx had argued:

. . . as man develop their productive faculties, that is, as they live, they develop certain relations with one another and the nature of these relations necessarily changes with the modification and growth of the productive forces. . . .

M. Proudhon has very well grasped the fact that men produce cloth, linen, silks. . . . What he has not grasped is that these men, according to their faculties, also produce the *social relations* amid which they prepare cloth and linen. Still less has he understood that men, who produce their social relations in accordance with their material productivity, also produce ideas, categories, that is to say, the abstract ideal expressions of these same social relations (Marx 1846, pp. 446–48).

who can be bought and sold; lords and serfs who are tied to the land, landlords and tenants who must pay a rent to those who monopolize the land; capitalists and free wage laborers who must sell their ability to labor or starve.

Although Marx's fundamental concept of class is purely objective—a class is defined by its relationship to the means of production and produced by the logic of the mode of production—Marx differentiates between a class "für sich" (a class for itself) and a class "an sich" (a class in itself). A class for itself is class conscious—that is, is aware of its interests and the social forces acting on it, thinks of itself as a group, and moreover, acts on the basis of this common feeling in pursuit of its collective interests. A class in itself is not class conscious, that is, neither understands its interests nor thinks of itself as a collectivity or class. In discussing the proletariat, Marx treats the difference between a proletarian class in itself and a proletarian class for itself:

> Economic conditions had first transformed the mass of the people of the country into workers. The combination of capital has created for this mass a common situation, common interests. This mass is thus already a class as against capital, but not yet for itself. In the struggle, of which we have noted only a few phases, this mass becomes united, and constitutes itself as a class for itself. The interests it defends become class interests (Marx 1847, p. 173).

Since classes are social relations, there can be no such thing as a class in isolation. In order for there to be a class there must be at least two classes. Each form of class society typically has two major classes, one the complement of the other—the class that produces the basic wealth of society, and the class that controls the producers. Moreover, according to Marx the basic class dichotomy is the axis around which society develops: "Freeman and slave, patrician and plebian, lord and serf, guild-master and journeyman, in a word, oppressor and oppressed, stood in constant opposition to one another, carried on an uninterrupted, now hidden, now open fight, a fight that each time ended, either in a revolutionary reconstitution of society at large, or in the common ruin of the contending classes" (Marx and Engels 1849, p. 34).

Although all class societies have been characterized by fundamental dichotomization, in capitalist society this dichotomization is purer than ever:

> Our epoch, the epoch of the bourgeoisie, possesses, however, this distinctive feature: it has simplified the class antagonisms. Society as a whole is more and more splitting up into two great hostile

camps, into two great classes directly facing each other: Bourgeoise
and Proletariat (Marx and Engels 1849, pp. 34–35)

The position of capitalist is defined by the appropriation of surplus value from producers by means of wage labor—a capitalist buys
labor power from those that can and must (because of their lack of
property) sell it in order to live. The capitalist-wage laborer relationship on the one side generates capital and on the other proletarianization.

The capitalist-proletarian relation constantly *reproduces* itself.
The proletariat is forced to sell its labor power in order to purchase
the necessities of life for themselves and their families. The capitalist
appropriates the difference between their wages and the value produced by workers. The capitalist thus acquires the means by which
to purchase more labor power (thus accumulating capital, and becoming ever richer), while the proletarians, having consumed their wages,
again have nothing, and thus must continue to sell their labor power:

> Capitalist production, therefore, of itself reproduces the separation
> between labour-power and the means of labour. It thereby repro-
> duces and perpetuates the condition for exploiting the labourer. It
> incessantly forces him to sell his labour-power in order to live, and
> enables the capitalist to purchase labour-power in order that he may
> enrich himself. . . .
> Capitalist production, therefore, under its aspect of a continuous
> connected process, of a process of reproduction, produces not only
> commodities, not only surplus-values, but it also produces and
> reproduces the capitalist relation; on the one side the capitalist, on
> the other wage-labourer (Marx 1867, pp. 577–78).

Although much has changed since Marx's day, including many
things about capitalism and its class structure, Marx's conceptualization of class is as valid today as it was in his time. Class
structure rooted in the capitalist mode of production continues to
permeate all aspects of contemporary society.

2

The Historical Development of Class Inequality

This chapter treats the historical origins of class inequality, slavery, serfdom, and the origins of modern capitalist class relations. Beginning with a discussion of the primitive equality of hunting and gathering societies (which were universal until about 10,000 years ago), it traces the slow evolution of social inequality through the chiefdoms of horticultural societies to the crystallized class structures of the early agricultural kingdoms. The economic origins of class inequality in the ecological necessity for water control as well as the role of transformed reciprocity networks in the process of creating classes, are examined. The conditions under which slavery arose as the predominate mode of production, both in the Ancient Greek and Roman world and in the Caribbean basin in modern times, are outlined, as is the nature of the master-slave relationship and its contradictions. The historical origin and nature of serfdom is treated, and the relative efficiency of slavery, serfdom, and wage labor are compared. Last, the contradictions in the peasant mode of production as well as the characteristics of politically decentralized European society that gave rise to the growth and eventual hegemony of capitalist class relations in that part of the world are analyzed.

PRIMITIVE EQUALITARIAN SOCIETY

The very first farmers were simple horticulturalists who began to use wooden digging sticks to cultivate the earth in the period 10,000 to 7000 B.C. in the river valleys of the Near East. This coincided with the beginning of the Neolithic age—the age of refined stone tools. Animals were first domesticated around 8000 B.C. Irrigation came into use around 5500 B.C. in the Tigres and Euphrates River valleys. The most primitive plows began to be used about 3500 B.C. The first cities grew up between 4000 and 3000 B.C. (see Harris 1971, pp. 182-83; Sahlins 1968, p. 2).

Before the rise of simple horticultural societies in the Near East everyone lived by hunting and gathering. Through the nineteenth century most human societies continued to be composed of hunters and gatherers.* Because of their very primitive technology, such societies were necessarily close to nature. Their average size was about 40 members, they had loose boundaries, with individuals regularly leaving and joining. Hunting and gathering societies were normally nomadic or seminomadic, and self-sufficient.

Hunters and gatherers tended to live in abundant environments with small population densities where more than adequate food can normally be had with minimal labor (in fact, few people went to bed hungry in the Stone Age). In most hunting and gathering societies the amount of time put into physical labor in pursuit of food or the other necessities of life has been found to be considerably less than in class society (including advanced capitalism). On the average, people in such societies worked about three to five hours a day to obtain a diet rich in proteins and other essential nutrients. In fact, they generally enjoyed relatively high standards of comfort and security. Further, their work pattern was generally sporadic and discontinuous. Individuals typically rested when they felt like it, and periodically worked very hard. Bushmen, for example, alternated periods of intense effort with hours or days of visiting, repairing, feasting, or just lying around. It should be noted that the amount of work per capita and the length of the work day as well as the regularity of work patterns has *increased* in proportion to technological development—the increase continued until it reached its physiological maximum in the mid-nineteenth century (Harris 1971, pp. 217-19; Sahlins 1972, chap. 1).

In hunting and gathering societies there is no systematic division of labor (except that between the sexes). All adults of the same sex normally perform all the basic economic tasks required by the society. There are no specialized crafts or division of labor. This means that all healthy adult males, generally without exception, hunt, build shelters, make their own tools, and so forth; while all healthy adult women, again generally without exception, gather, hunt small animals, process food, make clothes, and so forth (Lenski and Lenski

---

*It has been estimated that approximately 90 percent of human beings who have ever lived have lived in hunting and gathering societies (see Brown 1977, p. 124).

1978, p. 99). This applies to all members of the society *including* those who are most respected and who are most often looked to for leadership.

Almost no hunting and gathering societies have been discovered in which there is a high level of stratification in prestige or preroga- tives. In the Yale Human Relations Area files, which contain compre- hensive information on over 1,000 societies that anthropologists have studied, only 2 of 143 hunting and gathering societies were found to have highly stratified systems—and these 2 most likely were trans- formed before being studied by anthropologists through previous economic contact with Western traders (Lenski and Lenski 1978, p. 101).

Hunting and gathering societies in their pristine state do not have private property in the land—their most important resource. Anyone can hunt and gather wherever there are resources. There has never been a hunting and gathering society where private prop- erty in land was general; although a few have existed where, because of contact with European traders (who created economic dependency), a limited conception of private property in hunting areas developed, e.g., restrictions existed only on trapping fur-bearing animals that were traded to the Europeans (Lenski and Lenski 1978, p. 128; Leacock 1981).

The first simple horticultural societies (which at first continued to obtain much of their food from hunting and gathering) averaged only about two or three times the size of hunting and gathering societies, and like them consisted of only one community per society (Lenski and Lenski 1978, p. 97). While people tended to both work longer hours and more consistently in such societies (because of the demands imposed by cultivation), neither the total amount of labor nor the degree of labor discipline approached that of later class societies.

The land in simple horticultural societies normally belongs to the community (which allocates its use to individual families). Fam- ilies that have use of the land are typically entitled to continue to cultivate it. Further, *any* family is typically entitled to cultivate *any* unused piece of land. In the event a family ceases to cultivate a piece of land, it can then be used by anyone else who is willing to cultivate it (the earlier family retaining no rights in the land). No adult member of society can be deprived of a more or less equal share of their habitat. In conditions of relative land abundance (the norm in simple horticultural societies), this means that families are relatively equal in economic resources, just as is the case in hunting and gathering societies (see Harris 1979, chap. 4; Lenski and Lenski 1978, chap. 4; Sahlins 1968, chaps. 1, 2).

Often in hunting and gathering societies (but by no means always), and typically in simple horticultural societies, those that actually secure the food have some prior rights to it. Similarly, those that make (or have otherwise secured) tools, containers, weapons, clothing, ornaments, and other personal effects have prior claims on their use. However, in both hunting and gathering societies and in simple horticultural societies the community has strong rights in such objects (especially in food). For example, among the Eskimos established rules determine the distribution of the catch from the sea among members of a band. Among the Andaman Islanders all who have food are expected to share it with those who have none. All the food found during the day by Bushmen is shared by all in their camp. While the members of equalitarian societies usually believe that weapons, clothing, containers, ornaments, tools, and so forth ought not to be taken away or used without the consent of the owner, requests for use are normally expected to be, and are, honored. Most utilitarian items may be borrowed without difficulty when the owner is not using them. There is little accumulation of personal wealth. For example, it is unthinkable that any one Eskimo should have two harpoons while others have none (Farb 1968, chaps. 2-5; Harris 1971, chaps. 10, 11; Lenski and Lenski 1978, chap. 6).

There are strong social mechanisms in classless societies that ensure equal access to resources as well as the sharing of both food and personal effects on the basis of need. In environments of potential scarcity in which a component of luck enters into which particular hunter will secure a catch, as among the Eskimo, social norms that dictate sharing of food are particularly strong. No one hunter could consume an entire seal. On the other hand, unlucky or poor hunters and their families would starve without sharing the surplus of others. Further, from season to season different families might have a surplus while others were starving. It is obviously most rational for all members of such a society to share in the product of the hunt. Likewise, it is most rational for all to have access to the resources of the society. Only a limited amount of food can be stored or hoarded. An attempt by some to exclude others from hunting grounds or from unused land deprives some of food without the possibility of providing more to the excluders (not a rational proposition).

Equalitarianism is in part impelled by the necessity to maintain an ecological balance. Competitiveness manifested in boasting and differential status rewards among hunters, in a economy where hunting one or two days a week is sufficient to adequately feed all, would tend to produce waste and depletion of resources (which would in the long run destroy the basis of a society's wealth). Hunting and gathering societies thus generate pressures for hunters to be modest and reticent about their productivity (Harris 1979, p. 81).

The accumulation of wealth in hunting and gathering societies is also greatly inhibited by the geographical mobility of such societies. The amount of possessions held by an individual is limited to what he/she can carry on his/her own (mobility and property are in contradiction). This further facilitates equalitarianism.

In small societies (where everyone is related to everyone else, and knows everyone and their business very well) informal social sanctions, such as approval, disapproval, blame, praise, ridicule, gossip, warmth, reserve, and so forth are very powerful means of social control—mechanisms to reward those who share and punish those who do not, to reward those who work hard (and provide more food) as well as sanction those who slack off and try to survive by consuming more than they produce. The ultimate sanction in such communities is ostracism and exile—normally severe penalities given the intensity of group life. Another equalitarian mechanism is witchcraft. Unpopular individuals are frequently accused of practicing witchcraft and consequently penalized severely. One of the best protections against such accusations is to act in a generous, open, amicable manner, avoid quarreling, and do everything possible not to lose the support of one's kinsmen (Harris 1971 chap. 16).

Other factors that ensure equality in such societies include the ability to simply walk off, leaving one band and joining another (where one might well have relatives) in the event that a few individuals were to attempt to encumber the access of all to resources. The fact that resources to make tools and weapons are readily available and the skills to do so are virtually universal, is also a strong equalitarian influence that hinders the monopolization of resources.

It should be stressed that hunting and gathering societies as well as most simple horticultural societies are highly democratic in decision making and leadership. Decisions in these societies are typically made through formal or informal discussions in which all adults participate on a more or less equal basis (sometimes with men having greater weight in the majority of types of decisions, with women having greater weight in a minority). Decision making tends to be dispersed, with the various subgroups most affected often deciding for themselves what to do. The decentralized and often informal nature of decision making, together with the lack of clear and strict sanctions in most matters, results in considerable latitude for individual expression and tolerance of disagreements (so long as these do not threaten the existence of the group).

In these societies power and prestige are mostly a function of personal abilities and skills. One's leadership position must be continually validated. Incompetence or bad leadership is punished by loss of position, while those with demonstrated abilities in hunting, fighting, magic, and so forth normally gain respect, and thus leadership. The leaders of hunting and gathering societies and the more democratic of simple horticultural societies, the "headmen" or "big men," lack authority to speak for their society (as chiefs in wealthier horticultural fishing or herding societies are able to do). A headman is relatively powerless. Such a leader is incapable of compelling obedience. In order to get his way he must bargain, plead, and cajole. People do not fear or revere such leaders. To remain a leader one must generate respect. A successful headman must set an example and lead through respect won. This means he must work harder and be more generous than the average person. In leading a society headmen must intuit public opinion and act on behalf of a consensus that they may have helped develop through their strength of personality and persuasiveness (Lenski 1966, pp. 104-12; Sahlins 1968, pp. 22-24, 90-94; Leacock 1981, pp. 19-22, 42, 110).

Since the headmen or big men in hunting and gathering and in most simple horticultural societies must work harder and be more generous than the average, positions of leadership are not always actively sought. It is quite common for individuals in such societies to strive to *avoid* appointment to such positions because of the extra burdens entailed (burdens that have few compensations other than respect) (Lenski 1966, p. 175).

Goods are transferred among families and among communities in primitive societies on the basis of reciprocity. The product of one's labor is rather freely given to others, with the expectation that those who are given goods will reciprocate (either at the same time or at a future time). There is considerable variation in the accounting of the equity of such exchanges. Food is typically given on the basis of need without expectation of a more or less balanced counterflow, while durables and luxury goods tend to be exchanged in a framework of balanced reciprocity. Both unequal and delayed exchange are very important mechanisms that tie individuals, families, and communities together. Gifts create an obligation to return the gift. They thus put the recipient in the debt of the giver. The Eskimos have a saying that "gifts make slaves, just as whips make dogs." Reciprocity strengthens interdependence and thus overall social unity.

One of the principal ways of winning respect and obtaining a personal following is through generosity, of giving more than one receives, and thus both winning prestige and putting others in one's debt. Thus, unlike as in class societies, to gain leadership one must give more than one gets. This implies dual rules: first, people should help those who have helped them; and second, people should not impugn those who have helped them. The expectation that those with wealth will give it away is another important mechanism for ensuring equality in material possessions. (Harris 1971, chap. 11; Sahlins 1972, chaps. 4, 5).

In many primitive societies the products of different individuals or families are brought to a central place, sorted, counted, and given away. In some there are predetermined rules (based on kinship) of who must be given what. In others, especially in larger simple horticultural societies, the family units typically give a significant share of their product to the headman, who then in turn gives it away to others. In such societies the redistribution process is more institutionalized than in most hunting and gathering societies, with the headman functioning as custodian and dispenser of the collective product. Such headmen, further, are expected to provide for people in times of need. Generosity being the prerequisite of leadership, headmen who attempt to hoard, who hold back from redistributing goods provided to them; or who refuse to give to those in need, soon lose their leadership positions.

Many simple societies (especially wealthier fishing and simple horticultural societies) have institutions similar to the Potlach of the Kwakiutl, in which a man attempts to establish his status as a "big man" by throwing extravagant feasts, thereby putting others in his debt, a debt which if others can not reciprocate with an even greater feast will result in their humiliation. Those who can not reciprocate are forced to recognize the biggest feast throwers' higher status. One succeeds in such contests (and thus grows in status) by working harder than anyone else, by restricting one's own consumption, and by impressing friends and relatives by the seriousness of one's effort, thereby securing their help. Success at smaller feasts means the acquisition of a circle of followers who help the aspiring big man to throw ever greater feasts until eventually the highest status big man—the headman—is challenged. The successful big man, however, finds himself faced with a lifetime of dependency on those who helped him (the rule of reciprocity), requiring continuous toil to repay debts, i.e., it does not result in a higher living standard for those of highest status, if anything, just the opposite (Harris 1977, pp. 104-5).

Such processes, and the resultant bigmanship they generate, have a number of positive functions for a classless society. The big men act to intensify production (they cajole many to work harder), they use their prestige to organize trading expeditions, and they use their position to redistribute both locally produced goods and goods acquired in external trade.

Simple horticultural societies apparently develop out of hunting and gathering societies at times and in areas where the abundance of wild flora and fuana is undermined, thus providing an incentive to cultivate plants and domesticate animals in order to obtain more food from a given area. Since cultivation and domestication require considerably more work to obtain the living standard characteristic of hunting and gathering societies, it is to be expected that such a radical change in work patterns would only be undertaken in the face of potential starvation, or at least a considerable decline in living standards.

Most simple horticultural societies are virtually as equalitarian, democratic, and communal in property arrangements as are hunting and gathering societies. However, there is more private property in such societies (although it still must be shared). The headmen generally have more prerogatives and power (although they are still held closely accountable to the group). Unlike in hunting and gathering society, they are sometimes exempted from manual labor. They often wear special insignia or clothing and have special privileges such as the right to polygamy and larger garden plots (Lenski 1966, pp. 130–39).

THE DEVELOPMENT OF RANK SOCIETIES AND CHIEFDOMS

When the wealth available to a group becomes great enough, either because of the superabundance of its natural environment (as was the case among Pacific Northwest Coast Indians), or because technical innovations are forced by the need to maintain living standards under conditions of increasing population density, depletion of resources, or climatic change, *qualitative* changes begin to occur in the organization of societies. Primitive democracy is undermined as the headmen accumulate greater power. Inequalities in wealth come into existence and are aggravated through the distortion of reciprocity networks. The earliest societies with qualitative differences in wealth and power developed between 8000 and 3000 B.C. in the river valleys of the Near East. The development of horticulture with the metal hoe was a particularly crucial event (about 4000 B.C.). The considerable economic surplus that the metal hoe allowed to accumulate made possible societies composed of millions of people organized by complex bureaucratic machines led by a class that did not perform manual labor. Craft specialization and the social division of labor between laborers and planners/supervisors developed. Qualitative increases in social stratification in power, wealth, and prestige became institutionalized. Table 2.1 displays the relation between the division of labor and "stratification" and the various forms of early societies.

More efficient economies and the stratified economic, social, and political systems that organized them were a result of the drive for intensification necessitated by the gradual depletion of natural resources. It appears that until about 11,000 B.C. human populations

TABLE 2.1: Frequency of Craft Specialization and Status Stratification by Societal Type (In percentages)

Type of Society	Metalworking	Weaving	Leather Working	Pottery	Boat Building	House Building	Average	Percentage Having a Stratified System	No. of Societies in Sample
Hunting and gathering	—*	0	0	0	0	0	0	2	142–43
Simple horticulture	—	0	3	2	4	2	2	17	66–69
Advanced horticulture	100	6	24	24	9	4	28	54	243–224
Agrarian	100	32	42	29	5	18	38	71	84–88
Fishing	—	0	0	0	9	4	2	32	43–41
Herding	95	11	22	—	—	0	21	51	50–49

*The activity in question is seldom found in this type of society.
Source: Adapted from Lenski and Lenski 1978 pp. 99, 100.

were more or less in ecological balance with their environments. Marvin Harris argues that in early hunting bands the high protein/ low carbohydrate diet that was the norm together with lengthy 3 to 4 year periods of lactation of mothers served as effective contraception because such a diet prevented the accumulation of body fat (the signal for the resumption of postnatal ovulation), and consequently produced a 4 to 5 year period between pregnancies. This together with infanticide (conscious and unconscious) tended to keep the size of bands roughly constant and in equilibrium with their environments (Harris 1979, p. 82). But as the glaciers of the last Ice Age (which had covered much of the Northern Hemisphere) retreated, and the climate became less severe, forests invaded the grassy plains that had nourished the herds on which the early hunters had depended. The loss of grazing lands combined with increased hunting by humans (who were forced to hunt more extensively to make up for the decline of large animals) resulted in an ecological disaster. In the old world a number of formerly prolific giant mammals soon became extinct: the wooly mammoth, the wooly rhinoceros, the steepe bison, the giant elk, the European wild ass, many varieties of goats. Other species such as the musk ox and taiga antelope came near to extinction under the pressure of upper Paleolithic humans seeking animal protein. A similar process occurred at the same time in the New World. Between 11,000 and 7000 B.C. big game hunters in the Americas had hunted to extinction a total of 32 genera of large animals, including camels, mammoth, mastodon, giant ground sloths, giant rodents, horses, giant bison, oxen, and elephants (Harris 1977, pp. 30–31).

As the large species were hunted to extinction, hunting cultures everywhere tried to keep up their protein intake by improving their hunting techniques (e.g., lances, spear throwers, darts, and the bow and arrow) while both increasing the time spent on hunting and gathering and turning to smaller, more labor-intensive species. The collapse of lower Paleolithic big game hunting cultures was followed by the rise of Mesolithic peoples who obtained their protein largely from fish, shellfish, and deer, and increasingly from birds, snails, nuts, wild legumes, and grains. Eventually simple hunting and gathering was no longer able to produce sufficient food, and domestication of animals and horticulture had to be introduced in order to maintain living standards. As the labor costs of hunting and gathering increased, and as the benefit fell, sedentary horticultural economy became increasingly common (Harris 1979, pp. 87; 1977, pp. 34–35).

Hunting and gathering peoples had long known about plant cultivation. The reason for not engaging in cultivation had nothing to do with lack of knowledge. Hunting and gathering, given a plentiful environment, is simply the most labor efficient way of acquiring a comfortable life. Many hunters and gatherers engaged in such practices as refraining from stripping wild grains bare, weeding, watering, using fire to favor certain species, and so on in order to encourage the growth of their favorite wild species (Harris 1977, pp. 16–17 and 1979, p. 86). Similarly, it was not lack of knowledge that kept hunting and gathering peoples from domesticating animals—it was simply more efficient to hunt plentiful game than to put tremendous amounts of labor into domestication (many hunting and gathering peoples in fact domesticated pets such as dogs). Domestication occurred when species were on the verge of extinction, and consequently, domestication became the most efficient (and eventually the only) means of maintaining living standards (Harris 1977, chap. 3).

Just as pressures toward intensification and innovation occurred in hunting techniques when animal resources became depleted, the techniques of cultivation were subject to similar pressures as population density in settled communities increased. Harris argues that with the decline in average protein consumption per capita that occurred with the rise of horticulture, lactation lasted on average for a shorter period, and thus women became pregnant more often. Even intensification of the practice of female infanticide could not compensate for the resultant population explosion (a population explosion that accelerated the rate of intensification and innovation necessary to maintain living standards.) Simple horticulture with wooden sticks was thus superceded by horticulture with metal instruments, then by agriculture (the use of the plow), agriculture with beasts of burden, and then agriculture with systematic irrigation. Although agriculture with irrigation is on average five times more productive than simple horticulture per man-hour most members of such societies have on average a lower nutritional intake and work much longer hours than in simple horticultural societies. While agricultural societies were much more efficient, population densities were much greater than before (Harris 1977, p. 35).

The reason for the breakthrough to intensive agriculture in China and the Mideast, but *not* in the New World, would seem to be in good part due to the availability of domesticated animals in the former but not in the latter regions. The extinction of potential traction animals (through over hunting in the 11,000–7000 B.C. period) inhibited the development of both agriculture and the wheel in the New World. Although the wheel was invented by the Amerindians as both a toy and for making pottery it was never used for transport, for lack of horses, oxen, or equivalent beasts of burden. The New World, because of its limited ability to intensify agricultural production (imposed by the lack of beasts of burden), was left far behind the Old World, which did have sufficient domesticatable animals to harness both to the plow and to carts. This in good part explains why Columbus "discovered" America and Europe plundered it, rather than the Amerindians discovering and plundering Europe (see Harris 1977, p. 42).

Tribal societies or chiefdoms are transitional political forms between the equalitarian hunting and gathering bands and the more primitive simple horticultural societies with their big man systems, and the states of agricultural societies with their crystallized ruling classes. Chiefdoms are based on prosperous wooden hoe farming, herding, fishing, or more primitive metal hoe farming, i.e., economies that allow a considerable surplus to be accumulated by chiefs, but an insufficient surplus to allow full-fledged classes to develop.

There is considerable stratification in chiefdoms. The chief and often his retainers as well are excused from physical labor. Balanced reciprocity declines. Rank in such societies is a factor in almost every transaction among people, making exchanges imbalanced because of considerations of status. There is normally a system of graded *families* with differential claims to services and goods who are differentially in control of both wealth and force. Unlike, as in the case of big men in hunting and gathering and simpler horticultural societies, the chief is a true authority with structural power (independent of what he earns through his own activities). But there is no ruling *class* in fundamental control of the means of production or of physical coercion (as *is* the case in class societies) (Sahlins 1968, pp. 20-27).

Chiefdoms evolve out of the head man system through the gradual transformation of the system of reciprocity. The head man is able to use his position at the center of the society's redistribution network to delay reciprocity and to deflect incoming goods to secure loyal followers, and eventually to accumulate goods for his own use (i.e., to give away less than comes in). The asymmetrical reciprocity that develops provides the material means for the chief to coerce his followers into increasing their productivity.

However, the ability of a potential chief to divert part of society's wealth to his own use depends first on people's recognizing his importance to society (since an apparatus of coercion is absent). On the one hand, this means that the chief must be seen as responsible for increasing production (organizing people to produce more) and otherwise bringing benefit (perhaps by military leadership) to society; *and* on the other hand, he must appear very generous, both by redistributing large quantities of goods and sponsoring generous feasts (thereby putting people into his debt) (Sahlins 1968, p. 26; Service 1975, pp. 70-80; Harris 1979 pp. 92-93). Successful chiefs must still create feelings of obligation indicating that they expect to be repaid in both material goods and loyalty. The more extensive and important the redistribution network is for the economic life of a society, the more important the chief's role is, and thus the more likely people are to want to reward the chief by allowing him to skim off a part of what is given him, i.e., the less likely they expect to receive as material gifts from the chief as much as they give him. Gradually contributions to the redistributive portion of the economy (gifts to the chief) lose their voluntary character. They are transformed into a compulsory tax. But the economic basis of tribal power essentially remains generosity. The economic position of the chief is transformed into political inequality by gift giving according to the Eskimo adage that "gifts make slaves."

A chief has to toe a difficult path in pressing people to provide him with more goods (so that he has the means to consolidate his position through gift giving). Chiefs sometimes get too greedy. They press for more gifts, while cutting back on how much they themselves give away. They thereby risk losing their supporters and eventually their chiefdomship. Chiefly high-handedness is a dangerous game. Despotic chiefs can be overthrown relatively easily by new chiefs who skim off less and are more generous and fair in redistribution (Sahlins 1968, pp. 92–93).

Economic production for the most part is similar in tribal chiefdoms and simple horticultural societies still organized in bands (with big men as leaders). However, in tribal societies the people are occasionally mobilized by the chief to build temples, fancy homes for the chief, irrigation complexes, and other public works as well as for warfare.

The chief's enhanced position, his authority to increase production and to engage in somewhat imbalanced exchange with his people, is at first willingly granted and accepted by the people because of the important role they see the chief playing. But the chief through his enhanced position acquires the ability to reward and punish by differential distribution of goods. He is able to create an especially loyal group of followers and retainers by favoritism in the redistribution process (thus putting some in special debt to him). The chief is thus able to amass a group of retainers and a fund of power that enables him to exercise a degree of coercion against potential opposition. As a society grows and becomes more wealthy, the personal followers and retainers of the chief tend to be transformed into full-time officials. The basis of the chief's power comes to rest less on reciprocity, generosity, and voluntary support, and increasingly on coercion and the maintenance of a personal retinue.

In all primitive societies, families, not individuals, are the primary units of society. Thus it is quite natural for positions to tend to pass to different individuals in the same family. The principle of heredity of position is a consequence of the central role of kinship in the social structure of primitive societies. In bands the headmen are able to give their heirs only a slight advantage in the contest for success. Here an heir must prove he is up to the mettle of his predecessor, or else he does not consolidate his position. But in chiefdoms, chiefly position is normally strictly hereditary. The old system of kinship continuity is transformed into hereditary privilege.

THE ORIGIN OF CLASS STRUCTURES AND THE STATE

The chiefdom, under the right economic conditions, transforms itself gradually into a state. The chief and his relatives and retainers tend to transform themselves into a ruling class whose political and economic position is based on control of a state bureaucracy that supports itself by taxing the people (the voluntary gifts of the older redistribution network are gradually transformed into compulsory taxes). The transformation of tribal chiefdoms into kingdoms has occurred where the economic role of the chief was most important for the people.

Kingdoms have developed in areas where the chief's ability to mobilize the community's labor in productive public works such as irrigation have an obvious benefit to all. The primitive irrigation works that existed in chiefdoms grew into the elaborate water control works that became the state's central function. The function of labor mobilization became especially important where a chief was able to expand his control over other chiefdoms through conquest, and was, thus, in a position to coordinate many communities in common projects (especially in the river valleys in which the first states developed). Water control (dams to control river flooding and irrigation canals) was almost everywhere integrally tied up with the formation of classes. In fact, all six archaic class societies that independently developed a state had some kind of water control system (Service 1975, pt. 3; Claessen 1978, pp. 543, 643; Harris 1977, chap. 13; Wittfogel 1957).

Large-scale irrigation and drainage works in the river valleys led to the intensification of the coordination (managerial) function, and to the increasing separation of the emerging class of state managers from the people. The crystallizing managerial (state bureaucratic) class appropriated control over the most important means of production—water. In the absence of adequate rainfall, the control of waterworks by the state bureaucratic class gave it control over the living standards of the people (*and* the power to destroy political dissenters). The state apparatus, which grew up because of the important functional role it played in production, was gradually transformed into a mechanism for accumulating wealth for an owning and ruling class. It thus became essentially a means of exploitation.

Whether or not a chiefdom was successfully transformed into a kingdom (where a state exercises a monopoly over the means of coercion) was in good part a function of the ecology of the tribal environment. There are limiting factors besides the lack of the need for water control (the most important), such as the availability of domesticatable plants and animals, harsh climate, and the lack of space (e.g., islands) that could block the intensification of production and thus prevent the crystallization of sharp differences in wealth and power. A successful transition to a state requires the economic basis of the pristine kingdoms to be sufficient (in both size and intensity) to allow the emerging ruling class to sustain a permanent police force (of perhaps a minimum of several thousand individuals), thus securing a monopoly on the means of violence—the essence of the state. Such an economic basis implies at least intensive horticulture (with metallurgy and perhaps irrigation), or more commonly, full-fledged agriculture.

Another condition for the transition to crystallized class societies (and their concomitant states) is that the emerging class of producers is not able to escape from the increasingly demanding emerging ruling class by simply fleeing into adjacent less-populated areas without suffering a significant decline in their living standards. Early class crystallization and state formation occurred in areas with sharp ecotones (areas with sharp boundaries between fertile river valleys and deserts or mountains). This meant that dissatisfied producers within the emerging states would have to suffer a significant deterioration in their economic condition by leaving the river valleys (where class crystallization was occurring) to live as nomads, hunters and gatherers, or simple horticulturalists in the hostile terrain of deserts and mountains (Harris 1979, pp. 101-2).

Not only did all the early states arise in similar ecological conditions (where rainfall was scarce and river control necessary for large-scale intensive agriculture), but for thousands of years strong central states tended to be stable only in such regions. In areas such as Western and Central Europe where rainfall was regular enough to allow agriculture without irrigation, kings remained very weak in comparision with the powerful emperors of the large imperial states based in the river valleys. Kings, such as King John of England, who attempted to become despots were systematically frustrated (in John's case by his nobles who forced him to sign the Magna Carta) because they lacked the economic basis to secure compliance (Harris 1977, p. 255; 1979, pp. 104–5).*

The early "hydraulic societies" tended to develop a cyclical pattern of increasing intensification and centralization, followed by a period of corruption, decay, and decentralization, followed in turn by a revival of intensification and centralization. The rapacity of the ruling class tended to increase, while the reciprocal reward to the peasants (above all an effective and regular supply of water for irrigation) declined. Public waterworks were progressively neglected by the state bureaucratic class. Production consequently declined and the lot of the people worsened. Under these conditions the peasantry would increasingly become disaffected, and thus susceptible to being mobilized by rebels, or at least reluctant to be mobilized by their royal ruling class against external invaders. In either case, new dynasties (resulting from successful rebellion or external conquest) emerged that usually reconstructed the waterworks. They were at first generally sensitive to the needs of the people. Production would typically increase and the economy would once again function effectively. But gradually decline would again set in (see Harris 1977, p. 239).

It should be stressed that the consolidation of a propertied class and the creation of a massive state bureaucracy would not have been possible without the considerably enhanced ability of the laboring classes to produce more than they consumed. The introduction of the metal hoe allowed a given producer to produce considerably more than needed to feed himself/herself in the same time from the same amount of soil than was obtainable with a wooden digging stick. This created the possibility of a considerable "economic surplus" that could be appropriated (and in fact was) by a new ruling class. The size of the available surplus was again increased considerably with the invention of the plow (especially the plow harnessed to beasts of burden). In fact, the formation of fully consolidated social classes and massive state bureaucracies in the Old World pretty much corresponded to the development of agriculture. The consolidation of full-fledged class society and fully formed state bureaucracies

---

*The contrast between the highly centralized states (and highly crystallized class formations) that emerged in northern India (in and around the Indus and Ganges River valleys), which had a hydraulic basis, and the loose feudal character of the smaller kingdoms of southern India, where rainfall was adequate for agriculture, reflects the decisive role of water control (Harris, 1979, p. 108).

occurred for the first time around 3500 B.C. in Mesopotamia and Egypt coincident with the invention of the plow and the growth of the first cities (Harris 1977, chap. 13; Service 1975, chaps. 12, 13).

Chiefdoms were also transformed into class systems (organized by states) in areas of diversity in natural productivity that required the long distance exchange of goods or raw materials (especially metals). This process tended to occur *after* the formation of the first states (which were based on water control) in adjacent areas. Since the trade in such goods was not a traditional part of reciprocity networks, people had no standards of what equal reciprocity was. They rather greatly overvalued the goods obtained through long distance trade (often from the adjacent empires) through the organizational ability and contacts of the chief. A metal knife or ax obtained through trade is of almost incalculable value to those previously using only stone tools. The debt created by the gift of metal tools (and other such items) by a chief with connections to other regions is enormous. By trading furs or other raw materials to other peoples in exchange for advanced tools a chief is able to use the traditional reciprocity network to accumulate tremendous power (and wealth) *without* creating the feeling (at least at first) among his people that they are being treated unfairly in the reciprocity process. This is due to the tremendous increase in productivity associated with the chief's gifts, gifts which cost the chief much less in his exchange with others than is willingly given the chief by his own people for the same goods.

In areas around the periphery of the large empires (which grew out of the first kingdoms) distinctive trading peoples began to emerge whose primary activity was to engage in trade with the great empires (e.g., Phoenicians, Jews, the citizens of many Greek city-states). In these peripheral areas it appears that trade with the great empires induced the formation of a strong merchant class, the development of a landowning aristocracy (through foreclosure on mortgages), and a ruling class that displaced the weaker kings before they could consolidate strong state bureaucracies. But such a process of class formation (such as described by Engels for ancient Greece) seems to have been historically marginal. The primary process of class formation occurred in the emerging empires.

The early impact of metallurgy was highly undemocratic. The chiefs' early control over the trade in metals (especially bronze) enabled them to monopolize the distribution of efficient metal weapons and tools. The relative scarcity of the component raw materials of bronze and the difficulty of working them enhanced the power of the kings. However, it should be noted, with the development of iron smelting there were equalitarian transformations. Iron was plentiful, widely distributed, and easy to work. Since it was relatively easy for artisans to produce iron tools and weapons independent of royal monopolies, the dependence of *both* artisans and merchants on royal households and states was significantly reduced. The relative ease of manufacturing iron weapons also democratized warfare, hence somewhat reducing inequality (this was especially manifested in peripheral regions such as Greece) (Childe 1951, 1954).

It should be stressed that the evolution of kingdoms out of tribal chiefdoms was not effected through a process of coercion. There is no record of massive resistance or rebellion during the early period of kingdom and class formation (Service 1975, p. 271). The process of class formation occurred with the general consent of the masses of people because of the apparent considerable economic benefit it brought. The bureaucratic and coercive apparatus that the new kings were able to establish, however, gradually came to make the voluntary support of the masses less important. Coercion and manipulated religion, especially in areas conquered by kings, became increasingly important as mechanisms of power. Even in the most consolidated kingdoms, however, a king can only rule effectively with considerable support from the people—support which must in part be maintained by both the king's generosity in time of need and his contribution to the economic productivity of society through the maintenance of public works.

In many early kingdoms the kings still bore certain marks of their origin in chiefdoms (where power rested on reciprocity). Many of the peoples of western and central Europe that the Roman Empire conquered as well as those it came into trading relations with had in good part made the transition from chiefdoms to kingdoms (or at least were well advanced in the transition) by 500 B.C. (e.g., the Gauls, Teutons, Britons).* These early kingdoms in good part retained the reciprocity mechanisms characteristic of chiefdoms, but the kings tended to hold a monopoly on the means of military and police power (especially horses, body armor, iron swords, and war chariots). Peasants were typically required to provide the king with gifts of cattle and grain as well as to render labor services (Harris 1977, p. 252).

Many of the characteristics of chiefdoms continued to exist in the post-Roman European world (in good part brought by the conquerors of the empire who grafted their tribal traditions onto a weakened Roman economy and class structure). For example, William

---

*It is likely that the transition to primitive kingdoms in this area was in good part *induced* by trade with Rome and other advanced Mediterranean states.

the Conqueror in eleventh-century England still held great feasts reminiscent of those of great redistributor chiefs. He further regularly traveled around his kingdom taking temporary residence among his various "chiefs" or lords, living off their hospitality (Harris 1977, p. 115). The early European feudal system can thus in good part be considered a transitional (although rather advanced) form between chiefdoms and fully consolidated kingdoms.

Hunting and gathering societies and simple horticultural societies as well as fishing and herding societies and stateless advanced horticultural societies (all societies with headmen or chiefs) are organized through kinship networks—in which obligations and reciprocity are based on one's obligations to relatives. Not only are economic exchanges and welfare obligations handled through kinship, but justice is also administered through kinship networks. There are no police or prisons in such societies (and little need for them, since there is an abundance of resources and equality of distribution). In the event of theft or bodily harm to an individual, relatives are expected to take vengeance against either the perpetrator or a member of the perpetrator's family.

With the transformation of chiefdoms into kingdoms the kinship basis of primitive society was undermined and replaced by a class organization buttressed by a state composed of full-time officials and police who enforced taxation, maintained public works, established laws, and administered justice independent of kin obligations. This transformation of obligations and authority from kin through the personal retinue of the chief to a state bureaucracy occurred gradually. Probably at first in times of severe stress on resources the chief's closest relatives (with a higher rank and greater wealth) came to exert a stronger claim on resources than did the more distant relatives in the chief's lineage. Gradually similar political and economic position came to exert a stronger pull than did kin obligations (at least for distantly related individuals). The common interest of the wealthy came to exert itself in protecting privilege and wealth against the claims of poorer relatives. Kin obligations were gradually abrogated by the wealthy who came to rely first on the chief's retinue and then the state bureaucracy and police to maintain their wealth. Since they abrogated their economic obligations to their distant kin, the wealthy could hardly rely on these same kin to punish those that robbed or assaulted them, especially not against other poor people (who may well have acted out of dire economic circumstances). The old system of popular mobilization in time of war (where all men would be soldiers) was also gradually replaced by a (more or less) full-time professional army that could be relied on to repress domestic rebellions when necessary. The state apparatus came to secure a monopoly of force, consolidating and enhancing inequality in society. An increasingly centralized state developed with a large body of paid officials carrying out the orders of the king.

Fully developed classes formed for the first time in history. An unambiguous and sharp gulf developed between the laboring classes who produced the wealth of society—but who lost all power to control either how they labored, what they produced, or how their product was disposed as well as control over other aspects of society—and an owning and ruling class which lived a luxurious life-style on the basis of the exploitation of the laboring classes. A propertied class of roughly 1 percent of the population came to consume about half of society's product. Labor became compulsory and the laborers were obliged to increase their work under threat of physical punishment. The laborers lost free access to land and to raw materials—the ruling class came to appropriate the land and raw materials for itself, granting use rights to the laboring population on condition that they turn over a large part of their produce to the state. However, typically, details of production were left in the hands of the local villages, which still pretty much ran their own affairs according to principles similar to those that governed chiefdoms (a high degree of communality persisted, provided only that they paid their taxes and provided labor service when it was required).

The dichotomous class structure was manifested in social classes which for the first time had their own highly distinctive subcultures, distinctive architecture, home furnishings, diet, dress, domestic routine, sex and marriage practices, religious rituals, art, ideology, speech patterns, and so on. These differences were in good part enshrined in law. For example, in the Inca Empire only rulers could wear gold ornaments, in China only the nobility could wear silk dresses, and in feudal Europe only the lords could carry daggers and swords. In general, the laboring class came to be required to show their inferiority to the owning class. Commoners were required to perform subordination rituals such as lowering the head, removing the hat, averting the eyes, bowing, crawling, maintaining silence unless spoken to, and kneeling in the presence of the owning/ruling class. A chasm was created in life-styles, power, mode of labor, and social status. Such things were unknown in primitive society.

Both external and internal trade in the early kingdoms were the basic responsibility of the king (internal distribution generally continued to be handled through primitive reciprocity and kinship networks in the villages). There is no evidence from early civilizations of important private merchant activity (Service 1975, p. 382; Polanyi 1957). Foreign trade was carried on by official state representatives (who could be considered ambassadors) empowered to negotiate exchanges, with prices politically determined rather than established through markets. Merchants gradually developed in the cities of kingdoms to supply people with goods difficult to obtain through either the old kin-based reciprocity networks or from the benevolence of the kings (who progressively came to neglect the redistribution of goods obtained in taxes and trade). Throughout the Bronze Age (from roughly 3500 B.C. to 1200 B.C. in the Middle East), however, traders remained subordinate to (and generally agents of) the royal bureaucracy. Independent merchant classes slowly evolved out of rural laborers and urban artisans during the first millennium B.C. (Polanyi 1957).

Although the merchant and artisan classes became more important in the Iron Age (after 1200 B.C. in the Middle East) than they had been in the Bronze Age, the basic classes in the early empires and in their successor imperial states throughout the history of the Middle and Far East (through the nineteenth century) remained the rural peasants (who were the primary producers) and the ruling class of state bureaucrats (who controlled the economy and extracted massive tribute from the formally free peasants through control of a highly centralized and powerful state apparatus).

There was some variance in the class formation process among the six archaic civilizations where classes apparently developed independently: around 3500–3000 B.C. in the Indus River valley, around 1500 B.C. at the great bend of the Yellow River, and around B.C./A.D. in both the valley of Mexico and in coastal Peru (Service 1975, p. 5). One of the most important differences was that the class societies in the New World, unlike the old, were based on advanced horticulture. Although they never developed the plow pulled by beasts of burden, their economic surplus was nevertheless sufficient to develop full-fledged class societies and state bureaucracies.

Ancient Egypt probably carried the system of redistribution without a money economy the furthest. Trade there, unlike (at least late) Sumer (in lower Mesopotamia) seems to have played no important role in the villages. Land was opened and farmed collectively under the guidance of headmen who were responsible for turning over to the state the economic surplus of the laborers. Likewise, craftsmen in the cities were organized into groups led by a foreman who was allocated, and then distributed, clothing, raw material and food to the artisans (and who in turn collected and disposed of their products). The Egyptian state was an enormous and very complex redistributional bureaucracy. The division of labor within ancient Egyptian society was guided, and when necessary subsidized, at all important points (Service 1975, chap 13; Claessen 1978, chap. 10).

SLAVERY

Slavery is the system of relations of production in which the laborers themselves are a commodity, bought and sold by the exploiting class of slave masters. In contrast to capitalism where only *labor power* (the ability to labor of the producing class) is purchased, here the dominant propertied class buys and sells the very bodies of the laborers.

Slavery can arise out of primitive classless societies (in chiefdoms), out of semiconsolidated class societies, such as appears to have been the case in ancient Greece and Rome, or as a retrogression in areas of the world capitalist system, in response to the center's need for the production of commercial crops in areas of labor shortage, as was the case in the sixteenth through the nineteenth centuries.

Slavery first developed in chiefdoms out of the institution of adopting war captives. While in simple horticultural societies such "slaves" tended to pretty much have the same economic position as full members of the society, with the development of rank stratification (especially in advanced horticultural societies) slaves came to be used for accumulating wealth for the higher ranks.

Slavery as the predominant mode of exploitation has only prevailed for relatively limited and circumscribed periods, the most important of which included ancient Greece in the fourth and fifth centuries B.C., ancient Rome between the second century B.C. and the second centuries A.D. and the Caribbean region from the sixteenth to the mid-nineteenth centuries.

Slaves as a rule are recruited externally (and through the reproduction of existing slaves) by means of wars of conquest *or* purchase of slaves from others (who mostly acquire them in conquest). This was the case in ancient Greece and Rome as well as in the European-ruled Caribbean. Slavery, as the dominant mode of production, is thus a characteristic of highly commercial and expansionist societies.

Ancient Slavery

It was in ancient Greece that slavery was first transformed from an ancillary into a central mode of production. The previously existing as well as most contemporary and succeeding societies (e.g., the Hellenistic states) did not rely centrally on slavery. Further, slavery first became absolute in ancient Greece. The status of the producing class was reduced to that of beasts of burden. What became de facto the case in Greece was fully institutionalized in Roman law. The Roman legal conception of absolute property, including absolute property in human beings, contrasted with all previous legal conceptions of property, which considered property including property in humans, to be relative or conditional (including reciprocal obligations and reserved rights of others) (Anderson 1974a, pt. 1).

In the fifth century there were approximately 80,000 to 100,000 slaves in Athens, compared to 30,000 to 40,000 citizens (Anderson 1974, p. 38). At its peak, in the western half of the Roman Empire commercial agricultural production took place predominantly on slave-utilizing latifundia. Around 50 B.C. about 40 percent of the total population of Italy and perhaps 90 percent of artisans in Rome were slaves (Anderson 1974a p. 62). Virtually all economic activities in classical Greece were performed by slaves at one or another time or place including police, prison attendants, personal secretaries, supervisors, managers, and (more rarely) the liberal professions. However, slaves did not hold public office nor were they soldiers (Genovese 1973, vol. 1, chap. 2).

Since the enslavement of war captives was the primary source of slaves in the Roman world, the maintenance of the Roman economy required continuing expansion. Once this social formation ceased to expand, the source of slaves dried up. Further, the price of slaves skyrocketed and the condition of slaves improved (since the bodies of the slaves were now much more valuable), i.e., slavery became much less profitable as a means of production. The stagnation and decline of commerce in the Roman world (in good part a result of the lack of popular purchasing power characteristic of slave modes of production, and consequently the reduced commercial demand for the products of the slave-utilizing latifundia) gradually resulted in the ancient Roman slaves' being transformed into serfs. Serfs, although tied legally to the land and to their occupations, had considerable rights in the land as well as in other aspects of their lives (unlike slaves). The withering commercial economy of the ancient world undermined the profitability of slave production, resulting in the transformation of the old slave latifundia into increasingly self-sufficient manors with the producers bound to the land by serfdom.

The Development of Modern Slavery

Slavery as a mode of production developed in the ancient world because of its profitability in a labor-hungry expanding commercial imperialism. Slavery reappeared in the sixteenth and seventeenth centuries in the Caribbean region for the same reason. Plantation agriculture (that primarily produced sugar and cotton for export to Europe) required the reinvention of commercial slavery because of the extreme labor shortage in the Caribbean region and the high profitability of these commercial crops.

Although the reinvention and predominance of slavery in the Caribbean and adjacent regions from the sixteenth to the nineteenth centuries was a consequence of developing industrial capitalist relations in Europe (which created the economic demand for the goods produced by the slave system), the master-slave relations developed in the Caribbean region were qualitatively different from the emerging capitalist-worker relationships in Europe and the Northern United States. The slave relations of production that redeveloped in the Caribbean thus had much more in common with the relations of production in ancient Greece and Rome than they did with the developing worker-capitalist relations of the North. Consequently, the basic social and political institutions as well as the emerging ideology and social psychology of the Caribbean region came to have a great deal in common with similar institutions in ancient Greece and Rome. In fact, they increasingly grew apart from the emerging social, political, and ideological forms that were developing in western Europe and the U.S. North at the same time. Slavery gave the Caribbean region in general and the south in the United States, in particular, a distinctive social system and culture very different from that of the emerging industrial capitalist areas.

Commercial slavery was first used extensively in modern times by the Portuguese and Spanish who dominated both the African trading ports and the Caribbean until the early seventeenth century. African slaves were first used commercially in the islands off the coast of Africa (and to a limited extent on the Iberian peninsula itself) even *before* the discovery of the Americas. But in the sixteenth century slaves increasingly came to replace the indigenous Indian populations of the Americas as the primary producing population, especially in the least densely populated regions that had the greatest commercial possibilities. The import and utilization of slaves was greatly accelerated in the seventeenth century when the English and French seized some of the most profitable Caribbean islands from the Spanish and then intensively exploited them as sources of sugar (Fogel and Engerman 1974, pp. 14–19).

In the period 1500–1870, approximately 38 percent of all slaves imported from Africa initially went to Brazil, and about 17 percent each to the British, French, and Spanish areas of the Caribbean, with another 6 percent going directly to the United States (or the British North American colonies) (Fogel and Engerman 1974, p. 14). In 1825, however, 36 percent of all the slaves in the Americas were in the United States, and 31 percent were in Brazil, 15 percent in the British Caribbean, and 11 percent in Spanish America. These latter figures indicate the importance of American and Brazilian slavery for the world capitalist system in producing commercial exports (mostly cotton and sugar respectively) (Fogel and Engerman 1974, p. 28).

In 1860 there were approximately 4 million black slaves in the U.S. South. At the same time, there were approximately 8 million whites and 250,000 free blacks. Almost 400,000 white families owned slaves, although about 50,000 families (12 percent of all slave owners and roughly 3 percent of all white families) owned over half of all slaves. In the United States, many slaves were owned by relatively small white farmers who owned only one or two slave families. The relatively wide distribution of slave owning in the United States contrasts with the West Indies and Brazil, where the large plantation owners owned most of the slaves, and the typical plantation usually had more than 100 slaves. (Starobin 1970, p. 5).

Slavery was ideally suited to the plantation export economy. Under proper management on fertile soils it was significantly cheaper than available free labor (and more profitable). Slaves in the United States not only produced 90 percent of the cotton in the primary cotton-producing region of the U.S. Black Belt, but were also the primarily producers of Virginia tobacco, Kentucky hemp, Louisiana sugar, and Carolina rice. Slaveholding plantations dominated the export sector of the South (Starobin 1970, p. 5).

Commercial slavery developed in the Caribbean world because of the need for large quantities of cheap labor. In the sixteenth, seventeenth, and eighteenth centuries, sufficient quantities of cheap labor could be acquired in no other way except through forced transportation and enslavement. Coerced labor was necessary because, regardless of the contract terms initially entered into by free laborers, they had the relatively easy option of leaving for the plentiful open lands if they found conditions on plantations disagreeable. Forced transportation was necessary because conditions were not attractive enough to bring sufficient numbers of laborers willing to work cheaply to the plantation areas. Free workers will only work under the degrading and low wage conditions of plantation labor when no other alternatives are available. Indentured servants from Europe (who during the earlier years did provide the bulk of plantation labor in the English areas) could not be recruited in sufficient numbers. Further, indentured servitude had the disadvantage of requiring the training of new groups of workers as the terms of older workers expired. While it is certainly cheaper to indefinitely extend the terms of indenture than buy the contracts of new servants, the more this is done the more difficult it becomes to recruit new indentured servants (as well as keep those remaining from illegally breaking their contracts and fleeing to the mountains). In fact, historically, conditions for white indentured servants were gradually lightened in the attempt to encourage recruitment.

Given the imperatives leading to the redevelopment of slavery as the primary relation of production in the growing plantation system it pretty much followed that African blacks would be selected as slaves. The terms of whites could not be indefinitely extended because of the tremendous recruitment problems this would entail in Europe, as well as the increased resistance the plantation lords would face from both indentured and ex-indentured whites in the Americas. The forced transportation of Africans meant that there was no imperative to improve conditions to facilitate recruitment. Whites, unlike ethnically and visibly distinct blacks, could much more easily escape from servitute with the aid of relatives and friends, many of whom were already living in remote regions (thus making it much more difficult to successfully exploit them).

Indians early on came to be defined as making very poor plantation slaves. Other than the fact that there were not enough Indians to staff the developing plantations, the primary factors that made the lowlands Indians less desirable than forcibly transported blacks as slaves included: first, the relative ease with which Indians could escape, live off familiar land, and secure help from free Indians; second, Indian societies had the capacity to strike back against the white colonizers which were enslaving their members (thus increasing the costs of the slave owners); and third, most Indians the whites came into contact with (especially in the Caribbean region) were at the hunting and gathering or simple horticultural stages of preclass society. Except in highland Peru, Mexico, and the Yucatan, they were not sedentary peasants accustomed to highly class-stratified relations of production or to subsistence agricultural labor. Most of the consequent democratic Indian tribal traditions made them very difficult to successfully enslave. In contrast, most forcibly transported blacks came from fairly advanced rank-stratified or class societies (largely advanced horticultural societies with states, or at least highly stratified chiefdoms). Most had either been slaves or subordinate menial laborers in Africa. They had thus in good part already been broken to servile labor (Geschwender 1978, 120-25; Harris 1964, p. 14-15).

The difficulties with enslaving either whites or Indians meant that the next most available source of cheap labor would be utilized. The West Coast of black Africa lay directly across the Atlantic from the Caribbean region of the Americas. In fact, the Caribbean is considerably closer to Africa, than to Europe. Further, Africa was considerably more densely populated than were the Americas. Its states and advanced chiefdoms were willing and able to trade large numbers of war captives to European traders in exchange for metal goods, weapons, and other manufactures. The European trade in guns induced the African states and chiefdoms to engage in warfare with each other in order to secure sufficient captives to trade for more guns. Each state or chiefdom was forced to engage in such trade under penalty of losing wars to those with more guns, and then themselves being enslaved and transported to the Americas (see Davidson 1961). Last, the only cost to the Europeans of depopulating Africa was the slight undermining of the market for the manufactured goods traded for the slaves. There were no European investments or other economic stakes in Africa that suffered from the depopulation and labor export slavery required (the cost was borne by a different economic system).

It must be emphasized that the enslavement of Africans had nothing to do with any innate or preexisting white prejudice or antiblack racism. White plantation owners proved quite capable during the early years of both brutally exploiting the native Indians as well as their white indentured servants. Antiblack racism developed *after* and *as a result* of the enslavement of blacks, i.e., it was a consequence, not a cause, of African slavery. Africans were enslaved simply because they proved to be the most profitable to enslave, i.e., for reasons of nearness to the Caribbean, population density in Africa, unfamiliarity with the local population and the environment in the Americas, and the African class structure.

It took approximately a hundred years for the institution of chattel slavery to redevelop in the British North American colonies. The first blacks brought by the Dutch into Virginia were treated like the indentured servants brought from the British Isles. It was not until the 1660s that the status of blacks became distinct from that of white servants (Gossett 1963, p. 30). Blacks, like whites, were, at first, indentured for a fixed term (usually seven years) after which they were freed. Their children, like the children of whites, were not bound. Further, they retained many basic rights characteristics of the relations between masters and indentured servants. Gradually under pressure of the world market for more and more produced cheaper and cheaper, the rights of blacks were restricted until they were eventually reduced to virtually the status of beasts of burden. Not only were blacks enslaved for life, but the children of slave women became the property for life of their owners. Short of overtly killing a slave, the master class had legal power to do virtually anything they willed with their chattel.

It should be noted that in the less intensely exploited (and somewhat less integrated into the emerging world market) areas of Portuguese and Spanish America, the reappearance of slavery did not progress (at least in its legal manifestation) as far as it did in the British areas. In the Spanish and Portuguese areas black slaves retained many legal rights, such as the right to own property, to save money, to purchase one's freedom, to have Sundays and holidays off, to have free time, and to marry as well as protection from excessive and unjust punishment by masters. This contrasted with the legal condition of chattel slaves in the United States, where slaves had no civil rights, could hold no property, could make no wills, could not hire themselves out, could make no contracts, could not legally marry, could buy or sell nothing, could keep no cattle, horses, hogs, or sheep, and could not buy their own freedom (Elkins 1959, chap. 2).

Although the legal situation of slaves varied considerably between the Spanish, Portuguese, and French areas *and* the British colonial areas, the reality of treatment and the degree of exploitation of slaves *in fact* varied as a function of the world demand for the commercial crops slave labor produced. The legal situation reflected the general level of long-term economic demand in the various empires (which implemented the various slave codes on an empirewide basis) rather than the specific economic demand at a specific place at a specific time. The British areas, being thoroughly integrated into the most dynamic and developing capitalist economy, took the evolution of chattel slavery the furthest in both theory and practice; while the Spanish and Portuguese, being the least affected by developing capitalism, preserved, especially in their legal codes and ideology, strong elements of feudalism (with typically feudal guarantees for the producing class) in the forms of slavery that developed in their areas.

In spite of the formal rights of slaves in Brazil, in those areas most responsive to economic demand originating in the most dynamic capitalist areas, and during those times when demand was at its peak, the *actual* treatment of black slaves did not differ significantly from that in the British areas. In Brazil in the mid-eighteenth century it was common practice to initiate new slaves with a vicious whipping, to work slaves without rest, and to inflict punishment capriciously. In the nineteenth century slaves were whipped to death in the presence of other slaves (doctors fabricated death certificate for the authorities). Slaves that attempted to report violations of their rights to the authorities were generally not taken seriously, and in addition were often beaten by the police for reporting their masters (Genovese 1971a; Davis 1971).

The French slave code was especially humane and specified a number of rights and protections for the slaves. However, it was treated with contempt in the French West Indies during periods of sugar boom. By the 1780s the provisions of the 1685 *Code Noir* had become dead letters. In the Spanish areas, such as Cuba, slavery was traditionally mild and humane, with the rights of slaves fairly consistently implemented. However, after the successful Haitian slave insurrection removed the leading sugar exporter from the world market, Cuba was rapidly developed as a substitute. The rapid integration of Cuba into the world capitalist market—which occurred in the first half of the nineteenth century—produced a rapid deterioration in the treatment of Cuban slaves, with their traditional rights now ignored (Genovese 1971).

Once an area declined in economic importance (as occurred in much of the Spanish and Portuguese Americas) the slave system relaxed, with the legal rights of slaves once again coming to have some meaning. The oppressiveness of slavery fluctuated considerably in Brazil. It was most brutal during the sugar boom of the seventeenth century, the mining boom of the eighteenth century, and the coffee boom of the nineteenth century, and most relaxed during the periods of world recession in the commodities Brazil exported. The practice of slavery also varied considerably among the regions of the United States. Slavery was the most humane in the tidewater areas of Maryland and Virginia, and most brutal in the new areas of the Mississippi Delta and the Southwest, where high-pressure/high-profit agriculture was most central (Davis 1971, p. 118).

The conditions of slaves also varied by the availability of cheap replacements for slaves. With a cheap and abundant supply of slaves from Africa, slaves could be, and sometimes were, systematically worked to death (as in the early period of the development of the Mississippi delta). But with the closing of the slave trade (when the only source of new slaves became the surplus children of existing slaves), it became imperative to treat slaves decently enough to allow them to reproduce themselves as well as to protect the now considerable capital investment the masters had in their bodies.

Although the *legal* rights of slaves were traditionally much greater in the Portuguese and Spanish areas, as the sharp contrast between the percentage distribution of slave imports and slave population by country suggests, the standard of living of slaves in North America, at least in the nineteenth century, was better than in South America. American slaves in fact were generally better fed, clothed, housed, and worked than in the Caribbean and Brazil (Genovese 1971b, p. 302).

In fact, the food consumption of black slaves in the United States in 1860 compared rather favorably with that of the free population. Slaves consumed about 10 percent *more* food (in weight and in calories) than did the free population, about 10 percent less meat, and about 50 percent as much milk (Fogel and Engerman 1974, pp. 112-13). In 1850, the life expectancy of slaves was 36 years, compared to 40 years for white Americans (Fogel and Engerman 1974, p. 125).

There is strong evidence that the standard of living (food, clothing, shelter, medical care, sanitation) for slaves was, on the average, somewhat better than the standard of living of the new Irish immigrants to the Eastern cities in the 1840s and 1850s. By the end of the slave period in the United States, slaves had become especially valuable to their masters. Thus their material needs were adequately taken care of so that they would be lifelong productive laborers, and so that the master's capital investment would not be undermined by improper treatment (factors which did not apply to plentiful and cheap Irish free labor).

The Quality of the Master-Slave Relationship

Although modern slavery *developed* solely for reasons of profitability, the slave plantations (at least in the late period of American slavery) were not strictly organized (as are capitalist enterprises) according to profit-maximizing principles. A considerable amount of the slave's labor time went into feeding and providing for the owner and his family as well as providing the services that enabled the master class to live in a style characteristic of its station (as dictated by the requirements of masterhood). The acquisitiveness of the slave lords was channeled into the accumulation of slaves valuable *both* for the surplus value they produced and the leisure they brought, *and* military, political, and social honor, the most esteemed values.

Slavery was much more than simply a system of "extraeconomic compulsions" enabling an economic surplus to be squeezed out of the producing class.* The master-slave relationship permeated all aspects of Caribbean and Southern U.S. life, including the relationships among free whites. The prevalence of slavery determined the character of slave societies as a whole. Slavery generated an aristocratic class that was very different from a ruling class of merchants or industrial capitalists. A ruling class that bases itself in the ownership of other human beings must demonstrate its all-around social superiority. The master class had to clothe itself in the facade necessary to effectively control the poor white population (as well as the slaves).

The master-slave relation generated a distinctive psychology in the master class. A habit of command was inculcated that permeated relationships with both slaves and nonslaves. A distinctive aristocratic poise, grace, dignity, gentility, and graciousness were all class characteristics of the slave masters.

---

*This section relies heavily on Genovese 1967, 1968, 1969, 1971a, 1971b, and 1974.

The world view of the slaveholders also grew out of the master-slave relationship. Politically and ideologically the South came to develop a distinctive philosophy qualitatively different from that of the industrial capitalist world emerging around it. A distinctively anticapitalist ideology hostile to individualism, markets, the idea of a voluntary social contract, the callous exploitation of wage labor, and the single-minded pursuit of profit became pervasive. The slave owners recoiled from the notion that profit should be the sole governor of life, that economic pursuits should be strictly guided by rational maximizing principles, that thrift and hard work should be virtues, and that a society ought to be evaluated in terms of its rate of economic growth.

The slaveholders came to believe that slavery was the most humane and mild form of exploitation; the one from which all classes, the productive class as well as the ruling class, benefited the most. It was maintained that cultured civilization is impossible without a leisure class, and that slavery is most ideally suited to this end.

To the planters, slaves were a source of prestige and pride as well as power. Slave ownership was not only regarded as a privilege, but also as a social duty, responsibility, and societal trust. Slavery was seen by the master class as the essence of morality in human affairs. The slave owners defended slavery as a morally superior social system. The defense of slavery for this class thus was a defense of their honor. The Southern conflict with the North was seen as a moral conflict in defense of a superior system. Because their self-conception as well as their whole civilization was so tied up with the continuation of slavery, the plantation lords would resist a peaceful metamorphoses into capitalists. Even if wage labor could have been shown to be more profitable, the slaveholders would not have agreed to disband slavery for to do so would have violated their very raison d'être.

Slavery tended to generate a slavish, subordinate, overtly compliant, and childlike personality in the slaves. What has been called the "Sambo" personality was created and became prevalent in the Southern United States (but not in the rest of the Caribbean area). This personality type was characterized by irresponsibility, loyalty, laziness, humility, irrepressible lying and petty stealing, docility, infantile silliness and talk full of childish exaggeration. The Sambo personality seems to have been induced by the especially brutalizing and disorganizing experience of being enslaved.

Black slaves were systematically infantized by the slave system. Feelings of inferiority largely resulted from the traumatic experience of being made into slaves, which, as Stanley Elkins (1959) points out, bore many similarities to the shock of being incarcerated in a Nazi concentration camp, an experience that also resulted in the infantiza-tion of prisoners. Slaves, after their capture in Africa, immediately became subject to the most dehumanizing treatment in their imprison-ment and forced march to the sea. Approximately one-third of slave captives died even before being put on ships bound for the Americas. Starvation, thirst, and other brutalities of all kinds were the norm. The African ordeal was followed by the grueling two-month passage in the incredibly overcrowded, brutal, disease- and filth-ridden holes of slavers packed from floor to ceiling to maximize profits. Another one-third of the African captives died during the middle passage, leaving only about one-third of those originally captured to be sold in America. In the British and American regions, which systematically divided up slaves from the same tribes (rather than settling them together, as was the practice in Brazil), their language, customs, religions, and even names became irrelevant to the new slaves' life. Old standards no longer made sense in the New World, where forced labor under humiliating conditions, English, Christianity, and even a new name were all suddenly forced on one (typically breaking one's will to resist) (Elkins 1959, chap. 3). The required quick adjustment to absolute power in a totally different environment typically without the support of others of the same culture produced both a detachment from one's prior life and infantization. The British-American system of systematically and suddenly destroying the African culture of the slaves by splitting up people from tribes and firmly prohibiting the practice of African customs had a more lasting psychological effect than did the Spanish and Portuguese practices. In the light of the shock of America, it is not difficult to see how a paternalistic slave lord, as the source of all privileges, gifts, and necessities (as well as punishments) would be viewed with awe reminiscent of a father, and, thus, the ideology of paternalism become rooted in the personal-ities of the slaves as well as in those of the masters (Elkins 1959, chap. 3; Genovese 1971a; Fanon 1961).

However, it should be noted that once the initial shock of being enslaved was over, the conditions of life on the plantations were different from the ongoing life in concentration camps. The slaves who accommodated to their new life found considerable space within which to maintain some integrity *provided* they fundamentally accepted the paternalistic authority of their slave lords, i.e., at least *acted* like children. Slaves, unlike typical concentration camp pris-oners, did not normally systematically suffer from malnutrition or grossly inadequate clothing or shelter. Further, fairly adequate health and sanitation precautions were taken with slaves, if only to preserve the capital investment of the masters. Concentration camp prisoners were systematically denied basic human amenities, such as a social life, friends, sexuality, and so forth, that were *not* denied slaves. The Gestapo deliberately attempted to destroy the individuality and integrity of prisoners, while the planters generally accepted slave individuality. While the Gestapo was not interested in securing the loyalty of prisoners (only their unquestioning obedience) the slave lords *were* concerned with gaining the loyalty of their slaves.

Further, after the closing of the slave trade more humane standards of treatment developed (in order to ensure a regular supply of laborers). The subsequent growth of a Creole slave population narrowed the cultural and social gap between the slaves and masters (as well as other whites), resulting in the development of feelings of mutual affection and intimacy.

Paternalism, rather than cold exploitation, became characteristic of the way masters related to slaves. A fatherly, protective, but at the same time dominant and commanding, attitude came to be typical. Slavery required masters to see slaves as acquiescent human beings who had certain rights as well as duties and responsibilities. The masters came to feel certain responsibilities for the welfare of slaves as well as to believe that slaves had certain rights.

In sum, within the parameters of paternalistic authoritarianism, slaves, once they adjusted to the new world, were not generally subject to a constant state of terror (such as existed in concentration camps). Their inferiorization was thus only partial. The slaves maintained a sense of moral worth (Genovese 1974).

That most black slaves in good part acquiesced in their submission is demonstrated by the overwhelming evidence from the testimony of ex-slaves about conditions on the old plantations (which in some cases amounts to nostalgia) as well as the testimony of masters that they did not, as a rule, fear their slaves. In fact, neither the doors of plantation houses nor those of the slave quarters were usually locked at night. Even where there were panics among slave lords about rebellions, it was normal to feel that one's own slaves would protect against the rebellious slaves of other masters (Genovese 1974, p. 615).

In spite of the general inferioration and partial acquiescence created by slavery, there *was* systematic resistance on the part of slaves to their lot. Two of the chief manifestations of this resistance were systematic "soldiering," including lack of care for tools, laziness, and "stupidity" (as a tactic not to have to do things), and slave religion. The black transformation of the Christian religion (which was initially forced on them) allowed blacks to strengthen their pride and solidarity with each other, even while it acted as a safety value for the oppressions of this world (deflecting concerns to another life). Black Christianity, even while reflecting the hegemony of the master class, emerged as a means of resisting the moral and psychological aggression of that class (Genovese 1974, book 2). Resistance to slavery was also manifested in running away, fleeing to the North or Canada, occasionally in killing an overseer or even a plantation lord, and sometimes (although rather rarely in the United States, unlike in the Portuguese, French, and Spanish areas) in slave revolts. The largest slave revolt in the United States, that led by Nat Turner in the 1830s, involved only a few hundred slaves and lasted for only a few days, an event that would have gone virtually unrecorded in Brazil.

The Variety of Occupational Positions of U.S. Slaves

In 1850, about 7 percent of all U.S. slaves were in managerial posts (mostly as slave drivers), 12 percent were artisans and craftsmen (blacksmiths, carpenters, and so forth). In fact almost 80 percent of southern artisans were slaves—and about 7 percent were in semiskilled or domestic jobs as gardeners, stewards, teamsters, and house servants. About three-fourths of all slaves were simple laborers (mostly all in the fields) (Fogel and Engelman 1974, 39; Reich 1981, p. 21).

Black slaves were generally employed as foremen (slave drivers) in direct supervision of slave gangs working under white overseers. The drivers were given certain privileges such as whiskey and extra food, access to women, and closeness to the master. They often went with the master on hunting trips, discussed plantation business on mutually respectful terms, and took on trusted responsibilities. Drivers had responsibility for much of the punishment of recalcitrant slaves and were held responsible for maintaining the level of production. Many blacks preferred to work directly for whites rather than for the drivers. But some drivers also mitigated the harshness of the system and defended their people. Drivers often provided leadership to the slave quarters, gaining a degree of respect because of their position and ability to protect. But because they were so dependent on the masters they were mostly effective agents of order and discipline (Genovese 1974, pp. 365–88).

House servants represented another relatively privileged strata of slaves. House servants were especially trusted because of their daily personal associations with the master class. As with the drivers, they were especially dependent on the master class for their special privileges. But the master class was especially dependent on their house servants as well. The master class needed the support and trust of their house slaves far more than house servants needed theirs. The masters and mistresses needed personal servants they could depend on. This gave the house slaves considerable leverage to enhance their position. Considerable intimacy was often involved, especially in the relations between the mistresses and their personal female servants (who spent much of their time sharing with their servants the secrets of their love lives) (Genovese 1974, pp. 327-65).

However, for the most part, neither the drivers nor the house servants formed a distinctive subclass distinguished socially from the bulk of simple field hands. Male servants were generally youths under 15 or persons over 45. Children employed as house servants were sent to work in the field during their most productive years and then allowed to return to the house as their bodies grew weaker (many top field hands who did not become house servants in their later years were shifted into the crafts to become plantation artisans as a reward for good service) (Fogel and Engerman 1974, p. 220). It should also be noted that the typical house slave worked on either a small farm or a moderate size plantation where there were too few other house slaves to allow the formation of a separate social strata of house slaves even if the position was a lifelong one (Genovese 1971, p. 308).

A significant number of black slaves (approximately 5 percent in the 1850s) worked in industry, mostly in rural, small town, or plantation industries. Only about 20 percent of slaves employed in industries were located in cities (Starobin 1970, pp. 11-12). About 80 percent of industrial slaves were owned by industrial enterprises, with the other 20 percent being rented from their owners by the month or year (Starobin 1970, p. 12). The textile and especially the iron industries were heavily dependent on slave labor (slaves were the chief labor force in most upper South ironworks). It should be noted that southern iron production stagnated in the 1850s because of severe competition from Pennsylvania and Ohio (which used free white labor) (Starobin 1970, p. 14). But the trend in southern industry in the 1850s was toward the replacement of black slaves by white wage laborers.

Although most industrial slaves did not work in cities, it is of interest to note that the slave population of the largest Southern cities declined from 1850-60. The slave population of the ten largest southern cities dropped by 9,000 (or 12 percent). In a period when slavery was *expanding* in agriculture this suggests an incompatibility between slavery and urban enterprises, and thus a blockage on the expanded use of slaves in industry (Fogel and Engerman 1974, p. 98).

For industrial slavery to be consolidated, especially in the skilled occupations, it would have been necessary to provide the slaves with considerable incentives (perhaps including the right to purchase their freedom). To implement such a system, however, would have been socially dangerous because: first, it would bring privileges to the industrial slaves, thus raising (potentially explosive) expectations among the black population; and second, it would undermine the legitimating myth that blacks were inferior and capable of only menial tasks requiring close supervision. Employers thus resisted implementing a material incentive system functionally equivalent to wage labor. Consequently, while the northern factory workers had the fear of unemployment and the possibility of making more money as incentives to increase productivity, the slaves did not. They were thus not as efficient as wage workers.

The use of black slaves in many industries in the South in spite of their relative inefficiency was in good part a result of the quality of white labor available. White laborers were generally considered to have a status only slightly better than black slaves since the degradations encumbent on slave status tended to be generalized to all menial labor (which thus carried a considerable stigma). The logic of slavery, in which manual labor is the distinctive burden of the slave, dictated that manual labor *in general* would be considered menial and humiliating. White laborers were deeply affected by the ideology of the planter class and thus very much resented (and felt humiliated by) performing "slave" labor. Their consequent demoralization negatively affected their reliability and productivity. Because of the low status associated with industrial labor, the whites recruited to it tended to be the dregs of white society, often more "lumpen" than typically proletarian in attitude.

The Contradictions of Slavery

Slave economies are full of contradictions that prevent them from increasing their economic efficiency and maximizing capital accumulation. Although the introduction of slavery generally greatly increased the productivity of an area (because of the previous shortage of labor), the slave mode of production soon tended to economic stagnation, especially in comparison with capitalist economies with their internal dynamic of increasing efficiency. The economic backwardness and relative decline of the South's economy in relation to the North of the United States as well as to Great Britain was a product of the logic of the master-slave relationship.*

---

*Nevertheless, the Southern slave system was sufficiently profitable to survive and grow (even if more slowly than the industrial capitalism of the North). Southern plantations, controlling for size (and thus economies of scale), appear to have been approximately as efficient (in terms of value of output from a given input of labor, land, and capital) as Northern farms, indicating that the slave system was economically viable, even if profitability could be maintained only in the few crops that lent

Slave labor is notoriously low in productivity. Slaves generally work indifferently unless they are very closely supervised (which is only possible at great cost). Slaves do not have the efficient incentive structure of proletarians (they do not have the pressure of unemployment, demotions, promotions, and so forth driving them). They will eat, and eat pretty much the same, independently of how much they work. Since the master class has a capital investment in them, reasonable care will be taken of their bodies no matter how poorly they work. Slavery does not lend itself to motivating the producers by a close linking of how much they produce to their reward (see Genovese 1967, chap. 2).

There were, however, various incentive systems superimposed on the basic coercive framework of slavery to induce slaves to work. Whippings as well as deprivation of privileges (such as visits to town), and such punishments as branding, confinements in stocks, incarceration, and sale were also applied to recalcitrant slaves. Positive incentives were also implemented, in various degrees and various places. Some planters offered prizes for the individual or gang with the best performance, e.g., whiskey, tobacco, trips to town, or sometimes even cash. Year-end bonuses for working hard were sometimes offered (in either goods or cash). The most productive slaves were sometimes rewarded with patches of land that they could work on their own account. Slaves who performed well also increased their probability of eventually becoming artisans, house servants, or drivers (and the consequent rewards of higher status, better housing, better clothing, and cash bonuses these positions entailed) (see Fogel and Engerman 1974, pp. 144–49). However, such positive and negative incentives were of secondary importance compared to the immediate fear of sacking, hunger, and short-term prospects for pay increase that governed the behavior of industrial wage laborers.

Slaves, because of the deficiency of incentives, are typically careless in their handling of tools (e.g., in order to reduce breakage the typical Southern hoe used by slaves weighed three times as much as the hoe in use in the North at the same time) as well as in their care of animals (e.g., less efficient oxen and mules had to be used instead of the more efficient horses that required greater care), and in cultivation in general (e.g., fertilizer could not generally be used because

---

themselves to slave labor. This seems to have been the case in spite of the relative inefficiency of slave labor because the remuneration of slaves was less than the income of family farmers of the West, while the growing world demand for the export crops of the South kept prices relatively high as well as because slave labor was used more intensively than was labor on family farms (Fogel and Engerman 1974, chap. 6).

improper application could easily destroy the land's productivity). In general, technical innovations were inhibited and traditionally inefficient methods preserved. For the most part, slaves worked best doing simple repetitive tasks that required more brute strength than care or initiative (and required the minimum of supervision). Certain crops that required simple care, especially sugarcane and cotton, lent themselves well to slave labor. Because of the limited number of such crops, however, there could be little or no crop rotation. This together with the inhibition on the use of fertilizers tended to result in the depletion of the soil and put obstacles in the way of reclaiming worn-out land. As a result, the productivity of the land in slave areas declined, forcing the slave system to continuously incorporate new virgin soils (this was a major source of the imperialist impetus of the Southern slave system manifested in the U.S. annexation of Texas and the war with Mexico in the 1840s as well as in its imperial designs on much of the Caribbean) (see Genovese 1967, chaps. 2-5).

The inefficiency, laziness, and clumsiness of slaves was perpetuated and stabilized by the need of the master class to believe that slaves were inferior. They thus expected them to be lazy, inefficient, and clumsy, as this was validation of the myth that justified paternalism and the slave mode of production. The very ideology that justified slavery acted as a contradiction of the system.

Another major problem with slave labor lay in the inflexibility of the labor force. While capitalists can quickly and easily expand or contract the size of their work force simply by hiring or firing, the slave owners must purchase new human beings at great initial cost when they want to expand, and sell them (perhaps in a poor market) when they need to contract. As a result, the size of a plantation labor force tends to be much less flexible than that of a capitalist. While the capitalists can lay off during slack seasons or recessions, the slave masters generally must continue to feed and provide for their slaves the year around, and in spite of the condition of the market, in order to be sure to have a labor force during the busy season and when the market picks up. The problem with securing a labor force is not so great when a cheap source of new slaves is readily available, but it can become a major obstacle to increasing production when the source of cheap labor dries up. Not only does slave labor make for an inflexible, unmotivated, and very expensive labor force, it also provides little opportunity to select specially trained workers for specific tasks. Slaves are purchased for an indefinite tenure and must be flexible in the tasks they perform.

Slaves in fact were generally purchased for use, rather than speculation. Slaves once purchased were rarely resold. The slave's familiarity with conditions on a given plantation, personal attachments, and the economic loss encumbent on letting equipment and land lie idle because of insufficient labor as well as the general paternalistic mentality of the plantation lords prevented slaves from being treated like bales of cotton. The fact that during depressed conditions slave prices were low and during boom times high also inhibited the selling of slaves. After the end of the slave trade it appears that almost half of slave sales originated in the breakup of estates due to death or bankruptcy, rather than in plantation lords selling slaves in order to make a profit (Fogel and Engerman 1974, pp. 54–55).

In 1860, about 6 percent of slaves in rural areas were on hire. A good number, if not most, of these were artisans who were frequently allowed by their owners to hire themselves out on their own account, in return paying their owners a fixed percentage of their income. The renting of field hands played a minor, if not inconsequential, role in Southern agriculture. However, in the urban areas where there were concentrations of slave artisans, slaves on hire represented about 30 percent of the slave population (Fogel and Engerman 1974, p. 56). In summary, slaves tended to stay in place throughout their lifetimes irrespective of the ups and downs of the economic fortunes of their masters. This was very different from the norm for wage laborers in capitalist economies.

Slavery also resulted in a contradiction of domestic economic demand (which inhibited the development of industry). The low living standards of the slaves on the one hand, and the aristocratic living standards of the lords, largely satisfied by imports from abroad (together with the concentration of wealth among whites in a relatively few hands), on the other, meant that there was little in the way of a domestic market to stimulate local industry. The slave lords themselves preferred to invest their profits in more land and slaves (even if industrial enterprises appeared somewhat more profitable) because of the central importance of aristocratic status in the system, i.e., there was strong pressure to conspicuous consumption, rather than maximizing savings and accumulation.

Slaveholding planters were generally hostile to industry. The state apparatus they controlled was consequently used to tax commerce and manufacture to support the countryside, rather than vice versa (as has been done in both capitalist and socialist countries that have wanted to facilitate industrialization).

The policies the Southern U.S. slave lords advocated, and tried to get the U.S. federal government to implement, were determined by the logic of the master-slave relationship. They needed low tariffs to guarantee cheap imports of both their luxury goods and the goods necessary for the plantations as well as to avoid reciprocal high tariffs against their cotton exports. Unlike the Northern industrialists who wanted high tariffs to protect their markets, the Southerners could not care less if local industrial production was encouraged. In general they did not want the federal government to engage in internal improvements such as railroads and canals. Nor did they want it to engage in other measures that would have facilitated the growth of small farmers in the West or strengthened the economic power of the Northern states. They were thus opposed to granting homesteads to small farmers, encouraging European immigration, building railways to the West, and virtually all other state policies that benefited industrial capital (see Genovese 1967, chap. 1). In general, the predominance of slave relations of production inhibits industrialization and consequently, by blocking technological process, puts a slave society at a disadvantage vis-à-vis other societies (e.g., the capitalist North of the United States), whose modes of production facilitate industrialization.

That slave relations of production tend to cause stagnation and inhibit increases in efficiency and productivity in both agriculture and industry is borne witness to not only by the relative stagnation of the Southern economy in the United States, but also by the experience of the slave mode of production in the ancient world. During the eight centuries from the rise of Athens to the fall of Rome (when slavery predominated), there was very little technical innovation in the means of production. No major inventions occurred. Wherever slavery has been the dominant mode of production, there has been general technological stagnation (Anderson 1974, p. 26).

SERFDOM

Serfdom is the system of property relations in which the producing class is tied to the land but maintains important rights to their labor time as well as access to the land (and other vital resources such as wood and water) on condition that they provide a major part of their labor to a lord. The exploitation of the producing class in such societies, the serfs, is typically effected by the requirement of working so many days a year on the lord's estate or manor as well as so many days on public works such as roads or the lord's castle. There is a variation within serfdom in the degree to which the serf is bound to the lord (in contrast to the land) as well as in the relative rights of the serf and lord in the land. But in general, the lord has both political-legal and economic authority over the serfs (both of which are used to enforce exploitation).*

---

*The discussion in this section draws heavily on Anderson 1974; Bloch 1961; Critchley 1978; Pirenne 1937; Hobsbawm 1965; Hilton 1976; and Cheyney 1936.

As commercial relations radically declined in the late Roman Empire, the practice of binding most producers to their occupations developed as a way of ensuring the performance of economic functions. The former slaves on latifundia (which had once been oriented to sales on the world market) were largely reduced to serfdom by the fifth century A.D. This occurred considerably before the total system of feudalism with its vassalage system of personal homage (which organized relationships *within* the propertied class) developed (Bloch 1961, chap. 19; Anderson 1974, pt. 1, chap. 1).

The "barbarian" conquerors of the Roman Empire lived in essentially preclass tribal societies in which personal, usually kin-based ties, governed relationships. The tribal chiefs of the conquering barbarian tribes solved the problem of governing the conquered lands by assigning economic and political authority to their subchiefs in return for their continued provision of military services (i.e., the kings granted benefices to their ex-lieutenants). The old tribal war chiefs thus developed into sedentary kings, while the subordinate military leaders developed into feudal lords. The old tribal councils (within which decisions had been made) withered away, replaced by the retinue of the king (who made grants of the use of land and other gifts in return for services performed). The old protoserfs of the Roman Empire acquired new masters (Anderson 1974, chap. 2).

There had been some free peasants in the Roman provinces of western Europe. Many more free peasants were created from the settlement of the barbarian conquerors (the rank-and-file tribal warriors were rewarded with land). However, over the course of the Dark Ages neither the state, village, nor extended kin network could any longer provide sufficient military protection to the free peasantry, and thus they were gradually largely forced to voluntarily enserf themselves to local lords in return for military protection. The condition of the early barbarian peasantry also deteriorated because of the burden placed on them by continuing wars (to which they were recruited) and taxation. In fact, class stratification developed rapidly among the new barbarian settlers once the migratory tribal federations became territorially fixed. Serfdom, during the classical period of European feudalism from 900 to 1200, thus represented a convergence of the old protoserf system of the late Roman Empire with the newly enserfed descendants of the free peasants. Full-fledged serfdom had become general in western Europe by the late ninth century.

During classical feudalism serfs typically worked on the mostly self-sufficient manors of the lords. The serf would work so many days a year on the manor and so many days to feed his family on land allocated to him by the lords for that purpose. The serfs depended on their lord for basic social welfare as well as for police and military protection. The manors had their own artisans and there was little dependence on towns or trade.

Serfdom, even during this period, was not universal in western Europe. There were regions such as Sweden, Switzerland, and much of Normandy where the peasants were not attached to the land. In other areas there were patches of land not subject to serfdom. In such areas, some serfs held land on their own which was not subject to their lord. Some villages scattered around Europe almost entirely escaped servitude. The degree of dependence of serfs on their lords also varied by area. In the early period English serfs were more subordinate than were the French because the English state was stronger than the French (and was thus more effective in running down runaway serfs) (Block 1961, chap. 19).

Western European serfdom was associated with the system of decentralized and fragmented economic and political relations among the classes. There was profound stratification within the landowning class of nobles, with the kings at the top and the knights at the bottom. In classical European feudalism, the relations among the landowning nobility were governed by personal relationships of obligation (vassalage). The superior lord granted a fief to a subordinate in exchange for service. Typically, this involved the right to exploit peasants in a certain geographical area as well as the right to administer justice and pretty much make the laws. In exchange, the subordinate lord had to provide military service when called upon to do so by the superior lord. The grant of the political and economic rights of a fief were contingent on performance of duty and could theoretically be revoked for noncompliance. It would often happen that a given minor lord owed vassalage to two or more different superior lords because he held fiefs from more than one superior. A minor lord owed personal homage only to his immediate lord or lords, not to the lords of their lords. Thus, in the advent of rebellion by an intermediate lord, his vassals generally sided with him rather than with the lord's lord.

During the earliest period of feudalism fiefs were typically granted for the life of the vassal, but gradually the term was extended, with fiefs becoming the patrimony of the vassal, and the expectation of service less. Fiefs had pretty generally become inheritable by 850 (Anderson 1974, p. 142). The transformation of the fiefs into the patrimony of the lords was facilitated by the greater incentive for performance involved if the lord knew he could pass on his fief to his son as well as by the general deterioration of the economy, which weakened the authority of the central kings.

The class barriers between the landed aristocracy and the rest of the population crystalized in the twelfth century (at the same time as the rigidities of serfdom were being undermined). While prior to the twelfth century it was possible for commoners who had obtained sufficient wealth, or who had performed important services for the king, to become nobles, after this period it became very difficult. The nobility became virtually exclusively hereditary. The privileges and prerogatives of the nobility that formerly were mostly simply customary became legally enforcible and jealously guarded. Measures were taken that prevented the sale of fiefs, thus guaranteeing them as the more or less indivisible patrimony of the lords. These measures were taken in the time of expanded market relations in order to advance and consolidate the political and economic position of the landed class against both the rising bourgeoisie of the towns (whose rapidly accumulated wealth was becoming a threat to the traditionally economically dominant classes) and the serfs who were gradually being transformed into formally free tenants (Anderson 1974a, pp. 182–85; Bloch 1961, pt. 6).

After 1100 in the area west of the Elbe serfdom began to wither away (and was eventually abolished) because of expanding markets. The old essentially self-sufficient manor was gradually transformed into a unit producing for the market. The old feudal labor dues were transformed into rents. The serfs became formally free peasants (who could be pushed off the land if they did not work hard enough). In general, in the twelfth and thirteenth century, the revival of commerce transformed the feudal class structure.

Not only were traditional serf relations undermined west of the Elbe, but as the towns rapidly grew in size and economic importance, artisans and merchants became much more important than they had been during the earlier period of serfdom. The crafts evolved from small familylike operations in which most apprentices could eventually expect to become master craftsmen to highly commercial operations in which the journeymen artisans were systematically exploited by the masters. By the middle of the thirteenth century, class formation had proceeded to such a point in the new towns that sharp class struggle broke out in many of them between the economically and politically dominant merchants and the increasingly subordinated artisans (see Cheyney 1936, chap. 1–4).

Serfdom is a more efficient and productive mode of production than is slavery, although it is considerably less efficient than is wage labor. The period of predominance of serf-lord relations thus saw tremendous advances in the means of production as well as in the expanse of land under cultivation. The iron plow became general in tilling, the stiff harness was developed for superior horse traction, the water mill was developed for mechanical power, and the three-field system of agricultural rotation came into general use (Anderson 1974a, p. 183). In contrast, the period of the domination of ancient slavery saw almost no technical progress.

Feudal societies devoted a higher proportion of the surplus produced by the exploited population to reinvestment in the means of production and rather less to the conspicuous consumption of the ruling class, than did the Asiatic mode of production (state peasantry). On the other hand, capitalists tend to reinvest much more than do feudal lords. Moreover, the rate of innovation under capitalism is considerably greater (because of the pressure of forced commercial competition) than it is in feudalism (with its traditional economic practices).

Neither serfdom nor feudalism were unique to precapitalist Europe. Japan developed a feudal system that was very much like that of Europe in the wake of the gradual decay of its earlier Asiatic mode of production. Japanese feudalism also saw the combination of vassalage among the nobility with the legal binding of the serf to the land. There were minor differences with European serfdom/feudalism, however. In Japan the authority structure was firmer (with more acts of submission and less symmetry of obligations). Further, there was no plurality of lords (Anderson 1974b, pp. 413-18).

Serfdom, however, has been rather limited in geographical scope. In fact, throughout the central regions of the World Island, from the Balkans and Morocco through the Near East and India to China and Southeast Asia, serfdom has been rare. The most common class system in agricultural societies has been one of more or less free peasants with fairly secure rights in the land (which legally is usually state property) providing their surplus to the central state in the form of a tax. In the case of China, for hundreds of years before the twentieth century most of the land was private property, with free peasants either paying rent (usually in the form of a share of the crop) to a private landlord, or tax to the state. As early as the eleventh century in China perhaps as many as 60 percent of the peasants were small holders (Anderson 1974b, p. 527).

The peasants in the Asiatic societies had relatively secure and inheritable use rights in the land so long as they and their children used the land and paid their taxes to the central states. Peasants generally had the right to shift residence (although movement was often regulated in various degrees) (Anderson 1974b, p. 371). The Asiatic world had no stable hereditary nobility. Local administrators generally served at the pleasure of the central state and operated within the guidelines laid down by it.

The Oriental mode of production (state peasantry) and its attendant form of relatively free peasantry (exploited mostly through taxation) tends to arise and be stable in areas where water control, and hence a central state to supervise public works, are predominant. In contrast, feudalism and serfdom tend to arise and last the longest in areas where neither insufficient rainfall nor catastrophic flooding of river valleys is a major problem (and hence where a central state bureaucracy is not a precondition of intensive agriculture).*

PEASANTRY

Peasants are oriented to subsistence agriculture, have considerable direct operational control over their own labor in production, and are required to produce a surplus for the dominant agrarian class.† Within these parameters the degree of peasant autonomy, the specific land tenure system, the form, relative size, and distribution among different groups (i.e., landlords, state, church, merchants, moneylenders) of the economic surplus appropriated from the peasantry varies considerably.

Peasants typically have at least some rights in the land and can not in most cases easily be totally displaced by either their landlord or the state (when it is the ultimate property owner) so long as the peasant family continues to fulfill its obligations to cultivate the land and provide the surplus to the dominant class. (This is less the case in sharecropping tenancy than in other types of peasantry.) Unlike slaves or serfs, peasants are formally free. They are not rigidly tied to either the land or to a given landlord and, consequently, have a degree of flexibility in their location. They often have, however,

---

*It is important to note that there is not a universal association of state peasantry with a strong economic role for the state in managing public waterworks. However, the management of public works gives rise to state peasantries both in the immediate area of the public works where they are directly functional and in surrounding (often widely spread out) areas that the military and economic power of the states built on water control are able to conquer or otherwise dominate. Thus, state peasantry came to be prevalent throughout the center of the world, from the South China Sea to the Mediterranean, but not so common in western Europe, Japan, central Asia, central Africa, or regions on the edges of the World Island. The regions on the world center's margins, namely western Europe (and perhaps Japan), were relatively immune from the imposition of state peasantry and strong central empires; consequently, they were more likely to develop capitalism because of the relative weakness of the strong central political forces that block its development (see the last section of this chapter).

†This section on peasantry draws heavily on Stavenhagen 1975; Shanin 1971; Paige 1975; Stinchombe 1962; Wolf 1966, 1969. The peasant mode of production is usually referred to in the Marxist literature as "semifeudalism."

significant de facto constraints on their movement as well as formal and informal relations of subordination to the landowners and/or the officials of the state (including the lack of basic civil rights). Various studies have shown that in stable peasant societies with plow agriculture the surplus taken by the dominant classes amounts to roughly one-half of the peasants' total production (varying considerably according to population density and land productivity).

Three types of relationships between the peasant producers and the dominant (exploitive) class prevail in peasant societies: first, patrimonial domain, or subordination to lords who have hereditary rights in the land and who exploit the peasantry through rents (either in kind or in cash) and perhaps labor services; second, prebendal domain, or subordination to officials of a state that owns the land and exploits the peasantry primarily through taxes in kind or cash (the difference between a "rent" and a "tax" in the case where the state owns the land or where the landlord has juridical powers has no substantive meaning); and third, mercantile domain, where the land formally belongs to the peasants, rather than to the state or landlords, but where the peasantry is exploited largely through domination of markets by merchants and payments on land mortgages to moneylenders (here the surplus is extracted in the form of unequal exchange and interest).

In prebendal domain the officials who collect taxes for the royal bureaucracy either receive a set salary (as was traditionally the case in China) or a proportion of the taxes actually collected ("tax farming") as occurred in the Mogul Empire in India or the Ottoman Empire. But in either case the authority of officials over such state peasants is limited. It is exercised at the discretion of the centralized royal bureaucracy that maintains ultimate authority over the peasants (typically mediated by village headmen within semiautonomous villages). As long as the prebendal peasants continue to utilize the land and provide taxes they are generally secure in their use rights. In such systems use rights to land are often either periodically redistributed or redistributed on the death of a peasant.

Peasant proprietors generally maintain relatively self-sufficient households, i.e., they produce most of the goods they consume, build their own buildings, make their own clothing, grow most of their own food, and so forth. They are normally dependent on markets for only a few essentials such as salt, metal utensils, and tools. The typical peasant village is even more self-contained with its own artisans (e.g., blacksmiths, coopers, and so on) to provide much of what the household cannot itself produce.

Peasants do not regard their land as a means to make money. They are oriented rather to providing for the traditional (and more or less set) consumption of their family as well as to pay dues to the political and economic powers, not to accumulating wealth. Peasants run a household, not a business enterprise.

Since the goal of peasant production (beyond taxes and rents) is to meet the consumption needs of the household, peasants tend to allocate their labor over the year (the number and intensity of hours worked), so as to produce an output that meets their basic requirements. Thus, a decreasing return from increasing labor inputs ("decreasing marginal returns") does not generally affect the peasant's labor as long as the needs of the family have not yet been satisfied. This makes economic sense to the peasant, since in a self-sufficient household labor that is not expended, no matter how marginal the expanded output, would otherwise be idle. The peasant is not oriented to the rate of hourly remuneration or to the rate of profit, but rather to the aggregate remuneration of a whole labor year. Once a peasant household has produced all it needs to satisfy its traditional consumption requirements and pay the landlords, state, and creditors, it tends to cut back on its labor input, no matter how great the marginal returns of additional labor may be.

Normally, however, all able-bodied family members put in a full day of labor. This is the case because of the tendency of landlords, the state, merchants, and moneylenders (assuming all productive land is occupied) to adjust the levels of rent, tax, terms of trade, and interest to what the peasants can bear (without their rate of deserting the land exceeding the rate that is necessary to maintain cultivation).

Questions of comparative profitability of various expenditures do not usually arise in peasant economics. There would be no question, for example, of whether to grow grass or hemp, since the two are not substitutes for each other. A certain amount of grass for grazing and a certain amount of hemp for rope are both necessary. The crop(s) that must be provided as rent/tax (either directly or indirectly after being converted into cash in the case of more commercialized societies) are usually either dictated by tradition or by the directives of landowners or creditors, rather than by price fluctuations in markets.

Peasant land is generally farmed more intensively than is commercial land, since all able-bodied members of the peasant family are employed more or less independently of their marginal output. Therefore, there is generally a smaller output per worker, but a higher output per unit of land than is the case on comparable commercial land. The peasant family that rents land often rents it at a price higher than would be profitable from a capitalist standpoint so as to employ the surplus family labor that would otherwise be idle.

Commercialized peasantries are very often sharecroppers who provide a set *share* of their crop to the owners of the land, generally around 50 percent (more if tools, fertilizers, and seeds are provided, less if only the land). They may also be cash tenants who sell their commercial crop in order to pay a fixed rent.

Peasant income is often supplemented through handicraft production. Not only do peasant families make most of their own clothing, tools, utensils, and so forth, but in more commercial economies they very often produce such additional goods as can be sold in order to earn an income to help purchase the necessities they cannot themselves produce. This is especially the case in regions with a short growing season, and hence where there is much labor that would otherwise be idle in the off season. No matter how inefficient, so long as the price of the artifacts sold is greater than the cost of materials bought, it is rational for a peasant family to utilize labor that is not necessary in agriculture in producing handicrafts.

Another important source of supplementary peasant income in more commercial societies is part-time wage labor and temporary wage labor for unmarried children. Hiring out to commercially oriented farmers or rural enterprises is common (especially in industrializing economies). Sometimes sons may temporarily migrate to a city to secure employment either in the agricultural off season or for a few years, while daughters find employment in nearby towns working for a wage in light industry (e.g., textiles, electronics). Further, in many areas the wife may become a trader, engaging in market activities on a part-time basis to sell the produce of the family, and (perhaps) to secure extra funds by buying and selling other people's produce. Such forms of labor become increasingly important in the face of industrialization and declining agricultural prices (due to increased productivity in expanding commercial farms). Part-time or temporary wage labor, under such conditions, often becomes permanent (even while the myth of return to the land lingers on for decades).

With increasing commercialization, private landlords often transform land tenure, turning over legal title to the better-off peasants in exchange for money payment (the landlords assuming long-term mortgages), then loaning them money (and securing interest), obtaining fees for water, grazing, wood rights, and so on. The benefit of such a conversion lies in both the displacement of the risks of production to the peasant and to increasing the peasants' identification with the land (and hence their incentive to increase long-term productivity). The owning (but heavily indebted) landowning peasantry now must pay fixed fees to the agrarian upper class (landlords and merchants), rather than share risks with them (as in a share-cropping system). Under conditions of increasing commercialization there is also a tendency to transform the traditional peasant sharecroppers into cash *tenants* to take advantage of increasing population density and the consequent pressure to bid up rents as well as to shift risk to the peasants. Whether or not large-scale commercial agriculture, small holding, or cash tenancy grows out of traditional peasantry is a product of such factors as the capital intensity of production, the value of the land, the annual fluctuations in crops and their price, and population density (see the Appendix to this chapter).

The peasant family is typically very strong because it is the basic cooperative economic unit. Extended families are often the norm (with 20 to 40 members not being uncommon). The sense of family solidarity is high, with the family head having considerable authority over members. Social status and self-esteem are normally defined by family identification and loyalties.

Peasant communities differ considerably in the degree of inter-family solidarity among members of the same village or neighborhood. In traditional Slavic communities (e.g., Poland, old Russia) as well as in much of the Near East there was a well-developed sense of village solidarity and mutual neighborhood assistance, cemented by an often elaborate exchange of gifts. In southern European peasant commun-ities such as those of southern Italy, as well as in most Latin American peasant villages, attitudes of mutual distrust, hostility, and fear have been more common. Here there is little mutual help, a prevailing attitude of avoiding contact with strangers, especially authorities, and a sense of resignation about one's lot.

Anthropologist Harry Tschopik described a prototype of the dis-trustful, family-oriented, antisocietal peasant Bolivian Aymara as

> anxious, apprehensive, brutal, careless, closed, cruel, depressed, dirty, dishonest, distrustful, doubtful, drunken, dull, fearful, filthy, gloomy, hostile, ignorant, insecure, irresponsible, jealous, malevolent, malicious, melancholic, morose, negative, pessimistic, pugnacious, quarrelsome, rancorous, reticent, sad, silent, sinister, slovenly, stolid, sullen, suspicious, tense, thieving, treacherous, truculent, uncom-municative, unimaginative, unsmiling, untrustworthy, violent, and vindictive (cited in Paige 1975, p. 30).

These characteristics, typical of Central and South American as well as southern European peasants, reflect a peasantry brutalized and exploited as *families* for centuries. The attitude that valuable goods are always in short supply, and that therefore one's family can only improve its lot at the expense of others, reflects the reality of a situation in which resources in the land are limited, and probably declining, because of hacienda or commercial farmer land grabs and increasing population density as well as hundreds of years of exploitation and manipulation by outsiders, such as tax collectors, military recruiters, agents for the landed estates, and so on. Hence the lesson, learned again and again, that one can only trust one's own family. Edward Banfield has characterized the attitudes of such peasants as "amoral familism." He illustrates this world view with a story told to him by a southern Italian peasant:

> Dr. Gino tells a story about a peasant father who throws his hat upon the ground. "What did I do?" he asks one of his sons. "You threw your hat upon the ground," the son answers, whereupon the father strikes him. He picks up his hat and asks another son, "What did I do?" "You picked up your hat," the son replies and gets a blow in his turn. "What did I do?" the father asks the third son. "I don't know," the smart one replies. "Remember, sons," the father concludes, "if someone asks you how many goats your father has, the answer is you don't know" (cited in Paige 1975, p. 31).

The tradition of peasant sharing, a remnant of more primitive equalitarian relations, continues to exist in areas where the dominant class came to exploit the peasants as *collectives*, allowing their villages considerable local autonomy, thus utilizing the old institutions of cooperation to ensure exploitation (rather then destroying them). In such areas the ancient traditions of solidarity, mutual support, and equal distribution of the burden survived. In contrast, peasant distrust (outside of familial relations) became the norm in areas where the traditional communities were destroyed and where the peasants came to be *directly* exploited by the landlords and state.

Most traditional peasant communities, whether they are permeated by a sense of distrust or have highly developed mutual aid networks, have strong pressures against change and an emphasis on conformity (although certain types of tenure under commercial conditions promote radicalization). Peasant conservatism normally leads to resistance to social and technological innovation. New things upset the traditional precarious economic balance as well as result in increased visibility (and hence potential trouble). As long as the traditional family needs are met there is no incentive or desire to innovate. Technological change raises the possibilities of trouble from outsiders who may well demand increased tribute or even threaten to expropriate one's land or steal one's newly acquired wealth. In the case of cooperative peasant communities, characteristic of the Slavic countries and much of the area where the Asiatic mode of production prevailed, the same types of social pressures operative in tribal equalitarian societies acted to ensure relative equality (including periodic land redistribution) and discourage individual incentive to innovate. Some forms of tenure especially tend to promote peasant conservatism, e.g., cotton sharecropping as well as commercial estates or haciendas that have high levels of supervision and control by the agrarian upper classes.

Under certain conditions, however, certain types of peasants (e.g., wet rice sharecroppers, small holders under market pressure), especially in areas where community traditions of solidarity survive, are susceptible to rapid and militant politicization (e.g., such groups were the social basis of revolutionary movements in Ireland, China, Vietnam, northern Italy, and the Philippines). An important element here is lack of supervision (and hence social space) as well as the high level of social solidarity promoted by the class homogeneity (and physical isolation from the agrarian upper class) that such a system entails.

THE TRIUMPH OF CAPITALIST RELATIONS OF PRODUCTION IN EUROPE

There is a qualitative difference between merchants, and industrial or productive capitalists. Only the latter produce wealth by the use of wage labor, i.e., utilize distinctively capitalist relations of production. Merchants can and have thrived, buying and selling goods, and loaning money produced by the full range of types of commodity production. Merchant capital has been especially important in slave, Asiatic (state peasant), private peasant, *and* capitalist modes of production (i.e., wherever production has primarily been for sale in markets).

Merchant capital has little or no logic of its own. It does *not* tend to transform relations of production or social structures except to make them still more commercial, i.e., to undermine remnants of serf and primitive communal relations. Productive capital on the other hand, has a transforming effect on class systems and social structures. Unlike merchant capital its long run effect is to create a world after its own image, i.e., to spread wage labor throughout the world while transforming the forces of production (see Szymanski 1981, chap. 4).

Merchant capital became increasingly important in Europe after 1100. It became politically *dominant* in Holland around 1600, in Great Britain with the English civil war in the 1640s, and even earlier in many city states in northern Italy and around the Baltic. The ascendancy of mercantile capital, however, did *not* affect the underlying (postserfdom) peasant relations of production in Europe on which the accumulation of mercantile wealth was based. Private tenant and yeoman relations of production (which had sprung from the contradictions of the serf mode of production) persisted until their contradictions forced a transformation to distinctively capitalist productive relationships. Merchant capital did not play the leading role in their transformation. Merchants did, however, loan money (when they expected a high rate of return) to the rising class of productive capitalists who were being generated out of the peasant mode of production. They thus *facilitated* the capitalist transformation without being responsible for it.

Industrial capitalism as the *predominant* mode of production arose in parts of northwestern Europe in the late eighteenth century and grew to maturity in the nineteenth, not because of a series of fortuitous accidents but rather because of the logic of the preexisting modes of production.* It did *not* grow out of serfdom (the classical European feudalism of the middle Ages). Serfdom in western Europe was on the decline from the twelfth century, and had in good measure been eliminated west of the Elbe by the eighteenth. Capitalism rather grew out of the contradictions of the *peasant* (or private landlord) mode of production prevalent from the fifteenth to eighteenth centuries in western Europe.

The transformation of serfdom into tenancy (supplemented by yeoman peasantry) was a direct result of the contradictions of the inefficient serf-lord (classical feudal) mode of production. The tendency of the lords to demand more and more from their serfs would seem to be the primary motor of the transformation of serfdom into tenant peasantry. Growing competition among the feudal lords for superior military forces (required not only to grow but to survive) and status (high standards of conspicuous consumption) as well as by the tendency of each lord to have two or more sons each of which wanted to be provided with the means to live in an aristocratic manner would seem to have been the driving forces for the growing appetite of the lords. The traditional system of feudal labor service where the serfs worked so many days a year on the lord's lands was not amenable to increasing productivity (because of the lack of incentives in this system), nor was it to increasing the number of days worked on the lord's lands (since the serfs had to work so many days a year on their own lands in order to feed themselves). The transformation of serfdom into tenancy (which incorporated a strong incentive to increase production) was thus a rational solution to the lord's demands for more.

---

*The discussion that follows is based on a wide variety of sources, the most important of which includes Anderson 1974a and 1974b; Bloch 1961; Dobb 1963; Cheyney 1936; Hacker 1940; Hilton 1976; Hobsbawm 1965; Moore 1966; Pirenne 1937; Polanyi 1957; Wallerstein 1974; and Wittfogel 1957.

The characteristics of, or "contradictions" in, peasant (tenant and yeoman farmer) relations of production greatly facilitated the development of capitalist relations of production in the urban areas of western Europe. These included the fact that tenants and yeoman farmers as free laborers were able to migrate to the cities to work in capitalist enterprises when they were pushed off the land by expanding commercial agriculture. The desperation of displaced tenants and yeomen was manifested in the very low wage rates of early capitalism (rates of wages that enabled the early enterprises to rapidly accumulate capital).

The commercializing of agriculture also resulted in internal differentiation among tenants and yeomen. The generation of a class of rich peasants with capital allowed for investment in small productive enterprises *outside* of the guild system, which greatly facilitated the accumulation of capital through the generation of a capitalist class out of the peasantry. The existence of a free tenant and yeoman class also facilitated the accumulation of wealth in the hands of merchants and moneylenders who got rich from trade with, and moneylending to, the rural producers. Merchant and moneylender fortunes also contributed to the development of capitalism by being invested in industrial production.

Further, yeoman farmers, but also many tenants (those who are able to sell part of their produce), provided an economic demand for the growing capitalist production of the cities. This was especially important as a source of mass demand for the cheap mass-produced textiles and other goods produced *outside* of the guild system (which came to revolutionize production). Last, the peasant mode of production, unlike unfree labor, required a relatively high level of skills, both in agriculture and, more importantly, in handicraft production that became available for capitalist enterprises.

The development of a free peasantry, however, could have taken two basic forms: either the consolidation of tenancy (i.e., sharecropping or cash renting for a private landlord who held basic property rights in the land); *or* state peasantry, with heavy tax payments to the state which held ultimate rights in the land, but that guaranteed the peasantry use of the land (including inheritance of *use* rights by either individuals or the village community as a whole) on condition of tax payment. The first mode of development implies a relatively weak central state, while the second implies a strong one. In regions where a strong central bureaucracy developed, such as through most of Asia, private landownership by landlords was rare. In regions such as Europe without such strong central states, powerful and wealthy aristocrats owned the land and collected rent from the peasants. An account of why tenancy rather than state peasantry developed in western Europe must then account for the factors that inhibited the development of a strong imperial bureaucracy there.

Unlike as in China or the Islamic world (where until the fifteenth century the forces of production were more advanced), there was no single political structure in Europe (which consisted of a multitude of small and highly competitive states). The consequence of the coexistence of small competitive states was that each had to facilitate the development of cities (and their bourgeoisie) in order to guarantee to themselves the advantages (especially financial and military) that they could provide. The advantage in warfare between the aristocratic states tended to go to those with the most prosperous cities. The European lords were then forced to compete among themselves in encouraging the growth of rich merchants and prosperous cities (and eventually an industrial capitalist class). If a lord were to suppress urban and bourgeois development, he put himself at a distinct economic and military disadvantage, and was consequently likely to disappear.

Political decentralization was thus a decisive factor in capitalist development. Had a single state been able to conquer the others and create an empire comparable to that of China or the Ottomans the impulse to capitalism would have been stymied (as it was in these other empires). Restrictions would have been put on the growth of the merchant and industrial capitalist classes to prevent them from accruing enough power to challenge that of the state, e.g., in China there were limits on the number of workers a wealthy man could employ, in other parts of Asia, confiscation of wealth upon the death of a wealthy man was the rule. But in the absence of a continental empire, each local European lord and king was forced to produce "their own grave diggers," the rising bourgeoisie—at first the relatively nonantagonistic merchants, but eventually the dynamic and antagonistic industrial capitalists.

The degree of political decentralization in Europe must in turn in good part be attributed to the distinctive logic of its characteristic mode of production, private landlord peasantry (in contrast to the state peasantry characteristic of the empires). The ecological conditions in western Europe, specifically the presence of adequate annual rainfall, (unlike as in much of the region from the Mediterranean to the South China Sea) did not require massive state-managed irrigation and flood control projects. More or less self-sufficient production lends itself to political decentralization.

The reason for the breakthrough to capitalism in Europe and the failure of previous attempts under similar social and political conditions must be attributed to the level of the productive forces achieved in the world by the eighteenth century. Similar impulses to the hegemony of capitalist relations of production in other places and at other times had been frustrated by the development of strong states that limited such developments. In other places and other times the productive forces were developing so slowly that aspiring emperors had time to fight it out among themselves and consolidate before the commercial classes became powerful enough to assume control of the societies (and facilitate the establishment of predominantly capitalist relations of production). Such was not the case in Europe, however.

The development of technology, especially of the sail and the gun, resulted in a very rapid increase in the wealth of the European commercial classes as well as provided a decisive advantage to whomever was politically closest to the commercial classes. The decisive technical innovations of the late Middle Ages, many of which occurred in China or the Arab world, did not have a revolutionizing effect on the economies of their region of origin because of the strong central states there. But they did have a decisive effect in Europe, which adopted and developed these technologies without the inhibiting effect of central bureaucracies. These technical developments (which because of the geographical diffusion of technical innovations must be considered to occur at the world level) occurred when Europe was decentralized and politically weak. Had another part of the world with similar relations of production been in a similar situation at this time capitalism as the predominant relation of production would have probably developed there as well.

The development of the productive forces *on the world level*, the product of the slow technological advance of the ages, had reached a decisive point in the seventeenth to eighteenth centuries. The world was now sufficiently technologically developed for the "takeoff" of capitalism. Those that controlled industrial technology were now potentially in a position to assume the leading role in society. Exactly where capitalism would breakthrough and become the predominant relation of production was a product of what part of the relatively developed world was decentralized enough (lacking in large and strong political units) during the period of sufficient technological attainment. The role fell to western Europe.

It was not an accident that Europe fit the conditions of having access to the technological advances being produced in the central empires as well as being politically decentralized. Western Europe was on the margins of the relatively developed world, which ranged from Japan in Northeast Asia through the central regions of China, India, Persia, the Arab world/Ottoman Empire to western Europe on the other extreme. Its backwardness and relative poverty as well as its geographical marginality (unattractive climate, lack of resources, and low population density) protected it from the military expansionist thrusts of the central empires, while it was at the same time close enough to be in continual economic contact with them. Other possible candidates for the development of capitalism during this period might have been such equivalent regions as Japan or parts of central Africa.

Crossing the threshold of technological change with its consequence of greater possibilities of accumulation of wealth, and hence power, in the hands of first the merchants and then increasingly the productive bourgeoisie, tended to make these groups the hegemonic class. This occurred first in Holland and England in the seventeenth and eighteenth centuries (with the ascendency of the commercial bourgeoisie), then in France in the late eighteenth century, throughout western and much of central Europe in the nineteenth century. As the period of Europe's hegemony wore on, the relative position of commercial and industrial capital was reversed, with industrial capital decisively subordinating commercial capital (e.g., in England in the early nineteenth century).

It should be noted that the commercial domination of most of the rest of the world achieved by Europe by the eighteenth century did *not* play a *decisive* role in the development of capitalist relations of production in Europe, although it did, of course, *facilitate* that process. Other world systems such as that of ancient Greece, the Roman Empire, the medieval Arabs as well as most of the great Asian empires (which systematically sought tribute from surrounding regions) had the advantage of wealth accumulation from satellite regions without any of them developing predominantly capitalist relations of production as a consequence. It was quite normal for both the classical empires and earlier commercial societies to amass large quantities of wealth which were merely extravagently consumed by their ruling classes. What must be explained is why the appropriation of much of the world's wealth by Europe from the sixteenth through the eighteenth centuries became a "primitive accumulation" which facilitated the triumph of capitalism in Europe, when equivalent wealth transfers never had in previous times and places.

The technical ability of Europe to commercially dominate so much of the world after the fifteenth century was a product of the logic of the peasant mode of production in Europe with its demand for greater material wealth, together with the political decentralization of the region that gave it the incentive to adopt and develop technology. The world commercial domination of Europe in turn resulted in the rapid expansion of commercial fortunes in Europe. Fortunes which in those parts of Europe where the contradictions of the peasant mode of production were ripe facilitated the development of distinctively capitalist relations of production by being loaned to the aspiring capitalist class. Thus the contradictions *within* the peasant mode of production, not the exploitative relations with what was to become the European periphery, must be understood as the key dynamic force behind the triumph of industrial capitalism in Europe.

The size of the political/economic units the new European bourgeoisie were interested in creating was much different from that of the early contestants for empire. While the Kings were interested in becoming emporers by conquering as many other countries as possible, expanding their wealth and power extensively on the model of all previous empires based on state peasant production, the new bourgeoisie was interested in state units of a specific size. They sought state territories big enough to guarantee a sufficiently profitable common market, but not so big as to incorporate competitors that threatened to gobble one up.

It is in the nature of commercial societies (with either merchants or capitalists in control) to tend to aggregate small units up to a critical point because of the guarantee of protected markets involved in larger units. Hence the bourgeoisie supported the economic and political integration of France in the eighteenth century and the economic and political integration of Germany and Italy in the nineteenth. Throughout the European world in the seventeenth to nineteenth centuries units of roughly the same general size and population tended to be created. Far from being an accidental product of diplomacy, this was a result of the working out of the forces of markets in societies where the bourgeoisie was gaining hegemony.

There was a considerable destabilizing or centrifugal force operating to break apart units any bigger than this maximal size. Commercial economies continually suffer from inadequate markets (insufficient demand). Any one merchant or capitalist is constantly in competition with the rest. There is only so much to go around, and the rest must suffer if some prosper. Each regional group of merchants then tends to cooperate to control their state so as to use it against the others. The creation of a European empire would then at best have only been supported by a part of the bourgeoisie in any aspiring imperial country (specifically that segment of the commercial classes that stood to gain economically). It would be systematically and effectively opposed by the bulk of the commercial classes in all other countries as well as by a significant segment of the bourgeoisie in the leading country. Further, if one country succeeded in expanding beyond its maximal economic size, centrifugal forces would be generated internally by the competition among different segments of the expanded bourgeoisie. Civil war and secession would thus tend to be produced, initiated by those segments of the bourgeoisie (national bourgeoisies) that were losing economically from the new common market. The modern European nation-states are a product of the logic of bourgeois domination.

SUMMARY

It appears that capitalist relations of production matured and became predominant in most of Europe in the nineteenth century because of three factors: first, the contradictions and propensities of the peasant mode of production; second, the general state of the productive forces in the world in the seventeenth and eighteenth centuries; and third, the political decentralization of Europe prior to the maturation of capitalism. All three factors are manifestations of the mode of production prevalent in Europe *before* the triumph of capitalism. The development and predominance of capitalism in Europe then must be attributed to the logic and contradictions in the mode of production that predated it in Europe, and not to any logic of commercial or market forces operating on a local or world level. Likewise, the failure of capitalism to triumph in the central empires of the world island must be attributed to their modes of production, specifically to the logic of state peasantry (the Asiatic mode), and to the logic of strong central imperial states that occurs with this mode of production. In conclusion, the conceptualization of mode of production in terms of relations and forces of production, and of capitalism as a productive relationship where labor power is a commodity, appears to be more useful in helping us understand why industrial capitalism occurred when and where it did, than do conceptualizations focusing on the *purpose* of production or on market forces.

APPENDIX

The Determinants of Rural Relations of Production

Relations of production embodying unfree labor (serfdom or slavery) occur under specific conditions. The greater the real opportunity of rural producers providing for their needs *without* having to work for a lord or master, the greater the probability that *unfree* labor will be the norm. In agricultural societies this means that the more plentiful the land, the higher the land/labor ratio, the more underpopulated a

---

The arguments in this section are drawn heavily from Dobb 1963, Paige 1975, Stinchcombe 1962, Stavenhagen 1975, and Wolf 1966.

region, the greater the labor shortage, and the more alternative opportunities to agriculture there are to earn a living, the more likely, other things equal, slavery or serfdom will develop. However, these factors are operative only when they are not counterbalanced by the need to promote the growth of an urban working force, *or* when the opportunities for escape by the rural producers are uncontrollable.

In situations where the lords of the land want to encourage the growth of cities because of the value of urban produce, because of the trade goods cities make available, or because of the taxes they provide, the lords must allow the producers to leave the land and go to the cities. Historically, the conflict between the needs of the landlords to secure their own labor force and to promote the growth of cities led to a rule in much of feudal Europe that serfs that escaped to a town would be formally free a year and a day after their escape.

The very different interests of the lords of the land in the growth of cities in eastern and in western Europe produced opposite results in terms of the trends in unfree/free labor after the fifteenth century. The lords of western Europe needed cities within their domains as the best way to secure both luxury and military goods. They were driven to procure both, not only because of vanity and ambition but also by the competition with the multitude of other lords (who threatened to displace them), together with the tendency for the aristocracy to increase in size over time (because aristocratic women mostly gave birth to many sons). In eastern Europe, which was technologically more backward than western Europe, however, the most effective way for the lords to secure luxury and military goods was not to encourage the growth of cities in their domains, but rather to trade with western Europe where cities had already developed. The west was ready and able to provide what the lords wanted and to buy what they could produce using unfree labor. Here low labor/land ratios resulted in the development of serfdom, at the same time as it was being abolished in the west.

Whether or not the factors associated with a low labor/land ratio or a labor shortage manifest themselves in unfree labor also depends on the technical and political abilities of the lords of the land to prevent their producers from escaping to areas over which they have no effective control. This in turn is a function of the efficiency of their police and military and the degree of political coordination of large geographical units. These factors in turn are a function of both technical and legitimation factors. If there are accessible regions of wilderness where the lords exercise no effective control, or there are other domains hostile to the local lords and willing to accept refugees, then the feasibility of unfree labor is undermined by the lure of escape; likewise, if the lord's police are unable to control squatters on marginal land. Under such conditions a low labor/land ratio (or labor shortage) can have the opposite result, i.e., produce a lower, rather than a higher, probability of unfree labor.

Where the *market* power of the agrarian upper class is weak, but where they are *politically* powerful, either unfree labor systems or labor systems where the producers have little in the way of civil rights tend to develop. Where the upper class has little wealth outside of the land itself and can only afford to maintain the producing class at a level significantly lower than they could obtain in alternative employments (e.g., as urban or mine laborers), the political power of the landowning class is used to force the rural producers to stay on the land either through formal ties (serfdom, debt peonage, and so forth) or by restricting alternative economic opportunities (e.g., apartheid). This can take the form of prohibiting employment of rural producers in factories, reserving such positions for people of a different "race" (e.g., the system adopted in both South Africa and the South of the United States after the Civil War) or putting restrictions (formal or informal) on emigration.

On the other hand, where the market power of the agrarian upper class is strong, whether or not it is also politically powerful, wage labor or family small holdings with formal civil rights for the producers tends to develop. Control of credit, agricultural machinery, and supply and purchasing institutions by the agrarian upper class as well as a shortage of land held by anyone other than the agrarian upper class means that tenants or wage laborers have little option but to accept rents so high or wages so low as to guarantee land-owners a great profit. Further, under these same conditions small landowners must buy, sell, and borrow in markets where considerable monopoly power is held by the upper class, and hence considerable wealth can be extracted from them *without* political coercion.

Unfree labor can develop when the lot of the poor free peasants becomes desperate due to unstable political and military conditions (e.g., constant warfare among lords or pillage and plunder by outlaws or foreigners that is difficult to control), or a decreasing standard of living, which lead the free either to sell their relatives into slavery to improve their plight or to enserf themselves voluntarily in order to secure the protection of a lord and the right to work the land. This happens, however, only when the lord has an interest in preferring unfree labor over tenancy. Thus its occurrence must be attributable to the factors that produce the lord's preferences.

Unfree labor is best suited to production processes that require little skill or care, i.e., labor-intensive tasks that use a low level of technology, and in which efficiency and productivity are relatively unimportant. Unfree laborers typically have little or no incentive to do a careful job. The ideology of the inferiority of the producers, necessary to mystify unfree labor, has the contradictory effect of both encouraging and justifying "laziness," "stupidity," "clumsiness," and the lack of initiative on the part of the unfree. Therefore unfree labor is more prevalent the less developed are the forces of production and the more suited the crops and land are for labor-intensive unskilled production processes. Certain crops, such as sugarcane, which require very little skill or care when produced by traditional methods, are thus naturally suited to slavery. In general, the most productive land, which requires no fertilization or irrigation and produces well even with bad cultivation practices, lends itself to unfree labor.

Whether or not slavery (where the producers are bought and sold, and have no rights in the land or their tools) or serfdom (where the producers are bound to the land, but have rights in both the land and their bodies) develops depends on the role of markets in a region. Slavery as a *dominant relation of production* arises and is maintained only in highly commercialized economies with great demand for the export crops it produces. It is geared to extensive cultivation on plantations producing for the world market. Serfdom on the other hand tends to occur where there is relatively little market for export crops and where cultivation tends to be for subsistence with a surplus going to the lords. Serfdom, however, is intermediate between free peasantry and slavery, and thus movement from the one to the other typically passes through the intermediate stage of serfdom, as the pressure for one or the other form develops within a commercial economy. Thus, the "second serfdom" of eastern Europe in the seventeenth to nineteenth centuries transformed the former peasantry into virtual slaves (in Russia serfs could be and were sold separately from the land) because of the pressure of export markets. However, before full-fledged slavery became general in Russia, social forces began to operate to move the typical labor relationships on the land back to traditional peasantry, with reliance on taxes and rent instead of direct exploitation of slaves as the best way to profit from the producer's labor.

Serfdom is undermined by the growth of demand for goods, i.e., by the fact that it is a relatively inefficient mode of production. But whether or not it is transformed in the direction of slavery, peasantry, or wage labor depends on many different factors. It must be stressed, though, that there is nothing about increasing commercial demand that necessarily generates increasing freedom for the producers. Increasing demand can just as well take away the traditional rights of serfs, reducing them to slaves.

Peasant relations of production (with either tenants engaging in sharecropping or renting from a local landlord *or* producers having ownership or use rights in the land and paying a tax to the state) tend to develop under certain specific conditions. Peasantry can develop either out of serfdom (as it did in late middle ages in Europe), out of slavery (as it did in some areas of the Caribbean after the abolition of slavery, such as in the U.S. South), or out of tribally organized rural producers living in village communities (as apparently happened in most of the ancient empires of Asia).

Peasant tenancy tends to develop where taxes or rents (in money, in a proportion of the crop, or in a fixed quantity of the crop) brings in more to the landowning class or the state than a requirement of labor services with direct supervision and tying the producers to the land. This tends to be the case in areas where there is a high labor/land ratio (overpopulation or scarcity of land), i.e., where rural people are without alternative ways to secure a living independent of working for a landlord or the state. Under conditions of overpopulation it is to a landlord's advantage to release his serfs from their traditional ties and obligations as well as to eliminate their traditional rights in the land, since they have no alternative but to stay on the land. To stay on the land they must produce more surplus for the lord than was traditional because of the real possibility of being displaced by other (landless) tenants willing to produce more. Population pressure generates competition among free peasants for the scarce land of the lords, and hence allows the lords to increase rents. The increasing share demanded by the lords in turn provides a motive for the tenants to increase their productivity in order to maintain their level of living. Thus, while the direct supervision of serfdom is undercut, the pressure of increasing rents drives peasant tenants to increase productivity more rapidly than was possible under serfdom.

Peasant tenancy tends to arise in those areas with highly productive soils (and where land is expensive), and in crops that require more care and concern by the producers. It tends to develop where the most profitable crops are labor intensive and require little capital or mechanization, where there are no appreciable economies of scale, and where labor is cheap. Whether or not an adequate crop is produced depends much more on the self-motivation of the producers than it does in unfree labor systems.

The requirements of labor intensity and relatively low capital investment for peasant tenancy generally mean that tenancy is found where the crops are annuals and require only minimal processing, not in the areas of perennials like sugar, and tree fruits that require a significant capital outlay and year to year continuity of care. The insecurity of tenure (especially for sharecroppers) means that their interest lies in exploiting the soil and crops as fully and immediately as possible (at the cost of long-term productivity)' producing an affinity for tenancy (especially sharecropping) with annual rather then perennial crops.

Tenancy is most common in areas requiring a relatively high level of care in crop production, but which utilize a low level of technology, e.g., in wet rice and traditional cotton production. The higher the level of agricultural technology the more important both *skill* and *care* as well as the greater necessity for centralized control and supervision of the labor process. At low levels of the productive forces producers can be pretty much left to themselves even when great care is needed in the production process. However, with high levels of capital investment in advanced machinery, a complex division of labor that requires close supervision and control as well as care and skill is required to maintain profitability. Hence the development of modern agricultural machinery and techniques dictates the transformation of peasant agriculture into corporate plantations or farms utilizing wage laborers.

The degree of social differentiation among the peasantry, a result of the degree of development of market forces, is also an important factor in the prevalence of private landlord peasant tenancy. On the one hand, the rise of poor landless peasants generates a class of desperate people who must become sharecroppers or cash renters (if not wage workers) in order to maintain their traditional living standards. On the other hand, the development of a class of commercial farmers out of rich peasants means that a class of people with money can buy land to rent to the still subsistence-oriented poor peasants.

Sharecropping, especially in its purest forms (which is generally associated with an impoverished peasantry), is most common in areas of extremely high land values where population density is high, cultivation is intense, and (often) irrigation is common. With its relatively high tenant turnover and high rate of exploitation, sharecropping generally stabilizes only in those areas where the agrarian upper class has considerable political power over the producing class, i.e., where the producing class has few civil rights and where the upper class can use state power to hinder the emigration of croppers off the land (in pursuit of higher incomes elsewhere). Small holding is generally more efficient than sharecropping with the same crops and type of land since it provides better long-term incentives to the producers to improve the land; and, thus, providing the cost of land (and irrigation) is not prohibitively high, small holding tends to replace sharecropping under conditions of unrestricted competition (where there are no politically enforced constraints on sharecroppers).*

In the eighteenth and nineteenth centuries in Europe private landlord peasantry tended to grow into rural wage labor and petty bourgeois commerial farmer production. Commercial family farmers, unlike traditional peasants, are not subsistence oriented. They rather tend to produce almost entirely for the market where they themselves also purchase their necessities of life. They are not generally required to turn over a high proportion of their product in rents and taxes. To the extent their product goes to others it is in the form of a cash rent to a landlord, mortgage payments to a bank and the transfer of value to corporations because of the effect of monopolized markets in the commodities the farmer must purchase and competitive markets in the farmer's products.

Commercial family farmers tend to develop either out of a tenant peasantry after a revolution or land reform that takes ownership of the land away from the aristocracy or state and turns it over to the former tenants (thus transforming them into family landowners) *or* in regions of recent settlement on previously sparsely inhabited land, such as in the United States in the eighteenth and nineteenth centuries. It also tends to develop out of a peasantry (mostly from yeomen) under conditions of increasing commercialization that produces significant internal differentiation among the peasants (specifically the development of a rich peasantry that can afford to buy land and equipment).

Family farmers, even more than tenants, normally tend to relatively labor-intensive production with low capital requirements (since they have plenty of hands—all family members work—but normally have very little to invest in expensive equipment). Crops that are annual and methods of production without significant economies of scale tend to produce family farming. There is also a tendency for commercial family farming to develop in crops in which there are wide fluctuations in price (e.g., wheat, rubber, vegetables). Here the producers, rather than the agrarian upper classes, bear the cost of the fluctuations.

---

*It should be noted that small holders, either fixed cash renters or owners, can be efficiently exploited on highly productive, high-priced land through high rent or mortgage payments as well as through unequal exchange.

In regions of mixed forms of land tenure (e.g., wage labor, tenants, and family farmers, or slaves, tenants, and farmers) commercial farming tends to develop on the *least* productive, and hence least costly, land. Here the best land is incorporated into large estates (which rent it out) or plantations (which use slaves or menial wage labor).

Under conditions of high capital intensity and advanced means of production, which dictate relatively high levels of skill and care in production, and where there are significant economies of scale as well as the cost of land being out of reach of most producers, wage labor tends to be the dominant relationship in agriculture.

Wage labor develops in commercial conditions where wages can be low because of a population surplus on the land, in those crops and with those methods of production which are relatively capital intensive (in perennial and highly mechanized crops), where there are economies of scale (which facilitate large coordinated production units), and where a relatively high level of skill and care is required in crop production. Rural wage labor also tends to develop out of both unfree labor and peasantry when there is abundant cheap land or alternative employment at attractive remuneration *and* the land-owning class is either not willing or politically not able to keep the rural work force from moving except through offering attractive wages. In western Europe, with the rise of cities, there was a tendency to alleviate the economic burden on both the serfs and the peasants and in some places to go over to wage labor at a relatively high level of remuneration to keep the producers from leaving for the cities (here there was little interest in blocking the development of cities or prohibiting emigration to them, as there was in eastern Europe).

Other things equal, wage labor tends to be preferred over tenancy, not only in those crops that require greater capital investment and have economies of scale, but also in many animals and crops that are less labor intensive but amenable to supervision (e.g., wool, sheep, rubber, fruit, coffee). Wage labor is, of course, also facilitated by market-induced internal differentiation in the peasantry, which creates a class of landless laborers forced by their desperation to sell their labor power (and where the landowners are unwilling to rent them land because they see hired labor as more profitable than tenancy).

There might be considered to be four basic types of distinctively *capitalist* agriculture (landowners utilizing *wage labor*). The first type occurs on plantations that tend to operate on the most productive land, employ an unskilled, low-paid, and especially oppressed labor force (lacking in civil rights), require large capital investment (but are nevertheless labor intensive), and do not require high levels of skill or care in the production process. The antecedents of capitalist plantations generally used unfree labor (e.g., slaves in the Caribbean region) or contract or indentured labor directly supervised by the landowners.

Plantations utilizing wage labor are most likely to prevail in perennial (mostly tropical) crops that require a substantial bulk reduction (e.g., sugar, sisal, tea, oil palm) as well as a continuing labor supply for most of the year. Plantations are also common in crops which, although they do not require substantial reduction (and hence do not require substantial fixed capital investments in such things as sugar mills and cotton gins), require continuous 12-month harvesting (e.g., rubber). It should be noted that rubber—unlike sugar, tea, oil palm, or sisal—neither requires great amounts of capital investment, nor benefits from economies of scale. It can be produced just as efficiently by small holders as by plantations. Thus, plantations, rather than small holding, tends to prevail in rubber-producing areas only where the agricultural upper class has reduced the producing class to a distinctively inferior political position lacking in civil rights (and where often a degree of compulsion is involved in the owner-worker relationship).

The second type of capitalist agriculture is found on capital-intensive ranches that employ few workers on extensive and inexpensive grazing land (e.g., cattle, sheep). Labor on ranches is not closely supervised, requires more autonomy as well as care and skill, and hence is generally rewarded better than plantation or migrant labor.

A third occurrence is on farms using migrant labor, which require massive amounts of labor only for short periods, mostly during the harvest season (but sometimes during planting as well). This system is most common with perennial tree crops that are too valuable to be trusted to tenants, and generally need a few weeks of intensive labor (during the harvest) each year (e.g., coffee, grapes). Since the types of crops produced in this system could generally be produced almost as well by small holders (since they do not require inordinate capital investment or have great economies of scale) the prevalence of this system generally depends on an especially servile (often lacking in civil rights) labor force (i.e., since the market position of commercial farmers using migrant wage labor is weak). They must resort to political means (or at least to their political advantage) to maintain their labor supply. Such has been the case in the fruit and vegetable farms of the West Coast of the United States that have, since their inception, used a long succession of noncitizen or politically disadvantaged groups as their primary labor supply.

Migrant laborers either tend to move north and south with the harvesting season (often moving from crop to crop as well), or to work on commercial farms for only part of a year, working their own subsistence plots for the rest of the year. The first is most common in areas with many crops and very short harvesting seasons (e.g., fruits and vegetables), while the latter is most common in single-crop areas with long harvesting seasons. In many areas of Africa and Latin America a system has developed in which the rural producers maintain their traditional subsistence plots in areas (on the poorest land) far from the commercial crop areas (on the best land) to grow much of their own food during the off season. This system has the advantages of allowing wages to be low in the commercial sector (since the producer for part of the year, and his family for all of the year, are growing most of their own food), while at the same time establishing a reserve that provides extra labor in especially good years and absorbs redundant labor in bad years (thus keeping the labor force near the farms, rather than leaving for other regions in search of work). In this type of system commercialization produces a dual economy in which labor is performed by worker-peasants. A highly commercial, typically export-oriented, sector symbiotically coexists with a traditional subsistence peasant sector. It should be noted that the maintenance of worker-peasants in such dual systems, by inhibiting the development of a homogeneous rural proletariat, hinders the development of radical class consciousness.

A fourth type of capitalist agriculture, which employs full-time yearround workers, could be labeled industrial agriculture. It develops where agriculture is highly mechanized (especially at the harvest) and capital intensive, and where productivity differentials on large units utilizing advanced technology (compared to nonmechanized small units) are considerable. Here the difference between urban industrial workers and rural workers has essentially disappeared.

As the forces of production advance under pressure from capitalist markets there is a long-term trend away from the plantation and migrant labor variants of capitalist agriculture as well as away from ranches toward industrial agriculture. The potential productivity increases and greater profits obtainable from capital-intensive food and fiber production processes become increasingly manifest. There is a strong tendency for all aspects of farming to become highly mechanized and even automated (e.g., chicken and egg factories, tree farms, milk production, and so forth), with the consequence of the disappearance of the need for seasonal or migrant labor as well as unskilled politically disenfranchised workers and highly autonomous tenants. Rural producers are, thus, becoming homogeneous with the urban working class.

The displacement of peasant and small holder production by capitalist agriculture is a relatively recent development in the history of capitalism. It is not until the development of the productive forces in agriculture reached a very high level, thereby pushing the great mass of peasant tenant and family farmers off the land, that capitalist agriculture blossomed. During the period of the growth and consolidation of capitalism, precapitalist relations of production predominated in agriculture, i.e., unfree labor in eastern Europe and the Caribbean, and peasant tenancy and family farming in western Europe and the North of the United States, while various forms of peasantry/semiserfdom prevailed in Latin America, south Asia, and the South of the United States after 1865. The accumulation of capital in the cities was consequently greatly facilitated by the exploitation of serfs, slaves, peasants, and farmers from whom value was transferred to industrialize the cities. It was not until the advanced period of monopoly capitalism that capital came to transform rural relations in the world capitalist system (both in the industrialized and less-developed countries) into distinctively capitalist relationships.

3

The Class Structure of Advanced Capitalism

Classes are places or *positions* in the social structure of a society. They are neither a set of individuals, nor statistical aggregates of individual characteristics. Classes are the components of societies, not properties of individuals. Individuals occupy class positions within a social structure.*

It is the properties of classes, not of individuals, that are central to the logic of class, and hence of social structure. Individuals, then, can be referred to as "agents" of production, or carriers of productive relationships. As agents or carriers, given individuals can move from one class to another, while the class structure remains the same. Most individuals in a given society tend to fit fairly well at any given time into one or another class position, but some, because of multiple jobs or sources of income, or the intermediate status of their job, do not.

CLASSES AS RELATIONS OF PRODUCTION

Classes are relationships generated and reproduced within the productive processes or economic life of a given type of society or mode of production. Classes are, then, *relations of production*. Classes are relationships of power over labor within economic processes. Such power over labor encompasses: first, property or "real economic

---

*The discussion in this section is heavily indebted to the work of Carchedi 1977, Poulantzas 1974, and Wright 1978.

ownership,"—control over the means of production, including the power to assign the means of production to given uses (including *how much* and *what* is produced), to invest profits, and to dispose of the product; and second, "possession," or operational control, including *how* things are produced—the capacity to put the means of production into operation, and authority over supervision and discipline of workers within the labor process.

Real economic ownership can be *legal* ownership (ownership rights that can be bought and sold, at least in a commercial economy, and inherited by one's children or other assigned heirs). Legal ownership is generally more secure than real ownership that is not sanctified in law and, further, is considerably less constrained by the claims and demands of others. However, it is sometimes the case that those with legal title to property exercise neither real economic ownership nor operational control because legal ownership is widely dispersed. Here a few with control of the greatest concentrations of stock may well have real economic ownership. Some who have and exercise real economic ownership grant operational control over the means of production to others, receiving an income from their property without being involved in routine decision making (e.g., an absentee landlord or heir of a family fortune). In defining classes, real economic ownership is central, i.e., neither legal title nor operational control is a necessary criterion of class position.

The organization of control over the production process is structured to generate wealth for those in control, i.e., to secure an income as a result of the sale of the product of the production process that is greater than the payment for labor power (direct and indirect in the form of equipment and supplies) that had to be purchased in order to secure the product. The purpose of production in class societies, then, is to obtain "surplus labor" (or "surplus value"). Since relationships of control over the production process are inherently relations of exploitation, corresponding to the relations of ownership and non-ownership are the derivative relations of exploiters and exploited.

In a class society the basic classes are relations of opposition that exist in mutual antagonism. Since classes can not exist in isolation; it is impossible to have merely one class. The existence of a class with power over the labor power of others logically implies the existence of a class that labors, but does not control its own labor. The existence of an exploiting class logically implies the existence of an exploited class. Because classes are relationships of power and exploitation they are relations of domination and subordination. Because they are structures of domination and subordination, struggle and conflict between the classes are an inherent part of the class structure. To one degree or another on a day-to-day basis a subordinate and dominated class will attempt to reduce its subordination, domination, and exploitation, and increase its power over the productive process. Likewise, the dominant class will act on a day-to-day basis to increase its control over labor power as well as the degree of exploitation.

The very existence of an owning-exploiting class depends on class practices designed to increase power and exploitation. The very nature of powerlessness and exploitation, given the qualities of human beings pressed into such class positions, implies resistance and the attempt to improve one's condition. Class consciousness, or a coherent "discourse" that explicitly defends class interest, is *not* necessary for class struggle to take place. While such *might* be the case, simple day-to-day actions to limit output, break equipment, avoid supervision, and so forth are part of class struggle.

Classes are historically concrete. They are defined by the logic of a historically specific type of society, or mode of production, such as capitalism, slavery, or feudalism. They are not merely positions of power and exploitation in the abstract. Various exploiting and controlling classes are, thus, defined by their specific type of property (or mode of control over labor power): simple control over land (landlords); simple control over factories, mines, transportation equipment, and so forth (capitalists); control over unfree laborers who can be bought and sold (slave lords); control over land and unfree laborers attached to the land who can not be sold (feudal lords); and so on. Comparable historically specific exploited classes are implied within each of these modes of production, e.g., peasants, proletarians, slaves, and serfs. Each of the different exploiting classes has qualitatively different characteristics—economic, social, and political—from the others. Likewise, each of the exploited classes, while they share the lot of dominated menial laborers, has qualitatively different economic, social, and political characteristics. The character of both the exploiting and the exploited classes is a product of the mode of production that generates both.

A given society, or social formation, may contain more than one mode of production, e.g., slavery and capitalism might coexist as they did in the United States until 1867. Thus, slave lords, capitalists, proletarians, and slaves can coexist within the same social formation. Two systems can be mutually supportive, as occurred in the United States prior to 1867 where slaves produced cotton that was sold to be processed into cloth in capitalist enterprises (much of which was purchased by the slave lords).

Likewise, today, the independent commodity production of family farmers and artisans (although declining in importance) continues to exist side by side with capitalism, as it once did with feudalism and the peasant mode of production, thus generating an independent petty bourgeoisie. This does not mean that the independent petty bourgeoisie is economically independent of capital, for most of the product of the small family farms is sold to corporations, while other corporations provide most of the equipment they purchase, and the banks to which they are in debt oversee their decision making. Just as the modern slave system was a product of the capitalist world economy, so too contemporary independent commodity production is thoroughly a product of the capitalist world economy.

Class position is generally the most important factor in one's life. Daily life experience, life chances, and life-style are pretty much structured by individual class position, and that of the class positions of parents and spouse. Class position heavily influences all patterns of social interaction, including family life (marriage and children), friends (largely people with a similar class position), and neighborhood (and the interactions and life chances that these produce). In turn family life, friendship networks, and neighborhoods, together with income and other on-the-job experiences, pretty much produce patterns of leisure, political attitudes, and even religious involvement.

Class position, then, tends to give rise to organic social groups formed on the basis of common class position—social classes. Social class can, then, be defined as a socially coherent set of families based on a common class position which share a generally common life-style, social status, traditions, customs, and consciousness; *and* which feel socially comfortable with and have intimate access to one another—as manifested in a propensity to freely intermarry. Intermarriage is probably the best single acid test of comparable status as well as an important source of ties that bind a social class together through overlapping networks of kinship.

While it is individuals that occupy class positions, the composite units of social class are families. The intimate relations between people that are part of the same household, and who thereby share the most intimate aspects of their lives, means that the impact of the class position of those members of the family unit who work outside the home tends to permeate the consciousness and structure, the life-style, and social and political behavior of all members of the family. If more than one member of a nuclear family works outside the home, it tends to be the class position of the family member with the greatest power in the production process that overrides the impact of the class position of those other members with less power in the production process in structuring the consciousness, life-style, and social and political behavior of all members of the family. Thus, if one's spouse is an independent professional such as a doctor or lawyer and the other is a sales clerk or typist their life-style, the family income, their friendship networks, their neighborhood, the future class positions of their children, and so forth will tend to be petty bourgeois. Thus, social class is operationally defined in terms of the family member with the "highest" class position. Since it is difficult to obtain statistical data on the "highest" class position within each family, social scientists often approximate this by taking the class positions of married *men* as an estimate of the measure of social class. Such a practice produces results that differ little from the real social class structure since, because of the traditional assignment of women to housework and low-level menial jobs, there are very few families in which wives have a "higher" level job than the husband.

Some groups with very distinct traditions and culture who share a common class position may have their social role and customs, especially the rules of whom they marry and what occupations they and their children can and can not pursue, enshrined in law. Many societies have forbidden working people to adopt the clothing of higher groups as well as have forbidden the men of the laboring classes from having sexual relations (in or out of marriage) with women of the dominant class. It is not necessary that such prohibitions and customs are enforceable by the state; strong social sanctions and tightly organized social class communities can be sufficient to preserve a highly rigidified and hierarchical pattern of social classes. In such structures one's class (and typically occupation as well) is normally automatically inherited by one's children (to fully reproduce the class structure with all its sharp and elaborate social and cultural distinctions from generation to generation). Such crystallized social classes are called castes. Leading examples of caste structure include the traditional elaborate Indian class structure where each caste traditionally had a different class position; feudal Europe, which was divided into an aristocracy, peasantry, and the (Jewish) commercial caste, each of which had legal restrictions on its class practices and marriage patterns; and the Southern states of the United States, where the black ex-slaves formed a distinctive caste largely of share-croppers, menial domestics, and urban laborers reinforced in their caste position by bans on intermarriage and a multitude of caste-defining Jim Crow laws.

Classes vary considerably in the degree to which they share a common life-style, custom, habits, and so on as well as in the degree to which they intermarry and otherwise feel socially comfortable with others of the same class position. Some sets of families which share a common class position do not form a social class. They may not freely intermarry with others in the same class position, nor share common customs, traditions, consciousness, or life-style. In fact, they may not even share a common language. Such was the case in the multinational, multilingual, multireligious urban working class in the Northern cities of the United States between the Civil War and the 1930s, where there were many different ethnic groups each one of which tended to maintain its separate ethnic culture and identity rather than form part of a single social class. Thus, periods of very rapid immigration from diverse rural areas into rapidly industrialized regions tend to be periods in which the working class is not constituted as a social class. However, it should be stressed, a few generations in the same *industrial* area generally results in those in a similar class position losing their ethnic uniqueness, and consequently in the formation of a homogeneous social class (on the basis of the similarities in life experiences and interests generated by a shared class position).

Just as a periods of rapid social dislocation such as industrialization and massive immigration tend to be followed by periods of social class formation, periods of lengthy economic stability and slow geographical mobility tend to generate increasing rigidification or crystallization, as social class, with or without the legal sanction of the state, tends to assume a greater and greater role in the life of families. Castes are also formed through force, either when one group militarily conquers the territory of another (such as happened in India or in areas of East Africa), or imports another group to work as slaves (e.g., the Caribbean area from the seventeenth to nineteenth centuries) or menial laborers with few legal rights (e.g., East Indians or Chinese "coolies" who were brought into the Caribbean by the British after the abolition of slavery). Castes sometimes also form purely through the taking up of certain economic roles primarily by a given ethnic group, even when force or legal sanction is not employed to maintain them (for example, various ethnically based merchant groups throughout the less-developed countries—Indians in East Africa, Chinese in Southeast Asia, Lebanese in West Africa, Armenians in the Near East, and, formerly, Jews in central Europe).

The members of a well-formed social class are normally conscious of class. They can correctly outline the social class structure of society, recognize class boundaries and barriers, have a sense for the differences in power and status among the classes as well as identify themselves as being in a common economic and social position with other members of their social class.

However, a social class does not necessarily form what Marx has called a class for itself—a social class which is both conscious of its common class interest against other classes and which acts more or less as a coherent or organic social actor in pursuit of its correctly perceived interests.* Social classes might sometimes act more or less as a political unit, but around a false or erroneously perceived common interest, or sometimes might not, in fact, be mobilized to act as a unit even when it does have a generally correct understanding of its common class interest. To be a class for itself, however, a social class must have: first, class consciousness, i.e., have a *true* (correct or scientific) understanding of its class interests; and second be a coherent unit that is mobilized politically as an active force in pursuit of its interests. The members of a class for itself tend to identify their personal interests with their class interests and thus if necessary, put the interests of their class before those of themselves and their families.

False consciousness is in good part reproduced by the control of the dominant class of the means of *mental* production. Normally in a class society, the owning class controls the schools, dominant churches, the mass media, and other means by which abstract phenomena removed from the daily life of people are defined, such as the nature of other societies, the possibilities of alternative forms of social organization, the ultimate criterion of good and evil, and so on. The more abstract such understandings are (the more removed they are from the daily life of the common people), the more people are open to believing what they hear in the churches, schools, or media.

The state plays a central role in class society in preserving and reproducing the class structure. The ability of the dominant class to maintain its privileges rests largely on control over state agencies, whether as in slave or feudal society by making class position legally enforceable, and forcibly repressing any attempt at modifying the class structure, or an individual's attempt to change classes, *or* as in capitalist society by indirectly reinforcing the class system by institutionalizing the market (which generates class inequality), repressing attempts to radically modify class structure, controlling education and much of the media (which produces an ideology of legitimation of class structure), and so forth.

The probabilities of class consciousness are in good part determined by the degree of collectivity of labor. Structures that organize large groups of workers in a complex division of labor (highly socialized labor) under conditions that isolate them from the owning class and its agents are highly conducive to generating class consciousness. This process is facilitated if in addition industry is located

---

*By "interest" is meant that course of action which would rationally maximize the chances of obtaining the needs and wants of an individual or group in a given social position.

in a class-homogeneous city or in an isolated area (e.g., a mining town) that allows the workers to form fairly class-homogeneous communities isolated from cross-class pressures. The probability of developing class consciousness is also affected by such other structural factors as the ability to talk on the job (e.g., classical cigar makers), oppressiveness of labor (e.g., assembly line workers), and centrality in the overall productive process (e.g., transport workers).

The class structure not only pretty much determines the probability of developing class consciousness, and hence the *agents* of class struggle; but it also defines the potential *objectives* of class struggle (the feasibility of nationalization, increased wages, the reality of socialist revolution), the organizational *capacities* of classes, the training in discipline and leadership given by the production processes (which together with their size and geographic concentration produce their mobilizable strength), and hence the probable *outcomes* of class struggle.

The class structure itself is subject to the logic of the mode of production that generates it—in capitalist society, the dynamic logic and contradictions of the capital accumulation process as well as the development of the productive forces it induces. Thus, in the last analysis to understand the logic and dynamic of class struggle, one must understand the logic and dynamic of the mode of production within which it occurs.

Class struggle, while a product of the logic of class structure, itself influences the process of class formation, social class formation, and the development of class consciousness. For example, active struggle by a middle class in a social formation *could* result in the state's implementing measures to preserve small farmers and artisans against competitive pressures from monopolization, thus slowing down the shrinking of the independent sector of the middle class as well as the growth of the managerial sector. Similarly (working) class struggle could persuade capital to slow the construction of large modern plants (which tend to structurally generate a class-conscious working class) and resort instead to seasonal labor (e.g., as in South Africa) or greater reliance on petty commodity production. Class struggle can influence social class formation. In the process of class conflict the emerging social classes may develop traditions and build friendship networks among themselves and antagonisms to the owning class that give form to social classes (e.g., the struggles of European workers from the 1830s). Alternatively, because certain groups do not participate in the class struggle, the formation of social class may be hindered (e.g., the increased hostility to blacks who were sometimes used as strikebreakers in pre–World War I industrial battles in the United States).

Class struggle, furthermore, can influence the degree to which different segments of the laboring class or middle class come to see themselves as part of the working class or middle class (and hence in good part determines their role in the overall class struggle). This effect is probably particularly important for those intermediate in position between the three basic classes (e.g., police, elementary teachers, foremen) who can identify either with the middle class or the laboring class and, thus, are open to being mobilized by one or the other group.

Changes in class structure are in the last analysis a product of changes in the mode of production. Classes first arose in response to contradictions between tribal societies and their environments. Slavery arose and declined in response to the relative availability of labor and economic productivity. Serfdom arose in response to problems with slavery, and then declined because of the greater efficiency of free peasantry. Wage labor developed as the cheapest mode of production in areas of surplus population and expanding markets.

Within the capitalist mode of production during the twentieth century the processes that have produced the most basic changes in the class structure have included the increasing role of the large corporations whose efficiency has driven most small farmers and other independent artisans and proprietors out of business (to swell the ranks of both the working class and the managerial sector of the middle class), and the corresponding increased importance of coordination, sales, finance, supervision, planning, and so forth that has produced a large managerial stratum within the middle class on the one side and the large clerical-sales strata of the working class on the other.

THE CLASS STRUCTURE OF CONTEMPORARY CAPITALIST SOCIETIES

In the capitalist mode of production the relation between the owning and laboring class is one of wage labor.* Here the wealth of the dominant class is generated by hiring free laborers (laborers who are both free to work for whomever will hire them, and free of owning any significant means of production, and who, therefore, *must* sell their labor power in order to live) and by paying them less in wages than the value of what they produce. Wage labor, as opposed

---

*The discussion in this section is indebted to Carchedi 1977, Hill 1975, Loren 1977, Poulantzas 1974, and Wright 1978.

to slavery, serfdom, peasantry, or some other mode of exploitation, is, thus, the defining characteristic of capitalism.

The three basic classes of capitalist society are: the capitalist class (the bourgeoisie); the middle class (the petty bourgeoisie); and the working class (the proletariat). Contemporary capitalist society also contains people who have no class positions (i.e., no structured relation to production). This classless group (what has been traditionally called the "lumpen proletariat") can be referred to as the "excluded sector."

The capitalist class owns (either legally or de facto) the means of production and exchange (industrial, agricultural, commercial, and financial), but does not do a significant portion of the labor of putting these means of production and exchange into operation (instead employing wage laborers as well as supervisory employees to do so). Capitalists have the power to assign the means of production and exchange to given uses, to invest in different ways, and to dispose of the product. They also have the power (to directly exercise, or to allocate to others to exercise at the discretion of the capitalists) of operational control—to assign labor to different operations in the production process, to supervise and discipline labor, and to determine how things are produced.

The working class does the labor (manual in industry, service, and farm; nonmanual in clerical and sales), but does not have the power to determine what or how they produce or how their product will be disposed. The working class merely has some discretion about which particular employer they will sell their ability to labor (their labor power) to, and when to change employers. But once the decisions are made, their labor power is at the disposal of the capitalist class and its agents in the managerial middle class. Because the working class does not own sufficient means of production or exchange to survive, they must sell their labor power under conditions established by capital. They must agree, as a fundamental condition of employment, to produce more for the capitalists than they are paid in wages.

The middle class is intermediate between capital and labor in terms of both power and exploitation. They either control their own labor power but not to any significant degree that of others (i.e., independent proprietors, small farmers, artisans, independent professionals), have operational control of the labor power of others but not real economic ownership (i.e., managers), or are employees with considerable autonomy, greater in practice than is characteristic of even many independent middle class positions, but since they are employed and, thus, lacking in real economic ownership, they are still subject to the guidelines of capital. All these groups, because they have essentially the same degree of power over economic relations, share a similar class position and, thus, tend to form into a single social class.

Any system of two antagonistic classes, one exploiting and dominant, and the other dominated and exploited, necessarily generates intermediate class positions whose function it is to structurally mediate between them. It is impossible for those in the top positions of slave, peasant, feudal, or capitalist society to directly control and supervise all slaves, peasants, serfs, or workers. A society composed of only two classes is not viable. An intermediate class is, thus, a necessity of the requirements of exploitation and supervision. Such a class has in varying degree "possession" of the means of production, or operational control over labor, over *how* things are produced. It, consequently, has authority over supervision and discipline within the labor process (while being fundamentally constrained by the top positions, especially in assigning the means of production to different uses). Such an intermediate class may be exploited in relation to the owning class, i.e., the wealth that its labor allows the owning class to accrue is greater than its own income, while not being exploited in relation to the working class, i.e., its income is significantly greater than the wealth produced by the average worker. In other words, an intermediate class typically shares in part of the surplus labor extracted from the producing class. They, therefore, must be considered to have an antagonistic relation to the working class based in both domination and exploitation. But because they do not fundamentally control their own labor power, and are dominated by the owners of the means of production (as well as exploited in relation to them) they also have an antagonistic relation to the owners.

The excluded sector is composed of all those who are permanently unemployed and are neither part of a nuclear family with a full-time relation to the means of production nor whose life trajectory (student, job, temporarily unemployed, retired) is basically one of employment. The excluded neither owns (legally or de facto) productive property, nor do they regularly sell labor power. Thus, they are neither exploited, nor exploiters. The members of this group have no structural relation to the means of production. Consequently, their income as well as their skill level, education, and social status are the lowest of any group in capitalist society. This group includes, first, those who can not hold regular jobs because of emotional disturbances, drug addiction, alcoholism, and demoralization as well as beggars and dependents of the state. Many in this group are petty criminals, irregular street-walking prostitutes and pimps, and hustlers and part-time petty drug dealers of various kinds. These people are "broken." The pressures of society, of discrimination, and other humiliations, have been so great that they have "given up" and survive the best they can. Second, it includes those who are permanently disabled, many of the blind, crippled, mentally handicapped, and so forth who are unable to hold employment as well as longtime welfare recipients. Last, it includes those who could probably hold a regular job if they wanted to, but who *elect* to subsist from welfare programs (often illegally), part-time hustling of various kinds, and perhaps occasional prostitution or drug dealing, e.g., many hard-core "hippies" or "voluntary lumpen." All three segments of the excluded sector lack a structural relation to the means of production and exchange. They live off of society. Those in the excluded sector, further, share a common position in society that gives rise to a similar consciousness, life-style, attitudes, and so on. In a loose sense, then, they tend to form a (highly diversified and individualized) social "class."

Intermediate Positions in the Class Structure

In addition to a class society's generating a set of *middle* class positions, it also generates sets of positions intermediate *between* the classes: between the owning class and the middle class, and between the laboring class and the middle class. While middle class positions are fairly consistent and coherent, pretty much equally balanced in economic role between the owning and laboring classes, this is not true of locations intermediate between them.* Such positions are

---

*Considerable misdirected (and largely wasted) intellectual effort has gone into debates about categorizing those positions intermediate between the classes. Some authors such as Judah Hill (1975) as well as all those in the new working-class tradition put positions intermediate in control over labor between clearly working class and clearly salaried middle-class positions in the working class. Hill defines them as "semi-professional workers." Others such as Nicos Poulantzas put them squarely in the "new middle class." Indeed it is such occupations that because of their real ambiguity are most often the subject of controversy. Rather than either forcing such groups into one or another category (or alternatively attempting to create a new class category equivalent to the others for them) it makes considerable sense to explicitly recognize the intermediate class nature of such positions. The alternative is to split hairs and exaggerate arguments about whether such positions are working class with strong middle-class components; or middle class with strong working-class components.

The false debate that has gone on by focusing on class position, and largely ignoring *social* class formation, has unfortunately provided little real insight into the key questions of what class culture, institutions, and consciousness the various intermediate groups develop, and hence with which of the three basic classes they are most likely to identify and share common politics. The analysis in this section, although in part inspired by Wright 1978, differs in many respects from his notion of "contradictory class locations."

intermediate between the owning class and middle class or between the laboring class and the middle class in terms of power over labor, (and, hence, their economic interest as well). These positions near the top of society consist of those directly subordinate to the owning class, the second level managers of big corporations and state administrators as well as self-employed small capitalists who have control over only a small operation subject to markets dominated by monopoly corporations, or who, while having only marginal economic ownership or control over what is produced, have pretty much total operational control or possession. Such positions near the working class are those of foreman and lower level supervisors who have some degree of possession or control over the labor power of others and how production occurs, but only within rather narrow limits. Semiprofessionals who have only limited work autonomy (e.g., nurses, technicians, primary and secondary school teachers, social workers, rank and file police, reporters, purchasing and real estate agents, insurance salespeople, own-account salespeople, commercial artists) are also intermediate between the middle and working class.

In both the cases of higher level managers and of foremen the nature of their work is to supervise the labor of others, for the higher managerial stratum within limits so broad as to often include a share in real economic ownership (thus, blurring the distinction with real capitalists), and in the second case within limits so narrow as to blur the distinction with laborers. Higher level managers in capitalist society have possession of the means of production, decide how things will be produced, and pretty much exercise operational control over their own and other's labor power, but do not generally exercise fundamental economic ownership or control over investment resources (and further can be dismissed by those who do). Foremen (at least those with some real authority) and line supervisors (at least those with minimal prerogatives) have partial operational control over labor power, especially that of others.* As intermediates between the real decision makers and production workers they consequently feel the contradictory pressures of representing the lower ranks upward and the higher ranks downward.

---

*A few generations ago foreman *was* a middle-class position with considerable authority over the labor of others (often including the power to hire and fire) as well as with significantly more technical knowledge of production. The rationalization of production, however, has increasingly given the technical knowledge to the engineers and technicians, and the powers of hiring, firing, promotion, and discipline to personnel departments and lower level management. The position of foreman has been reduced to that of a transmission belt between the true management and the technical staff *and* the working class proper.

Semiprofessionals, which Erik Wright refers to as "semi-autonomous employees," are subject to considerable restraints and direction by supervisors, doctors, principals, engineers, and so forth in both the type of work they do and how they do it; but at the same time all have a degree of autonomy as well as, often, of supervisory power over others. The autonomy of such positions or the degree of control over others is insufficient to categorize these positions as middle class, while their degree of power of supervision is too great to categorize them as workers. Their categorization as intermediate in class position is supported by their intermediate positions in income and status between the two classes.

Positions such as rank and file police, primary and secondary teachers, and lower level social welfare workers are in many respects equivalent to factory foreman. While such employees have no say in *what* the police, schools, or welfare system will do in maintaining and reproducing the social order (through their role in repression and legitimation) they do have some degree of operational control over *how* those they deal with on the job behave. The role of the rank and file police is based on control over others, whether drivers of cars or criminals, while the role of a primary or secondary school teacher is based on control over the day-to-day activities of students, even while the guidelines of how the rank and file police and teachers exercise that control is fundamentally determined by higher authorities (just as is the case with foremen and lower level supervisors in production enterprises).

Miscellaneous Categories

The mode of categorizing class positions in terms of power over production (both real ownership, and possession or operational control) can be applied by analogy to positions in the noneconomic institutional orders of society, namely political and ideological apparatuses, such as the military, the civilian state apparatus, and the church. Different positions in these institutions have different relationships of control of labor and domination of others. However, normally, the occupants of the top positions in political and ideological hierarchies in a class society do not exercise fundamental power over what these institutions do, i.e., they have neither legal ownership nor real ownership. They generally have rather possession or operational control—the power to assign subordinates, to put the institutional processes into operation; to determine *how* they operate, including the authority over supervision and discipline. Normally, generals and other leading military officers, members of Parliament/Congress, state executives, and so forth must be considered to occupy middle class or at best intermediate (between the capitalist class and the middle class) positions within a capitalist society. Only if it can be determined that the generals, president, or dictator has assumed *fundamental* power (including essential power over economic institutions) can it be maintained that such positions are equivalent to, or part of, the possessing/dominant class (an atypical situation). Thus, the typical generals, parliamentarians, and state administrators within a class society must be treated just like managers in the private sector. The incumbents of all these positions have their careers advanced because they develop and administer policies that advance the capitalist system, and would be dismissed if and when their policies no longer serve that system.

It is common, however, that the individuals who occupy the top positions in the military, state, or church are part of the social class of the owning group by virtue of their own *direct* relation to the means of production as well as the class position of their parents and other relatives (in the case of career officials).

The intermediate positions within the army, government bureaucracy, and church must be treated as essentially petty-bourgeois positions intermediate in power between that of the generals or top officials and those of the rank and file; while the privates and corporals together with the lower levels of the civil service and religious apparatus (e.g., nuns) are the equivalents of the working class, since they exercise neither real economic ownership nor possession in any significant degree (rather they have their labor virtually totally controlled by those above them). Ministers, priests, and other clergy employed by religious institutions should be categorized mostly as salaried professionals.

Foremen in the economic order can be considered to be in an intermediate location between classes because while they have no real economic ownership they have a significant amount of possession (intermediate between that of the petty bourgeoisie and the working class), and so should sargents (or their equivalents) in the military and lower level supervisors in the civil bureaucracy. All of these groups feel conflicting pressures from above and below.

Students must be considered to have a *class background* (the social class of their parents) and a *class destination* (the class position for which they are training). The status of students then is *not* a class position. Retired people should generally be considered part of the social class of their former class position, unless there has been a significant and long-term collapse of their living standards and lifestyle, and, thus, a fall into the excluded sector. The temporarily unemployed must be categorized according to their regular occupation since, like the retired, their social life and consciousness is shaped by their past (and normal) relation to the means of production. Dependents (children, spouses, and so on) of an "economically active" person must be categorized according to the class position of the nuclear familiy member who normally has a direct relationship to the means of production, since it is this position that structures the social life and consciousness of the entire family.

Those that engage primarily in illegal activity should be categorized in the same manner as anyone else. Those that control large-scale criminal operations (e.g., Mafia chiefs) are capitalists since their wealth is based on control of other's labor power. Those who work on a regular and sustained basis for such "underworld bosses" are in the working class (as are the women who work in illegal houses of prostitution). Those who are independent operators and who work on a sustained and regular basis (including "call girls"), as well as the "second lieutenants" of the leaders of criminal syndicates are petty bourgeois. Only those who engage in petty crime (or prostitution) on an irregular and often spontaneous as well as incompetent level are truly "lumpen," or part of the excluded sector.

Short-term prisoners can probably best be categorized in terms of their class position before they entered prison (i.e., they should not be classified as workers just because they are made to perform prison labor, or as part of the excluded sector if they serve time without performing such labor) since prison status is normally temporary and artificial. Their social class position is also greatly influenced by that of their relatives on the outside, which is normally identical to that of their outside occupation. There is, however, a tendency for long-term prisoners to develop into lumpen (part of the excluded sector which is psychologically unable to hold regular working-class employment) because of the powerful social pressures existing in prisons that inculcate hatred of authority demoralization, cynicism, and a hustling attitude to work and life. The high density and confined quarters of prisons are hothouses of common value production in which a typically lumpen consciousness is generated.

Individuals sometimes have more than one class position, e.g., factory workers might also work on weekends, vacations, and after regular work on their own farm. Such individuals generally tend to form into the social class of the class position in which they spend *most* of their time or derive *most* of their income. When the two class positions have significantly different status, however, an individual usually forms into the position with *lower* status since status is normally degraded by participation in labor below one's position. Further, if one has two positions (one in the working class and one in the petty bourgeoisie) this is almost certainly the case because insufficient income is being earned from the petty-bourgeois position to allow the individual to quit the working-class job and assume a full-time, petty-bourgeois position. Hence one's friendship networks and intermarriage patterns are not typically those of the petty bourgeoisie, even while one of the two class positions (and normally the preferred one) is petty bourgeois.

It should also be noted that the social class factors that a family comes to acquire (relatives, friends, life-style, and so forth) do not change immediately upon a change in class position. One's social class tends to lag behind changes in class position, perhaps by as much as a generation (*especially* in the capitalist class).

Size of Various Classes in the United States

Table 3.1 roughly estimates the relative size of the various classes in the United States in 1970. Approximately 0.1 percent of the population can be categorized as large or medium capitalists (i.e., defined either as the number of millionaires or the number of families listed in the *Social Register*, see Chapter 4); and 2 percent as small capitalists (who derive most of their income from the labor of their employees, but who are largely socially integrated into the upper reaches of the middle class). Roughly 23 percent of the population (as estimated by the male occupational structure) can be categorized as middle class (9 percent self-employed, 14 percent salaried). Fifty-four percent are working class (45 percent blue collar, 9 percent white collar, again as estimated by the male occupational structure). About 13 percent of the population must be categorized as intermediate between the working class and middle class (e.g., primary and secondary school teachers, technicians, cultural workers, foremen, office managers, and such high level sales emloyees as real estate agents, insurance agents, advertising people, stock and bond sales-persons, sales representatives, buyers and purchasing agents, and credit people). Roughly 8 percent of the population can be categorized as in the excluded sector. This sector is defined as all those who are not in the active labor force and who are living below the poverty level (excluding those retired, after a lifelong occupational career, and those in school). The operational definition of this latter category is based on all husband-wife families below the official poverty level in which they men did not work at all during 1970, plus all poor single women (parents and not) who did not work in 1970. The number of female single-parent families and individuals is used to supplement husband-wife family data (rather than the equivalent category of men) because in the excluded sector single men are very likely to attempt to avoid census takers as well as all other forms of state authorities and, thus, not to be counted in official statistics. The single women in this group, who normally have the children and thus benefit from various government programs, are much less likely to have motives to avoid government counts, thus their number gives a much better estimate of the size of this stratum than do counts of single men.

Since, for the most part, the size of the various classes is estimated on the basis of the male occupational structure, it might be argued that the size of middle class and intermediate sectors could be somewhat exaggerated, this because single women more than single men are concentrated in working-class occupations. However, it must be noted that in 1970 roughly 85 percent of women aged 25-54 were

TABLE 3.1: Estimate of the Class Structure of the United States in 1970

Class	Percentage of Total
Large and medium capitalists (*Social Register* level or millionaires)	0.1%
Small capitalists	2.0
Middle class	23.0
Self-employed	9.0
Salaried	14.0
Intermediate sector	13.0
Semiprofessionals	4.4
(of which teachers)	1.6
(of which technicians)	1.4
Semimanagerial	4.1
(of which foremen)	2.9
Police	0.8
High-level sales	3.6
Working class	54.0
White collar	9.0
Blue collar	45.0
Excluded sector*	8.0
Total	100.0

*The excluded sector is operationally defined as all families below the poverty level in which the "head" did not work at all in 1970 plus all female unrelated individuals below the poverty less who did not work in 1970 less all families whose "heads" and all female unrelated individuals below the poverty level who did not work because they were in school, and less all male family heads who did not work because they were retired.

Source: U.S. Bureau of the Census, *Current Population Reports*, Series P-60 #81 Consumer Income. *Characteristics of the Low Income Population 1970*, 1971, Table: 20. See Tables 5.8 and 7.3 as well as Chapter 4.

married, and only about 5 percent of women aged 30–54 had *never* been married. Thus, the experience of single women is of much less weight than that of married women in influencing the *social* class structure. The vast majority of never married women are under 30, and are, thus, still heavily influenced by the social class of their parents. The vast majority of once married women (widowed and divorced) are either between marriages to men of the same social class or are relatively recently widowed or divorced and are, thus, still socially integrated into the class of their former husband (even if their income has radically decreased). Thus, the use of the *male* occupational structure to estimate the *social* class of the entire population should result in very little upward bias.

THE DISTRIBUTION OF WEALTH AND INCOME IN THE UNITED STATES

The capitalist class in the United States and other advanced Western industrial societies owns the bulk of the factories, mines, and other means of production. They hire the labor power of the working class on condition that the value of what this latter class produces is greater than the cost of labor power to the capitalists, i.e., that there is a positive difference (or surplus) between total wages (supplemented by overhead, raw materials, and depreciation, which are largely reducible, directly or indirectly, to the labor costs of those capitalists that supply these inputs) and the total sales of the capitalists. The survival and growth of the capitalist mode of production then depends on profit, or what amounts to the same thing, the exploitation of labor power (exploitation in the sense of the price of labor power being less than the value of what it produces). Out of profits come not only the consumption income of the capitalists, but also the funds to reinvest in capitalist enterprises. It is, thus, the power of capital to hire labor power, a power based in the concentration of productive property in the hands of a very few capitalists, that is the source of their income and wealth as well as of the expansion in that wealth, i.e., ownership of the means of production provides the ability to increase wealth. It is only in these terms that the income and wealth distributions of capitalist countries such as the United States can be understood. In this section it is shown that the logic of the private ownership of industry in the United States produces a great gap in the distribution of income as well as a much larger gap in the distribution of wealth. It is also shown that the income and wealth distribution in the United States have remained essentially constant over the course of the twentieth century.

The Distribution of Wealth

In the United States in 1972, 1 percent of *all* persons held 25.9 percent of all wealth (net worth), and just one-half of 1 percent held 20.4 percent. The top 1 percent also held 56.5 percent of all corporate stock, 60 percent of all corporate bonds, 52.7 percent of all debt instruments, and 89.9 percent of the value of all trust funds. The top one-half of 1 percent held 49.3 percent, 52.2 percent, 39.1 percent, and 80.8 percent respectively (see Table 3.2). There is an extreme concentration of wealth at the top levels of contemporary capitalist society. In 1972 the top one-half of 1 percent of wealthy individuals held 79 percent of all the net worth of the top 1 percent, as well as 87 percent of the value of their corporate stock. In 1969 those with a total net worth of $1 million or more (approximately 0.1 percent of all adults) held 9.6 percent of total net worth and 23.1 percent of corporate stock. Thus, the top one-tenth of 1 percent of wealthy individuals around 1970 held roughly 37 percent of the net worth and 41 percent of the corporate stock held by the richest 1 percent of the population (see Turner and Starness 1976, p. 43).

The concentration of wealth grew over the course of the nineteenth century until the end of the 1920s. In 1810 the richest 1 percent of families held 21 percent of all wealth and in 1900 about 28 percent. In 1929 the richest 1 percent of adults held about 36 percent of all wealth. After declining to about 20 percent at the end of the

TABLE 3.2: Personal Wealth: Value of Assets Held by All Persons in the United States

	1958			1972		
	Top 0.5%	Top 1%	Top 0.5% as % of Top 1%	Top 0.5%	Top 1%	Top 0.5% as % of Top 1%
Total assets	20.40%	25.50%	80.00%	18.90%	24.10%	78.40%
Corporate stock	66.60	75.40	88.30	49.30	56.50	87.30
Bonds	36.00	41.40	87.00	52.20	60.00	87.00
Debt instruments	28.60	37.30	76.70	39.10	52.70	74.20
Trusts	85.10	92.10	92.40	80.80	89.90	90.00
Real estate	10.10	15.10	66.90	10.10	15.10	66.90
Net worth (less liabilities)	21.70	26.90	80.70	20.40	25.90	78.80
Number of persons (millions)	0.87	1.74	0.50	1.04	2.09	0.50

Source: U.S. Department of Commerce 1981, p. 471.

1940s, the wealth concentrated in the hands of the richest 1 percent fluctuated around 27 percent through the 1950s, 1960s, and 1970s (see Table 3.3). It should be noted that the concentration of wealth in the United States has been approximately the same throughout the post-World War II period (with roughly the top 1 percent holding about 26 percent of the national wealth).

In 1953 the highest income percentile of families owned 51.7 percent of all corporate stock. It was 49.1 percent in 1964, 50.4 percent in 1969, and 51.1 percent in 1971 (see Table 3.4). There has been little change since the late 1950s in the concentration of corporate stock ownership, as measured by that held by those with the highest *income*. However, there has been a definite deconcentration of stock as measured by percent held by the *wealthiest*. Since there has been no decrease in the distribution of wealth, the lessening share of stock ownership in the hands of the wealthiest 1 percent means that the wealthy have been transferring their investments from corporate stock to other forms of wealth. The transfer appears to be in part to "debt instruments" (notes, mortgages, security credit, and similar assets) and bonds. For example, the proportion of all debt instruments held by the wealthiest 1 percent rose from 37.3 percent to 52.7

TABLE 3.3:   Share of Wealth Held by Richest 1 Percent of U.S. Adults

Year	Percentage of Wealth Held
1810	21.0
1860	24.0
1900	(26.0–31.0)
1922	31.6
1929	36.3
1933	28.3
1939	30.6
1945	23.3
1949	20.8
1953	27.5
1956	26.0
1958	26.9
1962	27.4
1965	29.2
1969	24.9
1972	25.9

Note: Data for nineteenth century is for families instead of adults.

Sources: Turner and Starness 1976, p 19; U.S. Department of Commerce 1981, p. 471.

percent of the total between 1958 and 1972, while the proportion of all bonds held rose from 41.4 percent to 60.0 percent (see Table 3.2). The fact that there has been no decrease in the percentage of corporate stock held by the top 1 percent of income receipients indicates that stock ownership remains as concentrated as ever (rather there has been only a change in the portfolio composition of the wealthiest).

The assets of the middle class and skilled working class consist mostly of their home. Those of the poorer working class consist mostly of their car and savings account. Those of the upper middle class are concentrated in their business and investments. The assets of the capitalist class predominantly consist of their investments (especially corporate stock). For example, in 1962 about 55 percent of the average wealth of all families in the $10,000-$25,000 range was equity in their homes, 5 percent in their automobiles, and 16 percent in cash (with 9 percent in their family business and 13 percent in investments). For families with less than $1,000 in assets, 48 percent was accounted for by their auto and 34 percent by cash. For families with $500,000 or over in assets, however, an average of only 5 percent was in equity in their home, 0.2 percent in their automobiles, and 4 percent in cash. For these families 50 percent of their networth was in investments—other than their own business or profession (see Table 3.5).

In 1976, 72 percent of the net worth of those who died with net assets of $10 million or more was in corporate stocks, 11 percent in bonds, and only 4 percent in real estate and 3 percent in noncorporate business assets. In strong contrast, those with a net worth of under $500,000 had only 18 percent of their net worth in stock and 6 percent in bonds, but 35 percent in real estate (mostly their own homes). In general, the greater one's net worth, the higher the propor-

TABLE 3.4: Percentage of Stock Value Owned by Families with the Highest Income

	1% of Income	1% of Wealth
1953	51.7%	86.3%
1958	50.5	75.4
1964–65	49.1	61.0
1969	50.4	50.8
1971	51.1	—*
1972	—	56.5

*Data not available.
Sources: Rossidies 1976, p. 131; Table 3.2 herein; Smith and Franklin 1974.

TABLE 3.5: Mean Value of Assets of Specific Types as a Percentage of the Mean Value of Wealth of All Types, by Wealth Class of Consumer Units, 1962

Wealth Class	Assets					
	Home	Automobile	Business or Profession	Liquid	Investments	Miscellaneous
All	26.9	3.1	18.4	12.7	33.4	5.3
$1–999	10.1	48.0	2.3	33.8	3.5	2.3
$1,000–4,999	47.7	16.4	3.0	25.8	6.2	0.9
$5,000–9,999	58.6	8.4	8.6	16.9	6.1	1.4
$10,000–24,999	55.1	5.3	9.3	16.3	12.7	1.0
$25,000–49,999	36.9	3.2	18.8	18.1	21.3	1.5
$50,000–99,999	20.5	2.2	24.2	15.7	35.5	1.7
$100,000–199,999	17.2	1.7	17.3	14.2	48.3	1.4
$200,000–499,999	8.6	0.8	24.1	7.0	56.3	3.2
$500,000 and over	4.5	0.2	23.4	3.7	49.8	18.4

Note: Total assets of each class equal 100 percent.

Source: Dorothy S. Projector and Gertrude S. Weiss, Survey of Financial Characteristics of Consumers (Washington, D.C.: Board of Governors of the Federal Reserve System, August 1966), p. 110, cited in Turner and Starness 1976, p. 27.

TABLE 3.6: Composition of Assets by Size of Net Worth, 1976 (in millions of dollars)

	Number	Total Net Worth	Real Estate	Bonds	Stock	Notes and Mortgages	Noncorporate Business Assets
Less than $500,000	187,954	$28,764	9,978 (34.7%)*	1,753 (6.1%)	5,153 (17.9%)	1,178 (4.1%)	650 (2.3%)
$500,000–1 million	8,694	5,881	1,500 (25.5)	630 (10.7)	1,892 (32.1)	242 (4.1)	159 (2.7)
$1 million–2 million	2,780	3,732	736 (19.7)	520 (13.9)	1,463 (39.2)	121 (3.2)	103 (2.8)
$2 million–10 million	1,240	4,346	588 (13.5)	702 (16.2)	2,035 (46.8)	110 (2.5)	114 (2.6)
Greater than $10 million	79	2,708	119 (4.4)	288 (10.6)	1,941 (71.7)	85 (3.1)	75 (2.8)
Total		$45,436 (100%)	12,921 (28.4%)	3,898 (8.6%)	12,484 (27.5%)	1,736 (3.8%)	1,101 (2.4%)

*As a percentage of total net worth.
Note: Data from estate returns.
Source: U.S. Internal Revenue Service, *Statistics of Income 1976: Estate Tax Returns,* 1979.

tion of one's wealth is concentrated in corporate stock and the less is tied up in real estate (see Table 3.6). It is clear that the wealth of the capitalist class is concentrated in ownership of the corporations.

The Distribution of Income

In 1978 the highest 5 percent of income earners received 15.6 percent of total money income (of families), the highest 20 percent, 41.5 percent of the total, and the lowest 20 percent, 5.2 percent. These figures were all essentially constant over the 1960s and 1970s (see Table 3.7). Gabriel Kolko has shown that the income share of the highest one-fifth and one-tenth remained essentially constant in the 1910 to 1959 period as well—although there was a slight tendency for these shares to rise before 1929, shrink until the end of World War II, and then increase again in the immediate post–World War II period (see Kolko 1962, p. 14). Kolko, however, also found that the share of income going to the lowest one-fifth declined in the 1910 to 1941 period from 8.3 percent to 3.0 percent of the total, rising again in the immediate post–World War II period to the 4 to 5 percent range (and as can be seen from Table 3.7), settling at slightly over 5 percent through most of the 1960s and 1970s.

Studies of the trends in income inequality since the end of World War II that take into account the entire income distribution (by using the Gini index) have shown little change between 1947 and 1973. Depending on the definitions used and whether income tax returns or Bureau of the Census sample data are used, somewhat different results are obtained. Using Internal Revenue Service (IRS) income tax return data, inequality appears to have increased somewhat. The Gini index (the bigger the index the more inequality, 0.0 indicates perfect equality, 1.00 total inequality) increased slightly from 0.42 in 1947 to 0.45 in 1971 (with the rate of increase being fairly constant over the 24-year-period). Using Bureau of the Census data, however,

TABLE 3.7: Aggregate Family Income

	1960	1965	1970	1975	1978
Lowest fifth	4.8	5.2	5.4	5.4	5.2
Second fifth	12.2	12.2	12.2	11.8	11.6
Middle fifth	17.8	17.8	17.6	17.6	17.5
Fourth fifth	24.0	23.9	23.8	24.1	24.1
Highest fifth	41.3	40.9	40.9	41.1	41.5
Highest 5%	15.9	15.5	15.6	15.5	15.6

Source: U.S. Department of Commerce 1981a, p. 454.

there was no apparent change. The Gini index stood at 0.42 in both 1947 and 1973, with only minor fluctuations between 0.40 and 0.42 between those years (see Zeitlin 1970, p. 112).

In 1978 the top 1 percent of income recipients received 7.5 percent of all income, i.e., the highest income 1 percent got about half of the income of the highest income 5 percent, indicating a fairly high degree of concentration at the upper reaches of the income distribution, but significantly less concentration than is the case with wealth (see Table 3.8). The top 1 percent of stock dividend recipients received 37 percent of all stock dividends (the top 10 percent received over 58 percent), while the top 1 percent of those with capital gain income received 32 percent of all net capital gains (the top 10 percent received over 54 percent) (computed from data in Table 3.8).

Those with the highest incomes in the United States received most of their income from corporate stock dividends and capital gains (in good part the selling of corporate stock initially purchased at a lower price). In 1978, 31.7 percent of the income of those earning over $1 million in that year was in the form of stock dividends and 26.2 percent in the form of net capital gains. Only 16.2 percent was in the form of wages and salaries. This is in strong contrast to those with incomes of less than $20,000. For these people fully 87.7 percent of their income was in the form of wages and salaries and only 1.3 percent in the form of stock dividends and 1.2 percent in net capital gains (see Table 3.8). In general, the higher the income, the higher the proportion accounted for by both dividends and capital gains and the less accounted for by wages and salaries. It is clear that the high incomes, and thus the ability to accumulate capital, of the rich come from the exploitation of the working class.

It is of interest to note that the proportion of business and professional (including partnership) income to total income is highest in the $50,000–$500,000 a year bracket where small capitalists as well as higher paid self-employed professionals are concentrated. In this income range business and professional income is more important than either stock dividends or net capital gains (salaries are more important still). But in the highest income brackets where the medium and large capitalists are found, it is corporate stock ownership not directly owned enterprises or managerial compensation that is the basis of wealth. The high income and wealth of the capitalist class in the United States is based on their ownership of the giant corporations, not in any entrepreneurial activity or managerial function that they themselves perform.

Because of the very different ways in which the different classes receive their incomes, the actual differential in wealth received is greater than the figures on money income reported to the Internal

TABLE 3.8: Types of Income by Income Size, 1978 (in billions of 1978 dollars)

1978 Income Size	Number of Income Recipients (in 1,000s)	Gross Income	Salary and Wages	Dividends	Net Capital Gains	Business, Partnership, and Professional Profits
0–$20,000	67,473.0	$566.8	$497.3 (87.7%)	$7.264 (1.3%)	$6.652 (1.2%)	$23.108 (4.1%)
$20,000–$50,000	20,474.0	576.6	501.0 (86.9)	9.197 (1.6)	8.394 (1.5)	32.105 (5.6)
$50,000–$100,000	1,471.4	96.3	61.7 (64.1)	5.692 (5.9)	4.391 (4.6)	18.593 (19.4)
$100,000–$200,000	285.3	37.5	20.9 (55.7)	3.989 (10.6)	2.793 (7.4)	7.512 (20.0)
$200,000–$500,000	59.9	16.7	7.4 (44.0)	3.051 (18.3)	2.064 (12.4)	3.012 (18.1)
$500,000–$1,000,000	6.6	4.4	1.3 (29.2)	1.176 (26.5)	.861 (19.4)	.720 (16.4)
Greater than $1,000,000	2.0	4.1	.7 (16.2)	1.302 (31.7)	1.077 (26.2)	.638 (15.5)
Total	89,772.	$1,302.4	$1,090.3 (83.7%)	$31.672 (2.4%)	$26.233 (2.0%)	$85.688 (6.6%)

Source: U.S. Internal Revenue Service, 1978 Statistics of Income: Individual Income Tax Returns, 1980, Table 1.4.

Revenue Service of the U.S. government indicate. One of the principal means to avoid progressive income tax rates applicable to high incomes is to receive income in kind rather than in money. Thus, higher level executives receive generous expense accounts (which pay for vacations, private planes, suites, meals, parties, yachts, cars, medical care, entertainment, gasoline, and so forth, none of which is considered "income" but rather "business expenses").

Another way the rich have to reduce the income they report to the IRS (and thus to make the income distribution statistics appear more equal than they are) includes having the corporations distribute less of their profits than they otherwise would. In the period 1923–29 the corporations withheld only 27 percent of corporate profits, but in the period 1946–59 (after the individual income tax rates were greatly increased) they withheld 51 percent, i.e., only distributed 49 percent to stockholders (see Kolko 1962, p. 23). This means that money that would be taxed if distributed as dividends accrues as a benefit to the stock owners in greater value on their investments, an increase in value that is only taxed (as capital gains) when stock is sold, and then only at much less than the rate of dividend income.

In conclusion, it appears that at best both the wealth and the income distributions in the United States have remained essentially constant throughout the twentieth century, and that the changes in them are basically cyclical or erratic. There is no trend toward greater equality. Thus, the popular myth that the New Deal, progressive taxation, inheritance taxes, and the welfare state have produced a significant reduction in economic inequality in the United States is mistaken. It would seem that the logic of the capital accumulation process within U.S. monopoly capitalist society generates a certain set income and wealth distribution independently of state role in the economy.

The taxation of incomes by the U.S. state has little effect on the income distribution. In 1972 the before-tax income share of the highest fifth in the United States was 44.8 percent, its after-tax share was 42.8 percent, while the before tax share of the bottom fifth was 3.8 percent and its after-tax share 4.5 percent—a slight, but not very significant change (Sawyer 1976, p. 14). The federal tax system in the United States, technically, is sharply progressive, i.e., the higher one's income, the higher the proportion of one's income theoretically paid in taxes. However, because of a systematic series of "tax loopholes" written into the income tax law from the beginning (with the intention of reducing the actually applicable rates), very few wealthy people ever pay anything approaching the official rate for their income class. In fact, the average effective tax on high incomes in the 1960s and 1970s was about 30 percent without any significant tendency to increase after about the $200,000 a year income level (in 1970 dollars) (see Stern 1973, p. 11). The story of federal tax loopholes, the regressive nature of state and local taxation, and the ability of the rich to pass taxes on to the working class in the form of higher prices has been told many times and will not be repeated here, since this book is concerned only with the effect of taxation on income distribution and this is negligible.*

The Poor

The U.S. Social Security administration defines the poverty level income in the United States as three times what the Department of Agriculture estimates is the minimum cost of a nutritious diet. The rationale for this estimate of the minimum it takes to maintain a healthy, no-frills standard of living is that food expenses have been empirically found to account for about one-third of the budgets of the poor. In 1978 in the United States the poverty level was officially defined as $6,662 a year for a family of four (32.6 percent of the median income of a family of four, down from 40.6 percent in 1965 and 35.2 percent in 1970). In 1978, 24.5 million persons in the United States were below the poverty level (and 34.2 million below the 125 percent of poverty level that is also often used to specify the poor). These figures represent 11.4 percent and 15.8 percent of the total U.S. population respectively. The poor in the United States can, thus, be defined as between 11 percent and 16 percent of the U.S. population (see U.S. Department of Commerce 1981a, pp. 464–65).

Since the poverty level is defined in terms of absolute nutritional requirements (instead of relative criteria), the percentage of the population below the official poverty line has decreased as the proportion of the median income that must be spent on a nutritious diet has declined (i.e., as the real wage level in the United States has risen, or, to be more precise, as the cost of basic foods measured in labor time has declined). Over the course of the 1960s the percentage of those below the poverty level declined from 22.4 percent of the population in 1959 to 12.1 percent in 1969 (this corresponded to the rise in real wages during this period). The percentage below the poverty line remained constant over the course of the 1970s, however, corresponding to the failure of real wages to rise over this period (see U.S. Department of Commerce 1981a, p. 464).

In 1978, 66.4 percent of people below the poverty line were white and 31.1 percent black (and 10.6 percent Ladinos). These figures

---

*See Stern 1973; Szymanski 1978, chap. 8.

represented 8.7 percent of all whites, 30.6 percent of all blacks, and 21.6 percent of all Ladinos respectively. (U.S. Department of Commerce 1981a, p. 466).

In 51 percent of the families below the poverty line the "head" (the man in the case of husband-wife families, the single parent, usually a woman, in the rest) was not in the labor force (i.e., neither employed nor looking for work), and in another 9 percent was unemployed (i.e., looking for work). Only 48 percent of such families had their head employed at some point during 1977, with 38 percent of these 48 percent, less than 27 weeks during the year (U.S. Bureau of the Census 1979b). In 42 percent of families below the poverty line in 1977 there was no one at all working or looking for work (U.S. Bureau of the Census 1979b). Thus, about half of the poor can be described as working poor and almost half as part of the excluded sector.

In the South 14.7 percent of all families were below the poverty line (including 34.1 percent of all blacks) as compared to 9.1 percent in the North Central states, 10.0 percent in the West, and 10.4 percent in the Northeast. In central cities in 1978, 15.4 percent of persons (and 31.5 percent of blacks) were below the poverty level, while in nonmetropolitan areas 13.5 percent of persons (including 37.2 percent of all blacks) were. Both figures contrast sharply with only 6.8 percent of persons (and 20.1 percent of blacks) in suburuban areas below the poverty line. In 1978, 38 percent of all persons below the poverty line lived in central cities and another 38 percent in nonmetropolitan areas; these figures compare with 28 percent and 32 percent of the total population living in such areas (U.S. Department of Commerce 1981a, 18, 464-66). The poor are disproportionately located in the South, in rural areas, and in the central cities.

In 1978, 13.9 percent of those 65 years and over, 16.5 percent of those under 14, but only 8.2 percent of those between 22 and 64 were poor (U.S. Department of Commerce 1981a, p. 466). A total of 13 percent of all those below the poverty level were over 65, while 31 percent were under 14; 38 percent were between 22 and 64. The poor are, thus, disproportionately old and dependent children (these latter heavily concentrated in mother-child families).

In 1978 the U.S. minimum wage (which represented 44 percent of the average earnings of production workers in manufacturing in that year) produced an annual income (assuming 52 forty-hour weeks) of 91 percent of the official poverty level for a family of four. The average Social Security payment to retired men represented 59 percent of the poverty level for such a family and the average Aid to Families with Dependent Children payments amounted to 47 percent

(U.S. Department of Commerce 1981a, pp. 342, 356, 425). These figures manifest the fact that people working at minimum-wage jobs, the retired without savings or investment income, and single mothers with young children are all very heavily represented among the poor. They also reflect the fact that the minimum wage as well as welfare and social security support levels are set at such a low level as to provide a tremendous incentive for people dependent on them to look for work (or in the case of minimum-wage jobs to look for higher paying work).

Of all families below the poverty line in 1977, 22 percent had an income entirely from their own earnings (wages, salaries, and self-employment income) and 29 percent lived entirely from various social security and public welfare programs. The rest (49 percent) had incomes that were a combination of earnings, income supplements from various Social Security and public welfare programs, and other unearned income (U.S. Bureau of the Census 1979b, p. 142).

The poor, both the working poor and those in the excluded sector, are a product of the logic of capitalist society. Poverty is a necessary condition for the maintenance of profitability within capitalist forms of economic organization. Capitalism needs a significant level of people (both low paid and without pay) who are actively looking for work at any given time (in order to put sufficient downward pressure on wages so as to maintain profits.) By increasing productivity, and hence layoffs, it continually reproduces their number as well. A low-wage sector, in addition to putting pressure on those with higher wages, also allows marginal and labor-intensive industries to survive and prosper. Further, it must be noted that protracted unemployment produces a significant number of physically and mentally broken and demoralized people unable to sell their labor power on a sustained basis, and who thus sink permanently into the excluded sector.

Poverty is not a matter of lack of education, insufficient "drive" or motivation, or faulty culture (a "culture of poverty"). Nor is it part of a "vicious circle" involving these three. If everyone had a Ph.D. and was motivated to work hard 12 hours a day at any job no matter how menial, the rate of unemployment as well as the wage structure between high- and low-paying jobs would remain the same if not deteriorate (as would the proportion of those eventually physically and morally broken by the system). So long as there are a significant number of unemployed willing and able to take the jobs of the employed, workers are constrained from demanding pay raises, from relaxing work discipline, or from resisting the authority of management. And for higher paid workers, the existence of low-paid workers anxious to move up to better paying jobs has the same effect. If there were no unemployed, wages would rise as capitalists bid the cost of labor up in order to secure scarce labor power even without unions (higher wages that could only be granted by decreasing profits). Further, workers would be inclined to slow down on the job, to perhaps not show up on Mondays or Fridays, and to ignore directives of foremen. If there is no one available to take one's job, one becomes rather indispensable, and can get away with a lot more than if one could be easily replaced. Thus, in times of very low unemployment, wages tend to rise and *real* productivity declines from its maximum. Workers are in a strong position to resist capital. But in times of high unemployment, wages decline as capitalists are able to reduce wages (it should be noted that in such periods profits often decline even more rapidly). If workers resist wage reductions there are always the unemployed who are willing to accept lower pay. Further, in times of high unemployment speedup tends to rise toward its technical maximum since workers now are under the imminent threat of being fired unless they produce (this occurs even though aggregate statistics of output divided by workers employed may not rise due to enterprises holding on to redundant workers). Without unemployment wages would rise to the point of threatening the very existence of profits, and productivity and work discipline would also seriously decline.

Unemployment and low-wage jobs are not the result of a conspiracy among capitalists. Rather they are structurally generated by the logic of capital. As the pool of the unemployed is reduced by capitalists hiring more and more workers to work in new factories and industries, capitalists must induce workers away from other capitalists to take new jobs in expanded enterprises by bidding wages up. At the same time employed workers also receive wage increases as an inducement not to leave for higher paying jobs elsewhere. Rising wages *tend* to reduce profits, giving capitalists a growing incentive to introduce *labor-saving* machinery to replace increasingly expensive labor power.

The introduction of labor-saving machinery results in workers being laid off, thereby increasing the pool of unemployed workers actively seeking work. As the pool of the unemployed grows there is increasing pressure on those still employed to accept wage cuts as well as to increase their output. With plenty of unemployed workers willing to work for less than those who are currently employed, capital is now in a position to reduce wages. If an employed worker quits as a result, there will be no difficulty in finding others to do the work. Wages, thus, decline to the point where labor power is so cheap that it is as cheap as introducing new labor-saving machinery

The rate of technical innovation, thus, slows down, as more and more inexpensive labor power is hired. The now considerable reserve of unemployed labor is consequently reduced. In fact, in normal times actual cycles of unemployment induced by this process are not that large, nor are cycles in the rate of introduction of labor-saving technology or wages. Rather, an equilibrium is normally reached between the rate of introduction of labor-saving technology and the unemployment rate, an equilibrium that generates a more or less large and stable pool of unemployed workers.

A similar process operates to maintain the differential between high-wage and low-wage jobs. Significant numbers of high-paid workers can be replaced by other workers in low-paid jobs when the differential between them becomes too great (this may involve a deskilling or automation of the labor process of higher paid skilled positions). If the differential is too small, there is little incentive for the slightly lesser paid workers to press for the jobs of the higher paid. As a result of the enhanced security of equalitarian wage policy, the compliance to capital, and hence productivity, is reduced. Pay differentials are also maintained as an inducement to receive training and develop skills as well as to motivate performance.

The Excluded Sector

The excluded sector is a product of the logic of the capitalist mode of production. Much of the excluded sector consists of the "human discards" of the system. Those who have become disabled or made permanently ill because of injuries and diseases associated with early job experience or class position as well as those who have been mentally damaged (made mentally ill) by the stresses and strains of lower class life, to the point of not being able to hold a job (this includes those driven to alcoholism and other forms of drug addiction). It also includes those subject to the high levels of frustration and strains associated with racism.

The maintenance of the excluded sector is also a product of state policy. Just as the working poor perform a necessary function in maintaining profitability for capital (both those actually employed at low-wage jobs and those actively seeking work), so too do those in the excluded sector (those unable or unwilling to actively seek work). The extremely poor conditions and generally degraded treatment received by those in the excluded sector serves to motivate the working poor to continue in their low-wage jobs and to keep actively seeking work (under the penalty of sinking to the level of those on welfare, or those living at a subsistence level through petty crime and other forms of hustling). The humiliations experienced by the excluded sector puts a fire under low-paid workers. Without the fear of slipping into the excluded sector, many of the working poor would reject the humiliating conditions of their low-paying jobs for the alternative of state support. The existence of the excluded sector together with the extremely low level of support available from the state (with the humiliation suffered by state clients) guarantees that labor-intensive, low-wage jobs (disproportionately in the service sector in such jobs as dishwashing, janitorial, domestic labor, and so forth) get filled. If the level of state support increased to the level of the minimum wage (or to the official poverty level) and the treatment accorded to all those that choose not to work were improved, profitability (especially in service sector industries) would be radically undermined. Therefore, state policy operates to ensure that the excluded sector continues to exist.

The welfare system in a capitalist society such as the United States is oriented to ensuring a labor force that is motivated to, *and* is able to, sell its labor power to capital *when* capital needs labor under conditions that *capital* finds profitable. This means that welfare payments must be kept significantly below the lowest wages offered by capitalists (the minimum wage) as well as significantly below the level necessary for a minimal but adequate standard of living (the poverty level). This ensures that there is great pressure on all those state-supported programs to actively seek work, no matter how menial, degrading, or low paid (see Piven and Clovard 1971).

The treatment of those on welfare (especially in times of labor shortage) of necessity must be so punitive and degraded as to instill in the working class a fear of the fate that awaits them if they should relax and be tempted to resort to relief rather than low-paid menial labor. It is structurally necessary to degrade even those who are physically incapable of becoming workers (e.g., the disabled, aged, insane) so as to emphasize the boundary between those who offer their labor power and those who do not.

The level of state welfare tends to vary as a function of the demand for cheap labor and political instability. In general, the greater the demand by capital for cheap labor, the less generous is public welfare, this in order to put maximum pressure on potential workers to offer to sell their labor power when it is needed the most. For example, the lack of demand for labor in the 1930s was a major factor in the expansion of welfare at that time, while the relative labor shortage of the 1940s and 1950s was responsible for its contraction. Generally, the more political unrest and the stronger the political movements of the poor, the more generous the welfare system (this in order to co-opt and contain their movements). Thus, in times of political stability welfare tends to contract, and in times of massive unemployment, to expand. In the 1930s and the 1960s in the United States, when there were significant movements among the poor, the U.S. welfare system expanded, while in the politically stable 1950s and 1970s, when this was no longer the case, it contracted (Piven and Clovard 1971).

Welfare tends to expand during times of massive unemployment in order to ensure that the reserve labor force maintains itself in a reasonably healthy condition (at state expense) without suffering from large-scale starvation or epidemic diseases until such time as labor demand picks up, and when it does, sufficient workers will be available to offer their labor power for sale. Once labor demand is up, every effort tends to be made to get potential workers off state programs so as to provide the necessary cheap labor as well as to put pressure on the employed so as to keep wages down and productivity and profits up.

The granting of relief varies by region within the United States as well as according to season and phase of the economic cycle in correspondence to the needs of capital for a labor force. Traditionally in the U.S. South it was virtually impossible for blacks to get on welfare during the cotton season (so as to force them into the fields at the very low prevailing rates of pay), but very easy for them to get on during the off-season (so as to give them an incentive *not* to migrate out of the area, thus ensuring the continuing presence of a cheap labor force).

COMPARISONS AMONG THE ADVANCED CAPITALIST COUNTRIES

Comparisons among the major advanced capitalist countries for which there are comparable data indicate that in general their class structure varies rather little, and that in particular the class structure of the United States is quite typical. The independent (or old) petty bourgeoisie is smaller in the United States than in any of the other comparison countries except Sweden. The U.S. figure of 10.9 percent compares with the average of the other seven of 14.2 percent (of the employed male population). This difference is almost entirely due to the very small number of independent family farmers left in the United States (2.3 percent—lower than in any of the comparison countries), which contrasts with the average of 5.2 percent for the others. Japan with 7.0 percent and France with 7.7 percent have the largest percentage of family farmers remaining. There is no great difference in either the percentage of self-employed professionals or self-employed business people and artisans between the United States and the other advanced countries. In fact, only Japan with 12.4

percent of its employed population who are self-employed business people or artisans, and perhaps Sweden, where only 0.8 percent of people are categorized as self-employed professionals, appear to be significantly out of line from the overall averages (see Table 3.9).

There is no significant difference between the percentage that are salaried professionals in the United States (13.6 percent) and the average for the other advanced countries (12.6 percent), although there is considerable variation among the advanced capitalist countries (from 21.5 percent in Sweden to 5.6 percent for Japan). The disparity in salaried professionals would appear in good part to reflect the differential role of the state in education, research, the military, and so forth among the advanced countries.

There does appear to be a considerable difference between the United States and the rest of advanced capitalist countries, however, in the percentage of employed administrators and managers. In the United States it was 11.6 percent while elsewhere it averaged 5.0 percent. It can be noted that the countries with the highest proportion of their employed male population categorized as managers tend to have the smallest categorized as clerical employees. In fact, the total of managerial plus clerical employees in the United States was 17.8 percent as compared to 14.9 percent for the other countries. This indicates that the apparent difference in percentage categorized as "managerial" employees among the advanced countries in good part reflects a difference in drawing the line between "managerial" and "clerical" employees within private enterprises and the state as well as differences in the relative importance of administration and management. It would seem that the first effect is the greatest and thus that there is probably only a slight real tendency for managers/administrators to be more important in the United States than elsewhere.

The tendency for the United States to categorize a higher proportion of managerial-clerical employees as managers and administrators seems to primarily account for the size of the middle class in the United States (36.1 percent) appearing larger than the average for the other seven countries (31.5 percent). If the total of all the self-employed and the employed professionals is *added* to the total of managerial-clerical employees the total is 41.6 percent for the United States and 41.7 percent for the other seven countries. If the number of employed managers and administrators is *deducted* from the reported figures for the total middle class, the figure for the United States is 24.5 percent and that for the others is 26.5 percent. Both comparisons are extremely close, indicating that in fact the true size of the middle class in the United States is virtually identical to the average of the other advanced countries (as well as the fact that the

TABLE 3.9: The Class Structure of the Advanced Capitalist Countries, ca. 1979

	France	West Germany	Netherlands	Sweden	Canada	Australia	Japan	USA	Average of the Other Seven
Self-employed professionals	1.9	1.6	1.1	.8	1.2	1.2	1.4	1.6	1.3
Self-employed farmers	7.7	2.8	4.5	4.4	4.5	5.2	7.0	2.3	5.2
Self-employed business and artisans	8.8	6.7	7.0	5.1	5.3	9.1	12.4	7.0	7.8
Total self-employed	18.4	11.1	12.6	10.3	11.0	15.5	20.8	10.9	14.2
Salaried managers and professionals*	16.5	15.4	17.4	24.9	20.8	16.3	11.7	25.2	17.6
(of which professionals)	13.2	11.8	14.8	21.5	11.7	9.4	5.6	13.6	12.6
(salaried managers plus clerical)	11.6	16.9	17.5	8.4	15.5	15.6	19.3	17.8	14.9
Total middle class	34.9	26.5	30.0	35.2	31.8	31.8	32.7	36.1	31.5
White-collar workers*	11.6	17.5	21.1	11.3	15.8	14.0	23.1	11.2	16.3
of which clerical	8.0	13.3	14.9	4.6	6.4	8.9	12.9	6.1	9.9
Blue-collar workers*	53.5	56.0	48.9	53.5	52.5	54.3	44.3	52.7	51.9
of which production	46.8	47.3	41.7	44.7	39.9	46.5	38.3	42.9	43.7
of which service	3.8	7.4	4.3	5.5	9.4	4.4	5.1	8.2	5.7
Total working class	65.1	73.5	70.0	64.8	68.2	68.2	67.4	63.9	68.3

*The definitions employed by the ILO are utilized here. Thus those who are categorized as intermediate in class position (e.g., semiprofessionals, high-level sales people, foremen, police) are distributed over the various occupational categories used by the ILO (e.g., professionals, white collar, production blue collar and service respectively). No attempt is made to estimate the relative size of either the excluded population or the capitalists. We would probably not be too far off to assume that 2 percent of the total are small capitalists (and thus should be deducted from the figure for the middle class) and roughly 5 percent of the total population is part of the excluded sector (and thus that the percentages reported for other groups should be reduced accordingly).

Note: Data from employed males.

Source: International Labor Organization, Labor Yearbook, 1980, Table 2B. All the major advanced countries for which data were reported in the 1980 ILO Labor Yearbook are included in this table.

size of the middle class in the advanced capitalist countries varies but little). However, even if the *proportion* of all managerial-clerical employees who are managers is the same in the United States as elsewhere (and thus the size of the total middle class is virtually identical) there are still significantly more managerial-administrative employees in the United States than elsewhere (about three percentage points greater in the United States). Apparently the managerial-administrative stratum is somewhat more important than the average in the United States than it is in other countries because of such factors as the greater role of the military and the location of so many financial corporate headquarters in the United States as well as a higher level of development of private-sector management than elsewhere.

If the relative size of the middle and working class are adjusted, assuming a constant managerial/clerical employer ratio, the working class (as well as the middle class) in both the United States and in the other countries is the same relative size (64 percent if U.S. standards are used, approximately 69 percent if the standards of the other countries are used). There is an even greater similarity in the internal structure of the working class than in the middle class. While a total of 52.7 of employed males in the United States were blue-collar workers, the average for the other seven countries was 51.9 percent (the range here is from 56.0 percent for West Germany to 44.3 percent for Japan). In the United States 42.9 percent of the employed males were production workers, while on average 43.7 percent were in the other countries (the range here is from 47.3 percent in West Germany to 38.3 percent in Japan). The proportion of service workers is somewhat higher in the United States (8.2 percent) than elsewhere (5.7 percent), apparently indicating the greater development of the service sector in the United States.

In general, both the overall homogeneity of the class structure among the advanced capitalist countries, and the representativeness of the class structure of the United States is most striking and indicates that the logic of capitalism tends to overwhelm all other forces (including tradition, differential requirements of legitimation, different types of political coalitions, and formal political institutions) to produce essentially the same results everywhere. The *minor* differences between the United States and the rest, i.e., the higher proportion of managers in the United States, the lower proportion of farmers, and the higher proportion of service workers, seems primarily to indicate the slightly more advanced development of capitalism in the United States than elsewhere. It is to be expected that the class structures of the other advanced countries will tend to converge on that of the United States, i.e., that their proportion of farmers will decline, while their proportion of service employees as well as the proportion of managerial and administrative employees will grow.

The income distributions among the advanced capitalist countries do not differ greatly except in the share going to the bottom income fifth. The United States is somewhat above the average in the share going to the highest income fifth (44.8 percent versus 42.9 percent) and is lowest in the income going to the bottom income fifth (3.8 percent as compared to the average of 5.7 percent). These facts combined means that the ratio between the lowest and highest income fifths is greater in the United States (11.8) than in any advanced capitalist country, while Japan (5.6) is the most equalitarian (see Table 3.10).

The somewhat higher than average proportion of total income going to the top 20 percent in the United States is probably in part a combination of the relatively lesser incentive to disguise real income in the higher income fifth (because of lower tax rates in the United States than apply in most other advanced capitalist countries), *and* the greater role of private sector employment of managers and professionals than elsewhere (where the state with its more equalitarian salaries plays a stronger role). The fairly sharp difference in the income share going to the lowest income fifth between the United States and most of the other advanced capitalist countries would seem to indicate *both* the relatively undeveloped system of public benefit programs for the poor in the United States as compared to

TABLE 3.10: Quintile Share Distribution of Total Pretax Income for Selected Countries and Years, 1966-73

Country and Year	Lowest Fifth	Second Fifth	Middle Fifth	Fourth Fifth	Highest Fifth	Ratio of Highest to Lowest Fifth
Australia, 1966-67	6.6	13.5	17.8	23.4	38.8	5.9
Canada, 1969	4.3	10.9	17.3	24.2	43.3	10.1
France, 1970	4.3	9.9	15.8	23.0	47.0	10.9
West Germany, 1973	5.9	10.1	15.1	22.1	46.8	7.9
Japan, 1969	7.6	12.6	16.3	21.0	42.5	5.6
Netherlands, 1967	5.9	10.9	15.8	21.6	45.8	7.8
Norway, 1970	4.9	11.6	18.0	24.6	40.9	8.3
Sweden, 1972	6.0	11.4	17.4	24.3	40.5	6.8
United Kingdom, 1973	5.4	12.0	18.1	24.2	40.3	7.5
United States, 1972	3.8	10.0	16.8	24.5	44.8	11.8
Average	5.7	11.4	16.8	23.2	42.9	7.8

Source: Sawyer 1976, p. 14.

most of the rest of the advanced capitalist countries, and the fact that until the mid-1970s the prevailing unemployment rate in the United States was much higher than that of the other advanced countries. The higher unemployment rate of the United States resulted in both low incomes for a higher proportion of the lowest income quintile (the unemployed or partially employed) *and* a generally greater downward pressure on wages manifested in an above-average size low-wage sector.

The comparative figures on income distribution support those on the relative size of different classes (and sections of classes). With minor variations, the logic of capital accumulation in the advanced countries generates a similar income distribution as well as a similar class structure. Again, this logic, for the most part, appears to overwhelm variations in traditions, the power of various coalitions, differences in need for legitimation, and so on. Thus, the class structure of the United States can be treated as illustrative of that of all the advanced capitalist countries. Analyses drawn on the basis of that structure, can, thus, for the most part be generalized to all advanced capitalist social formations.

In capitalist economies the higher income of those in managerial and professional class positions in comparison with the working class is *ideologically* necessary to demonstrate the superiority of those in these positions vis-à-vis the laboring class (while at the same time their significantly lower income in comparison with the owning class "demonstrates" their *inferiority* vis-à-vis this latter class). Higher status as well as higher income is an outward sign of the legitimacy of their greater economic power. Both are "proof" of their greater contribution and superior abilities and, as such, both facilitate their ability to successfully secure respect from and command the laboring class. It is *not* necessary to offer "semiautonomous employees," independent professionals, or even supervisory personnel an income higher than workers receive to get them to perform their jobs, since the inherent rewards of such labor in comparison to the hard, boring labor and the degradation associated with laboring class jobs is generally sufficient (although higher pay might well be a secondary factor in many cases, especially in initial recruitment of people from the working class for semiprofessional positions or to motivate supervisory personnel to greater efficiency). The superior skill, income, and status of middle-class positions vis-à-vis working-class positions within a class society is the outcome of the logic of the class structure, just as, in a different way, is the superior income and status of the owning class.

The very high incomes of the capitalist class are almost entirely a result of their ownership/control of the means of production. It is derivative from the "surplus value" obtained through their ability to pay those whose labor power they hire (directly or indirectly) less than the value of what they produce, i.e., it is a result of exploitation guaranteed by the competitive pressure among capitalist enterprises that are forced under threat of bankruptcy to expand sales, reduce costs, and maximize funds for reinvestment. The high status associated with capitalist class positions is partially a result of the great prestige associated with their economic power (and hence ability to determine events) and in part cultivated in order to legitimate their power.

SOCIAL CLASS FORMATION

Those in the same class positions tend to have similar degrees of skill, incomes, and social status because each of these are conditions of, or are derivative from, similar class positions. Noncraft working class positions are the least skilled, require the least training, receive the least income, and have the lowest status (are the most degraded). Propertied class positions, although they do not necessarily require much skill (they are most typically inherited), are typically associated with high levels of formal education. They have both the highest incomes and the highest status (because of the power associated with these positions). Salaried middle class positions as well as independent professionals and artisans normally have a greater skill (and hence training) associated with them than typically do either workers or capitalists because efficient performance in such positions requires it.

Those in a similar class position tend to coalesce into the same social class. A similar relation to the means of production produces a common social psychology, common leisure patterns, and a common life-style and culture, a strong tendency to intermarry with other members of the same class as well as a common sense of identity as a class. Common class position tends to erode traditional differences among ethnic groups of diverse peasant origin as well as the importance of "racial," religious, and other cultural differences; and, over time, results in a fairly homogeneous social grouping.

Each of the three basic classes as well as those in the excluded sector tend to form into distinct social classes sharing a more or less common consciousness and life-style. Those in intermediate positions in the class structure tend to be absorbed into one of the two basic social classes to which they are adjacent, rather than form a separate social class of their own. Large and medium capitalists tend to form into a very distinct social class defined by highly exclusive social institutions (at the heart of which are the exclusive men's clubs and the *Social Register*—see Chapter 4). Small capitalists, who are in fact intermediate between (the independent sector of) the petty bourgeoisie and the capitalist class proper, tend to form into the *middle* social class (whose other members afford them respect, while they are snubbed socially by middle and large capitalists). This fact is testified to by the fact that the majority (60 percent) of capitalists in the United States (the vast majority of whom are, of course, small capitalists) predominately identify themselves as "middle class"— only 10 percent identify as "upper class" (see Table 3.11). Likewise, upwardly mobile top managers who have obtained a significant amount of real economic power (and normally considerable material wealth as well) are excluded from the social institutions of the capitalist class and, thus, socially integrate with the middle class. Although they may be in transition from the middle class to the capitalist class proper, because they do not have the right ancestry, they are socially excluded, no matter how much they might try to imitate capitalist class life-styles.

Semiprofessionals as intermediate employees tend to be socially integrated into (the bottom reaches of) the middle class. Although the income of primary and secondary school teachers, most technicians, journalists, and so forth is little different from manual workers, their status (and self-conception) is higher. Thus, although they may engage in a bit of "value stretch" and economizing to put on a public show (while skimping considerably on less socially visable aspects of their lives), they generally strive to middle class practices and values, and further, are pretty much accepted by most middle class people as peers (if somewhat low-status ones). The middle class identification and practices of semiprofessionals are enhanced by the fact that they typically have four years of college (or in some cases two), the fact that they generally have a fair degree of autonomy on the job, and

TABLE 3.11: Class Identification, 1977

	Lower	Working	Middle	Upper
Capitalists	0%	30%	60%	10%
Old middle class	1	43	47	9
New middle class	1	22	68	8
Intermediate Employees	1	42	56	1
White-Collar workers	2	55	42	1
Blue-Collar workers	5	66	26	2
Total	3	52	41	4

Source: University of Michigan, Survey Research Center, *General Social Survey* (Ann Arbor: National Opinion Research Center, 1977).

the fact that their labor tends to be relatively unsocialized and little affected by mechanization (factors common to the middle class proper). In 1977 in the United States 56 percent of intermediate employees identified themselves as middle class, as compared to 42 percent who identified themselves as working class (see Table 3.11). Foremen, however, are part of the working social class. They typically come from working class families, have spent their lives before promotion in working class positions, usually have (and see) few possibilities of further promotion, have workers as friends, relatives, and neighbors, and continue with a fairly affluent but still working class life-style.

White-collar workers, although they tend to be influenced in a middle class direction, mostly share a working class culture and identification. In 1977, 55 percent of all white-collar workers identified as working class (and 42 percent as middle class). This compared with 66 percent of blue-collar workers who identified as working class and 26 percent who identified as middle class. It is of interest to note that a significant proportion of traditional middle class people identified as working class (43 percent), indicating that many small farmers, artisans, and marginal business people from working class or small farmer backgrounds who live in working class social environments are not socially integrated into the middle class proper. The class identification of this group contrasts sharply with that of the new middle class, where 68 percent identify as middle class (see Table 3.11). The processes of class formation that affect the three basic classes are examined extensively in the next four chapters.

The fact that those in the excluded sector do not produce anything of use for society, instead existing in an atmosphere of mutual suspicion, competition, and hustling, produces a social psychology of individualism, egoism, ruthlessness, and lack of sympathy for others. A distinctive lumpen social psychology and culture tends to develop that is very different from that of the working class (including the working poor). They do not feel the social pressures toward compliance with the prevailing norms and standards of respectable working class life. Personal relations, especially those in families, tend to be strained. Fighting, drinking, neglect of children, and functional illiteracy are common. Sexual relations tend to be casual and loose with consensual unions rather than legal marriage common. A woman tends to have a number of children by different men (for whom *she* assumes primary responsibility). Family life is more female centered, with men more marginal (this is reinforced by the welfare system that normally grants welfare only to women not living with men). Attitudes are characterized by fear, suspicion, and apathy as well as inferiority, fatalism, and cynicism. The politics of this group are highly unstable. One minute they may participate in a riot against state authority, and the next they might serve as informers or thugs to break up a union meeting or political demonstration.

It is clear that whether we are examining capitalists, the working class, the middle class, or the excluded sector, class structure is the basis for the formation of social classes. Common class position results in common attitudes and values, common life-styles and inter-marriage patterns, and in common class identification.

4

The Capitalist Class

This chapter examines the economically and socially dominant class in U.S. society, the capitalist class. Its historical development out of preexisting classes is treated, as is its consolidation as a distinctive social class in the last years of the nineteenth century. The various subcategories of the capitalist class are examined with emphasis on the predominant role of its monopoly (especially its financial) core. The economic basis of all sectors of the monopoly capitalist class is the giant corporations and financial institutions that dominate the world capitalist economy. The ties of the leading wealthy individuals and families to these institutions are examined closely. The role of the leading hired executives of the giant corporations is analyzed, and it is found that they, for the most part, can not be considered to be part of the core monopoly capitalist class; although many of them, because of either the partial discretion they obtain due to fairly diversified stock ownership *or* stockownership in their own right must be considered part of the capitalist class. Last, the various social institutions that shape and give coherence to the monopoly and middle levels of the capitalist class are examined in detail. It is found that the capitalist class is by far the most cohesive and conscious of itself as a class of all classes in the United States.

THE ORIGIN AND DEVELOPMENT OF THE CAPITALIST CLASS

The capitalist class (as with all contemporary social classes) has been shaped, and is continually being transformed, by the logic of the capitalist mode of production of which it is a manifestation. Historically, the capitalist class had a tripartite origin in: the old commercial bourgeoisie of merchants, moneylenders, and shipowners that dominated commerce during the precapitalist period; the precapitalist landlords in Europe and slave lords in America; and the small artisans and petty-bourgeois businessmen of both Europe and America. In the eighteenth century these groups were distinct both economically and socially; however, over the course of the nineteenth century old merchant wealth merged with landed fortunes and the rising sector of the old petty bourgeoisie to form a single economic and social class.

The early factories (which were heavily concentrated in textiles) tended to grow up either from an expansion of the workshops of artisans or from a centralization of the operations of small merchants who had formerly made their money in the putting-out system (they bought raw materials which they distributed to peasant households for transformation into finished products). The expansion and/or centralization of textile production (as well as metalworking and mining) was typically financed by the wealthy merchant class. Such financing was necessary because of the inadequate funds of the smaller merchants and artisans who generally initiated the new forms of business organization.

The fortunes of the rich merchants who financed much of early industrialization were often made in the overseas trade in slaves, rum, metal goods, and so forth. Once the industrial capitalist system got off the ground and proved its superior productivity and profitability, the older classes of landlords (who had previously existed on rents from tenants) and slave lords were undermined. They too came to invest their wealth in the expanding productive enterprises that employed wage labor.

The origins of the modern U.S. capitalist class are to be found in the period between the Civil War and the turn of the nineteenth century—the period of the transformation from competitive to monopoly capital. It was during this period that large trusts were first formed on a wide scale in order to set prices, share out markets, and control labor and the prices of raw materials. In the early period of capitalism there were hundreds or thousands of separately owned enterprises producing a given commodity. This was far too many for any one enterprise to have any control over the prices charged for their goods, or to have any systematic relation with other similar enterprises, except through the uninhibited competition of the market. By the early twentieth century competitive struggle among such small enterprises reduced their number in virtually every industrial sector to a relative handful of the most ruthless competitors and efficient producers.

Ancillary to the processes of competition, bankruptcy, and merger, which resulted in fewer but ever bigger businesses, were the revolutionary technological progress of industrial production and the expanding scale of marketing. These two factors were putting the initial investment required to open an industrial enterprise beyond the reach of any but the very richest individuals. Ever greater funds became necessary for investment, which meant that virtually anyone wishing to open an enterprise had to secure funding from finance capital (or at least assistance in floating stock).

In this environment the modern corporate form was developed, the most distinctive legal feature of which was limited liability. The corporation came to be treated as a legal entity that could sue, be sued, and otherwise have a legal identity independent of its owners, owners who were legally libel for the actions of such corporations only up to the value of the stock they held. The initiators of a given corporation were thus able to mobilize large sums of money from those who were willing to buy shares, but did not want to assume liability or responsibility. A few large stockholders could thus dominate a corporation on the basis of a rather small amount of stock. The formation of the corporations brought great personal fortunes to their founders. While in 1861 there were only three millionaires in the United States, by 1897 there were 3,800 (Baltzell 1958, p. 18).

It was typically the financial capitalists (whose money originated either in commerce, e.g., J.P. Morgan, or in the monopolization of a given commodity from the inside, e.g., John D. Rockefeller) who were in a position to mobilize smaller masses of wealth to establish the corporations. A financial capitalist, such as Morgan, would buy up a large number of smaller competitive enterprises (such as steel mills or railroads), create a monopoly, and raise the price of the goods produced or service provided to the public, thereby greatly increasing profitability (people had little or no choice but to purchase the new monopoly corporation's product at the new monopoly price). The financiers would then sell stock in the new corporation based on its new monopoly position (the aggregate value of which was set on the basis of its ability to make profits, which was considerably more than the worth of the physical equipment and resources initially purchased, or the amount the financial capitalists had recently paid to the previous separate owners). Through such processes large numbers of corporations, including most of the major corporations that continue to dominate the U.S. economy today (or their predecessors in the case of mergers and in a few cases divisions) were formed around the turn of the century. The consolidation of the monopoly corporations meant that a class of monopoly capitalists based in commerce, finance, and industrial production became the dominant class in the United States.

The founders of the modern corporations, those like the Rockefellers who rose up from the ranks of small business and those like the Vanderbilts and Morgans who transformed themselves from commercial merchants into productive capitalists and financiers, tended to manage their early enterprises themselves and thus to direct their operations (although the financial capitalists such as Morgan generally merely managed the banks, not the productive enterprisess they established). However, over the twentieth century, as the heirs of the great founding fathers took over the family fortunes, the operational control and management of the monopoly corporations has mostly been put into the hands of professional highly trained and skilled managers (whose social origins are predominantly in the petty bourgeoisie). As the technical problems of modern corporations have increased, and because there is no reason to expect that the children of the founders would be the most able to handle them, managerial functions have mostly devolved to experts. Those wealthy families who are able to hire the best managerial talent are in the position to make the highest profits on their investments. The role of the founding and owning families then, has increasingly been limited to hiring and firing management, and in varying degree, through participation on the boards of directors and voting their stock to control only the most basic corporate decisions. The course of the twentieth century has seen the decline of entrepreneurs or self-made millionaires, the rise of managers, and a consolidation of the position of the banks (who have become increasingly powerful as the still extremely wealthy founding families' economic power is diffused).

THE SPECIFICATION OF THE CAPITALIST CLASS

The capitalist class is composed of all those who have real economic ownership of the means of production (or power over what is produced) in capitalist society. Capitalists control the labor power of wage laborers, allocating it to various tasks and disposing of their workers' product as they wish. Their income comes predominantly from hiring the labor power of others. Real economic ownership implies that capitalists may either themselves exercise operational control (control over *how* production is carried out) *or* assign it to others, subject to compliance with the production goals of the capitalists. While being a capitalist implies that one has sufficient security in one's position not to be displaced by others as a result of following one or another policy (short of bankruptcy or long-term abuse of position), it does *not* necessarily imply the ability to transfer property to others (through inheritance, sale, or gift).

We might categorize five types of capitalists: first, those who have *legal title* to the means of production and themselves administer the means of production, thus exercising both real economic ownership *and* day-to-day operational control; second, those who have both legal title and real economic power, but hire others to manage their enterprises (i.e., do not exercise operational control), stepping in only when there is trouble or when they have fundamental disagreements with management; third, those who have partial legal title but because of wide distribution of their stocks are unable to exercise real economic ownership over any particular enterprise, and thus content themselves with receiving income from stocks and allocating capital through buying and selling stocks (these capitalists are a leisure class with legal rights to their income which influences major corporate decisions because of their power in the stock market); fourth, top executives (the highest level managers of mega corporations) who do *not* have legal title and, thus, can neither pass on title to their heirs or sell their positions to others, but nevertheless, because of a wide dispersion of stock ownership, have a significant degree of discretion (i.e., relative autonomy), and hence partial real economic ownership; and fifth, state capitalists who are in the top administrative positions of state-owned enterprises *and* have sufficient security in their positions not to be displaced from their general position because of public disagreement with their policies (although they may perhaps be transferred from one enterprise to another), and who thus essentially have real economic ownership of such enterprises.

There are two aspects to the real economic ownership of capitalists: first, the labor of coordinating and organizing labor power so that it can effectively produce; and second, the exploitation of (i.e., the securing of an economic surplus from) labor power. The first aspect of this function is productive, it is necessary in any type of economy (it must be performed by someone); while the second is a distinctive product of exploitative relations of class society. The content of the capitalist organization of labor power, thus, consists of: that part dictated by the logic of technology and the basic social laws of work organization; and that part required by the necessity of maintaining exploitative productive relations.

It should be noted that at a given level of the development of the forces of production it may be the case that the only practical way in which society's wealth can be increased is through private ownership of the means of production, and, thus, that the condition of fulfilling the first function (productivity) is the existence of the second (exploitation). But these two functions are not inextricably or logically linked. Either can occur without the other. They come together at a certain historical conjunction in the transition from peasant society to capitalism. But they gradually become disassociated in the latter phase of the development of capitalism, a period when private ownership and control of the means of production tends to produce an increasing antagonism between the two functions (with the exploitative tending to predominate over the productive function).

The income of the capitalist class comes primarily from hiring the labor power of others, rather than from their own labor. The capitalist class can, thus, be categorized according to the extensiveness of its control over the labor power of others (or the size of its wealth). The monopoly sector (or fraction) of the capitalist class is those who have power to significantly influence the economy of the country as a whole (and perhaps beyond) through controlling the major corporations and financial institutions (and buying and selling very large quantities of stocks and bonds). A rough guideline in the United States for distinguishing this sector from the rest might be those extended families that had an aggregate net worth of at least $100 million in 1982 (see Hill 1975, p. 5). The monopoly capitalist class in the United States consists of a few thousand families (the most prominent of which include the Rockefellers, Mellons, Fords, and DuPonts).

Below the monopoly capitalist sector of the capitalist class is the nonmonopoly middle sector, those who have considerable economic power but are not in a position to significantly influence the entire economy. These capitalists are either: in control of relatively small, but nevertheless, substantial, competitive sector enterprises; in control of enterprises that are not national in scope, but do have substantial control or influence over the economy in their region; or have a substantial, but not controlling, interest in monopoly corporations. The wealth of such capitalists could roughly be considered to be between a few million and 100 million dollars in 1982. Its size can be measured in the tens of thousands of families.

The nonmonopoly middle sector of the capitalist class (as well as the small capitalists) is being preserved and reproduced within monopoly capitalist society because of its vital role in the overall capital accumulation process. The monopoly megacorporations have largely appropriated the high profit, relatively low risk, and capital-intensive sectors of the economy, leaving a number of niches for smaller capitalists (from whom they can profit indirectly). The niches that continue to be occupied (although not exclusively) by competitive capital include the sectors of limited profitability (e.g., large farms, many retail stores, garment factories); sectors that pioneer in new types of production or lead in technological innovations and are, thus, normally high risk (such enterprises tend to be bought up by the monopoly corporations, or in a few cases join them, once they have demonstrated the viability of their innovations); and sectors that are especially labor intensive and involve relatively high risk because of fluctuations in markets (e.g., large fruit and vegetable farms, clothing manufacturers, construction firms).

There are also social and political reasons why this middle sector is tolerated by the monopoly corporations (effective through state actions favoring smaller business, e.g., subsidies, loans, contracts, and so forth). It serves as a buffer between it and the working class and petty bourgeoisie. The monopoly sector is able to mobilize tens of thousands of smaller capitalists all around the country (who typically have considerable political influence on the local level) in support of the monopoly capitalist system. The existence of a middle and lower strata of the capitalist class acts to defuse antimonopoly sentiments because it holds out hope to both the smaller capitalists *and* the petty bourgeoisie (the hope that they can be upwardly mobile into and in the capitalist class) as well as preventing the development of the considerable hostility that would result if the monopolies adopted a policy of driving the smaller capitalists out of business. (The existence of an independent petty bourgeoisie plays a similar role in relation to the working class—see Poulantzas 1974, pt. 2, chap. 1.)

Competitive sector middle level capitalist enterprises are often dominated by the monopoly sector through contracting agreements allocated by the megacorporations, the ownership of patents and licenses by the monopoly corporations, the monopoly position of the megacorporations vis-à-vis the competitive sector businesses as suppliers and purchasers, and not least of all, the position of the smaller competitive sector enterprises as debtors to the megabanks (from which they must borrow to increase their productivity in the competitive struggle). The competitive sector of middle capitalists thus tends to be organically integrated with the monopoly corporations. While there may be some resentment on the part of the members of this sector against the monopoly sector (or the "Eastern banks"), for the most part they profit quite handsomely by this integration, and fully identify with them as capitalists. Since they are not generally being driven out of business by monopoly capital (as is much of the independent petty bourgeoisie and small capital), they have no significant potential to oppose monopoly capital in a serious way.

The lowest level sector of the capitalist class is intermediate between the petty bourgeoisie and the middle sector of the capitalist class. These small capitalists employ only a relative handful of workers (roughly between 10 and 50) who were worth at the most in 1982 a few million dollars (but more likely less than a million).

Included here are the owners of small workshops, medium size stores, large farms, and so forth.

Both the small business and intermediate competitive sectors of the capitalist class are likely to pay their workers less than do monopoly capitalists as well as to provide them with less comfortable and secure work situations. Unlike the monopolies, these businesses do not have the ability to pass high wages or taxes on to consumers by informally fixing prices. When a wage increase is granted or a new tax imposed, prices of goods produced by a monopoly corporation are generally raised by a comparable amount. Such raises are not possible for a competitive enterprise that finds its prices in the market (and thus has no significant control over them). These sectors, then, tend to resist reforms and concessions to the working class more than does the monopoly sector.

The question of the separation between legal title and real economic ownership, and between ownership and operational control, is most relevant in the monopoly capitalist sector. Most enterprises in the competitive sector (and those of regional significance) tend to be controlled by their legal owners (an individual or coalition) and often managed by them as well. This is even more true of the small capitalists who typically manage their own property (if only because they are not wealthy enough to hire someone else to do it for them).

The capitalist class can also be categorized according to its various industrial functions. The basic divisions here being among: productive capitalists, who control factories, mines, transportation, communications, and large-scale agricultural enterprises; commercial capitalists, who control the means of distribution, of buying and selling commodities produced by the productive capitalists; and financial capitalists, who control the banks and insurance companies, which finance both productive and commercial enterprises. Although there is a basic identity of interest between these three sectors (since all exploit labor power), there are secondary antagonisms based on differences over the share of the product going to each sector, e.g., between the productive and commercial capitalists and the financial capitalists over the rate of interest and debt, and between the productive capitalists and the commercial capitalists over wholesale prices (e.g., monopoly producers will attempt to squeeze competitive distributors, while a monopoly distributor will attempt to squeeze competitive producers such as small farmers). There are also secondary antagonisms within the productive sector, e.g., between those that produce goods and those that transport them; between those that produce goods and those that produce power or handle communications, among those who produce commodities such as steel and those that produce such commodities as coal and iron ore on the one side and machine tools or automobiles on the other, and so on. Such antagonisms are rooted in the relative prices (and hence share in profits) accruing to one or another faction of the capitalist class. And last, within identical economic sectors, e.g., steel, auto, rubber, and so forth, there are, of course, significant antagonisms among the different enterprises based on competition over market shares (which usually in the monopoly sector does not take primarily the price form).

In all capitalist countries other than the leading one (or perhaps handful) the capitalist class can also be divided according to its relationsip to the corporations and financial institutions of the leading imperialist state(s)—in Europe in the post–World War II world largely U.S capital, in the rest of the capitalist world since the 1960s to U.S., Japanese, West German, French, and British capital. National, comparador, and internal bourgeoisie can be distinguished. The national bourgeoisie is that fraction of capital (monopoly, competitive, middle sector, or small intermediate sector) that is in direct competition with foreign-owned enterprises and companies and banks, and then has an interest in the exclusion of such foreign operations from the territory of the local state. The national bourgeoisie tends to be concentrated in the competitive and middle and small capital sectors as well as to be productive capitalists (rather than merchants). The comparador bourgeoisie in contrast, owes its existence (and hence its share of profits) to the presence of foreign capital within a country. It acts as the intermediary in one way or another for foreign capital (e.g., purchasers of the goods of small farmers or artisans, distributors or the products from the imperialist country, provider of essential services for the foreign corporations, and so forth). Because of its total integration and dependence on foreign capital, this sector of the bourgeoisie tends to be strongly supportive of the presence of foreign economic interests, including the general economic subordination of their country to foreign imperialism. They tend to be concentrated in the merchant sector.

A third sector of the bourgeoisie of countries other than the leading imperialist power is what Nicos Poulantzas has labeled the internal bourgeoisie. This class has become increasingly important throughout the capitalist countries (both the industrialized and less developed). This sector, while integrated most often in the form of joint enterprises or cooperative projects with foreign capital, also has a basis for autonomy. The internal bourgeoisie generally acts to acquire a larger share of the profits and to reduce the role of foreign corporations without excluding them entirely (and thus losing their technology, selling techniques, and so forth). While it might at times act to limit the role of foreign capital, and thus increase profits for itself, the internal bourgeoisie, understanding that its profit position is based on integration with foreign corporations thus fundamentally defends the foreign presence. This sector tends to be located among the larger enterprises in the productive sector, e.g., manufacturing, mineral and petroleum production (see Poulantzas 1974, pt. 1, chap. 2).

THE ECONOMIC BASIS OF THE U.S. CAPITALIST CLASS

The wealth of the monopoly capitalist class is, of course, rooted in their ownership rights and other claims to income in as well as their control over the monopoly corporations that dominate the capitalist world's economy (see Chapter 3). The largest of these corporations in 1980 had assets in the $50 billion to $100 billion range, greater than the GNPs of all but a handful of the richest countries of the world (see Table 4.1 and 4.2).

In 1980 there were approximately 600,000 millionaires in the United States. This represented about 1 percent of the families and 0.6 percent of the labor force with income in that year (*Money*, January 1981, p. 36). In 1977 the National Opinion Research Center Social Survey found that 1.8 percent of economically active males and females reported themselves as self-employed *and* supervising someone who supervised someone else. Given these figures, we would probably not be to far off to estimate the number of capitalists in the United States at approximately 1 to 2 percent of the population—let us, being liberal, assume the 2 percent figure, i.e., that in 1980 there were about 1 million individual capitalists in the United States.

In 1982 Forbes magazine estimated that there were 13 billionaires in the U.S. (see Table 4.3). The two richest individuals in the United States in 1982 were Daniel Keith Ludwig and Perry Richardsen Bass, both of whose fortunes exceeded $2 billion. The two richest individual fortunes in recent years have been those of J. Paul Getty and Howard Hughes (both of whom died in the 1970s), which in 1967 were evaluated by *Fortune* magazine at roughly $3 billion each (in 1982 dollars). *Fortune* has estimated that there have been about 46 individual fortunes in the United States between 1967 and 1978 whose worth exceeded $500 million. Many of these are third or later generation multimillionaires belonging to the richest families in the United States (whose founders' original fortunes are now dispersed among many descents). According to *Fortune*, these include six Rockefellers, four Mellons, and a DuPont (see Table 4.3).

George Lundberg estimated that in 1964 the DuPont family fortune as a whole (including all descendents of the founders of the

TABLE 4.1: Twenty Leading Industrial Corporations in the United States, 1980

Rank	Company	Sales (millions)	Assets (millions)	Employees	Rate of Profit[a]
1	Exxon	$103,143	$ 56,577	176,615	22.2%
2	Mobil	59,510	32,705	212,800	25.0
3	General Motors	57,728	34,581	746,000	—[b]
4	Texaco	51,196	26,430	66,745	21.1
5	Standard Oil of California	40,479	22,162	40,218	21.7
6	Ford Motor	37,086	24,348	426,700	—[b]
7	Gulf Oil	26,483	18,638	58,900	14.6
8	International Business Machines	26,213	26,703	341,279	21.6
9	Standard Oil (Indiana)	26,133	20,167	56,401	20.4
10	General Electric	24,959	18,511	402,000	18.5
11	Atlantic Richfield	23,744	16,605	53,400	22.2
12	Shell Oil	19,830	17,615	36,596	19.0
13	I.T.T.	18,530	15,417	348,000	14.3
14	Conoco	18,325	11,036	41,503	22.4
15	E.I. du Pont de Nemours	13,652	9,560	135,900	12.6
16	Phillips Petroleum	13,377	9,844	32,400	21.7
17	Tenneco	13,226	13,853	106,000	17.4
18	Sun	12,945	10,955	48,806	16.8
19	U.S. Steel	12,492	11,748	149,172	9.5
20	Occidental Petroleum	12,476	6,630	34,700	34.6
	Total	$1,650,263	$1,175,471	15,909,985	—[b]
	Top 500	$119,978	86,871	1,702,416	—[b]

[a]Rate of return on stockholders' equity.
[b]Data not available.
Sources: Fortune, May 4, 1981, pp. 324, 342; June 15, 1981, pp. 216-17.

dynasty) was the largest single *family* fortune in the United States, totaling $20 billion (in 1980 dollars), while the Mellon and Rockefeller families had approximately $13 billion each (in 1980 dollars) and the Ford heirs roughly $7 billion (Lundberg 1968, pp. 143, 151, 158). It has been estimated that in the mid-1960s there were 31 other familiy fortunes worth over $200 million (in 1980 dollars), including the following families: Dorrance, Phippse, Harkness, Reynolds, Milbanks, McCormick-Deering, Morgan, Whitney, Houghton, Waggoner, Lehman, Duke, Firestone, Pitcairn, Weyerhauser, Post-Hutton, Harriman, Guggenheim-Straus, and Fisher (see Menshikov 1969, p. 52).

TABLE 4.2: Twenty Leading Financial Institutions

Rank	Company	Assets (millions)	Employees
1	Citicorp	$114,920	53,700
2	Bank America Corp.	111,617	83,713
3	Chase Manhattan Bank	76,100	33,450
4	Prudential Life	59,778	62,453
5	Federal National Mortgage Assn.	58,470	1,142
6	Manufacturers Hanover Corp.	55,522	24,893
7	J.P. Morgan and Co.	51,991	11,325
8	Metropolitan Life	48,310	48,000
9	Continental Illinois Corp.	42,089	12,257
10	Chemical New York Corp.	41,342	18,223
11	Aetna Life and Casualty	35,753	39,100
12	Equitable Life Assurance	34,600	26,160
13	Banker's Trust New York Corp.	32,326	11,827
14	Western Bancorp	32,110	30,085
15	First Chicago	28,699	10,602
16	Security Pacific	27,794	25,069
17	Wells Fargo and Co.	23,638	17,460
18	Aetna Life	22,271	17,399
19	Travelers Corp.	21,637	29,339
20	New York Life	19,725	19,623
Total			
	50 largest commercial banking companies	$970,969	568,748
	50 largest life insurance companies	$370,899	429,131
	50 largest diversified financial companies	$364,748	612,417

Source: *Fortune*, July 13, 1981, pp. 116-21.

The very wealthiest families have been able not only to preserve their inherited fortunes but to increase their wealth significantly in spite of the various "redistributive measures" of the "welfare state." It is also of interest to note that about half of the wealthiest families are new wealthy who amassed their wealth mostly in the post-1930 period (54 of the 90 richest families) (Menshikov 1969, p. 54). But this is true of very few of the very richest families (who accumulated their wealth in the post–Civil War generation, and in some cases before). Some large fortunes were made during World War II and the economic boom that followed it in good part through military and construction contracts with the government as well as in petroleum. But for the most part, the newer wealthy, such as Howard Hughes,

TABLE 4.3: U.S. Billionaires, 1982

Individual	Primary Source of Fortune	Amount
Daniel Keith Ludwig	Ships	$2 billion +
Perry Richardsen Bass	Oil	$2 billion +
Gordon Peter Getty	Oil	$1.4 billion
Margret Hunt Hill	Oil	$1 billion +
Philip Anschutz	Oil	$1 billion +
Forrest Mars, Sr.	Candy	$1 billion +
William Herbert Hunt	Oil	$1 billion +
David Packard	Electronics	$1 billion
Caroline Hunt Schoellkopf	Oil	$1 billion +/–
Lamar Hunt	Oil	$1 billion +/–
Nelson Bunker Hunt	Oil	$1 billion +/–
Marvin Davis	Oil	$1 billion +/–
David Rockefeller	Oil/Banking	$1 billion +/–

Source: Forbes, September 13, 1982, pp. 102–5.

remained economically subordinate to the older and even wealthier interests concentrated in New York banks (see Fitch and Oppenheimer 1970; and Menshikov 1969, chap. 2).

Increasing Monopoly

The power of the largest monopoly corporations continues to grow as the economy becomes more concentrated (more in fewer hands) and thus centralized (increasingly coordinated). As a consequence, the relative position of the monopoly sector of the capitalist class is enhanced. The percentage of total value added in the manufacturing sector by the largest manufacturing companies has continually risen in the United States since World War II. In 1947 the largest 100 manufacturing corporations were responsible for 23 percent of the value added by all manufacturing companies and in 1958, 30 percent. By 1976 they were responsible for 34 percent. The largest 200 manufacturing corporations meanwhile expanded from 30 percent in 1947 and 38 percent in 1958 to 44 percent in 1976 (see Table 4.4). It should be noted that while the long-term trend in proportion of assets held has been in the same direction, there was no tendency for asset concentration to increase over the course of the 1970s. In 1950, the largest 100 manufacturing corporations held 39.7 percent of all manufacturing assets, while in 1979 they held 46.1 percent. The largest 200 in 1950 held 47.7 percent, and in 1979, 59.0 percent (U.S. Department of Commerce 1981a, p. 568).

The trend toward industrial concentration, and hence the enhancement of the position of the monopoly capitalist sector of the

TABLE 4.4: Percentage of Total Value Added by Manufacturing for the Largest Manufacturing Companies

	Largest 100	Largest 200
1947	23%	30%
1954	30	37
1958	30	38
1962	32	40
1967	33	42
1972	33	43
1976	34	44

Source: U.S. Department of Commerce 1981, p. 568.

capitalist class (both owners and top managers), has been general throughout the advanced capitalist countries. For example, in the United Kingdom the share of the largest 100 manufacturing companies increased from 30 percent of net output in 1958 to 40 percent in 1972. In West Germany the share of sales of the largest 100 companies grew from 21.7 percent in 1972 to 24.4 percent in 1975. In Canada the share of value added by the 100 largest manufacturing companies increased from 23 percent in 1947 to 35 percent in 1976 (New York *Times*, April 28, 1980, B-1).

Industrial concentration, and hence the role of the monopoly capitalist segment of the capitalist class, is more pronounced in some sectors of the economy than others. For example, in the United States in 1972 the top four companies accounted for 99 percent of passenger car production, 92 percent of flat glass production, 90 percent of cereal breakfast foods, 90 percent of turbines and turbine engines, 90 percent of electrical lamps, 85 percent of household refrigerators and freezers, 84 percent of cigarettes, 83 percent of television pictures tubes, 79 percent of primary aluminum, and 73 percent of tires and inner tubes (New York *Times*, September 28, 1980, B-1).

The tendency toward concentration is manifested in the absorption of some companies by others. Over the course of the 1960s and 1970s in the United States the tendency for larger corporations to merge with each other has accelerated. For example, in 1960 there were 51 corporate mergers of industrial corporations, involving a total of $1.5 billion in acquired assets. In the 1977–78 period there was an average of 105 such mergers a year, involving $9.7 billion in acquired assets (U.S. Department of Commerce 1981a, p. 575).

The Central Role of Financial Institutions in the U.S. Capitalist Class

Finance capital (banking and insurance) is more concentrated than is manufacturing. In 1979 the 50 leading commercial banks in the United States (which together held $517.1 billion in assets) accounted for 36 percent of all the assets of U.S. commercial banks (U.S. Department of Commerce 1091a, 535). The assets of just commercial banks in the United States in 1979 amounted to 33.5 percent of the reproducible, tangible national wealth of the entire business sector. There has been little change in this percentage since the 1930s. All banking institutions in 1979 accounted for 50.7 percent of the national wealth in the business sector (up from 44.2 percent in 1930 and 43.9 percent in 1950). All financial companies (banking plus insurance) accounted for 65.2 percent of the U.S. national wealth in the business sector in 1979, up from 56.4 percent in 1930 and 61.2 percent in 1950 (it should be noted that the short-term mid-1960s/late 1970s trend has been toward declining percentages) (see Table 4.5). In 1975 the ratio of the assets of all financial companies to those of all manufacturing companies was 1.92 (this ratio has been relatively constant since the 1930s). The center of power within the capitalist class is thus seen to be in financial institutions, especially the banks.

Banking institutions (especially commercial and investment banks) are extremely important power centers within the U.S. monopoly capitalist class. Their power is primarily exercised through both their control of credit to the industrial enterprises and their control over a high proportion of stock (held largely in their trust departments). In 1974, 33.3 percent of all corporate stock outstanding in the United States was held in one form or another by financial institutions (11.1 percent of the total in personal trust departments of banks, 9.9 percent in bank-held pension funds, 5.4 percent by investment companies, and 3.5 percent by life insurance companies). In 1929 all financial institutions held only 9.6 percent of total corporate stock, in 1952, 18.9 percent. The biggest source of growth in bank holdings has been in pension funds, where bank holdings grew from 0.9 percent of total bank assets in 1952 to 9.9 percent in 1974. While the personal trust stocks held by banks often do not give banks full voting rights, pension fund trusts do. This fact gives the commercial banks a rapidly growing role in the fundamental decision making of the corporate sector. Further, financial institutions are direct owners of stock in their own right. In the 1959–68 period net stock purchases by financial institutions were more than three times as great as the value of all *new* stock issues (Kotz 1978, pp. 64, 65).

A U.S. Senate study done in 1980 of 100 of the largest U.S. corporations found that J.P. Morgan and Company is effectively the

TABLE 4.5: The Role of Finance Capital in the U.S. Economy (assets in billions of dollars)

	Commercial Banks A	All Banking Institutions B	Life Insurance Companies C	All Insurance Companies D	All Financial Companies E=(B+D)	Manufacturing Companies F	G=E/F	National Wealth (Reproducible Tangible, Business Sector Only) H
1930	64.1 (34.1)[a]	83.0 (44.2)[a]	18.8 (10.0)[a]	23.5 (12.0)[a]	106.5 (56.4)[a]	69.2 (36.8)	1.53	188
1940	67.8 —[b]	85.4 —	30.8 —	35.9 —	121.3 —	60.5 —	2.00	—
1950	156.9 (35.1)	196.2 (43.9)	64.0 (14.3)	77.5 (17.3)	273.7 (61.2)	141.6 (31.7)	1.93	447
1960	243.3 (29.9)	355.4 (43.7)	119.6 (14.7)	149.7 (18.4)	505.1 (62.1)	262.3 (32.2)	1.93	814
1965	382.9 (38.1)	570.7 (56.7)	158.9 (15.8)	200.7 (20.0)	771.4 (76.7)	311.5 (31.0)	2.48	1,006
1970	581.5 (37.2)	836.9 (53.6)	207.3 (13.3)	265.9 (17.0)	1,102.8 (70.6)	612.9 (39.2)	1.80	1,562
1975	974.7 (36.5)	1,434.0 (53.6)	289.3 (10.8)	383.5 (14.3)	1,817.5 (68.0)	944.6 —	1.92	2,673
1979	1,437.7 (33.5)	2,174.9 (50.7)	432.3 (10.1)	620(est.) (14.5)	2,795 (65.2)	— —	—	4,288

[a]Percentaged on Column H.
[b]Data not available.
Sources: U.S. Department of Commerce, 1981, pp. 533, 536, 537, 550, 552, 567, 474; 1975b, pp. 1047, 1060.

first or second biggest stockholder (mostly through holdings it manages for others) in *25* percent (including IBM, Bank of America, Eastern Airlines, Citicorp, Mobil, General Motors, General Electric, Sears, and Westinghouse). This study found that the leading stockholders of virtually all of these 100 corporations are the 15 most powerful banks and insurance companies in the United States. Since 1945 stock ownership in the major corporations has become increasing concentrated in the hands of the major financial institutions (New York *Times*, February 5, 1981, p. 26).

Another study of the top 200 nonfinancial corporations in the United States found that Chase Manhattan (the leading Rockefeller bank) had a controlling interest (at least 5 percent of stock plus representation on the board of directors) in 16, the First National Bank of Chicago in 6, Bankers' Trust of New York 5, and the Mellon National Bank of Pittsburgh in 3 (Kotz 1978, p. 111). This study also found that 35 percent of the largest 200 nonfinancial corporations in the United States were under full or partial control of a single financial institution (Kotz 1978, p. 97).

The growing role of bank trust departments has given banks (which until 1981 could legally operate fully only within a single U.S. state) considerable control over other financial institutions around the country. Not only do the larger banks tend to dominate smaller regional banks and insurance companies, but they tend to be *each others'* major stockholders as well. For example, in 1980 the largest 11 banks collectively held 13.5 percent of the stock of Bank of America, 10.4 percent of Morgan Guaranty, 10.2 percent of Citicorp, and 9.4 percent of Continental Illinois (New York *Times*, May 2, 1980, D-9).

Control over bank trust departments is especially highly concentrated. In 1980 the Morgan Guaranty Trust Company, with $24 billion in trust fund assets, led all other banks. (In 1974 Morgan Guaranty held 5.4 percent of all bank trust assets.) In the same year First National City Bank was second with 4.8 percent of the total and Bankers' Trust Company was third with 4.5 percent. The ten leading banks together controlled 32.2 percent of all bank-held trust assets (Kotz 1978, p. 70).

An equally if not more important source of real economic power of the financial institutions lies in their role as the principal lenders to the nonfinancial corporations. Their ability to grant or withhold credit gives them considerable economic power. This power is in part manifested in the placement of bank-affiliated directors on the boards of the corporations to which they are tied (to look after their interests).

Although in the 1930s and early 1940s almost all of the industrial corporations' needs for new capital were obtained from internal sources, both before and after that period financial institutions supplied close to *half* of all money resources required by the corporations. In the period 1900–29 about 45 percent of the capital of nonfinancial institutions came from external sources; in the 1950–70 period approximately 40 percent (Menshikov 1969, chap. 5; Fitch and Oppenheimer 1970).

Financial institutions supplied about one-third of the *external* funds used by the nonfinancial corporations in the 1900–30 period, slightly over one-half in the 1946–55 period, and almost two-thirds in the 1956–65 period (Kotz 1978, p. 61). Life insurance companies as well as commercial and investment banks play a key role in financing the corporations. It should be noted that in the 1956-65 period life insurance companies acquired almost one-half of the new bonds issued by U.S. nonfinancial corporations (Kotz 1978, p. 62).

The banks can also exert power by threatening to sell stock in order to decrease its price, thereby undermining a corporation's credit standing and the confidence of other holders, with the consequence of the top executives losing money from stock options and bonuses as well as status and making it easy for alternative managements to win proxy fights (see Menshikov 1969, chap. 4).

The real economic power of the financial institutions over nonfinancial institutions is reflected in the fact that in the mid-1970s, 21 percent of all outside directors of the largest 500 industrial corporations were bankers—bankers were almost half of all outside directors with seats on *three or more* corporate boards (Castells 1980, p. 149). In 1980, Citicorp had the most interlocking directors. Members of the board of Citicorp occupied a total of 49 directorships on the boards of 100 leading corporations studied by a U.S. Senate subcommittee (New York *Times*, February 5, 1981, p. 26).

The Role of Family Wealth in Corporate Control

The holdings of the shares of the various corporations become more diversified over time. This happens both because of inheritance (many heirs, plus the need to sell stock to pay inheritance taxes) and because it is a wise investment strategy to diversify holdings to avoid risk (a rational strategy which is adopted as symbolic identification when the old family business withers). Consequently, real economic power comes increasingly to be exercised through the mediation of the financial institutions as well as to be shared with coalitions of other major stockholders (rather than being directly exercised by individuals and single families). Major financial institutions often tend to keep their equity and loans to a given corporation large enough to exert a degree of influence, but small enough so that risk is minimized (and so the financial institution can get out with a minimum of loss if they so desire).

Nevertheless, in spite of the continuing diversification of family fortunes and the growing role of the banks as the centers of real economic power in contemporary capitalism, the real unmediated economic power of wealthy families remains considerable. Family fortunes, often coordinated through family funds (which manage relatives' stock as a unit) and foundations, are able to keep the real economic power of a family intact. Such large blocks of wealth are considerably magnified in their influence because the institutions they control attract the smaller fortunes of the less wealthy.

A study of the top 200 nonfinancial U.S. companies in 1965 found that 35 percent were essentially under the control (real economic ownership) of wealthy families (Scott 1979, p. 57). Another study done in the mid-1970s found that an individual family held a partial controlling interest in at least 21 percent of the top 200 corporations (Kotz 1978, p. 97).

Further, and very importantly, given the growing real economic power of financial institutions, single families still have a controlling interest in a considerable number of major financial institutions. A 1980 study found that a single family interest held 5 percent or more of the stock in 42 major financial companies in the United States. The Mellon family, for example, was found to hold 18 percent of the stock of Mellon National Bank (New York *Times*, May 2, 1980, D-9). Chase Manhattan Bank has been controlled by the Rockefeller family since the 1920s. David, in fact, was its president or chairman (and for a good part of the time both) from 1962 to 1980 (Kotz 1978, p.87).*

Corporate boards of directors reflect the biggest shareholders (individuals and banks) as well as the principal financiers of a corporation. Although their role varies from corporation to corporation, they normally determine the general policies of a corporation and select the managers of the companies (thereby fundamentally determining policy, even when day-to-day affairs are decided by management), a management that would be replaced in the event it pursued policies disagreeable to the directors.

The hereditary wealthy families who make up the core of the monopoly capitalist class (together with the hereditary wealthy in the middle sector) seem to exercise considerable direct economic power over the leading corporations. In 1963 a study of the boards of directors of the 15 largest banks, 15 largest insurance companies, and

---

*Family control of the leading corporations seems to be more central in Europe than in the United States (see Scott 1979, pp. 70–72).

20 largest industrial corporations found that 53 percent of their 884 directors were members of the hereditary capitalist class—i.e., were listed in the *Social Register* (Domhoff 1967, p. 51). It should also be noted that in 1960 in over 141 of the 232 largest corporations the *directors* held enough stock to control the company—5 to 10 percent (Domhoff 1967, p. 49). The largest single categories of noncapitalist class people among the remaining 47 percent of directors in the 1963 study were hired executives (who rose to prominence because of efficient service to the corporate wealthy). It should be noted that the majority of hereditary wealthy major stockholders are directors of firms that are *not* under the control of a *single* family. Their position on these boards, then, reflects rather their (or their family's or associated financial group's) partial stake in a corporation or financial institution as just *one of many* major stockholding interests.

It should also be noted that direct supervision of management is not a necessary condition of real economic ownership by the leading individual stockholders (individual families or financial institutions) of a corporation. It is normally sufficient for real economic power to be exerted over management through subtle pressure and the knowledge that if an occasion were to arise, the leading stockholders could almost certainly muster a plurality of the stock to vote out recalcitrant managers, replacing them with others agreeable to their will. Actual interventions as well as "takeovers" through massive purchasing of stock by a given financial interest are most likely in crises situations or when those desirous of obtaining real economic power over an enterprise see an occasion to make a considerable profit by taking over the assets of an enterprise (see Scott 1974a, pp. 44, 45). Because of the relative ease a financial interest group (or wealthy individual or corporation) can (with the aid of financial institutions) acquire a controlling block of stock in the event of mismanagement, or what is perceived to be an exceptional profit opportunity (e.g., DuPont's takeover of Conoco and U.S. Steel's of Marathon in 1981), the economic power of top management in those corporations that have no apparent single source of outside control (in either major stockholders or financial institutions) is *most* fragile.

The 40 to 50 percent of the top 200 corporations that might appear (depending on the study—see Kotz 1978, p. 97; Scott 1979, p. 57) to be under "management control" because no *single* outside power center has a large enough block of stock are subject to the same general forces to which the rest of the corporations are subject. If they should behave differently than other corporations, their top management would eventually be displaced (if the normal pressures of the market and the penalties accruing to the top management, both financial and status—from lowered profits and slow or negative growth—should prove to be insufficient to produce changes in policy). Thus the real economic power of the top managers in corporations without a single outside controlling bloc (and where the managers themselves own an insignificant proportion of the total stock out-standing) is generally incomparably *less* than the real economic power of financial institutions and the leading wealthy families, whose real economic ownership (based on stock ownership, management of trust funds, and control of investment funds) continues to keep them at the center of the monopoly capitalist class.

It should be noted that, in contrast to corporate directors, the overwhelming majority of top executives have no big blocks of shares (all managers together hold less than 10 percent of the stock of the leading corporations). Hired executives rarely become principal share-holders in the major corporations. In 1955-65 there was not a single case of a hired executive of the top 100 corporations who advanced to become a leading stockholder (Menshikov 1969, pp. 110-11). This fact generally leaves managers in a weak position in disputes with major outside interests.

The board of directors of most corporations without a single controlling family or bank reflects a constellation or coalition of the wealthiest stockholders and leading financial institutions with a stake in the firm, no one (or often even two or three) of which has a predominant influence. While the lack of a single dominant interest often gives the top management considerably more discretion than they otherwise would have, if management consistently acts against the interests of the bloc with the greatest concentration of real economic power they tend to be replaced—if they should fail to heed the warnings of the outside directors and banks who monitor their results (see Scott 1979, p. 41).

It should be noted that recent years have seen a rise in both the relative numbers and the role of outside directors in most large corporations (coincident with the growing role of banks). A study done in the late 1970s of 600 major corporations found that in more than 80 percent outside directors represented between 63 percent and 75 percent of all directors. This study found that such outside direc-tors held nearly all of the audit committee seats plus about 90 percent of all positions on the powerful nominating and compensation committees (see New York *Times*, September 24, 1979, p. D6).

The *average* outside directors (in contrast to those representing powerful blocs of stockholders or creditors) exercise more authority in some areas of corporate decision making than others. A study done in the late 1970s found that most *outside* directors believed they had the greatest impact in areas of compensation of top management and mergers and acquisitions. They generally felt they had much less influence on selection of senior executives and only moderate influence on capital expenditures (New York *Times*, August 19, 1981, p. 30). The average outside director put in about eight hours a month on corporate activities for each board membership held (New York *Times*, September 5, 1981, p. 25).

The Managerial Sector of the Capitalist Class

The only managers who by virtue of their managerial *position*, rather than their stock ownership, are part of the capitalist class are those who, because of their structural position, have fundamental power over what is produced and the organization of production (i.e., at least a share in real economic ownership). This includes most of the top executives of the largest corporations who, although they typically have authority delegated to them by the banks or controlling families in real economic ownership, nevertheless have a circumscribed but independent power base that allows them significant discretion. These top executives have a limited power over tremendous resources and over the labor power of a great many employees. The aggregate of their power is roughly equivalent to that of the principal owners of small corporations who have few constraints imposed on them by financial institutions, or that of large shareholding families in medium-size corporations who have more of such constraints. All have less than full real economic ownership.

It must be stressed that legal ownership of the means of production is not a necessary condition for being part of the capitalist class. It is enough that one is a functioning capitalist, that the top executives perform the capitalist functions of control, allocation, and organization of production and disposal of the product, *without* being entirely the agents of others that hire them, i.e., have significant real economic power of their own.

The highest paid executives of the monopoly corporations in the United States in 1980 had salaries plus benefits in multiples of millions of dollars a year. In 1980, Thomas Pickens, president of Mesa Petroleum, was the highest paid executive of all with total compensation of $7.9 million. There were eight other top executives who made over $3 million that year (see Table 4.6). A total of 69 chief executives made over a million dollars in salaries and benefits in 1980 (*Forbes*, June 8, 1981, p. 115f). The *average* of salary and bonuses for the chief executives of the largest corporations (those with sales of over $5 billion in 1980) was $589,000. Managers, further, are entitled to very generous fringe benefits. A study in the early 1960s showed that corporations paid 87 percent of the costs of trips to professional conferences, 83 percent of the costs of professional journals, 82 percent of dues to professional associations, 83 percent of the costs of taking wives on business trips, 81 percent of entertaining clients in clubs and restaurants, 43 percent of entertainment in homes, and 48 percent of personal car expenses (Menshikov 1969, p. 111).

It is clear that the great proportion of the salaries of top executives of the monopoly corporations comes from the surplus labor of working people and can not be considered compensation for the labor they perform (even if the competition among the top corporations drives salaries so high because of the organizational abilities of these executives). This in itself, however, does not make them part of the capitalist class, merely extremely well-compensated petty bourgeois who live off other people's labor, since they have no rights (i.e., real economic ownership) in their salaries, as, for example, stockholders *do* have in their dividends, nor can they affect capital allocation by transferring their income to others, as (again) stockholders can by buying and selling stock.

In most cases, however, the top corporate managers *are* part of the capitalist class by virtue of their stock ownership in the corporations that they manage. A study of the stockholdings of the top five executives in the largest 50 manufacturing corporations in the United States in 1963 found that each on average owned $2.4 million worth of their company's stock (Lewellen 1971, p. 79). The result of such stock ownership is that the bulk of the annual income of these top corporate executives comes from stock income (dividends plus capital gains) rather than from their fixed dollar renumeration (or even from their fixed dollar renumeration plus stock-linked incentive plans). In the 1960–63 period the average fixed dollar (aftertax) compensation for the top five executives of the top 50 manufacturing corporations of the United States was $83,899 a year. Stock-based incentive renumeration (aftertax) that directly linked the executives' behavior to their success in maximizing other stockholders' interests averaged a further $47,583. In addition, these top managers secured an average of $26,559 in aftertax stock dividends plus an additional $544,340 in aftertax capital gains from the stock of the firms they managed. This meant that for these 250 top executives their direct income from stocks averaged 6.8 times their fixed renumeration and 4.3 times their fixed salary plus stock-linked incentives. Moreover, the ratio of all stock income (direct and incentive) to fixed renumeration averaged 7.1 times (Lewellen 1971, p. 90). The tremendous importance of stock income in comparison to fixed income from salaries, pensions, fringe benefits, cash bonuses, and so forth can be seen from the statistics on the top ten highest paid corporate executives in the United States in 1980 (see Table 4.6). For these ten individuals income from stock

TABLE 4.6: The Ten Highest Paid Chief Corporate Executives in the United States in 1980
(In thousands of U.S. dollars)

Executive	Corporation	Salary and Bonuses	Benefits	Contingent	Stock Gains	Total
Thomas Pickens	Mesa Petroleum	$416	$169	$45	$7,236	$7,866
George Scharffenverger	City Investing	569	12	121	4,464	5,166
Robert Charpie	Cabot	799	1,222	1,376	1,309	4,706
Walter Sanders	Advanced Micro Devices	538	28	8	3,707	4,281
Milton F. Rosenthal	Engelhard Minerals	1,825	477	1,699	—*	4,000
Clifton Garvin	Exxon	1,043	61	228	2,016	3,348
Fred Hartley	Union Oil	876	370	463	1,419	3,129
Ray Adam	NL Industries	662	22	247	2,162	3,093
David Lewis	General Dynamics	455	9	—	2,557	3,021
Robert Anderson	Rockwell International	865	19	920	1,163	2,967

*Data not available.
Source: *Forbes*, June 8, 1981, p. 115.

represented 62 percent of their total compensation. It is clear that most top level managers of the megacorporations are part of the capitalist class, *both* by virtue of their relative autonomy *and* by virtue of their direct stock ownership. Top managers are generally held accountable to the corporate wealthy through both their common interest in maximizing corporate profits and long-term corporate growth, *and* the normally greater real economic power of major stockholders and financial institutions.

In the process of reaching the top, managers are thoroughly conditioned to identify with, and serve, the interests of those who have real economic power (whether financial houses, founding families, or in a few cases self-perpetuating top executives). They, thus, come to single-mindedly pursue the interests of profit maximization that the controlling interests are structurally dedicated to (regardless of which of the three types of control—or hybrids thereof—exists). In addition, the incentive structure for top managers is geared to ensuring that they perform according to the principles of profit maximization. Options to buy stock at a discounted price in the future, in order to realize an immediate capital gain, compensation in "dividend units" geared to the price of stock, bonuses for outstanding performance as well as the possibilities of hefty salary increases (and alternative job prospects) and the actual ownership of corporate stock supplement simple pride in performance, identification with corporate profit, and growth position and status with peers as powerful economic incentives acting on managers to behave the same as legal owners in maximizing the profitability of their corporations. It has been found empirically that the principal determinants of the level of "executive compensation" are the corporation's level of profit and the rate of return on equity, i.e., the objective interests of top managers are tied to the interests of the leading stockholders (Castells 1980, p. 151).

In most respects corporations with and without a single identifiable center of outside real economic power behave in the same way. It has been found that the rate of profit as well as its fluctuations are the same in both types of corporations. Corporations without a single center of outside control, however, tend to have a higher dividend pay-out rate than those controlled by a single family—not at all surprising, given a family's greater stake in accumulating funds within a family-controlled enterprise (Castells 1980, pp. 150–51).

CAPITALISTS AS A SOCIAL CLASS

The monopoly and middle sectors of the capitalist class form a highly integrated social class. This class has a high consciousness of kind, the highest degree of social interaction, and the most distinctive class boundaries of any class or subclass in society. The capitalist class maintains a distinctive style of life and group solidarity that sets them off from the rest of the population. They share such things as accent and tone of voice, distinctive understatement in dress and behavior, common values and assumptions, and a characteristic sense of noblesse oblige. This social class is distinguished by its concern with ancestry, exclusive club membership, exclusive neighborhoods, distinctive sports (e.g., fox hunting, horse breeding and racing, dog showing, yachting, and, less today than previously, cricket and lawn tennis). The sense of solidarity, the "we" feeling of the capitalist social class, is national in scope. Their demeanor is marked by self-confidence, carefully reinforced by their education and based in their objective power (see Baltzell 1958, chap. 15).

This social class is roughly specified as those listed in the *Social Register*, of which until 1977 there were 12 city editions. In the late 1960s it contained about 38,000 nuclear families (unmarried children over 18 are listed with their families) and 108,000 names (and in which people from all 50 states were listed). (In 1977 the separate editions were consolidated into a single volume.) The *Social Register* lists families of old wealth (normally at least third generation or in a few cases second generation). It is a listing of families that are socially acceptable to one another, feel comfortable with each other because of their common background and upbringing, and have intimate access to another. With the exception of the old Washington, D.C., *Register*, which listed the president, Supreme Court justices, and senators regardless of class background, as a matter of courtesy, it is virtually impossible to be listed in the *Social Register* no matter how wealthy one might become, or how much political power one has achieved, unless one has inherited wealth, gone to the right schools, and belongs to the right clubs (and otherwise has already demonstrated *social acceptability* to the core capitalist class). However, since the *Social Register* pretty much excludes Jews, blacks, and other minorities (and discriminates against Catholics), excludes people who have been involved in public scandals and individuals who elect not to be listed, and is a bit prudish and excessively exclusive, the actual size of the *social class* of core capitalists (including its minority adjuncts) is actually larger than the 38,000 nuclear families listed. For example, in 1979 there were 600 Smiths, but only one Cohen listed (these are the two most common names in the New York telephone directory). The *Social Register* asks potential listees for their "Christian names." The first black was listed in 1970 (New York *Times*, February 2, 1980, p. 14). Considering all these factors we might estimate that the true size of the top and middle sector of the capitalist class is about double those listed in the *Social Register*, about 75,000 nuclear families (see Domhoff 1967, pp. 13-15).

The social class of capitalists, with monopoly capitalists at its core and with medium-size capitalists at its fringes (with small capitalists excluded and instead integrated socially with the petty bourgeoisie's upper reaches) was largely formed in the last two decades of the nineteenth century through a social merger of the traditional commercial wealthy with the new superwealthy founders of the corporations. During this period, New York City became the social center of upper class life in the United States. The *Social Register*, which became the criterion par excellence of social admission into the inner circles of the upper class, was founded in 1887. The first *Social Register*, issued for New York in 1888, contained a little less than 2,000 families. By 1912, however, a *Social Register* was being published for 12 different cities. By 1940, there were 38,500 families listed, with 13,200 in the New York edition alone (Baltzell 1958, p. 9).

It was during this period as well that the exclusive New England boarding schools and eastern universities became family surrogates, central in producing a socially integrated social class of capitalists in the United States. These schools became the means of bringing together the sons of the old commercial and landed wealthy from the South with the sons of the new wealthy, such as the Rockefellers and the other nouveau riche founders of the new corporations. The new centralized and monopolized economy of the United States generated a single national socially unified capitalist class.

The wealth of the core of the capitalist class is descended from fortunes made either before the Civil War, largely in trade and landownership, or in the generation after, in investment banking and manufacturing. Because of the exclusive nature of the institutions frequented by upper class children, and hence whom they meet socially, and because of the pressure put on capitalist class children to marry their own kind (both for reasons of social respectability and fears of outsiders marrying in for money), a high degree of inter-relationship has been achieved by the upper levels of the capitalist class: "Everyone is related to everyone else." There is, nevertheless, a tendency for "brains" and "beauty" to marry into the capitalist class. That is, capitalist class men sometimes marry the "most beautiful" women of the middle class (with whom they come into contact at school or work), while upper class women sometimes marry "the brightest" upwardly mobile managerial or professional men employed by their class (typically graduates of exclusive universities such as Princeton, Yale, and Harvard).

Members of the capitalist social class know each other. They are personal friends. Acquaintance patterns extend widely over the country, interlocking this class together (Baltzell 1958, p. 7). One study of top California families, for instance, showed that 91 percent of those in the San Francisco area and 64 percent of those in the Los Angeles area knew each other (Domhoff 1970, p. 86). The class consists of overlapping social cliques. Thus, although every individual does not personally know everyone else, everyone has friends and relatives who interact with people in other cliques to produce a tightly interwoven national class mosaic.

The core of the social class of capitalists (those listed in the *Social Register*) provides a highly disproportionate share of those in key power positions in American society. Roughly 25 percent of all those listed in *Who's Who* (a good indicator of positions of power, prestige, influence, and achievement) are also listed in the *Social Register* (Baltzell 1958, p. 8). Baltzell reports that for Philadelphia in 1940, 75 percent of all bankers listed in the *Who's Who* were in the *Social Register*, 51 percent of lawyers, 42 percent of businessmen, 42 percent of architects, 37 percent of physicians, 35 percent of museum officials, and 32 percent of authors. This contrasted with only 10 percent of church officials, 12 percent of musical artists, and 16 percent of educators. This provides a pretty good picture of the types of careers the children of old wealthy families pursue (Baltzell 1958, p. 33). Of the 532 directorships in industrial and financial institutions reported by those listed in *Who's Who*, 60 percent were those of individuals listed in the *Social Register*. The presidents and more than 80 percent of the directors of the six largest banks were listed in the *Social Register*, as were almost all the senior partners of the largest law firms (Baltzell, p. 386). This suggests the powerful and central role of financial institutions and corporate law firms as mediating institutions for the capitalist class.

The capitalist social class maintains a distinctive life-style and norms. Its language is British influenced, with many words pronounced with an English accent. This is because traditionally British nannies often raised the children of the upper class and because the Eastern seaboard heart of the capitalist class is Anglophile. The English have traditionally been imitated in clothes, sports activities, club ritual, and so forth.

Ritual is an important aspect of capitalist class life. The men are marked by a distinctive type of clothing (the Brooks Brothers' tradition) and various exclusive symbols such as club neckties, hatbands, little charms on lapels, or watch chains (while the women's dress is exclusive in style and the best in quality). Style tends to be both exclusive and conservative, typically understating one's position. There tends to be absolute conformity in personal cards, notepaper, and invitations. In general, conservatism in personal taste and respect for tradition are highly valued. The reverence of the past, characteristic of any aristocracy or hereditary elite, reflects the fact that wealth and position is a result of ancestral accomplishments.

Members of the cpitalist class do not generally purchase or consume in a conspicuous manner. Publicity and flaunting of wealth is frowned on by the core members of this class. Squandering money and flashy displays of wealth are characteristic of the new rich and upper middle class entertainers (i.e., those not socially acceptable to the true capitalist elite). Old black cars, baggy tweeds, and small private parties are common. Members of the hereditary capitalist class do spend lavishly on fine homes (although the sumptuous mansions characteristic of their grandparents around the turn of the century are no longer popular) as well as on art and leisure activities (horses, ski lodges, summer homes, and so forth). It should be noted that works of art not only give a distinctively upper class air to the interior of capitalist class residences, but that they are both good investments and a means of passing wealth on to heirs (see Vanfossen 1979, pp. 297-98; Baltzell 1958, pp. 50-58).

Peer norms and sanctions are strong in this class. A capitalist class member caught in an act of dishonesty or disloyalty fears the disapproval of his peers. Shared experiences based in common school ties, common club memberships, and so forth produce a closeness that is at least as strong as the ties of rational interest. The capitalist class is truly socially coherent.

The capitalist class tends to share a common religion—Episcopalianism. The Episcopal tradition in the U.S. upper class dates from the period 1750-1800, when many of the upper class descendants of Puritans, Quakers, Huguenots, and the Dutch Reformed converted to Anglicanism. After 1800 Anglicanism also recruited among the Southern slave lords. After the Civil War, new wealth was gradually converted from lower status Protestant denominations such as Methodist, Baptist, and Lutheran. The major exception to the Episcopal predominance within the U.S. capitalist class is the Boston area, where many of the descendants of the early Calvinists are Congregational and Unitarian (Baltzell 1958, p. 227). Baltzell found that for those in the Philadelphia *Social Register* in 1940, 65 percent of those who listed a religion were Episcopalians, compared to 21 percent of those listed in the *Who's Who*, but not in the *Social Register* (Baltzell 1958, p. 236).

The upper capitalist class child is very carefully socialized into the capitalist class. His/her education is both the best in quality as well as highly exclusive in order to inculcate feelings of superiority and class solidarity. During infancy and childhood, the upper class child is brought up by nurses and governesses so that his/her parents are free to pursue their careers and class obligations. The children then attend special preschools, often exclusive Episcopal church kindergartens. At primary school age they attend exclusive "day schools," which are very important in bringing the children to realize that they are set apart from the great numbers of other children who attend the state schools (Domhoff 1967, chap. 1; 1970, chap. 4). They take special dancing classes, riding lessons, and tutorials in foreign languages.

In adolescence the capitalist class child typically attends a boarding school, often far from home, seeing his/her parents only during the summer and school holidays. These exclusive (mostly Episcopal) schools take over the primary socialization of many upper class children at around the age of 11. In other cases, upper class children may only attend such schools for the last few years of their secondary education. The two richest and oldest of such schools for boys are Exeter and Andover (both also now admit a number of children from middle class families on the basis of promise, and even offer some scholarships for poor and minority children). New England is the traditional region for such schools, with the wealthy sending their adolescent children there from all over the United States. Exclusive New England boarding schools became important in the 1880s with the founding of Groton (1884). They soon became a vital part of creating a national consciousness in the U.S. capitalist class with more or less homogeneous behavior and values. Andover and Exeter founded in the eighteenth century and St. Pauls' founded before the Civil War experienced considerable growth in the 1880s and 1890s (Baltzell 1964, p. 127; 1958, p. 307).

At these exclusive schools the youth learn distinctive upper class values, manners, speech, and demeanor as well as consolidate the feeling that they are special. Attendance at such exclusive private schools ensures that the child will mingle with other upper class children from around the country, making lifelong friends and meeting suitable members of the opposite sex to eventually marry. These schools, typically segregated by sex, arrange social occasions with schools of the opposite sex, building acquaintance circles within which intermarriage takes place (see Domhoff 1970, p. 22 for a list of the most exclusive of the capitalist class boy's schools).

Attendance at exclusive boarding schools is supplemented by summers spent with the family at exclusive upper class resorts or at summer camps with rounds of social events the most important of which are debutante parties (coming out rituals for the girls of the capitalist class). Debutante balls remain a distinctive capitalist class institution. They continue to perform the important function of reinforcing the sense of belonging to a distinctive social group. Debutante balls are rites de passage that introduce the postadolescent into the upper class adult world, as well as protect upper class endogamy.

The capitalist class male children have historically tended to go to just three or four colleges: Harvard, Yale, and Princeton (and for West Coast youngsters, Stanford). In the 1960s, 67 percent of all those males listed in the *Social Register* who had graduated from college graduated from Harvard, Yale, or Princeton (Domhoff 1967, p. 18). Furthermore, at these three exclusive institutions, the children of the upper class are socially isolated from the intellectual elite of upwardly mobile middle class children, who make up a significant proportion of total enrollments, by a system of highly exclusive clubs and fraternities, e.g., Porcellian and A. D. at Harvard, the Fence Club, Delta Kappa Epsilon, Zeta Psi, St. Anthony Hall at Yale, and the dinner clubs such as the Ivy Club at Princeton (Baltzell 1958, pp. 330-31).

These three universities and the exclusive circles within them are the main arena in which upper class children from all around the United States become acquainted with their counterparts, consolidate their early socialization, and become full and active members of the capitalist class. Friendships are established here that become valuable business and political contacts for life. It should be stressed that these schools, especially Yale and Harvard, also function to co-opt or assimilate the most promising children of other classes. They provide a proving ground where the new and old rich smooth over their differences and the children of the new rich are gracefully assimilated.

It should be noted that for capitalist class children admission requirements to these exclusive institutions consist primarily of parental background criterion, not scholastic achievement or ability. Before World War II the typical entering class at Ivy League schools had an aptitude score of approximately the national average for all college freshmen in the United States. By the early 1960s with increasing middle class enrollments it has risen to about the top 10 percent (Baltzell 1964, p. 341). Special admissions programs, however, continue to allow admission to the children of the capitalist class who do not have scholastic abilities comparable with upwardly mobile middle class children. The most important of these is virtually guaranteed admission for the sons of graduates of these institutions.

It was during the period of the formation of the modern national capitalist class in the 1880s that the three schools began to become predominant in upper class education (displacing regional colleges). They became especially important as upper class accrediting institutions in the 1920s, peaking in this role around 1940. Baltzell found that of Philadelphians listed in the *Social Register* who graduated from college between 1870 and 1900, 24 percent went to Harvard, Yale, or Princeton, and 48 percent went to the local elite institution—

the University of Pennsylvania; but among those who graduated between 1920 and 1940, 57 percent went to the three elite national institutions, compared to 22 percent who went to the University of Pennsylvania (Baltzell 1958, p. 328). However, in the post-World War II generation a decentralization again occurred, with more and more children of the upper class going to other elite institutions such as Stanford, the University of California at Berkeley, and Ivy League colleges other than the big three. Of those persons listed in the *Social Register* attending college in the mid-1960s, only 45 percent were at Harvard, Yale, or Princeton (Domhoff 1967, p. 18).

In most of America's principal cities there are exclusive capitalist class metropolitan men's clubs, membership in which is essential for a socially integrated member of the capitalist class. Membership is evidence of confirmed prestige and acceptance by the core capitalist class. Admission is very rigorously regulated and limited to those of proper pedigree, i.e., at least second, and preferably third, generation wealthy. Virtually all gentlemen-businessmen of any importance belong to at least one such club. J.P. Morgan, Jr., in 1940 belonged to no less than 13 clubs in various cities around the country.

These elite clubs provide an exclusive atmosphere where members of the capitalist class can dine, relax, meet with acquaintances and friends from around the country, and if necessary spend a night away from women, scrutiny by servants, the press, and the hectic life of business. In addition to being essential proof that one is a gentleman, the clubs function to provide: first, an informal atmosphere in which new members of the upper class can be fully intitiated into the norms that govern capitalist class behavior; second, a tie to the national upper class for capitalist class members from smaller towns; third, a place where political and economic differences among capitalists can be smoothed over informally in a friendly manner; and fourth, (although formal and organized business conferences are as a rule forbidden) as a place where the groundwork for major business deals can be established. All in all, it would be difficult to function as a member of the capitalist class without access to the contacts that such metropolitan clubs provide (Baltzell 1958, chap. 13). Baltzell found that 90 percent of Philadelphians in the *Social Register* listed membership in an exclusive club (1958, p. 335).

The exclusive metropolitan clubs grew out of eighteenth-century English and American coffeehouses where influential men of business used to informally gather. They gradually evolved into permanent private establishments. The oldest American club was the Philadelphia Club, which was established in 1834. It was followed by the Union Club in 1836, the Century Club in New York in 1847, the Somerset in Boston (1851), and the Pacific Union (San Francisco) in

1852 (Baltzell 1958, p. 337). Thus the establishment of such metropolitan clubs predates the Civil War and the formation of a national upper class. In their first generation they were marks of local elite rather than national capitalist class status (as they became in the latter part of the century). But by the 1900s the metropolitan club had become *the* most critical social institution for the new national capitalist class, surpassing the country clubs, private schools and colleges, and exclusive neighborhoods as the mark of a member of the class (Baltzell 1964, p. 137).

Most of these clubs pretty much limit themselves to the old-line white Protestant wealthy. Traditionally, virtually all totally excluded Jews and heavily discriminated against Catholics, although some, like the Century Club in New York, opened themselves to top intellectuals and artists, including Jews. But most of the most prestigious clubs have been and remain very exclusive, e.g., Union League, Links, Knickerbocker (even while most now admit a few Jews). The major and most powerful clubs remain obsessed with exclusiveness (Baltzell 1964, pp. 137, 370-71). (For a listing of the most prestigious exclusive metropolitan men's clubs see Domhoff 1970, pp. 23-24.)

Some clubs, like the Century in New York, the Tavern in Boston, and the Frank Inn in Philadelphia are less exclusive. These clubs tend to recruit more members who have achieved rather than inherited their position; and, thus, to focus more on intellectual life. Likewise, with the Harvard, Yale, and Princeton clubs in major cities, which recruit accomplished graduates of these institutions regardless of parents' class position. There are also fairly exclusive athletic clubs. These are of two kinds: the racquet club, favored by wealthy younger men who are oriented to "keeping themselves in shape"—a rich man's YMCA, and the various "athletic clubs" (e.g., the New York Athletic Club or the Penn Athletic Club), which are somewhat lower status metropolitan clubs (Baltzell 1958, pp. 339-40).

In recent years, the country clubs, to which whole families belong (rather than just men), have become increasingly prominent as centers of upper class social activity (and the mark of family exclusiveness). The exclusive country clubs are in good part oriented to sporting and family social activities. The founding of the country clubs, like the rest of the distinctive capitalist class institutions, coincided with the formation of a national social capitalist class. The first was The Country Club in Brookline, Massachusetts (founded in 1882), followed by the Tuxedo in New York (Baltzell 1958, pp. 356-57; 1964, p. 113).

There are annual summer encampments of the wealthy, probably the most famous of which are Bohemia Grove in Northern California and Ranchero Visitadoes in southern California. For a couple of weeks each summer hundreds of upper class members come together in rural areas for horseback riding, partying, games, and "off the record" political discussions (Domhoff 1970, 1971, p. 79.; 1974).

The national upper class tends to vacation together. Again the institutionalization of national upper class resort areas was concentrated in the 1880s. In both summer and winter there are a few geographically circumscribed areas where they vacation. In winter, the Palm Beach–Hobe Sound area in Florida and Palm Springs in California, and in summer the New England coast between the Hamptons on the tip of Long Island and the Canadian border on the Maine coast (including Fisher's Island, Watch Hill, Jamestown, Newport, Martha's Vineyard, Nantucket, Hyannisport, Mt. Deseat Island, and North Haven). There are also a few other exclusive spots, including Rehoboth Beach, Delaware; and (for San Francisco) Lake Tahoe and the Monterey peninsula, and some little towns north of the Bay Area (Domhoff 1970, 1971, pp. 80-83). This coming together during the vacation season (especially for the annual summer vacation) of the hereditary wealthy from all around the country, helps cement the ties among the upper class as well as provides another opportunity for the young people of the class to get to know each other better, forming relationships (business and sexual) that last for life.

The women of the capitalist class have their own exclusive institutions and specialized functions. Women, as do men, have their exclusive schools and clubs. The most important upper class women's colleges are Vassar, Smith, and Wellesley; and also Hollins and Sophie Newcomb (for the South); Colorado Women's College and Sripps and Mills (for the West). Capitalist class women also attend the intellectually less demanding "finishing schools" (with normally two-year programs) as well as join exclusive elite sororities at elite universities, such as Kappa Kappa Gamma (Domhoff 1970, p. 37).

Women too have exclusive clubs, e.g., the Acorn (Philadelphia), the Chilton (Boston), the Colony (New York); the Friday and Fortnightly (Chicago) and the Sunset (Seattle) as well as the somewhat less exclusive but more influential Junior League chapters all around the country. The Junior League is meant for women under 40, but has "sustaining membership" for women over that age. It is a "service" organization composed of about 200 chapters and 100,000 members that involves itself in museum programs, foster homes, social services, tutoring, and so forth, as well as in exclusive social activities. Upper class women in general tend to be active in such things as opera and symphony associations, alumni associations, and garden clubs as well as various welfare activities (see Baltzell 1958, p. 584; Domhoff 1970, pp. 39-40).

Traditionally upper class women have not held salaried positions in the corporations, but in the last half of the twentieth century they have become increasingly active as authors and artists, journalists and academics (especially trustees and administrators of women's colleges). Upper class women still focus most of their activities in *volunteer* work (or as "civic workers," paid or unpaid) for such institutions as the Red Cross, museums, boys' clubs, and so forth.

Upper class women organize the social life of the upper class. They organize parties and plan charity and debutante balls, organize dancing classes, and serve as social secretaries (who counsel new rich families and plan the larger social functions of other wealthy families), all functions that help keep the upper class a socially homogenous and intermarrying social class of people who know one another. Upper class women tend to set the cultural and social standards for women of other classes. Upper class women have traditionally acted to smooth over some of the rough edges of the economic system through their involvement in welfare activities. Social work was originally an upper class volunteer profession originating in the settlement house movement in the new urban slums in the 1880s. The early settlement houses that helped the new immigrants survive and adjust to the industrial slums were run and financed by upper class women (Domhoff 1970, chap. 2).

Because of the racism of the exclusively Protestant and northern European stock upper class social institutions, Jewish wealth was forced to develop its own separate set of upper class institutions. It should be noted that the exclusion of Jews from the social class of capitalists did not occur until the 1880s and 1890s. Before this time prominent wealthy Jews were among the founders and leading members of some of the most exclusive clubs, such as Knickerbocker and Union League. However, after 1882, the old-time German Jews who predominated in the United States were overwhelmed by the new immigration of Jews escaping Russian pogroms. While in 1880 there were only 250,000 Jews in the United States, by 1920 there were 4 million. The new anti-Semitic prejudices of the Protestant wealthy were based largely on the stereotypes of the new lower class Jewish immigrants as well as worldwide growth of racism (the ideological support of the new imperialism that was dividing the world in this period). There was considerable resentment in the established Jewish community against the new immigrants for causing them to lose status. The term "kike" in fact was invented by the older German Jews as a term of derision to insult the new Russian immigrants.

The Jewish wealthy, further, were pretty much excluded from participation in the formation of the new national industrial corporations. They were forced into the more peripheral parts of the economy, e.g., consumer goods, retail, wholesale, entertainment, and communications. In response to their expulsion from metropolitan clubs, exclusive neighborhoods, and resorts *and* in order to set up social defenses against the new Jewish immigrants, they established their own exclusive clubs and resorts, neighborhoods, and charities (Baltzell 1958, pp. 276-91; 1964, pp. 55-59).

Socially, top executives from middle class families who hold their position because of their superior managerial expertise are ineligible for the *Social Register* or admission into the most exclusive clubs and, thus, are not part of the social class of capitalists. Their exclusion from the social network of capitalists means exclusion from a very important source of contacts and loci of decision making and, thus, reflects their general exclusion from much of the power center of the U.S. economy. They are often, however, able to accumulate considerable wealth, send their children to the right schools, and, thus, ensure their heirs' social integration into the capitalist class (in the *next generation*). Higher level managers often tend to be the best students and most promising individuals recruited from the middle classes by way of high-quality colleges and high-status business schools as well as through a rigorous career of highly competitive selective processes of promotion from lower management strictly on the basis of performance. The most creative, aggressive, energetic, dedicated, intelligent, ruthless, and organizationally proficient consequently reach the top, and, thus, acquire the ability to bring their children into the middle levels of the capitalist class.

It should be stressed that top managers tend to come from *upper* middle class and small business family backgrounds. In 1950, 69 percent had fathers who were either business owners or corporate officials (compared to 66 percent in 1925), while only 14 percent had fathers who were either manual workers, white-collar workers, or professionals (see Menshikov 1969, p. 94). Their recruitment to the major corporations and their promotion to the top typically receives a major boost by their graduation from the leading business schools (e.g., Harvard), a criterion whose achievement is highly correlated with one's *father's* financial success and orientation.

Small capitalists might be best considered to form an intermediate stratum between the capitalist class proper and the petty bourgeoisie. Their aggregate wealth as well as education, social background, friendship networks, and overall life-style are likely to be closer to that of a prosperous petty bourgeois than to that of a capitalist in the monopoly sector. Socially the small capitalists are more integrated into the petty bourgeoisie than into the monopoly sector of the capitalist class, i.e., tend to be part of the social class of the petty bourgeoisie. In class consciousness this stratum can identify with either class, i.e., it has antagonisms with monopolies who are its suppliers and often its distributors and competitors (and who may be threatening to drive them out of business because of their superior productive and/or sales apparatus). But it generally has solidarity with monopoly capital in questions of maintaining exploitation of its labor force.

SUMMARY

Wealthy families and individuals operating increasingly through financial institutions, rather than through direct ownership of traditional family businesses, continue to be the primary locus of real economic ownership. Increasingly, the major corporations and financial institutions are controlled by coalitions of leading stockholders (individuals, families, and financial institutions), with financial institutions (especially through their trust departments) coming to play an ever more important role. Top corporate executives are not for the most part a part of the core capitalist class. Mostly upwardly mobile from the upper middle class, they must operate within the parameters established by those with real economic power or be displaced by them. Further, they are excluded from the social institutions of the core capitalist class and, thus, from the networks where so much of the basis of fundamental decision making occurs. The monopoly capitalist class, largely rooted in the period of the formation of the major corporations around the turn of the century, has established itself as a distinctive and powerful social class with generational continuity unmitigated by the "democratic ethos" of U.S. society. Both its wealth and social exclusiveness have been well protected over the entire course of the twentieth century. The monopoly capitalist class continues to be the most socially coherent and class-conscious class in the United States as well as the center of real economic power.

5

The Middle Class

Intermediate between the capitalist class and the working class is the middle class (traditionally referred to as the petty bourgeoisie). This class is intermediate in power over the means of production or distribution, and thus in aggregate control over labor power (their own and others) between the two major classes. While there is considerable variation in this class between those who supervise many, but have relatively little discretion in the production process, and those who do not supervise anyone else, but have considerable discretion, the *product* of the number of those supervised and the amount of individual discretion falls within a relatively small range, thus defining the boundaries of this class.

SPECIFICATION OF A SINGLE PETTY BOURGEOISIE

We can perhaps usefully subcategorize the petty bourgeoisie by two dimensions. One dimension is *social function*: whether their role is, first, the production and transmission of capitalist culture, and thus indirectly capitalist class relations (e.g., social "scientists," literary apologists, social studies teachers, social welfare workers, and so forth); second, the direct administration and reproduction of capitalist class relations through supervising and directing labor power (i.e., managers, managerial consultants); third, the production of goods or adding to productivity (e.g., small farmers, artisans, engineers); fourth, the accounting and realization of value (e.g., high-level salesmen, advertising personnel, bankers, accountants, small retail businessmen); or fifth, the provision of general social services (e.g., doctors and other health professionals and lawyers). A second dimension is *employment status*: whether they are, first, self-employed; second, work for private corporations; or third, are employed by the state as civil servants. Each of the possibilities within these two dimensions has different consequences in terms of the life experiences and values of the various sectors of the single petty bourgeoisie.

The three most important distinct groupings of the middle class are, however, probably: first, the managerial sector of the middle class (both in the state and in private industry), which directly mediates between the owning and laboring classes through supervising labor power within the guidelines established by the owning class; second, those professionals employed by the state and corporations, who have considerable autonomy over their own labor powers so as to facilitate creativity (but who have little control over the labor power of others); and third, the traditional middle class of the old petty bourgeoisie, which is not directly employed by the state or capital, and thus is not directly controlled by them (and which thus has a rather wide degree of autonomy over their own labor, but relatively little over the labor of others). We can refer to the first two types of middle class positions as the salaried or new middle class (or new petty bourgeoisie) in contrast to the traditional self-employed middle class or "old petty bourgeoisie."

The amount of control over the labor power of others is *essentially* similar in the three groups. For example, while the managerial stratum has *direct*, although greatly delimited, power over the labor power of workers, the professional stratum, for the most part, does not. But professionals benefit from the services of secretaries, research assistants, and janitors, and have authority over students and clients (an authority while analogous to control of their labor, is not essential control). Professionals are not typically in a position to hire, fire, promote, or otherwise exercise fundamental control of the labor power of those who serve them. (The managers and administrators where professionals work have this power.) On the other hand, they typically have significantly more discretion over their own labor than do lower and middle managers. The traditional petty-bourgeois farmer, shopkeeper, or independent professional typically has some power over the labor of others (a few regular employees, workers during the harvest, schoolchildren on weekends, a bookkeeper or receptionist, their own family members, and so on), although the allocation (and hence, essential control) of their labor is in good part dictated by the constraints and compulsions put on small business by capital. Further, the independent petty bourgeoisie typically has considerably more discretion over their own labor power than does either major segment of the new middle class. On the other hand, the old petty bourgeoisie is largely dominated by capital: the banks (which hold their mortgages), railroads, grain elevator companies, slaughterhouses, supermarket chains, and food processing, distribution, and wholesale companies. Thus, while the old petty bourgeoisie has significant autonomy in their labor, they have been in good measure controlled (and indirectly exploited) by the logic of, and are thus subordinate to, capital.

Although the range is considerable, all three groups are intermediate in both the amount of control they have over their own labor, and that of others. It should be noted that the group with the greatest control over other's labor (management) has the least discretion over its own. While the forms of control (indirect versus direct) differ, the aggregate amount of autonomy and control by capital of the old petty bourgeoisie, and of the professional and managerial strata, is similar.

Corresponding to their similar positions of control over labor power are all three major social segments of this class's similar position vis-à-vis technical knowledge of production (position in the mental versus manual or technical division of labor) as well as their position vis-à-vis exploitation of the working class. All three major sectors of the middle class typically have qualitatively more general knowledge of the production process than do most manual workers. The managerial stratum's position rests in part on its ability to attain overall knowledge of the production process. The professional employees' (e.g., scientists, engineers) contribution is based on their technically superior education and knowledge of basic processes. The role of independent artisans, farmers, small businessmen, or independent doctors or lawyers requires mastery of a wide range of knowledge and skills to keep a necessarily multifaceted independent operation viable. In contrast, almost all sectors of the working class are kept, in good degree, *structurally* ignorant of the overall production process.

The managerial stratum of the new middle class mediates between the real economic owners (including some of the top managers of the major corporations—see Chapter 4) and the laboring classes who do the actual productive labor They distribute tasks within the work unit, decide when the work process is to be interrupted and modified, make judgments about the quality of output, schedule the rhythm of tasks, arrange for the raw material input and the distribution of the product, supervise the maintenance of machinery, study and redesign the work process, monitor the work performance of individuals, hire, fire, promote, transfer, and otherwise reward and punish personnel, direct the sales effort, direct purchasing, and so forth. The heart of their functioning, however, is to devise and administer forms of control and surveillance of the labor process. And to this end they make every effort to master general knowledge of the production and distribution process, reducing those who actually carry out the tasks to agents without general knowledge. The managerial stratum tends to concentrate in itself information about production and distribution, selecting problem areas to call to the attention of the owners or top managers of the large corporations. They receive general orders form above, specify and recast them in instrumental form, then implement them through the actual laborers. The principal function of the lower level managerial strata is to extract surplus labor from the laboring population (see Carchedi 1977, chap 4; Poulantzas 1974, pt. 2, chap. 4; and Braverman 1974, pt. 1).

Management can be subdivided according to its functions. The primary section of management (in industrial enterprise) is directly responsible for control and coordination of production workers, while the other most important sections of management are generally sales and advertising. The sales division manages promotion and creation of customers as well as most correspondence, sales analysis, and orders; the advertising division promotes the products of the firm. Other important subdivisions include finance, which watches over capital and checks and controls a firm's enlargement. It encompasses borrowing, extending credit, debt collection, supervising cash flow, and relations with stockholders. In summary, the managerial sector of the petty bourgeoisie has parceled out to it those bits of specialized knowledge and delegated authority necessary for the operation of the corporations (and the state).

The managerial stratum of the middle class normally can be counted on to have internalized the authority of the owners or those top managers with real economic ownership, to identify with the corporations' goals, and thus to exert itself enthusiastically to maximize profits within the guidelines established by those with real economic ownership. But to reinforce this internalization, managers are themselves evaluated, coordinated, supervised, and rated according to the performance of those under them. Raises, promotions, and bonuses accrue to those whose performance is most profitable, while demotion or firing await those who do not perform well. Thus an elaborate structure of inducements (both material and status) exists to structure managerial behavior in the interests of those with real economic power.

The salaried professional stratum of the middle class has special skills and expert knowledge important for those with real economic ownership (or in top positions in the state apparatus). It includes engineers and research scientists, architects, accountants who are employed by capital to increase profitability, computer experts, salaried doctors and lawyers, salaried intellectuals, authors and artists, social scientists, university professors, clergymen, and so forth. Virtually all of these occupations require considerable training (very often a doctoral degree or its equivalent in preparation time and energy); or in the case of many top entertainers and professional athletes, exceptional skills developed over considerable time. In all cases, although the salaried professionals typically have considerable autonomy, they are constrained within the parameters provided by those who pay their salaries.

In one sense, this section of the middle class could be considered equivalent to the independent middle class. Their expensively developed skills could be considered intangible means of production (more important than the physical means of production they employ, such as typewriters, calculators, law books, and so forth). Employed professionals might be considered to be selling their skills on a contract basis to a single customer, while self-employed professionals (such as doctors and lawyers) could be considered to be selling their skills to many customers. Moreover, in most cases salaried professionals function in a secondary role as managers in relation to nurses, medical technicians, legal assistants, research assistants, secretaries, computer programers, janitors, draftsmen, and so forth. In addition, in the case of such occupations as college professors, they have a role somewhat analogous to managers vis-à-vis their students, and in the case of medical doctors, to their patients.

On the other hand, salaried professionals establish neither the goals of what they do nor the broad parameters of how they do it. Owners and top managers set the conditions of intellectual life. Terms of employment are set up by the top editors, directors, managers, university administrators, and so forth, who in turn are accountable to the capitalist class. Salaried professionals are, in the last analysis, promoted, demoted, or fired, and otherwise rewarded and punished, to the degree to which their product complies with the requirements of those who pay their salaries, even when the reward structure is loose and it takes years for penalties to become effective (unlike as is the case with the much tighter control structure of managers). The autonomy characteristic of these jobs is a requisite for creative (and hence ultimately profitable) performance. The scientists, college professors, artists, architects, engineers, and so forth would not be able to perform well under too-specific directives. Besides, traditionally it has been impossible for the non–technically qualified managers and owners to give detailed instructions to this stratum (which has traditionally had more or less of a technical monopoly on expert information). They can generally only judge by results.

Scientific research and the production of knowledge should be understood as a production process encompassing both the scientists and engineers and the unskilled laborers who engage in the various physical tasks necessary for the production of information. Scientists and engineers have a managerial function in relation to many of these workers (technicians, janitors, laboratory assistants, secretaries, clerks, and research assistants of various kinds, machinists, computer keypunchers, computer operators, and so forth). Their technical information represents the exercise of relations of domination vis-à-vis technical support personal. But it is not only the actual information possessed by the individuals in the scientific-technical ideology that is materialized in the positions of dominant scientist-engineer and subordinate workers, positions of power legitimized by their being labeled "expert" and "laborers."

People in lower level salaried middle class positions are in balance neither especially exploited nor especially beneficiaries of exploitation. That is, they secure in income more or less the same share of society's labor product for which they are responsible. For the most part, they are not generally exploited even when they are employed because the immediate result of their economic activity is to ensure to capital more profit than would be the case without their employment (since most of their share in the surplus labor of those that they supervise is equivalent to the surplus the capitalists derive from the labor of the supervisors). This is also true for highly educated professionals, who likewise share in the surplus product of productive workers (which allows the capitalist class to pay them salaries higher than productive workers while still increasing their profit through their employment). The wealth returned to most employed professionals in salaries can be considered roughly equal to the value of the wealth or services their labor is indirectly responsible for creating. Further, it is also true of the independent middle class, who do most of their own labor themselves, and hence derive most of their income from their own effort, rather than through exploitation of the labor power of others.

Today in the Western capitalist countries all three principal segments of the middle class are central to the capital accumulation process. Thus, all are very much a product of contemporary capitalist class relations (even though the independent middle class historically originated in a precapitalist mode of production). Small farmers produce the bulk of the food that monopoly capitalists transport, process, and sell. Small businessmen sell the products produced by monopoly capitalist corporations. Small farmers and small businessmen are still central to capital accumulation. However, the role of these groups in the capitalist process is undergoing a fundamental transformation. There is an increasing socialization of the role of the independent petty bourgeoisie. Agricultural production is being appropriated directly and indirectly by corporate entities, while sales in all sectors are being taken over by giant chains. Expansion, sales, and production decisions are increasingly coordinated by financial institutions. The same functions continue to be performed, but now more and more by the managerial stratum, and less and less by the old independent petty bourgeoisie.

THE DECLINE OF THE INDEPENDENT PETTY BOURGEOISIE

Within the towns of feudal society a class of petty traders grew up alongside the artisans and craftsmen of the guilds. The majority of the class of petty traders and artisans were, together with the now free yeoman peasantry, intermediate between the wealthy landlords and big merchants on the one hand and the rural tenants and the small class of urban propertyless on the other. Most of the urban manufacture of material goods when the peasant mode of production was dominant in Europe (roughly 1400 to 1800) was by this intermediate class, a class which had considerable autonomy over its conditions of production.

From its revolution through the 1840s, the United States (outside of the South) was a society of mostly small proprietors (in 1780, roughly 80 percent of white families were propertied and worked for themselves). The predominant small landowning farmers who produced the bulk of the material product of American society were supplemented by the blacksmiths, coopers, carpenters, masons, barbers (who often doubled as doctors), and other self-employed artisans and small retail shopkeepers of the towns (Corey 1935, chap. 4).

In the 1840s capitalist industrialization began taking off in the Northern states of the United States, and the undermining of the small independent producers and distributors began. In the post–Civil War generation, the creation of monopolies progressively wiped out large sectors of the independents (especially artisans), while significantly infringing on retailers. In the first half of the twentieth century independent retailers went the way of independent artisans with the rise and consolidation of the big department stores and supermarkets. In the mid-twentieth century, what remained of the small farmers went down the same route, with increasing control by banks, processors, and distributors over the greatly enlarged and ever more capital-intensive, but still basically family-owned farms. Independent commodity production has progressively been undermined by the all-pervasive expansion of monopoly capital, with the consequence of the weakening of the independent middle class.

There has, as a result, been a radical transformation in the relative importance of the various sectors of the middle class. During the earliest period of capitalism, in the generation or two before and after 1800 in Great Britain, the generation before and after the Civil War in the United States, and the last half of the nineteenth through the early twentieth century in western and central continental Europe, most middle class people were self-employed independent farmers, artisans, retail businessmen, or professionals (the traditional petty bourgeoisie). But by the late twentieth century, throughout the advanced capitalist countries, the majority were either managers or employed professionals (the new middle class).

In the United States the number of self employed as a percentage of the total economically active population declined from 36.9 percent in 1880 to 8.7 percent in 1980. The decline was consistent until the 1970s. In each decade before this the proportion of self-employed was smaller than the last, even while the pace of decline has varied, being especially rapid in the 1960s (see Table 5.1). Most of the long-term decline has been due to the radical contraction of the number of small family farms over the twentieth century. In the nonagricultural sector, the decline in the self-employed has been much more gradual: from 12.7 percent of the total economically active population in 1940 to 7.3 percent in 1980 (see Table 5.1).

Examining the trends for men alone (the better indicator of social class position), it can be seen from Table 5.1 that the old petty bourgeoisie declined from 26.1 percent of the population in 1940 to 11.1 percent in 1980. Again, most of the decline has been a result of the rapid shrinkage of the agricultural petty bourgeoisie. While 14.8 percent of nonagriculturally active men were self-employed in 1940, 9.0 percent were in 1980. The decline in this percentage mostly occurred in the 1940s and, especially, in the 1960s.

The long-term decline of the self-employed middle class is generally characteristic of all contemporary societies (see Table 5.2). The exception to the trend, Great Britain, is, with the United States, the most advanced in this process. The slight increase in the size of the self-employed in Great Britain over the 1960–78 period as well as in the United States from 1970 to 1980 suggests that in these two countries, where the self-employed are the smallest of any major country in the world, the process of appropriation of the traditional petty bourgeoisie might be reaching its limits. It is notable that the U.S. proportion stabilized in the 1970s at approximately the same rate at which the British proportion stabilized earlier. It is more likely, however, that in both cases only a temporary plateau has been reached, rather than a permanent stabilization attained. It might well be the case that, at the prevailing level of technology and risk,

TABLE 5.1: Trends in the Independent Petty Bourgeoisie in the United States (self-employed as % of total employed)

	Employed Men		Nonagricultural Employed		Nonagricultural Men		Entire Labor Force	
	No.	% of Total	No.	% of Total	No.	% of Total	No.	% of Total
1980	6,246	11.1%	6,850	7.3%	4,800	9.0%	8,478	8.7%
1970	4,850	10.2	4,458	6.0	3,474	7.7	5,911	7.7
1960	6,834	15.7	5,443	9.0	4,396	11.1	7,901	12.2
1950	8,629	21.2	5,273	10.6	4,419	12.9	9,600	17.0
1940	8,837	26.1	4,635	12.7	3,844	14.8	9,781	21.7
1920	—*	—	—	—	—	—	9,739	23.5
1900	—*	—	—	—	—	—	8,716	30.8
1880	—*	—	—	—	—	—	5,441	36.9

*Data not available.

Sources: U.S. Department of Commerce, *U.S. Census, General Social and Economic Characteristics*, 1970, Table 80; U.S. Department of Labor, *Employment and Earnings*, January 1981, pp. 182, 183; Spurgeon Bell, "Productivity, Wages and National Income," in Edwards, Reich, and Weisskopf 1978, p. 180.

capital finds it more profitable to indirectly exploit small business until such time as there are major technological breakthroughs. Alternatively it might be the case that since the economic trends of the 1960s and 1970s were relatively unfavorable to what were in the immediate post-World War II period the most advanced capitalist countries (i.e., exceptionally high levels of unemployment existed), people were forced to create either their own means of survival or accept low incomes in their small businesses for want of alternatives.

The traditional petty bourgeoisie was largely destroyed by: first, great increases in productivity that occurred within the monopoly corporations (a result of the funds they had available to introduce the most efficient machinery and thus produce on a large-scale basis, taking advantage of economies of scale); second, the abilities of the monopoly corporations through national advertising, agreements for bulk shipments with commercial haulers and suppliers, and so forth to secure most of the market; and third, the use of their monopoly power to drive small proprietors out of business (e.g., by temporarily selling goods below their costs of production in order to drive marginal businesses bankrupt, then later increasing prices to make up the losses). The inability of the family proprietors to successfully compete against the wealthy corporations with their immense resources forced most to give up business and either become workers or merge into the rapidly expanding "new middle class" (this latter usually by sending sons to college).

The general business conditions of small business are given by external forces. Most of the goods sold by small retailers as well as

TABLE 5.2: The Independent Petty Bourgeoisie in the Advanced Capitalist Countries, 1960 and 1978

	Canada	U.S.	Japan	Australia	France*
1960	18.1% (1964)	17.3%	27.4%	18.6% (1964)	30.5%
1978	10.7	10.8	20.3	17.4	17.3

	West Germany	Italy	Sweden	United Kingdom
1960	15.6%	29.5%	14.7% (1967)	9.0%
1978	12.6	26.6	10.1	10.2

*Data for France are for all self-employed (of both sexes) plus unpaid family workers.

Note: Self-employed males as a percentage of the employed male population.

Sources: Organization for Economic Cooperation and Development, Labour Force Statistics, 1960–71 (1973) and 1967–78 (1980).

equipment and supplies bought are produced by monopoly corporations, which in good measure thus establish prices.

Further the conditions imposed by banks for the loans necessary to improve their operation puts considerable constraints on both types of small businesses. Small businesses, moreover, (unlike monopoly corporations) have no control over the prices they can charge (their prices are set by markets). They thus tend to be subject to a squeeze between the rising costs of supplies and the competitive price of what the market will bear. Stiff competition from monopoly enterprises tends to drive most such operations out of business (especially in times of economic recession).

Small retail businesses typically must, in good part, eschew modernization in favor of developing ties based on personal considerations (e.g., being on a first-name basis with customers, offering personalized advice). Such businesses can not afford large and diverse inventories, but must rather focus on those products with the highest turnover (thus resulting in overlapping inventories among competing small businesses). To survive, retail businesses must not only charge prices higher than large chain stores, but they must often sell inferior goods or skimp on services as well (this proves to be especially true in minority and poor areas where lack of good transport forces much of the local population to shop in such stores). Such practices quite naturally often result in tensions between the minority and poor clientele and the proprietors, (manifested in vandalism, shoplifting, and robberies on the one hand, and racism, enthusiasm for law and order, antiwelfare sentiment, and so forth on the other).

Small farmers, those who (with their immediate family) do (more or less) at least half of the physical labor on the farm themselves, survived relatively well (in comparison with urban artisans and retailers) through the mid-twentieth century. This has been the case in part because agricultural technology has lagged behind industrial technology, thus keeping ownership of farm equipment within reach of a significant number of family farmers (with heavy financing by banks), and because the state has heavily subsidized this sector through agricultural price supports and restrictions on corporate farming (for reasons of legitimation). However, fewer and fewer farmers are able to survive, and the corporations are increasingly taking over this sector as well. The surviving family farmers who still do most of the farming are ever more closely integrated into monopoly capitalist institutions. Basic production and expansion decisions must increasingly be approved by the banks and processers as most family farmers are gradually being reduced to the equivalent of franchise holders.

Business enterprises in the United States are mostly very small, with most sales concentrated in the hands of a small number of giant corporations. In 1976, 64.6 percent of all businesses in the United States *grossed* less than $25,000 (all these businesses together accounted for a grand total of 1.5 percent of total business receipts). Further 84.3 percent of all businesses accounted for just 5.3 percent of all business receipts. On the other hand, businesses that grossed over $1 million accounted for 80.9 percent of all business receipts (U.S. Department of Commerce 1981a, p. 556). The process of concentration is ongoing.

The concentration process in retailing is revealed in figures for sales and payroll per establishment. Sales per establishment increased from $807,000 in 1929 (in 1967 dollars) to $2,007,000 in 1977. Meanwhile the total payroll per establishment with wage and salaried workers increased from $11,200 (in 1967 dollars) in 1939 to $33,900 in 1977. The decline of the traditional petty bourgeoisie is reflected in Table 5.3, which shows the trends in retail businesses in the United States from 1929 to 1977. After increasing significantly during the Great Depression (when unemployed workers turned to establishing marginal retail businesses), the number of retail establishments in the United States has stayed virtually constant at 1.8 million. There has been a decline, however, in those stores that do not employ any workers (i.e., utilize only the labor of the owner and that of unpaid family workers). There were 753,000 of these latter enterprises in 1939 and 551,000 in 1977. It should thus be noted that while 43 percent of all retail stores were such exclusively family operations in 1939, this had declined to 30 percent by 1977 (see Table 5.3).

There has been a significant and continual decline since 1939 in the number of grocery stores as marketing comes to increasingly take place through supermarkets. While there were 388,000 grocery stores in the United States in 1939, there were only 179,000 in 1977. The number of restaurants, on the other hand has consistently risen, from 170,000 in 1939 to 274,000 in 1977.

A growing group among "independent businessmen" are the franchise holders (from oil companies, restaurant chains, grocery chains, hardware chains, and so forth). In 1980, roughly 25 percent of all retail businesses were franchises (and thus their owners were fundamentally accountable to the corporations that had real economic power). This includes almost 90 percent of gasoline stations and about 25 percent of all restaurants (but only about 10 percent of grocery stores). The number of franchises increased by almost 25 percent from 1970 to 1980. The growth of franchises has been the most rapid in restaurants (more than doubling from 1970 to 1980) and in grocery stores. On the other hand the number of gasoline

TABLE 5.3: Retail Businesses in the United States, 1929 to 1977 (all figures in thousands)

	1929	1939	1948	1958	1967	1977
Retail establishments	1,476	1,770	1,770	1,788	1,763	1,855
Retailers without payroll	—*	753	569	607	571	551
Grocery stores	307	388	351	260	218	179
Gas stations	122	242	179	206	216	177
Restaurants	134	170	194	230	237	274
Sales/establishments	807	807	1,045	1,180	1,557	2,007
(1,000s of 1967 dollars)						
Payroll per establishments with payroll	—	11.3	14.9	19.3	30.4	33.9
(1,000s of 1967 dollars)						

*Data not available.
Sources: U.S. Department of Commerce 1975b, p. 843; 1981a, p. 846.

franchises has declined, together with the number of gasoline stations (U.S. Department of Commerce 1981a, p. 847). Most franchise holders must follow strict rules set by their parent corporations concerning how business is to be conducted, what the product must look like, the architecture of buildings, pricing, and so forth. The parent corporation typically sets retail prices as well. Such franchises are eagerly sought after, however, because of the advantages national advertising and consequent brand loyalty brings as well as the cost savings involved in bulk buying and high productivity. Although a franchise holder has little basic control over his business, since profit depends on gross income, he is highly motivated to work long hours, give his all to increase sales, conscientiously supervise staff, and so forth.

The franchise form seems to be becoming the model for virtually the entire petty bourgeois business sector (except the services). In order to survive, small businesses must become integrated into, and subordinant to, the decision-making processes of the monopoly corporations and financial institutions. They become increasingly subordinate to their suppliers and distributors who are able to establish national product identification and monopoly power, in both supply and distribution markets, and to the banks that coordinate and regulate production through credit.

The medical and legal professional sector of independent business has been largely able to resist such dependence through development of a cooperative form—partnership as well as common ownership of law offices and medical centers. Nevertheless, the direct employment by corporations and the state of these professionals is expanding. Thus this sector too is slowly either being transformed into part of the new middle class or slowly becoming the equivalent of privileged vassals of the corporations (often working on a retainer basis).

A different picture is obtained when examining the service sector of the independent petty bourgeoisie. After growing only slightly more rapidly than the population from 1933 to the end of the 1960s, it grew very rapidly in the 1970s (from 1,188,000 service establishment in 1967, to 1,835,000 in 1977). The growth since 1948 in the number of such businesses that do not employ anyone other than the owner has been especially rapid (the opposite trend from retail businesses). From 535,000 service enterprises in 1958, one-person operations in this sector increased to 667,000 in 1967 and 1,110,000 in 1977 (while in 1958 55 percent of all service establishments were one-person operations, in 1977 61 percent were). It appears that it was the growth of this sector that accounted for the virtual stagnation of the decline of the independent petty bourgeoisie in the 1970s—the growth here compensating for the continual decline of agricultural and retail establishments (see Table 5.4).

TABLE 5.4: Service Establishments in the United States, 1933 to 1977 (all figures in thousands)

	1933	1939	1948	1958	1967	1977	Percentage without Payroll in 1977
Service establishments	502	646	665	975	1188	1835	60.5%
Number without payroll	—*	—	—	535	667	1110	—
Personal services	320	390	325	413	499	512	66.8
Barber/beauty shops	160	205	154	215	292	265	67.5
Business services	36	26	27	114	212	458	66.2
Auto repair	94	66	81	104	110	200	47.0
Miscellaneous repair	53	75	71	145	138	163	66.2
Amusement, entertainment (excluding motion pictures)	19	30	31	75	96	177	65.0

*Data not available.

Sources: U.S. Department of Commerce 1975b, p. 854; 1981a, p. 852.

The subsectors of the service sector that have experienced the most rapid growth have been amusement and entertainment (96,000 in 1967 and 177,000 in 1977), auto repair (110,000 in 1967, and 200,000 in 1977), and above all "business services" (advertising, managerial consulting, and so forth, with 212,000 in 1967 and 458,000 in 1977). For the most part these occupations are relatively labor intensive with small amounts of capital necessary for entry. In many cases (as in restaurants, the major expanding retail subsector) they depend on a considerable component of creativity, uniqueness, individual responsibility, and personal relations with customers for success. The rise of such independent businesses in the face of the decline of both the farming and retail petty bourgeoisie is, in part, a result of the significantly higher unemployment of the 1970s that drove many people to create their own alternatives to employment by others and, in part, a result of the increasingly technical and centralized corporations' inability to provide the certain special services as cheaply and conveniently as can individual consultants, entertainers, and repair people.

The Decline and Transformation of Family Farming

Over the twentieth century there has been a continual (and in the 1970s accelerated) concentration of agriculture in the United States. In 1920, the average farm size was about 150 acres, in 1950 about 200, but in 1980, about 450 acres (New York *Times*, February 1, 1981, ES). The average assets of a farm (land, buildings, equipment, and livestock) have increased dramatically over the course of the twentieth century. While in 1910 the average assets of a farm totaled $12,200 (1967 dollars) and in 1950, $21,500; by 1978 it had grown to $125,600 (see Table 5.5).

In 1974, 58 percent of all U.S. farmland was held in units of 1,000 acres or more by 6.7 percent of all farms. In 1900, 0.8 percent of all farms and 24 percent of all farmland was in units of 1,000 acres or more (see Table 5.6). There has been a steady tendency for the average size of farms to increase as well as for farmland to become concentrated in large capital-intensive units. In 1980, the largest 20 percent of farms accounted for 80 percent of all farm products sold (New York *Times*, February 8, 1981, p. 20). In California in the late 1970s 3.7 percent of all farms farmed 59 percent of the cropland (New York *Times*, April 1, 1981, p. 34). In 1962, about two-thirds of cattle slaughtered in the United states came from feedlots with less than 1,000 head; in 1973, two-thirds came from feedlots with over 1,000 head (Burbach and Flynn, 1980, p. 32). About 16,000 of the 300,000 egg-producing farms (5.5 percent) sold about 93 percent of all eggs in the United States in 1980 (New York *Times*, February

TABLE 5.5: The Decline of the Family Farmer In the United States

	Total Farm Population as Percentage of U.S. Population	Total Number of Farms (in thousands)	Total Family Farm Owners plus Unpaid Family Workers (in thousands)	Average Farm Assets (in thousands of 1967 dollars)	Ratio of Wage and Salaried Workers Total Family Workers
1910	34.9%	6,366	10,174	12.2	0.332
1930	24.9	6,546	9,307	19.8	0.343
1950	15.3	5,648	7,597	21.5	0.307
1960	8.7	3,963	5,172	45.1	0.364
1970	4.8	2,949	3,348	81.6	0.351
1978	3.7	2,672	2,097	125.6	0.464

Sources: U.S. Department of Commerce 1981a, pp. 420, 685, 686, 692; 1975b, pp. 457, 467, 480.

1, 1981, E3). In 1980, about 25 percent of U.S. farm production (including most seed crops, vegetables for processing, citrus fruit, chickens, and milk) was controlled by processors (either through vertical arrangements, contracting, or direct ownership of production).

The rural petty bourgeoisie has rapidly declined throughout the twentieth century. In 1910 34.9 percent of the U.S. population lived on farms, by 1950 this had declined to 15.3 percent. In 1978, it was only 3.7 percent. In 1900, there were 10.1 million farm owners and unpaid family workers laboring in agriculture in the United States. In 1950, there were still 7.6 million. But by 1978, they had declined to 2.1 million. The most rapid decline in the rural petty bourgeoisie has occurred since 1950. The number of farms in the United States has steadily declined since the 1930s. While there were 6.5 million in 1930 and 5.6 million in 1950, there were only 2.7 million in 1978 (see Table 5.5).

In spite of the concentration of agricultural production the ratio of wage workers in agriculture to total family workers actually declined slightly until the 1970s, when it increased significantly. While there were 0.307 wage workers in agriculture for each family worker in 1950, there were 0.464 in 1978 (see Table 5.5). The banks, corporations and large farmers have found it more profitable to preserve family farming (on an ever larger and more capital-intensive scale) than to directly take over; while the family farmers, for the most part, are willing to work considerably more hours for less pay than would wage workers (thus large numbers of family farmers are quite marginal).

A large number of the remaining farms are worked only on weekends and after work by workers who get most of their income from wage labor. Through the 1960s and 1970s approximately one-third of family farmers held wage jobs working for someone else. A significant number of small farm households in the 1970s received the majority of their income from off-farm sources. In 1979, approx-

TABLE 5.6:   The Increasing Size of U.S. Farms

	Percentage of Farms with 1,000 or More Acres	Percentage of Farmland in Farms of 1,000 or More Acres
1900	0.8%	23.8%
1930	1.3	28.0
1950	2.2	42.6
1959	3.7	49.4
1969	5.5	54.4
1974	6.7	58.1

Sources: U.S. Department of Commerce 1981a, p. 691; 1975a, p. 467.

imately 17 percent of all multiple jobholders in the United States were family farmers—mostly with their secondary job in agriculture (U.S. Department of Commerce 1981a, p. 401).

Family farmers' preference for the farm life and independence is shown by the gap between the earnings of self-employed farmers and other sections of the work force. In 1978 self-employed farmers' median earnings were about $7,500 per year. This contrasts with $12,133 for all workers in the United States (see Table 5.9). The willingness of small farmers to work for so little renumeration as well as to mobilize their wives and children as unpaid family workers in order to survive proves extremely profitable for the corporations. If they directly took over the operation of farms, their labor costs would increase considerably.

Agriculture has become increasingly capital intensive as ever more expensive equipment and expensive up-to-date feed, fertilizers, seeds, petroleum, and so forth have become necessary to survive. Given the competitive markets in which farmers must sell their goods, and the limited amount of their own resources, they are forced to turn to the banks to finance the innovations necessary to increase productivity, and thus keep their heads above water. The farmers that fail to innovate will soon find that their costs of production exceed the price of the commodities they produce. Each year large numbers of farmers find they are no longer able to meet their payments to the banks and consequently go bankrupt or sell out to their competitors.

Small farmers are increasingly indebted to the banks. They thus become ever more subordinate, losing control over the basic decision-making process. Total farm debt grew from about $25 billion in 1960 to about $55 billion in 1970 to almost $160 billion in 1980. The ratio of debt to gross farm income has risen significantly. While the ratio averaged roughly 2.5 to 1 through the 1960s and early 1970s, by the late 1970s it had grown to about 4.5 to 1. In 1980 interest payments accounted for 12 percent of the farmers' *total* production expenses (New York *Times*, February 8, 1981, p. 20).

Some corporate giants have come to exert control over family farms through contract growing, leasing land, and maintaining monopolies on equipment supply. The two leading farm equipment manufacturers, International Harvester and Caterpiller Tractor, have a virtual monopoly over modern farm equipment. Tenneco, the largest single corporate farm, owns more than a million acres of dry grazing land in the Southwest, most of which it leases out to tenant farmers. It leases another 125,000 acres of irrigated land (and farms 25,000 acres directly). It finds it more profitable to lease its land than to directly manage it (New York *Times*, February 1, 1981, E3; April 1,

1981, p. 34). Considerable real economic power is also exerted through contract farming. Tenneco, for example, handles and markets the produce of about 3,000 independent growers of fruit, vegetables, and nuts in the Southwest. It is the largest grower and shipper of table grapes in the United States, accounting for about 15 percent of the total shipments (New York *Times*, April 1, 1981, p. 34). In addition, Tenneco is a major supplier of fuel and equipment to farmers. Del Monte is another major corporation heavily involved in agriculture. But this corporation, too, concentrates on contracting, processing, and packaging, rather than on direct production.

Farm cooperatives, increasingly controlled by the biggest farmers (and increasingly acting like corporations), have also come to play a growing role in family farming. While the number of farms in the United States declined from 5.6 million in 1950 to 2.7 million in 1977, the membership of farm supply cooperatives increased from 2.5 to 3.1 million, while the membership of farm marketing cooperative declined from 4.1 million to 2.7 million (U.S. Department of Commerce 1981a, p. 704). In 1974–75, 75 percent of all dairy products, 40 percent of all grains and soybeans, and 25 percent of all fruits and nuts were sold through cooperatives. In 1980, about 25 percent of all production supplies purchased by farmers (e.g., fertilizers, chemicals, feed) were bought through cooperatives (New York *Times*, February 1, 1981).

The largest farmers' co-op is Farmland Industries (eighty-seventh on the *Fortune* 1980 list of the top 500 corporations). Farmland's enterprises include oil wells, refineries, pipelines, fertilizer plants, insurance agencies, a large pork-processing facility, and a marketing subsidiary (*Fortune*, April 20, 1981, p. 150). The fastest growing cooperative is Land O'Lakes (a marketer of dairy, poultry, and oil crops for 180,000 farmers in the north central states). In 1980 Land O'Lakes ranked one hundred forty-second on the *Fortune* list of the 500 biggest corporations in the United States (New York *Times*, February 1, 1981, E3).

The high risk associated with agriculture because of the variability of crops, combined with the still relatively semiindustrial and labor-intensive nature of most agricultural production (especially fruit and vegetable production) has inhibited the megacorporations from directly appropriating and running most farmland in the United States. The systems of supply, contracting, lending, and marketing mean that the small farmers absorb most of the risk, while working especially hard to keep their heads above water. The corporations are relieved of the difficult tasks of supervision of semiindustrial operations, while the labor of coordination is performed much cheaper (and in a highly self-motivated fashion) than corporate salaried executives and foremen would be able to perform the same operations. Family farming, through a combination of corporate penetration, bank supervision, and cooperation, has been largely reduced to a franchise operation in everything but name.

THE RISE OF THE NEW MIDDLE CLASS

From the early period of capitalism until the latter half of the twentieth century, the secondary component of the middle class was the salaried administrative and professional personnel in the offices of commercial and industrial enterprises. The typical small capitalist enterprise traditionally employed a handful of bookkeepers and clerks to keep records, manage correspondence, and help with purchases, sales, and supervision. Such early office workers were intermediate in their control over labor power. They shared in the power of the owner (as reflected in the real possibilities of succeeding the owner as proprietor or successfully establishing their own business). Their superior position was manifested in their high salaries and prerogatives vis-à-vis the workers, and in their superior all-around technical knowledge of the business. These early office workers shared in performing the function of the capitalists, coordinating the labor power of others.

Gradually, however, over the course of the latter part of the nineteenth century, a class of managers evolved out of the early office workers, a class which came to accumulate considerable power over labor power, while the vast majority were reduced to mere clerical and sales workers with no significant control over either their own labor power or the labor power of others. This latter stratum thus separated from the middle class, merging instead with the working class (as its clerical and sales sector), increasingly equivalent to the majority of blue-collar workers. (There is no longer a distinction in the nature of the labor process between a machine operator in an office and a typical factory worker.) The labor of this "white-collar proletariat" has been routinized and deprived of any supervisory role controlling the labor power of others. Thus, out of the early bookkeepers and clerks evolved a large and growing sector of the working class as well as both the managerial section of the capitalist class and the managers and supervisors who make up the managerial sector of the middle class.

The functions of the new middle class came to be in good part different from those of the old middle class. The old middle class was engaged primarily in producing material goods (foods, manufactures) and in sales. Under monopoly conditions these functions came to be performed by the expanded working class under the supervision of the managerial strata of the new middle class (with the technical advice of the professional strata of scientists and engineers). Thus, the traditional functions of the middle class were bifurcated, with the menial (manual and nonmanual) aspects accruing to the white collar working class. Other functions of the new middle class were created by the logic of monopoly capitalism and its state, and corresponded rather little to the traditional functions of the middle class. For example, the vast expansion of higher education, scientific research and development, the sales effort, finance, and the qualitative increase in the need to coordinate, allocate, and plan the labor process meant the creation of large segments of the new middle class that engaged in supervision, teaching, advertising, banking, research, design, and so forth.

The development of modern monopoly capitalism in the advanced countries has involved a number of processes that have led to the growth of both the managerial and professional subsectors of the new middle class. These include: first, the need to control the labor process of the working class in order to regulate and coordinate it in the interest of maximizing productivity and control (and hence profit); second, the rapid rate of technological innovation stimulated by the competitive pursuit of profit; third, the "realization problem," including the need for more advertising and redesign ("the sales effort"), the growing role of credit and financing, and the expanding role of the monopoly capitalist state in pumping money into the economy in order to counteract the tendency toward overproduction/underconsumption and economic stagnation (endemic in monopoly capitalism); fourth, the "legitimation problem," or the need to secure the loyalty of both the masses of the middle and working class through welfare programs *and* mass education and the mass media (and in case of failure, the police); fifth, in some countries (like the United States) much more than in others (like Japan) the militarization of society and the consequent need for more scientific and administrative personnel; and sixth, the greater wealth of all classes, which provides more discretionary income spendable on leisure, entertainment, books, professional services, and so forth. These structural trends have effected a rapid increase in both the new middle class and the semi-professional sector of the working class (e.g., technicians, primary and secondary schoolteachers, nurses, social workers, the rank-and-file police, and so on).

The logic of profit maximization in the ever-expanding monopoly corporations has dictated the rapid growth of the managerial stratum that functions to efficiently deploy and coordinate labor power. Complex hierarchies of supervisors and managers have been created to regulate all aspects of the labor process. This process has resulted in the rapid growth of the corporate managerial stratum of the petty bourgeoisie over the course of the twentieth century. The managerial sector of the petty bourgeoisie working for the corporations has increased greatly. In 1940 the private sector salaried managerial stratum represented only 10.8 percent of the entire petty bourgeoisie (as measured by the U.S. census categories rather than the reanalyzed categories used in Table 5.7), while by 1970 it had grown to 20.4 percent (see Table 5.7). The total number of nonfarm salaried managers and state administrators (as defined by U.S. Census aggregate categories) rose from 1.5 million in 1940 to 2.9 million in 1960 and 6.8 million in 1978 (see Table 5.7).

Monopoly capitalist society has an endemic propensity to produce goods valued at more than people are paid in wages and salaries (and thus are able to buy) because of the tendency for corporations to reduce costs (ultimately mostly wages) while increasing, or at least maintaining, profits. In order to combat this tendency the corporations increasingly engage in advertising (generalized propaganda to buy as well as propaganda to buy specific goods), expanding credit and financing as well as continuing style changes designed to induce people to go into debt rather than save money; the state facilitates consumer buying power by expanding social services as well as military spending and other forms of aid to the corporations, such as "foreign assistance," research and development support, and direct subsidies and loan guarantees to take up the slack left by the private economy. The expansion of the sales effort generates large numbers of advertising personnel, high-level salesmen, and sales managers as well as bank managers and others in finance. Meanwhile, government's efforts result in rapid expansion of welfare administrators as well as military officers and civilian bureaucrats, scientists, engineers, and college professors and administrators. In 1970, 5.9 percent of the petty bourgeoisie (1.4 percent of the employed male population) plus another 3.6 percent of the entire male population employed in the sales subsector of the intermediate strata, were engaged in performing finance, accounting, advertising, and sales functions (see Table 5.8). Reflecting the rapid growth of this sector of the petty bourgeoisie has been the total number of accountants and auditors in the United States, which rose from 23,000 in 1900 to 238,000 in 1940 and 713,000 in 1970 (U.S. Department of Commerce 1975a, p. 140).

The tremendous sums spent by the United States on the military, both to promote domestic prosperity (alleviate the endemic underconsumption problem) and to advance U.S. corporate interests around the world, result in the government spending vast sums on developing military technology and in maintaining a large standing army with an associated civilian bureaucracy in a supporting role (including intelligence services). This produces an expanded new middle class of

TABLE 5.7: Trends in the Major Components of the Middle Class (Occupational Structure of Employed Males)

	1940	1950	1960	1970	1978[a]
Professional	1,892.6[c] (16.1)	2,970.2 (22.6)	4,473.3 (33.1)	6,875.9 (43.2)	9,124 (43.3)
Self-employed	522.1 (4.4)	553.8 (4.2)	682.9 (5.0)	832.9 (5.2)	856 (4.1)
Government	484.1 (4.1)	714.1 (5.4)	1,206.7 (8.9)	2,058.8 (12.9)	
Privately employed	885.7 (7.5)	1,701.0 (12.9)	2,579.8 (19.1)	3,981.2 (25.0)	8,268 (39.2)
Managerial	3,326.5 (28.3)	4,340.7 (33.0)	4,627.8 (34.2)	5,325.9 (33.5)	8,186 (38.8)
Self-employed	1,832.6 (15.6)	2,223.2 (16.9)	1,721.2 (12.7)	1,427.0 (9.0)	1,393 (6.7)
Government	228.6 (1.9)	262.4 (2.0)	345.9 (2.6)	640.1 (4.0)	
Privately employed	1,263.1 (10.8)	1,852.9 (14.1)	2,555.4 (18.9)	3,247.2 (20.4)	6,791 (32.2)
Nonprofessional/mana- gerial self-employed	1,521.7 (13.0)	1,667.4 (12.7)	2,036.0 (15.0)	2,342.1 (14.7)	2,449 (11.6)
Craftspeople	717.4 (6.1)	728.7 (5.5)	807.1 (6.0)	938.7 (5.9)	—[b]
Sales people	198.3 (1.7)	327.4 (2.5)	500.1 (3.7)	553.8 (3.5)	—
Farmers and managers	4,996.8 (4.3)	4,189.7 (31.8)	2,392.3 (17.7)	1,355.2 (8.5)	1,314 (6.2)
Owners	4,959.3 (4.2)	4,157.2 (31.6)	2,368.9 (17.5)	1,328.8 (8.3)	—
Managers	37.5 (0.1)	30.7 (0.2)	22.4 (0.2)	26.4 (0.2)	—
Total middle class	11,737.6 (100.0)	13,168.0 (100.0)	13,529.4 (100.0)	15,899.1 (100.0)	21,073 (100.0)

% Government	6.1%	7.4%	11.5%	17.0%	—
% Self-employed	75.3%	65.4%	50.3%	37.0%	29.0%
% Nonfarm self-employed	57.5%	49.5%	39.8%	31.6%	22.3%
Middle Class as % Labor Force	34.4%	32.5%	31.1%	33.3%	33.5%
Nonfarm middle class as % nonfarm employed	25.7%	26.0%	27.9%	31.9%	32.8%
Salaried professionals and managers as % labor force	8.4%	11.2%	15.4%	20.8%	23.9%
Self-employed as % labor force	25.9%	21.2%	15.7%	12.3%	9.7%
Labor force employed	34,102.4	40,510.2	43,490.9	47,730.7	62,903.0

[a]Those with earnings in 1978, state and privately employed are combined for the year.
[b]Data not available.
[c]In thousands.
Note: Census definitions calculated as percentage on basis of total middle class.
Sources: U.S. Bureau of Census 1940, Table 6; 1950, vol. 2, pt. 1, U.S. Summary Table 128; 1960, Table 21; 1970c, Table 43; 1978, Tables 56, 59.

TABLE 5.8: The Structure of the U.S. Middle Class in 1970

	Salaried Private Sector	Salaried State Sector	Self-Employed	Total[a]
Administrators, managers, and proprietors	18.5%	4.7%	20.6%	43.8%
of which farm	0.2	0.0	9.9	10.1
Technical and Scientific professionals	10.4	3.2	0.4	14.0
Professionals who reproduce social relations[b]	5.7	2.8	2.1	10.6
Specialists in finance, accounting, and control	4.7	0.7	0.5	5.9
Total professional and managerial[c]	43.2	12.6	26.5	82.3
Nonprofessional/nonmanagerial self-employed	—[d]	—	17.7	17.7
of which sales	—	—	4.1	4.1
of which craftsworkers	—	—	7.0	7.0
Total[c]	43.2	12.6	44.2	100.0
Total in absolute number[c]	5,767,000	1,680,000	5,889,000	13,336,000
Middle class as % of economically active population in each category	16.5	25.0	100.0	28.0

[a]Excluding unpaid family workers.

[b]This category includes religious workers, lawyers and judges, labor relations experts, social scientists, social science and humanities teachers, authors, painters, public relations personnel, and so forth.

[c]Including occupations not listed separately.

[d]Data not available.

Note: Reconceptualized U.S. Census categories, male occupational structure.

Source: U.S. Bureau of the Census 1970c, Table 43.

civilian and military administrators, engineers, scientists, and university professors and administrators.

The competition among the giant corporations for markets and cost reduction, together with their immense resources, has resulted in considerable funds being allocated to technical improvement and innovation, both those designed to increase product performance, and those designed merely to sell goods (style changes). Technological innovation has become a planned and systematic process in which science has been integrated into the needs of capital accumulation with the development of organized research and development apparatus (both private and publicly funded or subsidized) to speed technological innovation. This process has resulted in the rapid expansion of engineers, scientists, architects, and so forth.

The technical and scientific sector of the petty bourgeoisie represented 14.0 percent of the middle class in 1970 (and 3.5 percent of the entire employed male population). In 1970 approximately 74 percent of this stratum were employed by private industry, while 23 percent worked for the state (and only about 3 percent were self-employed). The largest group here is comprised of engineers. While in 1900 there were only 38,000 engineers in the United States, and in 1940 there were 297,000, by 1970 there were 1.2 million (U.S. Department of Commerce 1975a, p. 140).

Last, in order to win and hold the support of both the middle and the laboring classes, the capitalist class (as the ruling class) has had to radically expand a wide range of welfare programs in response to the demands of the underlying population for a better life. Failure to do so would result in growing alienation from the capitalist system and the growth of massive disruptive and effective socialist movements, rather than the defusion and integration of oppositional forces into the system. As a result of massive government spending directed to removing the harsh edges of capitalism and ensuring a materially tolerable life for the majority, the number of medical doctors, social welfare administrators, administrators in farm support programs, and so forth has radically increased. Also in response to the need to secure and keep the loyalty of the masses of people in the face of potentially considerable skepticism about the justice of the monopoly capitalist system, the educational and public relations establishments have been radically increased. Primary and secondary education has become universal, higher education expanded, public relations departments developed by corporations, and state-sponsored radio and television (which in good part must be considered an attempt to persuade) promoted. Finally, active opposition to the business system in certain circles (e.g., youth, minorities) manifested in riots and "terrorism," increasing crime rates (and general disrespect for corporate and state property among the poorer laboring classes), has resulted in the expansion of the police. The need to secure legitimacy and social order has resulted in the rapid expansion of public relations personnel in industry, the development of a state-employed professional middle class of university teachers, administrators, media administrators, and a wide range of professionals as well as police officials and specialists (see Ehrenreich and Ehrenreich 1979).

The rapid expansion of the state's role in monopoly capitalist society (both for war and legitimation) has resulted in a corresponding growth in the number of state managers and administrators. In 1970 this group represented 4.7 percent of the petty bourgeoisie (and 1.2 percent of the entire employed male population). As measured by U.S. census categories, the number of state administrators grew from

229,000 (1.9 percent of the petty bourgeoisie) in 1940 to 640,000 (4.0 percent) in 1970 (see Table 5.7).

The growing importance of legitimation for monopoly capitalist society has resulted in the rapid growth of all three sections of those professionals whose social function is to legitimate, and hence reproduce, social relations. In 1970, 10.6 percent of the petty bourgeoisie (and 2.7 percent of the entire male population) were specialists in these functions. About 54 percent of these were directly employed by private business, 26 percent by the state, while 20 percent were self-employed (see Table 5.8). Social scientists grew from 36,000 in 1950 to 110,000 in 1970. Social workers grew from 77,000 in 1950 to 221,000 in 1970; personnel and labor relations personnel grew from 53,000 in 1950 to 296,000 in 1970 (U.S. Department of Commerce 1975b, pp. 140-41).

The new middle class as a whole in 1970 accounted for 56 percent of the entire petty bourgeoisie and 14 percent of the entire employed male population; while the independent petty bourgeoisie accounted for 44 percent of the petty bourgeoisie and 11 percent of the employed male population (see Table 5.8). As measured by the U.S. Census categories (which include semiprofessionals together with the true middle class), the professional and managerial strata increased from 8.4 percent of the employed male population in 1940 to 23.9 percent in 1978; while the independent petty bourgeoisie declined from 25.9 percent to 9.7 percent. In 1940 the traditional petty bourgeoisie was three times larger than the salaried managerial and professional sector, in 1960 the two parts of the petty bourgeoisie were about equal in size, but by 1978 the professional managerial sector (which here includes semiprofessionals) was twice the size of the independent sector—a radical reversal (see Table 5.8).

It is of considerable interest to note that the increase in the new middle class and the salaried intermediate strata has been approximately of the same size as the shrinkage in the old petty bourgeoisie. This is manifested in the total size of the petty bourgeoisie (plus salaried intermediaries) remaining relatively constant as a percentage of the total employed population. Men in middle class plus intermediate positions represented 34 percent of the employed population in 1940, 33 percent in 1950, 31 percent in 1960, 33 percent in 1970, and 34 percent in 1978 (as measured by U.S. Census categories). Applying the ratio of the salaried professional and managerial middle class as defined from the reconceptualized U.S. Census categories used in Table 5.8 to that defined by the aggregate U.S. Census categories (which include the intermediate strata) used in Table 5.7 (p. 73) reveals that the true middle class has averaged roughly 28 percent of the employed male population of the United States from 1950 to 1980. Declining from 32 percent in 1940, the (estimated) size of the true petty bourgeoisie (as a percentage of the *male labor force*) was 29 percent in 1950, 27 percent in 1960, 28 percent in 1970, and 27 percent in 1978. Considering the nonemployed underclass as well as differential unemployment, this means that roughly one-fourth of the U.S. people have been in middle class positions through the entire post–World War II period.

This constancy in the face of radical changes in its new and old components strongly suggests that the petty bourgeoisie as a whole is a single coherent class with a defined intermediate position in the class structure between capital and labor. The functions of the petty bourgeoisie formerly performed individually are being socialized (including the transfer of many functions formerly performed by the family farmer to such salaried professional and managerial positions as financiers, advertising experts, scientists, agronomists, managers of agricultural implement, fertilizer, food processing and distributing firms, and so forth) while their old more menial functions have come to be concentrated in the working class.

THE PETTY BOURGEOISIE AS A SOCIAL CLASS

Because of their common economic situation (vis-à-vis control over labor power), the various segments of the petty bourgeoisie (old and new) tend to experience life in essentially similar ways (essentially different from either capitalists or workers). Their similar class situation tends to put them in social contact with each other on more or less equal terms, while socially isolating them from workers and capitalists. They thus tend to establish friendship networks and intermarry across subclass lines (and relatively rarely with workers or capitalists) as well as to develop a common life-style, class culture, values, and policies. Nevertheless, there are significant variations among the various segments of this class in terms of class consciousness, income, life-styles, values, culture, and, not least of all, politics.

Professionals (both salaried and independent) and managers tend to be more socially coherent than most of the independent business sector. The former groups (together with the more successful of small businessmen) tend to live in more or less homogeneous middle class neighborhoods and to mix socially with people in similar positions. On the other hand, the majority of small proprietors and small farmers tend to live in more or less working class or heterogeneous farming communities. A percentage of independent proprietors (larger than either employed or self-employed professionals) come from working class families, have working class friends, and are socially integrated into working class networks (Hamilton 1972, chap. 9; 1975, chap. 2). In many ways then the highest level of the middle class (managerial, professional, and better-off independent business-men) tend to form relatively isolated class communities, often living in segregated neighborhoods on the edge of large cities (with their children attending the highest quality public schools and universities).

The greater social homogeneity of the salaried middle classes is manifested in a higher level of class consciousness in this stratum. Considerably more new middle class people than old petty bourgeois people identify themselves as "middle class." In 1977 in the United States 62 percent of new middle class people, in comparison with 47 percent of the traditional petty bourgeoisie (and 26 percent of manual workers) identified themselves as "middle class." On the other hand, only 22 percent of the new middle class, in comparison with 43 percent of the old petty bourgeois and 6 percent of manual workers identified themselves as working class (see Table 3.11).

There is a considerable variation in incomes within the petty bourgeoisie, both among its three major sectors and within them. On the average the highest income sector of the middle class is the self-employed professionals (e.g., self-employed doctors and lawyers), who in 1978 had a median income of $22,511 a year (that many did considerably better is reflected in the mean earnings of $28,132). The lowest earnings sector is farmers, who in 1978 earned an average of only $7,537 a year. Proprietors in the nonfarm sectors had a median income of $11,640 (and a *mean* income of $15,202, indicating a significant number of high incomes), while salaried managers and administrators averaged $19,380 and employed professionals averaged $15,202 (see Table 5.9). Salaried professionals are thus seen to be intermediate in income between the independent professionals and employed managers on the one hand and independent proprietors and family farmers on the other.

The relatively low income of so much of the independent middle class (both self-employed proprietors and family farmers averaged less than the median income for all employed persons) stems from the competitive pressure of banks, large farms, and monopoly corporations such as giant supermarkets, chain stores and assembly-line producers, who can produce the goods and services they supply more cheaply and thus force such small proprietors to live on marginal incomes. It is typical in the nonprofessional subsector of the independent middle class for the entire family to be employed (husband, wife, children) and for them to work long hours in order to keep the business viable (and prevent bankruptcy and consequent "descent" into the working class).

TABLE 5.9: Income in 1978 of Different Sectors of the Petty Bourgeoisie

	Salaried		Self-Employed	
	Median Earnings	Mean Earnings	Median Earnings	Mean Earnings
Professionals	$17,153	$18,988	$22,511	$28,132
Managers (nonfarm) and proprietors	19,380	22,447	11,640	15,202
Farmers	—*	—	7,537	10,075

*Data not available.
Note: Men with earnings in 1978 by occupation of longest job.
Source: U.S. Bureau of the Census, Consumer Income of Families and Persons in the United States: 1978 (Washington, D.C.: Government Printing Office, 1980), Table 56.

The different economic prospects of the various subsectors of the middle class are reflected in their differential attitudes about their future economic situation. Small businessmen tend to be pessimistic about their economic future (only 29 percent in 1968 thought that they would be better off in a year). This compared to all other segments of the middle class, where 50 to 55 percent thought they would be better off, and to the manual working class, where 35 percent thought they would be better off (Hamilton 1975, p. 41).

Middle class people (both old and new) tend to be more concerned with their status in the general community and, especially for salaried managers and most professionals, with status in relation to their peers than are working class people. Further they are often overtly more concerned with their status than capitalist class people.

Achievement is a key value in all segments of this class. It is generally regarded as a function of personal ability and initiative. Self-restraint and respectability are similarly regarded. Members of this class generally tend to assume that social opportunities are available to all those who want to take advantage of them; and that, therefore, the poor are responsible for their own plight. Those in the business sector tend to be future oriented, often tending to defer satisfaction of wants until sufficient money is accumulated.

In the business sector a high premium is put on thrift, with a strong tendency for most profit to be reinvested in the family business to increase efficiency and production. The salaried professional and managerial sectors who are on fixed incomes, on the other hand, tend more to be oriented to present comsumption (since their fixed income and job security minimizes risk and guarantees future consumption without the necessity for saving, as in the working class, or accumulation, as in the traditional petty bourgeoisie). For the salaried middle class their home, car, and the accomplishments of their children (as manifested in the quality of their education and in the jobs they obtain) are symbols of their success and serve as a basis for social status among members of this stratum. The intellectual abilities and competitive successes of their children in school, especially in the professional strata, are highly esteemed since university training is considered a prerequisite to high-paying and respectable jobs. Although competition and status in all sectors of the middle class are central, there is little evidence, at least since World War II, that this is manifested in "status panic," high levels of tension or particularly high levels of stress or anxiousness about its condition (Hamilton 1975, pp. 115, 266).

Individualism and anticollectivism (manifested in hostility to unionization, antisocialism, lack of solidarity with peers, highly competitive and "get ahead" behavior, and attitudes toward others) are characteristic of all segments of this class: the self-employed, the salaried managers and employed professionals. But perhaps the most extreme individualism tends to be found in the independent petty bourgeoisie (especially small retailers whose very possibilities of survival depend on beating the competition).

The highly competitive conditions of the petty bourgeois business sector tend to make such businessmen highly suspicious and distrustful of each other. Studies have shown that in fact such businessmen tend to socialize relatively little with each other. It has also been noted that the economic life of this stratum tends to promote aggressiveness and insecurity as well as a special concern with "responsibility." The employed professional and managerial sectors, while still very much sharing the general individualism of their class, tend more to be career oriented, measuring their success in terms of their "upward mobility" within the managerial stratum (largely a function of salary and prestige of firm), or within one's professional subfield (largely a function of prestige with one's peers). But as with the traditional petty bourgeoisie, success in management for an individual means knocking off competitors for the limited number of good higher level positions, just as success in the professions, especially science, university teaching, architecture, and so forth, means securing tenure over someone else, beating someone else into print, or establishing a reputation by undermining someone else's, and so forth. Success in the old petty bourgeoisie is largely a function of "hard work" and long hours (thus the high value placed on laborious work and sacrifice in this sector); but in the new petty bourgeoisie (especially in its professional sector) this is much less the case. Here careers are made much more through successful ideas, interpersonal style, and connections, than long hours and sweat (hence in the professional subsector, there is no especially high evaluation of hard work, in fact, the opposite is often the case, with leisure and consumption being more highly valued).

The individualism and career orientation of the salaried petty bourgeoisie (at the expense of extended family, community ties, and other collective commitments) as well as the high value they put on education stem from the role of their values for the monopoly corporations and the state that employs them. Individuals are selected and become successful on the basis of their motivation to train as well as be retrained to keep up with the latest developments in their field, to be flexible and adapt to new situations and technologies, and to be mobile in both geographical area and within their professions. The role of status is also a product of the distinctive class position of the new petty bourgeoisie. On the one hand it serves as a motive for performance (negative and positive) independent of income (the distribution of status operates to select those who perform best for capital or the state), and on the other, it operates to ensure compliance and deference from subordinates. This latter process is especially central for the managerial strata, where such feelings are vital to the successful supervision of others. It is also important for professionals in their dealings with clients (or others whom they perform services for). It is most useful in securing acquiesence (the ideology of professional expertise) when accepted by doctors' patients, lawyers' clients, teachers' students, and so forth.

The old petty bourgeoisie is generally the most conservative class, except on economic questions that directly reflect its hostility to big business (see Table 9.17). The more conservative strata of the old petty bourgeoisie tend to be independent businessmen while independent professionals tend to be the most progressive, at least in relation to general social questions. In 1968 this substratum was found to be the most conservative on questions having to do with government power (68 percent thought the United States government was too powerful, compared to 55 percent of independent professionals, 60 percent of managers and officials, and 62 percent of salaried professionals); federal aid to education (29 percent were supportive, compared to 47 percent of independent professionals, 36 percent of managers and officials, and 34 percent of salaried professionals); and federal assistance to maintaining job and living standards (26 percent of independent businessmen were supportive, compared to 43 percent of independent professionals, 22 percent of managers and officials, and 37 percent of salaried professionals) (Hamilton 1975, p. 55). Hamilton found, however, that when controlling for income, the salaried managerial stratum was more conservative (at each income level) than were independent businessmen. For example, he found that in the 1968 election 46 percent of independent business people (married, non-South) whose family income was between $8,000 and $15,000 voted Democratic, compared to 33 percent of managerials and officials in the same income brackets. Similar results were found for those with incomes of over $15,000. Here 30 percent of independent businessmen and 27 percent of managers and officials voted Democratic (Hamilton 1975, p. 65). Poorer and more marginal independent businesses (especially those without a payroll) tend to be relatively progressive (close to the working class in attitudes), while the larger small businesses tend to be especially conservative. The life experience of small independent business leads businessmen to fear the expansion of the public sector as a threat to their autonomy and privilege, while many salaried professionals and state administrators can welcome the expansion of the public sector as an opportunity to expand their authority and job prospects.

Another issue on which the independent petty bourgeoisie historically has been conservative has been the issue of civil liberties (see Table 9.17). Richard Hamilton and others have demonstrated that small business was the most supportive of McCarthyism in the United States and the most authoritarian as measured by support for banning leftists from schools and public speaking, just as they were the traditional basis for Fascist movements in Europe between the wars (see Hamilton 1975; Trow 1958).

Monopoly capital tends (somewhat differentially) to proletarianize the petty bourgeoisie. The independent business sector (especially farmers, retailers, and artisans) are driven out of business by the more efficient and wealthier corporations, the remaining independent professionals are increasingly coordinated with monopoly capitalist institutions, and salaried professionals tend to be regimented in both the conditions of their labor and in the purposes to which their labor is put. Scientists are not really able to determine what kind of research they will do or how their work will be used because of corporate funding and direction of their work; university professors are under pressure to mass-produce educated students without raising fundamental criticisms of the way things are; social workers are forced to act like police; architects are made to design monstrosities, rather than socially useful buildings; engineers are required to design cars with planned obsolescence and factories that pollute, and so forth. Only the managerial stratum, a product of monopoly capital (and subordinated from the beginning), is relatively immune from the pressure. Thus, all but this latter stratum of the middle class celebrates the ideas of security and autonomy (as they are being lost). Afraid of proletarization they have a considerable potential to oppose both monopoly corporations *and* strong labor unions and leftist movements. The teaching load of college professors and class size go up, architects and engineers are subjected to increasing productivity demands, social workers must take on higher case loads, and so forth.*

While the new petty bourgeoisie has fundamental antagonisms with the corporate capitalist class that controls and pressures them, it is *not* initially in as desperate a situation vis-à-vis this class as is the bulk of the independent petty bourgeoisie. On the other hand, the potential antagonism of much of the old petty bourgeoisie (namely those that employ a few workers) to the working class is more intense than is that of the new petty bourgeoisie (except perhaps its corporate managerial stratum). As the violently antiunion efforts of small growers in California and small farmers in northern Italy after World War I as well as the strongly antiunion efforts of small businessmen almost everywhere show, this class is badly hurt by unionization of its work force. Unionization results in wage increases which this sector can normally only meet at the cost of profits (it can not, like monopoly businesses, pass on wage increases to consumers by increasing prices). This class periodically becomes violently hostile to the socialists it sees as trying to take away the little property it has. The fact that the new petty bourgeoisie has already been "socialized," i.e., has no significant private property in the means of production, and does not directly depend on profits to survive, makes a fundamental difference in their attitude about both unions and the socialization of private business (although not of course about the preservation of their own relative privileges vis-à-vis the working class). Unionization and the improvement in the conditions of workers does not adversely affect the new petty bourgeoisie so long as they can maintain their pay differentials (which are often geared to increases in union settlements). The nationalization of enterprises and the expansion of social services do not hurt the new petty bourgeoisie, but positively help it by increasing its job opportunities and by raising its prestige and status by elevating the importance of the socialized sector and expanding funds available for scientific research, medicine, and so forth.

The new petty bourgeoisie, however, still tends to maintain a watered down ideal of a "third path" between monopoly capitalism and socialism. This is manifested in such things as the "small is beautiful" trend, fighting for secure tenure for teachers and other

---

*Although faulty as general analysis, in this context it is useful to examine Serge Mallet, *Essays on the New Working Class*; Andre Gorz, *Strategy for Labor*; and Thorstein Veblen, *Engineers and the Price System*.

professionals, and generally trying to increase job autonomy and minimize interference from administrators and owners, and so forth on the one hand, while preserving privileges vis-à-vis workers on the other. The general strike of professional workers in Sweden in 1971, whose goal was to *restore* the traditional pay differential with manual workers, is an important example of this latter tendency as have been various doctors' strikes around the world.

Both the salaried professionals and the independent petty bourgeoisie tend to feel superior to the working class and above all its organizational forms (labor unions). At the same time they have considerable potential to oppose encroaching corporate control of their lives. Thus middle class ideologies and movements traditionally have both anticorporate *and* anti-working class elements. They tend to celebrate "the little man." Reflecting this two-sided antagonism, middle class movements have tended to be hostile to both "big labor" and "big business." The idealic state of Jeffersonian Democracy with "every man a king" of his own farm, running his own business or being a successful doctor, lawyer, or professor, is their dream. Middle class movements, although often focused against the rich, are generally afraid of revolutionary transformation. They instead tend to support such demands as *"fair* competition" and "just criteria" for promotion.

In the period between the two world wars fascism became the leading political expression of the petty bourgeoisie (both its "old" and "new" sectors). The early Fascist movements attempted to find a third path that was both hostile to monopoly capitalism *and* socialism. The Fascists (out of power) never tired of directing their venom against Communists, socialism, unions, and workers' cooperatives, which were squeezing the petty bourgeoisie from the left, *and* the big banks, department stores, and corporations, which were squeezing from the right. Fascist programs throughout the world have promised *both* the destruction of independent trade unions and working class parties *and* the breaking up of the big corporations, banks, and landed estates, with redistribution to the petty bourgeoisie.*

Although the petty bourgeoisie has often given birth to Fascist movements (movements which are inevitably captured by the bourgeoisie whenever they achieve a massive following), the petty bourgeoisie also gives birth to progressive movements that focus their attacks against big business. Once the bankruptcy of their independent pursuit becomes clear, such movements have often merged with

---

*For good analyses of the middle class role in Fascist movements see Trotsky 1971; Corey 1935, chap. 12; Guerin 1973, chap. 2; Schweitzer 1964; and Tasca 1966.

working class movements. Such have been the paths of the left wing of the Populist movement in the United States, which after the People's Party right and center were captured by the big business-planter controlled Democratic party in 1896, merged into the Socialist Party; and the progressive movements of peasants and the urban petty bourgeoisie that have come in good part to accept the leadership of Marxist parties in China, Vietnam, and other developing countries as well as in Italy, France, Spain, and other European countries (especially at the time of revolutionary crises in such countries).

6

The Historical Development
of the Working Class

This chapter treats the origins and transformations of the contemporary industrial working class in the advanced capitalist countries in general and in the United States in particular. Four fundamental revolutions in the techniques of production are examined: the creation of factories to replace cottage industries, the development of machinery, the introduction of water- and steam-*powered* machinery, and the direct organization of the labor process by capital are examined, and their impact on shaping the evolving working class is treated. The evolution of the mode of control of the labor process from the traditional combination of master-servant relationships with autonomy for craftsworkers, through simple machine pacing (of which "Fordism" is the extreme form) and tight, simple supervision (of which "Taylorism" is an extreme example) and more sophisticated techniques of postive economic incentives and ideological manipulation, to the presently predominant systems of bureaucratic control by rules to which workers give their explicit and/or implicit consent and manipulated participation and responsible autonomy, are examined. Last, the specific history of the U.S. working class is examined from the introduction of the factory system in the 1830s and 1840s (which at first mostly employed women and children from farm families) through the successive waves of immigrant workers from displaced peasant populations (from Europe through World War I, the South of the United States through the 1960s, and now largely from Latin America). The focus here is on the effect that such a heavy reliance on immigrant workers has had on shaping the unique politics of U.S. workers.

THE SHAPING OF THE MODERN INDUSTRIAL WORKING CLASS

During feudalism and the predominance of the peasant mode of production in Europe, i.e., before the nineteenth century in England and before the mid-nineteenth century in the rest of Western Europe, industrial production took place either within the guild system (with its rigorous rules and restrictions) or through the putting out system, which utilized cottage industry. The putting out system consisted of a merchant supplying a peasant family with raw materials, the peasant family processing them into a finished product, often on equipment owned by the peasant family, and the merchant picking up and further disposing of the product, paying the family for their contribution. Thread, cloth, and finished garments were the mainstays of the system. The putting out system represented a transitional form between the guild form of production and industrial capitalist production. It allowed the merchants to circumvent the restrictions on production imposed by the guilds, thereby producing cheaper textiles and garments in larger quantities for expanding markets. The putting out system also had the advantage of giving the early merchant-capitalists a fixed unit cost (thus reducing uncertainty). The merchant-capitalists now purchased a set amount of labor, but labor over which they had no control.*

Four fundamental revolutions in the means of production occurred in the history of modern industrial capitalism, three in the period of the transition to capitalism and the other coincident with the rise of the modern monopoly corporations. First was the creation of the factory, in which the various handicrafts were brought together under one roof under the central supervision of the capitalist (with machinery now belonging to the capitalists). The factory system meant a qualitative decrease in the autonomy of workers who previously had been working in the putting out/home work/cottage industry system (mostly) or in the guilds. This system, which continued to use the same craft skills, labor processes, and tools as did handicraft production in the guilds and the home work system, can be called *man*ufacture proper (i.e., *hand*production).

With the introduction of factories the capitalists could ensure that their workers labored a set number of hours a day, and, perhaps, did not slack unnecessarily, but other than this they exercised little control over the work process. This was sufficient, however, for

---

*The discussion in this section relies heavily on Balibar 1968, Edwards 1979, Friedman 1977, Gutman 1976, Hobsbawm 1962, 1964, Kuczynski 1967, Polanyi 1944, Marx 1867, Stone 1975, and Thompson 1963.

production as well as profits to increase (compared to the putting out system). Profitability was also enhanced by the capitalists' ability to order the work process, centralize the supplies of material, and keep records of costs, payrolls, and sales (and the consequent ability to keep better records of profit and loss). These early factories were for the most part (at least in western Europe) set up by small merchants or wealthy artisans typically with money borrowed from wealthy merchants. The textile industry was the cutting edge of the new factory system. The first factories generally put the finishing touches on the textile product (e.g., dying) or processed crucial raw material (carding), but soon expanded into spinning and weaving.

The average size of factories continued to rise over the course of the nineteenth and early twentieth century. For example, in the United States in manufacturing in 1899 the average enterprise employed 22 nonsupervisory workers, in 1921, 34, and in 1939, 45. However, since the 1930s the average number of nonsupervisory employees in the U.S. manufacturing sector has stabilized at around 40. In 1958 it was 39, in 1972, 43 and in 1977, 38 (see the U.S. Bureau of the Census 1972, p. 3; U.S. Department of Commerce 1981a, p. 805).

The second revolution in the means of production consisted of the introduction of machinery to replace handicraft technology. This machinery in good part incorporated the skills and knowledge previously held by the skilled crafts workers. Craft skills were undermined and productivity was increased considerably. Although at first this new machinery was powered by workers, the use of machines simplified the labor process, while at the same time making the organization of the labor process in good part independent of human labor power. The introduction of the machine as the principal capitalist means of production revolutionized the production process even *before* the machine was attached to water and eventually steam power. The capitalists were able to increase considerably their intervention in the labor process, organizing production through controlling the allocation of labor to machinery.

Traditional artisan work habits in the early factories before the introduction of machinery caused considerable problems for capital. Craftsworkers traditionally alternated periods of intense labor with periods of idleness. They took irregular breaks, drank on the job, often took a extra day off to make a long weekend. Often little work was done on "Blue Monday" as workers recovered from weekend debauches (see Gutman 1976, p. 33-34).

The third revolution in the means of production consisted of the introduction of *externally* powered machinery. The introduction of powered machinery greatly increased output. The attachment of the machine regulated tool to an external source of power meant that the worker now lost control over the *pace* or *rhythm* of work. In the last half of the eighteenth century waterpower was used to run the new spinning and weaving machines, causing a revolution in output in the textile industry. In the 1780s the new spinning jenny as well as Cartwright's new power loom were harnessed to the steam engine for the first time. Cotton replaced wool as the leading raw material for textiles in the 1780–1810 period, and the cotton mill proletariat became the heart of the British working class. By 1830 cotton production in Great Britain exceeded wool production by a factor of three times (Kuczynski 1967, chap. 2).

The textile capitalists were now largely able to control the work process of the new relatively unskilled workers (largely women and children). The introduction of the machine-regulated tool to replace handicraft skills allowed the massive employment of women and children without prior skills. The use of external power freed production from both the limits imposed on productivity by human strength (further facilitating the use of women and children) *and* the limits imposed by human resistance to a rapid and constant pace of work, and thus the traditional peasant mentality. With the introduction of powered machinery and its qualitatively higher level of work discipline, workers were virtually reduced to "appendages" of the machines they tended. The modern industrial working class was created.

It is important to note that for most of the working class the introduction of powered machinery was in good part completed very early in the process of industrialization, i.e., around 1800 in Great Britain and in the next generation in the United States. The introduction of machine-guided tools meant that the working class became divided into a mass of relatively unskilled machine operatives and a smaller group of skilled craftsworkers. Formerly, almost all urban workers were craftsworkers or apprentices sharing or learning handicraft skills. The craftsworkers' skills were reproduced because of the continuing need of capital for skilled labor in certain occupations. Skilled craftwork continued to be necessary in machine repair, in the production of fine clothing, in much of construction, in the production of many non-mass market commodities, and so on. But most factory workers now became lifelong "operatives" or manual laborers.

The early industrial capitalists were generally, at first, unable to induce the skilled craftsworkers (who were entrenched in the guilds' traditions) to give up their protected positions and privileges and endure the humiliating and extremely disciplined conditions of unskilled labor in the new factories. Instead, the early factory operatives were recruited from the less stable and "less responsible" elements in the population (e.g., ex-soldiers, paupers, broken tailors, cobblers, and especially former peasant home-workers and artisans who had lost their property or were unable to secure positions in the guilds) and, especially in textiles, young women and children whose fathers were marginal peasants, farmers, or artisans. In the U.S. cotton industry in 1831, 60 percent of the workers were women and about 20 percent children. In 1835 30 percent of English cotton mill workers were women and about 40 percent children (Kuczynski 1967, pp. 62, 63). These early factory workers considered factory work to be temporary, and they, thus, resisted establishing roots in the new industrial towns. A more or less homogenous working class with its own distinctive traditions and identity was not consolidated even in Great Britain, until the 1830s (see Thompson 1963).

In England brutal legislation was enacted in order to press the peasants off the land (so the land could be turned over to more profitable uses by the landlords, such as for grazing sheep so that their wool could be sold to the growing woolen industry) as well as to transform the peasants into disciplined proletarians in the rapidly growing industrial cities. Traditional common grazing lands, rights to collect wood in forests, rights to water in the streams, and so forth were increasingly denied the peasants, while the traditional peasant rights to the land itself were in many cases declared invalid.

Unable to support themselves any longer on the land, the peasantry (which held on as long as it could through participation in the putting out system in cottage industries) was increasingly forced into the towns. Stiff legal penalties were enacted against vagrants, beggars, petty thieves, and others who attempted to survive without selling their labor power to the new industrial capitalists. A relief system developed that provided subsistence to the destitute under conditions which were little better than starving or prison, and which made work in the new mills as oppressive as it was profitable. The workhouse system provided barely enough to live on in exchange for very long hours of back-breaking labor.

Working and living conditions in the early factories, industrial towns, and slums were mean. Overcrowding (often with shift sleeping in beds), large families sharing single rooms (houses became mere sleeping quarters), few sanitation facilities, open sewers, and epidemics, along with deterioration in diet and clothes, became common. The early mills were unventilated, crowded, unsafe, and unhealthy. But with the alternative of starvation, the workhouse, execution, or deportation (for even petty stealing) the ex-peasants were compelled to sell their labor power.

The early factory laborers were unprepared for regular factory work, industrial discipline, and running the new powered machinery.

The laborers had to learn to work to the regular rhythm of the machine, a regularity they had not been used to as peasants or guild craftsworkers. The new working class also had to become accustomed to work for monetary incentives. The early tendency was for workers to work just long and hard enough to earn the money equivalent of a traditional week's labor and then stop. There was little or no incentive to earn more than was thought necessary to maintain traditional life-styles. Early capitalists generally interpreted the laborers' reluctance to respond to monetary incentives as laziness and reluctance to work. The feeling was common that "only hunger spurs" and only discipline keeps workers at it. Wage payments became low enough so that the workers had to work a six-day week with a 12- or 14-hour day in order to earn the traditional minimum.

In order to create a working class that worked in a disciplined and systematic matter draconian factory discipline had to be introduced. The state's master-servant code, which severely punished breaches of contract by workers, gave legal authority over the workers to the capitalists. Legislation prohibiting unions and strikes was enacted. A system of fines for failure to produce were implemented. The early factories developed a system of harsh and despotic methods to habituate workers to their tasks. Attempts were made at virtually the total economic, spiritual, moral, and physical domination of the workers, often with dormitories for single female workers, company houses for families, and the regulation of nonwork time.

From 1800 to 1850 in Great Britain, Germany, and other western European countries conditions became steadily worse for the unskilled working class as the intensity of work was speeded up and hours worked grew. The principal mode of increasing output and profits was to increase the hours worked in a week while decreasing the hourly wage. Real wages declined over the period. Per capita meat consumption declined as did consumption of milk and cheese. Mortality rates increased in Great Britain from 1810 through the 1840s (see Hobsbawm 1964, chap. 5, 6, 7). But after 1850 the length of the workday gradually decreased. Through the introduction of machinery and the increasing ability to reorganize the work process, capital was now able to raise productivity more rapidly by reducing hours and intensifying labor. Likewise, real wages began to increase and living standards rose. In Great Britain between 1850 and 1874, average real wages rose by 33 percent (Friedman 1977, p. 60).

Through to the end of the nineteenth century the condition of skilled craftsworkers in the main was quite different from that of the masses of unskilled labor (whether those employed by craftsworkers or those women, children, and men hired directly by the capitalist). They maintained considerably higher wages (about twice that of the unskilled), job security, dignity in work, and prospects for future advancement as well as general social standing (a significant number of nineteenth-century craftsworkers were still able to become small capitalists). These privileged craftsworkers—the aristocracy of labor—in Great Britain in the mid-nineteenth century represented perhaps 11 to 15 percent of the working class (see Hobsbawn 1964, chap. 15). The traditional industrial craftsworkers had considerable autonomy in the production process. Their labor was performed in the traditional way without close supervision by capital. Likewise, their rates of payment and output were governed by tradition. There were powerful collective pressures among craftsworkers to perform their jobs well and there was a moral stigma against slacking. It was not until the 1880s that the craft tradition of accepting customary payment for customary output began being undermined as skilled workers came to demand wage increases according to what the market would bear. It was also in the last decades of the nineteenth century that craftsworkers began adjusting their output to the level of wages, sometimes allowing their production to slack unless held up by incentives (Hobsbawn 1964, chap. 17; Friedman 1977, p. 59; Edwards, Reich, and Gordan 1975, pp. 30-1).

The early capitalists often used a labor contracting system in which skilled textile workers were hired and paid on the basis of their output with the skilled workers themselves hiring unskilled assistants (often children). In the 1870s in the United States and the United Kingdom, the subcontracting system was still the norm in textile mills. This transitional labor form declined rapidly in the last quarter of the nineteenth century. The early subcontracting system (as was the putting out system) was plagued by problems of irregular production, loss of materials, slowness, lack of uniformity, and the uncertain quality of production.

In the last years of the nineteenth century capital again began to radically reorganize (for the fourth time) the work process. This reorganization had the most radical implications for skilled craftsworkers. Although less traumatic, this transformation, nevertheless, had significant consequences for the unskilled and semiskilled mass of industrial workers as well. They were now increasingly subject to the rational supervision of management, rather than to the traditional (and often arbitrary) supervision of craftsworkers (and fairly autonomous supervisors). Capital now came to assume full and detailed responsibility for controlling and supervising the work process in the factories. In order to increase productivity, many of the traditional crafts were in good part broken up and reconstituted under the control of rationalized management.

Coincident with this transformation of the work process was naturally the relative increase in the number of managerial employees involved in the production process. The tendency for the number of supervisory personnel to grow in relation to production workers has continued over the course of the twentieth century. In 1909 the ratio of supervisory personnel to all employees in the manufacturing sector in the United States was 18.1 percent, in 1930, 21.9 percent, in 1960, 25.1 percent, and 1979, 28.4 percent. This tendency has been manifested throughout the manufacturing sector. For example, the ratio of supervisory to all employees in durable goods manufacture rose from 16.5 percent to 28.7 percent between 1940 and 1979; while in the nondurable goods sector it rose from 20.6 percent to 28.1 percent (see U.S. Department of Commerce 1975, pp. 137, 138; and U.S. Department of Commerce 1981a, pp. 413, 414).

The position of the privileged craftsworkers deteriorated significantly as changes in the methods of payment (increasingly piecework), direct hiring of all workers, expanding mechanization, and the development of modern management techniques of subdividing and detailed supervision of the labor process occurred. Capital launched an offensive against the traditional prerogatives of craftsworkers, reorganizing and subjecting the skilled crafts to their direct control. The craftsworkers' all-around knowledge of the production process in the factories was diminished and their skills largely appropriated by machines (as had happened to unskilled labor much earlier). Between 1890 and 1910 the daily earnings of skilled steelworkers in the United States fell as much as 70 percent (while the wages of the unskilled steelworkers increased by 20 percent) (Stone 1975, p. 38).

In the late nineteenth century piecework became common as a means to induce increased output.* As a working class culture developed (replacing traditional rural cultures) and workers became used to working for a wage rather than merely producing a traditional output, they became psychologically attuned to trying to increase their total payment so as to buy the many new things that they saw about them in the new industrial cities, e.g., better housing, fancier clothes, better food, and so forth. The undermining of the traditional peasant psychology was taken advantage of by capital as it replaced

---

*In the early factories closer supervision or "driving," not pay incentives, was considered to be the best way of increasing output when necessary. The introduction of piecework (payment by results) was at first not initially conceived so much as a means of increasing productivity, but as a means of stopping it from falling below the norm. Further, the strong customary standards of the craftsworkers (together with the subcontracting system) appeared to make positive incentives largely unnecessary.

the subcontracting system and crude supervision with monetary incentives and direct and rational supervision.

Craftsworkers (largely unsuccessfully) attempted to defend their traditional prerogatives (the bloody Homestead Steel strike of 1892 in the United States was a defensive strike against the owners' demands to increase their control over production). The rise and consolidation in the 1890s of the American Federation of Labor (a coalition of *craft* unions which was dedicated to preserving, and advancing, the privileges of craftsworkers) was another expression of the attempt to defend their position (see Hobsbawm 1964, chaps. 15, 16; Aronowitz 1973, chap. 3).

It must be stressed that the transformation in the work process that occurred around the turn of the century most radically affected the skilled the craftsworkers in the factories. The labor process of the mass of the proletariat has been largely simplified and routinized from the time of the introduction of powered machinery in textiles. In the early period of the development of capitalist industry, when women and children were the preferred laborers, very little skill was required in the highly routinized labor processes. Skills and job control were characteristic of artisan and craftwork, i.e., they were *never* properties of the working class as a whole. Thus the fourth transformation of the work process resulted not in a general *degradation* of the working class, but rather in the *homogenization* of that class, with its elite or "aristoracy of labor" being partially reduced to the conditions already the norm for the vast majority of workers.

The routinization of labor and increased supervision by foremen, preprogrammed machines, or assembly lines implies the socialization of the labor process. It undermines the individualized nature of craft production (work processes that are historically and analytically intermediate between independent petty-bourgeois artisan production and the fully proletarianized and socialized production of unskilled and semiskilled labor). Historically craftsworkers, more than most factory workers, have tended to work by themselves or in small groups with a limited division of labor, i.e., to work under the *opposite* of socialized conditions. Collective participation in the labor process tends to generate feelings of collectivity, discipline, and an appreciation of the power of cooperation, to undermine the individualism (characteristic of artisans), and to promote feelings of solidarity among laborers in an obviously common situation. The more the traditional crafts are broken up and the craftsworkers subjected to the same detailed controls as the rest of the working class (i.e., the more socialized their conditions of labor) the *more* likely they will be to adopt a *class*, rather than a craft consciousness.

The conditions of labor of the majority of the working class have *improved* in many ways over the last 100 years in tandem with the decline in the working conditions of craftsworkers. The high-pressure brutal routine of sweatshops, the back-breaking physical labor, the especially oppressive and unhealthy conditions, 12- to 14-hour days for low wages, the lack of unemployment sickness, or old age benefits that were facts of life for the early working class have been considerably mitigated over the course of the twentieth century. The undermining of the craftsworker's traditionally privileged position vis-à-vis the rest of the working class, together with the general improvement of the working conditions of the unskilled, has brought the working class to an increasingly common condition of skill, control, and technical knowledge. This has undermined the material bases of the traditional divisions within the class in general (destroying a major internal source of conservative ideology).

It should be noted that unskilled laborers in large highly mechanized plants in Russia in 1917, in most of Europe in 1918–19 as well as in most industrial areas at any time where the revolutionary Left is strong, disproportionately have supported revolutionary politics. Where the Left is strong, most skilled craftsworkers, while they may generally support the Left, tend to be less enthusiastic for revolutionary change. The mere fact of running a machine that they themselves could not build (or even fix) does not in fact give the workers the impression that the capitalist class is necessary in general for production to proceed. The mere fact of seeing that people just like themselves (increasingly including even the engineers and repairman) are the ones who actually make the thing work in fact generates feelings of the redundancy of the *owners* and *top managers* (who now appear to not have the technical knowledge to run the industry). In fact, the simplification of even the skills of repair workers and engineers demystifies their contribution, and is probably likely to *increase* rather than *decrease* unskilled workers' confidence in feeling able to run the enterprise. Industrial labor, unskilled as much as skilled, demystifies the relations of production.

THE TRANSFORMATION IN THE FORMS OF CONTROL OF THE LABOR PROCESS

Industrial capitalism has employed a very wide variety of techniques to control the quality and quantity of the industrial workers' product. At any given time more than one method tends to be used for a given set of workers and different methods tend to be used in different industries, in different occupations, and by different firms. Further, normally at any given time a change is taking place in the predominant method used in any given situation (because of the contradictions in that method of control). The forms of control of the labor process by capital can be categorized by both their degree of closeness/looseness and their form (simple, economic, and hegemonic). The historical tendency is for capital to move away from the traditional modes of labor control with craftsworker autonomy and relations with the unskilled governed by arbitrary, direct, and authoritarian master-servant principles (and whose production as well as remuneration tends to be set by custom). In the latter years of the eighteenth century in Great Britain capital began to move toward machine-paced work; a trend that spread beyond textiles and beyond Great Britain over the course of the nineteenth and early twentieth centuries until it culminated in the full-fledged assembly-line characteristic of the automobile industry. Machine pacing came to supplant both traditional craft autonomy and master-servant modes of control of the labor process. In the latter years of the nineteenth century, capital, especially in occupations not amenable to machine pacing or assembly lines, began to redesign and closely supervise the labor process as a means of gaining control over the pace and output of the labor process (Taylorism). At more or less the same time, it also began to introduce simple piecework, utilizing direct economic incentives to increase output. Faced with serious limits to all these early (rather direct and unsubtle) attempts to control the labor process capital began to resort to more indirect and subtle mechanisms. Attempts were made to win worker loyalty and generate identification with the firm (ideological manipulation), to make economic incentives more effective by reducing possibilities for negative peer pressure (e.g., annual bonuses, promotion of the most productive), and finally, after the 1930s explosion of industrial unionism, institution of fixed rules (e.g., promotion by seniority, set job definitions, fixed wages for a given job, job bidding, and so forth), which workers typically came to accept as legitimate—their unions often participated in the establishment and guarantee of these rules ("bureaucratic control").*

In recent years, as the limits to these earlier improvements in the mechanisms of control of the labor process have been reached, capital has turned increasingly to various forms of limited worker participation and allowing responsible autonomy of work groups as a means of indirectly establishing hegemony over the labor process as well as to "enriching" jobs to make them less boring and increasing

---

*The discussion in this section relies in good part on Braverman 1974, Burawoy 1979, Edwards 1979, Friedman 1977, Mayo 1933, and Stone 1975.

job security. These recent innovations are more resistant to worker sabotage than the more direct and less subtle forms resorted to earlier (see Table 6.1 for a schematic outline of the means of labor control).

Many of the earliest capitalist enterprises were founded by crafts-workers with financial backing from merchants or bankers. In such enterprises the ex-craftsworkers, now "entrepreneurs," continued and developed the traditional relation between employed craftsworkers (or guild workers) and their apprentices and assistants. The mechanisms of the small entrepreneur's control over his labor force were crude, informal, and often quite arbitrary (reinforced by traditional master-servant legislation as well as expectations). The early capitalist enterprises were, thus, in good part expanded and more authoritarian versions of the earlier craftsworker's workshops (see Edwards 1979, chap. 1).

As enterprises got too big for entrepreneurs to closely and directly supervise all their workers, they came to employ foremen to mediate between themselves and the production laborers. These early fore-men, in the tradition of the entrepreneurs, tended to be arbitrary, ad hoc, and authoritarian in a loosely structured mode of labor control. Judged by the entrepreneur in terms of the short-term output of those they supervised, foremen tended to be brutal in their direct (and typically noninnovative) supervision of the labor force. Foremen usually had the power to hire and fire as well as to promote and assign tasks, dock workers in pay, and sometimes even to beat workers (Edwards 1979, chap. 1).

The first major innovations in the traditional work relations within capitalist enterprises were a consequence of the introduction of powered machinery whose pace of operation was not under the control of those running the machines. The introduction of modern powered carding, spinning, and weaving machinery in the textile industry led the way. With technical control and machine pacing, the quantity and quality of workers' output tended to be very similar (since the skill and rate of output had largely been transferred to the machine) so long as the worker performed simple tasks at a minimum level of competence. The workers lost control of both the pace and rhythm of work and their traditional skills to the machines.*

---

*There is only one thing that motivates the capitalist and that is the maximization of profit. Because of competitive pressure, capitalists must choose the single method (or set of methods) of production that allows them to maximize profits. No capitalist who must operate in a market can introduce a non-profit-maximizing process for altruistic, idiosyncratic, or political reasons. Two factors enter into the determination of the most profitable method of production: first, the technical capabilities of a given machine/technique of production, i.e., its pure technical efficiency in being used to produce a maximum product with minimum input; and second, the opportunities that a given production process/machine gives the worker to "soldier," its propensity to facilitate wildcat strikes or other collective resistance, the room it provides for sabotage, and so on—in sum all those properties of the production process/machinery that aid the worker as against the capitalist in the class struggle.

For example, suppose production process A has the technical potential of allowing the worker to process 200 units per day while process B allows only 150 units per day. For the sake of the argument let us assume that the machinery and raw materials used in both processes have equal value. If the first production process was such as it necessarily gave the workers great discretion in production, thus allowing them to soldier or artifically constrict production, and the social relationships generated by that process facilitated strikes, slowdowns, and other forms of collective resistance, so that over the course of a year the actual output averaged only 100 per day (one-half of what was technically possible), while the second process allowed for the concentration of skill and knowledge in management and so isolated the worker that relationships of solidarity and collective resistance were hindered so that the actual production was 140 units per day, then the capitalist would, of course, actually utilize process B, even though it was less efficient technologically than process A. On the other hand, if process A resulted in an output of 160 units a day it would be utilized even though process B was "qualitatively" more efficient. In other words, it is neither "quantitative" nor "qualitative" efficiency that guides capitalists, but rather *profit*.

The requisites of the capitalist mode of production, by requiring control over the labor process in order to make a profit, may very well force the use of technologically less efficient machinery and production processes than would be the case in a society with workers' control over the means of production. Capital may introduce technologically less efficient work processes in order to better control workers and thereby increase profit efficiency. The requisites of the capitalist mode of production may also well require the introduction of technically efficient processes, even though such processes promote class consciousness and working class resistance (in fact, this would seem to be the most fundamental result of the introduction of the factory system). Capitalism is a contradictory system in which the pursuit of profits by the capitalist class forces them to organize production in such a way as to create a working class, creates socialized conditions under which that class becomes class conscious, and generates crises and other forms of oppression that propel this class into revolutionary action. The capitalists are forced to bring workers under one roof, to destroy craft skills and privileges, thus tending both to reduce all laborers to one common level and to educate workers in the socialized experiences of collective labor, promoting proletarian class consciousness. They can not act otherwise without suffering the fatal penalities of the market. The single-minded pursuit of profits, necessarily produced by the logic of the capitalist system, necessarily generates an effective opposition to this logic.

Although increasing control of the work process has been a contributing cause of work routinization, increasing technological efficiency has been the primary cause. Technological efficiency has been driven by the requirements of profit maximization dictated by capitalist markets. We might call that part of the routinization and simplification of the labor process (or the breakdown of craft skills) *above and beyond* that caused by the drive to increase technical efficiency *surplus routinization*. Surplus routinization is thus the difference in the degree of routinization and simplification of the labor process that would occur in a genuinely democratic workers' cooperative operating in a capitalist market, and a capitalist enterprise operating in the same market.

The success of powered machinery in radically reducing worker control of the labor process, however, did not find comparable success in all industrial sectors. The nature of the work process in many industries (e.g., those with small batch or single unit production) did not lend itself to machine pacing, as did the production process in other industries such as textiles, meatpacking, electrical products, and eventually automobiles (where the flow of production was more continuous). The introduction of powered machinery in shoemaking, steel, metal products fabrication, garmets, shipbuilding, railroad car construction, glassworks, sawmills, barrelmaking, and so on did not generally lead to overall machine pacing of the rhythm of work and output. While the introduction of machinery revolutionized the *techniques* of production in such industries (thus largely making the traditional craft skills obsolete as well as radically increasing productivity), the more traditional forms of shop organization, with loose forms of supervision in which worker largely continued to have the requisite technical knowledge of production as well as considerable detailed job control, continued to prevail through most of the nineteenth century. Because of the nature of the work process in these industries the technical introduction of powered machinery did little to change the social organization of the labor process (see Edwards 1979, chap. 7).

Even in industries where technical control and machine pacing were applicable and reasonably effective, there were limits to effective control. The new techniques of production not only led to worker resentment and resistance (often manifested in strikes, sabotage of machinery, poor quality of output because of worker morale, and the spontaneous generation of work norms that established the pace at which the machinery was run), but also to greatly increasing interdependence of the work process. This latter development facilitated collective working class consciousness and enhanced the workers' ability to effectively act as a class against capital. When the production line stops the whole plant stops. Thus, a few workers acting together can halt the whole production process. By undermining the traditional wide disparity of skill levels within industry (the tendency to reduce most workers to simple homogeneous labor) technical control created an exceptionally favorable environment for the development of class consciousness and class organization—in most countries workers in the industries where technical control tends to be the most effective tend to develop a high level of militant unionism, e.g., automobiles (see Edwards 1979, chap. 7).

With the redesign of the traditional craftworkers' jobs in the late nineteenth and early twentieth centuries, less extensive training in *generalized* skills became necessary for skilled workers to adequately

TABLE 6.1: The Forms of Control of the Labor Process by Capital

Mode of Control	Degree of Closeness of Control		
	Close	Intermediate	Loose
	Direct Despotic Supervision	Technical Control	Traditional Shop Organization
Simple Control	Detailed supervision with task fragmentation. Mostly negative sanctions (fines, threats of being fired, and so on). Repressive system.	Machine pacing. Designing of machinery to maximize exploitation of labor and minimize workers' autonomy in the labor process. Continuous flow of production.	Customary craft rules largely govern skilled workers' production, output, remuneration, hours of work, and so on. Traditional master-servant relations govern the position of unskilled.
Early	High discretion of entrepreneurs and foremen. Arbitrary authoritarian supervision.	Machine pacing with limited worker discretion, e.g., spinning and weaving machine tending.	Craftworkers hire own apprentices and assistants who are subject to arbitrary authority of craftsworkers. Craftsworkers themselves are very loosely supervised.
Late	Hierarchy of control. Concentration of knowledge of production in management. Extreme form—Taylorism. Limited discretion of foremen. Rational management.	Assembly line. Extreme form—Fordism.	Supervision of craftsworkers by entrepreneurs and their foremen. Encroachments on customary autonomy of craftsworkers.

	Piecework	Bonuses and Dividend Sharing	Promotion by Output
Economic Incentives	Direct tie between output during a period and remuneration. Pay strictly by output, or incentive pay scales and wage supplements.	Supplemental bonuses for exceeding output norms in addition to fixed wage. Also, annual stock dividend and profit sharing plans where *all* workers get a percentage of a company's profits or dividends.	Promotion to higher paying and better jobs on the basis of output rather than seniority. Evaluation of output by hierarchical management.
Hegemonic Domination (Consent to Authority)	"Industrial Relations" (Maoism): identification with firm. Capital manipulates conscious attitudes of workers or otherwise generates positive feelings among workers toward their work, e.g., stock ownership plans, gifts at holidays, company teams, slogans, group exercises, company newspapers, music, clean work environment, suggestion boxes, polite foremen, token participation, and so on. Most recently this has taken the form of "job enrichment" (either frequent rotation of tasks or widening of job definitions) together with increased job security (even in event of redundancy).	Bureaucratic Rules/ Collective Bargaining Rational work rules internalized and at least implicitly accepted by workers as fair. Promotion and layoff on basis of seniority. Set job definitions as basis of evaluation and grievances. Usually incorporated in collective bargaining contracts with unions. This has been the rule in basic U.S. industry since World War II.	Manipulated Participation/ Responsible Autonomy Manipulation of the quantity and quality of output and undermining of labor's collective resistance to management through engaging workers in decision-making processes and granting significant detailed authority to work groups. Creating the feeling that the workers in good part control production within the reality that profit maximization continues to structure the overall work process.

Source: Compiled by the author.

perform their tasks. While skilled work continued to be a necessary part of the production process, the skills required now tended to be specific to limited aspects of the work process (and often to the technology specific to a particular employer). Employers increasingly assumed control of apprenticeship programs so as to teach the new generations of skilled workers the new *specific* job skills they required—in good part for maintenance and repair work (see Stone 1975, pt. 2).

In the early stages of the reduction of the autonomy of craftsworkers, the capitalist entrepreneur's foremen were given considerable authority to supervise the new (narrowly) skilled and semiskilled workers. These foremen tended to act in the same authoritarian manner toward those in the trades that had traditionally been highly skilled, as they did toward those in the occupations that had traditionally been occupied by "servants." In fact, since the process of the reduction of traditional craft autonomy was accomplished more by recruiting and specially training ex-peasant immigrants to these new tasks (rather than by beating down those who had already established themselves as skilled craftsworkers), the attitude of early foremen toward those in the redesigned skilled trades often tended to be as authoritarian as it was toward unskilled fully menial laborers (in the United States the semiskilled, narrowly skilled, and unskilled workers were often from the same recent immigrant groups, while the foremen were typically of older native stock). Sanctions employed by foremen were largely negative in both cases (fines, insults, threats, firings, and so on).

Increasingly, however, management began to develop more rational and sophisticated methods of close supervision. The arbitrary authority of foremen was reduced, replaced by increased detailed involvement of higher management in establishing the rules of the labor process. More rational hierarchies of authority came to be established, with power, as well as generalized production knowledge, increasingly centered in management rather than with foremen. The new more rational hierarchical organization of industry produced a "chain of command" in which all (including the foremen) were closely supervised and evaluated by those directly above them.

The techniques of "scientific management" pioneered by Frederick Taylor ("Taylorism") were developed and employed. The labor process was analyzed by management to discover and enforce more efficient methods of production. The general knowledge of the production process that increasingly came to be concentrated in the hands of management enabled managers to increase their control over every step of the labor process. Management, in order to attempt to ensure that workers were working as close as possible to their maximum technical output without "soldiering" or otherwise resisting the maximum application of their energies to the production process, came to dictate to the workers the precise manner in which to perform their work (see Braverman 1974, pt. 1).

Both the new modes of close hierarchical supervision *and* the new techniques of scientific management (job redesign and deskilling) ran up against the barrier of workers' resistance, which proved to greatly limit the promise of these new managerial methods of controlling the labor process. As the regime on the shop floor became ever more harsh and oppressive (with sanctions mostly negative for not meeting management's expectations), an atmosphere of perpetual conflict and antagonism developed. Such naked use of power by capital made the oppressive nature of capitalist relationships increasingly obvious to workers, thus adding fuel to the development of working class consciousness and willingness to collectively oppose their conditions of employment (as well as capital in general). Sabotage, physical threats to especially oppressive foremen, and the outbreak of spontaneous and militant strikes as well as the maintenance and reinforcement of anti–speed up (solidering) norms were the fruits of naked power on the shop floor. Likewise, the introduction of scientific management was strongly resisted by workers. In fact, its potential (in its pure form) as a means to radically increase production had largely run its course by World War I because of the intense (organized and unorganized) opposition it generated among workers (Edwards 1979, p. 98).

In response to the limitations of the machine pacing and hierarchical/scientific management modes of labor process control, the corporations began to experiment with a wide variety of systems of *positive* incentives (incentive pay, annual bonuses, profit sharing, promotion on the basis of output) as well as attempts to get the workers to identify with their employers and to persuade them that their interests were identical with those of their company.

Although simple piecework was practiced widely, this system of remuneration soon ran up against strong barriers to increasing output. This system of payment, ironically, contains an incentive for workers to deceive employers and restrict output to what is considered a reasonable level by making jobs appear to take as long as possible, so that artificially high piece rates get set for them. The early history of piecework consisted of workers increasing their average wages above the customary level through increasing their output, and as a result, the capitalists lowering the piece rate, so that average worker's wages sank back to the traditional average (but now at a more intense rhythm of work). It did not take workers long to learn that working harder in the (futile) attempt to increase their wages amounted to the same thing as simple speed up. Their spontaneous response thus generally became putting intensive social pressure on any "rate busters" who attempted to produce more than what most workers thought proper. Rate busters came under intense pressure from other workers (even to the point of physical assault) because they demonstrated to management that the rates set were artifically low and, thus, caused a general speed up without an increase in pay for all. Faced with the control piecework (together with intense peer pressure) gave workers over the pace of their work, it was not long before it began to decline as a means of controlling worker output (in favor of machine-paced work, closer supervision, job redesign, and promotional possibilities in internal labor markets for the better producers as well as more sophisticated methods of labor control) (see Stone 1975, pp. 42-54).

Economic incentive schemes became more sophisticated than simple piecework. The possibilities of supplemental incentive pay granted to the most productive workers, collective bonuses granted to *all* workers if product norms were met as well as the system of promoting workers into higher paying and inherently more enjoyable jobs on the basis of their productivity tended to undermine the solidarity of workers and gave employers increased leverage to control the production process. The system of promotion within the firm ("internal labor markets") meant that to get ahead workers had to curry favor with their supervisors by playing by the rules and increasing their output. The better one's job and the higher one's wage the more stake one had in not rocking the boat or otherwise not offending management (for to do so would result in being bumped back to an entry level back-breaking position).

The attempt to increase managerial control of the labor process by gaining the consent of workers to the authority of management was, in good part, articulated by Elton Mayo and his "industrial relations" school. In this technique of control of the labor process the focus is on increasing "worker satisfaction" and, thus, undermining the work restriction norms of workers by getting them to identify with the company's goals of profit maximization. Mayo pioneered many of the techniques of industrial relations as a counter of Taylorism. Rather than stressing either simple control or economic incentives, the Mayo school attempted to manipulate the attitudes of workers to create positive feelings toward their work so as to get them to voluntarily (and with, if possible, enthusiasm) increase their output (see Mayo 1933). Stock ownership plans were initiated in which employees were encouraged to buy small amounts of stock at below market rates (to get them to identify with the firm's profitability). The work environment was cleaned up and made safer.

Plant newsletters, athletic teams, holiday gifts, suggestion boxes, retraining classes, token participation on advisory bodies, and so on became common. A new more humane and less authoritarian style of management as well as paternalistic welfare policies were instituted. Very important among these were pension rights contingent on long-term employment, which could be revoked in cases of "misconduct" as well as lost if discharged (see Stone 1975, pp. 49–53).

The various schemes of sophisticated economic incentives as well as the new techniques of industrial relations, while they were an improvement over earlier methods, also had their limits. The attempt to speed up production, without actually increasing wages (which occurred within the various systems of economic incentives) soon produced cynicism and resultant resistance by workers. Likewise, the new form of "management with a human face" did not generally result in much more than a superficial change in production relationships that continued to be marked by a high level of authoritarianism (improvements in working conditions that did occur were neutralized by the rising expectations of workers about what proper work conditions should be).

The mode of control of the labor process that became predominant in basic industry throughout the advanced capitalist countries in the post–World War II period has been based on fixed work and promotion rules for the most part consented to by the workers through the medium of collective bargaining ("bureaucratic control"). In the bureaucratic method of control workers are promoted (and if necessary reluctantly laid off) through a system of strict seniority, with a high probability of lifetime employment providing general economic conditions allow (contingent only on adequate performance). The "rule of law," thus, replaces arbitrary rule by management. The role of supervisors and foremen was transformed to judging the workers' performance according to formally set criteria (rather than the supervisors' personal standards). If a worker does not agree with a supervisor's evaluation, or otherwise feels unjustly treated (i.e., feels that there has been a violation of the "rules"), the subordinate can appeal (or "file a grievance") either through the union or through a company's own appeals process. Set job descriptions are established with workers becoming entitled to their pay on performance of stated duties. Further, in this method of control of the labor process feelings of identification with the firm are enhanced by a general reluctance to lay off or fine workers after a set probationary period, except for gross incompetence or because of severe economic problems (see Edwards 1979, chap. 8; Burawoy 1979, chap. 6).

Central to the new system of bureaucratic control is the system of internal labor markets with promotion to better jobs primarily on the *basis of seniority* within the plant (workers generally "bid" for better jobs as they become open). This system, just as much as internal promotion on the basis of *output* (the earlier system), encourages individualism and tends to undermine working class solidarity. But this newer system has its effect more by creating a commitment to the enterprise in which one has accumulated seniority (and thus relative privilege) than by pitting every worker against every other worker in a competition to be assigned the better jobs by management (as did the earlier form of internal labor markets). Further, when workers can transfer from job to job with relative ease this minimizes their resistance to job redesign and the setting of low standard rates for any given operation. This is the opposite effect from that which occurs in the system of internal promotion by productivity, where workers have a special stake in maximizing resistance to job redesign and the setting of high standards—which would make promotion *more* difficult.

Both because of worker union involvement in establishing or agreeing to the rules, and because they appear to be fair and honored by management (which allows promotion into better jobs on the basis of "reasonable" and "justly" applied criteria), the bureaucratic mode of control of the labor process gained large scale success in the post–World War II period. Control became embedded in the organizational structure of the firm (job categories, work rules, definitions of responsibilities, fixed disciplinary and promotion procedures, and so on). Capitalist relationships of exploitation became less visible as arbitrary authority was constrained by impersonal rules. Rewards and punishments came to appear to be a result of rules (and thus "legitimate"), rather than the arbitrary dictates of capital. Capital-worker relations shrank from sight as power was made invisible in the structure of work—and at the same time both rationalized and made more effective (Edwards 1979, chap. 11).

As Michael Burawoy (1979) vividly points out, the institution of the bureaucratic mode of labor control can be considered to have reconstituted the labor process as a "game" that workers play according to fixed rules—a game that involves the active participation of both the worker and management in the process of the worker attempting to maximize chances for rewards and promotion within the set limits established with workers' collective consent. "Making out" or winning at the work game not only brings job security, but also both intrinsic rewards for performance and the approval of one's work mates. Participation in the game, the parameters of which are established by the logic of the capitalist process, generates consent. The "lived relations" of the capitalist labor process legitimate it. Consent is reproduced on the shop floor and is, thus, not dependent on consent drummed into people's heads (a la Mayo's industrial relations school, or by the media and education) *nor* on the pure pursuit of economic gain (a la piecework and bonuses) (see Burawoy 1979, chap. 5, 6, 12).

The success of the bureaucratic mode of control of the labor process was manifested in the great increases in labor productivity as well as in the stabilization of worker-capital relations that occurred in the post–World War II generation (1945–1970). Indeed, this period witnessed the largest most sustained and significant long-term increase in productivity and real wages as well as the most peaceful period of labor relations that U.S. capitalism had ever witnessed. Similar results were obtained in most of Europe and Japan in the 1950–75 period.

Among the contradictions of bureaucratic control are its tendency to make wages more of a fixed rather than a variable cost of production (more similar to rent than to raw materials). The tendency to resist laying off workers and implementing wage reductions was a corollary of creating loyalty to the firm and reducing hostility toward its rules. But as a result the companies loose economic flexibility to deal with changing market conditions (which can result in high levels of losses in recessions). Another problem with this means of controlling the labor process is that workers increasingly come to consider that their job (as well as promotions to better jobs) is theirs as *a matter of right* (so long as they are not incompetent). This tends to result in both growing resistance to increasing output (since there is little fear of being fired or demoted) and to rising feelings that workers ought to have more say in establishing the rules by which the labor process is governed (the possibility of an internal challenge to the employers' power grows). Perhaps most seriously, however, was the fact that potentials of bureaucratic control appeared to become exhausted. In the latter part of the 1960s, and increasingly over the course of the 1970s, capital experienced increasing problems with productivity, maintaining work discipline, and quality of production. Absenteeism, cynicism among workers, shoddy performance, resistance to foremen, and so on became increasingly serious problems.

In an attempt to deal with this latter problem management in the advanced capitalist countries (with countries like Sweden taking the lead) began to adopt both "work humanization" and "worker participation" programs in an attempt to increase productivity by generating worker consent to the authority of capitalist relations by means more sophisticated than employed in either the bureaucratic or industrial relations methods of control. Earlier Taylorization and Fordism are reversed with "job enlargement" and "job enrichment" schemes to make work more interesting and to increase worker commitment by increasing the skill and the responsibilities of given positions. Workers are now more frequently rotated among menial tasks to reduce boredom. These techniques of increasing productivity by increasing "worker satisfaction" are very much in the tradition of Elton Mayo's industrial relationship school (although more sophisticated than earlier versions). Worker participation programs are in some ways a partial throwback to the traditional autonomy of craftsworkers. "Worker participation" has come to include both increasing autonomy of the work group (with workers in a given unit allocating their own labor power in ways they judge best to accomplish a goal provided by management) *and* representation on various decision-making, quality control, and administrative bodies within the plant or company. Worker participation has proven to be successful in quelling discontent among workers, increasing productivity, and increasing identification with the goals of the corporations (Friedman 1977, p. 101; Edwards 1979, p. 156). The principle involved here is to get workers to behave *as though* they were actually participating in a process structured by themselves (i.e., as if they were working for themselves), thereby greatly increasing worker morale (and productivity) when, in fact, the whole process is structured by capital to maximize profits.

Among the contradictions in the new work humanization/worker participation modes of labor process control are the decreased flexibility these modes give to management to allocate labor (changing work methods, moving workers around the plant, the introduction of new machinery, shifting production to meet changing quality and quantity demands and so forth become more difficult). Management finds it more difficult to either fire unproductive or disruptive workers or to reverse the humanization and participation schemes, since workers' expectations about the kind of jobs they have, their right to a job, and their rights to participate in the decision-making process tend to increase over time. Thus, firings and reversals risk provoking a "legitimation crisis" within the plant, with a consequent collapse of morale and rising hostility to management and its goals. To the extent that worker participation programs have some substance and are felt to be real but limited in impact by workers, they can create the expectation that the workers' role in decision making ought to be *increased* (and to feelings that capitalist management is *or* could be redundant). Worker participation plans can, thus, be "too successful" in increasing productivity by showing that workers can manage by themselves much more than the prevailing managerial ideology cares to admit, i.e., fundamental threats to the very nature of capital-worker relations can begin to arise. The limits to worker participation would, thus, appear to be *either* at the point where increased participation is resisted by management, and, thus, workers become cynical about "sandbox politics" and the schemes lose effectiveness; or the point at which further increases in participation begin to fundamentally challenge capitals' control over the labor process (by workers making decisions contrary to transnational profit maximization). It would appear that once such limits are reached, that management would be quickly forced back to reliance on earlier (and more authoritarian) modes of labor process control in order to recapture direct control of the shop floor.

THE MAKING OF THE AMERICAN WORKING CLASS

The industrial revolution began in the United States in the period 1835-45. Within a couple of decades the formerly dominant commercial capital had been eclipsed by industrial capital as the major economic force in the northeastern states. Factories employing machines powered by water and steam sprang up everywhere (largely, at first, in textiles). Before the 1840s most manufactured goods in the United States were produced in the home (much through the putting out system). But after the 1840s most manufacturing was done in factories.*

The creation of a modern industrial working class occurred much more rapidly in the United States than in Great Britain. While between 1820 and 1840 the percentage of gainfully nonagriculturally employed persons ten years old or over in the United States increased only slightly from 28.2 percent to 31.4 percent, by 1860 it had reached 41.1 percent and by 1870, 47.0 percent. By 1900, 62.5 percent were employed outside of agriculture. The watershed was 1880, when the population was divided almost equally between the two sectors (see Rosenblum 1973, p. 66).

In textiles, iron, and increasingly other sectors as the introduction of the techniques of mass machine-guided production replaced artisan methods, the demand for unskilled labor increased. In the 1840s in the United States it was principally women and children (whose fathers were typically farmers in need of supplemental income) who provided the labor force for the new mills. But by the 1850s it was primarily new immigrants who became the source of factory labor as well as the major source of workers on railway and canal construction.

---

*The discussion in this section relies in good part on Davis 1981; Kolko 1976, chaps. 3 and 5; and Rosenblum 1973.

The most important source of industrial workers during the 1850s was the Irish. The British had transformed Irish agriculture into a one-crop potato economy in order to profitably feed the rapidly growing urban population in Great Britain. When a disease affected that single crop, the Irish peasants found themselves in a catastrophic situation from which there was no option to starvation other than leaving their country and fleeing to Great Britain or the United States in search of work. Half a million Irish starved to death within a few years after 1845. The absolute desperateness of the Irish made them an ideal source of factory labor in both countries. They would work for next to nothing in order to keep their families alive. Further, they were amenable to factory discipline because they had no alternative other than death. The displaced Irish peasants (both men and women), like the young native farm women and children before them, generally lacked craft skills. But with the skill and the pace of work concentrated in the machines, this made little difference to capital. The introduction of machine technology allowed unskilled and semiskilled workers to occupy the central positions within the production process.

The defeat of the Southern plantation owners by the North in the Civil War removed the considerable constraints Southern political power had imposed on the development of industrial capital in the United States. In the interest of preserving and advancing the slave system, the Southern slave owners were able to exercise a veto in Washington over a wide range of policies advocated by the rising class of industrial capitalists, and were thus able to constrict the development of industrial capitalism. The Southerners prevented the implementation of protective tariffs high enough to allow Northern industrial capital to obtain a guaranteed domestic market for its products (products that were generally rather more expensive than British imports). Southerners had inhibited the state funding of railroads and canals connecting the North to the East, fearing that such transportation networks would undermine the use of the Mississippi River system (which linked the West with the South). They blocked the settlement of the West by small farmers economically tied to the growing Northern-based agricultural implement, railway, and marketing networks, so as to facilitate the occupation of Western land by slave-utilizing plantations. They vetoed government-subsidized colleges to train engineers and agricultural experts. They inhibited the encouragement of European immigration to the Northern industrial cities. In general, the Southern slave owners used their political position to advance the slave system and inhibit the growth of industrial capitalism.

The secession of the South in 1860-61 led to a more or less immediate change in federal policies toward industrial capital. The central state now became most supportive of the interests of the new industrial capitalists. High protective tariffs were implemented, the government gave land to new state colleges specializing in engineering and agriculture, it facilitated the settlement of the West, it heavily subsidized railroads, it facilitated European immigration, and so forth. In addition, the tremendous government orders for military equipment during the Civil War gave a great impetus to capital accumulation. Industrial capital emerged hegemonic from the Civil War in the United States. The power of the slave owners had been broken. Even in the South they became economically integrated with and subordinate to the economic power of industrial capital (see Moore 1966, chap. 3; Hacker 1940, pt. 3; and Genovese 1967, chap. 1).

Industrial capital dominated the U.S. state almost unchallenged for two generations after 1860. The U.S. state during this period facilitated industrialization in whatever way capital required. Virtually no regulations or restrictions of any consequence were put on capital, while at the same time state subsidies were given to industry—especially railroads. The state's police powers were systematically used against strikes, unions, and working class demonstrations. High protective tariffs were implemented to guarantee American capital a large home market for their goods.

The most rapid period of industrialization and the most rapid expansion of capitalism in the United States (and the most rapid the world had yet seen) occurred after the Civil War. In 1860 there had been more slaves than factory workers. Factories that employed less than ten workers were the norm. In 1869 one-half of manufacturing enterprises still used waterpower (Gutman 1978, 1976, p. 33). The 1871-99 period saw the most rapid expansion of capital and industry of any period in U.S. history (Kolko 1976, pp. 35, 73). By 1880 U.S. crude steel production equaled that of Great Britain. By 1913 U.S. steel as well as coal production exceeded that of Great Britain, Germany, France, and Belgium combined (Rosenblum 1973, p. 66). Increases in productivity proceeded apace as more and better machinery was introduced. Between the 1869 and 1914 the ratio of the horsepower of machinery to the number of wage earners increased 2.5 times. Output in manufacturing increased by two-thirds in the decade of the 1920s. The period 1914 to 1929 saw a productivity explosion (Kolko 1976, pp. 72, 101).

Cheap and easily available peasant labor encouraged the rapid development of highly capital-intensive advanced technological processes. Since it was impossible for peasants to quickly master traditional techniques and difficult for them to accustom themselves to factory work rhythms, simplified labor processes that regulated the paces of work by machinery had to be introduced even more rapidly in the United States than was the case during the first industrial revolution in Great Britain.

The labor force for rapidly expanding industrial capital in the post-Civil War period was largely drawn from displaced European peasants.* Irish immigration ebbed in the mid-1850s as migration from Germany increased. Unlike the Irish, many of the German migrants had crafts skills and many were *political* refugees from repression in their home country. These German workers thus carried with them *both* experience in organizing unions and socialist ideology. The German immigrants were untypical of most immigrant groups to the United States in this regard (although the British immigrants brought union skills and the Finns later brought socialism). The German migration ebbed in the 1890s because the now-rapid industrialization of Germany came to offer plenty of employment opportunities in their home country. The 1890s saw the beginning of a radical transformation in the ethnic composition of the U.S. working force (see Table 6.2). The major source of immigrants now became southern Italians and Poles and other eastern Europeans, mostly from the Russian and the Austro-Hungarian Empires. Peasants from southern and eastern Europe were now being driven off their land by extreme poverty induced by the commercialization of agriculture. They were becoming redundant on the land, much as had English peasants in the centuries before, and Irish and German peasants in the previous two generations. They were thus forced to migrate to the growing industrial cities both in their own countries and the United States in order to survive. Those with skills mostly stayed in Italy or Poland where they were able, because of their skills, to find work in the industrializing cities in their own country. It tended to be only those who had no real choice but to risk the uncertainties of life in the new world that went to the United States.

In 1880, about 80 percent of the people in the major cities of the United States were either immigrants or the children of immigrants (but as late as 1890 only 3 percent of all immigrants living in the United States were from either eastern or southern Europe—Gutman 1976, pp. 40-41). In 1909, 58 percent of the workers in the 20 principal mining and manufacturing industries in the United States were foreign born. The foreign born were 45 percent of all unskilled and 38 percent of all semiskilled laborers in the entire United States.

---

*In the 1850-1924 period about 90 percent of all overseas European immigrants migrated to the Americas, about two-thirds of these to the United States, which, thus, accounted for about 60 percent of the total (see Rosemblum, 1973, p. 46).

About 80 percent of the unskilled laborers in iron and steel were foreign born, mostly from southern and eastern Europe (Kolko 1976, p. 74).

The overwhelming importance of immigrants in the U.S. working class in this period is reflected in the fact that in 1910 only 45 percent of the immigrant male heads of households living in cities (and coming from non-English-speaking nations) could speak English. In iron and steel this was 31 percent (Kolko 1976, p. 75). In half of working class households in the major industrial concentrations of the United States, English was not the idiom of the house. By the 1930s the children of the foreign born were twice the number of foreign born. Together they accounted for 36 percent of the white population (Kolko 1976, p. 80).

Beginning slowly in the 1890s, accelerating during World War I (with the closure of European immigration) and again in the 1920s, slowing down but continuing through the depression, and accelerating once more during and after World War II, displaced Southern tenant farmers became an important source of recruits for the U.S. factory system. The continuing mechanization of Southern agriculture forced tenants as well as small holders off the land as large-scale farming with wage laborers became the rule. Millions of Southern rural blacks and whites (in about equal numbers) from the First World War through the 1960s (when the supply became virtually exhausted) migrated to the industrial cities of the Northeast and Midwest, especially Chicago, Detroit, Pittsburgh, Buffalo, New York, and other industrial areas of Pennsylvania, New Jersey, New York, Ohio,

TABLE 6.2: Areas of Origin of Immigrants to the United States

	Northern and Western Europe	Eastern and Southern Europe	All Other
1910–19	17.5%	62.1%	20.3%
1900–09	22.1	71.0	6.9
1890–99	49.4	47.5	3.1
1880–89	72.5	16.0	11.6
1870–79	75.8	6.3	17.9
1860–69	82.5	8.6	8.9
1850–59	90.3	2.8	6.9
1840–49	95.6	0.3	4.1
1830–39	77.5	1.1	21.5
1820–29	74.7	2.6	22.7

Source: U.S. Bureau of the Census, *Immigrants and Their Children: 1920*, Census Monographs VII, by Niles Carpenter (Washington, D.C.: Government Printing Office, 1927), p. 62. Taken from Rosenblum 1973, p. 71.

Indiana, Illinois, and southern California. Between 1910 and 1940 4 million Southerners migrated to the Northern cities (Kolko 1976, p. 80).

The massive immigration of displaced peasants caused a considerable degree of upward mobility for native-born Northern workers of western European stock. "Yankees" were recruited for foremen, clerks, and all white-collar occupations. The immigrants resented working for foremen of other immigrant groups, and thus there was a special inducement for capital to employ Yankees in this role (see Kolko 1976, pp. 80–82).

The immigrant workers found wretched conditions in the American factories. The 12- to 15-hour day was the norm in light industry. Steelworkers worked 12-hour shifts seven days a week without vacations. Child labor was common. Few safety or comfort facilities were available. Immigrant workers were further often subjected to the labor contracting system where contractors of their own nationality would mediate between them and their employers. These contractors took a percentage of wages in addition to their fee and, further, often held back the first week or two of wages until the end of the contract to ensure worker compliance. Arbitrary fines and cheating were common characteristics of the labor contracting system (see Feldstein and Costello 1974, pt. 4).

Before the Civil War, wages in the United States were considerably higher than they were in Europe. This historic differential was a product of abundant cheap land and, before the post-1850 rapid displacement of the European peasantry, a relatively low immigration rate. The wage differential, combined with the almost insatiable hunger for unskilled workers after the Civil War, caused millions and millions of peasants who were being displaced from the land in southern and eastern Europe (by the expansion of capitalist relations) to migrate to the United States in search of work. In 1870 wages in the United States were two to four times greater than in the United Kingdom, France, or Germany. Anthracite miners in the United States made two to eight times more than in Poland, Russia, Austria, Hungary, or East Prussia (Kolko 1976, p. 82). After the Civil War, however, the wage gap between Europe and the United States began to shrink as the massive transatlantic transfer of population acted to exert downward pressure on the wage level in the United States (as well as to alleviate downward pressure on wages in Europe). In the 1860–1913 period real wages increased by 50 percent in the United States, compared to 60 percent in Germany and France, 90 percent in the United Kingdom, and 200 percent in Sweden (see Rosenblum 1973, p. 22).

The wage differential between Europe and the United States had major consequences, other than attracting large numbers of foreign immigrants. It gave a capital bias to industrialization in the United

States (labor was dearer than machinery). Labor-saving innovations were introduced in the United States more rapidly than in Europe and their adoption became generally more rapid because of the higher wages in the United States (especially for unskilled labor). The considerably higher wages in the United States also acted as a conservatizing force. As oppressive as conditions were, the immigrant workers drew the comparison between their wages and what they could earn in the "old country," and thus felt privileged in many ways. In 1909 the average wages of southern and eastern European born workers were about two-thirds that of white native born workers (Kolko 1976, p. 83). But with a considerable wage gap between the new country and the old (their primary reference), it was not so important for the immigrant workers that they were on the bottom of American society.

The differential with the old country was especially salient since, except for the Jews who fled Russian pogroms, all the major immigrant groups to the United States in the 1880-1924 period came with the intent of working, saving money, and then returning to their native land. The psychology of gaining the means for a "second chance" back home, or reversing their marginal existence as peasants in rural Italy or Russia, prevailed.

In the 1880-1924 period about one-third did return home permanently, the rest continuingly putting off their return until they had established such roots (most were unable to save sufficient money to realize their dream) that they gave up the plan. In the 1880s and 1890s the rate of return was about one-third the rate of new immigration. From 1900 to 1914 it was about 40 percent. From 1914 to 1922 the rate of return was over half that of new immigration (Kolko 1976, p. 70). About two-thirds of all Rumanians and Hungarians returned, as did 56 percent of southern Italians, 40 percent of Poles, 46 percent of Greeks, 52 percent of non-Jewish Russians, and 21 percent of British (Kolko 1976, p. 70). A pattern of back and forth migration developed. In the 1899-1910 period 12 percent of European immigrants to the United States arrived for at least the second time. The intention to return home was reflected in the sex ratio of the immigrants. From 1899 to 1924 there were twice as many men as women immigrants.

The migration to the United States in search of work and fortune was seen as a tentative and transitory experience. As a result the new immigrant work force was oriented primarily to their own ethnic group and to developments back home (to which they would soon return). Their concerns were thus directed away from class consciousness or building organizations of working class struggle in the United States . The "old country" orientation that prevailed in the American working class until at least the 1920s was thus a major inhibiting factor in the development of socialist consciousness in the U.S. working class (see Kolko 1976, pp. 70-72). The largely young, single and male immigrant workers rarely protested in collective ways since they did not plan to stay long in the mills. Many immigrants responded to dissatisfaction and lack of employment opportunities by moving up their planned departure for their homeland, rather than joining organizations to fight for better conditions in the United States. Emigration, not social transformation, thus provided the easiest and most common solution to the problems experienced by foreign-born workers. Those who returned to Europe were often the most aggressive workers as well as the most militant and resistant to the demands of capital (some were in fact deported).

It is important to emphasize that with a few exceptions—such as the German immigrant workers in the 1850s and 1860s, and the Jewish and the Finnish immigrants after 1890—very few of the immigrants were socialists when they arrived in the United States. In fact, the mass of the peasant immigrants to the United States from Italy and Poland had been largely untouched by even the democratic mass movements that swept the urban areas of their countries in the mid-nineteenth century, and thus arrived in the United States virtually without politics of any kind. However, the experience of exploitation in the United States, the shock of realizing that the streets were not "paved with gold," radicalized many immigrants. The experience of the transformation from peasant to industrial worker resulted in the considerable growth of support for socialism in wide sectors of the immigrant communities. This was especially the case in mining, shoemaking, and the brewing industry, *and* after 1917, among immigrants from the old Russian Empire—many of whom were radicalized along with their relatives in the old country as a result of the Bolshevik Revolution (see Laslett 1970; Aronowitz 1973, chap. 3).

The fact that virtually all immigrants to the United States came with an overwhelmingly economic orientation had a considerable effect on the emerging social and political consciousness of the American working class. Desirous of accumulating as much money in as short a time as possible in order to return to the old country and establish themselves as successful petty bourgeois, the typical ex-peasant immigrant was very hard working, frugal, and compliant; and, further, was largely uninterested in the struggles of the established working class. The immigrant was less likely to be absent and more enthusiastic about long hours than the native born. Their normally zealous work habits often meant they were willing to take risks and put up with unsafe working conditions (as well as being generally reluctant to strike). The immigrants generally put up with oppressive working conditions both because the wages were so high, and because they considered themselves to be undergoing a temporary travail necessary to achieve the good life back home (Rosenblum 1973, chap. 5).

The hard work attitude of the immigrant workers was also facilitated by the radical uprooting, not only from rural peasant life, but also from a familiar national culture. The separation from tradition, routine, and friendship networks of the old life made the immigrants amenable to both work reorganization and to a more rapid pace of work than would have been possible in the old country (where informal work norms and social pressures would have operated in a higher degree in slowing increased productivity).

The economic orientation of most new immigrants, together with their clustering in ethnic ghettos isolated from the mainstream of American life (working class or otherwise) meant that their primary exposure to U.S. society was at work. Thus, as the union movement eventually developed among such workers it tended to be heavily biased in the direction of bread and butter business unionism, rather than a class-conscious radical working class movement. Unions tended to be seen, more than in Europe, as instruments of short-term economic improvement (the primary orientation of the immigrant workers). Longer term goals and broader social conscience continued to be displaced onto the gradually receding goal of a changed life in the old country, or were absorbed by ethnic-based institutions (including the churches).

The new immigrant sense of ethnic identity was considerably enhanced, if not created entirely out of whole cloth, in the United States. In Europe one was a peasant, a Catholic, or a native of a certain village or perhaps region, not an Italian or Pole. National identities for most groups of ex-peasants were created in the relatively ethnically homogeneous settlements in the United States and reinforced by the hostility demonstrated toward them by native-born Americans. Most new immigrants had little contact with people not of their nationality for some time after their immigration. Parochial localist peasant attitudes of the old country tended to break down as larger ethnic solidarities developed that served to overcome differences within an emerging national group yet at the same time served to increase isolation both from other national groups and the native American working class (see Rosenblum 1973, pp. 150, 151; Davis 1981, p. 35).

As urbanization accelerated and mass urban transport came into general use the larger cities became segregated into separate middle class suburbs, decent older housing largely occupied by native-born workers, and an inner core of tenements and overcrowded boarding houses for the new immigrant proletariat. These latter inner city areas became elaborately partitioned into ethnically (and linguistically) differentiated neighborhoods, each with a fairly self-sufficient (even if microscopic) life of its own. These communities shared common rituals and celebrated national festivals. Friendly and benevolent societies, sports, religious activities, and entertainment were all organized within such ethnic enclaves. The ethnic communities became a surrogate for returning home; they kept the hope of return as well as traditional culture alive, thus reproducing (and developing) ethnic rather than class identification.

Each ethnic community was from the beginning class stratified as the mass of immigrant workers was accompanied by a few petty-bourgeois labor contractors and merchants with money who used their ethnicity to exploit the overwhelming working class majority of the ethnic communities. The ethnic petty bourgeoisie came to provide political leadership, often integrating themselves into Democratic Party urban machine politics, gaining petty favors for their constituents in return for the votes of those who had been "naturalized" (see Kolko 1976, p. 90).

In the plants the workers were often organized on the basis of linguistic and ethnic groupings (supervised by unsympathetic native craftsworkers or supervisors). The ethnic divisions within the new U.S. working class were reproduced and encouraged by the policies of capital designed to keep different ethnic groups divided through giving some slightly more privileges, or at least different minor privileges, than others, or by segregating tasks by ethnic groups and sometimes mixing mutually hostile ethnics on the same job in order to make all more tractable (Kolko 1976, p. 75).

From the mass migration of the Irish and Germans in the 1850s through the ending of eastern and southern European immigration by the Immigration Act of 1924, the new immigrants faced the hostility of native-born workers who felt they were undermining their working conditions and wages. They were rioted against, refused admission into trade unions, and evicted from work places. Efforts were made to exclude them from the franchise. Periodically waves of xenophobia, such as that spearheaded by the American Protective Association in the 1890s, would sweep over the country, blaming unemployment, declining economic conditions, and so forth on the "flood of immigrants unloaded on America by papal agents" (Davis 1981, p. 34).

The working class movement came to reflect the fundamental ethnic bifurcation of the American working class between the native born who were concentrated in the skilled trades and the new immigrants of the rapidly growing mass-production industries. The major strikes of the later part of the nineteenth century (e.g., Homestead Steel) were *primarily* defensive strikes led by native-born craftsworkers attempting to hang on to their traditional skills and prerogatives against the offensive of monopoly capital that was attempting to increase its control of the production process, destroying the old craft unions in the process. The largest strikes of the pre–World War I period (the strike wave of 1909–13), on the other hand, were largely offensive strikes of the previously unorganized new immigrant proletariat. Just as the former were generally led by American Federation of Labor (AFL) craft unions, the new Industrial Workers of the World (IWW), a militant, class-conscious industrial union, frequently came to play a leading role in the latter. During this period there was great hostility between the AFL leaders and the IWW, with the craft unions of the native born regularly undermining and sabotaging the strikes of the immigrant proletariat (see Davis 1981, p. 40). The defeat of the strike wave of 1919, which had temporarily brought the native born and the new immigrant working class together, resulted in the retreat of native born workers to a gradually weakening craft unionism, and the immigrant workers away from unions and strikes altogether (until the mid-1930s).

The seeds of an emerging working class unity were drowned in the 1919–24 period in the most massive wave of nativist reaction and state repression the United States has ever seen. The Ku Klux Klan reached a membership estimated as high as 4 million, becoming a major force throughout the middle western industrial states where the new immigrants were concentrated. Its focus on anti-Catholicism, anti-Semitism, anti-Bolshevism, and the "American Way" had significant appeal to many skilled native-born (relatively privileged) workers who were led to believe that the largely Catholic and Jewish (the latter often Socialist) new immigrants were their enemy. Nativist hostility to the religions of the immigrants had the effect of strengthening immigrant religious identifications, just as nativist hostility to the persons and cultures of the immigrants forged developing nationalist identity among first-generation immigrants.

Nationality based groups became the primary institutions of emotional support—rather than broad class-based unions, parties, and their associated activities (as typically became the case in Europe at the same time). Even the leftist movement that did develop among immigrants (e.g., the foreign language federations in the Socialist and early Communist Parties) were largely organized along ethnic lines. By the time the second generation of eastern and southern European immigrants entered the labor force, the institutions of business unionism (mostly incorporated into the AFL) were firmly implanted (the industrial class-conscious traditions of the IWW never established firm roots) and were thus difficult to overcome. The Congress of Industrial Organizations (CIO) in the 1930s, in the face of a major crisis of capitalism, temporarily made major strides in the direction of class-conscious radical unionism, but soon fell back into the business unionism mold with the ending of the crisis and the patriotic and solidarity creating euphoria of the Second World War. In most of the rest of the capitalist world the shocks of rapid industrialization, economic crisis, and brutal exploitation characteristic of early industrialization provoked the formation of militant class-conscious unions and revolutionary oriented mass working class parties (e.g., the Marxist, anarchist, and syndicalist movements) that virtually everywhere became the dominant forces in working class politics during this period. The peculiar nature of the U.S. immigrant working class during the equivalent period in the United States resulted in its isolation from the effect of these forces during the crucial early years of institution formation.

The children of the immigrant workers were subject to very different pressures than were their parents. Unlike them, they were strongly oriented to the United States. Walls were structurally created between the immigrants and their American children. Compulsory schooling was in good part introduced during the period of the heaviest foreign immigration in good part to "Americanize" the second generation. The children were ridiculed for speaking their parents' tongue and for practicing the customs they had learned at home, and were induced to be ashamed of their parents and their national heritage. The limbo status of the children, their lack of full integration into either the old ethnic culture or the new American culture, facilitated familial breakdown, the destruction of the ethnic subcultures and communities, and the growth of juvenile delinquency. In fact, it acted to hinder the emergence of a unified cooperative working class culture transcending ethnicity. The second generation tended to totally accept American values just as strongly as the first held on to the old ways. The children were made to feel that to achieve recognition they must make themselves into "Americans." As a result, American patriotism developed very strong roots in the second generation. A patriotism grew that expressed the desire to be accepted and respected. A patriotism that was manipulated to persuade workers to endorse the "American ethic" of hard work, obedience to law and order, and respect for authority as well as to resist unions and radicalism as "un-American."

7

The Structure of the Contemporary U.S. Working Class

The working class is by far the largest social class in the United States. Its size as a proportion of the class structure has stayed relatively constant since the 1920s. In this chapter the components of the U.S. working class, i.e., type of occupation (industrial, white collar, service, and so on) and economic sector (manufacturing, farming, state, and so on), are studied. An examination of the economic position of the working class shows that there has been no tendency toward economic equality, and until the mid-1960s the standard of living of U.S. workers experienced a long-term increase. The culture and ideology of the working class is shown to be largely a response to the particular oppressions inherent in the distinctive relation to production of this class. Last, the origins, role, and effect of trade unions are analyzed as an aspect of the class response of workers to their position in capitalist relations of production.

THE SPECIFICATION OF THE CONTEMPORARY WORKING CLASS

The working class does the labor of capitalist society, without having the power to determine the conditions of that labor. Workers are free to sell their labor power to those who have the ability to buy it (i.e., those who own and control the means of production). But once they agree to sell, its disposition is in the hands of their employers and their agents in the managerial middle class. The working class in capitalist society is forced to sell its labor power because it does not own sufficient means of production to otherwise support itself.

Labor power is allocated according to the interests of capital. The worker is placed into the structure of capital in accord with the logic of profit maximization.

Over the course of the twentieth century the proportion of working class *occupations* (as defined by the U.S. Census categories of clerical, sales, craftsworkers, operatives, farm and nonfarm labor, and service) has stayed fairly constant at between 70 and 75 percent of the employed population (see Table 7.1). The proportion tended to rise slightly from 1900 to 1940 and slip somewhat over the course of the 1970s. In 1979, 71.8 percent of all occupations were working class, approximately the same level as in the 1900–20 period (see Table 7.1).

When we examine the class structure (remembering that social class position is generally determined by the higher status job of a married couple, i.e., normally the husband's job), we see that from 1920 to 1979 the working class (as measured by the proportion of working class occupations in the male occupational structure) held constant at between 70 and 72 percent of the population. In 1979 it was 70.9 percent of the total, approximately its level in 1970 (72.4 percent) and 1960 (69.8 percent) (see Table 7.2). Thus, it can be seen that there is a very strong tendency for the relative size of the working class to remain constant at roughly 70 percent of the employed population (as measured by the U.S. Census categories).

When the U.S. Census categories are reconceptualized to make them more compatible with our definition of class as relations of production (by removing the police, high-level sales employees, and foremen from the working class) in 1970 the size of the working class (as measured by the male occupational structure) was 60.0 percent of the employed population (see Table 7.3). The removal of occupations that are really intermediate in position between the middle class and the working class reduces the size of the class by roughly 17 percent. Assuming that these same reduction ratios applied in 1979, we can estimate the true size of the working class as a proportion of the employed population in 1979 as approximately 59 percent. Thus, we are struck by two facts: first, the substantial majority of the population is working class; and second, the percentage of the population that is working class has essentially been constant over the entire twentieth century.

The working class can be categorized in terms of relative degree of skill (i.e., skilled, semiskilled or "operatives", and unskilled laborers); economic sector (i.e., manufacturing, mining, agriculture, finance, and so on); type of employer (i.e., private corporations or the state); and type of labor (i.e., blue collar/manual, or white collar/nonmanual). The most commonly used categories, those employed by the U.S. census and the censuses of most countries, mix these distinct

TABLE 7.1:   The Occupational Composition of the U.S. Working Class, 1900–79 (percentage of total working class occupations)[a]

	1900	1920	1940	1960	1970	1979
Clerical	4.3%	11.0%	12.9%	19.2%	23.6%	25.3%
Sales	6.4	6.7	8.9	9.8	9.3	8.9
Total white-collar	10.7	17.7	21.8	29.0	32.9	34.2
Craftsworkers	15.1	17.9	16.0	19.2	18.4	18.5
Operatives	18.3	21.5	24.6	24.9	23.8	20.9
Nonfarm labor	17.8	16.0	12.6	7.6	6.2	6.7
Total industrial	51.2	55.4	53.2	51.7	48.4	46.1
Farm labor	25.2	16.1	9.4	3.3	1.7	1.3
Total production	76.4	71.5	62.6	55.0	50.1	47.4
Service (total)	12.9	10.8	15.6	16.1	17.0	18.4
Domestics	7.8	4.6	6.2	3.7	2.0	—[b]
Nondomestics	5.1	6.2	9.4	12.4	15.0	—
Total blue-collar	89.3	82.3	78.2	71.1	67.1	65.8
Total working class	100.0	100.0	100.0	100.0	100.0	100.0
Absolute number (1000s)	20,337	30,675	38,729	49,211	60,274	69,606
As a percentage of all employed population	70.1	72.7	74.9	72.4	75.5	71.8

[a]U.S. Census definitions.
[b]Data not available.
Note: Data for both sexes.
Sources: U.S. Department of Commerce 1975b, p. 139; 1981a, p. 418.

TABLE 7.2: The Changing Structure of the U.S. Working Class, 1900–79 (percentage)*

	1900	1920	1940	1960	1970	1979
Clerical	4.2%	7.5%	8.1%	9.5%	10.5%	8.9%
Sales	6.8	6.5	8.9	9.6	9.4	8.7
Total white-collar	11.0	14.0	17.0	19.1	19.9	17.6
Craftsworkers	18.8	22.9	21.4	28.3	29.4	31.6
Operatives	15.5	20.6	24.9	27.4	27.4	25.7
Nonfarm labor	22.0	20.0	16.7	11.2	9.6	10.7
Total industrial	56.3	63.5	63.0	67.4	66.4	67.9
Farm labor	28.0	17.2	11.6	4.2	2.4	2.0
Total production	84.3	80.7	74.6	71.6	68.8	69.9
Service (total)	4.6	5.3	8.4	9.4	11.3	12.4
Domestics	0.3	0.2	0.5	0.2	0.1	0.1
Nondomestics	4.3	5.1	7.9	9.2	11.2	12.3
Total blue-collar	88.9	86.0	83.0	81.0	80.1	82.3
Total working class	100.0	100.0	100.0	100.0	100.0	100.0
Absolute number (1000s)	15,836	23,518	28,327	31,893	35,781	38,752
As a percentage of all employed population	66.8	70.1	72.3	69.8	72.4	70.9

*U.S. Census definitions.

Note: Data for the male occupational structure.

Sources: U.S. Department of Commerce 1975b, p. 139; 1981a, p. 418.

TABLE 7.3:   The Structure of U.S. Working Class in 1970

Occupation	Percentage
Sales workers (less intermediate sector sales employees)	4.6%
Clerical workers	12.4
Total white-collar	17.0
Craftsworkers (less foremen)	27.2
Operatives	31.4
Nonfarm labor	10.5
Total industrial workers	69.1
Farm laborers (less foremen)	2.4
Total production workers	71.5
Service workers (less police)	11.3
Total blue-collar	82.9
Total working class	100.0
Absolute number (1000s)	28,548
As a percentage of all employed population	60.0

Note: Reconceptualized U.S. Census categories for male occupational structure.
Source: U.S. Bureau of the Census 1970c, Table 43.

dimensions. Thus, most of the data available have been compiled in terms of *manual* craftsworkers, operatives, and laborers, farm laborers (regardless of skill or type of labor); service workers (regardless of skill or type of labor); clerical workers (regardless of skill), and sales workers. Most of the statistical analysis used in this chapter will, thus, have to use these categories. Probably the most fundamental structural division within the working class is between blue-collar (manual) workers, which encompasses the census categories of craftsworkers, operatives, unskilled nonfarm labor, farm labor (these four together being *production* workers), and service workers (except the police), and white-collar (nonmanual) workers, which encompasses clerical and sales workers (excluding all managerial, professionals, and semiprofessional "intermediate" employees). Because the essential difference between production and service workers on the one side and clerical and sales workers on the other is less and less one of degree of physical strength versus mental work (as all segments of the working class increasingly are objectively becoming semiskilled machine operatives), the terms "blue-collar" and "white collar," which underline status differences, rather than "manual" and "nonmanual," which underline differences in the nature of work, are preferred.

Blue-collar occupations declined by 26 percent (measured as a proportion of all working class occupations) between 1900 and 1979, from 89.3 percent to 65.8 percent of the total. The proportion of all jobs that are industrial (craft, operative, nonfarm labor) has slowly declined from 1920 to 1979. In 1920 it was 55.4 percent of all working class occupations and in 1979, 46.1 percent. The total number of production workers declined more rapidly from 76.4 percent in 1900 to 47.4 percent in 1979 as farm laborers shrunk from 25.2 percent to 1.3 percent of all jobs. From 1940 to 1979 the most important changes in the occupational structure were the radical reduction in the size of farm labor and the radical growth in clerical labor, which increased from 4.3 percent to 25.3 percent of the total number of working class jobs.

Examining the figures for the class structure it can be seen that there was a decline in the proportion of the working class that was blue collar from 1900 to 1940 (from 88.9 percent to 83.0 percent of the population), while between 1940 and 1979 the proportion essentially held steady (it was 82.3 percent in 1979). The proportion of the working class that was industrial workers *grew* from 1900 (56.3 percent) to 1960 (67.4 percent), and then held steady through 1979 (67.5 percent). Production workers as a percentage of the working class declined from 84.3 percent in 1900 to 71.6 percent in 1960, holding fairly constant since. Between 1940 and 1979 the most significant changes in the composition of the *working class* were the decline of farm labor and the growth of the (nondomestic) service work sector, which increased from 7.4 percent to 12.3 percent. There was *no change* in the size of the white-collar sector (see Table 7.2).

When the U.S. Census categories are corrected (removing foremen, police, and high-level sales people) the blue-collar working class in 1970 was 82.9 percent of the working class, the industrial sector of the working class 69.1 percent, and production workers 71.5 percent. Thus, it is clear that the overwhelming bulk of the working class has been, and continues to be, blue-collar workers, with the great bulk of these being industrial workers (two-thirds of the working class from 1960 to 1980).

Blue-Collar Manual Workers

Craftsworkers have a considerable degree of control over their work process (relative to other workers). They typically work in conditions of relatively low mechanization of their particular craft, e.g., building construction, shipbuilding, printing, in which their skills, acquired over many years (in apprenticeship programs or vocational training programs), are a particularly important component of the production process, e.g., carpenters, electricians, painters, plumbers, jewelers, mechanics, machinists, tool and die makers, printers, and so forth. If the concept of a craftsworker were to be extended to white-collar occupations it can be considered to include such occupations as personal secretaries, computer operators, higher level salesmen, and the like.

Craftsworkers have significant control over the pace of their work. Their labor is usually relatively free from pressure as well as intrinsically relatively interesting. Craft jobs, more than others, involve the use of judgment and initiative. Craftsworkers generally consider themselves as good as their supervisors in both technical competence and social worth. The production process of craft labor tends to be less socialized and more individualized than that of semiskilled machine operatives. Craftsworkers typically have a relatively low degree of interdependence with other craftsworkers (in comparison to other types of worker's interrelations). This is manifested in the degree of solidarity developed on the job. A study of British factory workers found that 39 percent of craftsworkers compared to 60 percent of assemblers talked to their work mates on the job and during breaks "a good deal." The same study also found that only 13 percent of craftsworkers compared to 32 percent of assemblers and 41 percent of machinists would be upset by being moved away from present work mates (Goldthorpe et al. 1968a, pp. 50–51). The highly skilled nature of their work, however, does lend itself to cooperation for purposes of improving conditions of their labor, wages, and privileges, even against other parts of the working class (often of different ethnicity). Because it takes so much time to learn the skilled trades, such workers are in a position to monopolize their skills through *craft* unions and, thus, to protect their relative privilege both against capital and less skilled labor. Skilled workers have historically been the first workers to organize as well as to build effective (business) unions.

In 1970, 35.9 percent of those categorized by the U.S. Census as craftsworkers were in the manufacturing sector (compared to 40.2 percent in 1940) and 25.4 percent in construction (24.4 percent in 1940). In both years there was also a significant proportion of all craftsworkers in transport, trade, and the services (U.S. Bureau of the Census 1940, Table 82; and 1970c, Table 1). It should be noted that the reorganization and deskilling of the crafts has been most effective within manufacturing enterprises whose scale of operations and size of enterprises facilitates rationalization. Craftsworkers in smaller enterprises, and in economic sectors that do not lend themselves to a detailed division of labor or detailed supervision (e.g., construction), have experienced much less deskilling and work reorganization than those in large-scale, capital-intensive manufacturing enterprises. It should be noted that the ratio of all those classified as craftsworkers (plus foremen) to all industrial workers increased from 29 percent to 40 percent between 1940 and 1970 (see Table 7.1). This mostly reflects the inflation of the category of craftsworker (which now on average requires less generalized skill than before) as well as the more rapid automation of unskilled compared to skilled labor that has occurred over the course of the twentieth century. This statistic also reflects the fact that the census category of craftsworker also includes foremen (foremen increased from 10.4 percent to 14.4 percent of all those in this general category from 1940 to 1970, reflecting the generally expanded role of supervision).

Semiskilled workers or "operatives" run machines (including trucks and equipment) but are not so skilled that learning to efficiently run the machines takes more than a few weeks or months (i.e., does not require extensive apprenticeship or vocational training programs). Such workers tend to have little work autonomy and are pretty much subject to detailed work requirements imposed by both the routine of the machines they tend and a work organization administered by supervisors who have full knowledge of how the machines work and how to utilize them in the most efficient manner. In the case of white-collar workers, the equivalent would include keypunch operators, typists, and so on, and in the case of service workers operatives would include such occupations as gas station attendants, laundry workers, and so forth. Such labor requires little creativity, is typically exhausting, and often involves (for blue-collar positions) working in high temperature, foul air, or high noise, with unsafe machines, and so on. But more than skilled or unskilled workers this segment of the working class is trained by the socialized conditions of their work into patterns of interdependence, discipline, cooperation, and solidarity.

Some occupations such as miners and steelworkers especially lend themselves to the development of on-the-job work solidarity. Workers in steel mills, for example, have a strong tendency to generate work group solidarity because of the central importance of teamwork and cooperation (which is of central importance when the mill malfunctions). Mill workers are part of a complex team that performs as a unit before a large number of other workers. The knowledge of the idiosyncrasies of a particular mill takes years to acquire. The corresponding pride in workmanship and difficulty of being replaced contributes to an equalitarian spirit of solidarity among mill hands. Because of the physical danger, managers and non-mill hands stay away from the work area, making the rolling mill complex a private domain of manual workers (similar to a coal mine). Steel loading also tends to generate high levels of solidarity. Loaders are in an especially important position in the production process since it is their responsibility to move steel in and out of the plant as rapidly as possible. Their responsibilities, knowledge of loading, and discretion in handling many different types of products and orders puts them in a position to demand concessions from management because of the latter's inability to thoroughly rationalize the work process. Cooperation in both efficiently loading and in resisting management produces an especially high level of solidarity relationships (see Kornblum 1974, chap. 2).

The boring nature of semiskilled machine tending is reflected in the degree of worker dissatisfaction. One study found that 59 percent of all factory workers reported that they would prefer a different occupation, including 69 percent of all automobile workers and 65 percent of all ironworkers and steelworkers (Blauner 1964, p. 202). In the late 1960s the quit rate at Ford Motor Company reached 25 percent a year. At Chrysler in 1969 almost one-half of the newly hired workers did not complete their first 90 days. Absenteeism without explanation averaged about 5 percent in the auto industry, with the rate often reaching 10 percent on Mondays and Fridays (Braverman 1974, pp. 32–33).

The unrewarding and stressful nature of semiskilled operative labor tends to result in lack of identification with one's work. Instead, an "instrumental" orientation to labor tends to develop, a feeling that one works in order to earn a reasonably high income, instead of for an intrinsic reward (see Goldthorpe et al. 1968a).

Laborers or unskilled workers have traditionally been defined as those workers who work with their backs doing purely physical labor at tasks that take virtually no time to learn, e.g., ditchdiggers, garbage men, loaders, crop pickers, freight handlers, and so forth. Such labor tends to be backbreaking, strenuous, tiring, and typically low paying as well. It should be noted that today machines are used in virtually every occupation to perform the more physically strenuous labor, and, further, that most machines are now in good part self-regulating and require very little skill. Thus, unskilled physical labor has shrunk considerably in importance. Today only about 10 percent of the labor force has such jobs.

The distinction between skilled craftsworkers on the one hand and operatives and unskilled on the other is probably the most profound *within* the manual working class. The next most important distinction is probably that between production workers in manufacturing and mining who tend to work under highly socialized conditions and unskilled farm and service laborers who tend to work under more primitive and isolated conditions. These two lines of division within the working class tend to affect a wide range of social practices and political attitudes.

In 1970, 39 percent of the industrial working class were skilled craftsworkers and 61 percent unskilled or semiskilled operatives and laborers (see Table 7.3). The trend over time is for those categorized as skilled craftsworkers to rise as a proportion of all industrial workers (from 33 percent in 1900 to 46 percent in 1979, as measured by the standard U.S. census categories), while the proportion categorized as unskilled laborers has declined radically (from 39 percent in 1900 to 16 percent in 1979). These movements mostly reflect an inflation in job definitions, with the relatively less-skilled labor of machine tending categorized as "operative," even when it takes less time to master than "nonfarm labor" while other jobs, where most of the skill is in the machine, are nevertheless categorized as craftswork. Thus, these changing statistics hide the more essential process of relative deskilling of much of former craft labor as well as the process of virtually all industrial workers now becoming machine tenders of one form or another (with the strength as well as the skill of the jobs in good part now contained in the machine).

Agricultural workers, wageworkers in farming, stock raising on ranches, in a dairy, or fishing are generally isolated from centers of working class population. Although certain categories are located in more or less class-homogeneous communities that facilitate class consciousness (e.g., cowboys, fishermen, loggers), farm workers often live and work under especially oppressive (sometimes almost semi-feudal) conditions. Their pay and job security is generally much worse than that of most industrial workers. But mechanization of agriculture has proceeded apace, with these workers becoming increasingly like other machine operatives. Dairy farming, especially, has become mechanized, as has, to a lesser degree, logging and the harvesting of an increasing proportion of all commercial crops. Although the condition of rural workers is becoming increasing like that of urban factory workers, their work still tends to be more diversified, less mechanized, and socialized as well as situated in smaller work units.

There has been an accelerated pace of development of industrial agriculture that utilizes wage labor in a manner similar to urban factories, employing a more or less constant number of year-round workers to run expensive machinery. This has been associated with the most radical of all changes in the U.S. working class structure over the course of the twentieth century—the virtual elimination of the agricultural (or farm) sector of the U.S. working class. In 1900 almost 30 percent of the working class was on the farm, in 1940 about 12 percent, and in 1979 only 2 percent were agricultural workers (see Table 7.2).

The production sector of the working class is engaged in the manufacture of commodities, the extraction of natural resources, the processing of food, the operation of the transport and communications network, the production and transmission of energy, and construction. Generally the conditions of labor here are the most socialized and the level of cooperative labor is the highest of any sector. In addition, this sector is the most strategic in terms of its essentiality and centrality to the economy and the most transparent in terms of the role of production workers (versus management) in the output of goods. Labor here, especially in the larger production units, is highly integrated and tends to train workers to patterns of discipline, cooperation, and mutual dependence. It further results in low levels of identification with management (higher level supervisors and management are strictly segregated from the areas in which production occurs). Noncraftsworkers very typically come to function like part of their machines (especially in assembly-line work) with their every move regulated, regimented, and coordinated to the motions of the machines they tend. In smaller enterprises there tends to be a greater range of consciousness about employer-employee relations. In smaller businesses there is more likely to be a higher probability of identification with the boss (who is visible, and whose position often seems obtainable); but on the other hand, workers can become more bitter here because the smaller scale of operations makes more transparent their degree of exploitation (as well as because of generally worse conditions and lower pay in such typically competitive sector enterprises). Smaller work units tend to produce the feeling that the operation could be managed without the boss.

Service workers provide nonclerical and nonsales services. They are perhaps the most diverse of the census categories. They include janitors, cooks, waitresses, dental assistants, barbers, child-care workers, elevator operators, hairdressers, ushers, firemen, orderlies, stewardesses, bus drivers, cabbies, theater workers, car washers, painters, delivery people, phone installers, domestic servants, and so on. It should be noted that the U.S. census categorization of occupations as service workers is, in fact, in good part arbitrary, e.g., cooks in restaurants are considered service workers, but workers in food processing are considered craftsworkers, operatives, or unskilled; cleaners in factories are regarded as unskilled, but in hospitals as service workers. Similarly, some transport workers are considered to be service workers and others operatives.

Service workers can be divided between domestic laborers and those who work in specialized work places outside of private homes. Private household work is demanding and often humiliating. Servants are almost completely isolated and surrounded constantly by upper class, or in the case of part-time help, by upper middle class employers. There is, thus, a strong tendency to become identified with the master. Private household servants are today only a very small proportion of the labor force compared to what they were in the nineteenth century (when hired labor was very cheap for middle class families, and time- and labor-saving household appliances were as of yet undeveloped). In 1900 about 8 percent of all employed were domestics, but by 1970 only 2 percent (see Table 7.1). Labor formerly done by domestic servants has for the most part been mechanized (and, thus, displaced to production workers), and to a lesser degree socialized and, thus, performed by employees of specialized service corporations, e.g., caterers, gardening services, and so on.

The physical nature of service work is often much like production work. Both are more or less equally physical or manual. Workers of both types of jobs tend to be similar in income, education, and family background. Both types of jobs are typically hard, dirty, tiring, and poorly paid. For the most part, the essential difference is that production workers tend to produce material things while service workers do not (with the consequence that service workers are less likely to develop a consciousness of exploitation). Service work also tends to differ from production work in being more widely scattered in smaller work places through a city, and, thus, isolated from other workers (often serving mainly the middle class). Such labor tends to be less socialized, more compartmentalized, less mechanized, and less cooperative. Much work is done in close contact with the owners of the business (with no buffer of foremen), leading to either identification with the boss and the desire to start a small service business of one's own, or to high levels of friction (albeit often friction that is likely to be manifested in quitting). In general, the condition of most service work is less likely than that of production workers to give rise to class consciousness.

Service work is perhaps the least affected of all types of working class jobs by either automation-mechanization or the rationalization of labor. Most jobs in the service sector are less susceptible to technological change than are production jobs. Thus, while the labor force tends to shrink (relatively) in production, it tends to pile up in the services. Moreover, because of low capital requirements, competition among firms in the service industries tends to be reproduced and the labor force of this (in good part nonmonopolized) sector tends to be low paid and especially subject to petty humiliations. In addition to reflecting the relative difficulty of increasing productivity, the growth of the service sector has reflected the socialization of housework (formerly performed by unwaged homemakers). There is no evidence that the rate of increase in the "consumption" of services has increased more rapidly than that of goods over the twentieth century.

Nondomestic service workers have increased from 5 percent of total jobs in 1900 to 17 percent in 1979, a very significant increase (the number of domestic plus nondomestic service workers rose from 13 percent to 18 percent of the total). The rise of the service sector of the working class is almost as pronounced as the rise of service occupations (from 4.6 percent in 1900 to 12.4 percent in 1979).

In 1970, 35.7 percent of all those classified as service workers by the U.S. Census were food service workers, 23.8 percent cleaners, 15.2 percent in health care, and 15.0 percent in personal services (excluding domestics). Of all service workers 34.8 percent were employed in the professional service sector (mostly by educational and health care institutions), 26.5 percent by wholesale and retail establishments, and 9.5 percent by establishments that provide personal services (barbers, hairdressers, and so on). Other than the decline of domestic laborers, the most significant change in the sectorial distribution of service workers between 1940 and 1970 was in the number of jobs in professional services, which increased from 16.0 percent to 34.8 percent of the total (U.S. Bureau of the Census 1940, Table 82; 1970a, Table 1).

White-Collar/Nonmanual Workers

Clerical employees work in offices keeping records, preparing accounts, handling communications, doing simple calculations, and so forth. They perform the same tasks as those of the owner and bookkeeper in the era of small business. Clerical workers include bookkeepers, office machine operators, receptionists, secretaries, stenographers, telephone operators, typists, file clerks, and so on.

Although office work has become more dependent on machinery, machinery is often ancillary to work with its pace still largely under the control of the operator. Mechanization, thus, does not affect the social relations of the office as much as it does those of production. The average size of offices is as a rule smaller than production units, the division of labor within offices tends to separate office workers from each other more than the requirements of production separate manual workers; further, the nature of clerical work tends to be more varied, with a greater necessity for individualized production.

The office has traditionally been characterized by paternalism and its work relations permeated with personalistic and particularist ties (with less uniformity in standards of work and remuneration than in production work). Such relations cultivate a sense of solidarity vis-à-vis the boss as well as hinder identification with production workers.

Clerical workers have traditionally had a tendency to think of themselves as superior to production workers, to identify with management (borrowing some of their prestige). This has in part been produced by physical nearness to the boss, the nonphysical nature of the work, similar dress on the job, and the historical evolution of such jobs from petty-bourgeois positions that had significantly higher pay and more job control than average working class jobs. In the United States in 1977, 42 percent of white-collar workers as compared with 26 percent of blue-collar workers identified themselves as middle class (see Table 3.11). Lockwood found even more extreme results for England—70 percent to 25 percent (1958, pp. 126–27).

Working class consciousness among office workers is weakened by their identifications and status aspirations. Office workers have traditionally made invidious comparisons of status across the white-collar/blue-collar line. However, the income of office workers is insufficient to produce a middle class life-style. This often produces resentment against *both* workers *and* bosses. It should be noted that the feminization of office work (especially the employment of young, often single women) in place of men is undermining the traditional status difference between office and production labor, since such young women are more often than not from families with manual worker fathers and/or husbands. Not viewing their job as the principal definer of their social class they are, thus, more likely than male office workers to identify with a broader working class.

Office work has been radically transformed in the last 100 years. Before the closing decades of the nineteenth century few offices had more than a half dozen clerks and bookkeepers to assist the owner. Such assistants were exclusively male. They were the ancestors of modern management as well as of modern clerical workers. The early clerks generally acquired their jobs through personal contacts, family, or schoolmasters. The expectation was that the clerk would stay with his employer indefinitely with a real probability of becoming a junior partner or at least chief clerk. In the early office, duties were not precisely defined and salaries were not subject to a single scale. The gap between such managerial assistants and production workers was immense.

The development of the modern office began in the 1890s with the increased employment of low-skilled and low-status office workers under the supervision of the older clerks (who were now being transformed into managers). Clerical work was divided into departments, and work organized in a systematic and compartmentalized manner with detailed supervision becoming general (even before the introduction of machinery). Office machinery came into wide use in the

1910s. After 1900 the income gap between office and production workers shrank (as well as the income differential among office workers) while the income gap with emerging management radically increased. At the same time, office work became increasingly female—in 1977 in the United States 76 percent of all clerical workers were female compared with only 24 percent in 1900 (see Mills 1953, chap. 9). While office workers' pay has sunk below that of manual workers (especially in the monopoly sector and where there are unions) and job control has in many cases sunk to the level of a manual machine operator, their job security is typically still greater, as they are rather less likely to be laid off than are manual workers. For the office worker, greater job security is a partial alternative to ownership and, thus, produces a difference in consciousness compared to production workers. Such workers have also traditionally felt that their chances of upward mobility are greater than others. Conditions of work in offices (although they have become even more centralized and socialized through the twentieth century) are less socialized than is production labor. Hence, office work tends less than production labor to give training in cooperation.

There has been a tremendous expansion of office work as well as of the division of skills and labor in the office generated by the changing requirements of monopoly capital (e.g., the vast expansion of the sales effort, the great expansion of credit, the increasing control of the productive labor process, the increasing rationalization of all aspects of production, the increasing importance of planning). Office work is not only expanding in relative importance as compared to production work, but there is an increasing division of labor within it, as tasks become divided, specialized, and standardized.

Office work is tending to become more like factory labor. The traditional difference between factory operatives and office workers is declining as both now spend most of the day tending machines that require no physical exertion. The work process of offices is now tending to become one of continuous flow (the flow of information), with the different parts of the work process parceled out among many workers, no one of which has a comprehension of the process as a whole. Each job in the process is rendered more repititious and routine, with tasks tending to be compartmentalized and simplified (in order to increase productivity). Shorthand has been made obsolete by dictating machines, most of bookkeeping and payroll has been computerized, standardized letters are composed by word processors, addressing occurs by addressographs, and so on. Secretarial labor has been streamlined with executive links to stenographic processes through phone and recording equipment and the stenographic pool, the use of canned texts and phrases, automatic typewriters, and administrative support centers that handle nontyping duties (see Braverman 1974, chap. 15).

Computerization and other modern machinery that allows mechanization and standardization has resulted in increasing centralization of office operations. Word processors, small desk-top computers, and other aspects of automation have been pouring into offices. It has been estimated that between 1980 and 1985 the ratio of office computers, terminals, and electronic offices machines will rise from 15 percent to 30 percent of the number of white-collar workers (*Fortune*, April 20, 1981, p. 70). Increased mechanization and rationalization produce an increasing sense of isolation, impersonality, and a machine dominated tempo of work.

New office centers are now often set up away from the front office in low rent areas outside the central business district (this facilitated by modern communications). Shift work is being introduced to operate the new machines around the clock. As contact with the front office declines, the basis for the traditional identification with and deference to management is also declining (see Hamilton 1972, pp. 349–52). However, although office and factory labor are becoming more alike, they have not become identical. Office labor generally continues to involve more responsibility and less work alienation as well as to be less socialized, and hence it still does not generate class consciousness to the same degree as manual labor.

Along with the radical decline in farm and domestic labor, the other major occupational shift within the working class that has taken place in the twentieth century has been the rapid increase in the number of clerical jobs—from 4.3 percent of *all* jobs in 1900 to 25.3 percent in 1979 (see Table 7.1). Almost all the growth in white-collar workers from 10.7 percent of all working class jobs in 1900 to 34.2 percent in 1979 is due to this increase (sales jobs increased from only 6.4 percent in 1900 to 8.9 percent in both 1940 and 1979).

That the large increase in clerical jobs since 1940 has occurred concurrent with its feminization is reflected in the statistics on the relative growth of the white-collar (and clerical) sectors (and subsectors) of the working class. While the clerical subsector grew from 4.2 percent to 8.1 percent of the total between 1900 and 1940, it has stagnated since (see Table 7.2). In 1979, 8.9 percent of the working class was in the clerical sector. Likewise, there was no growth in the sales subsector of the white-collar segment of the working class. Overall 17.0 percent of the working class was in the white-collar sector in 1940 and 17.6 percent in 1979. It is clear that the great bulk of the working class has been and continues to be blue-collar (mostly industrial) workers. What might be taken for the growth of the white-collar segment of the working class (the growth in clerical jobs) has since 1940 been totally manifested in massive numbers of former homemakers (mostly with blue-collar working class husbands) entering the labor force. There is no reasonable sense in which such a transformation from the isolating experiences of working class housework to low level clerical labor can be taken as a social indicator of the weakening of the blue-collar sector of the working class.

About one-fourth of all clerical workers in 1970 in the United States were employed in the service sector (about 75 percent of these in "professional services," especially educational institutions and medical establishments). About one-fifth of clerical workers were employed in retail and wholesale trade establishments. Only 18 percent were employed in manufacturing, while 14 percent were in finance, insurance, and real estate and 12 percent in public administration (see U.S. Bureau of the Census 1970, Table 1).

The ratio of clerical employees to all workers in an economic sector can be taken as an indicator of the degree of organization and control characteristic of that industry, i.e., the higher the ratio of paper workers to production workers, the more monopolized, the more technically advanced, the larger the production units, and so on. There is a tremendous variation in the ratio of clerical workers to all workers in the various sectors of the economy. Agriculture (1.9 percent) and construction (6.3 percent) have the smallest proportion of clerical workers (reflecting the small size of enterprises, competitive markets, and relatively labor-intensive nature of production in these sectors). The very high proportion of clerical workers in finance, insurance, and real estate (48.2 percent) and public administration (39.9 percent) reflects the nature of these sectors—they neither produce nor physically transfer any material good, but rather act on the sectors that do. Within the manufacturing sector the most labor-intensive and competitive enterprises employ the fewest clerical workers (e.g., apparel 7.8 percent, textiles 8.8 percent), while the more monopolized and technically advanced employ the most clinical workers (nonelectrical machinery 13.6 percent, and electrical and electronics goods 13.6 percent).

The rapid growth of clerical workers has, not surprisingly, been closely associated with the growth of those economic sectors that have an especially high ratio of clerical to production workers, i.e., public administration, finance and insurance, and trade (as well as the professional services such as medicine and education) and the decline of agriculture (which employs very few). Since only about one in six clerical workers were in 1970 employed by manufacturing companies, it is clear that it could not be the expansion of clerical tasks within this sector that has been primarily responsible for the growth of clerical workers.

Sales workers tend to labor under relatively isolated conditions that separate them from other workers, putting them instead in contact with clients and patrons (often of middle class or of diverse class backgrounds). The individualized nature of selling tends to limit the development of collective consciousness. Their role as distributors, rather than as producers, makes it harder for them to see clearly the nature of exploitation (which tends to be more transparent to those who actually produce the goods they sell).

Salespeople often tend to identify with their customers (especially in smaller stores with regular clientele). Under such conditions salespeople tend to "borrow prestige" from middle (or upper) class customers, thus hindering class consciousness. But in larger stores without regular customers, the sales effort is much more impersonal. Here conditions are more likely to produce resentment against more wealthy customers who buy the goods that the salespeople themselves can not afford as well as hostility against management and owners. Salespeople often resent the requirement of having to "package their personality," having to be cheerful, efficient, and polite. The conditions of labor of some categories of sales workers are rather like semiskilled blue-collar workers, i.e., grocery clerks who spend most of their time stocking shelves, sweeping floors, bagging groceries, and so forth, rather than actually waiting on customers (see Mills 1953, chap. 8).

A number of structural factors are responsible for the rapid increase in clerical and sales in relation to production workers in the United States over the course of the twentieth century. Most of the structural transformations in the nature of work corresponding to the changes in the needs of capital are discussed in Chapter 5. Here it need only be pointed out that the following factors have played a major role: first, the tremendous increase in the role of marketing, advertising, and credit required to sell the goods produced by corporations; and second, the great expansion of state services, such as medicine, education, post office, social work, police, military, and so forth, all of which have produced a considerable increase on the one hand in the salaried middle class, and on the other in clerical and service work jobs.

The Distribution of Employment by Economic Sector

The relative size of employment in the different economic sectors of the U.S. economy has undergone considerable change over the course of the twentieth century. The most rapid expansions have occurred in the government sector (from 5.4 percent to 17.3 percent of the total between 1900 and 1979); finance, insurance, and real estate (from 1.5 percent to 5.5 percent of the total); services (from 8.6 percent to 18.9 percent of the total), and trade (from 12.3 percent to 22.3 percent of the total) (see Table 7.4). The most radical declines have occurred in agriculture (from 25.2 percent to 1.0 percent), mining (from 3.1 percent to 1.1 percent), and transport and public utilities (from 11.2 percent to 5.7 percent). Unlike all the other major sectors, the relative size of the manufacturing sector has held constant over the course of the twentieth century (it was 26.9 percent in 1900 and 23.1 percent in 1970), although it declined significantly in the 1960 to 1979 period (see Table 7.4).

These changes in employment patterns within the U.S. economy reflect radical changes in economic organization and productivity. The increase in agricultural productivity combined with the natural limits to food consumption has meant that very few people are employed any longer in this sector. Similarly, tremendous increases in productivity in mining together with a much slower growth in demand for raw materials has meant the decline in employment in this sector. The rapid expansion of the role of the state in monopoly capitalist society (reflecting primarily its increasingly central role in both the economy and social legitimation) has naturally brought with it a rapid expansion in employment in this sector. The intensification of the sales effort and the growing centrality of large corporations in both the wholesale and retail trade has been responsible for the expansion of employment here. The growth of professional services, especially education and health care, has been primarily responsible for the growth of service sector employment (see Table 7.5). As banks and insurance companies have come to play an ever more central role in the economy, employment in this sector has, of course, significantly expanded. The relative expansion of the state, trade, and service sectors in relation to the manufacturing sector reflect the difficulty of increasing productivity (output per worker) in the latter three sectors, compared to the former, and not a tendency for the consumption of services or commerce to rise more rapidly than the consumption of manufactured goods. This is demonstrated by the fact that between 1940 and 1979 manufacturing output (measured in quantity terms) increased by a factor of 5.96, while between 1940 and 1979 employment in the government sector increased by 3.72 times; in trade by 2.98 times; in finance, insurance, and real estate by 3.30 times; and in the service sector by 4.62 times (see Table 7.4 and U.S. Department of Commerce 1975b, p. 667).

TABLE 7.4: Changes in Number of Employees by Economic Sector in the U.S. Economy

	1900	1920	1940	1960	1979
Mining	637 (3.1%)	1,180 (3.6%)	925 (2.6%)	712 (1.3%)	957 (1.1%)
Construction	1,147 (5.6)	850 (2.6)	1,294 (3.6)	2,885 (5.2)	4,644 (5.1)
Manufacturing	5,468 (26.9)	10,702 (33.0)	10,985 (30.5)	16,796 (30.1)	20,972 (23.1)
Transport and public utilities	2,282 (11.2)	4,317 (13.3)	3,038 (8.4)	4,004 (7.2)	5,154 (5.7)
Trade	2,502 (12.3)	4,012 (12.4)	6,750 (18.7)	11,391 (20.4)	20,137 (22.3)
Finance, insurance, and real estate	308 (1.5)	902 (2.8)	1,502 (4.2)	2,669 (4.8)	4,963 (5.5)
Services	1,740 (8.6)	3,100 (9.6)	3,681 (10.2)	7,423 (13.3)	17,043 (18.9)
Agriculture (excluding forestry and fishing)	5,125 (25.2)	4,948 (15.3)	3,632 (10.1)	1,604 (2.9)	930 (1.0)
Government	1,094 (5.4)	2,371 (7.3)	4,202 (11.7)	8,353 (15.0)	15,612 (17.3)
Total Employees	20,303	32,382	36,008	55,838	90,412

Note: Data are for both sexes
Sources: U.S. Department of Commerce 1975b, pp. 137, 139; 1981a, pp. 413–15.

A somewhat different picture is seen when the distribution of classes (as indicated by the occupation of men) among different economic sectors is examined. Here it is seen that the tendency for employment in manufacturing to decline as a percentage of all the employed is a result of women entering the wage labor force (largely as white-collar and service workers), rather than as a result of a decline in employment in that sector. While in 1940, 24.5 percent of the employed male population was in the manufacturing sector, in 1978, 29.8 percent was (see Table 7.5). Similarly, the large increases in employment in trade, finance, and public administration are mostly accounted for by ex-homemakers entering the labor force, and consequently have had no significant effect on the *class structure*. The two significant changes in the class structure have been those of agriculture, which has radically declined in importance, and the nondomestic services, which have considerably increased in importance (see Table 7.5).

Within the manufacturing sector some industries have been increasing their share of all manufacturing employment. From 1960 to 1979 the share of fabricated metals rose from 6.9 percent to 8.7 percent of the total, electronics and electrical machinery from 7.9 percent to 9.2 percent, and rubber and plastics from 2.3 percent to 4.0 percent. On the other hand, some industries have significantly decreased their share of employment. Primary metals (especially steel) declined from 7.9 percent to 6.5 percent of total manufacturing employment, while the food industry declined from 9.6 percent to 7.8 percent, textiles declined from 6.6 percent to 5.2 percent and apparel from 8.7 percent to 7.5 percent (see Table 7.6). In general, it tends to be the high technology monopolized industries that have been increasing their share of all manufacturing sector employment, while the competitive-sector light industries (which mostly face sluggish increases in demand) have been declining.

Employment in the nondomestic service sector of the economy has been expanding particularly rapidly (from 1940 to 1970 by a factor of 2.89). However, this growth has been very uneven. For example, personal services, including hotel/motel, restaurant workers, laundry workers, barbers, hairdressers, and so forth, experienced a growth of 1.18 times from 1940 to 1970. This is significantly less than the average for all employment in the entire economy (which was 1.70 times). Likewise, employment in recreation and amusement increased more slowly than the national average, as did many of the

TABLE 7.5: Economic Sector of U.S. Men

	1940		1978	
Mining	902	(2.7%)	643	(1.4%)
Construction	2,022	(6.0)	4,038	(8.5)
Manufacturing	8,250.6	(24.5)	14,126	(29.8)
Transport and public utilities	2,768.3	(8.1)	4,344	(9.2)
Trade	5,509.3	(16.3)	9,150	(19.3)
Finance, insurance, real estate	1,013.3	(3.0)	2,078	(4.4)
Services	3,709.6	(11.0)	8,787	(18.5)
Agriculture (excluding logging and fishing)	7,886.8	(23.3)	1,041	(2.2)
Public administration*	1,414.1	(4.2)	3,268	(6.9)
Total labor force	33,577	(100.0)	47,473	(100.0)

*Not identical with the government sector (many government employees are classified elsewhere).

Sources: U.S. Bureau of the Census 1940, Table 82; 1980b, p. 236.

TABLE 7.6: Distribution of Nonsupervisory Employees in the U.S. Manufacturing Sector

	1960	1979
Lumber	4.5%	4.3%
Furniture	2.5	2.7
Stone, clay, glass	3.9	3.7
Primary metals	7.9	6.5
Fabricated metals	6.9	8.7
Machinery (except electrical machinery)	8.2	10.8
Electrical and electronics	7.9	9.2
Transportation equipment	8.8	9.4
Food	9.6	7.8
Textiles	6.6	5.2
Apparel	8.7	7.5
Paper	3.8	3.6
Printing	4.7	4.7
Chemicals	4.1	4.2
Rubber and plastics	2.3	4.0
Total manufacturing	100.0	100.0
Absolute number (1000s)	12,586	15,010

Sources: U.S. Bureau of the Census 1970c, Table 1; U.S. Department of Commerce 1967, pp. 222–24; 1981a, pp. 413–15.

traditional business and repair positions (e.g., auto services increased only 1.18 times in employment). The radical increase in the services was located in professional services, mostly the educational and health care industries. Overall employment in the professional service subsector grew by 4.08 times between 1940 and 1970, while service employment in educational institutions grew by 3.95 times and in health care establishments by 4.17 times. In 1970 fully 71.5 percent of all those classified as employed in the service sector were in professional services (32.6 percent of all those employed in service industries were in education and 22.4 percent in health care). This was up from 50.7 percent—23.9 percent and 15.6 respectively in 1940 (see Table 7.7).

The private sector of the economy can be considered to be divided into two fundamental sectors: the monopoly/capital-intensive sector and the competitive/labor-intensive sector. For the most part, industries with high ratios of machinery and plant to the number of workers employed tend to be dominated by a few firms (since it is very difficult for new firms to enter such sectors because of the tremendous capital requirements necessary). Likewise, firms with relatively small capital per employee ratios tend to be in competitive

TABLE 7.7: Changes in the Service Sector of the Economy

	1940		1970		
	Number (in 1000s)	Percentage of Total Service Workers	Number (in 1000s)	Percentage of Total Service Workers	Ratio of 1970/1940
Business and repair	864	13.2%	2,428	12.8%	2.81
Auto services	480	7.3	568	3.0	1.18
Personal services (excluding hotels)	1,418	21.7	1,674	8.8	1.18
Hotel services	553	8.4	663	3.5	1.20
Amusement, recreation	395	6.0	632	3.3	1.60
Professional services	3,317	50.7	13,540	71.5	4.08
Educational	1,564	23.9	6,171	32.6	3.95
Medical	1,019	15.6	4,248	23.4	4.17
Charitable religious	385	5.9	1,168	6.2	3.03
All nondomestic services	6,547	100.0	18,937	100.0	2.89
All employees (all sectors)	45,166	(14.5%)*	76,805	(24.7%)*	1.70

*All nondomestic service workers as a percentage of the total.
Note: Data are for total employment of both sexes, excluding domestics.
Source: U.S. Bureau of the Census 1940, Table 82; 1970c, Table 1.

markets (since it takes relatively little capital to open a new enterprise here). Table 7.8 displays some of the basic characteristics of operatives (or other basic manual workers) in each of the major economic sectors of the U.S. economy (excluding agriculture, trade, and finance), ranking them by their ratios of assets to nonsupervisory employees.

Although workers in the capital-intensive sector are very slightly older and more educated than workers in the labor-intensive sector, these differences are minute. There is no significant difference between these two sectors on these factors. A higher percentage of the labor-intensive than capital-intensive sector workers are Ladinos and blacks, 20.0 percent versus 16.3 percent. There is not a major difference between the two manufacturing sectors, however. It appears that blacks and Ladinos are almost as concentrated in the monopoly sector as in the competitive sector industries. Excluding service workers, capital-intensive industries tend to be only slightly more unionized than competitive-sector industries (70 percent versus 64 percent). But industrial workers as a whole tend to be far more unionized than service workers (67 percent versus 12 percent), a rather radical difference.

The two factors on which the capital-intensive and labor-intensive sectors appear to diverge the most is in basic male operative pay,

TABLE 7.8: Monopoly/Capital-Intensive and Competitive/Labor-Intensive U.S. Economic Sectors, 1970

	Capital Invested per Employee (in $1,000s)	Annual Wages of Operatives	Ratio of Union Members to Nonsupervisory Employees	Median Age of Male Operatives	Median Education of Male Operatives (years)	Women as % of all Operatives	Blacks and Ladinos as % of all Operatives
Capital-intensive sector							
Chemicals	48.6	$8,163	0.60	37.2	12.2	17.1%	15.1%
Mining	70.1	7,253	0.78	38.8	10.5	2.9	9.6
Primary metals	55.2	7,514	0.75	40.0	10.8	7.1	21.4
Paper	39.3	7,420	0.83	35.3	11.5	23.7	14.7
Food	23.1	6,383	0.75	38.9	10.5	35.0	23.0
Rubber and plastics	18.8	7,072	0.61	34.2	11.6	35.1	16.6
Transportation equipment	23.1	7,849	0.89	36.4	11.5	16.0	17.7
Nonelectrical machinery	22.7	7,432	0.42	36.2	11.9	16.1	12.2
Average	37.6	7,386	0.70	37.1	11.3	19.1	16.3

Labor-intensive sector							
Construction[a]	10.6	7,679	0.91	42.1	11.2	1.7	10.1
Fabricated metals	18.6	6,639	0.87	36.7	10.8	23.2	19.0
Printing	12.8	6,909	0.55	30.4	12.1	45.6	11.4
Lumber	15.6	5,016	0.44	38.4	9.8	15.5	22.2
Electronics	14.9	6,964	0.82	36.3	12.0	55.1	16.5
Textiles	17.1	4,709	0.22	34.8	9.9	65.5	30.2
Apparel	4.8	4,762	0.71	35.0	10.4	77.7	22.5
Service industries[b]	—[c]	—	0.12	—	—	—	—
Personal services	—	5,072	—	40.3	11.9	66.4	15.4
Cleaning services	—	4,636	—	47.3	9.9	32.4	32.1
Health services	—	4,488	—	31.6	12.2	87.9	25.2
Food services	—	2,899	—	27.0	11.0	68.7	16.1
Average (excluding services)	13.5	6,097	0.64	36.2	10.9	40.6	18.8
Average (including services)		5,434	0.44	36.3	11.0	49.1	20.0

[a]Data for craftsworkers (the large majority of all construction workers) instead of operatives.

[b]Data for all employed in these subsectors.

[c]Data not available.

Sources: U.S. Bureau of the Census 1970c, Tables 1, 44; U.S. Department of Commerce 1975a, pp. 347-49; 1975b, pp. 927-31; 1981a, pp. 430, 561.

and in the proportion of operatives (or other basic workers) who are women. In 1969 operatives in the more capital-intensive manufacturing industries earned 21 percent more than operatives in the more labor-intensive industries (excluding services) and 36 percent more including services. There is an especially great differential in the proportion of operatives that are women. In 1970, 19.1 percent of operatives in capital-intensive industries were women, compared to 40.6 percent in the competitive sector excluding services and 49.1 percent including them. Thus, it is clear that the lower paying labor-intensive sector, for the most part, has a strong preference for female workers (who can be hired at lower wages) and tends to pay its male workers less. It appears that industries in which wages represent the greatest part of outlay (i.e., are labor intensive) and are at the same time in competitive markets (which force costs down) are forced by market conditions to pay less to men as well as hire a higher proportion of workers who can be paid less (i.e., women). In the capital-intensive sector, on the other hand, wages represent a relatively small proportion of total outlays and, further, because monopoly conditions tend to prevail, wage increases can be passed on to consumers relatively easier (through implicit collusion in raising prices). Thus, this latter sector can afford to pay its male operatives higher wages as well as to employ a disproportionately male labor force.

The state sector greatly expanded its share of total employment in the U.S. economy over the course of the twentieth century. From a total of 5.4 percent of the civilian labor force in 1900, government employment expanded to 17.3 percent in 1979. If the military were to be included in these figures, in 1979 government employment accounted for 19.5 percent of all employment (see Table 7.4 and U.S. Department of Commerce 1981a, p. 376). In 1979 only 18.0 percent of all civilians employed by the U.S. state were employed by the federal government. Over half, 58.9 percent, were employed by local governments and 23.2 percent by state governments. It should be noted that the long-term increase in public employees as a percentage of the labor force ceased in the 1970s. In 1970 it was 17.7 percent of the total and in 1979, 17.3 percent. The number of civilian federal employees was constant over the course of the 1970s (at 2.8 million)—thus declining as a percentage of total civilian employment from 4.1 percent to 3.2 percent of the total (U.S. Department of Commerce 1981a, pp. 318, 413).

State employment plays a specially important role for some sectors of the working class and very little for others. For example, in 1970, 21.7 percent of *all* clerical workers were employed by the state as were 25.2 percent of *all* service workers. The expansion of these two occupations over the 1900 to 1970 period must in part then be attributed to the growth of the public sector (especially public administration, health care, and education) during this period. On the other hand, industrial workers are overwhelmingly in the private sector. Only 2.9 percent of all nontransportation operatives were state employees (U.S. Bureau of the Census 1970c, Table 43).

The overwhelmingly greatest concentration of government workers is in education. In 1979 there were 6.8 million public employees in the educational sector (42.4 percent of all government employees at all levels). About 55 percent of these were teachers. The number of educational employees has risen rapidly. In 1965 there were only 4 million (37.5 percent of total public employment). Other major concentrations of government workers are in health care and the police force (in 1979, 10.2 percent and 4.5 percent of the total). Those employed in health care rose slightly from 9.4 percent of the total in 1965, as did the percentage accounted for by the police, which increased from 4.0 percent (U.S. Department of Commerce 1967a, p. 437; 1981a, p. 318).

Traditionally the public sector was less unionized than the average. In fact, in 1970 only 18.5 percent of public employees were unionized as compared to the national average of 27.5 percent of the nonagricultural labor force. The 1970s witnessed a significant growth of public sector unions while union membership in the private sector shrank. By 1978 membership in public sector unions had grown to 23.4 percent of state employees, the same proportion as was the case in the private sector (U.S. Department of Commerce 1981a, pp. 429, 430). This reflects both the increasing size of government units and the fact that the need for the state to perform the legitimation function (winning and keeping the support of the majority of the population) leads it to enact legislation and follow policies that now facilitate union organization in the public sector.

State workers can be considered to have four subsectors. First, production workers who essentially perform the same function as production workers in private enterprise, e.g., workers in state-owned coal mines, steel mills, railways, buses, the post office, utilities, and so forth. Such enterprises, at least in Europe, are often run to make a profit, if not for the state itself then to subsidize private profit making through providing goods or services to business at below cost. Production workers also include those state employees providing productive services to capitalist enterprises (e.g., airline controllers, science researchers and teachers, statistics gatherers, and so on). The second subsector includes those performing repressive functions, i.e., the police and the military. A third subsector is comprised of state employees whose activities are essentially directed to general social needs (even when distorted by capitalist society), e.g., firemen in residential neighborhoods, health workers, and so on. Those performing essentially legitimation functions (e.g., social science teachers, social workers) make up a fourth subsector.

The latter three types of state workers are not exploited in the same sense as are private sector production workers. No owners, stockholders, or controlling group of managers makes a direct profit from their labor. The administrative stratum in this sector does not derive material benefit from the labor of those they supervise, and, thus, they do not have the same incentive for speedup and profit efficiency as do managers in private industry (or profit-oriented, state-owned enterprises).

Because these latter categories of state workers generally provide services needed by both business and the public, their role in class struggle is less clear than that of production workers, e.g., strikes in this sector often hurt the public more than private business (and as a result antagonism is often generated in other sectors of the working class against public employees). Moreover, since pay raises normally come out of taxes, taxes mostly borne by working people, rather than out of profits there also tends to be a potential antagonism here, with many production workers tending to oppose pay raises for state workers such as teachers, while state workers tend to develop resentment against those workers concerned primarily about their tax rates. The indirect relations of state workers to the economy tends to inhibit the development of a class consciousness (of solidarity with other workers based on the transparency of exploitation), instead facilitating a general hostility to "the public" and/or feelings of oppression in "racial" or sexual terms (see Hill 1975, p. 72).

WORKING CLASS ECONOMIC POSITION

From the middle of the nineteenth century in both the United States and Western Europe there was a long-term tendency for real wages to rise. From this time workers received a share of the growing wealth that they were producing. In the United States in the 1900-10 decade real earnings of employees rose by 22.4 percent, from 1910 to 1920 by 10.7 percent, and from 1920 to 1930 by 24.1 percent (the most significant increase until that time); even in the 1930s real earnings increased by 13.1 percent. The period of the most rapid increase in real earnings, however, was the 1940s and 1950s. Between 1940 and 1950 real earnings increased by 40.8 percent, and between 1950 and 1960 by 31.8 percent. These decades saw the incorporation of the majority of U.S. workers into the "affluent society." After the mid-1960s, however, the long-term trend for real wages to increase came to a halt. Between 1960 and 1970 real earnings increased by only 13.2 percent. Between 1970 and 1980, for the first time in the twentieth century, there was a *decline* in real earnings of 7.7 percent (see U.S. Department of Commerce 1975b, p. 164; 1981a, p. 422). Real wages peaked in 1973. In that year a nonagricultural private sector employee had a gross pay of $109.2 a week (in 1967 dollars) and a worker with three dependents brought home $95.7. By 1980 gross pay had declined to $95.1 while take-home pay for a worker with three dependents had been reduced to $83.5 (declines of 12.9 percent and 12.7 percent respectively).

The long-term rise in real wages within the capitalist system has been possible because of the long-term trend of rising productivity. The working class has shared in the wealth of capitalism, however, because of a number of factors. The continuing expansion of capitalist enterprises meant a continuingly growing demand for labor, and consequently a relative labor shortage that has acted to bid wages up over the century. As the new working class lost its roots in the peasantry (and subsistence agriculture) it became increasingly reliant on only the wage to provide all the necessities of life (thus producing pressure for wages to rise). At the same time, commercial agriculture experienced an explosion of productivity resulting in the decreasing real cost of basis foodstuffs (i.e., "wage goods"), and consequently a rise in real wages. As the U.S. working class was formed and a degree of craft and class consciousness developed, unionization became a more important force. Strong unions, especially active in the 1940s and 1950s, were, thus, a major contributing cause of the rapid increase in real wages during these years. From the 1930s the U.S. state has been active in regulating the economy and providing expanding social benefits to the working class (as well as institutionalizing collective bargaining). This intervention of the state, instituted as part of its legitimation function to defuse the crisis of the 1930s and prevent its reoccurrence, has acted as a major force in increasing real wages.

Finally, the closing of large-scale immigration from the rest of the world to the United States in 1924 meant that capital now had to find most of the additional workers it needed from within the United States, thus driving up wages more than would have occurred with the unlimited immigration of poor peasants that had been the case before. The most rapid rise in real wages in U.S. history took place in the 1940-60 period when the United States was closed to the immigration of cheap foreign labor and U.S. industries were overwhelmingly hegemonic in the world's markets (the economies of its chief competitors having been largely destroyed in World War II).

The intensive pace of investment in this period, together with the relative labor shortage that it, together with immigration restrictions, produced was manifested in a relatively low unemployment rate and consequently strong upward pressure on wages. In the 1946–59 period in the United States the unemployment rate averaged 4.5 percent, compared to the 1970–80 rate of 6.2 percent (see U.S. Department of Commerce 1981a, p. 407; 1975b, p. 135).

It can be speculated that the reversal of the long term-trend of increasing real wages that occurred in the period after the mid-1960s in the United States has been a result of the reversal of many of the factors that were the cause of the long-term trend. The increase in productivity of U.S. industry stagnated during this period. Further, U.S. industry came under great pressure from other advanced capitalist countries whose costs were less (especially West Germany and Japan). The tendency to export operations overseas, together with an accelerated pace of immigration from Latin America and East Asia (the restrictive immigration law was loosened in the mid-1960s) during this period have also acted to increase the rate of unemployment (i.e., the size of the reserve army of labor), and hence to put downward pressure on real wages. The power of unions in the U.S. economy has declined considerably, thus weakening organized labor's ability to gain a proportional share in the growing wealth of the country. While in 1955, 33.2 percent of all nonagricultural employees in the United States were in unions, in 1965 28.4 percent and in 1978 only 23.6 percent were (U.S. Department of Commerce 1980, p. 429). Finally, in the mid-1970s the U.S. economic intervention to ensure relative prosperity (increasing productivity and economic growth) peaked, and in the Carter years began to decline (this tendency was, of course, accelerated during the Reagan administration).

Over the course of the 1970s the long-term historical disparity in wages between the United States and northwestern Europe largely disappeared. In 1978 average wages in manufacturing in the United States were $6.17 an hour, compared to $8.14 in Denmark (the highest in the world), $6.90 in Sweden, $6.23 in Norway, $6.18 in Switzerland, $5.87 in Belgium, $5.75 in the Netherlands, and $5.84 in Germany. Further, wages in Japan were almost as high as was the norm in northwestern Europe and North America—$5.39 an hour. (It should be noted that both the United Kingdom and France were significantly below the average North American and northwestern European norms with hourly wages of $3.55 and $3.92 respectively (see Business International Corporations, *Bi-Data*, January 1980). The spread in workers' real standards of living is even more striking than the figures for pretax wages indicate. While a higher proportion of a worker's paycheck is deducted for taxes and other social benefits in northwestern Europe than in the United States, the working class in the former countries receives a considerably higher wage supplement (or "social wage," in both proportionate and absolute terms) in the form of free or heavily subsidized social services than in the latter. The differences between the two areas include the existence of free medical care, heavily subsidized housing, and a higher degree of subsidized higher education (along with a whole range of other social benefits) for workers in northern Europe.

The equalization in the living standards of workers throughout the advanced capitalist countries has been largely a result of the international market in both industrial exports and industrial capital. In export markets the lowest wage countries have a competitive edge over high-wage producers, resulting in both expanded unemployment in high-wage countries and rapid wage increases (to induce an expanded labor force) in low-wage countries. Capital also leaves high-wage areas for more profitable low-wage areas, again creating unemployment (and hence downward pressure on wages) in the former, and new demand for labor (and hence upward pressure on wages) in low-wage areas. The homogenization of the working class in both skill levels and income throughout the advanced capitalist countries is, thus, a product of the logic of the *world* capitalist market.

Between 1949 and 1978 the income differential in the United States between professionals and managerial personnel on the one hand and operatives in manufacturing on the other has been constant at about 1.5. The middle class–working class differential in incomes, thus, has been maintained throughout the postwar period (the class gap here is as important as it ever was). It should be noted, however, that although operatives in the highly unionized manufacturing sector held there own, the position of operatives outside of the manufacturing sector deteriorated significantly (see Table 7.9).

One of the most significant changes in the 1949–78 period was the convergence of the income of sales and clerical workers with that of manufacturing operatives. Averaging 13 percent more pay in 1949, these groups had drawn virtually even with manufacturing operatives by 1978, thus undermining the traditional income advantages of white-collar over blue-collar workers (a process significant for the possibilities of the development of a broader class consciousness encompassing both segments of the working class). It should also be noted that the traditionally great disparities among factory operatives (e.g., between workers in durable and nondurable goods sectors) also declined during this period, again increasing the structural possibilities of broader class consciousness.

On the other hand, the differential between craftsworkers and operatives was maintained throughout the 1949–78 period, while the

TABLE 7.9: Annual Median Earnings of those with Earnings in the United States

	1949		1969		1978	
Professional	$3,958	(1.48)	$10,617	(1.39)	$17,391	(1.43)
Managerial	3,944	(1.48)	11,012	(1.45)	18,234	(1.50)
Sales	3,028	(1.13)	8,447	(1.11)	12,061	(0.99)
Clerical	3,010	(1.13)	7,259	(.95)	11,909	(0.98)
Craftsworkers	3,125	(1.17)	8,176	(1.01)	13,583	(1.12)
Operatives	2,607	(0.98)	6,793	(0.89)	10,980	(0.90)
Manufacturing	2,671	(1.00)	7,059	(0.93)	11,780	(0.97)
Durable goods	2,742	(1.03)	7,005	(0.92)	11,841	(0.98)
Nondurable goods	2,573	(0.96)	7,166	(0.94)	11,656	(0.96)
Laborers (nonfarm)	1,961	(0.74)	4,614	(0.61)	4,476	(0.37)
Service (nondomestics)	2,195	(0.82)	5,086	(0.67)	5,505	(0.45)
Farm labor	863	(0.32)	2,513	(0.33)	2,744	(0.23)
Farmers	1,455	(0.55)	4,869	(0.64)	7,537	(0.62)
Total	2,668	(1.00)	7,620	(1.00)	12,133	(1.00)

Note: Data are for males only.

Sources: U.S. Bureau of the Census 1950, Table 129; 1970c, Table 1; 1980b, Table 56.

differential between the service, unskilled, and farm labor sectors and the rest of the working class grew considerably. While in 1949 operatives made 32 percent more than unskilled nonfarm laborers, in 1978 they made 143 percent more. Likewise, while operatives in manufacturing in 1949 made 22 percent more than service workers, in 1978 they were making 111 percent more (see Table 7.9). Although the number of farm and nonfarm laborers has been reduced to a virtually insignificant proportion of the U.S. working class, the large numbers of both craftsworkers and service workers suggests that the income differentials between these groups and operatives will continue to act to undermine a broad class consciousness (especially between low-paid service workers and the rest of the working class).

A particularly nasty aspect of working class life is unemployment. In the working class to lose one's job raises the more or less immediate specter of losing one's house as well as one's car (because of the inability to make payments). Further, it often means being forced to move, perhaps to a different town or part of the country, severing lifelong ties, worrying about how to feed the family, and the disruption of one's entire work and leisure patterns. Unemployment (and the fear of unemployment) are, thus, major sources of worry in working class life (especially in times of economic recession and crisis).

Unemployment varies considerably by both occupation and economic sector. Unemployment disproportionately effects unskilled, semiskilled, and service labor, and is especially pronounced in agriculture, construction, and trade. On the other hand, professionals and managerial personnel, almost all of those in government employment as well as those in finance, insurance, and real estate are relatively free of the threat of unemployment (see Table 7.10). In the 1975-79 period operatives (nontransport) had an average unemployment rate of 10.3 percent, while laborers had a rate of 12.6 percent and service workers a rate of 8.0 percent. This contrasts sharply with the rate of 2.9 percent for professionals and 2.7 percent for managerial personnel.

THE WORKING CLASS AS A SOCIAL CLASS

The relationship of workers to the means of production shapes their whole social existence.* It tends to result in a common *economic* relationship growing into a common culture, consciousness, and participation in class institutions.

A corporation essentially decides whether to hire or fire (as well as allocate) workers on the same basis as it would build or abandon a plant. In both cases it is a matter of cost accounting and profit maximization, of how much money can be made from hiring or firing workers versus buying a new plant or equipment. On the books of a corporation labor power appears as the equivalent of any other input into the production process. The working class is, in general, treated as an object more or less equivalent to raw material, plant, or overhead.

Workers sell their labor time in order to secure the material means necessary to survive and attain a reasonable standard of living. Once sold, labor power is at the disposal of capitalists. Workers forfeit fundamental control over their work, over what they produce and how they produce it, in return for their wages. They are subject to the detailed commands and supervision of others throughout the workday.

Their domination during their labor time has a deep effect on workers. Most work (much of crafswork aside) is both inherently boring and often physically exhausting. More importantly, most labor is debasing and dignity denying as well. Constant supervision designed to secure maximum output leaves a stigma manifested in all of

---

*This section relies heavily on Hamilton 1972 and 1975, Sennett and Cobb 1972, and Shostak 1969.

TABLE 7.10: U.S. Unemployment Rates: 1975–79 Average by Occupation and Industry

Occupation	Unemployment Rate	Ratio to Average
Professionals	2.9%	0.41
Managerial	2.7	0.39
Sales	4.9	0.70
Clerical	5.7	0.81
Craftsworkers	6.0	0.86
Operatives	10.3	1.47
Transport operatives	6.7	0.96
Nonfarm Labor	12.6	1.80
Service workers	8.0	1.14
Total	7.0	1.00

Industry	Unemployment Rate	Ratio to Average
Agriculture	10.2%	1.46
Mining	4.3	0.61
Construction	13.4	1.91
Manufacturing	7.3	1.04
Transport	4.5	0.64
Trade	7.7	1.10
Finance, insurance	3.9	0.56
Service industries	6.4	0.91
Government	4.0	0.57
Total	7.0	1.00

Note: Data are for all in labor force.
Source: U.S. Department of Commerce 1981a, p. 410.

their relations. It tends to leave feelings of humiliation, inadequacy, and hurt (see Sennett and Cobb 1972).

Manual work, no matter how well performed, is generally stigmatized. The dirtier and harder the job, the worse the stigma. Workers are subtly taught that they do low-paid manual work because of lack of education, ambitions, or ability. At the core of the American myth is the idea that hard work produces upward mobility and success, and, therefore, those who do not make it must be inferior, i.e., it is their own fault, not that of the system, that they are on the bottom.

In spite of this pervasive ideology there is, nevertheless, a tendency for poorer people to blame either fate or the social structure for their poverty, and for high-income people to attribute their success to hard work (or other self-serving factors). In the mid-1960s a study found that of those with a family income of under $4,000 a year 25 percent gave "fatalist" and 28 percent "structuralist" explanations of poverty, while of those with a family income of $10,000 and above only 12 percent gave fatalist and only 16 percent structuralist explanations of poverty. Poverty, thus, tends to generate feelings of either demoralization and hopelessness or (to a lesser extent) radicalization, while success tends to be rationalized in terms of support for the system (Jeffries and Ransford 1980, p. 376).

Workers' feelings of inadequacy, hopelessness, and demoralization are reinforced by both treatment on the job and experience in school and with the mass media. The schools expect submissiveness from working class children. They are often assumed by the schools to be lazy, stupid, and so on. Working class education focuses on teaching respect for authority, respect for experts, hard work, and so on. The rebelliousness and juvenile delinquency of working class children must in good part be understood as a reaction against such expectations and emphases.

Working class consciousness, culture, institutions, and political behavior are in good part a reaction to humiliation experienced on the job, mediated by the structure of employment as well as by neighborhood and friendship patterns generated by relations of production. Working people strike back in a wide variety of ways in an attempt to establish their dignity. This often takes the form of soldiering or "putting one over" on the boss, i.e., convincing the boss that one is working as hard as possible (generating the maximum output) when, in fact, one is producing much less than is technically possible. It can be manifested in high rates of absenteeism, quit rates, sabotage of production, shoddy workmanship, wildcat strikes, use of drugs on the job, defiance of foremen, and so on. It can take the form of deflecting hostility generated on the job to other situations, such as identification with a powerful sports team, dominating women, and racist attitudes and behavior toward minority ethnic groups.

The attempt to reestablish one's dignity and feelings of selfworth is also manifested in the ethic of manhood, encompassing expertise at fishing, fixing cars, sporting statistics, and so forth as well as with women. To accumulate detailed expertise about sports, to be asked to settle a refined point about batting averages or racehorses, or to have many female friends is especially ego gratifying and compensatory for lack of respect on the job.

Working class leisure time tends to be a reaction against the boredom and humiliation of work. It is, in good part, oriented to escapism (especially for male workers to aggressive macho activities such as hunting, repairing powerful automobiles, watching adventure programs on television, or following superior sports teams). Spending a season identifying with a team that eventually wins a championship can become a validation of one's existence. Vicariously hitting a home run, breaking through the line, or winning a race confirms one's manhood, a manhood denied on the job. Identification with a sports hero (including fantasies about the sexual prowess of prominent athletes) as well as identification with rough and tough macho television characters offers compensation for the dignity-denying experience of daily life.

The attempt to establish dignity can be manifested in hostilities against certain groups of people. Hostility against those on welfare can reflect, on the one hand, contempt for people who have given up (or do not even try to win respect through work)—who do not suffer the on-the-job humiliations workers suffer in order to survive. On the other hand, it often reflects a secret *titillation* for those who are seen as trying to beat the system (a tempting titillation that must be emotionally guarded against). The attempt to establish dignity was manifested in hostility in the 1960s to campus radicals, who were seen as morally offensive for rebelling against the very life-style manual workers wanted their children to achieve. They are often either unable to realize a college education for their children because of the expense involved, or are able to attempt to realize it only by making the protracted sacrifice necessary to save enough to put one's children through school. Student militance represented a threat to the whole orientation of working class parents.

Working class people, especially once they realize that they will be spending the rest of their own lives in the factory, and will therefore "accomplish little" in their lives, typically come to focus their hopes and aspirations on their children achieving a better life. They, therefore, come to adopt a philosophy of sacrifice, sacrificing their own lives for the sake of their children. The essence of this ideology of sacrifice for the sake of children is the attempt to redeem what is often seen as the waste of one's own life (Sennett and Cobb 1972, chap. 2). Parents aspire to the jobs for their children that are *both* materially rewarding and inherently attractive. Working class parents do not want their children to suffer the same on-the-job humiliations that they have suffered. It is for this reason, as much as for material rewards, that they push them to achieve such respected and relatively creative careers as those of engineering, business management, and high school teaching. College education for children thus has a different meaning for working class parents than it does for the middle class.

While their relatively low income forces working class people to skimp on many necessities, it is common for them to spend considerable sums (usually financed by credit) to purchase a fancy car or other expensive high status consumer durables. Such behavior is, in good, part a compensation for the meaninglessness of work time and the humiliations that are suffered on the job. Consumption of a car, of a television, of a snowmobile, recreational vehicle, or a suburban house represents an assertion of one's worth as well as a compensation for the pain of earning money.

The working class and the middle class tend to see different symbols of success. While upper middle class people tend to stress a quality college education for their children, working class people tend to stress more home ownership. A study done in the 1960s found that 41 percent of poorer working class people as compared to only 8 percent of upper middle class people viewed home ownership as the primary mark of success (the corresponding figures for having a college education were 21 percent and 61 percent respectively). The relatively greater importance of home ownership for working class people reflects the importance of security and material achievement for this class (something that is pretty much taken for granted in the petty bourgeoisie; see Heller 1969, p. 298).

The importance of home ownership for the working class must be also understood in the context of class subordination. Domination all day long on the job gives workers a strong desire to have something they can control, something they can be in charge of, something they can fix up and have pride in. Home ownership and independence from landlords tends to be very important in the working class as an escape from humiliation and for the establishment of identity. Home ownership symbolizes dignity and accomplishments; it means being a *real* person.

A second aspect of the working class relation to capitalist production that has a considerable impact on working class culture, consciousness, institutions, and behavior is the relatively high degree of socialization on their labor process. They tend to work in large production units within which there is a high degree of division of labor *among* workers within the production process. Such working conditions tend to condition workers to the importance of mutual dependence, cooperation, and discipline since such workers are mutually interdependent on each other's coordinated performance in producing the final product. The work attitudes necessarily taught within the capitalist production process quite naturally spill over into the worker's all-around attitudes toward individualism and cooperation as well as discipline and responsibility. Although such habits and attitudes are structurally inculcated because of their profitability for capital, they tend to have contradictory results for capitalist institutions since the discipline and sense of mutual dependence taught in the capitalist labor process is generalized to a sense of disciplined class solidarity among workers (which tends to be manifested in unionism, job actions, strikes, political attitudes, and feelings toward political parties). The social psychology of cooperation that is structurally induced on the job tends to become manifested in collective bargaining and militant solidarity during strikes as well as in notions of the desirability of collective ownership and control of production (and support of disciplined political parties that support such goals). The feelings that results are gotten by working together rather than as individuals and that power is a result of cooperation are developed by the very process of capitalist production.

Not only do highly socialized labor processes tend to generate feelings of discipline, cooperation, and solidarity, rather than competitiveness, individualism, and irresponsibility, they also tend to give workers a feeling for their tremendous potential strength vis-à-vis capital. This is in contrast to individualized production, e.g., of artisans or home workers, which lends itself to feelings of isolation, weakness, and the inevitability of things (i.e., the impossibility of changing the "naturally ordained" order). Workers in the highly socialized production process of modern factories are able to see that workers like themselves are directly responsible for all aspects of the production process, from providing the raw materials to distribution of the final product. They, thus, have a tendency to feel that those who own the factory as well as the top managers seem to play no essential role in the production process other than ensuring that everything is run in the interest of profit maximization (seemingly often against the interests of the actual producers). Further, workers tend to develop the feelings that they collectively have all the necessary skills to run both their particular production process and the productive processes in general, i.e., the conditions of working class life tend to generate a socialist political consciousness among workers. The highly socialized conditions of labor in modern industrial enterprises thus demystify the class relations of production, including feelings or understandings that a worker's lot is not a product of luck, fate, individual qualities, hard work, and so forth, but rather a product of the economic structure within which the working class is located; and, further, that the working class, acting collectively, has the power to change it.

In contrast to the conditions of labor of most productive workers, those of most service, clerical, and sales workers do not tend to demystify or make transparent the nature of their relations of production. In these sectors it is not easily clear to the workers what the relationship is between their job activity and the wealth of managers (as it *is* where workers are producing concrete goods, the sale price of which workers can compare with their wage to understand the nature of exploitation). Further, the conditions of labor here tend to be much less socialized (less dependent on an advanced cooperative division of labor), and workers tend to be isolated from other workers and closer to management (thus the development of a distinctive working class consciousness and culture tends to be defused rather than facilitated). Thus, even though the conditions of many service workers, and often clerical and sales workers as well, may result in just as much if not more humiliation (as well as exploitation), workers in these sectors are less likely to develop attitudes of discipline, solidarity, and mutual dependence. Thus, they are less likely to form unions, engage in effective collective bargaining and militant strikes, or develop socialist political attitudes (or in a crisis follow revolutionary organizations).

Working class people disproportionately support Communist and Socialist Parties where they exist in any strength because they appear to offer working people an alternative to the exploitation and humiliations of working class life. Their programs and analyses promise the elimination or restriction of the wage labor system as well as of a class society that is divided into the wealthy who control the economy and state and the subordinate working poor who do the physical labor. Traditionally, socialists and communists have held up an alternative vision of a world in which the working people run the enterprises where they work, the economy as a whole, and the state. They promise the elimination or containment of the profit system where economic decisions are made on the basis of profit maximization, and its replacement by rational planning for human needs. Whether or not in the last analysis one judges the communist and socialist projects as realistic (which the present author *does*) is irrelevant to understanding why it is that working class people join such parties and otherwise give their political support to them. What is relevant is to understand the *meaning* that the Communist and Socialist programs have for people exploited and humiliated by capitalism.

In spite of the absence of a significant degree of socialist political consciousness in the U.S. working class in the post-World War II period, the evidence for the natural association of workers, especially industrial workers, with socialism is overwhelming. In every other advanced capitalist country *without exception* there is a large (if not virtually class hegemonic) working class party (or in some cases parties) that has in one degree or another a socialist (or socialistic) orientation—either as in Finland, France, Italy, Greece, Spain, Portugal, and Japan where this takes the form (at least in part) of a Communist Party; or in Scandinavia, the low countries, Austria, and West Germany where it takes the form of support for a Social Democratic Party, or in Great Britain, Ireland, Canada, Australia, and New Zealand where it takes the form of a very moderate, but still nominally socialistic, labor party. The differential working class support for such parties wherever they exist with any degree of strength is overwhelming. For example, in France in 1956, 49 percent of urban manual workers as compared to 1 percent of large business-men and executives supported the Communist Party. In Italy in 1958, 62 percent of urban manual workers as compared to 1 percent of large businessmen and executives supported either the Commun-ists or the leftist Socialists. In West Germany in 1967, 5 percent of professionals and 14 percent of businessmen as compared to 49 per-cent of urban manual workers supported the Social Democrats. In Great Britain in 1968, about 9 percent of large businessmen and executives versus 52 percent of urban manual workers supported the Labour Party. In Canada in 1965, 47 percent of urban manual workers supported the union-organized New Democratic Party as compared to 21 percent of professionals and businessmen (see Szymanski 1978, p. 29).

Although the conditions of working class life in the post–World War II period have not resulted in the reproduction or formation of large-scale socialist consciousness in the U.S. working class they, nevertheless, have consistently produced a relative equalitarianism and progressive orientation on class-related issues. For example, manual workers in the United States tend to be most supportive in comparison to middle class and capitalist class people toward the government spending more money on social welfare (especially on national health insurance). They also tend to be among the least supportive of big business (see Table 9.16). Further, they tend to be relatively more supportive than other classes of federally guaranteed jobs (Hamilton 1975, p. 55).

The high degree of manual working class identification with the Democratic Party must also be understood in these terms. Correctly or not the Democratic Party is perceived by most workers as "the party of the common man" and identified with the pro–working class measures of the New Deal (while the Republicans are seen as "the party of big business," and identified with the policies of Herbert Hoover). In 1968, 70 percent of manual workers outside of the South in contrast to 25 percent of independent professionals identified them-selves as "Democrats" (Hamilton 1975, p. 47).

The attitudes toward cooperation and discipline taught by the capitalist industrial process are also generalized to other aspects of workers' lives besides their class solidarity, manifested in unioniza-tion, strikes, and a tendency toward socialist politics and (in crisis situations) participation in revolutionary activities. These attitudes are also manifested in more generalized attitudes to "conformity" or toleration of idiosyncratic people, a sense of loyalty to friends and relatives as well as to sports teams (and in general a sense of teamwork, and fair play/trustworthiness within friendship networks). They tend to make close friends more rarely than do middle class people, but once formed, their friendships tend to last longer and be more supportive than do those of the middle class. In general, working class culture stresses discipline as well as mutual aid considerably more than does middle class culture, and, considerably less than middle class culture, individualism and competition (values that are induced in the middle class by the particular conditions of its relation to production).

Other aspects of the working classes' relation to production also affect the development of working class consciousness, culture, and behavior. Among the most important of these are the level of the wage, the physical qualities of the work process, the residence pattern induced by the necessity of working at a given location, and the possibilities of being fired (and hence unemployed, with all the trauma this entails, especially for a working class parent). Workers' wages are the principal determinant of their material consumption patterns, including the food they eat, the size and location of the house they rent or own, the type of vacations they take, and so forth, as well as a source of frustration in aspirations and strain in marriages when goods desired can not be bought.

The traditionally relatively low pay of workers combined with their legitimate fear of unemployment has tended to promote a greater concentration on the specifics and concretes of daily life (i.e., economic and practical day-to-day survival) than is the case at least in the more affluent and secure middle class. These structural facts also tend to give workers a shorter time frame in which to concretely plan their life (i.e., more of a "present" orientation) as well as often (but not always) a greater degree of pessimism and cynicism about the future. It should be noted, however, that in times of social crisis, the tendencies toward pessimism and cynicism can be radically transformed into considerable optimism and enthusiasm about the possibilities of qualitative change that can be brought about through unions and political action.

The physical nature of manual labor (which is often dirty and dangerous) tends to develop attitudes of ruggedness, emphasis on physical characteristics (especially strength), and a propensity for risk taking. In contrast, the requirements of both clerical and sales labor as well as of most middle class occupations induce polished social skills (which are quite often lacking in manual workers, who tend to be more direct, blunt, loud, and expressive).

Historically both the low wages of workers and the necessity to live within walking or trolly distance of work (together with the positive and negative social forces that tended to group people of similar ethnic identity together), produced class-homogeneous working class neighborhoods. People that worked under similar conditions, thus, tended to live together as well. Living in the same class-homogeneous neighborhoods had the important consequence of structuring friendship and leisure patterns. Neighborhood working class taverns and clubs developed. Acquaintance networks and long-term friendships were in good part formed within such neighborhoods. The local schools also tended to be class homogeneous, with the consequence that working class children found their friends and usually their marriage partners within the same working class neighborhood in which they grew up. The consequence of both living and working in a class homogeneous environment meant a strong tendency to develop and reinforce a distinctive working class culture and consciousness isolated from personal contact with the middle, and especially the capitalist, class (see Gans 1962).

With the development of the mass-produced inexpensive automobile after World War I, the physical constraints that forced workers to live grouped together within the industrial cities were considerably loosened. Individual commuting meant that workers from a given factory or industrial district could now live scattered over a much wider region. In the post–World War II period in the United States there was a mass movement out of the traditional inner city ethnic neighborhoods close to the places of work to the suburbs by the children of the "new immigrants" of the 1895–1914 period. Their old neighborhoods were taken over by the newer immigrants from the South and Latin America (who increasingly came to fill the low-paid "dirty work" occupations). Their wage level, however, put considerable constraints on the kind of house workers could afford (and consequently the kind of neighborhood they would move into). Blue-collar suburbs, typically consisting of inexpensively constructed nonelaborate single houses became the norm (see Berger 1960 and Gans 1967). Although now a given neighborhood contains relatively fewer people working in the same factory or industrial sector than before, it still tends to contain mostly people in similar class positions. Such neighborhoods, thus, continue to serve (although somewhat less than before) as the basis for the formation and reproduction of a distinct working class culture in their taverns, parks, schools, and so forth.

Because of the continuity in the working conditions of manual workers, the continuing on-the-job humiliations, the highly socialized conditions of labor and the maintenance of the traditional income differential with the middle class, the considerable increase in real pay that occurred (especially in the 1940s and 1950s) did not undermine the structural conditions for the reproduction of a distinctive social class based on those in a proletarian relation to the means of production.

What has appeared to some to be an "embourgeoisment" or undermining of a distinctive working class culture and the adoption of middle class values by the working class is, in fact, principally a manifestation of the merger of blue- and white-collar culture (which has been occurring as white-collar work becomes increasingly proletarianized), together with the natural development of working class social and cultural patterns in response to the changes in economic and social conditions over the course of the twentieth century. The old peasant-based ethnic values of the 1895–1914 generation of immigrants have been largely lost in the process of the formation of a homogeneous white native-born working class culture. The increase in absolute living standards that occurred through the middle of the 1960s significantly altered the material culture of class. And along with all classes, the working class has been influenced by the transformations in production and consumption as well as by the ideological and cultural developments that have occurred over the course of the twentieth century. Further, events have occurred that have effected the destruction of the secondary current of anticapitalist and socialist sentiment that was part of the U.S. working class from the 1870s through to the end of the 1940s, not the least of which was the efficient political repression of the 1947–56 period in the United States (the effectiveness of this repression would seem to have been a product of the rapidly rising living standards of workers in this period as well as the legitimation effect of the euphoria of winning World War II and the United States consequently becoming the hegemonic country on the earth). There has also been a tendency for attitudes and values to develop within the working class that have a surface similarity to middle class attitudes and values, but, in fact, have a different meaning for the working class. The modification of middle class values by very different social circumstances and opportunities has been called "working class value stretch." This phenomena is especially salient in education and housing, where apparently similar behavior (e.g., desire to send the children to college or to buy a house) has both a different meaning and a different result in the two classes. Working class culture has evolved over the course of the twentieth century (as has middle class culture to a somewhat lesser degree).* But the social and cultural practices of the two

---

*It should be noted that much of the "culture of poverty" characteristics of marginal and poor workers has been a continuation of the common European peasant traditions of fearfulness, suspicion, and apathy toward the state and major social

classes remain distinct because the life experiences out of which they grow remain qualitatively different.

Unions

In order to resist treatment as mere labor power, in order to exercise some say in how they are treated (the conditions of their labor as well as its remuneration), to mitigate exploitation and humiliation, working class people have long tended to form themselves into unions designed to deal collectively (and hence effectively), rather than individually, with capital. Originally unions were formed to express the interests of their working class members (in varying degrees) for increased wages, shorter hours, safer and more pleasant working conditions, and more benefits such as health plans, and so on; and an improved position for working class people in the society *as a whole*, e.g., social welfare benefits through pressing for legislation designed to improve the economic conditions of workers as well as (in varying degrees in different industries, times, and countries) pressing for worker control over both the economy and the state. While initially unions grew up in order to express the interests of the working class *against* capital, again in varying degrees in different places and times, unions have become integrated into capitalism. In the stable and affluent post–World War II period the class struggle in which they were initially formed has been largely channeled into forms that are not harmful to the profits of capital.

In 1930 in the United States labor union membership stood at 11.6 percent of all employees in nonagricultural establishments in the United States, in 1935 at 13.7 percent. In the last half of the 1930s

---

institutions. It has also been further shaped and reproduced by the humiliating and demoralizing experiences of marginal working class life in urban America. Although, to a degree, the difference in values between the marginal and the mainstream working class stems from learning different values and attitudes, in good part it is a result of learning the same attitudes and values but being exposed to a very different reality as the mainstream. It, thus, represents pragmatic and realistic adjustment to the stresses and deprivations of lower class life. Lower class culture is a response to the conditions of poverty, an adaptation and reaction of the poor to their marginal position, an effort to cope with or explain feelings of hopelessness and despair. It arises from the realization of the improbability of achieving success in terms of prevailing values and goals. The peculiar institutions and attitudes of marginal working class life (such as juvenile gangs, gambling, fighting, and so on) are attempts to meet needs or express feelings that otherwise are not realized. They tend to be ways to maintain a modicum of dignity and to express frustrations against a system in which they are largely left out (see Ferman, Kornbluh, and Haber 1971, chap. 5; Harris 1971, chap. 20; Roach, Gross, and Gursslin 1969, p. 202).

and during World War II, union membership rapidly expanded, at first in response to the deepening dissatisfaction with the effect of the protracted Great Depression on workers (in this period the new Congress of Industrial Organizations movement was a true mass movement of working people), and then in response to government encouragement and the labor shortage of World War II. By 1939, 28.6 percent of nonagricultural employees were unionized and by 1946, 34.5 percent. Declining slightly in the immediate postwar years union membership stayed fairly constant at around 33 percent of the non-agricultural labor force until the end of the 1950s. Over the course of the next decades it declined from 31.4 percent in 1960 to 27.5 percent in 1970 and then to 23.6 percent in 1978 (see U.S. Department of Labor 1971, p. 339; U.S. Department of Commerce 1981a, p. 429).

The low union membership in the United States as compared to most other advanced capitalist countries is undoubtedly caused by the same factors that have resulted in a low level of working class socialist consciousness in the United States: first, the ethnic hetero-geneity of the working class, manifested in the growth of ethnic consciousness and mutual antagonism based on ethnicity; and second, the higher living standards experienced by the American working class through the mid-1970s than existed in Europe (the comparison for most of the industrial working class whose roots were there).

The decline in the membership of organized labor has been caused by the sectoral shift in the U.S. occupational structure from production workers in mining and manufacturing (traditionally highly organized) toward the services and finance (traditionally with a very low level of organization) as well as by the rapid entry of women into the labor force (who have historically tended to be somewhat less responsive to unionization than men). It does *not* reflect a decline of union membership among production workers (U.S. Department of Commerce 1981a, pp. 413, 430). The decline in union membership then must be attributed to the inability/unwillingness of the union movement to expand into the growing economic sectors and occupa-tions (the major exception to this general inability to expand has been in the public sector). The decline of unionism was a result in part of the less socialized conditions of labor in most rapidly expand-ing economic sectors and occupations, of the lack of effort and enthu-siasm on the part of organized labor, and of the relative prosperity and lack of crisis of the 1960s and 1970s (and the relative working class conservatism this bred).

Unions have been quite effective in improving the wages, job security, and fringe benefits of their members. Most union contracts have seniority clauses that make it difficult to fire a worker (a matter of great importance given the traditionally greater disruptive effect of unemployment on a worker's life). Unions have been especially effective in securing pension and health plans as well as paid vacations and other such supplemental benefits. A study done in 1974 in the United States found that unionized establishments in the manufacturing sector had 2.2 times a greater value of fringe benefits than nonunion establishments (Mitchell 1980, p. 82). This same study found that straight wages were 1.3 times higher in such establishments as well. Numerous other studies of the effect of unionization, comparing both firms within a given industrial sector and different sectors contrasted by their degree of unionization have found that unionization has a substantial effect on increasing wages even when all other relevant factors that influence wage levels are controlled for (e.g., sex composition, ethnic composition, capital intensity, degree of monopolization, and so on). Most such studies conclude that unionization results in, on average, a 20 to 40 percent higher level of wages than would otherwise be the case (Mitchell 1980, chap. 3). The differential is even higher when the effects of fringe benefits are considered. It should be noted that the effects of unionization within a given sector within a given region or city are often masked by the practice of a nonunion firm paying union wages (won by workers in a competing firm) in order to prevent the unionization of their employees.

Unions are generally more effective in preventing wage reductions than they are in securing wage increases above the rate of inflation. Thus, their greatest effect on workers' incomes has tended to be in times of recession and depression rather than in times of high prosperity, when the shortage of labor forces up the wages of both unionized *and* nonunionized workers (see Mitchell 1980, chap. 4).

For the most part unions have been most successful in improving the economic conditions of workers in capital-intensive, monopoly-sector industries. In this sector high and increasing wages and fringe benefits can for the most part be passed on to those purchasing the products of such enterprises. Since a handful of corporations dominate output, they can implicitly collude to raise prices at least enough to cover their increased labor costs, e.g., when the United Automobile Workers win a 10 percent pay increase, all the major U.S. automobile companies raise the prices of their cars by an amount at least sufficient to cover their increased wage bill. It should be noted that while the existence of unions in this sector allows such workers to make significantly more than the average wage, workers and others in the nonmonopoly sector who must purchase the goods of the monopoly sector have their real income reduced by this process. Thus, unions have relatively little effect in actually redistributing income from the monopoly capitalist class to the working class. In the last analysis their effect would seem to be primarily to transfer income from competitive sector workers and small business people to the organized working class in the monopoly sector.

In some relatively competitive sectors (e.g., construction, dock work, mining, apparel) unionization has been effective in increasing both job security and wages because of the effect that widespread unionization in these sectors has had on improving the profitability of capital. In industries like construction and garments, which are highly competitive and, thus, subject to wild fluctuations in wages, employment, and demand (and thus the growth and bankruptcy of firms) unionism has come to stabilize conditions by establishing standards of labor that are acceptable to most employers, thus equalizing wage costs while ensuring a regular and nondisruptive labor source. Unionization has, thus, in good part, eliminated some of the worst aspects of competition for the capitalists while in fact, at least in construction, mining, and on the docks, achieving pay and benefit levels comparable to that of workers in the monopoly sector.

Although they have improved the economic conditions of U.S. workers in many ways, most contemporary U.S. unions have become virtual extensions of the labor relations departments of the corporations through the institutionalization of collective bargaining. Through a process of negotiations between the unions and management under the guidance of the state, labor contracts are signed for a period of a few years that typically stipulate in great detail what the workers must do in return for their wages and fringe benefits. In the U.S. union officials become *legally* responsible upon signing a labor contract for seeing that the workers live up to the terms of the contract, i.e., workers come to have two sets of "managers" guaranteeing their compliance with industrial discipline. Wildcat or non-official strikes are repressed by union officials because they are violations of contract promises not to strike. Grievances against management about working conditions have become bureaucratized, with workers "filing grievances" with union officials who then take them to management often to eventually only "trade them off" for other concessions. Unions almost never challenge management prerogatives in running production, or in personnel allocation (other than in guaranteeing seniority and other forms of job security). Long-term labor contracts further serve the corporations in making wage costs a known and stable factor as well as in ensuring against unanticipated strikes or other disruptions to production. The bureaucratized collective bargaining process functions to channel the broad range of (potentially disruptive) rank and file grievances and compliants into formalized demands mostly for increased wages and benefits that the corporations *can* meet without threatening their control over production or profits.

Management not only tolerates but in most basic industries in the post-World War II period (as part of the managerial strategy of bureaucratic control of the labor process) actually supports a degree of union autonomy and militance. In order to maintain essential labor peace and worker commitment to the rules that govern the labor process (and that are often embodied in the periodic collective bargaining agreements unions sign with management), it is essential that unions be regarded by workers as a legitimate expression of their interest. Too close an identification of the union and its leaders with management and the companies can produce a delegitimation of both the union and the contracts it signs, and thus of the whole strategy of bureaucratic control (sweetheart contracts and company unions, techniques popular in the pre-World War II period, generally caused more problems for business than they solved) (see Burawoy, 1979, Chap. 7).

Union leaders in the post-World War II period have typically become far removed from the shop floor. They mostly receive very high salaries comparable with those of management rather than with the wages of the workers they represent. Their life-style, thus, tends to approach that of management as they lose touch with the problems of rank and file workers. In many ways they objectively become executives, somewhat like the labor contractors of old. Their role has been to ensure a certain guaranteed result for the capitalists in exchange for a set wage (of which they can be considered to get a percentage). Their transformed class character (into essentially petty-bourgeois managers from working class spokespeople) is reflected in the fact that when they fail to get reelected to office they mostly take up managerial or administrative positions with the corporations or state and rarely ever return to the shop floor from which they came. However, to stay in their positions of privilege and power they must perform a function for their working class membership. They must secure at least a modicum of material benefits and protections for the workers or they jeopardize their own position. Thus, even the most bureaucratized and corrupt of unions (even while they are operating to defuse class conflict and not pressing for all that could be obtained) normally still produce benefits for their members.

The bureaucratization of unions is facilitated by workers taking them for granted (as well as by relative affluence). In periods of prosperity and stability, such as the post-World War II period, participation in unions tends to decline. With the exception of a few craft unions with small locals such as the printers, few union members regularly attend meetings. In the large locals of the major industrial unions, perhaps one or two percent of the membership shows up for anything other than a strike vote or a vote on a dues increase. Only a small percentage of members normally even bothers to vote in most union elections.

Even strikes have come to serve a number of functions for big business. Big strikes with national publicity act to create acceptability in the public for price increases, which when following a strike can be blamed on the workers rather than on the corporations (even when they are considerably greater than what would be necessary to merely pay the increased wages granted after a strike). Periodic strikes, especially when the corporations have large inventories that they need to dispose of anyway, or when they can easily meet demand from other (perhaps overseas) sources, can also serve capital by letting workers "blow off steam." They can serve as a safety valve that gives workers the feelings they have "done something." Strikes allow workers to express their hostility against their company. After venting their hostility and experiencing a few weeks or months of strike benefits and the resultant economic difficulties, they come to appreciate the company once again.

Which aspect of unions is predominant at any place, industry, or time (i.e., integration into or opposition to the dominant economic order) is a product of the level of crisis in a society, the conditions in an industry, the state of politicized class struggle in a country as a whole, the ability of the corporations and state to co-opt militance, and the ability of the corporations to grant increased wages and more pleasant conditions. Many of these determining factors are complex. For example, economic depression with its massive unemployment, on the one hand weakens unions because of the greater difficulty of recruiting members or winning a strike (due to the large number of unemployed willing to work under worse conditions than the employed will tolerate, union members or strikers can easily be fired and replaced). Depression especially undermines "business unionism," which is oriented to short-term defense of economic interests. On the other hand, "social unionism," concerned about broader social change that is more militant and involves rank and file members, tends to grow after a number of years of bad economic conditions because of the accumulated rage of workers. For example, in the post-1929 Depression unions at first lost members, while strikes became rare. Beginning in 1934, however, a wave of militant strikes occurred, and unions, especially those associated with the more radical social unionism of the Congress of Industrial Organizations, snowballed. We might expect that the effects of a future major economic downturn, whether manifested in economic stagnation, and hence the reduced ability of corporations to grant wage increases (thus, to defuse other grievances with the system) or in massive unemployment, would eventually be manifested in a rebirth of militant class struggle oriented social unionism comparable to that of the late 1930s.

Unions have two aspects. Which is dominant is a product of the social conditions in which they operate, not the will of union leaders. Union leaders who keep their positions must produce the policies structured by the situation in which they find themselves, lose their positions, or have their rank and file members desert their union for another. In times of radical working class ferment, conservative bureaucrats, thus, either change, are fired, or are deserted as new unions form. Likewise, in times of prosperity and stability, radical leaders are either co-opted, gradually becoming conservative union bureaucrats acting just like the rest (the most common course), lose their position, or are deserted by the rank and file, who now feel more comfortable with more conservative, less socially oriented policies (e.g., the expulsion of Communist leaders from some CIO unions in the 1940 to 1949 period and the decimation of radical unions like the United Electrical Workers after 1949) (see Kolko 1976, chap. 5; and Aronowitz 1973, chap. 4).

But their membership is still working class. Unions have formal democratic procedures for selecting their leadership, if not for making basic decisions. Their self-proclaimed goal is to advance the interests of workers. The potential is there for class struggle to once again emerge under conditions of crisis or a pushing back of past achievements that have so improved working class life.

CONCLUSION

The U.S. working class has long remained fairly constant at about 70 percent of the employed population. Within the working class, manual workers are as important as ever. Conditions for nonindustrial workers, especially those in clerical and to a lesser degree service and sales, are becoming more proletarianized. Craft work has in part been deskilled and made more like industrial labor. Meanwhile, unskilled purely manual labor has been pretty much mechanized. More and more the typical condition for almost all working people is to operate machines that require relatively little skill and perform only part of the total labor process. The general conditions of labor within the working class are becoming increasingly homogenized as the varied skills, knowledge, and abilities of workers are reduced to the common denominator of simple labor power disposable at will by capital.

Small independent family farmers have in good part been pushed off the land and most forced to enter the urban working class. Likewise, many small independent family businesses have been driven bankrupt with their owners also forced into the working class. Domestic labor with its highly isolated and individualized relations of production has been almost totally eliminated. Sharecropping and other highly labor-intensive modes of rural labor have been largely eliminated by the introduction of industrial techniques based on the operation of machinery in large, often corporate units. All forms of labor are becoming more socialized.

Reflecting the homogenization of the working class relations of production and role in the production process is the increasing homogeneity of working class culture and life-styles. The traditional ethnic and religious differences inherited from the European peasantry or the U.S. South have been undermined and a common class culture is now largely shared by most native-born white workers regardless of country of European origin, or whether or not one's parents were from the South. It should, however, be stressed that the new immigrants from Latin America especially continue to maintain a separate life-style, language, and culture that sharply differentiates them from the rest of the working class.

The declining internal (economic and social) differences within the bulk of the U.S. working class make the contrast with the capitalist class even greater than before. Given the continuing realities of working class life this suggests the growing possibility of the development of class consciousness in the U.S. working class and, consequently, the potential of increasing hostility to the capitalist system (which is especially likely to develop in a time of crisis).

8

The Reproduction of Class Position

There is a high degree of continuity in class position throughout one's lifetime as well as from generation to generation. People who begin life in the working class or in the capitalist class are especially likely to finish their lives in the same class. Similarly, one is very likely to be in the same class position as one's parents. Working class children generally become workers, capitalist class children generally become capitalists (the richer a capitalist is, the more certain this outcome), and middle class children are most likely to become middle class. The two principal mechanisms for the intergenerational transmission of class position are the inheritance of property and the ability of those with middle class (and of course capitalist class) position to secure a quality college education for their children.

SOCIAL MOBILITY

There are two types of social mobility: intragenerational mobility, or the movement between classes that takes place during the lifetime of a person; and intergenerational mobility, the movement between classes that takes place from one generation to the next in the same family. Mobility can be upward, e.g., from the working class or poor rural groups to the middle class or capitalist class *or* downward, e.g., from the capitalist class or middle class to the working class. Studies of mobility have tended to focus on movement from the working class or rural poor to the middle class, and to a lesser extent on movement from either the working class or middle class to the capitalist class.

Change in rates of *upward* mobility over time and variations by regions or countries is principally a result of the following structural factors: first, changes in the relative number of middle class or upper class positions; second, a relative change in the fertility of middle and upper class families in relation to the lower classes; third, a change in the relative number of directly inheritable middle and upper class positions, namely in the number of privately owned businesses and landed properties; fourth, a change in legal or social restrictions on the lower classes entering middle class and upper class positions; and fifth, changes in educational opportunities for lower class children (e.g., free education, scholarships, geographical proximity of good schools).

There are generally higher rates of upward mobility in cities than in rural areas and small towns because: first, there are a higher proportion of managerial and professional jobs in urban areas; second, cities generally grow more rapidly than other areas; third, the birth rate of all urban classes is significantly less than that of rural groups; fourth, cities generally have less rigid status systems and lesser discrimination against lower class groups than do rural areas because of their industrial economic base; and, fifth, there are generally better educational facilities in cities.

Parental property is the chief determinant of a child's future class position in the capitalist class. If a father owns millions, it will be passed on to his children, and along with it membership in the capitalist class, totally independent of quality or quantity of a child's education. For the shrinking portion of the middle classes (small farmers and small businessmen) who still own their own property, and for the capitalist class, property continues to be as important as ever, as virtually the only criterion by which class position is passed on. The pattern remains that the family farm or business is passed on from father to son, and with it middle class position, this independent of the educational attainments, or lack thereof, of the son.

After parental property, educational attainment is the principal determinant of the reproduction of class position. As property ownership becomes less important as the economic basis of the middle class, educational attainment is becoming an even more important determinant of the job patterns of working class and middle class youth, especially in the professional and managerial strata of the new middle class.

Traditionally, a route of upward mobility into the middle class for some working class people was to somehow accumulate enough wealth to open a small business (this route is far more famous than actual). Likewise, a route of upward mobility for the middle class businessman was to be successful enough in business to gradually grow into a full-scale capitalist (this process too has been increasingly rare). With the increasing monopolization of business, and consequent decline of small business, more and more of the upward mobility that occurs takes place through the educational system. Either lower class children attain an education suitable for higher class positions, or middle class children attain a quality education, allowing them to stay in the position of their parents. Mobility from the middle class to the capitalist class now occurs mostly through the intragenerational career mobility of successful managers who are able to use their positions to accumulate wealth, and thus transmit positions to their children (both by passing on wealth and by providing a superior education beginning in the right prep schools).

In the United States in 1962, 55 percent of the sons of professional-managerial fathers were themselves in middle class positions, while only 24 percent had blue-collar jobs. On the other hand, only 22 percent of the sons of blue-collar workers were in middle class positions (6 percent as proprietors), while 53 percent remained in blue-collar jobs. Sixty-three percent of the sons of self-employed professionals were in middle class positions as well as 53 percent of the sons of managers and 52 percent of the sons of proprietors (16 percent as proprietors). In contrast, 21 percent of the sons of manufacturing operatives and 15 percent of the sons of manufacturing laborers (3 percent as proprietors) were in middle class positions (Blau and Duncan 1967, pp. 28, 496). The son of a self-employed professional has about a 4.3 times greater chance of becoming middle class than does an unskilled working class son.

Today most of this differential is caused by factors that operate through differences in class-based educational opportunity and differential motivation and discrimination in educational institutions rather than through barriers put on working class children's mobility by middle class proprietors passing most available middle class positions on to their children through inheritance.

Most movement out of *manual* (blue-collar) jobs is not to the middle class, but to relatively low status clerical and sales and "semiprofessional" (white-collar) jobs that often pay less than do skilled working class or manual jobs with a good union, jobs in which the worker has little or no more control over his/her labor than a factory worker, but jobs that are often socially defined as more prestigious and are, in addition, usually less exhausting or degrading. In any event, such movement from blue-collar to white-collar occupations can *not* be considered to be upward mobility between classes.

Some people who start life in manual working class jobs end up in middle class positions. In 1962, 13 percent of those who had started out as laborers in manufacturing made it into the middle class (10 percent as professionals or managers and 3 percent as proprietors). Further, 19 percent of those who had started out as semiskilled factory workers or operatives made it into the middle class (6 percent as proprietors and 12 percent as professionals or managers). Of skilled workers in manufacturing, 30 percent made it into the middle class (12 percent as proprietors and 17 percent as professionals or managers). Thus we see that the higher the level of one's original working class job, the greater the likelihood of making it into the middle class (by a factor of 2.3). The differential is particularly high in the relative probability of making it as a small businessman, here the differential between those who begin as unskilled and those who begin as skilled workers was 4.2 times (Blau and Duncan 1967, p. 31).

While the actual chances of upward intragenerational mobility out of the blue-collar working class are rather slim, the hope, and for the young workers, the expectation, of making it out of "the class" tends to be high. A study by Chinoy (1955) showed that most workers in their twenties and early thirties define their factory jobs as temporary. These young workers assume that they will eventually either succeed at a small business or in some cases make it as white-collar employees. Almost no young workers think they will be in the working class at the age of 60 (although almost all of them will be). Virtually all think that eventually they will succeed at a small business or go back to school and become some kind of professional (or at minimum at least get into a highly skilled trade or become a foreman). The longer workers stay in a plant and the older they get, the less they hold out a serious hope of making it out of the working class, and the more likely they are to displace their desires for upward mobility to their sons, who they hope will make it into the middle class through a college education.

Although very few working class people are ever able to make it out of the working class by saving money and opening their own business, many try. Approximately 25 percent of manual workers in the United States have at one point or another in their lives been in business for themselves, and about 40 percent, at one point or another, have at least attempted to set up a business (Lipset and Bendix 1959, p. 179).

The Chinoy study (1955, p. 82) found that approximately three-fourths of automobile workers had at one point or another in their work lives thought about getting out of the factory and setting up a business of their own. However, of those workers interviewed less than one-third (mostly younger workers) stated that they realistically expected to make it out of the factory (p. 87). Of the workers who stated that they definitely thought they would be able to leave the factory, less than half had actually taken any concrete steps to begin the process of setting up their own business (p. 87). The ideal of setting up an independent business is generally regarded by workers as an escape from the factory, rather than as an attempt to make significantly more money. The hope of becoming an independent businessman, of becoming "upwardly mobile" is mostly a stabilizing (conservatizing) myth, rather that a reflection of reality, that acts as a safety valve for releasing the accumulated discontent of workers. The vast majority of attempts to set up small businesses fail, usually within a few years of their establishment (with their proprietors returning to working class jobs). It is of interest to note that between 1900 and 1940 16 million new businesses were set up in the United States while there were 14 million business failures (Lipset and Bendix 1959, p. 102).

The average rate of mobility from unskilled manual fathers to nonmanual (white collar working class plus business and the professions and semiprofessions) in five major studies done in the years between 1900 and World War I was 20 percent. This compares to 23 percent for four major studies done from 1945 until the mid 1950s (Thernstrom 1969, p. 218). Thus, the balance of these studies (both national and regional) show very little difference in mobility rates. However, studies of Indianapolis *white males* at the three time periods of 1910, 1940, and 1967 show an increase in mobility from manual to professional-business jobs over these periods. While in 1910 only 6.3 percent of semiskilled or unskilled white fathers had professional or business sons, this increased to 8.7 percent in 1940 and 15.8 percent in 1967. Meanwhile, the percentage of manual sons of semiskilled and unskilled manual fathers decreased slightly from 80.6 percent in 1910 to 74.7 percent in 1940 and 75.4 percent in 1967 (see Table 8.1).

On the other hand, the Indianapolis studies show a hardening of class lines in the professional and business class. While in 1910 only 33 percent of the sons of white professionals or businessmen were themselves in this category, by 1967 55 percent were. Conversely, while in 1910 40 percent of this class's sons became manual workers, by 1967 only 29 percent did. Most of this hardening of position occurred from 1940 to 1967.

It should also be noted that these Indianapolis studies are based only on white men, i.e., they exclude both blacks and women, two groups that have moved into the Indianapolis labor force in great numbers over the twentieth century (especially since 1940). Both groups, especially blacks, have moved into manual level jobs, displacing the sons of white workers who, given expanding higher level job opportunities (which expansion of the labor force allows), find it

TABLE 8.1: Occupations of Indianapolis White Males by Father's Occupation: 1910, 1940, and 1967

| Occupation of Respondent's father | Year | Occupation of Respondent (as Percentages of Row Totals) | | | |
		Professional or Business	Clerical or Sales	Skilled Manual	Semiskilled or Unskilled
Professional or business	1967	54.9	16.3	7.1	21.7
	1940	33.0	29.1	15.2	22.6
	1910	33.1	26.7	20.4	19.8
Skilled manual	1967	22.4	10.7	41.2	25.8
	1940	10.5	19.2	32.4	37.9
	1910	7.6	15.3	49.0	28.1
Semiskilled or unskilled	1967	15.8	8.8	39.7	35.7
	1940	8.7	16.7	17.8	56.9
	1910	6.3	13.1	29.2	51.4

Source: Coxon and Jones 1975, p. 120.

easier to move into professional or managerial positions. A true test of changes in mobility rates over time would have to control for this factor, either by including blacks or by excluding the functional equivalent of blacks in the earlier time period (Slavs and southern Europeans). When this is done, it is most unlikely that a case could be made for any increase in upward mobility over time. In fact, all things considered, the weight of the Indianapolis evidence is that there has been a slight hardening of class lines.

That there has been something of a hardening of class lines in the United States in the last generation is supported by sample survey data. While in 1952 52 percent of young workers (up to age 24) had working class fathers (and 24 percent farmer and 20 percent middle class fathers), in 1964 63 percent had working class fathers (and 17 percent farmer and 8 percent middle class fathers). (Hamilton 1972, p. 310). The manual working class is increasingly recruited from its own ranks. This is apparently, at least in part, a result of the source of new domestic recruits from the farms drying up (as the farm population dwindles), and the upper middle class's consolidation of its position (by ensuring the best education for its children). Mobility from the manual working class to the middle class in the United States has been declining over the years.

Mobility from the working class to the capitalist class has always been and continues to be miniscule, while mobility from the middle class to the upper class is rather small and declining over time. Studies of U.S. capitalists and top managers done by generation show that for those born between 1891 and 1920, 74 percent were from upper class families and only 3 percent from manual families. The percentage of top business people recruited from the middle class decreased somewhat from the period of the last part of the nineteenth century to the twentieth century, while the percentage from the working class was consistently tiny (see Table 8.2).

Studies of the social origins of the richest individuals (capitalists) shows that an ever increasing percentage of them come from upper class families: 82 percent in 1970 as compared to 39 percent in 1900. While in 1900, 39 percent came from lower class background, by 1970 only 4 percent did (see Table 8.3).*

TABLE 8.2: Percentage Distribution of the American Business Elite Born in Specified Years, by Father's Occupation

Father's Occupation	Year of Birth				
	1771–1800	1801–30	1831–60	1861–90	1891–1930
Businessmen	40	52	66	70	69
Gentry farmers	25	11	3	3	5
Subtotal	65	63	69	73	74
Master craftsmen and small entrepreneurs	9	4	3	1	—*
Professions	3	12	11	12	11
Government officials	4	7	3	3	3
White-collar workers (includes foremen)	7	2	2	3	6
Subtotal	23	25	19	19	20
Farmers	12	11	10	6	4
Manual workers	—	2	1	2	3
Subtotal	12	13	11	8	7
Total	100	100	100	100	100

*Data not available.
Source: Lipset and Bendix 1959, p. 122.

---

*In 1962, 34 percent of individuals with $500,000 or more in wealth had inherited a substantial proportion of it (in contrast to about 15 percent of those with a net worth of between $100,000 and $500,000). The higher one's net worth the greater the probability of having inherited a substantial part of it (Beeghley 1978, p. 222).

TABLE 8.3: Social Origins of the Superrich, 1900–70

Social Origin	1900	1925	1950	1970
Upper class	39%	56%	68%	82%
Middle class	20	30	20	10
Lower class	39	12	9	4
Not classified	2	2	3	4

Source: Dye 1976, p. 180.

Studies of the class origins of corporate executives (as distinct from the very wealthy) between 1900 and 1950 show a slight decrease (from 70 percent to 62 percent) from upper class backgrounds, a slight increase (from 4 percent to 8 percent) in those from working class backgrounds, and a slight increase (from 26 percent to 31 percent) in those from middle class backgrounds (Rothman 1978, p. 221). This reflects the increasing stress on ability rather than family as the qualification of the top hired executives. What is most striking about these figures is not this slight change, but rather the fact that almost two-thirds of top corporate executives are still recruited from the capitalist class and petty-bourgeois proprietors rather than from the children of professionals and lower level managers.

The rate of "upward" mobility from manual to nonmanual positions in the United States is little different from that of the rest of advanced capitalist countries. The U.S. rate of approximately 29 percent compares to 30 percent for France, 31 percent for Belgium, 24 percent for Japan, 24 percent for Australia, 25 percent for Great Britain, 26 percent for Sweden, 20 percent for West Germany, 24 percent for Denmark, 23 percent for Norway, and 20 percent for the Netherlands (see Table 8.4).

On the other hand, the rate of *downward* mobility from nonmanual to manual of the United States is among the lowest in the world. Here the U.S. rate of about 21 percent compares to 24 percent for France, 30 percent for Japan, 28 percent for Sweden, 29 percent for West Germany, 29 percent for Norway, 42 percent for Great Britain, and 37 percent for Denmark (see Miller 1969, p. 329). This again suggests a hardening of class boundaries in the United States, where middle class people have just about the best guarantee in the world of passing on their middle class position to their children.

Although the ideology of the United States as the land of opportunity, the "Great American Myth," has undoubtedly played a role in hindering the development of a socialist consciousness in the United States, there is in fact no basis for the idea that the United States is

TABLE 8.4: Rates of Intergenerational Mobility

Country	Percentage of Children of Parents In Nonmanual Occupations
Australia (Melbourne)	24.1%
Belgium (Mont-Saint-Guibert)	30.9
Denmark	24.1
Finland	11.0
France I*	30.1
France II*	29.6
Great Britian	24.8
Italy	8.5
Japan	23.7
Netherlands	19.6
Norway	23.2
Sweden	25.5
USA I*	28.8
USA II*	28.7
West Germany	20.0

*Roman numerals indicate different studies of the same country.
Source: Miller 1969, p. 327.

qualitatively different than Europe in the possibilities of working class children "making it" into the middle classes. In fact, U.S. middle class parents are better able than the middle classes almost anywhere else in the world to *preserve* their class privileges for their children, hardly what we would expect in a society where every individual tended to find his or her own level on the basis of ability and accomplishments.

The lack of a significant difference between the rates of upward mobility in the United States and the rest of the capitalist world appears to have been the case since at least the years of the great pre-World War I migrations from eastern and central Europe to U.S. industrial areas. For example, the rate of mobility from manual to nonmanual occupations in Indianapolis in 1910 was 21 percent while that in Rome in 1908 was 22 percent (Lipset and Bendix 1959, p. 37). Theories that suggest there was more opportunity for the poor in the United States than in Europe during the period of rapid industrial growth between the Civil War and the Great Depression of the 1930s are without empirical foundation. While drawing an image of a rapidly expanding industrial society open to merit, they forget that western and central Europe were industrializing at more or less the same rate at the same time and thus also drawing in a large population from the eastern and southern parts of the continent as well as from the rural sections of their own countries. Similar capitalist processes produce similar results. The process of capitalist industrialization produces a much higher rate of upward mobility than existed in preindustrial capitalist societies, and thus any variations among the advanced capitalist countries are largely attributable to differences in their rate of economic growth as well as differentials in class fertility, the relative size of the independent petty bourgeoisie, and state spending for education.

Studies of the movement of working class and of middle class people into the upper class show very different results depending on the operational definition of "upper class" used. Table 8.5 summarizes many of the major international studies of upward mobility, grouping them according to the size of the "upper class" or elite used in the operational definition. Here we see that 3.4 percent of the children of manual parents made it into the U.S. "elite" while 9.5 percent of the children of middle class parents did so (operationally defining the elite as about 7 percent of the population). This compares with about 2.5 percent and 11.5 percent respectively for France, 2.2 percent and 8.6 percent respectively for Great Britain, 3.9 percent and 8.3 percent respectively for Japan, 3.5 percent and 18.1 percent for Sweden, and 1.7 percent and 7.5 percent for Italy. Thus the rate of mobility of either working class or of middle class into the capitalist class and upper middle class is close to the average for all capitalist countries, although the U.S. rate of mobility from the working class, miniscule as it is, is a little higher than the average.

EDUCATION AND THE INTERGENERATIONAL TRANSMISSION OF CLASS POSITION

After the inheritance of significant amounts of property and wealth, differential educational advantage is the main mechanism by which class position is passed on from generation to generation. With the decline of the traditional petty bourgeoisie and the rise of the new middle class of professionals and managers, access to quality higher education and class-transmitted motivation to do well have become the primary means by which the middle class assures its children of middle class status (and in the process blocks upward mobility from the working class).

Education varies considerably by class position. Children of middle class and upper class families get a far higher quality education than do children of the working class (especially its poorest and minority segments). On the one hand, because of the geographic concentration of the different classes, middle and upper middle class children enjoy the best in *public* schools (high quality education with low student to teacher ratios funded by taxes on expensive property),

TABLE 8.5: Intergenerational Movement into the Upper Class from Various Other Classes

Size of Elite	Middle Class	Working Class	Manual Class	Independent Farmer	Farm Worker
2.5% to 4.6%	%	%	%	%	%
Denmark	4.6	—[a]	1.1	—	—
Netherlands	2.6	—	1.2	—	—
West Germany	8.3	1.6	1.5	2.1	0.6
6% to 8.5%					
France I[b]	12.3	4.2	3.5	1.9	2.0
France II[b]	10.5	2.0	1.6	1.7	0.4
Great Britain	8.6	—	2.2	—	—
Italy	7.5	—	1.7	—	—
Japan	8.3	—	3.9	—	—
Sweden	18.1	4.4	3.5	2.6	1.0
US	9.5	—	3.4	—	—

[a]Data not available.
[a]Roman numerals indicate different studies of the same country.
Note: These figures represent the percentage of the children of each class that make it into the "elite."
Source: Miller 1969, p. 334.

while children in poor neighborhoods attend schools funded at a much lower level and thus have higher student to teacher ratios, far less supplemental equipment, and generally worse teachers because of the low value of property that serves as the tax base. On the other hand, middle and upper middle class children can afford to send their children to quality *private* schools, especially when, because they live in urban areas, the public schools are not very good, while working class people have no choice but to send their children to low-quality public schools.

Moreover, within the school system students are systematically tracked into college, vocational, business, and other preparatory programs, with the children who are judged to show the most promise, or who have the pushiest parents, placed in the upper college-bound tracks (which have the best teachers and best all-around environment for success). Working class children, on the other hand, especially those from the poorer minority groups, are channeled into the lower vocational or business tracks designed to train them for working class jobs as well as to "cool out" any expectations of upward mobility (thereby reconciling them to their lot in life). Guidance counseling in the public schools typically functions to encourage students to have "realistic expectations." There is a pervasive tendency for working class children to be encouraged to train for working class jobs. On the other hand, the children of professional families (who are also likely to vehemently protest if their children are not assigned the highest tracks) are actively encouraged to prepare for college.

It is not simply that considerably more is spent per pupil in middle class schools than in working class schools, and the best resources within a given school are provided to middle class children; teacher turnover, regularity of student attendance, school dropout rates, participation in clubs and parental participation in parent-teacher committees are all class correlated (favorably to middle class students). Even remedial classes and subsidized milk and food programs benefit middle and upper class children more than lower class children (Rossidies 1976, chap. 6).

The fact that most teachers are part of a generally middle class milieu results in discrimination against working class children. Teachers have an image of the ideal student as well as an ideology of education that is highly disadvantageous to working class children. Teachers tend to favor and disproportionately support the child who behaves according to the norms of middle class respectability. It might even be the case that teachers often behave in ways so as to actually elicit from lower class students the low achievement that they expect on the basis of their stereotypes, while eliciting from middle class students the high achievement expected from such children (Rossidies 1976, p. 207).

There is a considerable difference between working class schools and middle class schools (and between the middle class and the working class tracks within schools) in terms of the attitudes and orientation inculcated in children. The more working class a school's composition, the more likely that discipline, punctuality, neatness, following instructions, standing in lines, not talking unless asked a question, and so on are stressed. While the more middle or upper class a school's composition, the more likely creativity, flexibility, and initiative are stressed. Thus the various types of schools (or tracks) are designed to produce those character traits in the various classes of children that are most suitable to the types of jobs they will find themselves in. Factory and low level office and service work require people who have disciplined work habits, who are punctual, who follow orders well, and so forth—not people who are creative, used to flexibility, and take initiative. The opposite is the case for professional and managerial jobs where initiative and creativity are at a premium. The urban public and Catholic parochial schools, which are disproportionately working class, must thus be understood in terms of the type of jobs they are training people for, and thus in terms of their role in reproducing the class structure, i.e., in transmitting the class position of parents to their children.

Bad education is functional (i.e., good) for the capitalist system. Working class schools are in good part structured for failure. If everyone were given a quality education, it would result in a majority having career expectations higher than the system could allow to be realized. Because of the nature of the occupational structure, most students eventually end up in menial blue- or white-collar jobs. To function well in these jobs, they must be discouraged from thinking they are too good for such work. They must come to think that they are naturally suited for such labor. For workers in menial jobs to think of themselves as capable of being a professional or manager is likely to be disruptive by: first, causing a high degree of employee turnover, as people keep looking for better jobs; second, undermining work discipline (people with high aspirations are less likely to follow orders or work hard at jobs they hate); third, producing a potential source of militant unionists and political agitators. Thus education that is so bad as to get a good proportion of working class kids to drop out of school, voluntarily giving up aspirations for professional or skilled jobs, and otherwise to be so "turned off" to education as to not want to go to college or be professionals is, in fact, most useful for the system.

Blue-collar workers have considerably less education than do capitalist class and middle class people. In 1977, according to the annual social survey of the National Opinion Research Center, 52 percent of blue-collar workers in the United States had never finished high school and only 12 percent had ever been to college. This contrasts sharply with only 15 percent of capitalists who had not finished high school and 50 percent who had at least some college. The blue-collar working class contrasts even more sharply with the new middle class, where only 4 percent had not finished high school and fully 71 percent had at least some college (52 percent had at least four years of college). The traditional independent petty bourgeoisie shows a wide diversity in educational level: 40 percent in 1977 had not finished high school but 31 percent had at least some college (15 percent having had at least four years of college).*

The probability of a student's graduating from high school, attending college, and graduating from college is a product of the student's aspirations and motivations, which are in turn in good part a product of class background, and the quality of past education the student receives, again in good part a product of the class of his/her

---

*It should be noted that in 1972 the expected lifetime earnings of a college graduate were 1.9 times that of a high school dropout and 2.7 times that of a grade school dropout (see Jeffries and Ransford 1980, p. 119).

parents (as manifested in the type of school and track within the school). Middle class and upper class parents expect their children to go to college and become professionals, pressure their children to adopt professional aspirations, and provide an intellectually stimulating home environment (books, intellectual games, role models, intellectual conversations, and so on) as well as special classes and tutors if necessary. This gives such children considerable advantage over working class children. Working class parents are generally content if their children become skilled workers or low level semi-professionals. They generally spend far less energy in attempting to develop middle class aspirations in their children. Their home life is much less intellectually stimulating. Working class parents are also much less likely to provide special classes or tutors for their children. All this means that middle class children are considerably more motivated to attend college, and thus obtain professional or managerial jobs than are working class children.

A study done in the late 1950s in an Illinois town found that only 1.4 percent of high school dropouts were from upper or upper-middle class families, while 47 percent were from low income working class families. In contrast, 12 percent of high school graduates were from upper or upper middle class families, while 20 percent of high school graduates were from lower income working class homes (Howard and Logue 1978, p. 38).

A study of Wisconsin youth in the 1957–64 period found that about 20 percent of working class children as compared to about 40 percent of middle class children and 67 percent of higher class children planned on attending college (Rothman 1978, p. 224). This same study found that approximately one-fourth of working class youth had at one point or another attended college as compared to 45 percent of middle class youth and about three-fourths of higher class children (Rothman 1978, p. 224). In 1970 in the United States, 88 percent of upper and upper middle class children entered college. In contrast, 40 percent of the children of higher income workers and only 15 percent of lower income workers did so (Blumberg 1980, p. 47). In 1977, 59.8 percent of children with parents earning $15,000 a year or over aged 18–24 were in college, in contrast to 22.6 percent of those whose parents earned less than $15,000 (U.S. Department of Commerce 1981, p. 169). Similar results have been found for other advanced capitalist countries (see Parkin 1971, p. 110; Reid 1977, pp. 192–95).

In the mid-1950s, 43 percent of the children of professionals were graduating from college, in comparison with only 8 percent of the children of manual workers (Kahl 1957, p. 207). A study of Wisconsin male youths showed that only about one-tenth of the children of working class parents graduated from college in the mid-1960s as compared to about 40 percent of the children of higher class parents (Rothman 1978, p. 224).

The forces facilitating entry into college (and hence into professional careers) for middle class children operate not only through the differential motivation and aspirations transmitted from their parents, and the greater financial resources of middle class parents that ensure a quality education for their children, but also through the higher grades and scores on aptitude and achievement tests (including IQ tests and college boards) obtained by middle class students (because of their home environment and better schooling). Nevertheless, even when controlling for the ability of students (as manifested in achievement and aptitude testing), higher class students at all ability levels for both men and women have a considerably higher probability of going to college. A study of college freshmen in 1960 showed that while 48 percent of lower class boys who were in the higher quarter of their high school classes went on to college, 87 percent of higher class boys in the same quarter did so; on the other hand, while 6 percent of lower class boys in the lowest quarter of their high school class went on to college, 26 percent of higher class students did so (see Rossidies 1976, p. 222).

The discrimination against working class children in probability of college graduation works independently of "ability" and "potential" as measured by IQ tests. One study of high school seniors in 1957 showed that 20 percent of children with high IQs from low level working class homes had graduated from college by 1965 as compared to 64 percent of higher level middle class children with similar IQs (Duberman 1976, p. 208).

As with primary and secondary educational institutions, tertiary education varies considerably in its quality and purpose. Some universities and colleges are designed to educate upper class children together with those from other classes selected on the basis of extraordinary ability to be trained for top level professional and managerial positions (e.g., Harvard, Princeton, Yale, Stanford). Others are designed to train ordinary professionals and managers; other low level professionals such as engineers, nurses, and teachers; and still others to train skilled workers (and "cool out" those children of workers with professional aspirations). Each type of educational institution is not only designed to train students for a certain range of social positions, but also tends to heavily recruit from the appropriate class backgrounds, i.e., from children of parents of similar social positions as those for which they will be trained.

In 1971, 42 percent of the students attending private universities in the United States came from families with an annual income of over $20,000; this compares with 22 percent for public universities, 15 percent for public four-year colleges, and 12 percent for students at public two year colleges. On the other hand, 62 percent of the students at public two-year colleges came from families that had an income of less than $12,500, 57 percent of the students at public four-year colleges, 45 percent of the students at public universities, and 31 percent of the students at private universities (Bowles and Gintis 1976, p. 210). In the mid 1960s, 75 percent of the students at Ivy League colleges were upper or upper middle class in their background and only 5 percent working class. On the other hand, only 20 percent of the students at state colleges and 5 percent of students at junior and community colleges were from upper or upper middle class backgrounds, as compared to 30 percent and 55 percent respectively from working class backgrounds (Rossidies 1976, p. 211).

As we would expect, far more money and better teachers, lower student to teacher ratios, and better auxiliary facilities exist in the elite colleges than in the average state and community colleges. The elite private and public schools emphasize liberal arts and creativity, while the lower status working class schools emphasize vocational programs (even if for low level professional jobs such as teachers and nurses).

An important secondary function of state colleges, and especially the two-year junior and community colleges, is to "cool out" the upward mobility aspirations of students from working class backgrounds. In order to avoid rebellion and disillusionment with the system it is important to keep alive the notion that anyone can make it if they work at it, and that the United States is the land of opportunity. If only a small percentage of high school graduates were allowed to continue on to higher education, while many willing applicants were turned down, this would undermine that myth. Community colleges and state colleges allow the avoidance of firm selection points for those who will be upwardly mobile, substituting instead pressures on the student to drop out or to willingly transfer to a vocational program designed to make them skilled workers, i.e., designed to get the aspiring student to blame themselves for failing and thus deflect hostility away from the system (Rossidies, 1976, pp. 213–16).

Just as there are tracks within the secondary school system within which different classes of children are heavily concentrated, there are similar tracks in the higher educational system—majors. Those preparing for law and medical school tend to be from higher class backgrounds, while those in nursing, engineering, and teacher training tend to be from working class backgrounds. Further, students in liberal arts programs, especially the humanities, are from higher class backgrounds, while students in more practically oriented subjects such as the sciences (and especially the applied sciences) tend to be from upper level working class backgrounds.

CONCLUSION

In summary, it is clear that one's class position is strongly related to that of one's parents, i.e., there is a strong tendency for class position to be hereditary. Further, when social mobility occurs it tends to occur over only a slight social distance (i.e., from the manual working class to the lower middle class or intermediate strata). It is extremely rare for anyone born into a working class family to become a successful capitalist. The two major mechanisms by which class is passed on to one's children are the inheritance of property and the ability of parents to ensure a quality education for their children. The United States is very far from being a land of equal opportunity.

9

The Personal Effects of Class Position

The impact of class in contemporary Western societies such as the United States is all pervasive. Class is a major determinant of virtually all aspects of our lives. One's class in good part determines how long one will live and what one will die of. Emotional stress, the quality of health care, the relative safety of our jobs, and such factors as nutrition and housing all impact one's susceptibility to disease and violence. Mental as well as physical health is in good part a product of class position. The most intimate aspects of our lives, such as our sexual preferences and practices, are significantly class related, as are the number of children we have, our child-rearing practices, the age we marry, and the probability of divorce. The probability of committing crimes, our treatment by the criminal justice system, and our attitude to crime are all greatly class correlated. Our deepest beliefs, such as our religions (both denomination and the intensity of religious practice) are highly associated with class. Consumption and leisure practices vary greatly by class as do the kind and degree of newspaper and magazine reading as well as watching television. Alcohol and drug use (and attitudes toward both) vary by class. Even patterns of friendship, the degree to which we socialize with relatives, neighbors, and work associates, and prefer to spend time by ourselves is associated with class position. Virtually all attitudes about social and political issues are class related, including liberalism/conservatism, attitudes about women's liberation, the environment, civil liberties, communism, big business, and race relations. This chapter investigates these various correlates of class.

LIFE EXPECTANCY AND HEALTH

The number of years one can expect to live, i.e., the probability of dying at any given age, is correlated with class position. Because of differentially available medical treatment, diet, occupationally related accidents and diseases, sanitary conditions related to housing, susceptibility to violent crimes, and above all greater emotional stress, the poorer one is the less is one's life expectancy and the greater the probability of death at any given age. Innumerable studies in the United States and in other countries have documented this phenomenon (see Reid 1977, p. 124; Blumberg 1972, pp. 482–85).

It should be noted that part of the variation in death (and health) rates with class is caused by the downward mobility of chronically ill people. If one becomes sick or disabled for an extended period, one's income will almost certainly suffer. It is also possible that one may drift into a more menial occupation. But it will not affect past educational attainment. Thus different indicators of class position are more or less susceptible to picking up the effect of downward mobility versus class factors that produce illness and differential death rates. Measures of income levels are obviously the least effective measures of the effect of class-generated factors (since annual income will probably decline because of sickness), while educational attainment is a superior measure (since it indicates the level of preparation for different level jobs). Measures of occupation are probably as good as measures of education because chronic illness or disability is more likely to result in lack of advancement or working part time within one's broad occupational area (the professions, craftswork, clerical work, and so on) than actually changing one's occupation to service, white-collar, or lower-level manual labor. Because occupation tends to be a better indicator of class position than education (since it indicates one's actual job, rather than merely preparation), statistics correlating health and death rates with occupation should be treated as as valid as the correlates of education. Statistics based on income levels, however, must be treated with caution and considered more or less valid depending on the nature of the ailment (e.g., they should be considered reliable for accident rates, but suspect for deaths from cancer) unless corroborated with data based on occupation and/or education.

Statistics utilizing family income (which is what most studies, in fact, use) are a considerably better indicator of the effect of class on illness and death than individual income since it dampens the effect of disability or illness on annual earnings by including the income of all members of a family. This is particularly important for children and nondisabled/nonchronically ill family members for whom statistics on family income would seem to clearly reflect the effect of class on illness and death rates (even if the disability or chronic illness of the father, or other major breadwinner, *had* resulted in the family becoming downwardly mobile).

In 1950 in the United States nonfarm (white male) laborers aged 20-64 had a death rate (standardized mortality ratio) 60 percent greater than professional people; 37 percent of the deaths among laborers were caused by the poorer medical care, diet, work and living environment, and greater emotional stress experienced by menial laborers as compared with professionals. In any year, being a laborer kills almost 2 out of 5 of those who die in this group, i.e., if these people had the advantages of being a professional they would not have died. White male service workers (except private household) had a standardized death rate 41 percent higher than professionals, and operatives 15 percent higher. The differentials between occupations tend to be highest for those in the 30- to 40-year-old range. Here the death rate for laborers is over twice that for professionals while that for service workers is about two-thirds greater and operatives about one-third greater (see Table 9.1).

In 1960 white males in the United States who had completed between one and three years of high school who were between the ages of 25 and 45 had a 63 percent greater chance of dying in a given year than those with at least one year of college. Those between the ages of 45 and 65 with some high school had a 22 percent greater chance of dying (Kitagawa and Hauser 1973, p. 17).

The same effect is observed when death ratios by family income level are examined. In 1960 for the United States as a whole white male family members with a family income of under $2,000 had a 1.80 greater chance of dying in any given year than those with a family income of $10,000 or more. For white women family members the equivalent ratio was 1.40 (see Table 9.2). The greater differential for men than for women is, in part, caused by the fact that family income is generally more a product of what men contribute *and* that many deaths occur after a protracted period of disability (and thus decreased family income). But the range of death rates as measured by income groups as well as by occupational categories and educational level (which are much less affected by protracted disability) indicates that the bulk of both the male and female mortality differential is, in fact, a result of factors differentially present in different classes, rather than of downward mobility or decreased earning power.

The class differential in probability of dying has been carefully studied for the city of Chicago over the years. In 1960 in Chicago white men under 65 from the lowest socioeconomic classes (as

TABLE 9.1: Annual Death Rates per 1,000: White Males, by Age and Major Occupation Group, United States, 1950

Major Occupation Group	All Ages SMR* (25–29)	(20–24)	(25–29)	(30–34)	(35–44)	(45–54)	(55–59)	(60–64)
All occupations	93	1.7	1.6	2.0	3.9	10.1	19.4	28.8
Professional, technical, kindred	82	1.2	1.2	1.5	3.2	9.4	18.9	29.2
Managers, officials, proprietors, nonfarm	85	1.3	1.5	1.5	3.3	9.5	18.9	28.9
Clerical, kindred	83	0.9	1.3	1.5	3.3	9.6	18.2	26.9
Sales	94	1.1	1.1	1.7	3.6	11.0	21.7	31.8
Craftsworkers, foremen, kindred	94	1.8	1.6	2.0	4.0	10.1	20.8	32.1
Operatives, kindred	94	1.8	1.8	2.2	4.1	10.3	19.4	28.6
Service, except private household	116	1.2	1.6	2.4	5.1	13.8	22.4	29.2
Laborers, except farm and mine	131	2.6	2.8	3.6	6.5	14.5	23.8	34.9

Age-Group

*Standardized mortality ratios (SMRs) are computed on the basis of the entire population. Since nonwhite are excluded in this table, SMRs can fall below 100.

Source: Guralnick 1962, p.82.

300

TABLE 9.2: Mortality Ratios by Family Income Level for White Family Members Aged 25–64: United States, May–August 1960

Family Income	Men	Women
Under $2,000	1.51	1.20
$2,000–3,999	1.20	1.12
$4,000–5,999	0.99	1.00
$6,000–7,999	0.88	0.98
$8,000–9,999	0.93	0.92
$10,000 or more	0.84	0.86
All	1.00	1.00

Note: The mortality ratio is the ratio of the death rate of a given category to the death rate of the entire population.
Source: Kitagawa and Hauser 1973, p. 18.

measured by neighborhood) had a 2.15 times greater chance of dying in any given year than white men in the suburbs, and the equivalent ratio for white women was 2.04. Nonwhite men in the lowest socioeconomic neighborhoods had a 1.88 times greater chance of dying in a given year than nonwhite men in the suburbs, while nonwhite women in the lowest socioeconomic neighborhoods had a 1.84 times greater chance (see Table 9.3). It can be seen that most of the differential between blacks and whites is clearly a result of the concentration of blacks in the lower classes, since the differential is considerably reduced when comparing similar neighborhoods.

In 1960 white men from the poorest neighborhoods had a life expectancy at birth of 60.0 years as compared with 67.4 years for white men in the highest socioeconomic class neighborhood. The differential life expectancy between these two groups did not change between 1940 and 1960. White women in the lowest socioeconomic neighborhoods had a life expectancy of 67.7 years as compared to 73.6 years for women in the highest socioeconomic class neighborhoods. The differentials here did decline from 1940 to 1960. The class differential among blacks (both women and men) was *greater* in 1960 than it was among whites. Among black men the differential increased between 1940 and 1960, while among black women it stayed roughly the same (see Table 9.4). In general, while the class differentials in life expectancy in the United States peaked in the nineteenth century, significant narrowing of the gap between the classes ended after the first decades of the twentieth century (Rossides 1976, p. 194).

If the white male death rate for the suburbs applied to all white men in the lowest socioeconomic neighborhoods, it can be established

TABLE 9.3: Age-Adjusted Death Rates for Chicago by Socioeconomic Status of Neighborhoods, 1960

	Male		Female	
	White	Nonwhite	White	Nonwhite
SE 1 (low)	8.6 (2.15)	10.9 (1.88)	4.7 (2.04)	8.1 (1.84)
SE 2	6.0 (1.50)	8.5 (1.47)	3.4 (1.48)	6.3 (1.43)
SE 3	5.2 (1.30)	5.7 (0.98)	2.9 (1.26)	4.8 (1.09)
SE 4	4.5 (1.13)	—[a]	2.4 (1.04)	—
SE 5 (high)	4.7 (1.18)	—	2.5 (1.09)	—
Suburban ring	4.0 (1.00)	5.8 (1.00)	2.3 (1.00)	4.4 (1.00)
All Chicago SMSA[b]	5.0	8.1	2.8	6.1

[a]Data not available.
[b]Standard metropolitan statistical area.
Note: Data are for under age 65 population. Parenthetical numbers indicate the ratio of a category's rate to that in the suburban ring.
Source: Kitagawa and Hauser 1973, p. 53–55.

that 55 percent of all deaths in these neighborhoods would not have occurred; if applied to the lowest strata black neighborhoods 65 percent of all deaths in these neighborhoods would not have occurred. If the age-specific death rate for white women in the suburbs were applied to white women in the lowest socioeconomic category it can be seen that 52 percent of white women and 73 percent of black female deaths in these poor areas would not have occurred. Thus it can be said that approximately 60 percent of the deaths among the urban poor (between ages 25 and 64) are attributable to their poverty and would not have occurred had they been upper middle class (and white). It is clear that class kills (see also Kitagawa and Hauser 1973, p. 173).

The considerably higher overall mortality rates among the poor and the working class are manifested in the differentials for specific causes of death. White men in Chicago in 1960 aged 25–64 with less than eight years of education were 8.8 times more likely to die of tuberculosis in any given year than men with at least some college. This same category of men was 1.3 times more likely to die of heart disease, and 1.8 times more likely to die from hypertensive disease. White men aged 25 and over were 1.6 times more likely to die of influenza and pneumonia and 2.3 times more likely to die of accidents than white men with at least some college. White women with less than an eighth-grade education were 1.2 times more likely to die of cancer, 2.4 times more likely to die of heart disease, and 2.6 times more likely to die of hypertensive disease than white women with at least some college. Women aged 25 and over with less than eight

TABLE 9.4: Differential Expectation of Life at Birth: Chicago 1940 and 1960 by Socioeconomic Status of Neighborhoods

| | Male | | | | Female | | | |
| | White | | Nonwhite | | White | | Nonwhite | |
	1940	1960	1940	1960	1940	1960	1940	1960
SE 1 (low)	57.8	60.0	47.4	56.7	62.7	67.7	53.2	62.5
SE 3	64.2	66.5	53.6	65.1	67.6	72.8	59.1	68.1
SE 5 (high)	65.3	67.4	—*	—	70.2	73.6	—	—
All in city	62.6	65.2	51.0	60.9	67.1	72.0	56.7	66.5

*Data not available.
Source: Kitagawa and Hauser 1973, p. 71.

years of education were 3.5 times more likely to die of diabetes than white women with some college (see Table 9.5). Similar results have been found for other advanced capitalist countries (see Reid 1977, p. 115).

Infant mortality, perhaps the best indicator of the health of a group, varies greatly by class position. In the 1964-66 period in the United States the male infant mortality rate for families with an income of $10,000 a year or over was 22.1 (for whites only 21.4) as compared to 36.2 for families with an annual income of less than $3,000 (32.0 for whites only). For couples where the father had 8 years or less of education the male infant mortality rate was 36.3 per 1,000 as compared to 20.2 per 1,000 where the father had 16 or more years of education (U.S. Department of Health, Education, and Welfare 1972, p. 12). Thus the chances of a boy dying during the first year of life were roughly 60 to 80 percent higher for the poor than for the middle class.

One's class position in good part determines the probability of getting killed in war because in the absence of a good job children of poorer families are more likely to enlist in the military (or alternatively are less likely to avoid the draft) and are more likely to find themselves as foot soldiers once in the army. A study of who died in Vietnam showed that soldiers of poor families were 1.8 times as likely to get killed in Vietnam as the average (Zeitlin 1977, p. 146). During the Korean War the ratio of casualties per capita in the poorer census tracks of Detroit, Michigan (with a median income of under $2,500) to the ratio of casualties per capita in the richest census tracks (with a median income of over $5,500) was 3.2 (Vanfossen 1979, p. 4).

TABLE 9.5: Mortality Ratios by Level of Education for Various Diseases: Chicago 1960

	Less than 8 Years	8 Years	High School 1–4 Years	College	Ratio of the Rates of the Lowest to those of the Highest Educational Levels
Tuberculosis					
Males (25–64)	1.84	1.19	0.80	0.21	8.76
Malignant neoplasms					
Males (25–64)	1.09	1.12	0.94	0.83	1.31
Females (25–64)	1.13	1.05	0.94	0.92	1.23
Diabeties mellitus					
Females (25 and over)	1.48	0.96	0.77	0.42	3.52
Arteriosclerotic and degenerative heart diseases					
Males (25–64)	1.01	1.01	1.07	0.81	1.25
Females (25–64)	1.41	1.16	0.84	0.59	2.39
Hypertensive disease					
Males (25–64)	1.27	1.05	0.92	0.71	1.79
Females (25–64)	1.52	1.26	0.75	0.59	2.58
Influenza and pneumonia					
Males (25 and over)	1.20	0.98	0.81	0.75	1.60
All accidents					
Males (25–64)	1.45	1.16	0.92	0.64	2.27
All causes					
Males (25–64)	1.15	1.06	0.97	0.77	1.49
Females (25–64)	1.30	1.08	0.89	0.81	1.60

Note: Data are for whites only.
Source: Kitagawa and Hauser 1973, p. 91.

Suicide is class correlated, only here it is those at *both* the top and bottom of the class structure who kill themselves the most often. Both professional-managerial people *and* unskilled laborers have suicide rates approximately three times those of clerical and sales and skilled manual workers (Roach, Gross, and Gursslin 1969, p. 460). Apparently a combination of lesser social sanctions on suicide and the lesser social integration into community and extended family life (i.e., more individualized life-styles) gives professionals and managers an especially high suicide rate. On the other hand, it is probably mostly the greater stress associated with the lowest level working class jobs that drives this latter group to suicide (although factors of lesser social integration and lesser involvement in community life might be operating here as well).

Differential mortality is affected not only by class position, but also by the variations over time in stress and living standards experienced by working class people. For example, the higher the unemployment rate, the higher the rate of suicide, the greater the admissions to mental hospitals, the greater the number of homicides, the higher the number of deaths from heart attacks and from alcoholism (cirrhosis of the liver). In the 1970–75 period it has been calculated that a 1.4 percent increase in the unemployment rate caused an additional 51,570 deaths, i.e., a 2.7 percent increase in mortality (see Table 9.6).

The most important factor in both the higher death rates among the working and underclasses is the greater emotional stress implicit in their position. Studies of the relationship between emotional stress and health have shown that the death rate of widows and widowers is *ten* times greater in the year after the death of one's partner than it is for others of the same age. Divorced persons have a *12* times greater incidence of disease in the year after divorce than do married persons of the same age. Studies have indicated that perhaps as many as 80 percent of serious physical diseases develop at a time when the person feels hopeless or helpless. Those who suffer from chronic anxiety, hostility, and depression are much more likely to

TABLE 9.6: The Cumulative Impact of a 1.4 Percent Rise in Unemployment on Social Stress Indicators, 1970–75

Social Stress Indicator	Percentage Increase in Incidence	Numerical Increase in Incidence
Suicide	5.7%	1,540
Admissions to state mental hospitals	4.7	5,520
Admissions to state prisons	5.6	7,660
Homicide	8.0	1,740
Mortality from cirrhosis of the liver	2.7	870
Mortality from cardiovascular disease	2.7	26,440
Total mortality	2.7	51,570

Source: U.S. Congress, Joint Economic Committee 1976, Table 2.

become victims of cancer (Conrad and Kern 1981, p. 458). Since working class and underclass people generally experience considerably greater emotional stress in both their work and home life, the factors that operate in general to associate stress and disease operate with greater potency in these classes than in the middle or upper classes.

Not only do the pressures of working class and underclass life on the job, at home, and at leisure generate significantly higher levels of day-to-day stress than in most other class positions, but such people experience greater life trauma as well. Persons living in working class and underclass situations tend to get divorced more often, experience the death of close relatives more frequently, are more subject to violent crimes, are much more likely to lose their jobs and their homes (through fire, eviction, and so on), and suffer other types of trauma or qualitative change in life patterns that are highly associated with increased emotional stress.

Hypertension is significantly related to education level (and by implication with class). In the United States in the early 1970s white college graduates had a 42 percent lower incidence of hypertension than whites who did not complete ten years of school. Among blacks the differential was 37 percent. The differential exists in all age-groups among both blacks and whites, although the differentials are stronger among younger people. When controlling for age, the black differential was generally higher than that of whites. It should be noted that college-educated blacks between the ages of 30 and 39 had a rate of hypertension 50 percent *lower* than blacks with less than ten years of education (Conrad and Kern 1981, p. 109). Studies of the relationship between hypertension and income reveal an even stronger relationship than with education. One study found that in the early 1970s among those aged 35–49 hypertension was three times more common among those with an annual income of less than $5,000 a year than among those with an annual income of $15,000 or more (Conrad and Kern 1981, p. 109).

Stress increases death rates by increasing the propensity to be involved in accidents, lowering resistance to diseases, and being a direct (psychosomatic) cause as well as by producing certain types of coping behavior that put one more at risk. People under stress are more likely to smoke (or resume smoking), and smoking has been shown to be positively correlated with a wide range of ailments. Likewise, drinking and overeating are basic responses to the emotional stress working people and the poor disproportionately experience. It is of interest to note that in 1976, 45 percent of men with an annual income of less than $15,000, but 35 percent of men earning $25,000 or more were smokers (there was no correlation among women). Fifty-three percent of male operatives and laborers and 47 percent of service workers were smokers, in contrast to 30 percent of male professionals and 41 percent of managers. Among women 39 percent of blue-collar workers and 35 percent of clerical workers were smokers, in contrast to 29 percent of professionals (U.S. Department of Health and Human Services 1979a).

The greater emotional stress that working and poor people suffer is revealed in the use of sleeping pills. In 1976, 10.3 percent of all those with a family income of under $5,000 a year (and 9.6 percent of those with less than nine years of education) regularly used sleeping pills at least once a week, in contrast to only 4.8 percent of those with family incomes of $25,000 or more (and 3.3 percent of college graduates). Among operatives 3.8 percent regularly used sleeping pills and among service workers 4.0 percent; in comparison, 2.4 percent of professionals and 1.9 percent of craftsworkers did (it should be noted that 4.2 percent of managerial and administrative people regularly use them). There is a similar distribution for the regular use of aspirin. In 1976, 28 percent of those with a family income of under $5,000 (and 29 percent of those with less than nine years of education) in contrast to 22 percent of those earning over $25,000 a year (and 18 percent of college graduates) reported using aspirin at least once a week (U.S. Department of Health and Human Services 1979a, p. 28).

Another cause of the differential mortality, disability, and illness rates between the working class and the upper and middle class is the hazards associated with manual labor. In 1978 there were 13,000 on-the-job deaths in the United States and 2,200,000 disabling on-the-job injuries. The incidence varied considerably by economic sector. The on-the-job death rate was highest in mining, with 63 deaths per 100,000 workers, construction with 57 deaths per 100,000, agriculture with 54, and transportation and public utilities with 29. The death rate was lowest in trade, with a rate of 6 per 100,000, and the services at 7 per 100,000. The rate of disabling injuries was highest in agriculture, with 54.3 per 1,000; construction with 52.2 per 1,000, mining with 50.0, and transportation and public utilities with 33.3. It was lowest in trade and the services with rates of 1.80 and 1.57 respectively (National Safety Council 1979, p. 23).

In the 1975–76 period in the United States, 6.6 percent of all professionals and 4.4 percent of all managers per year experienced some kind of an accident on the job (disabling or not). This contrasts with 21.0 percent of all blue-collar workers. The average numbers of workdays lost because of disabilities per year was 3.7 for male professionals and 3.4 for male managers as compared to 6.0 for all male blue-collar workers and 6.7 for all male service workers (U.S. Department of Health and Human Services 1980, p. 35).

Occupationally related illness is defined as any abnormal condition or disorder other than one resulting from an occupational injury caused by exposure to environmental factors associated with employment. In 1976 there were approximately 168,000 new cases of occupational illnesses. Their incidence varied greatly by occupation from a rate of 8 per 1,000 full-time employees per year for agriculture and 5.3 per 1,000 for manufacturing to 0.7 per 1,000 for finance, insurance, and real estate, and 1.1 per 1,000 for the wholesale and retail trade. Almost half of occupational illnesses are skin diseases or disorders (43 percent) while about 13 percent are caused by physical agents and another 13 percent associated with repeated trauma (National Safety Council 1979, p. 23).

In 1972 it was estimated that there were approximately 100,000 deaths from job injuries and occupationally induced diseases combined (Reiman 1979, p. 65). Clearly, then, many more people die from occupationally induced diseases than from on-the-job accidents. Among the most notorious of occupationally related diseases are black lung disease (silicosis) caused by breathing coal dust in the mines, radiation exposure (especially for uranium miners), cancer, and asbestosis for workers who work with asbestos, and the brown lung disease (byssinosis) of textile workers.

In the mid-1970s at least 100,000 ex-coal miners suffered from fully developed black lung disease (which makes it very difficult to breath and consequently impossible to work). About 10 percent of active miners have the disease in its early forms (Reiman 1979, p. 68; Lejeune 1972, p. 47). Around 1970 about 17,000 active cotton, flax, and hemp workers had brown lung disease. A study of asbestos workers who worked in the 1943 to 1971 period found that 11 percent have died of asbestosis and another 38 percent of cancer. It is estimated that 3,000 ex-asbestos workers die each year in the 1970s and 1980s from "excess respiratory, cardiopulmonary deaths and cancers of the lung" (Reiman 1979, p. 68). Workers who have worked in coke ovens for five or more years die of lung cancer at a rate 3.5 times higher than the average for all steelworkers. Approximately 800,000 people suffer from occupationally related skin diseases a year (Reiman 1979, p. 69). It has been estimated that between 20 percent and 40 percent of cancer deaths are caused by on-the-job exposure (Berman 1978, p. 46).

One cause of the differential mortality and chronic illness rates among the classes is the quality of medical care obtained. In countries like the United States where medical care is largely private and must be paid for, poorer people find it difficult to get quality medical care, and when they do obtain it through state-sponsored programs they usually receive the poorest quality available. In most other advanced capitalist countries where there is state-financed medical insurance, private practice exists for those with money, who thus get the best medical care, while those who cannot afford it must be content with often second-rate, state-funded care. In the United States private insurance policies that pay for hospitalization and major illness are most common in the middle class and among better-off people who need it the least. In 1970 only 47 percent of those below 125 percent of poverty level income had hospital insurance and only 14 percent had major medical insurance. This is in contrast to 85 percent and 49 percent respectively who were above the 125 percent of poverty income level (U.S. Department of Health, Education, and Welfare 1977, p. 53). In 1976 in the United States 35.2 percent of service workers and 27.8 percent of blue-collar workers with a family income of less than $10,000 were not covered by private hospital insurance, while only 3.3 percent of professionals and 6.1 percent of managers earning over $10,000 were not covered (U.S. Department of Health and Human Services 1980, pp. 49–50).

Although far more susceptible to disease and with a considerably greater risk of dying, the working class and poorer people spend considerably less (in absolute terms) on medical care than do the better-off groups that are the healthiest. In 1975 blue-collar workers earning less than $10,000 a year averaged total medical expenses of $209 a year and service workers $212, compared with $290 a year for professionals and $323 a year for managers earning over $10,000 (U.S. Department of Health and Human Services 1980, p. 59). Although they spend less on medical care, the burden of medical expenses is much greater on poorer families. In 1970 those earning $7,500 and over spent on average 3.5 percent of their aggregate family income for personal health services. This contrasts with 5.7 percent for those earning between $5,000 and $7,499; 7.3 percent for those earning between $3,500 and $4,999; 9.0 percent for those with incomes of between $2,000 and $3,999 and 12.9 percent for those with family incomes of less than $2,000 (U.S. Department of Health, Education, and Welfare 1977, p. 47).

Although they feel sicker, have a greater incidence of disease, are more likely to die, and worry more about sickness, poor and working class people are less likely to visit a doctor than are better-off people. In 1975 and 1976 in the U.S. an annual average of 78.0 percent of all professionals and 74.7 percent of all managers with family incomes of $10,000 or over in contrast to only 34.3 percent of blue-collar workers and 38.6 percent of all service workers earning less than $10,000 a year visited a physician (U.S. Department of Health and Human Services 1980, p. 44).

Poorer people are significantly less likely than higher income people to participate in preventative medical care. For example, 39 percent of women over 17 whose family income in 1973 was under $3,000 a year and 28 percent of those whose family income was between $3,000 and $5,000 never had a pap smear, compared to only 15 percent of those whose income was above $15,000. Fifty-one percent of people over 40 whose family income was less than $3,000 a year, and 46 percent of those whose family income was between $3,000 and $7,000 never have had a glaucoma test, compared with only 32 percent of those whose family income was over $15,000. Nineteen percent of persons with a family income of under $5,000 in 1973 never had a routine physical examination, compared to only 4 percent of those over $15,000. Of those earning less than that $7,000 a year in 1973, 15 percent never had a chest X ray, in contrast to 10 percent of those with incomes of over $15,000. Of persons over 40, 38 percent of those earning less than $3,000 a year as compared to 32 percent of those earning over $15,000 never had an electrocardiogram (Howard and Logue 1978, pp. 52–55).

The poor and working classes have a greater inclination to consider pain and body malfunction normal or inevitable. One study showed that in the 1950s in the United States blood in one's stool was recognized as a symptom needing medical attention by 98 percent of the upper middle class, and 60 percent of the poorer working class; swelling of the ankles by 77 percent of the upper middle class and 23 percent of poorer workers; persistent headaches by 80 percent of the upper middle class and 22 percent of poorer workers; a lump in the breast by 94 percent of the upper middle class and 44 percent of the poorer workers; pain in the chest by 80 percent of the upper middle class and 31 percent of poorer workers, and so forth (see Table 9.7).

Even in societies with free medical service, the poorer a group the less likely they are to utilize them. For example, in the United Kingdom around 1970 upper middle class people were almost 50 percent more likely than lower level working class people to immunize their children against smallpox and were about 15 percent more likely to immunize them against diphtheria or to bring their children to a dentist (Reid 1977, p. 146).

Other important factors in the differential death rates by class are differential diet and the quality of one's living environment. Poorer people do not eat as well as richer people. They are more likely to be malnourished or overweight, thereby increasing their susceptibility to disease as well as their ability to recover from accidents (see U.S. Department of Health, Education, and Welfare 1977, p. 449). Overcrowded housing and unsanitary apartments in neighborhoods (which are, of course, more common among the poor)

TABLE 9.7: Percentage of Respondents in Each Social Class Recognizing Specified Symptoms as Needing Medical Attention

Symptom	Class I (N = 51)	Class II (N = 335)	Class III (N = 128)
Loss of appetite	57	55	20
Persistent backache	53	44	19
Continued coughing	77	78	23
Persistent joint and muscle pains	80	47	19
Blood in stool	98	89	60
Blood in urine	100	93	69
Excessive vaginal bleeding	92	83	54
Swelling of ankles	77	76	23
Loss of weight	80	51	21
Bleeding gums	79	51	20
Chronic fatigue	80	53	19
Shortness of breath	77	55	21
Persistent headaches	80	56	22
Fainting spells	80	51	33
Pain in chest	80	51	31
Lump in breast	94	71	44
Lump in abdomen	92	65	34

Note: Class I is upper class, class II is middle, and class III is lower.
Source: Koos 1960.

increase exposure to contagious diseases. The higher crime rates of poorer neighborhoods increase the rates of homicide and disability from acts of violence. The relative lack of playgrounds and organized play activity increases the rate of accidents among poor children, while a parallel lack of affordable entertainment and overcrowded housing increases involvement in street life and adventuresome activities that increase the accident, homicide, and disability rates among such people. The inability of the poor to afford adequate heating leads to death during cold spells in the winter. Likewise, inability to afford ventilation (e.g., fans, air conditioners) can lead to deaths from heat prostration during heat waves in the summer.

Health in general is highly class correlated. In the United States in 1973, 60.7 percent of all persons with a family income of $15,000 and over were in "excellent health" and only 5.5 percent in "fair" or "poor" health (as defined by the persons themselves). This contrasts sharply with those whose family income was under $5,000 a year, 32.4 percent of whom were in "excellent health" and 25.6 percent of whom were in "fair" or "poor" health. The difference between the two groups was strongest among those from 45 to 64 years of age.

Here 18.4 percent of the poorer group and 47.3 percent of the better-off group were in "excellent health"; while 45.8 percent of the poorer group in contrast to only 10.5 percent of the better-off group were in "fair" or "poor" health (Conrad and Kern 1981, p. 443).

The incidence of diseases varies considerably by class (see Table 9.8). About 1970 for those aged 45–64 arthritis was about twice as prevalent in families with incomes below $5,000 than in those with family income above $15,000; asthma was 2.4 times as prevalent; chronic bronchitis 1.5 times; diabetes 2.4; heart conditions 2.1; hypertension 1.6; hearing impairments 1.9; and vision impairments 2.3 times more prevalent.

Although they spend significantly less on medical care, visit physicians less and are less likely to participate in preventative medicine, working class and poorer people are (because of the greater incidence of serious diseases and accidents) considerably more likely than middle class people to be hospitalized. In 1970 people with a family income below $10,000 were admitted to hospitals at a rate about 1.5 times that of people with incomes of $10,000 and over (Howard and Logue 1978, p. 50). In 1973 persons with a family income of under $5,000 received on the average 2.30 days of hospital care per year, those with an income of from $5,000 to $9,999, 1.35; those with a family income of between $10,000 and $14,999, 0.87; and those with family incomes of over $15,000, 0.80—a quite substantial difference (U.S. Department of Health, Education, and Welfare 1977, p. 309). In the 1975–76 period 8.3 percent of all professionals and 8.7 percent of all managers with a family income of $10,000 or over were hospitalized at some point during the year. This contrasts with 9.2 percent of blue-collar workers earning under $10,000 and 10.2 percent of all service workers earning less than this amount (U.S. Department of Health and Human Services 1980, p. 43). The fact that poorer people are less likely to be admitted to a hospital for relatively minor problems than middle class people and are generally admitted for serious ailments more than is the norm in the middle class is reflected in the statistics on average length of stay. While those with family incomes of under $5,000 had an average stay of 9.6 days, and those with family incomes of between $5,000 and $9,999, 7.9 days, those with family incomes of $15,000 and over had an average stay of 6.4 days (U.S. Department of Health, Education, and Welfare 1977, p. 309). In the 1975–76 period the average length of stay in hospitals was 6.3 days for professionals and 6.6 days for managers with a family income of $10,000 or over a year as compared with 8.0 days for blue-collar workers earning less than $10,000 and 7.7 days for service workers earning less than $10,000 (U.S. Department of Health and Human Services 1980, pp. 43–44).

TABLE 9.8: Chronic Disease by Family Income for Ages 45–64, 1969–73

	Arthritis (1969)	Asthma (1970)	Chronic Bronchitis (1970)	Diabetes (1973)	Heart Conditions (1972)	Hypertension (without Heart Involvement) (1972)	Ulcers (1968)	Impairment of Back or Spine (except Paralysis) (1971)	Hearing Impairments (1971)	Vision Impairments (1971)
Total number per 1,000 persons 45–65 years	204.2	33.1	35.4	42.6	88.8	126.7	33.4	68.2	114.1	63.0
Family income										
Under $5,000	297.8	53.5	44.2	74.1	139.3	172.7	45.2	102.8	158.9	114.1
$5,000–$9,999	200.3	33.5	38.7	43.8	92.5	125.4	31.8	67.2	118.1	57.4
$10,000–$14,999	163.7	23.7	29.0	37.8	74.3	121.3	28.3	62.3	107.3	45.9
$15,000 and over	159.8	22.7	30.3	30.5	66.6	105.3		52.2	85.9	48.9
Ratio of incidence in lowest income group to incidence in highest	1.86	2.36	1.46	2.43	2.09	1.64	1.60	1.97	1.85	2.33

Source: U.S. Department of Health, Education, and Welfare 1977, p. 487.

Dental health is also class correlated. In the 1966 to 1970 period 38 percent of those with a family income of less than $5,000 a year had decayed or missing teeth, compared to 17 percent of those with incomes of from $10,000 to $15,000 and 10 percent with incomes of over $15,000 (Howard and Logue 1978, p. 59). The condition of one's teeth reflects dental care. In 1973 the number of visits to the dentist for children aged 6-16 in the United States varied from 1.1 per year for children with family incomes under $5,000, 1.4 per year for those with family incomes between $5,000 and $9,999, 2.2 for those with family incomes from $10,000 to $14,999, and 3.1 for those with family incomes of $15,000 or over (U.S. Department of Health, Education and Welfare 1977, p. 425). In the 1975-76 period the percentage of adults 17 and over visiting a dentist per year varied from 34.3 percent for blue-collar workers earning less than $10,000 and 38.6 percent for service workers earning less than $10,000 to 68.9 percent for all professionals and 63.4 percent for all managers with a family income of $10,000 or over. The average number of visits per year showed a more significant spread. While among blue-collar workers earning less than $10,000 the average number of visits was 1.0 per year (and among service workers in the same income range it was 1.3), for all professionals it was 2.2 and for all managers it was 2.2 (U.S. Department of Health and Human Services 1980, pp. 43-44).

HAPPINESS AND MENTAL HEALTH

Not surprisingly, the higher one's social class the less likely one is to be unhappy, the less likely one is to be dissatisfied with one's present situation, and the more likely one is to experience joy than pain in their life, and, as has already been seen, the higher the level of emotional stress.

In the 1977 National Opinion Research Center (NORC) General Social Survey (a national U.S. sample) 51.0 percent of (self-employed) independent middle class people said they were "very happy," compared to 41.5 percent of salaried middle class people and 30.3 percent of manual workers. The results of an Italian study done in the immediate post–World War II years demonstrate the class correlation of happiness even more sharply. In 1948 in Italy 26 percent of workers stated they were "unhappy at the moment" as compared to 10 percent of managers and employers and 14 percent of employees. While 64 percent of manual workers reported that they were "dissatisfied with their present situation," this was true of only 31 percent of business owners and 35 percent of salaried managers. Further, 48 percent of manual workers stated there was "more pain than joy in their lives" as compared to only 23 percent of managers and 32 percent of employers (Tumin 1970, p. 183).

Satisfaction with one's job varies greatly with social class. Professionals, owners, and managers generally have few if any complaints about their jobs, and mostly would choose the same occupation if they could start over. Working people, especially those in unskilled jobs, generally have considerably more complaints about their jobs and would generally choose a different occupation if given the chance. A study of male workers done in the early 1960s showed that only 16 percent of unskilled auto workers, 21 percent of unskilled steelworkers, and 24 percent of all blue-collar workers stated that if they could start over again they would choose a similar type of job. This contrasted with fully 93 percent of urban university professors, 91 percent of all mathematicians, and 83 percent of all lawyers (Blumberg 1972, p. 429).

In 1977 in the United States 67 percent of those in traditional independent petty-bourgeois positions reported that they were "very satisfied" with their job, as did 57 percent of those in salaried professional and managerial positions, while only 40 percent of manual workers and 43 percent of white-collar workers reported that they were "very satisifed." When asked what was the single most important thing they valued about a job 28 percent of manual workers as compared to 15 percent of independent petty bourgeois and 14 percent of the new middle class said it was "income." In contrast, 68 percent of the new middle class and 56 percent of the traditional independent petty bourgeoisie as compared to 37 percent of manual workers said that having "important work" was the most important thing about a job (computed directly from the 1977 NORC General Social Survey). What different people see as the most desirable characteristic of a job varies considerably by class. Relatively higher class people see congeniality as the most desirable characteristic, while lower class people see economic benefit.

In a survey of industrial workers in the United States in the 1960s it was found that among younger workers 25 percent of those in skilled and high-level semiskilled jobs reported "ever being bothered by nervousness," compared to 45 percent of those in lower level skilled occupations. Twenty percent of those in repetitive semiskilled occupations reported that they "do not wake up rested" as compared to 11 percent of those in skilled and highly semiskilled occupations. Eighty percent of those in repetitive semiskilled positions as compared to 53 percent of those in skilled and high-level semiskilled occupations reported that they sometimes "boil inside without showing it." Among those in repetitive semiskilled occupations 37 percent felt "optimistic about their own future" as compared to 69 percent in skilled and highly semiskilled occupations (Kornhauser 1965, Table 4-3). Among the more skilled younger workers 11 percent reported being often worried and upset as compared to 28 percent of those in repetitive semiskilled jobs. Of those in repetitive semiskilled occupations 46 percent reported sometimes feeling "ever so blue and that nothing was worthwhile," compared to only 22 percent of those in more skilled positions (Kornhauser 1965, Table 4-3).

A study by the U.S. government's National Center for Health Statistics (NCHS) found that in the 1974–75 period experiencing periods of depression was strongly related to class position. The mean score on the NCHS depression scale for those who did not graduate from college (and who were aged 25–74) was 10.9, while that for those with some graduate school in the same age bracket was 5.5 (half that of the less educated). Similar results were found with measures of annual family income and occupation. The average score on the NCHS depression scale for those in families with less than $5,000 in annual earnings was 12.5 and for those in families with between $5,000 and $9,999 annual family income 9.3. This compares to a score of 5.5 for those with family incomes of over $25,000. Male professionals had a score of 5.3 and male managers a score of 5.4, in contrast to the 8.0 score of male operatives and the 11.9 score of farm laborers. (U.S. Department of Health and Human Services 1980, pp. 13, 19).

Mental health is strongly correlated with class position for two reasons: lower class people are diagnosed and assigned treatment by upper middle class criteria; and more importantly, the stresses, strains, and tensions of lower class life are considerably greater than those of upper middle class life, consequently, people in the lower classes are more likely to break under the pressure. It should be noted that there is generally a sharp rise in mental hospital admissions during a recession (see Table 9.6). A study of factory workers in the 1960s showed that 58 percent of young skilled workers and 56 percent of middle-aged skilled workers, in contrast with only 10 percent of young and 26 percent of middle-aged semiskilled workers doing repetitive work were ranked high on mental health (Kornhauser 1965, Table 4.1). Lower class people are much more likely to become psychotic than middle class people. Table 9.9 shows the distribution of some of the major forms of psychoses by class as found in a mid-1950s study by August Hollingshead and Frederick Redlich.

A thorough study of mental illness in mid-town Manhattan in the mid-1950s confirmed Hollingshead's findings of an association of mental illness with class. This study found that in the highest status group only 18 percent had symptoms that impaired the individual's

TABLE 9.9: Class and the Rate of Different Types of Psychoses per 100,000 of Population

Type of Disorder	Prestige Class			
	I-II (high) (n = 53)	III (n = 142)	IV (n = 585)	V (low) (n = 672)
Affective psychoses	40	41	68	105
Psychoses due to alcoholism and drug addiction	15	29	32	116
Organic psychoses	9	24	46	254
Schizophrenic psychoses	111	168	300	895
Senile psychoses	21	32	60	175

Note: Data are adjusted for age and sex.
Source: Hollingshead and Redlich 1958, p. 233).

functioning, while in the lowest stratum 33 percent were incapacitated. The results of the midtown Manhattan study are reported in
Table 9.10.

Since it certainly is the case that many people fall in their
contemporary class position because of their impaired functioning it
is more important to look at the relation between the class in which
one started life and one's contemporary mental condition in order to
determine the impact of class position on mental health (rather than
vice versa). Studies of schizophrenia and parental class background
show that unlike other forms of psychosis this mental disease is *not*
related to class *background*, but rather that the correlation between it
and class position is essentially a product of the downward mobility
of schizophrenic victims (Reid 1977, p. 117; Rossidies 1976, p. 198).

Those categorized as neurotic (minor impairment of social functioning) as opposed to psychotic (severe impairment of social functioning) are much more likely to be from the higher classes (the opposite
of the distribution of psychosis). This is apparently because working
class people tend not to seek treatment for neurosis, but rather
generally interpret neurotic behavior as "nerves" or simply normal,
and thus do not seek out treatment from counselors or psychiatrists,
while on the other hand upper middle class people often *pride* themselves on going to and talking about their "analyst." While psychiatric help is typically considered something to be ashamed of in the
working class, more often than not, it is considered quite normal in
the salaried middle classes. Further, the higher the class, the more
sympathetic and tolerant are attitudes, especially the attitudes of
authorities and medical people, toward neurotic disturbances and the
greater the likelihood that deviant behavior will be attributed to

TABLE 9.10: Distributions of Respondents on Mental Health by Parental SES Strata for ages 20-59

Mental Health Categories	*Parental SES Strata*					
	A (Highest)	B	C	D	E	F (Lowest)
Well	24%	23%	20%	19%	14%	10%
Mild symptom formation	36	38	37	37	37	33
Moderate symptom formation	22	22	23	20	20	25
Impaired	18	16	21	25	29	33
Marked symptom formation	12	9	12	13	16	18
Severe symptom formation	4	5	8	8	10	10
Incapacitated	2	3	1	3	3	5
Total	100	100	100	100	100	100

Note: Socio-Economic Status (SES) index is a popular indicator of social position composed of measures of income, education, and occupational prestige.
Source: Srole and Fisher 1975, p. 289.

mental illness, rather than considered as something to be punished, as in the lower classes (Rossidies 1976, p. 197). While the defining of people as "neurotic" is highly arbitrary, both on the part of the family and friends of the people concerned and on the part of persons in authority, there is relatively little room in the case of psychotic or mentally incapacitated people for the operation of socially flexible definitions. It is very hard for family, friends, and authorities to overlook a psychotic, and the psychotic individuals to avoid some type of treatment or institutionalization, i.e., the statistics of psychosis can thus be considered to fairly accurately reflect the real social distribution of psychotic breakdowns, while the figures on neurosis must be considered to mostly reflect the highly variable social definitions prevailing in different social classes. It should be noted that the poorest working class people are three times more likely than professional or managerial people to become psychotic (Hollingshead and Redlich 1958, p. 210).

The type and quality of therapy received by mental patients varies greatly by class. While 47 percent of upper and middle class "neurotics" (in Hollingshead's prestige Class I and II) received psychotherapy, only 5 percent of lower class patients (classes IV and V) did (Hollingshead and Redlich 1958, p. 267). Fifty percent of upper and middle class psychotics received psychotherapy, compared to 8 percent of those in the lower classes. While 84 percent of lower class psychotics received nothing but custodial care, this was true for only 50 percent of the upper and middle classes (Hollingshead and Redlich 1958, p. 290). According to Hollingshead, around 1950 total expenditures per psychotic patient in the upper and middle classes was 3.0 times greater than that for the lower classes (Hollingshead and Redlich 1958, p. 309).

MARRIAGE, SEXUALITY, CHILD REARING, AND FRIENDSHIP

Marriage, divorce, fertility, sexuality, child rearing, and friendship are all heavily class related. Men and women seek out members of their own social class to marry. There is a strong tendency for people from middle class backgrounds to marry others from middle class backgrounds, for people from working class backgrounds to marry others from working class backgrounds, and, above all, for the sons and daughters of the capitalist class to marry each other. This is not at all surprising since people from the same social class backgrounds grow up in the same class-segregated neighborhoods, go to the same schools (and within the same schools tend to take similar programs), have overlapping relative and friend networks, tend to work in similar jobs, belong to similar churches and clubs, and so forth. Further, middle and especially capitalist class parents are very status conscious. They generally press their children to find marriage partners of at least as high a social class as their own. To marry people of a lower "status" is normally regarded as degrading for both the individual and their family.

Age at marriage varies by class. Middle and upper class people marry later than do working class people. Although people have a strong tendency to marry within their class this is more true of upper class women and lower class men than of upper class men and lower class women. Consequently, in relative terms, the upper class has fewer unmarried men and more unmarried women than does the working class (which has relatively fewer unmarried women and relatively more unmarried men). This latter fact is the case because of the tendency of "more attractive" working class women "marrying up" to middle class and sometimes even upper class men who, because of their money, have a wider range of potential mates to choose from, than do upper and middle class women. Higher class women "lose status" by marrying a working class man, no matter how "attractive" (Rossidies 1976, p. 177).

The number of children desired and number of children actually had varies by class. Generally the poorer the family the more children the parents want and the more children the mother has. This is especially the case for the rural poor and for people from rural backgrounds. Working class families traditionally have had bigger families than the middle class, although this has become less the case over time (see Table 9.11).

Poor people, especially the rural poor, have traditionally wanted larger families because of the economic advantages of large numbers of children. Children both supplement the family income (or do necessary chores around the farm or family business) and (especially before state-supported social security) were vital for supporting parents in their old age, or in the case of disability or other crisis. The more children, the larger the family income, the more unpaid family laborers, and the greater one's economic security. To have many children was traditionally a most rational decision. The situation of the salaried middle class family contrasts sharply with the condition of the rural poor (or the traditional independent small businessmen). Here children are a major financial liability. The children of this class do not generally ever supplement family income, instead they are supported, not just until they are 16 or 17, but typically through the end of their college years. Supporting children through college, especially at elite institutions, can be a very expensive proposition, whose return normally comes only in the form of increased family prestige. Further, this class has relied much less than either the working class or the rural poor on children as social security (instead depending on their own wealth and/or various pension and benefit plans). The declining differential between the working class and the petty bourgeoisie in number of children is a result

TABLE 9.11: Average Number of Children Ever Born to Wives Aged 35-44, by Spouse's Occupation

	1950	1970
Professional, technical, and kindred	2.941	1.825
Managers, officials, proprietors (except farm)	2.941	1.949
Sales	2.891[a]	1.827
Clerical and kindred	2.841[a]	1.827
Craftsworkers, foremen, and kindred	3.119	2.313
Operatives and kindred	3.179	2.523
Service workers[b]	3.018	2.103
Laborers, (except farm and mine)	3.367	3.004
Farmers and farm managers	3.578	3.204
Farm laborers and foremen	4.296	3.796

[a]The 1950 census combines sales with clerical and kindred workers.
[b]Includes private household.
Source: Abrahamson 1976, p. 218.

of the increasing distance from rural life of the working class, the decreased role of child labor (as a supplement to family income) in the working class, the increased probability of working class children going to college or at least vocational school (and thus being a long-term financial burden on their families), and the prevalence of social security and private pension plans and institutions to take care of the basic needs of working class families in their old age and in times of crisis.

The happiness of one's marriage is influenced by one's class position. In 1977 in the United States 72 percent of those in the independent middle class and 70 percent of those in the new middle class as compared to 63 percent of manual workers reported that their marriages were "very happy" (computed from the NORC General Social Survey for 1977).

Divorce as well as marriage is in good part class determined. in 1970, lower level working class people had a ratio of (currently) divorced to married men over twice that of the nonprofessional middle class. Service workers (excluding domestics) had a ratio of 5.4 percent and nonfarm laborers had a ratio of 5.0 percent. This contrasts with a ratio of 2.4 percent for managers and administrators, and 3.5 percent for professional men. The ratios for other occupations in 1970 were sales and clerical 3.9 percent, craftsworkers 3.3 percent, operatives 4.0 percent (U.S. Bureau of the Census 1970c, Table 31). Similar findings have been found for most countries (Tumin 1970, pp. 163–68; Reid 1977, p. 133). It should be noted that desertions and separations without formal divorce are considerably more class related than are divorces (Roach, Gross, and Gursslin 1969, p. 440).

The considerably greater instability of poorer working class marriages probably mostly reflects the higher levels of emotional stress and the consequently lower level of happiness in such families. The problems of poverty and working class life are displaced into hostilities toward one's mate. The greater divorce and separation rates of lower class families also reflect the lesser economic stake in such unions, in comparison with upper middle class marriages. When the wife is not so dependent on her husband's income (either because she works or can sustain herself without a drastic decline in living standards from state welfare programs) unhappy wives are less likely to stay in unhappy unions.

Sexual activity is strongly class correlated. Working class people traditionally begin active sex lives earlier, and are more likely to engage in intercourse (rather than achieving orgasm in other ways) than are middle class people. Kinsey found that in the United States in 1948 upper middle class young single men were considerably more likely to masturbate than lower level working class men. They were also more likely to engage in "petting" to climax. On the other hand, working class single men were considerably more likely to have intercourse with prostitutes as well as more frequently have sexual relations with female friends. Higher level working class men were more likely to have homosexual relations than either lower level working class or middle class men (see Table 9.12).

Married upper middle class men were found by Kinsey to be significantly more likely to masturbate than working class men, while working class men were more likely to have intercourse. Otherwise there was not a great difference in the sexual behavior of married men by class (Kinsey et al. 1953, Table 2).

In San Francisco in 1969-70 it was still the case that working class youth began active sexual lives earlier than youth from the middle class. The mean age for initial experience with sexual intercourse for men who had never been to college was 16.7 years compared to 18.9 for college graduates. For women who had never been to college it was 18.1 and for college graduates 21.5 (Weinberg and Williams 1980, Table 2B). The San Francisco study also found that there was a slight negative correlation between class and number of sexual partners by men, but *not* by women. Male high school graduates reported having slept with a mean of 12.8 women, while male college graduates reported having slept with a mean of 7.7. This comparies with Kinsey's 1948 sample where the mean for high school graduates was 18.9 and for college graduates 9.6 (Weinberg and Williams 1980, Table 3B). This study also found that in 1969-70

TABLE 9.12: Sources of Orgasms for Single Males Aged 21-25, by Educational Level, 1948

	Level 0-8	Level 9-12	Level 13+
Masturbation	20.15%	29.67%	53.30%
Nocturnal emissions	5.02	8.10	15.67
Petting to climax	1.23	2.77	7.50
Intercourse with companions	52.84	38.02	18.45
Intercourse with prostitutes	12.55	4.66	1.27
Homosexual outlet	8.06	16.31	3.72
Animal contacts	0.15	0.47	0.09
Total outlets	100.00	100.00	100.00
Number of cases	361	263	1,898
Total solitary outlets	25.17	37.77	68.97
Total heterosexual outlets	66.62	45.45	27.22
Total homosexual outlets	8.06	16.31	3.72

Note: Data are for percentage of total orgasms.
Source: Kinsey et al. 1953, p. 303.

there was *no* class correlation between educational level and the relative frequency of various forms of heterosexual sex or masturbation. The significant difference in forms of heterosexual sex is not found in its relative occurrence in the different classes, but rather in the age of first experience. For example, mean age at first experience with oral-genital sex performed by a woman was 17.3 years for men without college and 19.5 years for male college graduates. For women, performed by a man, it was 20.0 years for those without college and 24.2 years for women college graduates (Weinberg and Williams 1980, 39).

Working class men are less likely than middle class men to read pornography, are more likely to endorse the double standard, and to receive less satisfaction from sex (Rossidies, 1976, pp. 176-77). The lower the social class, the less enjoyment and interest both wives and husbands get from sexual intercourse. A study done in the late 1950s found that 78 percent of middle class husbands as compared with 44 percent of "lower lower class" husbands expressed "great interest and enjoyment" in sexual relations. The same study found that 50 percent of middle class wives, in contrast to 20 percent of "lower lower class" wives felt great interest and enjoyment. It should be noted, however, that there was no significant difference between the middle class and the "upper lower class" on this dimension for either husbands or wives (Grey 1969, p. 121).

There are significant differences in child-rearing practices among the social classes, differences that become manifested in the different types of personality characteristic of the adults of the various classes. Traditionally working class people were more likely than middle class people to breast-feed their children; since the mid-1940s this tendency has been reversed—middle class people are now more likely than working class people to breast-feed. This change, however, is due entirely to the decreasing tendency for working class people to breast-feed. In the principal studies of the frequency of breast-feeding done before 1948 it was found that on the average about two-thirds of all working class people breast-fed, while in those studies done after 1947, it was generally found that approximately half did. On the other hand, studies done in both periods showed that on the average about two-thirds of middle class mothers breast-fed (Bronfenbrenner 1970, p. 211).

Traditionally working class people breast-fed longer than did middle class people. Again this was reversed in the late 1940s. Working class people now breast-feed for shorter periods than middle class people. While both middle class and working class people now breast feed for a shorter period of time, the greatest decrease has occurred among working class people. While the average amount of time children were breast-fed before 1948 (as reported in various studies done before this date) in the working class was approximately 5 months, after 1947 it was 2 months. On the other hand, in the middle class the average was four months before 1948 and three months after 1947 (Bronfenbrenner 1970, p. 212). Here again we see a rather major change in working class practices together with little or no change in middle class practices.

Average age at weaning (from both breast and bottle) has been a constant for the working class, averaging about 13 months both before and after 1948. On the other hand, middle class children's age at weaning has increased. The average found in pre-1948 studies was 11 months, and that found in post-1947 studies 13 months (Bronfenbrenner 1970, p. 213).

The decline in the probability of working class women's breast-feeding their children as well as in the length of time this class breast-feeds appears to be caused by fundamental shifts in the traditional role of working class women that occurred concurrent with this change. While working class mothers traditionally stayed home as full-time housewives/mothers, this pattern broke down in the post–World War II generation. There has been a radical increase in the probability of married women, especially mothers (driven by economic necessity), working outside of the home. This trend has been much less the case in the middle class, where a much higher proportion of women continue to be full-time mothers, at least until their children are all in school. Working women have much greater difficulty than do nonworking women in breast-feeding, consequently as working class wives have entered the labor force, the traditional class differential has been reversed.

Evidence from studies done before 1945 show that middle class people began and completed toilet training (both bowel and bladder) earlier than did working class people. However, the evidence from post-1945 studies shows the reverse. In recent years working class people have been shown both to begin and complete toilet training before middle class people (Bronfenbrenner, 1970, p. 213).

There are significant general differences between the two largest classes in the overall character of the child-parent relationship. Contemporary U.S. middle class disciplinary practices tend to be more oriented to the granting and withdrawal of approval and praise than are the disciplinary practices of the working class, while working class disciplinary patterns tend to be more reliant than middle class patterns on physical punishment as well as on threatening and cajoling. (Bronfenbrenner 1970, p. 216). Middle class people are more likely than working class people to deal with their children through ignoring infractions, reasoning, or talking with their children (Bronfenbrenner 1970, p. 216). Generally working class parents in the post-World War II period have put greater restrictions on their children's activity than have middle class parents (e.g., fixed bedtimes, restrictions on how far a child can go away from home). However, studies done before 1945 tended to show the opposite was the case in this period (Bronfenbrenner 1970, p. 217). Middle class children are generally allowed to express more aggression toward their parents (or other children) than are working class children (Bronfenbrenner 1970, p. 216). Middle class children are treated more permissively in their sexual behavior. They are less likely to be disciplined for touching their sex organs, and are more likely to be allowed to play unclothed and to see their parents naked (Bronfenbrenner 1970, p. 216). Middle class children are also significantly more likely than working class children to be told the "facts of life" by their parents as well as be told at an early age (Reid 1977, p. 150).

Working class child rearing in the post-World War II period has been generally characterized more than in the middle class by emphasis on obedience, neatness, cleanliness, and honesty, while middle class child rearing is characterized more than working class child rearing by stress on curiosity, self-control, consideration for others, and happiness. Middle class parents in general have higher expectations for their children (see Table 9.13). There are even differences in the language children acquire. Middle class children's language is organized more to facilitate comprehension of a wide range of symbols and social relationships, while that of the working class is organized more around a less abstract level of conceptualization and causality. The latter tends to emphasize more affective responses to immediate situations (Rossidies 1976, p. 182; Bernstein 1975).

In general, the middle class mode of child raising is geared to training adults suited for professional and business life—creative, self-directed personalities, while the working class mode is geared to producing adults better suited to subordinate menial labor, where workers respect authority, rather than demonstrate independence and creativity.

Friendship patterns are very different in the working class and the middle class. The lower one's class the more likely one is to regularly visit one's neighbors and the stronger are extended family ties. In 1977, 39 percent of manual workers in the United States reported that they "frequently" socialized with their relatives as did 40 percent of those in the capitalist class, while only 26 percent of those in the new middle class and 34 percent of those in the traditional middle class did so (computed from the NORC General Social Survey for 1977). A study done in the 1960s found that 43 percent of working class people, in contrast to 18 percent of upper middle class

TABLE 9.13: Mothers' Socioeconomic Status and Choice of "Most Desirable" Characteristics in a Ten- or Eleven-Year-Old Child

Characteristic	Socioeconomic Stratum				
	I (high) (N = 51)	II (N = 43)	III (N = 80)	IV (N = 128)	V (low) (N = 37)
Obedience	0.14	0.19	0.25	0.35	0.27
Neatness, cleanliness	0.06	0.07	0.16	0.18	0.27
Consideration	0.41	0.37	0.39	0.25	0.32
Curiosity	0.37	0.12	0.09	0.07	0.03
Self-control	0.24	0.30	0.18	0.13	0.14
Happiness	0.61	0.40	0.40	0.38	0.30
Boys		0.48	0.40	0.27	
Girls		0.54	0.40	0.45	
Honesty	0.37	0.49	0.46	0.50	0.65

Note: Data are for proportion who select each characteristic, by socioeconomic strata (on Hollingshead index).
Source: Kohn 1968, p. 155.

people were more likely to have relatives rather than either neighbors or friends over to their house for parties or visits. In contrast, 83 percent of upper middle class people as compared to 43 percent of working class people were most likely to have friends over. Working class people are more likely to visit with neighbors than are upper middle class people. The same study reported that the mean number of visits per month with friends was 2.1 in the upper middle class and 3.5 in the working class. Working class people are twice as likely to have their relatives for their closest friends than are upper middle class people (Blumberg 1972, p. 207). The working class is much more family and neighborhood oriented than is the middle class. The middle class is much more likely than the working class to be socially integrated with nonrelated friends who share a similar occupational situation. Further, working class people tend to maintain old friendships longer as well as to be more resistant to forming new friendships (i.e., friendships are generally deeper and more reliable in the working class).

Working class people tend to be more involved in close kin networks. These can act as a conservative force with strong sanctions against idiosyncratic ideas or deviance in normal times, or act as a strong force against "scabbing" in a strike situation, as well as in moving the class as a whole left in a crisis situation. Family life is generally more important for working class people. Feelings of family loyalty and obligations even for fairly distant relatives tend to be stronger than in the middle class. Traditionally sons tended to find employment in the same place as the father (or an uncle) while daughters tended to live near parents, continuing to maintain close relationships with them (especially with their mother). In the post-World War II period, however, the trend has been away from living near parents as well as for sons to work in different places than fathers. The strength of traditional family ties in the working class represents a continuity with the peasant family that prevailed in the recent past of most working class families. As that past recedes and the logic of industrial capitalism with its high degree of mobility and high tendency toward individualization proceeds, the remnants of the extended family with its strong kin solidarity are dissipated (see Shostak 1969, pt. 3).

Membership in organizations also varies considerably by class. In 1977 in the United States 38 percent of manual workers reported that they belonged to more than one organization. This compared to 45 percent of the independent petty bourgeoisie, 62 percent of the new middle class, and 80 percent of capitalists (computed from the NORC General Social Survey for 1977). Similar results have been found by many researchers (Duberman 1976:154; Reid 1977:220; Roach, Gross, and Gursslin 1969, p. 119).

RELIGION

Religious domination (especially within Protestantism in the United States) as well as the intensity and form of individual beliefs is strongly influenced by class position. Within Protestantism, the three denominations of Episcopalian, Congregational, and Presbyterian are the upper middle class religions. Their members have the highest average incomes and social status. The Baptists and the fundamentalists are the lower class Protestant religions. When a Protestant family becomes upwardly mobile it generally changes religion, first from Baptist or another of the relatively low status Protestant denominations to Methodist (or another of the respectable middle class Protestant denominations), and finally to one of the three upper middle class denominations (see Table 9.14).

The class basis of the different Protestant denominations is reflected in the character of both their services and rites, and in their theologies and beliefs. The "fire and brimstone" fundamentalist churches offer salvation and hope to the poor and oppressed—an offer of a better life in the hereafter, and justice and retribution for the sufferings of this life. Their ceremonies, rituals, and sermons are highly emotional and deeply involve their congregations. On the other hand, the upper middle class denominations preach an ethical religion that more often than not is focused on living a better and happier life

TABLE 9.14: Religious Denomination and Class

	(1) Median Family Income (1966)	(2) Median Occupational Status (1966) (0–100)	Percentage in Each Stratum			
			(3) High	(4) Intermediate	(5) Low	(6) Total
Protestants						
Congregational	$17,500	82.7	23.9%	42.6%	33.5%	100%
Episcopal	13,000	59.9	24.1	33.7	42.2	100
Presbyterian	11,667	60.3	21.9	40.0	38.1	100
Methodist	10,703	45.0	12.7	35.6	51.7	100
Lutheran	10,375	42.9	10.9	36.1	53.0	100
Baptist	9,311	28.6	8.0	24.0	68.0	100
Fundamentalist	8,290	24.8				
Roman Catholic	9,999	43.2	8.7	24.7	66.6	100
Jewish	14,688	65.0	21.8	32.0	46.2	100
No preference/ no religion	10,357	55.0	13.9	26.6	59.4	100
Grand total	10,177	45.2				

Source: For columns 1 and 2, Lauman 1969, p. 186, Table 2; source for columns 3, 4, 5, Schneider 1952, p. 228.

in *this* world, rather than on salvation and retribution. Moreover, their sermons and rituals tend to be intellectualized and not intensely emotional. Each of these types of religions speaks to the experiences and needs of their respective congregations, so it is no surprise that as a family rises in society its need for salvation and redemption decreases at the same time as its desire for social respectability (which membership in the higher status denominations brings) grows.

The traditionally relatively low income and social status of Roman Catholics in the United States is a result of the fact that the bulk of working class foreign immigrants—from the Irish in the 1840s to the 1880s through the Poles and Italians from the 1890s to the 1920s to the recent Latin American immigrants—have been of this faith. These groups, with the exception of the Irish, continue to be heavily concentrated in working class occupations. Although the ancestors of most U.S. Jews migrated to the United States from eastern Europe in a condition of poverty between 1882 and 1914, the bulk of their descendants have achieved professional or other middle class status because of their traditional middle class "pariah" (or "middleman minority") status (see Chapter 10 for a full discussion of the Jews and class).

Among all major religious tendencies in the United States, the higher one's social class the more likely one is to attend religious services. In 1977 in the United States manual working class people were the least religious (as measured by frequency of church attendance). While 33 percent of both the new and old middle class reported attending church at least once a week, only 22 percent of manual workers reported doing so. On the other extreme, while 35 percent of the independent petty bourgeoisie reported attending church once a year or less, 40 percent of the salaried professionals and managers and 42 percent of manual workers reported being equally irreligious (computed from the NORC 1977 General Social Survey).

A study done in the mid-1960s in the United States showed that among Roman Catholics 82 percent of the upper middle class attended church weekly, compared with 61 percent of poorer workers. Among liberal Protestant denominations 35 percent of upper middle class people, in contrast to 30 percent of poorer working class people, attended church regularly. Among conservative Protestant denominations 63 percent of upper middle class people, in contrast to 40 percent of poorer working class people, reported attending church weekly (Thielbar and Feldman 1972, p. 496).

Small but positive correlations have also been found between social class and frequency of praying, tithing, attitudes about the importance of religion, belief in a personal god, belief in life after death, and probability of being married in a religious ceremony (Thielbar and Feldman 1972, p. 499; Reid 1977, p. 205). One study found that in 1950 among U.S.-born whites 88 percent of all professionals in contrast with 67 percent of all laborers were married in a religious ceremony (Roach, Gross and Gursslin 1969, p. 440). Another study found that in the 1960's among moderate denomination Protestants 83 percent of the lower class believed in a personal god, compared to 87 percent of the upper middle class (this slight difference held among liberal Protestants, conservative Protestants, and Roman Catholics as well) (Thielbar and Feldman 1972, p. 499). Significantly more upper middle class people, both Protestant and Catholic, believe in life after death. Among the Catholic upper middle class 87 percent believed in life after death as compared to 72 percent of poorer workers. Among moderate Protestants, 84 percent of the upper middle class believed in life after death, in contrast to 66 percent of poorer workers (Thielbar and Feldman 1972, p. 499).

On the other hand, when we examine most religious phenomena that reflect salvation, retribution, temptation, and sin, we see a different picture. Here it is lower class people that report greater religious involvement than higher class people. Among Protestants, lower class people are significantly more likely to believe that the devil exists. The mid-1960s study reported 60 percent of poorer workers in contrast to 32 of the upper middle class believe in the devil. This difference holds with about equal strength both within liberal and conservative Protestant denominations (Thielbar and Feldman 1972, p. 499).

Lower class people are also significantly more likely to have had a religious experience than are upper middle class people. The mid-1960s study found that 41 percent of upper middle class Catholics were "high on religious experience" compared to 62 percent of poorer working class Catholics. Among liberal denomination Protestants the equivalent range was from 38 percent to 59 percent, and among moderate denomination Protestants 52 percent to 67 percent. Among conservative denomination Protestants the spread was only slight, 85 percent versus 90 percent (Thielbar and Feldman 1972, p. 493).

In general, religion for upper class people is more of an intellectual and ethical phenomenon, in good part focused around the social life of the congregation; while for poorer people religion is a more intensive emotional experience, not necessarily oriented to a congregation but focused on salvation and active spiritual forces, often of an evil kind, that influence daily life. These two views of religion are very much a product of the differential experiences of the classes.

CONSUMPTION, LEISURE, AND MASS MEDIA

Working class and middle class people have rather different spending and consumption patterns, in good part dictated by the amount of money each has available to spend to satisfy their families' needs. On the most fundamental level this is expressed in the type and quality of food bought, the quality of housing purchased or rented, and the quality of clothing worn (or made). For example, in the 1971-74 period, about one-third of persons living above the poverty level ate meat, on the average, more than once a day. This was true of only 22 percent of persons living below the poverty level (U.S. Department of Health and Human Services 1979b). The differences in consumption patterns ramify throughout all aspects of material life.

While most families above a very low minimum are likely to own an automobile, most middle class families, unlike working class families, own two cars. And, while working class people, no matter how poor, are as likely as middle class people to own a television, middle class people are more likely to have a *color* set than are working class people. Middle class people are more likely than working class people to own washing machines and clothes dryers, and are considerably more likely to own a dishwasher and an air conditioner (see Table 9.15).

The proportion of income spent on different categories of items varies by class. Poorer people, for example, spend a significantly higher proportion of their income for food, tobacco, and medical care than do middle class people, and a somewhat lesser proportion for clothing, automobiles, and recreation. In 1974 the lowest income decile in the United States spent 47 percent of its *gross* income on food as compared to 11 percent for the highest income decile. In 1974 the second lowest income decile spent 18 percent of its *net* income on energy as compared to 6 percent for the top income decile, 37 percent on shelter as compared to 12 percent, and 13 percent on medical care as compared to 5 percent. (Blumberg 1980, pp. 182, 184). In 1957 people with an income of over $10,000 spent 14 percent on clothing and 13 percent on recreation, compared with 11 percent and 11 percent respectively for people with an income under $3,000 (Shostak and Gomberg 1964, p. 76).

The different classes spend their leisure time differently. Middle class people are slightly more likely than working class people to regularly attend the cinema and are far more likely than working class people to attend the live theater or the other performing arts such as ballet, orchestra, or opera (Reid 1977, pp. 218, 219). Spectator sports are more important for the working class than for the middle class, but participant sports are engaged in more by the middle class than the working class. Spectator sports that are particularly more popular in the working class than in the middle class include boxing and horse racing, while participant sports that are especially more popular with the middle classes than the working class include swimming, golf, tennis, and table tennis (Reid 1977, pp. 223, 225).

In the United States hunting, fishing, auto sports, and gambling are especially important for men in the working class (as opposed to middle class). All of these activities can be considered to be an assertion of "manhood" (or dignity), an outlet for hostilities generated on the job, a source of creativity and achievement denied in work, and a chance to prove oneself and gain the respect of others, again opportunities difficult to achieve at work.

Gambling is especially popular in the lower levels of the working class. Gambling offers a number of rewards independent of actual payoffs. It holds out the hope of striking it rich, but probably more importantly, of gaining the respect of friends that comes from working out a method to "beat the system." Far more respect goes to those who win as an apparent result of a well-developed "system" than to those who appear to win merely because of luck (Shostak and Gomberg 1964, p. 451).

TABLE 9.15: Households Owning Cars and Appliances, 1971: Percentage Distribution by Income Level

Annual Family Income	Cars (1972)		Television		Washing Machine	Clothes Dryer	Refrig-erator	Freezer	Dishwasher	Air Conditioner
	One at Least	Two at Least	Black and White	Color						
Under $3,000	40.6%	5.3%	77.0%	16.1%	51.6%	13.9%	76.5%	21.0%	1.9%	13.5%
$3,000-$4,999	68.0	12.6	79.7	26.5	62.0	24.0	80.4	25.3	4.4	21.1
$5,000-$7,499	84.2	23.2	75.3	39.7	68.3	38.2	80.8	30.1	9.5	25.6
$7,500-$9,999	91.3	32.2	74.5	50.3	77.2	51.6	84.4	33.7	15.5	32.8
$10,000-$14,999	94.9	45.6	77.7	58.4	83.4	64.5	88.2	38.9	29.1	43.5
$15,000-$24,999	96.5	58.4	81.8	68.3	86.6	75.2	90.4	43.3	50.7	52.2
$25,000 and over	93.0	66.6	82.1	79.5	89.7	83.9	94.0	56.3	74.8	69.3

Source: U.S. Department of Commerce 1975a, Table 646.

Alcohol use varies considerably by class. In 1978 approximately 42 percent of people with family incomes of between $3,000 and $6,999 and 50 percent of those with family incomes of less than $3,000 were total abstainers, in contrast to only 18 percent of those earning over $15,000 and 21 percent of those earning between $10,000 and $15,000. While 53 percent of those with only a grade school education and 29 percent of manual workers were total abstainers, only 17 percent of college graduates and 16 percent of professional and business people were total abstainers. Further, there is a tendency for problem drinking to be more prevalent among the better educated and higher income groups. While 38 percent of college graduates and 39 percent of those earning over $15,000 a year reported that they sometimes drink more than they should, this was true for only 24 percent of those with only a grade school education and 27 percent of those with family incomes of between $3,000 and $7,000 (U.S. Department of Justice 1980, p. 391).

Lower class people are somewhat more tolerant of drug use than are upper class people. While 13 percent of upper middle class people in a U.S. national sample approved of the use of at least three illegal drugs (contained on a list of the principal drugs in use in the United States), 16 percent of working class people and 22 percent of lower class people did so (*Playboy* 1979, p. 27). Marijuana use does not vary significantly by income level. In 1977, 23 percent of those earning $15,000 or over a year as compared to 20 percent of those earning less than $5,000 and 25 percent of those earning between $5,000 and $15,000 reported that they "ever happened to try marihuana" (U.S. Department of Justice 1980, p. 396).

Lower class peole watch far more television than do middle and upper middle class people. One study found that in the early 1960s while "lower working class" people watched television for an average of 180 minutes a night, and middle level working class people 100 minutes, upper middle class people watched television for only 31 minutes and upper class people for 16 minutes (Hodges 1964, p. 161).

The higher one's class the more likely one is to regularly read newspapers (Roach, Gross, and Gursslin 1969, p. 119). The type of newspapers read varies considerably by class. For example, during the mid-1950s in the New York area 51 percent of upper middle class people regularly read the New York *Times* as compared to 4 percent of the lowest level working class. On the other hand, only 1 percent of upper middle class people read the New York *Daily News* as compared with 15 percent of lowest level working class (Hollingshead and Redlich 1958, p. 404).

The higher one's class the more likely one is to read both news and nonnews magazines (Roach, Gross, and Gursslin 1969, p. 119).

The type of magazine favored varies considerably by class. Upper middle and middle class people favor news magazines,digests, educational literary magazines, hobby and craft magazines; while lower class people, who read magazines at all, favor escapist, hobby and sport magazines (see, for example, Hollingshead and Redlich 1958, pp. 403–4).

Some magazines are much more widely read by higher class people and others by working class people. For example, in 1969, 52 percent of the *New Yorker* male primary readership as well as 31 percent of the male readership of the *New York Times Magazine*, 56 percent of the male readership of *Fortune*, and 35 percent of the male readership of *Newsweek* earned $15,000 or over a year. At the same time 26 percent of the primary female readership of *Cosmopolitan* had a household income of over $15,000. This contrasts with only 18 percent of the primary male readership of *Field and Stream*, 19 percent of the primary male readership of both *Popular Science* and *Mechanic Illustrated*, 14 percent of the male readership of *Parade Magazine*, 21 percent of the male readership of *Readers Digest* and 18 percent of that of *TV Guide*, and with 4 percent of the primary female readership of *Modern Romances* and 14 percent of that of *Modern Screen* (*Demographics*, 1969).

Working class people are more likely than middle and upper middle class people to get their news from the television rather than from newspapers or news magazines, and when they do get information from newspapers, to get it primarily from the sensationalist, scandal-ridden, and right-wing press, rather than from somewhat more objective and in-depth sources.

Book reading is especially highly correlated with class position. One study found that 48 percent of upper middle class people and 26 percent of lower middle class people had read at least one book within the previous three months, compared to 10 percent of working class people (Rothman 1978, p. 192).

CRIME

Class enters into criminality at many different levels: first, the definition of what a crime is; second, the probability of breaking the law; third, the probability of being arrested for a crime; fourth, the probability of being convicted for violating the law; fifth, the harshness and length of a sentence; and sixth, the probability of parole or pardon. At each of these six points the criminal justice system is organized against the working class and the poor,and in favor of the wealthy and middle classes. Further, class greatly affects the probability of victimization by crime.

The very definition of what legally and socially is a "crime" is very much a product of class forces. Whether or not an act is defined by the state as illegal varies tremendously among types of societies depending on how harmful or useful that act is judged to be to the dominant system of social relations. For example, in many societies charging interest on a loan is considered to be criminal. Such was the case in both feudal Europe and in traditional Islamic societies. Such interest was regarded as theft, just as surely as breaking into someone's home and taking an equivalent amount of money. However, in highly commercial and capitalist societies interest is necessary to make the economy work, therefore, here, charging interest is legal.

The concept of "stealing" or improperly taking something that belongs to someone else is a very elastic concept. Its elasticity is demonstrated both by the variability of the legal definitions of stealing in different societies, and by the variability of what is regarded as proper (and property) by different classes in the same society. In socialist societies such as the USSR and China it is regarded as stealing, and it is punishable by law, to hire (sometimes more than a very limited number of) people and pay them less than the worth of what they produce, i.e., it is illegal to make a profit from the labor power of others. It is also often illegal to charge rent for the use of housing. Such activities are not only legal in capitalist societies, but are the very essence of economic relations.

Although the law in capitalist societies defines the foreclosure of a person's home, farm, or family business as legal (and necessary for the operation of the credit system) people who may own a farm or home that had been in their family for generations may well regard the property as theirs in spite of legal definitions that dictate that when you can not make mortgage payments the bank then owns your property. However, in capitalist societies the police enforce the legal opinions of the banks against the sentiments of the small farmers and homeowners.

There are actions that are both illegal and generally socially defined as criminal, such as murder, robbery, rape, and so on; other actions that are illegal, but generally not socially defined as criminal such as much white-collar crime, e.g., price fixing, tax evasion, corporation's producing dangerous products (e.g., drugs, automobiles) that violate federal regulations; and actions that are not illegal but, among at least wide segments of people, are regarded as criminal, such as massive foreclosure of small farms in times of depression. In general, actions of poor people in taking what had been in the possession of others are much more likely to be both legally *and* socially defined as criminal, than parallel actions of wealthy people.

Moreover, the law is biased in a business-oriented society to the interests of the wealthy. The law generally favors landlords over tenants (in eviction proceedings, procedures for repair of a house, and so on); owners over workers (workers have little legal right to their job, little legal say in the production process, and so on); landowners over the landless (landowners, unlike the landless, have access to criminal trespass legislation). The effect of many laws is to enfringe on the prerogatives only of the poorer classes. As was once said about France, the law treats all classes equally, it prohibits both the rich *and* the poor from sleeping under bridges. Much the same thing can be said about stealing food or other necessities of life, or the money to procure them.

Working class and poorer people are more likely than are upper class and middle class people to commit acts that are defined by the state as criminal. The difference is especially pronounced in the class difference in crimes against persons. A study found that nine out of every ten murders in Philadelphia involved lower class people. A study of assault in St. Louis found that about 80 percent of both the offenders and the victims were working class (Clinard and Meier 1979, p. 199). Homicides are rare in the middle and upper classes. A study of five police districts in Chicago in 1965 found that the crime rate against persons was 5.5 times higher in a representative low/middle income white district than in a representative high income white district. But crimes against property were only 1.7 times more likely in the low/middle income district. The same study found that the rate of crimes against persons was over 30 times higher in very low income black districts than in high income white districts, while crimes against property were only 2.5 times more prevalent (Lane 1968, p. 217).

The poorer classes are more likely to commit both crimes against property and crimes of violence because: first, property crimes are in good part attempts to obtain the standard of living of middle class America that impacts the poorer classes from every television show and billboard (and thus becomes regarded as desirable and proper); second, crimes of violence are in good part a product of the stress, hostility, and bitterness generated by menial labor, poverty, and the humiliations of lower class life; and third, both types of crimes are encouraged by the "deviant subculture" or counterculture common among many lower class people, a culture of defiance and disrespect for property, law and order, and the better-off classes, a culture within which it is regarded as more or less all right to commit many acts regarded by the dominant institutions as criminal.

A U.S. Presidential Crime Commission's special study of approximately 10,000 households in the United States in the early 1970s found that "91 percent of all Americans have violated laws that could have subjected them to a term of imprisonment at one or another time in their lives." Sixty-four percent of all males in this sample as well as 27 percent of the females admitted to committing at least one felony for which they had never been arrested (Reiman 1979, pp. 100–1). It is clear that although legally defined crimes (especially crimes of violence) are more prevalent in the working class and underclass, crime is widespread in all classes.

Yet police are far more likely to arrest working and underclass people for crimes than they are middle or upper class people. On the one hand, the police image of the "criminal type" is a lower class person; such people are, thus, more likely to get picked up and charged for an offense whether or not they committed it. On the other hand, police are reluctant to arrest respectable middle class people unless they have strong evidence against them. A 1977 study found that 14 percent of manual workers and 7 percent of professional and business people reported that they had ever been picked up or charged by the police for anything other than a traffic violation. While 8 percent of those earnings over $15,000 reported that this was the case for themselves, this was true for 16 percent of those earning less than $5,000 (U.S. Department of Justice 1980, p. 491). One study reported that working class people (unemployed, semiskilled, unskilled, and laborers) were arrested in 1965 26 times more often for the major (FBI index) crimes as were white-collar workers and professionals (Duberman 1976, p. 175).

A study showed that 29 percent of middle and upper class people admitted to committing a major theft as a youth, while 40 percent of lower class people admitted doing so. Although there is relatively little difference in the actual rates of juvenile delinquency, lower class children are far more likely than middle class children to get into trouble with the police because the police do not like the behavior and attitude of lower class children and because of the relative powerlessness of their parents (Mandell 1975, p. 176; Roach, Gross, and Gursslin 1969, p. 485). A study of arrests of youthful criminals showed that the arrest rate in upper middle class and middle class neighborhoods was one-third that of poorer working class neighborhoods (Roach, Gross and Gursslin 1969, p. 477).

It should be emphasized that the working class and the underclass are the principal victims of violent crime. In 1977 the estimated rate per 100,000 persons of rape and attempted rape was 59 per 100,000 for white women with family incomes of over $15,000 a year while it was 185 per 100,000 for white women with family incomes below $3,000, 159 per 100,000 for those between $3,000 and $7,500, and 105 per 100,000 for those between $7,500 and $10,000. The incidence of robbery in 1977 was 373 per 100,000 for whites with a family income of over $25,000, while it was 1,106 per 100,000 for whites with a family income of less than $3,000 and 657 per 100,000 for those whites with a family income of between $3,000 and $7,500. The rate of victimization for robbery at *all income levels* for blacks was approximately twice that for whites at the same level. The incidence of assault for whites earning over $25,000 in 1977 was 2,409 per 100,000. This contrasts with a rate of 4,225 per 100,000 and 3,115 per 100,000 for those with family incomes of less than $3,000 and between $3,000 and $7,500 respectively (U.S. Department of Justice 1980, p. 359).

The incidence of all crimes of violence against all persons 16 and over in 1977 was 28.4 per 1,000 for professional people, while it was 54.6 per 1,000 for laborers, 59.0 per 100,000 for service workers, and 44.6 per 100,000 for operatives (excluding transport). The incidence of rape was 0.5 per 1,000 for professionals and 2.0 per 1,000 for service workers and 1.3 per 1,000 for clerical workers. For robbery it was 5.2 per 1,000 for professionals, 8.8 for laborers, 9.8 for service workers, and 7.8 for operatives (excluding transport). For assault, 22.7 for professionals, 47.1 for service workers, 45.1 for laborers, and 36.2 for operatives (U.S. Department of Justice 1979, p. 30).

The greater incidence of crime in poor and working class neighborhoods is reflected in a greater fear of victimization among these people. In 1977, 38 percent of persons with incomes over $15,000 stated that there were areas within a mile of their residence where they would be afraid to walk alone at night. This compares to 56 percent of those earning less than $5,000. While 23 percent of those earning less than $7,000 a year reported that they did not feel "safe and secure" in their homes at night, this was true of only 9 percent of those earning over $20,000 (U.S. Department of Justice 1980, pp. 227, 259).

The fact that it is working class and lower class people that are disproportionately both the victims *and* the perpetuators of violent crime tends to produce contradictory effects on attitudes toward harsher law enforcement against criminals. In 1977 there was no significant difference among the social classes on the question of whether or not the courts should be harsher on criminals—87 percent of both the manual working class and the new middle class as well as 89 percent of the independent middle class and 91 percent of white-collar workers maintained that the courts were *not* harsh enough (calculated from the NORC 1977 General Social Survey).

There is a tendency for the working class and the poorer people to least support capital punishment and for professionals and higher income people to most support it. In 1978, 68 percent of professional and business people in comparison with 63 percent of manual laborers stated they favored capital punishment for convicted murderers, while 72 percent of those earning over $15,000 a year as compared to 43 percent of those earning under $3,000 and 59 percent of those earning between $3,000 and $7,000 favored it (U.S. Department of Justice 1980, p. 293). Attitudes about the police also tend to be slightly class correlated. A study of attitudes in the United States in 1970 found that 58 percent of those with incomes under $5,000 as compared to 68 percent of those with incomes of $10,000 and over had a favorable evaluation of the local police (Beeghley 1978, p. 170).

Once arrested the chances of conviction are greater for poorer and working class people than for middle class people because judges and juries are less likely to believe the testimony of poorer people (who are typically presumed guilty) and more likely to believe that of middle class and upper middle class people like themselves, whom they have come to understand, trust, and respect from their day to day friendly relations with such people, and because middle class and upper class people, unlike poorer people who must often rely on overworked and unenthusiastic public defenders (or court-appointed attorneys), can secure the best legal defense. Very often the only advice poorer people who can not afford their own lawyer are given by a court-appointed attorney or public defender is to cop a plea (i.e., plead guilty to a lesser offense in a deal with the prosecution), thus guaranteeing a punishment for a crime less than that anticipated if convicted of the original offense. It has been shown that the chances of a jury returning a guilty plea are dependent on such factors as personal appearance, race, prior record, work and school history, and whether or not the defendant has a private lawyer (Mandell 1975, p. 176). All these factors work against the lower class defendant. Juries are generally biased in the over inclusion of middle class people and typically shunned by poorer people. Further, jurors with higher level occupations than the average jurors are typically selected as foremen, participate more in discussions, and have more influence in the final decisions (Rossidies 1976, p. 105).

Working and underclass defendants are more likely than middle class defendants to be unable to pay for a lawyer and as a result be assigned a counsel. In 1974 in the United States 83 percent of robbery defendants were assigned counsel as well as 63 percent of burglary defendants (both are disproportionately lower class crimes). This contrasts with 48 percent of defendants in tax fraud cases (a distinctively middle class crime) (Howard and Logue 1978, p. 45). One study showed that assigned counsels got dismissals for their clients in only 6 percent of cases, compared to 29 percent for retained counsels. The rate of acquitals/dismissals for privately retained lawyers was double that for those appointed by the courts (Reiman 1979, pp. 133, 114).

Once found guilty for the same crimes, poorer people are on the average given longer sentences than middle class people, are less likely to receive suspended sentences or probation than are middle class people, and are more likely to be sentenced to capital punishment (Rossidies 1976, p. 405). Those convicted of typically working class and underclass crimes are much more likely to get sentenced to prison than to a fine and/or probation. In 1971, 91.9 percent of convicted robbers received prison terms (only 8.1 percent probation) as compared to 21.9 percent of convicted embezzlers and 35.1 percent of those convicted of tax fraud (Howard and Logue 1978, p. 45).

The crimes typically committed by the poor are assigned longer sentences than those typically committed by the middle and upper class. In 1978 the average sentence (for whites) for federal prisoners for robbery was 176.5 months, burglary 88.9 months, securities violations 74.3 months, fraud 50.4 months, and counterfeiting 68.0 months (U.S. Department of Commerce 1980, p. 198). The greater harshness shown to the lower classes is also reflected in the fact that in 1978 the average sentence for a federal crime was 99.0 months for white convicts and 122.1 months for nonwhites. This is mostly a result of blacks much more often than whites being convicted of crimes of the poor that carry greater penalties—rather than a result of stiffer sentences for equivalent crimes. As a further illustration of the systematic bias against the lower classes in the criminal justice system it is of interest to point out that 55 percent of all executions in the twentieth century in the United States have been of black people, a people overwhelmingly concentrated in the lower level working and underclass of American society. In 1978, 41 percent of prisoners under a sentence of death in the United States were black. Only 7 percent had ever been to college. Sixty-seven percent had never finished high school (U.S. Department of Commerce 1980, p. 198).

In 1974 in the United States the state prison population was made up of 9 percent of persons of professional and managerial background (compared to 27 percent of the nonprisoner population). Eighty-three percent of the prison population reported that they most recently had worked as manual workers (this compared to 48 percent of the nonprison population). In the same year 9 percent of all state prison inmates had completed at least one year of college (compared to 22 percent of the general public) while 61 percent had not finished high school (compared to 45 percent of the general public). Only 10 percent of local jail inmates in 1972 had incomes exceeding the U.S. median income in the year before their arrest. Of all state prisoners less than 30 percent had been defended by a private lawyer. A study for the U.S. government has shown that a 1.4 percent increase in the

U.S. unemployment rate results in a 5.6 percent increase in the prison population (see Table 9.6; Reiman 1979, p. 127; Howard and Logue 1980, 1978, p. 44).

The lighter treatment for white-collar crime and for middle class criminals is *not* due to the lesser cost of their crimes. It has been estimated that the total cost of all state-defined robberies in the United States in 1965 was $27 million and of burglaries $251 million. On the other hand, the total cost of embezzlement was $200 million and tax fraud $100 million (Wright 1973, p. 29). The U.S. Chamber of Commerce estimated that the total cost of all white-collar crimes (including corporate crimes) in 1974 was over $40 billion—over ten times the total amount involved in all types of thefts included in the FBI index of major crimes (Reiman 1979, p. 106). Of this about half was estimated to be a result of consumer fraud, illegal competition, and deceptive business practices. These together resulted in a loss of $5.5 billion to consumers, $3.5 to other businesses, and $12.0 billion to the government in revenue (Reiman 1979, p. 107).

The criminal justice system treats the corporate rich very differently from the poor. White-collar crime, especially those crimes committed in pursuit of profits (price fixing, rigging bids, violations of federal drug regulations, and so on) are commonplace and persistent in corporate circles.

A study of the 70 largest U.S. corporations over a 40-year period found that every one of them had been convicted at least once for a crime during that period, and that the average number of convictions was 14 per corporation. There were a total of 307 adverse decisions on charges of restraint of trade, 222 convictions on charges of infringements of copyrights, trademarks, and patents, and 158 convictions for violating the National Labor Relations Act. About 90 percent of the 70 largest U.S. corporations are habitual criminals, having been convicted at least three times (Reiman 1979, p. 108).

Among the crimes that corporations commit (some of which they are occasionally prosecuted for and convicted of, and others that are not technically considered to be crimes or at least are not generally treated as such) include dumping of carcinogenic and other harmful chemicals, the production and sale of unsafe cars, the burning of buildings to collect fire insurance, deceptive advertising, deceptive testing of new products, maintenance of hazardous working conditions, nursing home frauds, securities frauds, price fixing, antitrust violations, tax frauds, land frauds, bribes, and illegal (and sometimes violent) attempts to prevent unionization. The major automobile companies have marketed cars, e.g., the Ford Pinto and General Motors Corvair, that were known to have deadly defects (the Pinto, an exploding gas tank, and the Corvair, defective brakes and a tendency to roll over) in order to rush these compacts into the market. It has been estimated that gas tank defects in the Ford Pinto caused the death of at least 500 passengers (Clinard and Yeager 1980, p. 160).

Executives who commit crimes in the pursuit of corporate profit are not generally regarded as criminals in business circles. When arrested and convicted of such crimes top executives are typically let off with a slap on the wrist. In a famous case of price fixing in the electrical equipment industry, involving sales of equipment worth over $1.7 billion, seven top executives received 30 days in jail each. In another case against the William S. Merrill Company, tried for selling a drug with many dangerous side affects (a drug cleared by the Food and Drug Administration on the basis of fabricated information), three executives got six month's probation and the corporation received a token fine. Civil suits brought by injured patients were given token settlements on the basis that the company would suffer "extraordinary financial strain" if the substantial compensation asked for by injured patients were awarded (Mandell 1975, pp. 178-79).

A study of 582 large corporations in the 1975-76 period found that 60 percent had at least one criminal prosecution brought against them during this period, and that almost half engaged in repeated violations. Of those corporations convicted of crimes, the most frequent penalty was a warning, with the second most common a token fine (80 percent of all fines were for $5,000 or less, less than 1 percent for one million or more). Of the 56 corporate executives of the 582 large corporations convicted in the federal courts for corporate crimes in the 1975-76 period 63 percent received probation and 21 percent suspended sentences (only 29 percent were incarcerated). Of those who served time for their offense the average sentence was 37 days (Clinard and Yeager 1980, chaps. 5, 8). Clearly, the justice system is far more sympathetic, and thus lenient, toward even legally defined criminals of similar backgrounds to judges and juries, and far harsher to the lower class, whose culture and behavior is alien to them (and whom the law is largely designed to control).

GENERAL ATTITUDES

A higher percentage of salaried middle class people label themselves liberal *as well as* conservative, than is the case in any other strata. While 34 percent of new middle class people in 1977 called themselves liberals, only 24 percent of the traditional petty bourgeoisie and 25 percent of capitalists did so. (See Table 9.16.) This contrasts with 30 percent of both manual and white-collar workers.

While 42 percent of new middle class people called themselves conservatives (as did 40 percent of capitalists, and 37 percent of the traditional petty bourgeoisie) only 27 percent of manual workers and 30 percent of white-collar workers did so. Manual workers had the greatest propensity of all groups to refuse to categorize themselves as either liberals or conservatives; 43 percent either defined themselves as moderates or refused to classify themselves at all, compared to only 24 percent of the new middle class. It seems that the new middle class is both the most politicized and the most polarized of all.

The new middle class is the most supportive of environmental conservation; 60 percent of this group, in contrast to only 30 percent of capitalists and 41 percent of the traditional petty bourgeoisie, felt that the government ought to spend more on improving the environment (50 percent of the manual working class supported more government spending in this area). The new petty bourgeoisie is the most likely to feel that premarital sex is all right. In 1977, 52 percent of this stratum held this opinion in contrast to 30 percent of the capitalists, 34 percent of the traditional petty bourgeoisie, and 40 percent of the manual working class. This stratum is also the most supportive of women working outside of the home; 80 percent of the new petty bourgeoisie, in contrast to 62 percent of the traditional petty bourgeoisie and 53 percent of the manual working class, did not agree that a woman's place is in the home. The new petty bourgeoisie was more likely than any other group to feel that communism is a good form of government at least for some—34 percent, compared with 15 percent for the traditional petty bourgeoisie and 19 percent for the manual working class. The new petty bourgeoisie also holds very liberal attitudes on the black movement and civil liberties for Communists. On the other hand, the new petty bourgeoisie has the most confidence in business of any stratum—43 percent, as compared with 23 percent of white-collar workers and 26 percent of manual workers. They were also the most antiwelfare of any group other than capitalists—73 percent favored a reduction in state spending in this area, in contrast to 62 percent of the manual working class (who were the *least* antiwelfare) and 63 percent of the traditional petty bourgeoisie. The new petty bourgeoisie also ranked below the national average on support for increased state moneys for national health. While 57 percent of the new petty bourgeoisie supported more money for national health in 1977, 61 percent of the manual working class did (the largest percentage of any class). The traditional petty bourgeoisie was the most conservative on this issue (49 percent supported more money).

Data from the Gallup poll for the United States in 1979 show that it is middle class people who are most supportive of nuclear

TABLE 9.16: General Attitudes by Class and Class Strata, 1977 (percent agreeing)

	Capitalists[a] (N = 20)	Old Petty Bourgeoisie[b] (N = 104)	New Middle Class[c] (N = 143)	Intermediate Strata[d] (N = 149)	White-Collar Employees[e] (N = 193)	Manual Workers[f] (N = 519)	Total (N = 1,128)
Self-defined liberals	25%	24%	34%	31%	30%	30%	30%
Self-defined conservatives	40	37	42	36	30	27	32
Support more state funds for the environment	30	41	60	54	57	50	52
Premarital sex is OK	30	34	52	37	41	40	41
Communists have a right to speak	85	52	80	70	70	48	60
Communism is an OK form of government at least for some	30	15	34	19	23	19	22
A wife's place is *not* in the home	70	62	80	77	76	53	65
The courts should be more harsh on criminals	84	89	87	84	91	87	87
Support more arms spending	15	30	24	26	17	30	26

344

Blacks should push even if not wanted	42	26	42	42	31	18	28
Whites *do not* have the right to keep blacks out of their neighborhoods	74	59	76	68	64	49	60
Have great deal of confidence in business	35	33	43	32	23	26	29
Support more state funds for national health	60	49	57	63	55	61	59
Support less money for welfare	90	63	73	71	64	62	66

a Anyone who reported that they were self-employed, *and* supervise subordinates who themselves supervise others.

b All self-employed people who are not capitalists as defined in Note a.

c All employed people who supervise others on the job who themselves supervise others (managers and administrators) *or* who have a high degree of job autonomy and do nonmanual labor (professionals).

d All employed people who supervise others and are not part of the new middle class as defined in Note c (e.g., foremen) *or* who do nonmanual labor and have an intermediate-level of job autonomy (e.g., technicians, nurses, police, primary/secondary school teachers, reporters, pharmacists, high-level salespeople).

e All people who do not supervise others, do nonmanual labor, and who have a low-level of job autonomy (e.g., clerks, low-level salespeople, secretaries, typists, bookkeepers, and so on).

f All employed people who do *not* supervise others and do manual labor (industrial, service and farm, skilled and unskilled).

Note: Percentages on all questions except those on self-defined liberals and self-defined conservatives are based only on those *with opinions* on the given question.

Source: Computed from the 1977 NORC General Social Survey data.

power. In that year 37 percent of the college-educated as compared to 23 percent of those with only a grade school education felt that it was extremely important to have more nuclear power plants built. Thirty-three percent of those with a college degree as compared to 16 percent of those with a grade school education felt that nuclear power stations were safe (Gallup 1980, pp. 112–14). Attitudes about legal abortion vary considerably by class. In 1979, 32 percent of those with college degrees and 31 percent of people in the professions or business thought that abortions should be legal "under *all* circumstances," in contrast to only 10 percent of those with only a grade school education and 18 percent of manual workers. Only 10 percent of those with college degrees and 12 percent of professionals and managers, compared to 39 percent of those with a grade school education and 17 percent of manual workers, thought that abortions should be *illegal* under all circumstances. It should be noted that there was no significant difference between men and women in attitudes toward illegal abortion. Eighteen percent of men and 19 percent of women thought that abortion should be illegal under *all* circumstances (Gallup 1980, pp. 132–34).

Not surprisingly, attitudes about trade unions are significantly class related. In 1979, 55 percent of people earning over $20,000 (with an opinion) approved of labor unions, compared to 80 percent of people earning between $7,000 and $10,000 and 74 percent of those earning less than $3,000 (Gallup 1980, pp. 180–81).

The picture that emerges is that the salaried petty bourgeoisie is the most liberal on nonclass questions, e.g., the environment, civil liberties, civil rights for minorities, tolerance of different political systems, and sexuality. However, on class or economic questions, it is more conservative than average, with the manual working class being the most progressive. The manual working class is among the most supportive of increased spending for national health and the least opposed to more spending on welfare as well as low on confidence in business and high on support for unions. It should be noted that in 1977, it was *only* in the working class that there were more self-defined liberals than conservatives. The greatest conservatism of the manual working class is manifested on questions of the role of women, abortion, civil liberties, attitudes on communism, and lack of support for the black movement. On most questions the traditional independent petty bourgeoisie was the most or next to most conservative on both economic *and* noneconomic questions, e.g., state spending on health, the environment, civil liberties for Communists, intolerance of other forms of government, hostility to the black movement, women in the home, premarital sex, arms spending, and making the courts tougher on criminals. It is clear that on noneconomic questions, but *not* on economic questions, there is a considerable difference between the two segments of the petty bourgeoisie. It should be noted that capitalists, not surprisingly, have the highest ratio of conservatives to liberals of any class or stratum, and that they are the most opposed to both state spending on the environment *and* spending on welfare. It is of interest to note that they rank very high on both civil liberties tolerance questions, and questions about civil rights for blacks. They also were the least supportive in 1977 of increased military spending. On the other hand, they are the most traditional about premarital sex.

There has been a long-standing discussion in social science about whether the working class or the middle class has the strongest "authoritarian" propensities, i.e., is most receptive to "extremist," "heavy-handed" and "inappropriate" measures, intolerant of minority groups and minority viewpoints, and supportive of militarist and forceful measures to solve problems. Before World War II most discussions of authoritarianism and class argued that the life experiences of middle class people generated hostility, which in turn produced aggression, which was then channeled into authoritarian politics such as anti-Semitism and fascism as well as manifested in highly authoritarian middle class child-rearing policies that produced authoritarian (or emotionally blocked, and hence, potentially aggressive) personalities in their children. There were numerous studies of the Nazi and Fascist movement that attempted to account for both their middle class base and their extreme authoritarian form within such a discourse. This approach generally saw the life of the shopkeeper, small farmer, or professional, especially in times of depression and unemployment, as one of extreme tension produced by being on the losing side of the intensified competitive struggle. A struggle to survive, which for the independent petty bourgeoisie meant long hours for the entire family, a cutback in consumption, and ever present anxiety about competition, foreclosure, and securing customers; and for professionals, increasing job insecurity, unemployment, and lower salaries. Unlike the working class, the middle class response to such crisis was intensified individualism ("Every family for itself"), since the survival of one shopkeeper in the competitive struggle meant the bankruptcy of another. Likewise, the promotion or survival of one salaried professional or manager often meant the demotion or firing of another. In a world of scarcity the condition for a few to survive was the defeat of others. Such intense competition was thought to promote considerable anxiety, tension, hostility, and aggression—a condition that predisposed such people to look for "extremist" and "unrealistic" solutions to their problems and to be intolerant of those imagined to be their persecutors. Such families,

families in which the parents (especially the father) ruled with in iron hand, and in which emotional warmth was at a premium (because of the frustration of the parents) produced children who had a strong predisposition to subordinate themselves to strong authoritarian father figures as leaders, while at the same time enjoying dominating the relatively powerless as a way to release their own frustrations (e.g., the Nazi S. S. mentality).

However, in the early 1950s, as the "enemy of America" shifted from fascism (with its middle class base) to Marxism (with its working class base,) studies of authoritarianism began appearing that argued it was the *working class*, not the middle class, whose life experience predisposed it to authoritarianism. In these arguments it was maintained that the frustrations of unemployment, poverty, and menial uncreative labor together with limited educational opportunities and isolated occupational communities produced intolerance, a propensity to look for "simplistic" and "unrealistic" solutions, and an attraction to undemocratic and violence-prone organizations and political solutions. It was further maintained that the frustrations and insecurities of working class life led working class parents to disproportionately use physical punishment and express less emotional support for their children, and hence produce children with authoritarian tendencies (Lipset 1960, chap. 4).

The leading empirical support for the "working class authoritarianism" thesis came from sample survey studies of attitudes toward civil liberties, especially for Communists (somewhat ironically) in the United States in the early 1950s. The central study in this literature found that only 27 percent of manual workers, as compared to 41 percent of proprietors and managers, were willing to allow an "admitted Communist" to speak in their community, while only 36 percent of manual workers as compared to 58 percent of proprietors and managers felt that an "admitted Communist" should not be put in jail. Although the class differences were sharpest on the Communist questions, they were also noticeable on questions dealing with atheists and socialists. Only 36 percent of manual workers, compared to 48 percent of proprietors and managers, would allow an atheist to speak, and 64 percent of manual workers as compared to 78 percent of proprietors and managers would allow a socialist to speak (Hamilton 1972, pp. 436–37).

Richard Hamilton did a sophisticated reanalysis of this original study, looking separately at each region (south, nonsouth) and at farm and urban backgrounds. When this was done, he found that most of the differences between working class and middle class people disappeared, i.e., among working class and middle class people of similar class background in the same region, there was relatively little difference in intolerance. For example, outside of the South 77 percent of working class married persons in 1956 from nonfarm backgrounds were "tolerant" in comparison with 81 percent of middle class people not of farm background (Hamilton 1972, p. 441).

Hamilton found that it is farmers, not manual workers, who are the most intolerant (especially white Southern farmers). As farmers and white Southerners have migrated to the cities they have brought their intolerant attitudes with them into the working class. It is not working class life or personality traits that generate intolerance but rather something about rural life and the social history of the South. Hamilton also suggests that the remaining degree of intolerance is in good part accounted for by a tendency for the downwardly mobile to be less tolerant and the upwardly mobile more tolerant. There is, therefore, a transfer of people between the two classes that acts to concentrate people with more tolerant propensities in the middle class, while concentrating people with less tolerant propensities in the working class. An operating mechanism here could well be attitude about college education. It has been shown that the more tolerant one's attitudes, the more likely one is to want a college education for one's children and thus the more likely one's children are to make it into the middle class (Hamilton 1972, p. 44).

However, there is probably still a small but significant tendency for people of working class backgrounds to be more intolerant of Communist viewpoints than middle class people. This fact is probably mostly due to the way communism has been portrayed to working people by the schools and mass media. Working class life is characterized by many fears and insecurities. It is entirely realistic for working people to be on guard against the preceived threats to their life, reflecting stresses that impinge on them more directly and more often than has been common in middle class life in the postdepression period. When the government and the media began a massive and hysterical campaign against the international and domestic "Communist threat" in the late 1940s, which portrayed Communists as a new version of Nazis set on destroying freedom thoughout the world and subverting the "American way of life" by every devious and manipulative means possible, it was not surprising that working people responded with concern and alarm feeling a need for decisive action to oppose the apparent "Communist threat."

In general, it is true that the more oppressed people are, and the less they are "cross-pressured" by conflicting interests and forces, the more likely they are to support clear and decisive solutions to their problems, i.e., blacks are more likely than whites to believe that *all* discrimination against blacks should end immediately, while whites are more likely to think that discrimination ought to be eliminated one step at a time through a series of compromises utilizing "balanced solutions" that take into account the "complexities" of the situation. Similarly, working class people in most countries are more likely than middle class people to feel that capitalist institutions ought to be totally restructured, since they have the most unambiguous stake in such restructuring (Szymanski 1978, p. 29). When communism was presented to the U.S. working class as repressive rule by a power-hungry elite worse than what they were already experiencing they reacted in a way that had nothing to do with any characterological propensity to authoritarianism.

In fact, although working class people in the 1950s were slightly more intolerant of civil liberties, in Wisconsin, Joseph McCarthy's home state, the McCarthy vote was concentrated in middle class and traditionally Republican areas, while most working class people voted for the Democrats, the party they perceived as the defender of their economic interests. This is hardly the pattern we would expect if working class authoritarianism were mobilized behind irrational extremist solutions (Hamilton 1972, p. 450).

It can well be argued that the real "authoritarians" were those in the upper class who were responsible for the anti-Communist hysteria of the 1950s as well as the demagogues like McCarthy who latched onto the "anti-Red" issue for their own careerist ends (McCarthy very much wanted to be president and saw the anti-Communist issue as one he could ride to the White House).

It is of interest to note that in 1977 the manual working class was considerably more willing to let a Communist speak in their community than they had been in the 1950s. In 1977, 48 percent of manual workers and 70 percent of white-collar workers as compared to 80 percent of those in the new petty bourgeoisie and 52 percent of the independent middle class were willing to let a Communist speak. Two things should be pointed out: first, there was no significant difference between the manual working class and the independent petty bourgeoisie on civil liberties; and second, the growth in tolerance was more pronounced in the working class than in either segment of the middle class. This gives support to Hamilton's argument that it has been the carrying out of traditional rural conservativism into the working class that was responsible for its traditionally greater level of intolerance of political dissent (the rural-urban migration within the United States has slowed considerably in the last generation). The fact that the traditional petty bourgeoisie has a high level of intolerance, especially in comparison to white-collar workers and the new middle class, lends support to many analyses of this group's having been the traditional basis of anti-

Communist, nativist, and semi-Fascist movements (e.g., Trow 1958). It should also be noted that the especially high level of tolerance toward Communist speakers (as well as towards Communist regimes in other countries) in the capitalist class in 1977 indicated both a high level of confidence in the stability of U.S. capitalism (and thus the lack of feeling that their interests are threatened by leftists) *and* the lack of credibility in this class of the media-propagated myth of the Communist "danger," a myth that *has* considerably greater credibility in the manual working class, which in good part identifies their feelings of self-worth and dignity with "America" (a result of immigrant socialization).

Two additional types of attitudes that have often been cited as indicators of a generalized "authoritarian dimension" are attitudes about racial minorities in the United States, specifically blacks, and attitudes about the use of force (one aspect of which is support of militaristic foreign policies and another, support for capital punishment).

Evidence on white attitudes toward blacks indicates relatively little difference between middle class and manual working class people on attitudes toward black rights, integrated schools, feelings that blacks are as intelligent as whites, government laws guaranteeing equal access to jobs for blacks, and willingness to go to a black doctor (although on most of these questions there is a *slight* tendency for working class people to be more racist).

Hamilton found in 1968 (at the peak of the "white backlash") that 80 percent of manual workers (outside of the South) as compared to 89 percent of nonmanual workers supported integrated schools; 81 percent of manual workers as compared to 89 percent of nonmanual workers felt that blacks were "just as intelligent" as whites; 83 percent of manual workers as compared to 88 percent of nonmanual workers would "not mind" if a black of similar income and education moved into their block; 89 percent of manual workers as compared to 88 percent of nonmanual workers supported fair employment laws that required white employees to hire "qualified" blacks; and that 76 percent of manual workers as compared to 81 percent of nonmanual workers said they would go to a black doctor if they were referred to one (Hamilton 1975, pp. 153–54).

On questions that relate to close personal contact or the black movement, however, there is a more significant tendency for manual workers to be more negative than middle class people. In 1968, while 13 percent of nonmanual workers outside of the South stated they would not object to their teenagers dating a black, only 6 percent of manual workers agreed. While 60 percent of nonmanual workers said they favored open occupancy laws that make whites rent or sell to "qualified" blacks, only 49 percent of manual workers favored such legislation (Hamilton 1975, pp. 155-56). In 1977, only 18 percent of manual workers felt that blacks should "push even where they are not wanted," compared to 42 percent of both the new middle class and the capitalist class. The old petty bourgeoisie was slightly more supportive than the manual working class (26 percent). While 76 percent of the new middle class and 74 percent of the capitalist class in 1977 stated that they did not think whites had a right to keep blacks out of their neighborhoods, 49 percent of manual workers thought whites did not have such a right (59 percent of the independent petty bourgeoisie shared this opinion).

White working class support of fair employment laws as well as lack of opposition to blacks of similar income and education moving into their block indicates an acceptance of black workers as a part of the working class entitled to employment on the same basis as whites. Negative attitudes on personal relations with blacks indicates that black workers are not part of the mainstream social class of workers in the United States and that traditional white chauvinism persists (even while black workers' rights are accepted).

Although on questions relating to close interpersonal relations such as interracial dating and intermarriage, working class people are significantly more racist than middle class people, given the relatively tolerant attitudes of white working class people toward blacks on other issues, however, it is questionable whether white working class resistance to interracial sexual activities reflects either a generalized racist or an especially authoritarian character structure. It is also important to note that white working class attitudes are becoming increasingly tolerant over time.

The persistence of white chauvinism in the working class would seem to be largely a residue of the history of the blacks' introduction into capitalist industry as competitors of the working class of European descent. Blacks, as the Poles, Italians, and Irish before them, and as the Ladinos after them, were introduced into the urban capitalist economy as low-wage menials who undermined the economic position of the established working class, thus causing considerable hostility among native-born whites.

White working class opposition to the black movement and their assertion of "white rights" would seem to reflect resentment at what is often felt as "special privileges" granted by the state and corporate affirmative action programs to blacks, while the oppressions of white workers are ignored. The feeling is prevalent that other ethnic groups made it by hard work, so why don't blacks do the same, instead of complaining so much. This feeling is reflected in the fact that in 1978, 89 percent of whites (and 56 percent of nonwhites) with opinions on the question *opposed* preferential treatment for women and minorities in college admissions and job hiring (Gallup 1980, p. 105). This attitude is compatible with both the general white working class willingness to accept ("qualified") blacks as co-workers and neighbors, *and* a feeling that blacks are inherently as able as whites. White worker attitudes about the black movement or affirmative action programs for minorities can neither be taken to indicate a generalized racism (or racist beliefs) nor the prevalence of some deeply rooted "authoritarian personality." The high level of support for integration among capitalists indicates the high level of acceptance in this class of a single working force in which black and white workers compete on equal terms for all working class jobs, thus lowering the overall wage rate (and perhaps undermining working class solidarity), while increasing the supply of workers, especially in the less skilled positions where it is difficult to find sufficient numbers of white Anglos.

On attitudes related to militarism such as support for increased military spending, "getting tough on Communism" overseas, and support of U.S. overseas military activities such as the wars in Korea and Vietnam, middle class people are generally more militaristic or "authoritarian" than are working class people. During the Korean War (1952) 56 percent of upper middle class people outside of the South favored "a stronger stand" as compared to 45 percent of manual workers; on the other hand, 47 percent of manuals supported a negotiated end to the war as compared to 36 percent of upper middle class people (Hamilton 1972, p. 453). In 1968, 26 percent of people earning under $5,000 a year favored an immediate pullout of U.S. troops from Vietnam, compared to 16 percent of those earning over $6,000. Similarly, 38 percent of those earning over $6,000 favored a stronger stand, compared to 25 percent among those earning less than $6,000 (Hamilton 1975, p. 195). In 1979, 81 percent of people with only a grade school education and 75 percent of those with a college education *approved* of the ratification of the SALT II treaty with the USSR (among those who had an opinion on the question) (Gallup 1980, p. 124). These facts, together with the fact that working class and poorer people are the least likely to support capital punishment (U.S. Department of Justice 1980, p. 293), would seem to be strong evidence against the thesis that working class people have a greater internalized aggression that manifests itself in an authoritarian character structure and a disproportionate propensity to support military adventures and harsh treatment of criminals.

In 1977, 30 percent of manual workers thought that the United States ought to be spending more on the military as compared to 24 percent of the new middle class and 30 percent of the independent petty bourgeoisie. These figures *do* indicate, at least in the late 1970s, that a significant segment of both the manual working class and the traditional petty bourgeoisie accepted the media-promoted notion of the importance of a stronger military (in good part because of their identification with American patriotism). But the differences on this question among the classes and strata are rather small, and the most important fact is that 70 percent of workers with opinions felt either that too much or enough was already being spent on the military— hardly a sign of an authoritarian propensity to violent solutions. The results on this question, compared to attitudes on the Korean and Vietnamese wars, however, suggest that the slight tendency for manual workers to be more promilitary in times of peace is reversed once casualties start occurring (casualties that are disproportionately suffered by the sons of the manual working class).

CONCLUSION

Class is an extremely powerful force. Our position in the class structure largely determines (or at least very heavily influences) virtually all aspects of our lives (including the most intimate and personal). Our health (physical and mental) as well as the probability of dying in a given year (and hence our life expectancy) are largely a product of class position. Likewise, family life, sexuality, friendship patterns, religious beliefs and practices as well as consumption and leisure patterns are strongly class related. Both the propensity to be defined and prosecuted as criminal and the probability of being victimized by violent and property crimes are heavily associated with class. Our political beliefs and ideologies are heavily class determined. In sum, class (although it is often mediated by "race," religion, and so on) is in the last analysis the most important single factor affecting our lives.

10

The Structure of Race and Class

The logic of the world capitalist system transforms and integrates (or destroys) preexisting social groups (tribes, nations, castes, peoples, social classes); and further, generates and reproduces new nations, castes, social classes, and peoples. Some of the transformed pre-existing social groups as well as some of those newly created come to play special economic roles in the world capitalist class structure that come to be legitimized in terms of the discourse of inherently inferior or superior (or at least, specially suited for their economic role) "races." Races are an outcome of the logic of capitalist class formation, not of biological evolution.*

---

*Social groups that get falsely defined as races are in fact either essentially social classes, castes, peoples, or nations. By nation is meant an historical evolved stable community of common language (or other means of intercommunication); common territory; common economic life, i.e., an all-around differentiated class structure; and common psychological makeup, common traditions, and culture. By people is meant an historically evolved stable community of common language (or other means of inter-communication), and common psychological makeup, traditions, and culture, which does not share a common territory nor possess an all-around class structure. Classes and castes are defined in Chapter 3. In this book the terms "subordinate group," "ethnic group," "racial group," "minority group," "racially oppressed people," and so on are used interchangeably to describe groups that are commonly defined as "inferior races."

355

A BRIEF HISTORY OF RACES AND RACIALIST IDEOLOGY

Just about every imaginable criterion has been used in characterizing racial groups.* Further, the hegemonic conceptions of race have changed very rapidly over time (i.e., people in different races at one period find themselves in the same race a few years later, and vice versa). Linnaeus, the Swedish naturalist, in the mid-eighteenth century attempted to classify humankind into four "races" on the basis of skin color (European, Asiatic, African, and American). Blumenback around the turn of the eighteenth century used a five-part classification (Caucasian, Mongolian, Malay, Ethiopian, American) on the basis of color, hair, skull, and face (shape of nose, eye color, shape of eyelid). In the mid- and late nineteenth centuries the most important criteria of race became hair, color, form of nose, and shape of skull. Various theorists have differentiated between 2 and 35 separate races using these criteria. Thomas Henry Huxley found 11 races (later 5 major and 14 secondary). Deniker in 1900 found 17 races. Sergi in 1911 found 2 (long head and round head—Euroafricans and Eurasiatics). In 1885 Topinard announced that there were 19 races. Haeckel in 1879 claimed there were 34 (Snyder 1939, pp. 8–9).

Although characterization of "races" in the nineteenth century and since has often been primarily by physical characteristics, linguistic as well as cultural, religious, historical, and geographical variables are also commonly employed to explicitly and implicitly classify "races" (see Snyder 1939, chap. 1). The tremendous variability of the different attempts to classify the single human race into allegedly separate races, and the total inability to approach a consensus around anything other than the superiority of one's own ethnic grouping, reflect the fact that there is, in fact, little if any correlation of the various types of physical characteristics offered as criteria of race (skin color, skull shape, nose size, hair type, stature, and so on) among the different peoples on the earth as well as the fact that there is never a consistent overlap of race as defined physically (by whatever criteria) and actual linguistic, cultural, political, intellectual, and economic characteristics (see Gossett 1963, chap. 4). Racialist theories scientifically have been a complete bust— obvious rationalizations for the dominance of whatever nation or class that subscribed to them at a given time, not ideas to be evaluated on scientific merit.

Racialism as a theory to legitimate the subordination of classes and people, although it has very ancient historical antecedents, did

---

*This section relies heavily on Gossett 1963, Snyder 1939, and Montagu 1953.

not become the predominant or hegemonic mode of legitimation of exploitation or imperialism until the middle of the nineteenth century. In ancient Greece, for example, there was little racialist justification of the slavery on which Greek society was based. The Greeks regarded all non-Greeks contemptuously as "barbarians," but did not develop a biological foundation for their felt superiority. They instead, for the most part, tended to use purely cultural grounds, i.e., the superiority of Greek culture (a culture that could be transmitted to other peoples as happened on a grand scale in Hellenism). Barbarians, by adopting Greek culture, could become the equals of the Greeks. Similarly with the Romans, for the most part they also failed to put forth a biological foundation for their world conquest or to legitimate the slavery on which their economy was based by racialism. Again, they legitimated their system on the grounds of the political and cultural superiority of Roman civilization, a characteristic that could be adopted by others through the adoption of Roman citizenship, language, culture, and political forms (Montagu 1953, pp. 10, 11).

Aristotle appears to have been the only Greek philosopher of consequence to have argued that slaves were biologically inferior (putting forth his theory as a late attempt to rationalize slavery at the end of the period of the flowering of Greek civilization when slavery was coming under increasing attack). Plato, for example, referred to the ideology of innate differences between people as the "Phoenician lie." What was true of the Greeks and Romans appears to have been generally true of almost all peoples down through the nineteenth century. Throughout history, although here and there a biological argument for the superiority of a particular group has been offered, until the mid-nineteenth century such a mode of thought never caught on to become the predominant mode of legitimation— generally, as with Greece and Rome, ideologies of cultural or religious superiority have sufficed (Gossett 1963, chap. 1; Montagu 1953, chap. 1).

In the sixteenth and seventeenth centuries a few individuals put forth notions of separate human races (often arguing that there had been separate creations). The Roman Catholic church, however, strongly condemned all such theories, maintaining both that there was only one creation for all human beings, and that all human beings, including the Indians, had been part of that single creation (and thus had souls). Advocates of the idea of a separate creation of primitive peoples were even burned at the stake for their heresies (Gossett 1963, p. 15). The church, as well as the ruling classes and dominant nations behind it, felt that the notion of the superiority of the Christian religion and European culture was fully adequate as a theoretical justification for feudal class forms in Europe as well as for early imperialist expansion overseas (imperialism was good because it brought Christianity and civilization to the pagans of the world). Indeed the long-term missionary zeal of Christianity (as well as Islam and other world religions) is theoretically based on the notion of the unity of the single human race. Paul said, "God hath made of one blood all nations in the earth to dwell." St. Augustine also rejected the notion of separate races (Gossett 1963, p. 9).

While the Jews in Europe were continually the subject of hostility and occasional persecution, the theoretical manifestation of anti-Semitism was essentially social, cultural, and religion (not biological). The Jews killed Christ, they refused to be converted, they murdered Christian children using their blood for ritual purposes, they were infidels, usurers, and so on (Montagu 1953, p. 12). A biological foundation for anti-Semitism was not logically consistent with Christian theory, the fundamental basis of societal legitimation in the eighteenth century.

Christ, the central figure in Christianity as well as his mother Mary and all the Apostles including Peter (the first pope) were born Jews. It was also acceptable for Jews to convert to Christianity. The lack of a hegemonic racialist theory underlying anti-Semitism, however, did not prevent the circulation of certain popular myths, e.g., some Jews had horns, Jews had an unpleasant odor, Jewish men menstruated, Jewish children were born with their rights hands attached to their heads (Gossett 1963, p. 11). Such notions, however, never gained acceptability as part of a hegemonic theory of anti-Semitism.

Most great pre–nineteenth century independent thinkers gave the notion of separate human races little serious consideration. Leonardo da Vinci, for example, accepted the prevailing Christian notion that humankind is really one race, arguing that physical differences among people were a product of their different environments. For example, he thought people born in tropic areas were black because they do most of their work during the night (when it is cool), thus absorbing the cool of the night; while peoples in northern regions are blond because they work during the day (Gossett 1963, p. 16). During the whole of the seventeenth century only five known books speaking to the question of varieties of humankind were published. Theories of separate races were extremely rare at that time. Leibniz writing at the end of the seventeenth century argued:

> I recollect reading somewhere, though I cannot find the passage, that a certain traveler had divided man into certain tribes, races or classes. He made one special race of the Lapps and Samoyedes, another of the Chinese and their neighbors, another of the Caffres or Hottentots. In America, again, there is a marvelous difference

between the Galibs, or Caribs, who are very brave and spirited, and those of Paraguay, who seem to be infants or in pupilage all their lives. That, however, is no reason why all men who inhabit the earth should not be of the same race, which has been altered by different climates, as we see that beasts and plants change their nature and improve or degenerate (Montagu 1953, p. 20).

The English word "race" was first used at the beginning of the sixteenth century. The term race was not introduced into the scientific literature until 1749 when Buffon began to employ it in his zoological classifications (Montagu 1953, p. 2). Much of the romantic literature of the eighteenth century as well as French enlightment thought, in fact celebrated the "noble savage" uncorrupted by European society (hardly a notion compatible with racialist thinking).

Although racist relations ("lived relations") of economic domination came into existence in North America between the dominant whites on the one hand and the indigenous peoples and the imported African slaves in the sixteenth and seventeenth centuries on the other, there was little felt need to justify them in terms of racialist theory. During the formative stages of slavery Africans were not generally regarded as biologically inferior (though they were treated as chattels and lived the experience of racism). The records of most early English and American slave traders show that they often felt the Africans to be their mental equals. Similarly, seventeenth-century observers generally concurred in describing the Indian abilities and intelligence in very high terms (Montagu 1953, p. 13). The extermination and displacement of the Indians as well as the development of the institution of slavery both occurred with a minimum devlopment of theory. It was not until these relationships came under attack in the nineteenth century that elaborate racialist theories were developed and gained intellectual hegemony. Until that time Christian notions of saving souls and civilizing "savages" sufficed to justify the lived relationships of racism (see Gossett 1963, pp. 17, 29).

In the last years of the eighteenth and early years of the nineteenth centuries racialist theories gained a certain currency and respectability, but were not yet intellectually predominant (during these years they were fighting an uphill battle). Voltaire, for example, defended racialist theory, as did Thomas Jefferson. Voltaire maintained that Indians and blacks were separate species unrelated to Europeans, arguing that both were "greatly inferior" to whites (Gossett 1963, p. 44). Jefferson argued about blacks that, "In memory they are equal to the whites; in reason much inferior. . . .in imagination they are dull, tasteless, and anomalous" (Gossett 1963, p. 42). Theorists like Voltaire and Jefferson however, were in a distinct minority in their time. Throughout the eighteenth century most informed and scientific opinion still supported the notions that blacks and other nonwhite groups were the intellectual equals of Europeans (Gossett 1963, p. 53).

The popularity of racialist theory (the idea that humankind is composed of distinct races which inherit superior or inferior character- istics) as a socially important theory is of recent development. Its rise and hegemony in fact coincided with the rise and triumph of modern capitalism and capitalist imperialism. The idea of "race" developed both as a defense of slavery during its last years and, increasingly, as a product of the need to justify the colonial subordination and inten- sive exploitation of the entire non-European world, as well as a justification of the special exploitation of the various displaced peasantries which became the labor force of the rapidly expanding capitalist industrial enterprises. The decline of Catholicism as an important ideology of legitimation along with the rise of the Darwin- ism theory of evolution lent credibility to the new racialist theories (which were often based on notions of different evolutionary paths). Herbert Spencer's social Darwinism and its thesis of cultural advance through "the survival of the fittest" provided an intellectually respectable framework within which to present racialist theory.

Racialist theory in the United States (more or less paralleling developments in Germany and England) has gone through a number of phases. Around the middle of the nineteenth century racialist theories, offered as a defense of the slave system (which was coming under increasing attack), achieved predominance in the form of the acceptance of the Aryan theory developed in Europe. Aryanism at this time argued for the essential unity of most Europeans and other speakers of Indo-European languages, including Persians, Kurds, Afghans, and perhaps Hindustanis (descendants of the speakers of Old Sanskrit) as supposed common descendants of the original Aryan race. To justify the enslavement of Africans (as well as European expansion into Africa and Asia) and the oppression of indigenous peoples in Australia and the Americas this theory served fine (see Gossett 1963, chap. 6; Snyder 1939, chap. 3).

In the last third of the nineteenth century the notion of a Teutonic or Germanic race (English, Dutch, Germans, Scandinavians, Franks) sometimes, as in the Anglo-Saxon variant with the English the finest example, became predominant. This notion served con- veniently to legitimize the devastation of the racially inferior Celtic Irish, who were subjected to mass starvation, special exploitation, and displacement to serve as cheap labor in England, America, and Australia as well as to justify a reinvigorated English imperialism active in areas occupied by people previousy defined as Aryans (in the Near East and Mediterranean as well as elsewhere). In the early years of the twentieth century Teutonism/Anglo-Saxonism was elaborated as the theory of the Nordic race that became dominant at that time. In the Nordic theory slavs, Italians, Spanish, Greeks, and so on were considered to be racially inferior Alpines and Mediterraneans. European Jews were considered to be part of the Semitic race. This racialist theory legitimated U.S., British, and German world predominance as well as the treatment of the massive Alpine (slav), Mediterranean (Italian), and Semitic (Jewish) immigrants in the United States.* The Nazi race theory was essentially of this type (although they employed the term Aryan). The Irish, it should be noted, while clearly excluded from the Teutonic and Anglo Saxon races, were often included in the Nordic Race.†

Although academic racism largely faded from the scene after the 1920s, latter day racialist theories came to talk about the Caucasian race, from which Jews were often excluded, but all other people of European descent were included. Most recently a vague concept of the "white race" has gained a certain currency in progressive as well as racist circles that includes Jews and all Europeans and European immigrants to North America and Australia (but usually excluding those to Latin America). In contrast to the white race are all "people of color," a category that usually includes Latin Americans as "brown." Although the ethnic composition of Argentina and Uruguay is similar to that of the United States, their populations are generally considered to be "Hispanics," as are the more or less purely European upper classes throughout Latin America. The rule of racial classification here appears to be one of geography and language (people living south of the Rio Grande or who are Spanish-speaking are people of color). Also included are usually Turks, Iranian, and northern Arabs who are virtually indistinguishable in physical characteristics from other peoples of the region (e.g., Armenians, Georgians, Greeks) who are classified as white (the implicit rule of racial classification here

---

*One of the chief articulators of the Nordic theory, although he (as did the Nazis) used the term Aryan to describe them, was the French Count Arthur de Gobineau (1816-82). In Germany the most prominent Nordic theorist (on whom Hitler directly built) was Houston Steward Chamberlain (1855-1927), in the United States, Madison Grant (1865-1927). Gobineau argued that the French upper class was descended from the racially superior Germanie Franks, while the peasants were descended from the racially inferior Gauls thus providing both a justification of French imperialism *and* class rule in France (Snyder 1939, chaps. 6-8; Gossett 1963, chap. 14).

†Some versions of Nordic theory not only include Scots and Irish as Nordics (e.g., Madison Grant), but especially around 1914-19 during World War I *excluded* Germans on the grounds that that country's original Nordic stock had been largely exterminated in the Thirty years' War of the seventeenth century, with most of the remainder migrating to America (Gossett 1963, pp. 357-58).

seems to be that populations that are predominantly Islamic and poorer are people of color while those predominantly Christian and slightly richer are white).

Racialist theories reigned almost unchallenged in academic and leading political circles in the period 1880 to 1920 (a period of most intense imperialist expansion as well as massive immigration to the United States). In this period the idea of Nordic superiority (with its corollary of Anglo-Saxonism) achieved hegemony or near hegemony in much of biology, sociology, history, literature, and political science. In 1980 Nicholas Murray Butler, president of Colombia University, argued that it was the "extraordinary persistence of the Anglo-Saxon impulse" which was the "chief cause" that "brought the United States of America into existence. For the origin of that impulse one must go back to the Teutonic qualities and characteristics of the people so admirably described by Tacitus" (Gossett 1963, p. 122).

The developing Aryan/Teutonic/Anglo Saxon/Nordic racialist theories predominant in England and the United States from the mid-nineteenth century through the 1920s served well to legitimate both the internal exploitation of much of the working population (blacks, Irish, Italians, Slavs, and so forth) and to justify the imperial expansion of both powers (see Snyder 1939, chap. 13). Defenders of U.S. imperialism in this period argued that some races (e.g., the Filipinos) were inherently incapable of self-government. In 1885 Josiah Strong, a prominent Congregationalist clergyman, speaking of the Anglo Saxon race argued: "this powerful race will move down upon Mexico, down upon Central and South America, out upon the islands on the sea, over upon Africa and beyond. And can anyone doubt that the result of this competition of races will be the 'survival of the fittest' " (see Snyder 1939, p. 230). Theodore Roosevelt argued that fitness for self-government "comes to a race only through the slow growth of centuries, and then only to those races which possess an immense reserve of strength, common sense, and morality" (Gossett: 1963, p. 329).

Racialist speculations about blacks became more derogatory in the 1880-1930 period than at any previous time (apparently justifying the pushing back of black rights won during Reconstruction and the servile caste status as sharecroppers and domestics of this group in this period as well as the conquest of Africa). Almost all writings about blacks during this time argued that intellectually blacks were racially inferior and that their temperament was racially determined and inherited. The failure of Black Reconstruction, the high rates of black crime, poverty, and disease, as well as low scores on "intelligence tests" and generally poor educational achievement were all taken to be evidence of racial inferiority—as similar indicators were taken as evidence of the racial inferiority of the Jews, Slavs, and Italians at the same time (see Gossett 1963, chap. 11).

In the 1890s a strong movement to restrict non-Nordic (sometimes still expressed as non-Aryan) immigration to the United States developed. In general, the racialist arguments for the exclusion of non-Nordics argued that the immigrants from the backward areas of Europe threatened to undermine American civilization by displacing the superior Nordic stock that made the country great (Snyder 1939, pp. 242–44; Gossett 1963, chap. 12).

For example, in 1895 the prominent Columbia University political scientist John Burgess argued:

> What folly, on the part of the ignorant, what wickedness, on the part of the intelligent, are involved in the attempts. . . to pollute [the United States] with non-Aryan elements. . . . We must preserve our Aryan nationality in the state, and admit to its membership only such non-Ayran race-elements as shall have become Aryanized in spirit and in genius by contact with it, if we would build the superstructure of the ideal American commonwealth (Gossett 1963, p. 307).

H. H. Laughlin, who worked closely with the U.S. Congress House Committee on Immigration as its leading expert on racial qualities, argued that the disproportionate percentage of southern and eastern European immigrants in American mental institutions, prisons, and poorhouses reflected their "inborn socially inadequate qualities" (Gossett 1963, p. 401). A "scientific" study of race and IQ done in this period (by A. H. Arlitt of Bryn Mawr College) concluded that there was a direct correlation between racial origin, socioeconomic status, and intelligence. She found that blacks had an average IQ of 83, Italians an average IQ of 84, and native-born Americans an average IQ of around 105–10; and further, that the semiskilled and unskilled native born had an IQ of 92 as compared to an average IQ of 125 for native-born Americans of high social status. She drew the conclusion that Mediterraneans and blacks were racially inferior, and further that the purest (racially superior) Nordics among the native born found their way into the top positions of society (Snyder 1939, p. 239).

The Bolshevik Revolution and its reverberations in Europe and among eastern European immigrants in the United States added fuel to the racialist fire. The "turbulent and anarchic" inferior Slavic race was now judged as especially dangerous to incorporate into the U.S. population (Gossett 1963, p. 341).

Racialists were found on both sides of the immigration controversy. Those desiring a continuation of the immigration of easily exploited European workers from eastern and southern Europe argued that these peoples were ideally suited for the hard menial labor and miserable conditions of the industrial slums of the U.S. For example, the prominent historian Frederick Jackson Turner argued that the Jews were "a people of exceptionally stunted stature and deficient lung capacity" and thus naturally suited to survive in the tenements and sweatshops of New York City (Gossett 1963, p. 29). The movement to radically restrict the immigration of inferior (non-Nordic) races culminated in the passage of the 1924 immigration act (which effectively excluded "Alpines," "Mediterraneans," "Semites," and Asians from further immigration into the United States).

It must be emphasized that the intellectual hegemony of racialist theory has had no necessary relationship to the intensity of racist structures. There have been many different ideological justifications for the extermination and displacement of indigenous peoples, the special exploitation of various groups, and the hostility toward groups in middle class positions. Not only has history witnessed a plenitude of nonracialist legitimations for the economic domination of groups in these three types of racist structures, but those in the dominant economic class have had a variable need for any consistent intellectual defense at all of their economic interest. In fact, the most sophisticated conservative theories of legitimation (not only racialist) generally arise and are adopted in periods when structures of special economic domination (racist structures) are most under attack (and are about to be transcended or modified). Indeed, slavery was more vicious in the eighteenth century than in the nineteenth, although there was little racialist justification in the earlier century as compared to the latter for the institution. The extermination of the Indians was more direct (e.g., the practice of scalp bounties) in the seventeenth and eighteenth centuries when genocide was not generally justified by racialist theories, than in the nineteenth when, although more Indians were killed and displaced than earlier, this was done in more circumspect ways, now justified by an ideology of *racial* superiority. Sometimes, however, the most vicious treatment of a group *does* correspond to a period of hegemony of racialist ideology, e.g., the extermination of central European Jews in the 1943–45 period. Although racialist theories were no longer intellectually respectable in most intellectual circles after the 1920s, there was little corresponding change in the structures of special exploitation to which blacks were subjected. Theories of the "melting pot" (assimilation) into which blacks (and later Ladinos) would eventually merge (or no special theories at all), coexisted with the maintenance of racist structures. This reality underscores the importance of understanding racism as a structure, *not* as a consciousness ideology.

Further, the lack of association of racialist ideologies with racist structures (special exploitation, exclusion, mediation) does not mean that feelings of superiority/inferiority were not induced in those in dominant and subordinate economic structures. Nor does it mean that these racist structures were in any way weaker than when they were legitimated by racialism. In fact, the very strength of racialist ideology may well indicate the weakness and vulnerability of racial structures, since racialism is so often ascendant when racist structures are most under attack.

It made little difference to the black slaves or American Indians whether they were treated the way they were because the dominant whites believed that they were racially inferior or their biological equals. Likewise, it seems to have made no difference to the dominant whites. Slavery induced feelings of humiliation and inferiority in the slaves while inducing feelings of superiority and paternalism in the masters. Likewise, genocide and displacement of Indians induced feelings of outrage and eventually demoralization among the Indians, as well as feelings of superiority and arrogance among the dominant whites. These structurally induced feelings seem to have functioned quite adequately for the vast majority of whites in lubricating the objectively racist economic structures of special exploitation and exclusion.

The Althusserian conception of ideology as a "lived relation" and as a structure ("ideological state apparatus") rather than conscious ideas enhances our understanding of the persistence of racist structures (see Althusser 1969). Racist structures of economic domination and the concomitant ideologies ("lived relations") must be considered to exist wherever a distinctive social group is in the structural position of exclusion, special exploitation, or mediation, regardless of whether or not this distinctive group is thought of by themselves or others as a race or whether or not they are consciously regarded as biologically inferior. Thus, ancient Greek and Roman slavery as well as early Caribbean slavery, which were not justified by racialist ideology, must be considered to be equally racist structures with latter day North American slavery.

RACE AS A STRUCTURE

The use of the term "race" to describe ethnically distinct groups implies that the essential differences between or among the various races are biologically rooted, i.e., that the social, cultural, psychological, or economic variations among groups are a result of inherited genetic differences in intelligence, innate creative potential, aptitude for menial labor, morality, inherent consciousness of kind, and so on. In fact, however, only one human race has inhabited the earth since the extinction of the Neanderthals about 40,000 years ago and that has been Homo sapiens sapiens. There are no scientifically demonstrated socially significant biologically rooted differences among the different people of the planet. Regardless of the degree of skin pigmentation, shape of the nose or head, type or amount of body hair, or physical size, all peoples, whether originating in Africa, Asia, or Europe, have the same average innate intelligence, creative potential, aptitude to labor, and so forth. The differences between societies and among groups are primarily a result of position within the world capitalist system and the class structure.*

There is no innate "consciousness of kind" or inborn primordial sense of ethnicity that leads people of similar surface physical characteristics (skin pigmentation, nose shape, body hair, and so on) to prefer association with each other and to feel hostility toward others. That this is, in fact, the case is borne witness to by the experiences of the children of one group being adopted into and growing up in another group, in the process fully adopting the identity of their parents' group. It is also manifested in a number of social phenomena. The boundaries of an ethnic groups are obviously socially, and not biologically, defined. For example, different societies define the children of "mixed parents" variously as full members of the subordinate group (the United States), a member of the mother's ethnic group (the Jews), or a member of a third ethnic group (mulattos, mestizos, coloreds) intermediate in status between the ethnic groups of the parents. "Races" or ethnic groups rather quickly disappear into other "races" or ethnic groups, and others are continually created anew. For example, immigrants from southern Italy to the United States in the pre–World War I period had no ethnic identity as Italians (they identified instead as Calabrian, Sicilian, and so on.) The Italian race was not created until after the arrival of distinctive groups in the United States. In the twentieth century, a new ethnic group, the Asian-Americans, has been created out of groups that were not only very different from each other, but in Asia had a long history of mutual antagonism (e.g., Koreans, Japanese, Chinese), including racism as intense as the racism experienced by them in the United States from those of European background.

That there can not be an innate "consciousness of kind" or inherent ethnic solidarity which inhibits intraethnic group conflict and facilitates hostility toward and exploitation of out-groups is shown by the plenitude of cases of vicious exploitation and oppression of members of an ethnic group by others of the same ethnic

---

*The discussion in this section relies in part on Bonacich 1973, 1980; and Burnbaum and Wing 1981.

group and civil wars within ethnic groups (e.g., the civil wars of England, France, the United States, Russia, China, Vietnam, and so on). Chinese and Jewish businessmen have exploited the members of their own groups just as harshly as have members of other groups. Likewise, such treatment has been resisted just as sharply by those affected as they have resisted similar treatment by members of other ethnic groups (e.g., the Chinese Revolution). Intraethnic conflicts are in fact quite prevalent, just as is interethnic solidarity.

The tremendous variation in the degree of out-group hostility and in-group solidarity over time and space is further proof that these phenomena can not be innate. Anti-Semitism and Jewish identity have varied immensely through the years as well as in different parts of the world capitalist system. There was tremendous racism against the Irish when they first migrated to England and the United States in the mid-nineteenth century, but very little was left by the mid-twentieth century. German immigrants to the United States have lost their sense of German identity, although their cousins who remained in Germany rather recently manifested a tremendous outpouring of consciousness of kind.

Finally, the notion that ethnic group differences are biologically based is refuted by the highly variable (and extremely arbitrary) criteria by which races are defined. In the United States and southern Africa the most important racial distinction has been skin pigmentation (or more accurately in the United States, whether or not one had *any* ancestor with dark skin pigmentation). The difference between the Ladino (or Hispanic) race and Anglos is defined in terms of cultural characteristics, including language. In other places, religion seems to be the kernel of "racial" differences. Some of the most vicious "racial" conflicts have, in fact, occurred between groups who have differed imperceptibly if at all in physical characteristics (and, in fact, whose ancestors had "interbred" for hundreds of years), e.g., Germans and Jews, Jews and Poles, Armenians and Turks, Protestants and Catholics in Northern Ireland, Christians and Muslims in Lebanon, French and English-speaking Canadians, Ibos and other tribes in Africa, and so on.

In class societies generally, and in capitalist societies specifically, what are defined as races are, in fact, generated and reproduced because of their distinctive role in the class structure. Generally, most (but seldom or never all) members of such a group play a distinctive economic role in the logic of production. A group's most distinctive cultural traits (including what are labeled in racialist theory as innate intelligence, creativity, ability to labor, and so on) are, in fact, a product of location in the class structure and the distinctive role the group plays.

Three fundamentally different types of racist structures or relationships can be distinguished: first, relationships of superexploitation/disorganization of the working class; second, relationships of exclusion (and appropriation of natural resources); and third, relationships of mediation between dominant and subordinate classes ("middleman minorities").

Racism, then, is in essence an economic structure (of exploitation, mediation, or exclusion) and *not* either a product of innate differences *or* an attitude (e.g., prejudice, bias, stereotypes). Racism is a structure that implies domination as well as all-around degradation (including cultural and interpersonal humiliations). Racist *structures* should be distinguished from racist or racialist theories claiming that social, cultural, and economic differences are biologically based (which are used to legitimate racist structures), and from dominant-group chauvinism (e.g., white chauvinism), the interpersonal behavior of members of the majority group toward members of subordinate ethnic groups or peoples that is generated by the racist structures in which both participate. (This can take the form of either malicious expressions of contempt, arrogance, and superiority *or* nonmalicious paternalistic/patronizing behavior or unconscious acceptance of the prevalent stereotypes of the minorities.)

Racist structures, then, can be considered to be any structures of economic domination that assume a castelike character, i.e., in which economic position is passed on through the generations with sharp lines of status and privilege associated with class position (whether or not there are sharp linguistic, religious, cultural, or physical differences between those in different positions). Thus, the various castes in the traditional Indian social structure must be understood as objectively racist structures, as too must the caste system of early feudal Europe with its three castes of nobility, peasants, and merchants (Jews). The validity of considering European feudalism as a racist structure was reflected in the nineteenth century when the various racialist theories that became hegemonic were not only directed to justifying the international position of England, France, Germany, and so forth and the subordination of Africans, Asians, Indians, and Jews, but also to rationalize the continuing domination of the aristocracy and other ruling classes in Europe as they came under increasing attack. For example, it was argued that the French aristocracy was of a racially superior Nordic stock, while the French peasantry was Alpine (i.e., racially inferior). In the nineteenth and early twentieth centuries in Europe and the United States such arguments gained considerable currency in justifying existing domestic class relations in spite of the fact that both the peasants (and workers) and the upper classes in France, Italy, Germany (where these theories were most often applied) tended to have the same physical characteristics, the same religions, speak pretty much the same language as well as shared a fairly similar culture.

The importance of seeing racism as essentially a relationship, and not an attitude or idea, can not be stressed too much. Hypothetically it might well be the case that leading capitalist employers of black labor do not themselves believe in the theory of superior/ inferior races (but only encourage such an ideology in white workers). It might even be the case that they do not share in unconscious stereotypes or engage in paternalistic behavior in their interpersonal relations with minorities. But nevertheless, they are the *real* racists. This is true both in the sense of being responsible for the system of exploitative race relations *and* the beneficiaries of that system, *and* because their system generates the conscious and unconscious racist ideologies and chauvinistic practices on the part of large segments of the majority group population that affect minority group peoples in all aspects of their lives (not just in on-the-job economic relations) including cultural and interpersonal humiliations.

Racist structures of exploitation are reproduced through both institutional discrimination *and* objective structures and politics which, although not discriminatory, nevertheless reproduce the class (or excluded) position of a group. Institutional discrimination is the explicit or implicit policy of admittance to training programs, schools, and universities; hiring and promotion policies of corporations; eligibility for government programs, and so on that differentially favor members of the relatively privileged group, who on all relevant criteria have the same objective qualifications as do subordinate group members, i.e., minority group members with the same or higher aptitude test scores or grade records, physical abilities, and so forth as majority group members, do not get admitted to school, hired for a job, or promoted when majority group members do. Such institutional discrimination is generally only a minor part of the total structure of exploitation of the subordinate group. Generally, more important are the objective structures and policies that differentially hurt the life chances of the subordinate groups as compared to those of the relatively privileged group. For example, the social forces and state policies that lead to the decline and decay of cities (especially the loss of industry) disproportionately negatively affect blacks and Puerto Ricans in the United States since they are heavily concentrated in the inner cities. Cutbacks in job training and creation programs as well as in the provision of basic welfare benefits are also instances of such factors. Immigration rules that act to exclude those without resident relatives or skills (thus disproportionately affecting people from Africa and Latin America) and that consequently lead to illegal immigration (and thus workers with no legal protection from special exploitation) should also be included here. These factors all function objectively as structures that facilitate exploitation because they all act to reduce the economic level of minorities (higher urban unemployment, greater economic desperation, lack of legal status) and their ability to organize and improve their condition.

It is, of course, true that rarely, if ever, are all members of a "race" or ethnic group in the class position defining that group. But it is, of course, in the nature of racialist theory to attribute the alleged characteristics of any "race" or ethnic group to *all* members of that group, whether or not they share the distinctive economic role of most group members. Racialist theories define groups as biologically suited for menial labor, inherently "sly" and "crafty," or innately impossible to "civilize" (and thus necessary to exterminate), i.e., they define a group by alleged biological and inherent characteristics that must logically apply to *all* group members. Thus, all members of a "racial" or ethnic group will necessarily experience the dominant group chauvinism associated with racialist theories whether or not they themselves as individuals are specially exploited, play a mediating role, or are excluded.

At a given time a specific ethnic group may be defined by more than one position in society's racist structure. One position might be dominant, or, at least for a time, two might be of more or less equal importance. Moreover, a group's primary structural definition might change over time from one to another category. Lastly, if a group loses its primary structural definition in a racist structure, it will eventually disappear as a distinctive racial group. For example, the Mexicans in the Southwest of the United States, after the conquest of the area in 1848, were both an excluded population (whose land was mostly stolen over the course of the rest of the century by Anglos) *and* a source of cheap, specially exploited labor. While at first the aspect of exclusion was predominant (in order to gain the land), eventually, once most of the resources were in the hands of Anglos, the aspect of cheap labor became predominant. A similar thing can be said about the indigenous inhabitants of the Republic of South Africa. A case can be made that the structural position of blacks in the United States increasingly is being defined not by the still dominant relation of special exploitation/disorganization but by the piling up of "redundant" urban blacks of the excluded sector (similar to the redefinition of central European Jews in the post-1880s period from their essential role as mediators to that of a redundant population in urban ghettos in the 1920s and 1930s).

A given position in a racist structure can be occupied by more than one ethnically distinct social group. For example, in much of the

Ottoman Empire Greeks, Armenians, and Jews all were concentrated in the position of petty traders and merchants, and all indefinitely remained ethnically distinct from each other as well as from mainstream Turkish culture. Likewise, in parts of Southeast Asia (e.g., Malaya, Singapore, and Burma), Indian merchants and moneylenders compete with the Chinese, with both maintaining their ethnic distinctiveness. In industrial capitalist societies it has been quite normal for a number of different ethnic groups to occupy the specially exploited working class position, even while one or two groups tend to dominate. In Germany, for example, while Turks have been the largest ethnically distinct group, there are also large numbers of ethnically distinct Greeks, Portuguese, Italians, and Yugoslavians. In the United States this position is largely shared by blacks and Ladinos.

Quite distinct peoples who happen to share the physical/linguistic characteristics by which a large minority group is culturally defined tend to experience the same type of racism as do the latter. For example, Haitian or Jamaican immigrants to the United States are part of a very different culture than that of native-born blacks (whose culture was formed in the experience of Southern slavery and its aftermath, where blacks were a minority and caste lines firm). Black African immigrants who have petty-bourgeois backgrounds are even more different (they do not share the crucial formative experience of slavery). Yet, antiblack racism, especially on the interpersonal level, as well as popular racialist ideologies apply indiscriminately across the board to all people with even a drop of African blood (with the irony that people who have grown up treated as whites or mulattos in the Caribbean, are suddenly treated as blacks in the United States). Similarly, different groups of Asian immigrants (Chinese, Japanese, Koreans, Filipinos) who in Asia are very distinctive groups without a common identity as Asians (and, in fact, with long histories of mutual antagonism toward each other) come to be treated in the United States (at least after the first generation when they have largely adopted the English language and U.S. culture) as essentially all simply "Asians". American Indians, particularly after they become detribalized (move to cities or outside of their traditional tribal areas), likewise come to be treated as "Indians" regardless of their very diverse cultures, languages, and traditions. A similar process appears to be occurring among Latin American immigrants. In spite of distinct national identities as Puerto Ricans, Mexicans, Salvadorians, Colombians, Dominicans, and so forth, they are often grouped as a distinct race of "Hispanics" on the basis first of common Spanish/Latin American language and traditions and second, even when in the second or third generation their distinctive national minority characteristics are lost, on the basis of physical characteristics or last name ("Spanish surnamed").

Because they are largely treated according to rules established for the large preexisting groups, smaller groups like Haitians, Jamaicans, Dominicans, Colombians, and so on tend to be amalgamated into the dominant (or emerging) racial categories (e.g., blacks, Hispanics) while losing their national distinctiveness. Such groups, thus, tend to be assimilated *nationally* into minor variants of the predominant mainstream national U.S. culture, while assimilated at the same time into the appropriate racial category (and, thus, to come to assimilate the secondary linguistic and cultural characteristics of these groups). Racial categories, but not separate national or tribal cultures, are thus reproduced within contemporary relations of production.

The pattern in industrial capitalist societies such as the United States is to draw in peasants from other areas or nations as a pool of specially exploited labor and to pretty much annihilate most of their traditional national or tribal characteristics within a generation or two (e.g., distinctive language, dress, foods, customs, and so on), assimilating the various ethnic groups into larger racial, and to a lesser extent, religious categories, i.e., white Protestants, white Catholics, Jews, blacks, Asians, Indians, Hispanics, in the process amalgamating all traditional national/tribal differences (i.e., Polish language, Irish customs, Italians peasant dress, and so on). All the distinctive racial groups in an advanced industrial society such as the United States have largely adopted the same language and similar customs (a product of the tremendous homogenizing force of industrial capitalism that requires a mobile, flexible population literate in a single language even while maintaining distinct identities). Secondary cultural characteristics (and perhaps accents or minor dialects in the case of more rural or excluded sections of a racial group) are reproduced along with racial identification as a product of the residential and cultural segregation of minorities and the resultant continuity in a high level of group interaction and relative social isolation from majority groups this results in.

It should be noted, however, that the small middle class segments of peoples defined by specially exploited or excluded relations as well as the salaried employee (new middle class) and independent professional sector of peoples defined essentially by their mediating relationship tend to adopt for the most part the accent and customs of the middle class of the majority group rather than that of the predominant specially exploited, excluded, or self-employed sectors (which tend much more than the former to maintain the traditional isolation from the majority group). Salaried middle class and independent professional people from all ethnic minorities are under tremendous pressure to conform to the standards of mainstream middle class life, not the least of which are pressures to speak with the same accent, be highly mobile geographically, and aspire to the same material goods. Further, they share a common higher education and work environment.

The fact of the common experience of dominant group chauvinism (shared by *all* members of a minority group) is a basis for group solidarity that at different times and different places may be more or less important as a basis of political unity than class solidarity with people in equivalent class positions belonging to other ethnic groups. The sentiments of group solidarity generated by a common experience of humiliation and discrimination can be manipulated by the wealthier segment of a minority group to lead (and themselves exploit) the poorer members of the group, or they can be used by the working class, or perhaps the intelligentsia segment, to primarily advance the interest of the poorer people in such groups.

RELATIONSHIPS OF EXCLUSION

As capitalism expanded through imperialism to subordinate virtually all corners of the globe, it came into contact with native peoples such as the American Indians and Australian aborigines who for the most part could not (outside the Mexican and Peruvian regions) generally be made to work profitably. Such peoples then became mere obstacles to the profitable exploitation of the natural resources and land of the areas they inhabited. Successful development of agriculture in Argentina, Australia, Brazil, or North America thus implied the elimination of the indigenous inhabitants through either physical extermination (genocide), which has been widely practiced, or forcible removal and relocation to remote and barren areas (reservations). Imperialist and capitalist relationships to such indigenous and "superfluous" populations can best be referred to as relationships of *exclusion*—exclusion from the land as well as from the class structure. A distinctive form of racialist ideology developed to justify the physical extermination and forcible relocation of such peoples and the consequent appropriation of their land and resources by expanding imperialism. This racialist ideology legitimated extermination in terms of indigenous peoples not being fully human, and relocation in terms of their inherent inability to productivity and creatively utilize resources. American Indians have and continue to suffer great oppression, not because their labor was exploited, but because their resources were necessary for the expansion of capitalism.

In economic, health, and standard of living terms, excluded peoples tend to be the worse off of the three types of oppressed ethnic groups. For example, in 1969 in the United States, American Indians had the lowest per capita income of any ethnic group—46 percent of white Anglos and 87 percent that of blacks. In 1970 only 63 percent of Indian males between the ages of 16 and 65 were in the civilian labor force and 11.6 percent of these were unemployed. This compares with 76 percent of white and 73 percent of black males in this age-group who were in the labor force, and the white male unemployment rate of 4.0 percent and the black unemployment rate of 7.3 percent. Further, 56 percent of employed Indian males were menial laborers, compared to 36 percent for the national average (U.S. Department of Commerce, 1975a, p. 336; U.S. Bureau of the Census, 1970a, Tables 6 and 7; Perlo 1975, p. 37.) In general, displaced indigenous populations suffer the most from disease and malnutrition as well as from the demoralization and mental stress associated with the destruction of their traditional ways of life and no systematic alternative. It should be noted that by 1970 the indigenous populations of the United States had been reduced to 0.4 percent of the total population. In Australia, aborigines in 1980 were 1.2 percent of the population (New York *Times*, November 8, 1981, p. 8).

The native North American Indians were systematically exterminated and forcibly displaced so that white settlers involved in the expanding world market could incorporate their land. Bounties were put on Indians (confirmed by Indian scalps). This practice of killing Indians on commission was first initiated by the Dutch in New Amsterdam in 1641 and continued through the early part of the nineteenth century. The last American scalp bounty was offered by the state of Indiana in 1814 as an "encouragement to the enterprise and bravery of our fellow citizens" (Gossett 1963, p. 229). For a century after the expiration of the last scalp bounties, killing Indians in most parts of the West was rarely prosecuted successfully as murder in court. The attitude of "the only good Indian is a dead Indian" shared by most commercial farmers, miners, and state officials served the expanding market system well. Indians who managed to escape extermination were largely displaced into territories thought to be without value to the expanding market system. For many years Indians were concentrated in the Indian Territory of Oklahoma, sometimes by forced marches in winter in which thousands died because they had no adequate protection from the weather (as occurred when the Cherokee nation was marched to Oklahoma after their expulsion from Georgia in 1838). Primitive bacteriological warfare was practiced on the Indians. It was not unusual for "gifts" to be made to unsuspecting Indians of blankets that had been contamminated with deadly contagious diseases (e.g., smallpox) against which Indians had few immunities. There were also massacres of whole Indians groups (warriors, women, and children). Some of the more notorious of these included the massacre of the Cheyenne at Sand Creek, Colorado, in 1864 after the discovery of gold on their land and of the Sioux in 1890 at Wounded Knee, South Dakota, after the discover of gold in the Black Hills.

The Indians were displaced again and again to more undesirable territory, each time losing more of their land as the ever expanding capitalist system demanded their resources. Although many formal treaties were signed by the United States and the Indian tribes, these were systematically ignored by the U.S. state. Large numbers of Indians forcibly and by treachery concentrated in the most barren and inhospitable regions (not wanted by the whites) died from exposure and starvation. The U.S. government attitude toward treaties with the indigenous people that guaranteed their reserved areas was well summed up by the U.S. commissioner of Indians affairs, General Francis C. Walker, in 1871: "When dealing with savage men, as with savage beasts, no question of national honor can arise. Whether to fight, to run away, or to employ a ruse, is solely a question of expediency" (Gossett 1963, p. 234).

During the oil boom in Oklahoma (formally the Indian Territory) white "guardians" were appointed by the U.S. courts to look after the financial interests of the Osage Indians (on whose lands considerable oil wealth was found). It has been estimated that between 1915 and 1931 90 percent of the royalties due these Indians on their oil was appropriated by the white "guardians." Until 1933 Indians were prohibited from incorporating or organizing politically. Indian tribal funds were appropriated to pay the cost of the Indian Bureau (between 1900 and 1930 $100 million was appropriated for this purpose). The Indian Bureau, appointed by the U.S. president, has virtual total power over Indian lands. It could, for example, expel from Indian lands any journalists or "agitator" without giving any reason (see Gossett 1963, p. 451). The condition of Indians in the United States, as was also the case of Jews and postbellum blacks, reached its all-time low point in the early 1920s.

Once an indigenous population has been largely excluded from their original land and resources, many of them come to work in the capitalist economy as wage laborers (or in earlier times as slaves, serfs, or tenant farmers). However, large numbers become demoralized by the process of genocide, displacement, and destruction of their traditional ways of life. Alcoholism, mental disease, drug addiction, and all-around demoralization became quite common. Thus, excluded populations tend to develop a large "redundant" population—

redundant in the sense of performing no useful economic function for capital, either special exploitation or mediation. Redundant populations may be left alone so long as they "starve quietly," but are most vulnerable to repression (or even further genocide) if either they cause the system trouble, or if the system needs a scapegoat for other problems.

Redundant populations have also been created out of groups that historically were defined by their positions of special exploitation or mediation in racist structures. Such processes can be referred to as secondary exclusion (in contrast to the *primary* exclusion of indigenous peoples). The commercialization of central European society beginning in the 1870s pushed the Jews out of their traditional mediating positions; and with the avenues to conversion to new middle class status as well as immigration largely closed in the 1920s and 1930s, a large population of unemployed Jews piled up in the ghettos of the larger eastern European cities (a true excluded population).

Redundant populations can also result from the discarding of a population formerly defined primarily by the relationship of special exploitation. This occurs when capital finds it more profitable to locate and utilize a new group of ex-peasant workers who will work harder for less than the second generation of an older group (or perhaps when technological change or economic stagnation makes a population largely redundant). This appears to be happening to blacks (as well as to many Puerto Ricans) in the North of the United States. Redundant populations, whether a result of *primary* or *secondary* exclusion, because they perform no profitable economic function, are extremely vulnerable to scapegoating (displacement of hostilities against capital toward them), and in the extreme case to physical removal or even genocide (their maintenance often represents a considerable economic cost to the system).

Appropriate theories have always been generated to legitimate the extermination and displacement of indigenous peoples. In the seventeenth century religious ideology was used. In New England, quickly forgetting how the Indians around Plymouth helped the Pilgrims through their first hard winter with gifts as well as by teaching them survival skills. Cotton Mather justified genocide by categorizing Indians as "the devil's minions," damned by birth by God and incapable of redemption. In the nineteenth century, racialist justifications of the inherent biological inferiority of Indians were used. Indians were now considered *biologically* incapable of civilization, an inferior breed of people, more or less savage beasts (Gossett 1963, p. 229).

RELATIONSHIPS OF MEDIATION

Most commercial class societies, including the Asiatic mode of production and feudalism as well as imperialism in its overseas manifestations tend to generate a distinctive group (or groups) of "middlemen" who act as buyers and sellers, moneylenders, lower level administrators, and so on between the propertied class/imperialist and the peasants.* Before the era of contemporary monopoly industrial capitalism it was common for a "middleman minority" ethnic group both to dominate petty trade and, for the majority of the middleman minority group, to be concentrated in these pursuits.

Middleman minorities in petty bourgeois trading occupations serve a number of functions for the dominant class structure. First, they (rather than the imperialists or the wealthy) absorb the hostility of the underlying population which deals with them on a day to day basis in buying, selling, and moneylending. Second, they allow the upper class or imperialists not to lose status by having to haggle with the lower classes (business and trade have traditionally been regarded as degrading by the upper classes). Third, they do the job cheaper (work longer hours for less remuneration, work harder, and so on) than members of the privileged classes or imperialist nation would. Fourth, by excluding members of the peasantry from such occupations, the problems associated with rising expectations are avoided, while maintaining a sharp class boundary between the upper and lower classes (important for legitimizing class relations). Fifth, the international ties of the middlemen provide a network that greatly facilitates trade and commerce. Ethnic solidarity facilitates trade and, moreover, petty trading tends to hold the ethnic group together. Their "alien" status also allows them to be objective in their dealings with the dominant group peasants and workers. They do not have familial or community ties that might intrude on business considerations. Sixth, in times of severe social tension, such middlemen can be scapegoated by the dominant class in order to absorb the energy of its opponents in both the working class/peasantry *and* among the petty bourgeois of other ethnic groups, e.g., periodic manipulated outbursts of anti-Semitism in the czarist empire, anti-Armenian sentiment in the Ottoman Empire, anti-East Indian sentiments of Africans in South and East Africa (from Durban to Uganda), and anti-Chinese sentiment in Southeast Asia that have included expulsions, violent pogroms, and "final solutions." Seventh, the hostility between the majority group of peasants/workers and middlemen that

---

*The discussion in this section is indebted to Bonacich 1973.

keeps them from developing solidarity also of course facilitates the general domination of the landlord/large capitalist class or the imperialists (the divide and rule strategy).

Racist feelings against middleman majorities come from the feelings of exploitation (high prices for goods bought, low prices for goods sold, high interest rates) of the majority group workers and peasants, from competition with petty-bourgeois members of the majority ethnic group (who often feel that the minority petty bourgeois are unfair "foreign" competition because they work longer, harder, use illegal or fringe methods, and so on); and from feelings of contempt by the upper classes, who look down on the petty, monetary orientation of these groups. Sometimes there is also resentment among majority group workers whose employers are faced with low-cost competition from middleman employers who are able to use ethnic solidarity, combined with worker desire to save money and become petty bourgeois (and consequently the feeling that their time in the working class is temporary), to pay their workers less while getting them to work harder (e.g., in restaurants and sweatshops) as well as keeping them out of majority group worker unions and otherwise obstructing class solidarity. Racist feelings against middleman minorities often become the most vicious of all forms of racism (not infrequently resulting in systematic pogroms and genocide).

The combination of inner group cohesiveness generated by their economic role and the economic interests of the richer members of the minority middleman community, which promotes nationalism in order to secure the domination and exploitation of the poorer members of the middleman minorities, is typically manifested in the maintenance of a separate religion (Judaism, Armenian Christianity, Buddhism, Islam, and so on), customs, neighborhoods, and community institutions as well as distinctive culture.

The typical middleman minority business is a family enterprise that often relies heavily on unpaid family labor. If the enterprise requires more labor, members of the extended family or nonrelatives from the ethnic group, who often come to be treated somewhat like kin, are preferred (they often live with the owning family above or behind the store). Both paid and unpaid employees tend to work long hours for low pay and have a personal loyalty to the owner. Most in the smaller enterprises have a not unrealistic hope of either becoming partners in the business or receiving sufficient assistance to eventually set up their own business. Labor costs in such enterprises tend to be especially low, enabling them to survive and grow where majority group businesses go bankrupt.

Middleman minority businesses are not always found in retail trade and moneylending. They also tend to concentrate in other sectors of small business that do not require the tying up of large amounts of capital for any significant amount of time (i.e., are easily liquidated or transportable—alien status encourages liquidity). Among such occupations are truck farming, which has been a common agricultural occupation for Japanese in California, Indians in Natal, and Chinese in New Zealand. Trades such as goldsmith, shoemaker, barber, jeweler, tailor, restaurant owner, and launderer in which Armenians in Syria, Jews in eastern Europe, and Chinese and Japanese in North America have tended to concentrate are also typical middleman minority trades (Bonacich 1973). The independent professions are a common occupational specialization for North American and Western European Jews.

The ethnic groups that become middleman minorities (e.g., Chinese, Asian Indians, Jews, and Armenians) tend to develop similar occupational structures wherever they go, suggesting that their role must be defined by a *combination* or some cultural/social background traits of these groups as well as by a functional need for such a group in the recipient countries.* It is probably the case that the typical middleman minority immigrants originate in an area astride major trade routes, and thus where commerce was especially important (e.g., Palestine, Armenia, South China, coastal India), and come from a downwardly mobile petty-bourgeois or middle or large peasant milieu in the "old country," and migrate overseas in order to restore or surpass their family background (in the process most typically temporarily engaging in manual labor in order to accumulate sufficient capital). These groups have historically been able to reassert their traditional middle class position, in spite of a generation or two of poverty, through the use of strong collective discipline, mutual assistance, and cooperation, manifested in strong extended family ties, trade associations, regional associations, and revolving credit societies. Thus, traditional middle class values embodied in distinctive institutions that promote sacrifice, saving, mutual support, and a strong sense of ethnic honor are able to bridge the generational gap in actual class position (see Light 1972; Bonacich 1973). Because host societies are so receptive to having a special ethnic group perform the middleman functions, once a group gets institutionalized in this role, its position is reinforced by both internal and external pressures which reproduce that role. New immigrants are, thus, better able to succeed in restoring their family background with the aid of their ethnic community reinforced by the expectations of the majority group.

---

*Before the First World War Armenians, together with Jews and Greeks, monopolized the internal commerce of Turkey. In the mid-1950s Asians (from India and Pakistan), while waking up only about one percent of the population, dominated trade from Durban to Uganda in East Africa (Bonacich 1973).

Because of the qualitatively different role of middleman minorities (old or new) in comparison with excluded peoples or specially exploited workers, income levels and health or living standards do not normally distinguish middleman groups from members of the dominant ethnic groups. Once they become established their income level generally becomes *higher* than the average for the majority group, as do their health and living standards.

There are two basic types of structures of mediation: the old petty-bourgeois position of classical middleman minorities, and the new salaried middle class professional positions, intermediate between these two is the transitional status of independent professionals (e.g., self-employed doctors, lawyers, dentists) in which many middleman minority groups (e.g., Jews) tend to be heavily concentrated. Before the era of industrial monopoly capitalism, in all forms of commercial societies (the slave mode of production of the ancient world, feudalism, the Asiatic mode of production, early European capitalism, capitalist imperialism in the less-developed countries) there was a strong tendency for a distinctive ethnic group to become defined as shopkeepers, moneylenders, and so on. But in the industrial capitalism of the monopoly capitalist era the independent petty bourgeoisie in all its manifestations is being replaced by corporate and state institutions that employ salaried professionals and managers. Everywhere the survivers of the traditional petty bourgeoisie (many were expelled or exterminated when they were displaced from their traditional roles by majority group members desirous of appropriating their traditional petty privileges) have transformed (or are in the process of transforming) themselves into part of the professional middle class through the mechanism of educating their sons (using accumulated family wealth to build up "human capital" in children). Thus, while traditionally Jews were overwhelmingly petty traders and moneylenders, today in North America and Europe they are overwhelmingly professionals. A similar process is underway for Chinese, Asian Indians, and Armenians (the degree to which this process has been completed is a function of the level of development of monopoly capitalist industrialization in the regions in which they reside).

The traditional position of middleman minority is highly visible since peasants must interact on a daily basis with people of obviously different cultural, linguistic, religious, and often physical characteristics. They are, thus, obvious and easy targets of racist hostility as well as discrimination. On the other hand, those in the new position of professional/managerial mediators come to speak the same languages (with the same accent) as the majority group, as well as adopt the dominant culture and religion of the majority middle class. The nature of professional work requires a linguistically and culturally homogeneous middle class in each country, while the traditional middle class structure of trade and moneylending requires international ties facilitated by cross-national cultural/linguistic homogeneity of the middle class group (and, thus, a contrast with any particular group of peasants). As a result, those in the new structures of mediation are much less visible to the working class to which they minister and supervise (as well as to the capitalist class for which they work). Consequently, in times of prosperity and stability, they tend to draw relatively little racist hostility, and to suffer relatively little discrimination (certainly in comparison to the past of these groups).

However, the professional middle class positions are objectively just as much positions of mediation as are the traditional middleman minority positions, and as such have the same potential to define groups with common ancestry (who often have different physical characteristics than the majority group) as a distinct *race* and to generate racist hostility and discrimination (especially in the form of restrictive quotas in universities and professional jobs) as well as to produce the other forms of racist oppression to which the traditional middleman minorities were subject. In times of economic stagnation and contraction, when the children of the majority group find it difficult to get into college or to get professional jobs, times when average working people accumulate hostility that can be directed by the upper class at an obvious (and relatively privileged) target, such as the Jews (read Chinese, Asians, Armenians, Asian Indians, and so on) who are "monopolizing" positions in the colleges, professions, and so forth, the economic definition and role of any that can be defined as a distinct "race" in the new positions of mediation becomes precarious. The conversion from old to new mediation status (which was largely complete for the German Jews by 1933) does not protect against anti-Semitism (or its equivalent for equivalent groups). As long as an ethnic group is heavily concentrated in a given economic position (whether old or new middle class) it is objectively in a racist structure (regardless of the degree of its cultural assimilation or surface visibility).

The Jews

The Jewish people were dispersed over the Hellenic world of the East hundreds of years before the conquest of Jerusalem by the

Romans.* It has been estimated that only about one-fourth lived in the independent Jewish kingdom of Palestine in this period. Hebrew had already ceased to be a spoken language. Most Jews in Palestine spoke Aramic (the language spoken by Christ), a major trading language of the Near East. Many others scattered around the Near East spoke Greek as their native language. Most of the Jews that still lived in Palestine in the seventh century A.D. were converted to Islam, just as were other neighboring peoples. (Most of the Palestinian Arabs of the twentieth century are, thus, descended from pre-Islamic Jews.) The Jews in the area who did not convert to Islam were mostly merchants. Throughout their long history whenever Jews failed to constitute a distinct commercial class they assimilated. For thousands of years to be Jewish meant to be engaged in commerce.†

Their location astride the major trade routes between Egypt and the Mesopotamian and Syrian worlds together with an environment rather unsuited for agriculture led the Jewish people into commerce and related occupations that carried them far and wide through the Mediterranean world and the Near East. It should be noted that the immediate northern neighbor of the Jews, the Phoenicians, also became a trading people, albeit sea traders rather than land traders, for much the same reason. Lebanon, unlike Palestine, had both forests of cedar for shipbuilding and many good harbors (thus accounting for the difference between the two). The dispersion of the Jews was facilitated by the fact that most of the common peasants through the Mediterranean world and the Near East were involved in a natural, noncommercial economy. Such peasants (who provided their surplus production to the state as tax) needed only a few necessities such as salt and metals from outside and thus welcomed the foreigners who provided such goods. Their position was also consolidated by the fact that the ruling classes of first Greeks then Romans generally despised trade. Contrary to popular myth, Jewish culture and identity has been preserved down through the ages (longer than any other West-

---

*This section relies very heavily on Leon 1950 and Pinson 1946.

†It is clear that there are no physical features held in common by Jews that could specify them as a distinct biologically based group whose traits are primarily a product of common descent from a homogeneous group originating in Palestine. Jewish people throughout the world take on the physical characteristics of the people among whom they reside for any length of time (both because of sexual relationships and conversions). European Jews look like Christian Europeans, Asiatic Jews like other Asians, Ethiopian Jews like other Ethiopians, and so on. The Jews of the Mediterranean basin, where a majority of the population is brunette, are also dark-haired. In northern Europe where the population is mostly blond the Jews are also predominantly blond. One study found that the Jews of southwestern Germany were 60 percent blond (Snyder 1939, p. 305).

ern tradition) not in spite of their diaspora but precisely *because of it*. This is because of the vital, distinctive, and continuous economic role performed by the Jews, a function that could only be performed in diaspora throughout the commercial world.

There were many wealthy Jewish traders at the peak of the Roman Empire. Most of the rest of the Jews in the Roman world were smaller traders, artisans, and peddlers. As trade declined, especially after protoserfdom was instituted around A.D. 300, the relative economic position of the Jews was enhanced. The ruling classes still needed luxury products from the East, and the Jews, utilizing their wide-ranging commercial network, became practically the sole intermediaries. Being Jewish and being a merchant became even more synonomous.

In the first part of the Middle Ages (especially from the ninth to the twelfth century) with the full development of the natural economy of serfdom and manors, the Jews dominated commerce. At this time, as wealthy merchants Jews were considered to be part of the upper class, with a juridical position not much different than the nobility. In feudal society the landlord class needed the Jews and the Jews needed the landlords (as protectors). Their communities in France (and Spain) became the international centers of Jewish life. People desirous of attaining wealth sometimes converted to Judaism, while Jews who became landlords came under great pressure to become Christians or Moslems. In general, Jews who became agriculturalists or entered other occupations soon gave up Judaism. The Jews were the caste of merchants, with Judaism the religion of this caste.

But with the general revival of commerce in the European world in the thirteenth century, the Jews were pushed out of their traditional monopoly of trade by a rising Christian commercial bourgeoisie. The commercial monopoly of the Jews was an obstacle the nascent bourgeoisie had to overcome. As they were forced to abandon their commercial role, the Jews applied their accumulated fortunes to moneylending (usury). (Jews had traditionally practiced usury as a supplement to their commercial business.) Usury is a necessary supplement to the natural economy of peasants who must rely on loans to purchase necessary seeds or equipment in exceptional times. The lords and kings were reliant on Jewish moneylenders. The Jews fleeced the nobles and the kings fleeced the Jews. The Jews became a mechanism by which wealth was transferred to the king.

As money became more abundant, the nobility's reliance on Jewish moneylenders decreased. Kings now renounced their debts to the Jews and often expelled them from their countries as "parasites." The role of usurer became unbearable because it became unnecessary. Kings established other mechanisms to acquire money. This happened in England in 1290, in France a number of times but decisively in 1392, and in Spain in 1492. Some Jews became assimilated as part of the rising national bourgeoisies, others became petty usurers in Italy and Germany (especially in their more backward regions). Others moved to the eastern empires, and by way of Germany eventually to Poland and adjacent eastern European countries. The economic collapse of the Jews in the West brought an era of persecution.

The Jews came to thrive east of the Elbe, where serfdom was instituted in response to the growth of economic demand from western Europe for agricultural exports. The institution of feudal relations of production after the fifteenth century in eastern Europe required a caste of geographically mobile traders and moneylenders intermediate in status between the nobility and the immobile and recently enserfed peasantry.

The logic of the world capitalist system and its differential requirement for a distinctive commercial caste was thus responsible for the movement of the Jewish center of gravity from France and Spain to Poland and western Russia by way of Germany. In eastern Europe the Jews assumed the roles of traders and moneylenders that they had held for hundreds of years in western Europe, both to the peasantry and to the upper class. And, as in western Europe, the vital economic functions they performed ensured their protection by the nobility and its state. Jews also frequently came to manage the commercial, and sometimes even the agricultural, enterprises of the nobility. Many Jews became artisans, especially in the production of goods for Jewish traders (e.g., furriers, tailors, goldsmiths, jewelers, and so on).

A significant portion of Polish Jews in the eighteenth century were located in the smaller villages, operating under the protection of the nobility as innkeepers, traders, and stewards of the noble-owned mills, estates, distilleries, dairy farms, bridges, breweries, and so on. In some areas, the nobles farmed out entire villages to Jews to rule and extract income from (in exchange for a fee). Polish landlords were generally eager to have Jews settle in their towns so as to stimulate the development of handicrafts and commerce as well as to increase the profitability of the nobles' enterprises through their managerial skills.

Excluded from the craft guilds, Jewish artisans in Poland operated outside of their restrictions. Before the nineteenth century Jewish artisans were thus at the forefront of developing new methods of work (e.g., the production of standardized articles) as well as new methods of organization (capitalism).

Until World War II the Jews played the central role in commerce in eastern Europe, occupying both the higher and lower level positions. Jews made up about one-third of the urban population and controlled about 60 to 75 percent of the commerce and 40 to 50 percent of industry and handicrafts as well. In 1818 in the Ukraine 87 percent of Jews were in commerce and another 12 percent were artisans. In Budapest 62 percent of all Jews in 1900 were in business, this declined to 51 percent in 1920 and 40 percent in 1935. In 1910, 47 percent of all those employed in Hungarian business and banking were Jews; in 1935, 30 percent. In Warsaw in 1882, 79 percent of all Jews were engaged in business; in 1921, 60 percent; and in 1935, 48 percent. In 1897, 75 percent of all those engaged in business and banking in Poland were Jews; in 1935, 58 percent. In Lithuania in 1897, 86 percent of all those in business and banking were Jews; in 1935, 55 percent. In Latvia in 1897, 45 percent were Jews, and in 1935, 32 percent (Weinryb 1946, p. 32; Leon 1950, p. 195). It is clear that the Jews of central and eastern Europe were defined by their middleman minority status as traders and small businessmen.

The destruction of feudal relations of production and the process of all-around commercialization and the growth of capitalism in eastern Europe in the last half of the nineteenth century wreaked havoc with the Jewish people. From the 1860s the Jewish domination of trade in central Europe came under a growing challenge from the increasing number of Christian competition. A strong anti-Semitic movement grew up coincident with the general rise of nationalism (and anti-foreign sentiments) throughout Europe. After the emancipation of the Russian serfs in 1861, many peasants as well as small landlords were displaced by commercialization. The general economic trends of the last third of the nineteenth century manifested in lower prices for agricultural commodities and economic concentration resulted in the displacement of many peasants from the land throughout central Europe and their concentration in cities, in many cases as petty traders and handicraftsmen in competition with the Jews. New industrial and commercial cities came to supplant the small towns and fairs that the Jews traditionally dominated. The relatively economically well-off position of many Jews in the latter part of the nineteenth century was increasingly coveted by their competitors.

Increasingly squeezed out of commerce many Jews immigrated to the rising cities and larger towns where they came to live in distinctively Jewish ghettos. In 1847, 5 percent of Russian Jews lived in cities; in 1897, 28 percent; and in 1926, 50 percent (Leon 1950, p. 216). The increasing exclusion of Jews from traditional commercial monopolies (a repeat of the process that had occurred a half a millenium before in western Europe) induced by the transition to capitalist relations of production caused class differentiation to occur among Jews. Many Jewish artisans were reduced to wage laborers in those industries where their skills were appropriate (typically working for Jewish capitalists, who themselves evolved from the merchants selling the traditional goods manufactured and sold by Jews). In the latter part of the nineteenth century a significant Jewish proletariat was created for the first time in almost 2,000 years. Jewish capital and a Jewish proletariat grew up in garments, furs, jewelry, and other light consumer goods, generally in small shops rather than factories. These enterprises suffered disproportionately from seasonal unemployment, bad working conditions, and low wages. In Poland in 1921 about 25 percent of Jews were workers or employees, in Germany in 1907 about 62 percent, and in Russia in 1925 about 15 percent. During these years about two-thirds of Jewish workers, however, worked in shops (compared to about 25 percent of non-Jews). In 1930 about 45 percent of European Jewish workers were in the clothing trades (compared to 9 percent of non-Jews). In Poland in 1931 about 59 percent of Jewish workers were artisans (compared to 33 percent of non-Jews). And 23 percent of non-Jews worked in medium or large industry, compared to 4 percent of Jews (Leon 1950, pp. 218, 220).

The hostility against the Jews in eastern Europe was immense. The peasants hated them because of their role as traders, money-lenders, and purchasers. The rising capitalist class was anti-Semitic, both because they resented the Jews' low-cost competition, and because anti-Semitism deflected criticism away from them. The Slavic and other Christian petty bourgeois despised them most of all because of the rigorous competition in those sectors into which increasing numbers of non-Jews were being forced by economic dislocations. The landed upper classes, meanwhile, became less dependent on the Jews' unique economic contribution as other groups and institutions came increasingly to play their role. Thus without their traditional protector in the nobility, and with rising popular hostility, anti-Semitism blossomed.

In areas of central Europe such as Silesia and central Poland (e.g., in Lodz and Bialystok) where industry was especially despised by both landlords and peasants, Jews came to own considerable amounts of *industrial* capital. Such early capitalist activities were sufficient to give a certain amount of credibility to the anti-Semitic claim that capitalism was a "Jewish invention," thus facilitating the channeling of much hostility against capitalism into anti—Semitism (which the Socialists tended to combat with the slogan "anti-Semitism is the socialism of fools"). As time passed the non-Jewish capitalists, which comprised the predominant segment almost everywhere, found it convenient to scapegoat Jewish capital, thereby deflecting hostility from themselves, while at the same time restricting their competitors.

But it is exactly because the Jews no longer played the role as a major commercial force that was attributed to them that anti-Semitic persecution was able to assume such a magnitude in the 1930s and 1940s. No longer playing an important role in the dominant economic system, the myth of the Jew as "exploiter" could be safely resurrected and the Jews easily destroyed, all in order to deflect hostility from the capitalist system that was, in fact, the real cause of the bankruptcy of the independent petty bourgeoisie (where anti-Semitism was the most venomous), the unemployment among the salaried petty bourgeois (where anti-Semitism was equally vicious); and the unemployment and destitution of working people and peasants—who too often fell for the "socialism of fools."

There had periodically been violent pogroms against Jews in the late Middle Ages in the more commercial areas of western Europe. Pogroms again became institutionalized now in the czarist empire after 1871. The first of the major modern pogroms was initiated by Greek merchants who wanted to eliminate Jewish competition in Odessa during Easter week of 1871. There were three days of massacres, synagogue defilings, and plundering of property, with both Greeks and Russians participating. The czarist government, at first somewhat apprehensive about pogroms, within a few years became complicit in them, not only ordering the police and militia not to suppress them, but often itself initiating them as a way to deflect hostility away from itself in times of depression or rebellion—and "blame the Jews." Especially severe official and officially sanctioned persecution of the Jews set in after the assassination of Czar Alexander II in 1881. During 1881 there were 215 recorded pogroms against Jews that the authorities either instigated or sanctioned by their refusal to protect Jews (Vishniak 1946).

The interwar period in eastern Europe saw a continuation of strongly anti-Semitic activities. With a decline in markets in the 1930s, competition for customers became all the more intense, and hence anti-Semitism among the petty bourgeois greatly intensified, playing the same role for this class as imperialist nationalism did for the large bourgeoisie (both justified a vigorous fight for markets). Newly independent Poland passed restrictive legislation against Jews. They were forbidden to acquire land, required to pay special taxes, and were eliminated from certain industries such as salt, tobacco, and matches (Mahler 1946).

The systematic Nazi-organized genocide of the Jews in the 1940s must be understood as a product of the logic of the world capitalist system. Expelled from their traditional vital economic role, there was no room for them in the crisis-ridden capitalism of the 1930s (except as scapegoats for the hostility of the desperate masses of that decade).

Jews were the first to be eliminated by decaying feudalism and the last to be integrated into capitalism, making their position extremely precarious. Pushed out of their traditional commercial occupations and forced to stay on the margins of capitalist enterprise, the Jewish people in eastern Europe attempted to transform themselves into part of the new and rapidly growing professional petty bourgeoisie. But here too, especially in the 1930s, they met extreme resentment from others scrambling to obtain petty-bourgeois status, and as a result they were largely excluded. In the 1923–33 period, 25 percent of Polish university enrollment was Jewish (Jews were about 10 percent of Polish society), but in the 1933–36 period it was 13 percent. In Hungary Jewish university enrollment declined from 32 percent in 1918 to 11 percent in 1931 (Leon 1950, p. 230). Pushed out of commercial life, denied access to the professions, and with emigration out of eastern Europe partially closed (after 1924 the United States would no longer take eastern European immigrants) massive unemployment, economic destitution, and despair set in for what was becoming increasingly a redundant (excluded) population.

The high level of anti-Semitism generated by the distinctive Jewish economic role in eastern Europe was reflected in the differential treatment of the Jews by the anti-Nazi resistance movements during the World War II period. In western Europe (e.g., France, the Netherlands, Denmark) the local population generally helped the Jews and opposed Nazi anti-Semitic measures. But in eastern Europe (especially in Poland, Lithuania, and Latvia), the anti-Semitic pogroms of the Nazis were generally popular with the local population (who in some cases actively assisted the Nazi extermination effort). Even after the defeat of the Nazis, the relatively few surviving eastern European Jews returning to their native cities and villages often received a hostile welcome. In the two years *after* liberation about 1,000 Polish Jews were killed by anti-Semitic Poles (Mahler 1946, p. 171).

The systematic persecution of the Jews drove many to leave the czarist empire for the United States (until immigration was closed first by the war in 1914 then by U.S. legislation in 1924). While in the 1871–80 period approximately 8,000 to 10,000 Jews a year emigrated from the czarist empire, between 1881 and 1900 between 50,000 and 60,000 did so. In the 1901 to 1914 period the annual average rose to about 150,000 (Leon 1950, p. 200). Although many immigrated to western Europe, Canada, and Latin America, the majority came to the United States. The systematic persecution combined with their increasingly destitute economic position forced more and more Jews to leave the Russian Empire.

Anti-Semitism in the United States did not become a significant force until the beginning of the massive immigration of impoverished eastern European Jews in the 1890s. This early anti-Semitism was based in hostility toward a specially exploited people, since most of these Jewish immigrants were workers (largely in the clothing industry). Anti-Semitism peaked in the United States both intellectually and in its popular form in the early 1920s (at the time of the greatest strength of the Ku Klux Klan and the movement for immigration restriction). The Klan stressed the supremacy of the white Nordic race against the "Semitic" Jews, and the Catholic and racially inferior "Alpine" and "Mediterranean races" (all of which were at that time overwhelmingly concentrated in the working class). Beginning in 1920, Henry Ford launched a virulent anti-Semitic campaign. Ford argued that, "The founding fathers were men of Anglo-Saxon-Celtic race. . . . Into the camp of this race comes a people [the Jews] that has no civilization to point to, no aspiring religion, no universal speech, no great achievement in any realm but the realm of 'get'. . ." (Gossett 1963, p. 372). In the early 1920s Columbia University instituted an admissions quota to limit the number of Jewish students (as did Princeton, New York University, and Williams College). Residential restrictions that prevented Jews from buying property in certain neighborhoods as well as a wide range of exclusionary covenants and practices became general in this period (see Gossett 1963, p. 372).

Arriving in the United States typically economically destitute, most Jewish refugees began life as menial laborers, heavily concentrated in the garment industry (especially around New York City) where they could use their traditional artisan skills and find employment (at especially low wages) often working in small Jewish-owned shops. In 1920 in the United States 75 percent of Jews were workers and employees (Leon 1950, p. 218). The vast majority of the immigrant Jewish workers from east Europe had recently been in the petty bourgeoisie and very much retained the desire to return to that status, if not for themselves, then for their children. They generally worked exceptionally hard, built a strong and militant trade union movement, and, in fact, within two generations were able to fully restore the traditional Jewish petty-bourgeois position, although now mostly in the independent and salaried professions rather than as petty traders and moneylenders.

In 1971, 70.0 percent of all employed Jewish men in the United States were professional and managerial, and only 11.0 percent were manual working class (craftsworkers, operatives, service, or laborers). Fully 72.3 percent of Jewish men between the age of 25 and 29 were college graduates and another 16.5 percent had at least some college education. Of all Jewish men, 60.4 percent had at least some college (American Jewish Committee 1973, pp. 280, 284).

It should be noted that the heavy concentration of Jewish people in the salaried professions, while it essentially restored the traditional petty-bourgeois Jewish position, has had different results than their traditional near monopoly on trade and moneylending. The ethnic integration of salaried professions implies *cultural* assimilation. There is no longer an economic basis for a distinctive Jewish language (such as Yiddish) or for distinctive customs. Intermarriage is now common. A study of Jews in Boston in the 1960s found that among families in which at least one partner was Jewish and in which the husband was 51 and over, only 3 percent were in mixed marriages, but in families in which the husband was 30 or under, 20 percent were (Sklare 1971, p. 190).*

Judaism as a religion is dying out. It is now practiced much less frequently than are the Christian denominations prevalent in the working class. A study of Boston Jews in the 1960s found that 62 percent never attended religious services except perhaps on High Holy Days (this compares with 24 percent for the general population). Another study in New York City found that 12 percent of native-born Jews and 34 percent of foreign-born Jews attended religious services at least once a month, compared to a citywide average of 55 percent (62 percent among blacks, 67 percent among Puerto Ricans, and 90 percent among the Irish) (Sklare 1971, pp. 118, 120, 121).

However, we should not dismiss the possibility that anti-Semitism could once again become a major force in the West. After all, the most intensive persecution of the Jews happened in the middle of the twentieth century in one of the most advanced capitalist countries of the world, where, it must be stressed, most Jews were culturally assimilated into German society (unlike as was the case in eastern Europe). The high concentration of Jews in the professions could well once again target them by the rest of the petty bourgeoisie in a time of economic crisis and a shortage of professional positions, especially if scapegoats are needed to deflect the hostility of the middle and working classes away from capital (and if the excluded segment of blacks proves not to be adequate for the purpose). There may well once again be a need to construct a racialist conspiracy theory involving the "cunning" Jews who are allegedly behind both the big banks and the radical Left, e.g., a resurrection of the Protocols of the

---

*It should be noted that in pre-1930 Germany, intermarriage rates in major German cities were, for newlyweds, higher. For example, in Berlin in the 1901–4 period, 15 percent of all marriages involving Jews were mixed marriages; in 1929, 29 percent (Leon 1950, p. 223). This, together with a high concentration of German-born Jews in the professions, indicates a high level of Jewish assimilation in German (unlike Polish) society.

Elders of Zion, a forgery of the czarist secret police dating from the 1880s that was designed to show how the Jews were responsible for all the ills suffered by the masses of the Russian people. The future of anti-Semitism is open.

The Chinese

The impact of the expanding world capitalist economy on China, especially its southern coastal area around Canton, disrupted traditional rural life. Millions of small landowning peasants and artisans were displaced from their traditional occupations. The inhibition of industrialization (imposed by the coalition of foreign imperialist interests) desiring only to export their manufactured goods to the lucrative Chinese market, and local landlord-comprador merchant interests, blocked the absorption of most of the displaced peasants and artisans into alternative urban occupations. As a result there developed a massive surplus population of people with more or less petty-bourgeois backgrounds and orientations subsisting at a near starvation level, desperate for any means to stay alive. Millions of this surplus population did die in the periodic mass famines that increasingly engulfed China through the 1940s. Millions of others looked overseas for employment, selling their labor (for the most part as contract laborers, or "coolies") to labor contractors who auctioned them off to labor-hungry capitalists all around the Pacific rim (especially in Southeast Asia). Their desperate condition (equivalent to that of the displaced Irish of the post-1840s famine migration) led them to accept the most humiliating employment at extremely low wages. Those Chinese that were forced by starvation to become contract laborers, as was true of almost all those who left Europe to secure jobs overseas, left mostly with the intention of earning money, remitting it to support their families in China, and eventually returning with enough savings to reestablish themselves as petty-bourgeois small landowning peasants or urban small businessmen (Simoniya 1961, p. 13).

In the last half of the nineteenth century, and through the 1930s, large numbers of economically desperate Chinese were displaced into Southeast Asia to provide contract labor for the rapidly expanding plantations and mines operated by British, French, Dutch, and, eventually, American capital. The typical labor contract arrangement involved a "deduction" from the workers' wages for the costs of transport and the commission of the brokers as well as for the use of barracks, clothes, and food. This arrangement often left the laborers in long-term relations of debt peonage to those who had bought their contracts. It was not unusual for the coolie to have a status little different from a slave (at least for the duration of the labor contract).

In 1880 the Dutch in Indonesia introduced a coolie statute that gave the plantation owners in most of the islands (Java excluded) the right to administer justice and legally inflict punishment on the contract laborers for the duration of their legally binding contracts. While initial labor contracts were generally for terms of between one and three years, a wide range of ruses and manipulations, as well as the occasional use of force, was employed to extend the contracts. Between 1912 and 1932 a quarter of a million Chinese contract laborers were imported into Indonesia (Simoniya 1961, p. 91).

In some areas the Chinese have continued to be a significant percentage of the working class, most notably Singapore (where the Chinese became the overwhelming majority of the entire population), Burnei, Sarawak, and Thailand (at the end of the 1930s about two-thirds of the urban Thai working class was Chinese) (Simoniya 1961, p. 95).

But in general the experience of the Chinese in Southeast Asia (as well as in the rest of the world) paralleled that of the Jews. After a generation or so of hard menial labor they were generally able to reestablish their traditional position as petty bourgeois, mostly as middlemen in the retail trade, moneylending, and related activities. They came to operate between the dominant Western-owned capital and the local populations (performing the function of mediation).

The function of buying up raw material from the indigenous petty producers (peasants and artisans) and selling wholesale to Western-dominated big business became almost exclusively the prerogative of immigrant middlemen ethnic groups, predominantly Chinese, but also including (especially in Burma) Indians. Neither Europeans nor the local populations played much of a role in the intermediate trade (with the partial exception of Indonesia, where many Dutch did play such a role). The Chinese also came to predominate in retail shops. The Chinese thus became an essential part of the reorganization of traditional Southeast Asian social structure by imperialism. As a result of their mediating position (just as happened to the Jews in Europe and the Armenians in Turkey), they experienced considerable hostility from the indigenous populations. Further, the Europeans felt contemptuous toward them. They regarded themselves as superior to the caste of petty merchants and moneylenders (Simoniya 1961, pp. 42, 81).

In Cambodia in 1962-63, 95 percent of all those engaged in commerce were Chinese, while 84 percent of all economically active Chinese were engaged in commerce. Although perhaps a bit more concentrated than the average for Southeast Asia this pattern was typical for most of Southeast Asia from Burma and Vietnam to Indonesia and the Philippines. The Chinese in the Philippines in 1932 conduced about 75 percent of all retail trade. At the beginning of the 1930s over 80 percent of the retail trade in South Vietnam was handled by Chinese (who were concentrated in the more commercial south of the country). In Java in 1930, 58 percent of all Chinese were in trade and commerce in 1931. In Thailand Chinese traders represented 87 percent of the Chinese population in 1937. Chinese merchants have traditionally dominated the Thai rice trade. The Chinese came to perform a good part of the petty trading function in the Caribbean basin.

For example, in 1943 64 percent of all Chinese in Jamaica were engaged in commerce (this represented one-fourth of all male wage earners in trade). In addition to being petty traders and moneylenders, the Chinese were also often granted special commercial rights by the local rulers and colonial powers, including the right to collect taxes (on commission), and monopolies on the sale of salt, tobacco, alcohol, gambling houses, and so on (Bonacich 1973; Simoniya 1961, pp. 57, 59).

The explanation of the development of the Chinese position as middlemen throughout Southeast Asia (as well as in other parts of the Pacific rim and Caribbean) is to be found in an overdetermination of supply and demand factors. A surplus population was being pushed out of the most commercialized areas of China—a noncolony in which there was relatively little foreign direct investment in plantations or mines, and consequently little concern about keeping a surplus labor force in China. The displaced population was especially commercial (petty bourgeois) in orientation because it came from the traditionally most commercialized areas of South China where land had long been a commodity and markets were well developed (unlike most of the rest of the non-European world). The colonial powers badly needed an ethnically distinct middle caste group to mediate between themselves and the local people (for all the reasons elaborated above), and found the Chinese the most available source for the region. Last, the pre-European strong Chinese role in trade and commerce that they had achieved in their own right provided a preexisting network into which the new Chinese laborers could integrate (sources of loans, preferred customers, sources of experience, "role models," and so on). The hostility of both the indigenous populations as well as the contempt of the colonial masters (both against the preexisting Chinese traders and against the new coolie laborers, both of which were now associated with imperialist domination) forced both the old and new Chinese together, reproducing (if not creating) a separate ethnic identity as Chinese, and a consequent willingness to help each other.

There was a Chinese presence in much of Southeast Asian commerce before the trade of that region came to be dominated by

European capital. From the middle of the seventeenth century the Chinese played an important part in the commerce, the trades, and mining in the region. Chinese immigrants to the Philippines as well as Java introduced sugarcane production. They opened up mines in northern Vietnam, Burma, Malaya, and Thailand. Chinese traders first organized tobacco, pepper, and vanilla plantations in a number of Southeast Asian countries. As the European commercial presence in the region grew stronger, the Chinese were increasingly crowded out of the more lucrative markets of the region and displaced into retailing (consolidating their position as intermediaries between the more lucrative Western-run enterprises and the indigenous populations). The Chinese also expanded their position in both moneylending and in marginal productive enterprises (e.g., mining) that had been abandoned as not sufficiently profitable by Westerners. As late as 1910 Chinese capital still accounted for 78 percent of Malayan tin output but by 1929 only 39 percent). Between 1906 and 1937 their share of Thai tin production was reduced from almost 100 percent to 38 percent (Simoniya 1961, p. 39, 48, 66).

Large numbers of Chinese contract laborers were imported into the western United States in the 1850s and 1860s (largely as construction laborers for the railroads). With the completion of the cross-country line in 1869, and the forced exclusion of Chinese from mineral mining that occurred at about the same time, the Chinese became concentrated in California as agricultural labor.

In 1854 Chinese were barred from giving testimony in court cases involving whites (this had long been the case with American Indians). In California, racial hostility against the Chinese grew after the 1860s. In 1870 the first popular demonstrations against Chinese immigration were held and in 1871 the first Chinese were lynched. In 1876 the state of California asked the U.S. Congress to bar further Chinese immigration. The first Chinese exclusion act was passed by the U.S. Congress in 1882 (further legislation in 1888 and 1892 closed the loopholes in this law and effectively barred all further Chinese immigration until the 1960s) (Gossett 1963, pp. 290–91). Chinese and other Asians were prohibited from acquiring U.S. citizenship through naturalization. Although the big agricultural farmers who used cheap Chinese labor fought it, a coalition of small farmers, capital-intensive manufacturers (concerned about cheap competition), and organized labor was able to implement the anti-Chinese legislation. This, together with mob actions, eventually resulted in the exclusion of Chinese from agriculture and industry, and the actual expulsion of many from the country. The peak of anti-Chinese pogroms was reached in the early 1890s. The Chinese were physically run out of most towns and cities of the West. It was not until 1943 that Chinese could be naturalized as U.S. citizens (for Koreans and Japanese becoming a citizen was not possible until 1952).

The Chinese were, however, soon replaced by Japanese immigrants, at first in the new (and especially menial) sugar beet industry, particularly in northern California (Mexicans at this time came increasingly to be used as menials in southern California). The Japanese were mostly displaced peasant farmers in Japan who had the skills and motivation to establish themselves as small farmers in California. Well organized and persistent, considerable numbers of Japanese succeeded in saving enough money to become small landowners as well as urban small businessmen (see McWilliams 1935, chap. 7).

The Japanese utilizing the traditional methods of middleman minorities (e.g., especially hard work, thrift, community support, drive to reestablish themselves as petty-bourgeois farmers) began to purchase farmland and transform themselves into efficient labor-intensive small farmers. In 1900 the Japanese held less than 5,000 acres of California farmland; in 1905, 62,000; and by 1910, 195,000. By 1914 they held 300,000 acres and in 1920, 458,000 (Bonacich and Modell 1981, p. 42).

As long as the Japanese were concentrated as rural wage laborers little hostility developed toward them—they threatened neither the Californian European work force (that did not compete for the same especially menial jobs as the Japanese were taking in California agriculture in the 1890-1910 period) nor the small farmers (the first Japanese landowners tended to buy waste land and convert it to rice production). Increasingly, however, hostility developed against the Japanese as they came to buy the better agricultural land from the European small farm owners facing competition from the Japanese (who were often willing to work longer hours and more intensely for less profit than Europeans, and were driving up the value of land both because of the increases in productivity they were responsible for and because of the numbers of Japanese attempting to become landowners) and from the big growers who did not want their cheap labor force to leave the fields. Pressure against the Japanese farmers mounted until 1913 when California passed its Alien Land Act, which prohibited most Japanese (as well as other Asians) from buying land. Hostility against the Japanese peaked in the 1941-45 period when all Japanese west of the Mississippi River (90 percent of all U.S. Japanese)—native born, citizens, foreign born and noncitizens alike—were "relocated" in concentration camps throughout the Western states. Given between two days and two weeks to liquidate all their property, the Japanese suffered catastrophic economic losses during this period.

As the Japanese laborers left the fields they were in good part replaced by Hindus (who came to California largely by way of British Columbia). But they too, although excellent menial laborers, tended to save their money and attempted to transform themselves into small landowners. Most of California Hindus returned to India after the passing of the Alien Land Act in 1913 and the exclusionary immigration act of 1924. In the post–World War I period (until the Depression) Mexicans became the primary labor force in Californian agriculture (see the latter part of Chapter 11).

The Chinese remaining in the United States after the 1880s became heavily concentrated in retail trade, especially in restaurants and laundries. By 1920 approximately half of all economically active Chinese in the United States were in these latter two economic sectors (Light 1972, p. 7). In the state of Mississippi the Chinese obtained a near monopoly of rural grocery stores through much of the state. As late as the 1960s, 97 percent of all Chinese in Mississippi ran grocery stores (Bonacich 1973).

After Japanese exclusion from small farming became effective, large numbers of Japanese transformed themselves into an urban petty bourgeoisie. In Los Angeles County in 1941, 47 percent of all Japanese males were self-employed—19 percent of the total as proprietors and 14 percent as farm owners (Bonacich and Modell 1981, p. 40). In 1919, 47 percent of Seattle hotels and 25 percent of Seattle grocery stores were run by Japanese (Light 1972, p. 10). In 1900, 11 percent of *all* East Asian men in San Francisco were self-employed retail shop owners (compared to a 4 percent of all native-born whites). In 1920, 12 percent of all East Asian men in Los Angeles were self-employed retail shop owners (compared to 5 percent of the native-born whites) (Light 1972, p. 13).

Although most migrated pennyless to the United States, like the Jews, the Chinese and Japanese were able after two generations largely to work themselves *back* into the middle class, at first in good part in traditional petty-bourgeois occupations, but recently (again paralleling the experience of the Jews) into the salaried middle classes.

In 1980, 1.3 percent of the U.S. population was Chinese, Japanese, Filipino, Korean, Vietnamese, or Asian Indian (compared to approximately 2.7 percent that was Jewish). The Chinese represented the largest single Asian group with 0.36 percent of the total, Filipinos were second with 0.35 percent, the Japanese third with 0.32 percent, followed by the Koreans with 0.16 percent (New York *Times*, July 30, 1981, p. 9). The Asians (except for the Filipinos), similarly to the Jews, tend to be in an economically better-off position than the majority of ethnic groups. For example, in 1969 the median family income for Chinese in the United States was $10,610 and for Japanese

$12,515. In the case of the Chinese this was 7 percent higher than white family income and 1.75 times greater than black family income. In the case of the Japanese it was 36 percent higher than white family income and 2.06 times black family income (U.S. Bureau of the Census 1970b, Tables 5, 6, 7, 9, 18, 19, 23, 24).

The Chinese and Japanese in the United States are heavily middle class. In 1970 in the United States 40.4 percent of all Chinese men aged 16 or over were either administrators or professionals. This compares with the U.S. average of 25.4 percent. Further, 9.7 percent of all economically active Chinese (and 10.1 percent of all economically active Japanese) as compared with 7.7 percent for the entire population were self-employed. The median number of years of education for Chinese men in 1970 was 12.4, for Japanese men it was 12.6 (compared with the average for whites of 12.2).

In 1970, 67 percent of all second-generation Japanese males born after 1934 (and over 25 years of age) were middle class (54 percent professionals, 7 percent farm owners, and 6 percent managers and proprietors). Of those born before 1915 an identical percentage were middle class, but the occupational composition was quite different— 14 percent were professionals, 29 percent farmers, and 25 percent managers and proprietors (Bonacich and Modell 1981, p. 137). In 1965, 60 percent of all employed male third-generation Japanese-Americans were professionals, 2 percent were farmers, and 7 percent managers and proprietors (Bonacich and Modell 1981, pp. 239–40).

Before World War II Asians were heavily concentrated in the traditional positions of middlemen; however, since World War II they have been largely transformed into professionals. It is of interest to note that 20 percent of the undergraduates at the University of California at Berkeley in 1980 were Asians (while 9 percent of the population of the Bay Area counties that produce the majority of Berkeley's students were Asians). In 1966, 5.2 percent of Berkeley's students were Asian. University of California administrators have predicted that the student body will be 40 percent Asian by 1990. At the same time, 16 percent of UCLA's undergraduates were Asian. Thirty-nine percent of the Asians graduating from California's high schools in the late 1970s were in the upper 12.5 percent of their class (and thus were automatically admitted to one of the University of California's campuses). This compares with 16.5 percent of whites, 5.0 percent of blacks, and 4.7 percent of Ladinos (New York *Times*, April 9, 1981, p. 10). The experience of the Jews, Chinese, and Japanese is strikingly similar. All three groups have successfully converted their traditional independent petty-bourgeois position into that of new middle class professionals, thereby preserving their structural position as mediators between capital and the working class.

It should be noted, however, that 38.6 percent of all Chinese men in 1970, compared with 36.0 percent of the national average, were in menial occupations. This reflects the post-1965 immigration of large numbers of relatively unskilled Chinese into the United States. There is, thus, a considerable gap in the Chinese community reflecting the intergenerational upward mobility of the Chinese who have been in the United States for some time on the one hand and the mass of menial laborers and shopkeepers who have recently immigrated on the other.

Although, like the Jews, disproportionate numbers of Chinese and Japanese in the United States have attained petty-bourgeois status and relatively high income levels, this does not immunize them from either racist hostility from those who resent their advance, or from future intense outbreaks of racism in a crisis situation. In fact, it targets them. The fact that the Jews, Chinese, and Japanese can be targeted because of their distinctive economic position (however minor their contemporary differences with the dominant culture) means that their position remains precarious if a serious economic crisis were to break out and strong competition develops for scarce professional jobs. The fact that Asians, unlike Jews, are easily recognizable by slight physical differences from the majority group (even while middle class Asians are as totally assimilated culturally into the dominant middle class culture as are the Jews) holds out the possibility of future outbreaks of racial hostility directed against them because of their heavy and increasing concentration in relatively privileged salaried middle class positions.

RELATIONSHIPS OF SPECIAL EXPLOITATION/ DISORGANIZATION

There are two varieties of the racist structure of special exploitation/disorganization: the system of job reservations and separation of racial groups (castelike systems), and the open competition for all (or most) working class jobs by members of different ethnic groups (and the consequent mutual hostility and disorganization that this results in). In the castelike system of job reservations majority group workers are guaranteed the better higher paying jobs, while members of the racially subordinate group are assigned the more menial lesser paid jobs (usually according to the principle that the "worst off" majority group worker has a better position than the "best off" minority group worker).

The system of castelike job reservations is profitable for capital as long as the racial line is drawn at a level where there is a sufficient number of members of both ethnic groups to ensure that wages are low enough and productivity high enough in *both* sectors. Work discipline is in part maintained for majority group workers by the threat of hiring minority group workers in the reserved jobs if the former should demand too much. Structural changes in the economy as well as differential rates of growth in the different populations are handled by redefining jobs at the margin between the two sectors so as to ensure an adequate supply of labor at profitable rates in both. The special advantage of the castelike job reservation system is that it tends to stabilize strong racial antagonisms among both ethnic groups of workers. The majority group workers tend to be thankful to capital for their privileges as well as threatened if they should get too militant or insufficiently productive, while the minority group workers tend to resent the privileges of majority group workers. The resultant mutual hostility tends to maximize disorganization of the working class as a whole.

The advantage of the second racist structure of special exploitation/disorganization (open competition for jobs) is that it results in maximizing the number of those competing for all jobs. This has the double advantage for capital of minimizing the total wage bill (largely through the reduction of the prevailing wage from what it would be in a system of racial job reservation), while at the same time securing the maximum availability of skilled workers in any given occupation or area. Disorganization of the working class (at least in the short run) is accomplished through the antagonistic competition for the same jobs in a scarce job market. Industrial capital tends to move away from the first structure of special exploitation/disorganization to the second because of the pressure of market competition, which dictates a minimization of wage costs (as well as maximum flexibility in hiring). Thus, virtually everywhere in the industrial capitalist world the older castelike system of job restrictions for some groups has given way to open competition (in which the minority groups are at a disadvantage).

Most people in the advanced capitalist countries who are today identified as distinct races, peoples, or ethnic groups and are reproduced by the logic of the dominant mode of production are specially exploited wage laborers. These ethnically distinct workers typically have migrated from poorer rural areas of the world capitalist system in search of higher wages (or work of any kind) with generally (in the first generation) the intention of saving money and returning home.

Ex-peasant immigrants are typically willing to do hard menial labor in a dead-end job in order to save money with which to start over at home. They tend to have a short time frame orientation to their role as industrial workers. Generally, minority group workers are willing to accept a wage lower than would majority group workers because the historically and morally defined *standard* of living is lower in their rural areas of origin than in the urban areas of the advanced countries, e.g., housing standards are lower, expectations about eating meat are less, entertainment customs are less costly, standards about supporting children through college or through secondary school are much lower (here children typically work to supplement family income). This factor dissipates as the frame of reference for the ethnic group becomes the "new" country—as the goal of returning retreats from consciousness. It generally plays little role in the second generation which comes to compare their lot to members of the majority ethnic group (and not to their cousins back in the old country). In the second generation (and in the first as well when and if they lose their orientation to the old country), they come to feel increasingly the indignity of their work and demand to be integrated into better jobs (in the primary labor market).

Further, part of the costs of reproduction of their labor power (maintaining themselves and their families at a socially defined acceptable level of subsistence) is often borne by their part-time participation in nonwaged labor (e.g., subsistence gardening, a few farm animals tended after work or in the off-season). Often the man is separated from his wife, who remains in a rural area producing food to feed the family rather than being an extra mouth to feed in the city. Among peasant/rural families, the wife traditionally performs productive labor in food production (or other economic activities) and thus the men do not expect to be able to support them. Often menial workers are simply single (men or women) and thus only need to feed themselves. In contrast, majority group workers more often live with their families and must thus either totally support them or at least provide the bulk of their support. The fact that immigrant workers are typically young, single, and male also allows the capitalists to pay them less, while at the same time minimizing welfare costs (they are the healthiest, will not take child leave, and so on), work the hardest, and do not require the standard "family wage." These men often live in overcrowded conditions and subsist on a minimal diet.

Subordinate ethnic group workers also serve as a reserve labor supply that can be pushed out of the labor market in the off-season, in recessions, or during other times when they are not needed (without a serious legitimation crisis or political opposition) and can be rapidly called into the labor force when it is expanding. In bad times the "dirty workers" go back to the old country, to rural areas, or subsist on welfare, precapitalist commodity production, or through kin networks, without generally producing trouble for the dominant class. Their role as a reserve army of labor provides not only a flexible pool of menial laborers, but also puts pressure on the wages of the majority ethnic groups, forcing down the general wage level through an oversupply of labor.

Since the orientation of the first generation of dirty workers is to return to the old country after saving up money, they tend (at least at first) not to be especially interested in local politics or in class solidarity with majority group workers—they look on themselves as sojourners. Consequently, such groups generally are more easily exploited, i.e., more labor power can be obtained from them at a lower wage and with less trade union or political resistance than with workers from the dominant group.

Very often such groups of menial workers do not have full legal rights (e.g., they are "guest workers" ineligible for citizenship," are foreign born who do not yet meet the conditions of citizenship such as language and literacy, are "illegal" (i.e., without proper documentation), or are special contract laborers (e.g., "braceros"). Even when they do have full formal rights, they are typically not effectively organized in unions or political organizations in a way in which they could protect themselves as effectively as majority group workers (in good part because they have come from peasant/rural areas where there was little political or economic organization of the poor or militant traditions). Further, to maximize their performance in the role of workers, it is necessary that their status as "foreigners" (either as an inferior "race" or "aliens") be reproduced, thus ensuring that they remain isolated from the rest of the working class as well as from other potential allies.

The political exclusion of industrial workers (in South Africa by the maintenance of the myth that they are immigrant workers from other countries—the Bantustans, "illegal aliens" in the United States, or "guest workers" in Switzerland, Germany, and elsewhere in West Europe) has definite advantages in securing a degree of special exploitation that would otherwise not be possible. On the other hand, the lack of basic political rights and elementary social security for a significant segment of the working class has historically eventually led to political disruption as well as industrial inefficiency. Modern industrial labor and high levels of productivity as well as political stability require the eventual granting of formal civil rights to most workers. Once the costs of the lack of citizenship rights for a significant segment of the industrial working class become clear, industrial capital becomes increasingly willing to abolish caste barriers in favor of racial competition (effective both in keeping wages down and in reinforcing the legitimation of capital—by distracting attention away from the capitalist class).

A further disadvantage of this latter mode of special exploitation for capital is that once race relations settle down and workers from both ethnic groups have accumulated experience of working side-by-side at the same jobs, the logic of cooperation inherent in the process of capitalist production comes to transcend the historical ethnic antagonisms, laying the basis for working class solidarity across ethnic lines. It should be noted, however, as the older ethnic lines in the working class are dissolved by the logic of capital new ethnic groups are brought into the capitalist system to renew both the racial structures and racist attitudes.

The Function of Racialist Ideology in the Working Class

Racialism is a legitimating ideology for an exploitative structure. Racist ideology propagated in the media, educational system, and other institutions, together with the actual distribution of relative petty advantage within the working class serves to disorganize the entire working class including the ethnic majority, thereby allowing capital to more effectively exploit most majority group workers.

Majority group workers are sometimes led to attempt to exclude minority workers from the relatively better and higher paying jobs. When this occurs mutual hostility and distrust is generated among *both* segments of the working class, which in turn results in the deflection of the anger of both groups away from capital and its displacement onto the other segment of the working class. Minority group workers tend to fight back against majority group worker attempts to preserve their slight advantages, tending to lump all majority group members together as oppressors, rather than making a distinction between their potential allies (the majority group workers) and their real exploiters. Often, the minority group feeling of being temporary sojourners with the goal of saving money and returning home is reinforced. As a result of such displacement and deflection, class action is inhibited. Strong unions that incorporate both segments of the working class are difficult to organize or maintain. Strong class-oriented political parties and other forms of political action that require a high level of working class solidarity to be effective are undermined. Because of this disorganization, the working class's ability to defend and advance its interests against capital are considerably less than it would be in the absence of racial devisiveness. Most segments of the working class, including those in the higher status ethnic group, thus suffer from lower wages, worse working conditions, fewer state social benefits, poorer education, and so on than would otherwise be the case.

The displacement of the anger of the higher status group workers generated by the oppressive relationships of exploitation they experience onto minority group workers is manifested in racist jokes, caricaturing of menial workers as racially inferior, chauvinism in personal interactions with minorities, exclusion from social situations, harassment of fellow workers, arrogance, contempt, being condescending, and so on as well as occasionally in actual interracial violence (either small group fights or race riots). In addition to affecting the disorganization of the working class, such displacement of anger also serves a scapegoating function in allowing the frustration of majority group workers to be dissipated against a relatively powerless target, rather than against capital. The deflection of frustration and anger toward minority group workers thus functions to *stabilize*—rather than destabilize, as it would if it were directed against the dominant classes—the social structure of power and privilege. Chauvinistic behavior thus acts as a "safety valve" for the release of otherwise potentially anticapitalist energy.

Racialist ideology also often functions (or is intended to function) to disorganize the *minority* group itself. An attempt is often made (e.g., in slavery) to get the dominated group to internalize a sense of inferiority in relation to the majority people and culture. Such a sense of inferiority propagated in the media, education, and through personal interactions with majority group members can be validated through the actual experience of differential treatment during the performance of menial labor alongside relatively privileged workers. To the extent that the ideology and experience of the subordinate group affects feelings of inferiority, such groups are much less likely to actively resist their situation, more passively accepting their lot as menial and docile laborers.

The Succession of Racial Groups in the Working Clan

As time progresses, any given group of dirty workers gradually comes to organize itself and to increasingly effectively demand improvement in its condition. Especially in the second generation, they come to identify with the country (or area) where they find themselves rather than with the old country or the South. The dream of returning is lost and their orientation changes to doing well in the new country. The standard of comparison for doing well changes from the peasant norm in the old country to the working class norm in the new country. At the same time they begin to organize economically and politically into unions, political parties, political machines, and so on as well as otherwise resist their condition (e.g., in riots, mass strikes, industrial sabotage). As a result of these pressures, it becomes increasingly costly (economically and politically) for the capitalist class to keep the same people in the most degrading and menial positions. The cost of relying on the same source of dirty workers increases over time, especially in the second generation.

It should also be noted that often the primary sources of dirty workers either "are up" because most peasants from a given country or region have already left the land, *or* is closed off by either rapid industrialization or revolution in the country of origin. This has the effect of both requiring the capitalist system to look elsewhere for new sources of menial laborers, and of closing off the reinforcement of peasant/old country sentiments in the ethnic group workers in the new country (thus facilitating both their organizating and the development of broader working class consciousness).

Capitalism throughout the Western world has *tended* to deal with its continuing need for a group of ethnically distinct menial workers through a dynamic system in which a succession of groups become the primary victim of racist structures within the working class. This is not to say that capitalism allows all ethnic groups that come into its system to "rise to the top." Barriers to top level positions generally remain long after the older group of dirty workers is released to compete fairly freely for the full range of *working class* jobs. Moreover, often the former group of dirty workers, rather than being integrated into the mainstream of the working class instead becomes an excluded population, either physically expelled from the country (e.g., Mexicans in the 1930s, Hindus after 1913, Chinese in the 1890s from the United States) or piling up as part of the excluded sector in urban ghettos (increasingly the experience of U.S. blacks).

Further, it is not always the case that capitalism necessarily succeeds in replacing one group with another. It might be the case that first, changing economic requirements associated with rapid automation and displacement of jobs by greatly reducing the demand for unskilled labor means that significant numbers of new immigrants were not needed during a given period; second, prolonged economic stagnation with its associated lack of growth in demand for menial laborers could have the same effect; third, the supply of conveniently located and nonpoliticized displaced rural populations within the world system could become exhausted; or fourth, the necessity to legitimate the rule of the dominant class could require the exclusion of a new group of immigrants from the system for political reasons (this latter because new immigrants carry political radicalism or because maintaining the loyalty of workers already in the system demands immigration restrictions).

Any of these factors hypothetically could lead to the closing off of significant numbers of new ethnic minorities willing and able to do menial labor for the modern capitalist economy, and as a result "freeze" the last group(s) entering the system more or less permanently in the lower level jobs (even if their organization and resistance to their special exploitation were to grow and, as a result, their continued exploitation become more costly).

Menial Laborers, Racism, and the World Capitalist System

The logic of the world capitalist system dictates continuing population shifts as capital of different degrees of labor intensity accumulates in different regions. During the early period of the development of capitalism, when the early peasantry was forced off the land in Great Britain, Germany, and other areas of Western Europe much more rapidly than the new industries could absorb them (more or less before 1850), there was a massive out-migration of economically desperate displaced peasants to North America and, to a lesser extent, Australia. Before 1860, about two-thirds of *all* the overseas migrants from Europe came from Great Britain (the country most advanced in developing capitalism). Another 20 percent came from Germany. In the third quarter of the nineteenth century, the source countries of European migration began shifting to the relatively more backward areas as the forces that rapidly commercialized agriculture and consequently drove peasants off the land (without the creating of a significant number of industrial jobs to absorb them) spread to the more semiperipheral regions: southern Italy, Spain, Poland, Russia, the Austro-Hungarian Empire, Greece. By the closing years of the nineteenth century, the rate of expansion of industrial jobs in Britain and the core countries of the rest of western Europe came to approximate the number of peasants commercialization was pushing off the land. Within a short time, these areas were transformed from being primarily exporters of their surplus population to importers of the surplus population of the adjacent "semiperiphery." The outlying regions of Europe now came to supply primarily the relatively docile ex-peasants willing to work in the low-paid menial occupations (Castles and Kosack 1973, pp. 15–17).

Until the mid-1890s, more European immigrants arrived in the United States from Great Britain (excluding Ireland), Germany, Scandinavia, Low Countries, and France; than from Italy, Poland, Russia, Austria-Hungary, and the rest of southern and eastern Europe. In 1890, there were 233,000 immigrants from the former set of countries and 160,000 from the latter. It was not until the first years of the twentieth century that the massive migration from eastern and southern Europe took place. In 1900, there were 68,000 from the former and 321,000 from the latter. In 1910, there were

724,000 immigrants from these regions and 172,000 from the former (U.S. Department of Commerce 1975b, pp. 105, 106).

Between the last decades of the nineteenth century and the outbreak of World War I, the displaced populations of Ireland, Poland, and Italy went in roughly equal numbers across the oceans to North America and the southern cone of Latin America *and* to the rapidly industrializing areas of western Europe. About as many Irish peasants settled in industrial England as came to the United States. Of the 15 million Italians who immigrated between 1876 and 1920, almost half went to other European countries. Many southern Italians also migrated to the industrial north of Italy. Large numbers of Poles immigrated to the Ruhr, northern France, and Belgium to become miners and metalworkers, while many others migrated to central and eastern Germany as agricultural laborers. By 1886, there were more than a million foreigners in France (about 3 percent of the entire population). It has been estimated that immigration accounted for 57 percent of the French population increase between 1891 and 1901. In Germany, the industrialization process, which was concentrated in the Ruhr, first drew away German landless laborers from east of the Elbe, then Poles (at first those within the borders of the Reich, then later those from Russian-occupied Poland). By 1913, 40 percent of Ruhr miners were Polish. At the same time large numbers of Italians were recruited into the construction trades, particularly in southern Germany. In 1907, 4.1 percent of the German work force was foreign (Castles and Kosack 1973, pp. 16–19).

In the 1920s immigrants from southern and central Europe continued to flow toward the industrializing regions of northern Italy, Germany, France, Argentina, and to a lesser extent Canada and Australia (immigration to the United States was closed off in 1924). Emigration from Russia was largely closed by the 1917 revolution. Between 1929 and 1950 immigration of displaced peasants to the industrializing areas of the world system was cut off almost entirely by depression (and the consequent lack of expansion of industrial jobs), nationalist restrictions on immigration, war, and the aftermath of war.

In the 1950s the traditional pattern once again resumed, with a restoration of the "normal" pattern of rapid industrial capital accumulation (now over a wider area than ever) together with a more rapid displacement of the peasantry than before (e.g., in southern Italy, Greece, Portugal, Spain, Turkey, Yugoslavia, Algeria, Mexico, Bangladesh, and India as well as the West Indies). Menial laborers once again began to flow into the most rapidly industrializing regions. Algerians, Portuguese, Italians, and Spanish into France; West and East Indians along with more Irish into Great Britain; Italians,

Yugoslavs, Greeks, and Turks into Germany. In 1975 the major countries of northwestern Europe averaged about 10 percent of their labor forces composed of "foreign" workers (Kudat and Sabuncuoglu 1980, p. 10).

The number of foreign workers in Germany, the leading industrial capitalist country in Europe, grew from 95,000 in 1956, to 507,000 in 1961, to 1.3 million in 1966, and 3.5 million in 1974, (Kudat and Subuncuoglu 1980, p. 11). In Germany in the late 1960s immigrant workers were about 7 percent of the total labor force. They were equally central in the French and British economies, where they represented at the same time about 6.5 percent of the labor force. They were far more important to the Swiss economy, where they were 30 percent of the total work force (Castles and Kosack 1973, p. 61).

Guest workers were heavily concentrated in the lowest paid most menial occupations. In the German iron and steel industry 59 percent of immigrant male workers were employed in unskilled occupations, compared to 17 percent of German workers. In construction 40 percent of immigrant workers were unskilled, compared to 17 percent of Germans; in electrical goods 30 percent were unskilled, compared to 11 percent for Germans. Very few were in the skilled positions: 3 percent in iron and steel as compared to 36 percent of Germans, 19 percent in electrical goods as compared to 54 percent of Germans. Of the male guest workers 34 percent were unskilled manual workers, 36 percent semiskilled manuals, and 29 percent skilled manuals. In 1969 guest workers were especially important in the metallurgical industries, where they represented 11 percent of the total: plastic, rubber and asbestos processing (17 percent); earth, stone, ceramics, and glass (12 percent); leather, textiles, clothing (12 percent); and construction (12 percent) (Castles and Kosack 1973, pp. 73, 82, 83). In 1978 26 percent of foreigners in Germany were Turks (39 percent female), 16 percent Yugoslavs (41 percent female), 14 percent Italians (34 percent female), 7 percent Greeks (46 percent female), and 5 percent Spanish (40 percent female) (Kudat and Sabuncuoglu 1980, p. 11).

In France 32 percent of all male immigrant workers in 1967 were unskilled manuals, 37 percent semiskilled manuals, and 25 percent skilled manuals. Algerians (the largest single ethnic group) were especially heavily concentrated in unskilled and semiskilled tasks (49 percent and 39 percent respectively) (Castles and Kosack 1973, p. 80). Thirty-six percent of all male immigrant workers in France in 1968 were in building and public works, and 14 percent in engineering and electrical goods (Castles and Kosack 1973, p. 63).

In Great Britain in 1966, 21 percent of male West Indians were in unskilled manual jobs, compared to 8 percent of all male workers;

as were 31 percent of Pakistanis and 20 percent of those born in Ireland. Ninety percent of male West Indians and 87 percent of Pakistanis, in contrast to 66 percent of the general population, were in manual occupations. Twenty-one percent of male Pakistanis were employed in the textile industry as compared to 2 percent of the total working population; 9 percent of West Indian men as compared to 3 percent of the total male population were employed in metallurgical industries; and 31 percent of those men born in Ireland were in construction as compared to 12 percent of the general population (Castles and Kosack 1973, pp. 75, 88).

Germany, as did the other European capitalist countries, came to regulate the flow of guest workers from the less-developed areas through official recruiting agreements with the major supplier countries. It is very difficult for such immigrants or their descendants, even when born in Germany, to gain German citizenship. Nevertheless, large numbers of guest workers have become permanent residents (as reflected in the large percentage of women among them). Their children are growing up in the German language, losing their ties to their parents' countries (as has happened to so many immigrant groups before them). Similar rules apply in most host countries (with exceptions sometimes made for immigrants from former or present colonies).

Over time the capitalist source of menial laborers has expanded geographically to ever wider regions, regions in which the process of capitalist accumulation has come to increasingly displace the peasantry. As older sources dry up because the rate of absorption into industry comes to exceed the rate of peasant displacement, new sources of displaced peasants must be sought. The pattern observed in Europe is identical to that observed in North America (or Australia, Argentina, or Brazil). There seems to be a general logic characteristic of all advanced capitalist economies (applying with modifications to Japan, where groups like the Burakumin, Ainu, and Koreans, although relatively small in number, face intense racism). Capitalism continually generates racism against the specially exploited menial laborers who are ever drawn into the lowest rungs of the economy.

The racialist theories generated to justify the treatment of Polish workers in Germany or Irish workers in England before World War I were identical to the racialist theories generated in the United States, at the same time (and incorporated into the 1924 U.S. restrictive immigration act). In all cases, certain ethnic groups were felt to be inferior and naturally suited to menial labor. Popular racialism as exemplified in ethnic jokes, slurs, and attitudes against West and East Indians in Great Britain; Portuguese and Algerians in France; Italians, Greeks, Turks, and Spanish in Switzerland and West

Germany; or against Koreans and the Burakumin in Japan do not differ in any significant way from the equivalent racialist attitudes expressed in the United States against ex-Southern blacks and Ladinos (the groups who have played the equivalent economic role in the United States in the post–World War II period).

In North America, Western Europe, and Japan, social and economic discrimination as well as objective racism manifested in low-quality education, second-rate public services, poor housing, and often lack of full citizenship rights (e.g., the "undocumented" workers in the United States, "guest workers" in Switzerland, Germany, and so on) as well as secondary (if any) status in the unions, seems to have an identical effect on the ethnically distinct displaced peasants and their descendants. Such discriminatory barriers and objective racism function to keep these menial workers in their economic position.

Native-born western Europeans seem to be more chauvinistic in their attitudes toward immigrant workers than are white Anglos toward blacks and Ladinos in the United States. A 1967 study in England found that 37 percent of the general population thought that white workers should be given preference over "coloured" in job promotions. A poll in France in 1966 found that 62 percent of the population thought that there were too many North Africans in the country. Another study of Parisian workers found that 65 percent manifested racist attitudes toward Arab workers. A 1966 study in Germany found that about two-thirds of the population would like to expel the guest workers altogether (lower paid workers were the most in favor of exclusion) (Castles and Kosack 1973, pp. 432–33).

In Great Britain, racist sentiments have run the highest against the Pakistanis (who are mostly "white") rather than against the black-skinned West Indians. Racist sentiments in France run stronger against Arabs (especially Algerians), than against black Africans, and in Germany and Switzerland racist feelings against white-skinned Turks and Portuguese are as intense as traditional German racism against Poles (or as intense as the racism of other nations against Arabs, Asians, Ladinos, or blacks). It is clear that having white skin or originating within the geographical confines of Europe has nothing to do with the intensity of racist exploitation, racialist attitudes, or dominant group chauvinism. Theories, attitudes, and behavior in relation to menial workers are manifestations of the underlying political economy of the world capitalist system.

NON-EUROPEAN RACIST STRUCTURES

In this section the racial structures of Latin America, Japan, Israel, and black Africa are examined briefly to demonstrate that racist relationships are a product of class society (and hence that racist structures are not specific to white Europeans), and that people who have been the victims of intense racism themselves can be just as racist as anyone else, as well as to illustrate the diversity of racialist definitions of economically dominated classes and peoples.

Latin America

The racial system of most of Spanish- and Portuguese-speaking Latin America contrasts in many ways with that of English-speaking North America. In some important ways it reflects the region's recent feudal heritage and in other ways it reflects the absence of a large European immigration (outside of the southern cone) as well as the failure to import an ethnically distinct third group to serve as a middle class (as was done in most of the nineteenth-century colonial world).

In the Latin American highlands the principal racial distinction is between the Ladinos, defined primarily by their Spanish language (spoken without an Indian accent) and Western dress and customs, and the Indios, defined by their traditional Indian languages (or Spanish with an Indian accent) and traditional Indian culture that usually includes living in a traditional Indian community. Although the Ladinos claim "Spanish blood," affirm their "whiteness," and make use of physical stereotypes (all characteristic of racialist ideological justifications of racism), in fact almost all Ladinos have Indian ancestors (the large majority with demonstrably Indian physical characteristics). Many Ladinos could easily by mistaken for Indios if it were not for their dress and speech, while most Indios could physically pass as Ladinos with little difficulty. It is possible to publicly admit that one has an Indian ancestor and still be regarded by others as Ladino (unlike in North America, where the admission of any African ancestor automatically defines one as black, no matter how white one's skin). In parts of highland Latin America (e.g., Mexico City's middle class) to have an Indian ancestor is a mark of pride for a Ladino, but through most of the highlands it is regarded as a mild deprecation (Harris 1964, pp. 38–39).

Behind the Ladino-Indio dichotomy is a sharp class division in highland Latin American society. The Indians represent both the indigenous (and in part excluded) population and a specially exploitable source of labor (both as wage laborers on the plantations and commercial farms and as peasants who are exploited through unequal trade, rent, and taxes). Indians are rooted in traditional Indian communities and villages typically on the worst (least productive) land in the highlands. Through a process of gradual encroachment that has gone on for 450 years (and that accelerated in the nineteenth century and continues today), Indians have been pushed off of the most valuable land as it was appropriated for commercial uses by the expanding market system. The plantations and large commercial farms continually expand (in good part by extralegal methods) in proportion to the demand of the world market for export commodities, thereby displacing the indigenous population into ever more undesirable lands (and consequently forcing them to sell ever more of their labor power to the capitalist farmers in order to survive). Most typically this occurs in a pattern of labor migration, with the Indios maintaining themselves for part of the year in the mountain villages where they engage in subsistence agriculture with the men migrating to the commercial areas to work for the rich Ladinos as their labor power is needed. Of course, not all Ladinos are capitalists, or even middle class, but Ladino workers occupy higher positions and receive higher salaries than do Indios. Ladino workers would never be supervised by an Indio foreman (Stavenhagen 1975, p. 179).

The Ladinos also relate to the Indian peasants in a relationship of mediation. The middlemen—traders, creditors, purchasers, sellers— are generally Ladinos (except perhaps for the most petty commodities sold in traditional village markets). The Ladino middlemen thus effect an exploitation of those Indios who do not engage in wage labor by charging high prices for the goods the subsistence peasant can not produce as well as charging high interest on the loans the subsistence peasants often require (Stavenhagen 1975, p. 187). Thus, in the highlands of Latin America where Indians are the majority of the population, Ladinos perform the functions of both the Jews, Chinese, Armenians, and so on, and that of the exploiting landlords and capitalist class, i.e., there are not three distinctive racial groups. Upper class Ladinos are usually "whiter," have more "Spanish blood," look less like Indians, and so on; and consequently have somewhat higher prestige than do middle and urban working class Ladinos. But the only *qualitative* gap is the dichotomy between Indio and Ladino.

The Indio-Ladino dichotomy has all the characteristics of racist relationships elsewhere in the capitalist world. Ladinos consider themselves as superior to the Indios. They are contemptuous of Indian culture and harbor derogatory stereotypes of "inferior" Indians. Ladinos in Guatemala normally refer to Indians as "like children," "dishonest," "without shame," "stupid,' "not deserving of respect," and so on (Harris 1964, p. 86; Stavenhagen 1975, p. 195). In general, Indians are subject to all the stereotyping, chauvinism, and discrimination that similar groups face elsewhere in the capitalist world system. In highland Ecuador, the tradition is that Indians yield their seats on trains and buses to Ladinos. In highland Guatemala, it is common for Indians to step off the sidewalk to make way for Ladinos. Segregation in recreation, housing, fiestas, school functions, religious ceremonies, and, of course, marriage is widely practiced (Harris 1964, p. 36). The consequences of the excluded/specially exploited position of the Indios in the Latin American highlands, just as for similar groups elsewhere, are higher rates of infant mortality, general mortality and morbidity, substandard living conditions, and so on. As a lived relation, for the Indios, racism is the same as in other regions of the world capitalist system.

In the Latin American lowlands black slaves were imported to serve as the labor force on the commercial plantations that grew up in these areas (the indigenous peoples were concentrated in the highlands, where they were effectively forced by the Spanish conquerors to provide the labor force there). Because there were so few European immigrants to serve in intermediate positions between the black slaves and the landlord class a separate caste of mulattos, free people of mixed European and African ancestory, was created to perform these tasks. (In North America the same tasks were performed by poorer whites; here there was such a shortage of unfree black labor that all those with any black ancestry were treated as one single group—the set of those to be specially exploited.)

Very few Portuguese migrated to Brazil in the sixteenth century. In the seventeenth century Portugal adopted a state policy of restricting emigration out of fear of depopulation. Between 1509 and 1790 only about 150,000 people emigrated from Spain to the entire new world (in contrast in the eighteenth century alone half a million British emigrated to North America) (Harris 1964, pp. 82, 86). The centrality of Great Britain in developing capitalist relations created an immense surplus population there that emigrated to North America to serve (in the southern regions) as intermediaries between the slaves and the slave owners. In fact, a surplus of "poor whites" eventually developed in the slaveholding regions. These poor whites in good part became an excluded population, forced off the good land and into the Appalachian Mountains as well as out of the South altogether to settle much of the Midwest and West. Spain and Portugal, on the other hand, on the periphery of the European region of capitalist expansion, maintained traditional noncommercial agriculture through the latter part of the nineteenth century (when a major emigration out of the Iberian peninsula, in good part to the Southern cone of South America, finally occurred). (In the Southern cone there are relatively few blacks *or* Indians.)

In Brazil in 1720 only one-third of the population was of European origin—in contrast to the four southern English colonies of

North America where 60 percent was. In 1819 less than 20 percent of Brazilians were white, compared to 80 percent in the United States (the black population of the Southern states of the United States never exceeded 38 percent of the total) (Harris 1964, pp. 84–85).

Among the vital mediating functions performed by the distinct caste of mulattos in the Latin American lowlands were the tasks of overseeing black slaves, tracking down fugitive slaves, capturing Indians for slaves (in Brazil), and exterminating and displacing Indians where they could not be profitably enslaved. One of the major functions of the mulattos in Brazil was to serve as the armed forces and police of the landowning class. Free mulattos were also the basis of the cattle industry (vital for providing power and transport as well as meat to the sugar plantations). Cattle raising grew up outside the plantation zone (on open rangeland unsuitable for plantations). Mulattos became the cowboys (vaqueros), a position in which it was not possible to employ slaves (Harris 1964, p. 87).

Just as most Ladinos in the Latin American highlands have some Indian ancestry (there were too few Spanish immigrants to have made it otherwise), most "blancos" in the lowlands have some African ancestry (for the same reason). Centuries of sexual relations between those of European and African ancestory in Brazil has produced a *continuum* of both color and racist attitudes reflecting the postslavery continuum of social-economic position, with no sharp qualitative social dichotomies (such as exist in the highlands or in North America). The Brazilian system is not legitimated by a consistent racialist ideology such as developed in North America to justify the sharp line between the black and white "races" (reflecting the sharp caste divisions between the two groups). The original sharp differences between pure African slaves, mulattos, and whites have been totally blurred. A study done of perceived "racial types" among the Brazilian people elicited descriptions of 40 different classifications, mostly specifying skin color along a somewhat vaguely defined continuum from pale white to dark black. These racial categories are significantly influenced by the class position of those with a given skin pigmentation, according to the principle "money whitens" (i.e., the richer a dark person becomes, the lighter will be the racial category to which the person is assigned by associates, friends, and relatives). Similarly, people with lighter skin who are very poor and hold low-level jobs are commonly categorized by skin color terms darker then their actual pigmentation. There is, of course, no descent rule, such as exists in North America, that defines one's race as that of one's parents. Thus, it is possible for individuals to change their race *during* their lifetime by increasing their income, securing a good job, and adopting the appropriate mannerisms and culture (without necessarily changing residence or friends) (Harris 1964, pp. 58–59).

Japan, Israel, and Africa

Being, or once having been, a "racially" oppressed group is not a prophylactic against being racist. The Japanese, who suffered intense white racism in California, are largely, in Japan, themselves racist in their attitudes toward other Asians (e.g., Chinese and Koreans) as well as to such internal minorities as the Burakumin (an outcaste group), the Ainu (the indigenous people), and Koreans (who in Japan are concentrated in specially exploited positions). In 1979 Japan refused to take any significant number of Vietnamese "boat people" on the grounds that they would not fit into Japanese culture.

In the later part of the nineteenth and early twentieth centuries the Japanese developed a racialist theory to justify their imperialist expansion throughout East and Southeast Asia. Japanese students in Europe and America in the later years of the nineteenth century brought back to Japan the latest in Western racialist theory.* Relying on traditional Japanese notions of the superiority of the Japanese (who, myth has it, were of divine descent) maintained that the present inhabitants of Japan are descended from the original race of Yamatos (Seeds of the Sun). Hirata, a Japanese scholar, argued that "from the fact of the divine descent of the Japanese people proceeds their immeasurable superiority to the natives of other countries in courage and intelligence" (Synder 1939, p. 291). The Japanese War Office in the 1930s maintained that it was "the great mission of the Japanese race" to bring together all the races of the world into one happy accord (Synder 1939, p. 29).

In the Jewish state in Palestine—Israel—Arabs form the inferior race, consigned to the specially exploited and most menial jobs (Jews

---

*Since the industrialization of Japan, Western racialist theorists have had to deal with an anomaly. How could a "racially inferior" Asiatic people achieve such predominance? The Nazis (the allies of Fascist Japan in the 1930s and 1940s) accorded the Japanese race a special status as a kind of minor Nordic people who are Asiatic only in outer form. After the Japanese ambassador to Berlin protested to the German government about Nazi party officials' public polemics against all non-Aryan races, Nazi speakers were instructed to always say "Nordic and related races" so as to include the Japanese (see Snyder 1939, p. 197). The Nazis also argued about their Italian Fascist allies that the best Italian blood was Nordic. It should be noted that in the Republic of South Africa the Japanese are accorded the status of "honorary whites" under the apartheid laws, while all other Asians are placed in an inferior status.

from Asia and Africa are also heavily concentrated in lower-level blue collar and service jobs, with Jews of European descent concentrated in professional and managerial positions). In 1977, 12.5 percent of all Israeli Jews were scientific and academic employees and administrative personnel, in contrast to 1.3 percent of all Israeli Arabs. In contrast, 22.9 percent of all Arabs in Israel, but only 5.7 percent of Jews, were in construction; while 16.7 percent of Arabs and 5.2 percent of Jews were in agriculture. In 1975–76 urban Jews averaged an annual per capita income 2.9 times higher than Arabs living in the same areas (Lustick 1980, pp. 161–63). Arabs in Israel are, thus, in the equivalent position of blacks and Ladinos in the United States, Algerians in France, and Turks in Germany.

For the most part Arab workers live in Arab villages or separate Arab quarters in Jewish cities, while almost all jobs are located in areas of Jewish population concentration. In the early 1970s this meant that more than two-thirds of Arab wageworkers commuted each day to Jewish areas to their jobs (Greenberg 1980, p. 49). In 1971 Arab-owned industries employed less than 1 percent of all workers employed in Israel (Lustick 1980, p. 159). The geographical and residential isolation of Arabs means that Arabs are the first to be laid off in a recession and the last to be rehired after a business upturn, since labor exchanges that are located almost exclusively in Jewish cities are required by law to give preference to local workers (Lustick 1980, p. 233). A Israeli law prohibiting the use of nonunionized workers, combined with the Jewish trade union (Histadrut) pre-1957 policy of not organizing Arabs, gave Jewish union officials (before 1957) the legal apparatus for demanding the dismissal of Arab workers and their replacement by Jewish workers whenever the latter wanted Arab jobs (Lustick 1980, p. 165). Although Arabs are now allowed into the Histadrut, not one of its thousands of collectively owned enterprises (as of 1977) was located in an Arab village (Lustik 1980, p. 96).

The Palestine Arabs, of course, are just as much an "excluded" group in Palestine as they are a source of cheap labor for the Israeli economy. Beginning in the 1880s European Jewish immigrants progressively displaced the indigenous Arab peasants. The process of exclusion was accelerated after World War I, when Palestine passed from Turkish to British rule. A flood of Jewish refugees emigrated from Europe immediately after World War II and large-scale emigration continued through the 1950s (from the 1950s the bulk of Jewish emigration was from Africa and Asia). Before Israeli independence in 1948 European Jews (who had considerable financial backing) progressively bought Arab land. With the independence of the Jewish state great quantities of Arab-owned land were confiscated mostly on the pretense that the owners had deserted it (to flee the fighting of the 1948 war). Many of the owners of the land confiscated by the Israeli state from the Arabs and turned over to Jews were, in fact, nonrefugees (who continued to be legal citizens of the Israeli state).

A number of legal ruses reminiscent of similar methods used to displace indigenous populations throughout the colonized world (e.g., South Africa, The United States, Australia) were employed. For example, an area encompassing Arab-owned farm land is declared a "closed area" for security reasons by the military (and Arabs are prohibited from entering the areas for any reason). After three years the Ministry of Agriculture declares all uncultivated lands expropriated. The Arab land, thus, passes into the general land reserve for Jewish settlements.

Arabs through the 1960s were required to demonstrate unchallenged possession of their land for 15 to 25 years by producing records from the British colonial period. Many of the hereditary occupants of the land were never issued official papers by the British during the mandate period, and many who had official papers had lost them during the hostilities of 1947-48 (facts well known to the Jewish authorities). Thus, large numbers of Arabs who remained in Israel and on their land were forced off it. Much of the remainder of nonrefugee Arab land was confiscated for reasons of "security" or "vital development." Although many violations of due process were later admitted by the Israeli state, no improperly seized land has been returned to the Arabs (Lustick 1980, pp. 175-78).

As is true of the "excluded" and "specially exploited" populations everywhere in the capitalist world, the Arabs living in Israel suffer the humiliations and poverty associated with these positions. For example, in 1974 the infant mortality rate for Jews in Israel was 19.2 per 1,000; for non-Jews 37.0 (Lustick 1980, p. 159). The gap grew from a ratio of 1.76 in 1960 to 1.93 in 1974. In 1976, 58 percent of all Arab families lived more than two persons to a room, compared to only 9 percent of Jewish families. Welfare payments made to the Arab poor as a matter of policy are 60 percent of the level provided to the Jewish poor (Lustick 1980, p. 185).

Jewish settlers in Israel generally express the same types of racist attitudes toward the indigenous and specially exploited population as is characteristic of European settlers in North America toward Indians, blacks, and Ladinos. A survey of Jewish attitudes toward Arabs taken in 1968 found that 86 percent said they would refuse to rent a room to an Arab and 67 percent would not agree to have an Arab as a neighbor. Another survey in 1976 found that 71 percent of respondents declared that Arabs will not reach the level of progress of Jews and 76 percent rejected the possibility of having an Arab superior at work. Everyday language in Israel uses the adjective "Arab" to denote undependable performance, faulty work, laziness, and stupidity. It is also common for the Hebrew term for "dog" to be used as epithet for Arab (Lustick 1980, p. 85). It would appear that the long Jewish experience of persecution has had no impact on Jewish racism toward the Arabs. The economic imperatives of exclusion and special exploitation seem to easily and quickly override any such autonomy of ideas.

The experience of Africans and people of African descent, no more than that of others, has immunized them from racist feelings. Blacks in East Africa have expressed tremendous hostility (often in the form of riots and expulsions) against the East Indians, who are mostly merchants (Indians were expelled in mass from Uganda in the 1960s). A similar racism has been expressed against the Arabs (which took the form of a bloody pogrom in Zanzibar in the early 1960s). Similar sentiments have also been demonstrated against Chinese and Jewish merchants in the Caribbean and in the black ghettos of the United States. There has been considerable hostility between the blacks in Jamaica, Guyana, and Trinidad against the East Indians (who were brought in as contract laborers by the British after the abolition of slavery, since they would work for less than the black freemen), who tend to both be middleman merchants and the lowest paid most menial agricultural labor. In the larger countries of the English-speaking Caribbean people of African descent tend to be concentrated in urban better paid and more unionized jobs and thus tend to resent cheap competition as well as what are perceived as gouging merchants.

Since independence there has been considerable hostility *among* Africans of different states and tribes (which has produced a number of expulsions of various groups). Ugandans were excluded from Kenya; Nigerians and Togolese from Ghana; Malians from Zaire and Upper Volta; Togolese and Dahomeans from the Ivory Coast, and so on (Wallerstein 1979, p. 172). In most of Nigeria there is considerable racist hostility against members of the Ibo tribe (who are heavily concentrated in middle class positions throughout the country). Anti-Ibo feelings are the equivalent of anti-Semitism in Europe, anti-Chinese feelings in Southeast Asia, or anti-Indian sentiment in East Africa. It is economic position, not skin color, language, religion, or geographical location that produces races and racism.

RACIST STRUCTURES AND CLASS DIFFERENCES

Different classes within the majority ethnic/racial group have different interests in different forms of racist structures. They vary in regard to racist attitudes and chauvinistic behavior as well as acceptance of racialist theory. Similarly, the various classes among minority peoples have different interests in as well as strategies for mitigating the racist structures by which they are defined.

Class Differences within the Majority Group

The capitalist class is the most consistently and thoroughly supportive of racist structures. Within this class, the more marginal, competitive, less productive, and technologically backward capitalists, historically, especially agricultural (and to a lesser extent mining) capital, have been the most insistent on *caste* orders (with firm lines between the occupations in which "racially inferior" groups could obtain employment, and those occupations reserved for "racially superior" groups). This has been the case because of this group's need to ensure themselves an abundant pool of cheap and compliant labor that is forced to provide its labor power in greater numbers and at lower remuneration that could be the case with a free labor market.

By supporting racial barriers to migration to cities, commercial farmers can establish a surplus of labor in the countryside that is forced to sell its labor power very cheaply. By establishing barriers to skilled occupations (predominantly in the technically advanced sector) marginal and competitive sector capitalists ensure themselves of an oversupply of cheap labor. The enforcement of a rigid caste order also has advantages for *both* sectors of capital in politically excluding the specially exploited sector of the working class from the political process (thus allowing parliamentary forms to function without disruption), the prohibition or strict regulation of trade unions among "racially inferior" workers, and the disorganization of the "racially superior" group of workers.

Majority group workers are led to support the capitalist class because of the *relative* advantages they have compared to the racially inferior caste (to which they feel superior and with whom they, thus, lack solidarity). Strict caste segregation of occupations, with the better jobs reserved for the racially superior, thus functions to legitimate capitalist institutions. Sometimes conscious racialist ideology is supplemented by considerable economic concessions to the skilled or technically advanced sector workers (as in South Africa). Sometimes no real concessions are granted, with capital relying instead on the *illusion* of concessions that comes from relative advantage compared to the subordinate caste to accomplish the *same* ideological effect (as in the South of the United States). This latter ideological effect (imaginary "white skin privilege") based on *relative* advantage is clearly a "lived relation" of racism.

The maintenance of caste barriers within essentially capitalist or semicapitalist relations of production is a continuation of the logic that led to commercial landlords institutionalizing slavery in the Caribbean basin as well as serfdom in eastern Europe in the sixteenth through nineteenth centuries (i.e., the necessity to secure a cheap labor force that was bottled up on the land). In the United States for two generations after the end of slavery the ex-black slaves were kept on the land through an interrelated system of semifeudal controls (e.g., de facto debt peonage, physical threats, differential law enforcement, lack of education) combined with exclusion from other economic opportunities. Blacks were excluded from the primary post-Civil War industrial sector—textiles—until the 1960s (see M. Reich 1981, p. 246-47) as well as from employment in most Northern industries (until World War I and the end of European immigration led to their massive entry). In the South blacks were employed in some industrial occupations outside of the central textile industry (e.g., turpentine, dock work, lumber) as well as in the most oppressive jobs in the new steel industry of northern Alabama. The caste exclusion of blacks from most alternative pursuits and their consequent bottling up on the land and in a few less-skilled occupations and more marginal Southern industries proved extremely profitable to both Southern landlords and much of small-scale Southern capital, who thereby secured an abundant and cheap labor force. Textile capital (much of it of Northern origins) was structurally *indifferent* to whether or not both blacks and whites, or only whites, were to be employed in the mills. But as long as an abundant source of cheap white workers was available, the system of racial exclusion proved very profitable. Textile capital, however, positively benefited from the racial exclusion rule since it operated to disorganize the white proletariat (through the threat of black strikebreakers as well as the continuing propaganda about the "privilege" of working in the mills), thus preventing the unionization of the textile industry and the formation of a distinctive working class oriented political force in the South (thereby resulting in highly favorable state policies for capital).

A similar process operated in South Africa. The Afrikaner (Dutch) farmers had maintained slave, serf, and semiserf relations with the native blacks since the settlement of the Cape Colony in the mid-seventeenth century. Through a process of displacement from the land, the Afrikaners appropriated both the best land and the cattle of the native populations in their continuing expansion from Cape Town toward the north and east. The native African people (although many were also killed or removed) were at first largely reduced to an unfree labor status on the land as slaves and serfs. In the nineteenth and early twentieth centuries this took the form of tenancy (and semiserfdom), with the blacks laboring for the white farmers in exchange for a plot of land for subsistence cultivation (together with grazing rights and other necessities) (Greenberg 1980, chap. 4).

The apartheid system developed in counterpoint with the expansion of capitalism in the republic. Gold was discovered in 1884 and the mining industry rapidly expanded, developing a huge appetite for cheap native labor. Urban industrialization, which began in the 1890s, was accelerated by World War I. This too produced a growing demand for cheap labor. The response of the increasingly commercially oriented Afrikaner farmers was to demand strict controls over the labor force, which prevented blacks from leaving the predominantly semifeudal tenancy relationships on the land for more lucrative alternative employment in the mines and urban areas. At first the pass laws were reinvigorated and "master and servant," vagrancy, and contract laws were strengthened and strictly enforced in an attempt to resist the logic of wage labor. As these proved inadequate, a series of legislative acts were passed beginning with the Native Labour Regulation Act of 1911 to construct an elaborate state-enforced system of labor controls that ensured a cheap supply of wage labor to Afrikaner farmers (Greenberg 1980, chaps. 5, 8).

As capitalism and modern agricultural techniques penetrated Afrikaner farming over the first half of the twentieth century, the old semifeudal tenancy relations gave way to the more efficient wage labor system. Rural wage labor not only allowed *all* the land to employ modern cultivation methods (the old system of subsistence farming for the tenants took much of the land out of commercial cultivation), but also allowed the farmers to utilize only young healthy males driven by the need to earn money (and the threat of being fired, and consequently sent to the desperate poverty of the native reserves) (Greenberg 1980, p. 95). The evolving apartheid system progressively excluded blacks from either landownership or tenancy in 87 percent of the country (including virtually all the best farming land, mineral resources, and cities). It became state policy to prohibit tenancy (and thus ensure modern agricultural relations and technology) in the countryside. The evolving black rural proletariat came to be legally defined as citizens of semiautonomous "Bantustans" (located on the largely barren other 13 percent of the country), to which their families were often forcibly displaced. By 1973 only 16,000 rural black tenants remained (all in the province of Natal) (Greenberg 1980, p. 93).

Rather than relying on the traditional elaborate system of labor controls that ensured semifeudal relations (such as the masters and servants acts, or legal restrictions on quitting), the new system of labor controls was much simpler. The system of pass laws, labor bureaus, prohibitions on landownership, and exclusion from high-wage occupations now forces the black proletariat to sell its labor under very favorable conditions for the commercial farmers as well as provide an adequate (and low paid) supply of black labor to industry (Greenberg 1980, pp. 104-5). In general (not only in South Africa), the interest of commercial farmers in preventing the development of free labor markets (and their support of semifeudal and wage labor systems based on caste distinctions) has been the norm until *industrial* capital becomes dominant (Greenberg 1980, chap. 3).

The evolving system of apartheid, whose primary motive thrust was the economic interest of the Afrikaner farmers for abundant and cheap African labor, was supported by the vital mining industry (owned by British capital), which also required a cheap and abundant labor force unhindered by the class conscious and militant unionism that characterized mine workers through most of the rest of the world. Rather than rely on a permanent proletariat settled around the mines, the mine owners developed a system of labor migration in which blacks both from the "Native Areas" (the 13 percent of the country reserved for black landownership and "permanent" residence) as well as adjacent countries (especially Mozambique), would come to work for half a year to two years, then return to the "Native Areas" or Mozambique, replaced by other "migrant laborers."

Especially in the early stages of mining development, when techniques were particularly labor intensive and few laborers could be induced to voluntarily leave their tribal and relatively abundant environments (where horticultural or pastoral modes of production predominated) mine owners relied on state-directed labor recruitment policies. These policies included the displacement of native peoples from their land and the separation from their cattle (which forced them to sell their labor power to survive), the corvée (or labor tax) in French areas, and the imposition of a "hut tax" requiring natives to pay a tax in European money (money which for most could only be earned by selling their labor power). The mine owners were faced with the fact that no wage rate, no matter how lucrative, was normally able to get those organized in tribal societies to sell their labor power to capital. It normally takes strong state intervention and/or displacement from the land to establish the conditions under which precapitalist producers will become wage laborers (Greenberg 1980, p. 134).

Not only was a repressive state labor system necessary to create a labor force for the mines, but the labor-intensive nature of mining (and commercial farming), together with the competitive conditions of the world market where the products were sold, exerted strong pressure for the wage rate paid in the mines (and commercial agriculture) to be considerably below that which would prevail in a truly free labor market (in fact, often at a below subsistence level). The caste system that closed certain occupations (including most urban employment) to natives, by creating an oversupply of native laborers attempting to sell their labor power to the mines and commercial farms, succeeded in accomplishing this. A below subsistence wage was made possible by employing young males for only part of the year, keeping their family on the land performing subsistence agriculture the year around—with the young men helping part of the time (see Magubane 1979, pp. 123, 143).

As long as there are sufficient laborers for both types of industries (as there were in the Southern United States in the pre-1960s period), and the majority group workers do not ask for too much, castelike systems have proven quite viable, especially in areas where general social legitimation has required the political support of majority group workers (e.g., South Africa).

Industrial capital, however, especially that in the technically most advanced sectors, has little or no special economic interest in maintaining caste orders (in contrast to commercial farmers and technically backward miners). First, by the time that significant industry has developed, there are normally adequate supplies of labor available from those who have been displaced from the land by earlier commercialization of agriculture. Second, employing generally more productive means of production than agriculture (and often mining as well) industrial capital can afford to attract plenty of labor in a free labor market (attracting free laborers away from the less-efficient commercial farms and mines). Third, rather than giving the majority group workers a monopoly of employment, thus ensuring them an artifically high wage as well as facilitating trade union consciousness among employed workers, industrial capital finds it considerably more profitable to open up all occupations to competition from all comers including subordinate ethnic group members who both drive down the wage (by competing for the same jobs as majority group workers), and disorganize the working class as a whole through the mutual ethnic antagonisms this competition for jobs between different ethnic groups generates (especially when one group tends to be concentrated in slightly better jobs, without any guarantee that it will keep them). The substitution of cheaper subordinate group workers for more expensive majority group workers, especially in industries and occupations that do not require a high level of skill and which are relatively labor intensive, is especially profitable for industrial capital.

It is sometimes the case that capital in the relatively more labor intensive, less skilled occupations employs all comers, creating the maximum, working-class disorganization, while in those jobs requiring high levels of skill an agreement with the *craft* unions (of the majority ethnic group) is struck to exclude minority group workers in return for high levels of productivity and loyality, i.e., stable relations with majority group workers. In such agreements the threat of the use of minorities is ever present if the majority group skilled workers should ask for too much.

Either mode of racially dividing the labor force—castelike job reservations with threats to undermine the privilege of majority group workers, or actual competition among all comers regardless of ethnic status—provides capital with tremendous freedom to manage the labor force, and to generate considerable profits as a result (see Greenberg 1980, p. 138). Often the particular mode of labor control adopted by industrial capital depends purely on the shape of their political alliance with mining interests and commercial farmers (and to a lesser extent organized skilled workers). When the constellation of forces changes (e.g., when agricultural capital becomes politically weak, or its needs for castelike labor systems change) industrial capital can rather quickly and easily make the transition to totally free labor markets (dropping all caste barriers). This was the case in the Southern U.S. textile industry. South African industrial capital appears willing to make such a transition.

Factory labor, unlike commercial farming, normally requires continuity in its labor force. Continually rotating migrant labor is inefficient in machine technology where industrial skills and discipline must be taught over a rather lengthy period, and gradually improved through a process of learning and promotion. Further, labor control in modern industrial conditions depends in good part on continuity and employee loyalty generated through promotion opportunities, internal labor markets, bonuses, acceptance of work rules, and so on. All these factors are lost in a system where migrant laborers are forced to return to their "homelands" every six months to two years. Industrial capital thus tends to promote and support a permanently settled labor force within reasonable daily commuting distance of their factories—a goal in conflict with traditional commercial agriculture and mining industrys propensity not to create a permanent proletariat (see Magubane 1979, p. 131).

It should be noted that both sectors of capital are structurally racist (those that rely on castelike segmented labor markets as well as those that rely on ethnically heterogeneous labor). However, technically backward capitals support of castelike structures must be judged more racist because of its especially detrimental effect on subordinate group workers. It should also be noted that technologically backward sector capitalists, much like slave owners and serf and semiserf employing landlords before them, tend to be especially paternalistic in their personal relationships with their subordinate group workers (rationalizing their inferior caste position as one of protection). Both types of capital have often consciously generated majority group ethnic solidarity or "nationalism," and used it to mobilize the people of the majority ethnic group (including the working class, petty bourgeoisie, and farmers/peasantry) to support its economic and military interests; and to prevent interethnic group class solidarity from developing that would act against the economic interests of the wealthy.

Majority group workers have two structural responses to subordinate group workers: first, to attempt to exclude them from the labor force (or at least from the better jobs), thereby reserving the better positions for themselves; or second, to help organize them into the *same* working class organizations into which they are organized (insisting that the position of majority group workers *not* be undermined by paying minority group workers less). Both responses have been common in the history of organized labor. The first has most often been the response of *skilled* workers who have found themselves in a position where their monopoly on skills (as well as their relatively small number) has allowed them to effectively strike, disrupt production, or otherwise organize to prevent integration; while the second has been the most common response of the unskilled and semiskilled workers (who are rarely in a position to affect the decisions of capital about whether or not to recruit workers of other ethnic groups). Among these latter workers an "interracial" organizing effort (e.g., industrial unionism) objectively offers the best hope of maintaining and advancing their position. Futile attempts to exclude workers of other ethnic groups normally results only in disorganization of the class, and consequently in a deterioration of the position of *all* workers because of the intensification of mutual hostility among its different segments. Industrial unions (that are unable to effectively create a job monopoly) composed of majority group workers who work side by side with minority group workers would be most hard pressed to successfully organize on any other basis than by incorporating *all* similarly placed workers. The attempt to organize only some workers at a given work place makes it most difficult to effectively strike or exert other power against capital (Greenberg 1980, pp. 284–86; M. Reich 1981, p. 271).

It should be noted, however, that in conditions of a very strong monolithic block of capital (e.g., commercial farmers, miners, and industrial capital) that is committed to a racial caste system excluding ethnic minorities from industrial employment, the dominant group unskilled working class unions mostly tend to support exclusionary policies. Under these conditions they do not face direct competition from minority group workers (only the underlying threat that capital might employ them in the event of a strike or if productivity does not rise, and so on). Providing there are sufficient numbers to profitably staff capitalist enterprises, appeals to the "white skin privilege" of majority group workers can well secure their political loyalty (even when interracial working class unity might have the result of fundamentally redistributing wealth and power to the mutual benefit of workers of *both* racial groupings).

It must be emphasized that relatively unskilled industrial workers are *never* powerful enough to effect the exclusion of other ethnic group workers against the will of their employers (as much as they sometimes might like to). They are simply too weak politically and economically. Decisions about the inclusions of various ethnic groups in different industries and occupations are primarily a result of the dynamic of the various sectors of *capital*.

Not only is "interracial" solidarity in the class interest of industrial workers (at least the less skilled), but the very structure of industrial production tends to create "interracial" solidarity within the working class (as well as to undermine racial categories). Studies of relationships among workers within industry show that relationships of solidarity are generated by the necessity of cooperation within industrial labor (Burawoy 1979, pp. 140–45; Kornblum 1974; chap. 2). The racial chauvinism and social exclusiveness of racially defined groups that exists *within the work relations* of industrial capitalism seems to be largely carried over from relationships outside of production (residence, culture, and so on). It is not uncommon to find work-generated relationships of mutual respect and friendship on the job, which are *not* generally continued after working hours (when each "racial" group retreats back into its own social environment). The divergence between the conscious and unconscious racialist stereotyping and chauvinism brought to the point of production by workers and the "lived relation" of interracial solidarity *on the job* is often resolved in favor of intraclass solidarity in industrial unionism as well as other forms of class action. It is also manifested in "joking relationships" across racial lines, where the racialist attitudes of both groups are expressed in the form of playful antagonisms that both allow the expression of hostility *and* affirm solidarity (in the form of a "friendship that takes no offense at insult," according to Alfred Radcliffe-Brown). The structural solidarity across "racial" lines (reflecting the lack of racism as a "lived relation") thus seems to be considerably more important than the conscious racialist attitudes manifested in racial jokes among majority group workers and the expression of other forms of chauvinist attitudes. There seems to be a qualitative difference in the structures and effect of racism between dominant group workers who work side by side with minority group workers for any length of time (and who thus must cooperate to survive), and those who are separated in castelike structures (and who thus do not have to cooperate in their daily labor).

There are contradictions in the racist structure of an integrated labor force. The process of integrating a labor force in order to create competition for jobs and disorganize the working class to maximize profits tends to result in creating "interracial" solidarity that comes to defeat the purpose of capital (as well as to eventually undermine the significance of the racial categories themselves, e.g., the difference between Irish and Anglo-Saxons, Italians and Nordics, and so on). This process, however, rather than resulting in the *general* undermining of racism, merely creates the need for the import of new ethnically distinct groups (which can be defined as racially inferior) to do the dirty work of capitalism.

However, the process of creating working class solidarity only need succeed in undermining the racialization of any specific groups within the working class when no strong counteracting pressures are acting. For example, if a significant and growing proportion of a racially defined essentially working class people are in a position of mediation (e.g., the Chinese), exclusion/redundancy (e.g., ghetto blacks or Puerto Ricans) racial lines can not only be maintained but even intensified. In such cases the racism generated in other contexts, through residential friction, hostility against merchants or other middlemen, resentments against paying taxes to support an excluded population in the ghettos, and so on, could counteract or even override the solidarity generated between the working class segments of the majority and minority group peoples generated on the job.

There is a long history of industrial unions in the United States that has emphasized the organization of all unskilled/semiskilled workers regardless of ethnicity. Indeed the Industrial Workers of the World as well as the Knights of Labor were based on such principles, likewise with the Congress of Industrial Organizations in the 1930s and 1940s (one of its slogans was "Black and White, Unite and Fight"). Even in the postbellum U.S. South (in the generation after the Civil War) there was a considerable history of blacks and whites working together in industrial unions. Dockworkers in New Orleans collaborated across racial lines, especially in the 1892 general strike. The same collaboration was found in the Alabama coalfields and the new Birmingham Steel industry. Around the turn of the century the United Mine Workers (UMW) were probably the most integrated organization in the United States (a concerted effort by capital to crush the union movement in the coal mines destroyed the UMW's initial interracial solidarity in 1908) (see Greenberg 1980, pp. 330, 343-45; M. Reich 1981, pp. 240-45). The history of industrial union-ism in the Republic of South Africa (through the 1930s) demonstrated many examples of "open" industrial unions that opposed the develop-ing racial exclusion system insisting on organizing both blacks and whites (see Greenberg 1980, p. 319). There has, in fact, continued to be a significant current of white trade union opinion, manifested in the leadership of unions such as the Garment Workers, which remains opposed to the system of job reservations and is willing to organize all comers (Greenberg 1980, p. 320).

While unskilled and semiskilled workers might often be the most chauvinistic in their *personal* relationships and attitudes (especially outside of the work environment), structurally they are the *least* racist of all classes in capitalist society (and as such are the natural allies of minority group workers).

Both structurally and in interpersonal behavior in relation to groups that are primarily in the mediating role, the petty bourgeoisie is normally the most racist of all classes. Both the old independent and the new salaried middle class segments of this class in Europe historically have been most anti-Semitic. Likewise, it is this class in Southeast Asia, East Africa, and Turkey that has expressed the greatest anti-Chinese, Indian, and Armenian sentiments. Limitations on their economic activities (including quotas in higher education and the professions) or their exclusion altogether (including their total expulsion from a country) benefit most those who would be in their place (in both trade and the professions). Thus, especially in times of crisis, when it is especially difficult for the majority group small shopkeeper to avoid bankruptcy or the children of the middle classes to find professional jobs, anti-Semitism, anti-Chinese, anti-Armenian, and similar sentiments as well as structural restrictions tend to grow (such was clearly the case in Europe in the 1930s).

Petty bourgeois farmers tend to be structurally (and interper-sonally) the most racist in relation to the excluded groups such as the American Indians (with whom they engaged in a rather unequal competition for the farmland of North America for 300 years). Often the majority group shopkeepers and professionals see the specially exploited workers as their potential customers and clients and, thus, have no special structural reason to express hostility to them. On the other hand, small farmers in a rural economy dominated by larger capitalist farms employing laborers from the racially dominated group as well as artisans or trades people in competition with urban ethnic enterprises using cheap labor often tend to see specially exploited "racially" distinct workers as the source of their problems (and are, thus, especially strong advocates of exclusion). This was the case for small farmers in California in the latter part of the nineteenth and twentieth centuries in their attitudes toward Asians as well as the case for the poor landowning white farmers of the Southern United States toward blacks in both the prebellum and postbellum periods.

Because of their structural desire to exclude competitors from other ethnic groups (from either business or the land), the interpersonal racism of this sector can be and has been especially vicious. Not uncommonly in the capitalist epoch it has manifested itself in systematic genocide (e.g., against the American Indians, against the European Jews). The majority group petty bourgeoisie has often used majority group ethnic solidarity or nationalism in order to mobilize popular support in their attempt to exclude competitors and potential competitors from their relatively privileged positions in small business and the professions.

In South Africa it was the alliance between the Afrikaner petty bourgeois (urban and rural), small capitalist farmers, and the skilled working class that developed the apartheid system. The three-class Afrikaner alliance always looked with suspicion on the overwhelmingly English (and now increasingly American and other major imperialist power owned) basic industries. It was this coalition that has been behind the Nationalist Party (which governed South Africa after 1948) and its central policy of constructing total apartheid (however inconvenient for industrial capital). All three segments of the Afrikaner people saw that their relatively privileged position would be threatened if the process of proletarianization and urbanization of blacks were allowed to continue.*

The Afrikaner petty bourgeoisie was the leading force in the rise of Afrikaner nationalism and the construction of the apartheid system. From 1910 when the British granted self-rule to the republic, the Afrikaner petty bourgeoisie actively cultivated nationalism based on "race," language, and religion, appealing to all Afrikaner farmers and workers to buy from Afrikaner shopkeepers, participate in Afrikaner cultural and religious activities, invest in Afrikaner businesses, and so on (see Magubane 1979, p. 167). The wealthier segments of the Afrikaner petty bourgeoisie strove to convert themselves into capitalists. After the Nationalist Party came to power in 1948 a

---

*The institution of apartheid meant the relocation of all "racial" groups including Indians into different zones. It should be noted that the massive uprooting and displacement of the Indians (the traditional commercial caste, along with the Jews, in the republic) opened up considerable commercial opportunities for the Afrikaner petty bourgeoisie (Magubane 1979, p. 177).

wide range of measures was adopted to assist this development. Afrikaner industrial capital (virtually nonexistent before World War II) became a major force after a generation of Nationalist Party rule (Magubane 1979, chap. 7). The reliance of Afrikaner capital on the Nationalist Party controlling the state (and the special economic benefits this provided) has given this class a special stake in the maintenance of the apartheid system (which materially benefits the Afrikaner petty bourgeoisie, commercial farmers, and skilled workers more than it does industrial Afrikaner capital).

Class Differences within the Minority Group

Although a specific "racial group" is normally defined by the class position of the bulk of its members (i.e., whether it is essentially in a relation of special exploitation, mediation, or exclusion) there is almost always a degree of class differentiation (or at least a range of positions in terms of privilege) within a given group. Thus, although blacks in the United States before the Civil War were defined by the relationship of slavery, there were both a small number of free blacks (a few of which were even slave owners) and a stratum of relatively privileged black slaves (slave drivers and some house servants). After emancipation a small (and since the 1960s rather rapidly growing) petty bourgeoisie developed among blacks on the one hand; while, on the other, in the post-World War II period a growing excluded sector has accumulated in the urban ghettos, even while blacks have remained defined by their central relationship of special exploitation. Among Jews, Chinese, Armenians, East Indians, and so on who have been defined primarily by the relationship of mediation, there has always been a differentiation between a few wealthy capitalists and rich merchants on the one extreme and large numbers of very marginal petty bourgeoisie (lumpen petty bourgeois) as well as low-paid employees of the wealthy on the other. Likewise, among the excluded there are usually a few who have a special privileged relationship with the majority ethnic group as well as those who have relative power and privilege among the remnants of tribal/band societies.

The different classes and strata within a given ethnic group or people have somewhat different interests as well as different propensities to accommodate to racist structures, transform them, ally with groups in the majority community, and so on. For example, it is very common for the most privileged classes and strata (the black petty bourgeoisie, the richest Jewish/Chinese merchants, American Indian chiefs, and so on) to accommodate to racist structures since they in fact (in spite of certain interpersonal insults and cultural discrimination) fare rather well (unlike the majority of their peoples). For example, traditionally the small black petty bourgeoisie actually profited from racial discrimination. Blacks who could not obtain the services of a white barber or undertaker were forced by the discriminatory structures to use the services of black barbers and undertakers (see Frazier 1957). The wealthiest Jews, Chinese, Armenians, and so on historically were normally well protected by the dominant landlord and imperial interests because of the vital economic functions they perform (vital and most profitable functions that would evaporate without the traditional caste privileges of these groups).

Ethnic identity or "nationalism" is the ideology that members of a nation, people, ethnic group, or "racial" minority have more in common with each other than the various constituent classes of the group have with other people in similar class positions. Further, "nationalism" dictates that because of their postulated overriding common interest, all classes within the ethnic group, people, or "racial" minority should work together economically and politically to advance their collective interests *against* other "nations", "races", ethnic groups, or peoples (even against those who are in the *same* classes). Nationalism is the advocacy of ethnic or "national" solidarity and action over class consciousness and action. It is, thus, the opposite of class consciousness that argues solidarity should occur and political alliances be formed primarily along *class* lines (even against the relatively privileged groups within one's subordinate ethnic group). Nationalism and class consciousness are, thus, alternative strategies of political action for gaining improvement in one's life.

In fact nationalism is a product of class forces. Although different kinds of nationalism differ qualitatively in their effects, *all* serve some classes within a given racial group as opposed to others. For example, the capitalist class, rich merchants, or the petty bourgeoisie of the dominated nation or people have often generated ethnic solidarity or nationalism and used it to attempt to mobilize the poorer segments of the minority group behind the former's interests and leadership, i.e., to preserve these groups' relative privilege. This has often been manifested in attempts to maintain the conditions of exceptionally cheap labor for the small capitalist enterprises of mediating groups (e.g., Jews, Chinese) Nationalism has also been used by the petty bourgeoisie of the Ladino and black peoples in the United States in the post-1960s period in their fight for affirmative action programs and quotas in universities, business, and the professions (which mostly benefit this class).

Similar uses of nationalism (here more often referred to as tribalism) have also occurred in the postindependence period in Africa. The relative overproduction of educated people combined with the surplus of petty business people especially in times of economic recession, has produced considerable ethnic or tribal conflict. This has taken the form of the relatively privileged (mostly petty bourgeois) professionals and small business people in many of the new states, or in some cases regions of the new states, attempting to mobilize tribal, national, or racial sentiments among the peasants and working class in order to gain allies for the exclusion of their competitors for scarce petty-bourgeois positions (many of whom have been from different tribes, states, ethnic groups, and so on). Some of the more successful efforts along these lines have resulted in the expulsion of the East Indians from Uganda, the massacre of Arabs in Zanzibar, and the exclusion of Malians from Upper Volta and Zaire, of Ugandans from Kenya, of Togolese from Ghana and the Ivory Coast, and of Nigerians from Ghana (see Wallerstein 1979, p. 172).

CONCLUSION

The capitalist nature of racist structures, racialist ideology, and interpersonal racism must be stressed. Although racism as a "lived relation" has existed (mostly without an articulated racialist ideology) from more or less the origins of class society, all three structures of racism were considerably intensified at the height of the capitalist epoch (as were racialist theories and interpersonal racism).

It should be noted that slavery was generally the most brutal in the English colonies, and most humane in the Portuguese and Spanish, i.e., the more closely slavery was related to rising industrial capitalism the more brutal it was. Likewise, the treatment of the American Indians was the most brutal in North America, where genocide and forced displacement was the most systematically practiced—again because of the drive of the expanding industrial capitalist system to incorporate new land and resources.

The last half of the nineteenth and early twentieth centuries, the period of the triumph and consolidation of capitalism, can perhaps be considered the most racist era in human history. During this period the systematic extermination of the indigenous peoples of North America and Australia reached its peak, and the enserfment of the highland Indians of Latin America reached its greatest intensity. The caste structure that forced U.S. blacks into sharecropping, denied them basic formal political rights, and imposed apartheidlike restrictions on them (the Jim Crow system) developed in the 1890s. Chinese and other Asians were transported around the world as indentured labor as well as massively assaulted and expelled. Jews and Armenians in the latter years of the nineteenth and early twentieth century were uprooted from their traditional occupations, displaced by the millions, and subjected to what must be considered two of the most systematic and cold-blooded genocides in human history.

All three basic structures of racism have partially mitigated in their intensity in the post–World War II industrial capitalist world. Primary structures of exclusion have largely withered away with the peoples against whom they were directed, e.g., American Indians, Australian aborigines (which made it functionless). Almost all land of value has been appropriated from the indigenous peoples and incorporated into the world capitalist system. However, it should be noted that secondary exclusion, e.g., that of redundant blacks, is increasing in significance. Antagonism against those in structures of mediation (middlemen minorities) has declined in importance as these groups have either been exterminated/expelled (the Jews in central Europe, the Armenians in Turkey, the East Indians in much of East Africa, and so on) or transformed into less visible (for the time being) middle class professionals. The viciousness of racial structures of special exploitation/disorganization has been mitigated somewhat by the long-term trend of rising prosperity and the associated all-around expansion of basic rights and social welfare that have, in part, trickled down to the racially oppressed groups (even to the new "guest workers," and "illegal aliens"), as well as by the withering of caste-like structures.

There is no special reason, however, to expect the post-1920s trend of mitigation of racist structures to continue either for those in positions of special exploitation, or in secondary positions of exclusion. In a period of economic contraction with an "oversupply" of college graduates seeking professional and managerial jobs, hostility against the extreme concentration of Jews and Asians among college students and in the professions could very easily manifest itself in considerable hostility against these groups (as it did in Germany, eastern Europe, and the United States in the 1920s and 1930s). Likewise, in a period of rising unemployment and declining real wages, competition for better jobs could well result in an intensification of racist sentiments in the working class as well as in capital increasingly using racial divisions to disorganize the working class in order to further reduce wages and increase work discipline (e.g., by increasing the immigration of Latin American workers, many as part of "bracero" type programs that limit their contact with majority group workers). Last, the growing secondarily excluded population piling up in the black ghettos of the United States could very well serve as a scapegoat to deflect the hostility of the masses of white working people away from the system responsible for their ills (similar to what happened to eastern European Jews in the 1930s). It must be underlined that racism is a *capitalist structure*, a product of the logic of capital.

11

The Position of Blacks and Ladinos in the U.S. Class Structure

This chapter examines the historical development of racist structures by which blacks and Ladinos are defined in the United States. Until the World War I period, blacks were heavily concentrated in the South as menial rural laborers—first slaves, then sharecroppers. After this period blacks were expelled from the land and pulled into the cities as urban menial laborers within fully capitalist relations of production. Since the 1960s new immigrants from Latin America have displaced Southern blacks as the primary source of new recruits for the most menial occupations within the capitalist system.

BLACKS AND U.S. CAPITALISM

After a period of struggle between the newly freed blacks and progressive (largely up-country and Republican) poor whites (who, with the support of the Union Army, instituted Reconstruction governments in the defeated Confederacy), the old planter class had by 1877 once again achieved political supremacy everywhere in the South. Although the slaves had been freed (without compensation) over the 1863-67 period, their former owners continued to pretty much monopolize both the land and the material means to work it. They were, thus, able to recapture their labor force and institute a system of semiserfdom on the land—a system that proved to be even more profitable than the former slave system (see Greenberg 1980, chap. 6).

The problem of maintaining an adequate supply of menial rural laborers on the land was solved through a variety of "extramarket" measures. The sharecropping system developed in which the tenants paid the landlords between one-third and one-half of their crops (depending on who provided the equipment, mules, and fertilizer). A series of laws were passed that forced most blacks into this labor system. "False-pretense" laws requiring the faithful carrying out of the contracts entered into by the croppers were instituted. Desertion of the land was, thus, made punishable by the state. Since the tenants often accepted "advances" for their crop they were bound to stay on the land to work off their debt, i.e., a system of de facto debt peonage was instituted (see Greenberg 1980, pp. 112-17; Reich 1981, pp. 230-31). Most croppers were kept in constant debt, and, thus, locked into a system that forced them to grow the cash crops (mostly cotton) that the owners of the land required. Lien laws were instituted that gave the landlords the first claim on the tenant's crops.

The system was reinforced by the planters' control over the state (including judges, sheriffs, and other local officials), which became an instrument of labor control for the commercial planters. Both real and contrived debts, frame-ups, and heavy charges for petty offenses were systematically used against those who resisted the system of tenancy (black convicts were leased out by the state to commercial farmers). The local state did little or nothing against individual and mob actions that drove blacks out of independent farming. To keep blacks from leaving the land antivagrancy laws were implemented and strictly (and sometimes fraudulently) enforced against those attempting to migrate. Groups of blacks waiting to cross rivers as well as black leaders were beaten up by mobs, often with the collaboration of local "law enforcement" officials. Finally, the lack of alternative employment opportunities, either in the rapidly growing textile mills of the South (where most employment was reserved for whites) or in Northern industry (outside of domestic labor and a few exceptionally menial occupations), further reinforced the semifeudal system of the South in which black tenant labor was central to profitable cotton production.

As long as there was a surplus of displaced European peasants (Irish, Poles, southern Italians, and so on) willing to perform the necessary menial labor in the low-paying occupations, and as long as the Southern plantation economy was financed by Northern banks and provided cheap raw materials for Northern industry, Northern capital supported the policy of keeping the black population on the land in the rural South.

In 1910 89 percent of all blacks were living in the South. Seventy-three percent of all blacks were living in rural areas. Blacks comprised 30 percent of the entire population of the South, compared to only 2 percent of the Northern and north central states (see Table 11.1). Between 1890 and 1910 there was only a minor migration out of the South—about 17,000 persons a year (see Table 11.2).

Beginning around World War I, the mechanization of the Southern plantation system began to push black sharecroppers off the land. The system of cotton tenancy was gradually replaced by mechanized farming of large units (a process that required much less labor than tenancy). Further, cotton itself was largely replaced by soybeans, cattle, poultry, tobacco, peanuts, and other crops that were generally less labor intensive than cotton (see Greenberg 1980, chap. 6). Thus, the semienserfed black population of the South became available as a labor pool for the urban factory system of the North. The increasing availability of this pool of surplus labor coincided with the closure of European immigration by the world war in the 1914-18 period as well as with the rising agitation against further European immigration that culminated in the 1924 Immigrant Exclusion Act (legislation made possible by the development of alternative sources of menial laborers now available among both the blacks *and* poor whites of the rural South). From 1914 through the mid-1960s the South was the primary source of new menial laborers for the expanding industrial capitalist system of the United States. Poor Southern blacks and, until the late 1940s, poor whites made up the *fourth* wave of peasants displaced by ever more pervasive and expanding world capitalism (the first three were: the British, predominant before 1850; the Irish/German/Scandinavian, predominant between 1850 and 1895; and the Slavic/Italian/Jewish, predominant between 1895 and 1914).

The industrialization of Italy, Germany, and parts of Central Europe (which provided job opportunities closer to home) combined with the withdrawal of one of the principal sources of peasant immigrants to the United States (Russia) from the world capitalist system (together with nationalist-motivated obstacles to emigration in Europe) reduced the supply and perhaps *more* importantly increased the price of labor power (the wages necessary to induce sufficient migration from Europe) relative to that for which those pushed off the land in the South were willing to accept menial industrial employment. The economically desperate, displaced Southern black peasants (as well as many whites) were willing to work for less than were new European immigrants.

Another significant factor in the switch from displaced European to displaced Southern peasants was the relative degree of disorganization of the two groups. European workers were becoming increasingly organized, and thus resistant to manipulation by capital. This was

TABLE 11.1: The Distribution of the Black Population of the United States

	Percentage Living in the South	Percentage Born in the South	Percentage Farm	Percentage Rural	Blacks as a Percent of the Total Population		
					in the South	in the North	of the U.S.
1890	90	93	—*	80	33	2	12
1910	89	93	—	73	30	2	11
1940	77	88	35	51	24	4	10
1950	68	83	21	38	22	5	10
1960	60	75	8	27	21	7	11
1970	53	49	2	19	19	8	11
1975	52	—	—	—	19	9	11

*Data not available.
Source: U.S. Bureau of the Census 1979a, pp. 13, 14.

TABLE 11.2: Net Migration of Blacks out of the South

	Number	Blacks as Percentage of Total Net Outmigration from the South
1880–90	70,000	20
1890–1900	168,000	—[a]
1900–10	170,000	72
1910–20	454,000	48
1920–30	749,000	55
1930–40	347,000	54
1940–50	1,599,000	75
1950–60	1,473,000	—[a]
1960–70	1,380,000	—[a]
1970–75	–44,000[b]	—[b]

[a]Net migration of whites into the South.
[b]Net migration of blacks into the South.
Sources: U.S. Bureau of the Census 1979a, p. 15; U.S. Department of Commerce 1981a, p. 27; Wilson 1978, p. 66.

manifested in the growing prevalence of militant strikes in industrial areas, (e.g., Lawrence, Massachusetts, in 1912; Patterson, New Jersey, in 1913; the wave of strikes of female garment and textile workers in New York City from 1908, all of which culminated in the strike wave of 1919—two of the most militant manifestations of which were the Great Steel Strike and the Seattle General Strike). Displaced Black peasants, in contrast, had for over a generation been politically docile, beaten down first by the overthrow of the Reconstruction governments, then by the institutionalization of the Jim Crow system and disenfranchisement. Their consequent lack of political skills and organizational experience made them ideal as docile labor who would resist unionization and willingly participate in the ongoing processes of reorganizing working class occupations (as preceding generations of ex-peasants without industrial experience had before them).

The availability of black peasants to replace European peasants as the primary source of new menial laborers in Northern industry was facilitated by the policy of the rapidly growing Southern textile industry to utilize only displaced poor whites as industrial labor (part of the "white supremacy" strategy of providing minor advantage to those with white skin in order to secure their loyalty to the system; see M. Reich 1981, pp. 246-50). As long as there were sufficient displaced white peasants there was no economic cost to the policy of black exclusion.

The social situation of blacks was radically transformed in the halfcentury after the beginning of World War I as a consequence of the radical transformation of their economic position within the world capitalist system. In the 1910-20 period there was an annual average net migration out of the South of 45,000 blacks a year, and in the 1920-30 period of 75,000. After slowing down in the 1930s, the black Northern immigration became much greater than ever with World War II. From 1940 to 1970 the net migration of blacks out of the South averaged about 150,000 people a year (see Table 11.2).

Beginning in 1914 black men were systematically recruited by Northern industrial capitalists for low-paying, unskilled, or semi-skilled work in the steel mills, packinghouses, foundries, automobile plants, and construction. Black women were increasingly drawn into the unskilled branches of the needle trades, food industries, and commercial laundries. The barriers to black employment in unskilled occupations outside of the service industries and domestic labor rapidly came down as black workers were drawn into the mainstream of the industrial working class by the logic of capital accumulation and its voracious hunger for low cost (and disorganized) labor.

Popular hostility in the North against the relatively few blacks in this region before 1914 was considerable. Traditionally, it was most intense in the lower portions of the states of the Midwest that had been settled by poor whites who had been pushed off the good land of the South by the plantation system. While still in the South these poor whites were unable to compete with the low-cost operations of the slave-owning plantation lords. As farmers, artisans, and free laborers, they were undercut by both slave and free black labor. These migrants settled in the old Northwest because slavery was not permitted there. They had no intention of allowing the legalization of the slave system in these states. Further, they fought for excluding free blacks from migrating to these areas *and* excluding those who were already there from occupations in which they competed with whites (Wilson 1978, pp. 48-49).*

With the general rise of racism within the world capitalist system after 1890 (an effect of both the expansion of capitalism into Africa and other regions and the massive migration of displaced peasants to the North of the United States), discrimination against blacks in the Northeast increased. Most integrated white churches expelled their black members, and hotels, restaurants, and theaters in the North came to exclude blacks or establish their own Jim Crow

---

*Abraham Lincoln's family was typical of this class of poor whites. Born in slaveholding Kentucky, his parents took him first to southern Indiana, then to downstate Illinois, where he made his political career in the new Republican Party.

rules (paralleling those established in the South at the same time). The first two decades of the twentieth century saw the most intense discrimination and racial hostility, as well as the firmest caste crystallization, of any period in the history of race relations in the Northern states since the abolition of slavery.

There were good reasons for the capitalist class of the North to encourage the racial hostility of first the Irish, then the Slavs, and finally Italians against blacks. Those blacks who could be recruited as strikebreakers during the strikes of European workers as well as those potentially competing with European workers for skilled jobs and the capitalist responsibility for excluding blacks from certain occupations (thereby giving the European workers petty privileges) served admirably as a deflector of class hostility away from capital, just as the Jim Crow white supremacy system instituted by the Democratic Party in the 1890s served in the South. The over-whelmingly racist portrayal of blacks in the upper class controlled media (which intensified in the 1890s) encouraged the displacement of the class hostility of white workers against the almost insignificant numbers of Northern industrial blacks.

Beginning in the 1890s Northern employers began the practice of using black scabs to replace white workers during strikes (blacks were otherwise not normally hired by industrial capital in this period). This practice generated considerable hostility among workers of European background as well as undermined possibilities of united class action along black-white lines (see M. Reich 1981, pp. 244-55). The mutual antagonism of black and white workers was manifested in the immediate post-World War I period in race riots (which took the form of white mobs attacking black neighborhoods) in and around the industrial cities into which black workers had recently flooded. In good part these riots represented the hostility of unemployed whites and older immigrant groups against the newest group of menial labors willing to work harder for less money.

The inclusion or exclusion of minorities is primarily a result of what is profitable for capital, not a result of the power of the relatively privileged working class (no matter what the dominant group workers may be led to believe by those who control the means of mental production). Although many might have liked to exclude blacks from industrial jobs, workers (especially the unskilled or semiskilled) did not have such power. White workers could express their anger in rioting, but were not able to offer any effective resistance to the increasingly massive employment of blacks. The Irish might have appeared to be able to force blacks out of certain occupations in the 1850s and 1860s, but in fact it was the logic of industrial capital that dictated the economic assignments of *both* groups. The inability of the Slavs, Italians, and Jews to exclude blacks from industrial occupations after 1914 is proof that it is the need of capital for a cheap labor force (combined with its desire to disorganize the working class as a whole) that has been behind the exclusion of minorities from better paying jobs, not the pressure of relatively privileged organized workers.

Confronted with the massive presence of blacks in unskilled positions in basic industry, the predominantly white new industrial union movement of the 1930s, the Congress of Industrial Organization (CIO), adopted a nonexclusionary policy of "Black and White Unite and Fight" to successfully organize most of the basic industries in which blacks were concentrated. The 1938 Constitutional Convention of the CIO passed a resolution that read in part: "Employers constantly seek to split one group of workers from another, and thus to deprive them of their full economic strength, by arousing prejudices based on race, creed, color or nationality, and one of the most frequent weapons used by employers to accomplish this end is to create false contests between Negro and white workers" (cited in M. Reich 1981, p. 257). It is no coincidence that when the traditional racist policies of the old AFL craft unions (that organized only the skilled and largely native born) went by the board, sufficient class-wide solidarity was generated to effectively organize steel, auto, rubber, and so forth.

The successful policies of the CIO in organizing all industrial workers into one union regardless of skin color or ethnic origin proved to bring considerable economic benefit to black and white alike as well as to significantly diminish the pre-1930s level of racial hostility (that had burst out so violently during and after World War I). The successful union organization of basic industry (in which large numbers of blacks were concentrated) in the 1930s and 1940s, together with state-sponsored equal employment legislation (instituted from the World War II period) meant that there was a considerable improvement in the economic position of what was becoming a distinct Afro-American *industrial* working class.

The older explicitly discriminatory practices of systematic exclusion from better paying jobs and lower pay scales for minorities were generally ended in basic industry. The dual labor market was superseded by a single labor market in which black and white industrial workers competed on the basis of who would be employed most profitably by capital. With the removal of most explicit discriminatory barriers, the relative advantage of white workers was now maintained through their superior education, skill levels, and past experience rather than by "white supremacist" discriminatory hiring policies (see Wilson 1978, pp. 110, 152).

The considerable improvement in the conditions of life of those ex-Southern peasants who formed the black industrial proletariat came to contrast increasingly with both the new black salaried petty bourgeoisie and the black underclass (which after World War II increasingly became a massive component of the Northern central cities). The emerging new black petty bourgeoisie has been helped considerably in consolidating a respectable economic position through state policies that have resulted in their disproportionate hiring in white collar, professional, and administrative jobs by the state, where from the 1960s effective affirmative action programs governing both recruitment and promotion have been applied. By the 1970s it was clear that three very distinct social classes had emerged and consolidated among blacks: the salaried petty bourgeoisie, the industrial working class, and the underclass of the central cities.

BLACKS AS DEFINED BY THEIR WORKING CLASS POSITION

Blacks are overwhelmingly a working class people. In 1977 only 12.7 percent of employed black men as compared to 30.2 percent of white men were professionals or managers while only 4.9 percent as compared to 11.3 percent for whites were self-employed. The black middle class is much smaller than the white middle class. Blacks are heavily concentrated in manual working class jobs. In 1977, 75.1 percent of employed black men and 46.1 percent of black women as compared to 53.7 percent of white men and 31.9 percent of white women were urban manual workers. It should be noted that very few blacks are employed any longer in agriculture. In 1977 only 3.5 percent of black men and 1.1 percent of black women as compared to 4.1 percent of white men and 1.0 percent of white women were so engaged. It should also be noted that blacks are heavily concentrated in state jobs. In 1977, 21.8 percent of all black men and 28.3 percent of all employed black women were working for the government, compared with 14.3 percent of white men and 19.7 percent of white women. (See Table 11.3.)

Table 11.4 shows that the occupational concentration of blacks decreased rather radically for both males and females in the period 1940-77. This change was most marked among men for clerical workers, craftspeople, and operatives—three of the most central occupations in the modern industrial economy—and among women for professionals, clerical workers, and operatives. For men the greatest barriers remain for professionals, managers, and sales-workers, while for women they persist for managers and sales-workers. In general, it is the most privileged occupations that have

TABLE 11.3: The Occupational Structure of Whites, Blacks, and Ladinos in the United States, 1977

	Whites		Blacks		Ladinos	
	Male	*Female*	*Male*	*Female*	*Male*	*Female*
Professional-managerial	30.2%	22.6%	12.7%	14.4%	14.5%	11.7%
Urban manual[a]	53.7	31.9	75.1	46.1	71.0	47.9
Menial labor[b]	32.2	32.2	59.6	54.0	50.4	50.5
Service workers	7.9	20.0	16.8	35.4	12.4	22.7
Industrial workers[c]	45.8	14.4	58.4	19.9	58.6	29.5
Agriculture	4.1	1.0	3.5	1.1	5.8	3.2
Clerical/sales	12.0	42.4	8.7	29.1	8.8	32.8
State workers	14.3	19.7	21.8	28.3	12.5	17.2
Self-employed	11.3	5.0	4.9	1.5	5.5	1.8

[a]Craftsworkers, foremen, operatives, nonfarm labor, nondomestic service workers, including the self-employed.
[b]Laborers (farm and nonfarm), operatives, service workers (including domestics).
[c]Craftsworkers, foremen, operatives, nonfarm labor.
Source: U.S. Bureau of the Census 1979c, Table 53.

been the most resistant to integration, while the central industrial occupations have become the most integrated. It is to these latter occupations that the largest numbers of new black immigrants to industrial areas have been recruited.

The data on trends in industrial composition support those for occupations. Within the manufacturing sector, 31.4 percent of (employed) black males (compared to 29.7 percent of white males) and 15.7 percent of black females (compared to 20.1 percent of white females) were employed in 1970 (U.S. Bureau of the Census 1970d, p. 394). Blacks are only slightly over or underrepresented in all the major industries except for both electrical and nonelectrical machinery, where they are significantly underrepresented compared to whites, and primary metals, where they are significantly overrepresented (see Table 11.5). Blacks are well integrated into the industrial proletariat and not just concentrated in a few industries.

The post-World War II period has seen a fundamental improvement in the income position of blacks in relation to whites. While the ratio of the annual median income of black men with reported income to the similar category of whites remained more or less constant at

TABLE 11.4: The Ratio of the Percentage of All Economically Active Blacks to the Percentage of All Economically Active Whites in Each Occupational Category

	Females			Males		
	1940	1970	1977	1940	1970	1977
Professionals	0.29	0.68	0.81	0.31	0.37	0.46
Managerial	0.16	0.34	0.50	0.12	0.24	0.33
Clerical	0.03	0.53	0.69	0.20	1.00	1.30
Sales	0.06	0.29	0.29	0.12	0.25	0.33
Craftsworkers	0.14	0.72	0.50	0.28	0.65	0.72
Operatives	0.30	1.10	1.50	0.67	1.50	1.50
Domestics	5.40	7.30	5.00	18.20	4.00	—*
Service	0.91	1.60	1.60	3.20	2.00	2.00
Farmers	2.70	0.50	—	1.50	0.24	0.33
Farm laborers	10.60	2.00	1.00	2.80	2.10	1.50
Laborers	0.90	1.40	1.00	2.80	2.50	2.30

*Data not available.

Note: Numbers greater than one mean that blacks are favored for these occupations; numbers less than one mean that whites are favored.

Sources: U.S. Bureau of the Census 1940, Table 62; 1970d, p. 375; 1979a, p. 248.

TABLE 11.5: **The Ratio of the Percentage of All Black Workers in Manufacturing in Each Industry to the Percentage of All White Workers in Manufacturing in Each Industry**

	1950	1970
Primary metals	1.71	1.43
Fabricated metals	0.60	0.75
Machinery (except electrical)	0.31	0.42
Electrical machinery	0.29	0.54
Motor vehicles	1.12	1.14
Food and kindred	1.16	1.20
Textiles	0.63	1.33
Chemicals	1.32	0.84
All manufacturing industries	1.00	1.00

Note: Numbers greater than one mean that blacks are favored in these industries; numbers less than one mean that whites are favored.
Sources: U.S. Census 1950, Table 2; 1970d, p. 394.

0.52 from 1950 to 1963, since that time there has been a steady improvement. From an average of 0.56 in the 1964-67 period, it rose to 0.61 in the 1968 to 1972 period and to 0.63 in the 1973-79 period. (See Table 11.6.) This represents a significant, but not radical improvement, apparently reflecting the corporate and state response to the black riots of the mid-1960s as well as the organized civil rights and black movements of the 1960s. A more significant improvement in the relative income position of black men is noticeable in the trend for year-round, full-time workers. Here we see that there has been a steady tendency for blacks to close the gap with whites since 1955. The ratio of the annual income of year-round, full-time employed black to white men averaged 0.61 between 1955 and 1959, 0.64 between 1960 and 1964, 0.66 between 1965 and 1969, 0.71 between 1970 and 1974, and 0.75 between 1975 and 1979. About 40 percent of the income differential disappeared over the 24-year period (a major improvement for black men). The significant difference between these statistics and those for all with income reflects the growing gap between the black poor and the black working and middle classes. At the same time blacks have been integrated into the mainstream of the industrial working class as well as since the 1960s into the lower levels of the salaried managerial and professional petty bourgeoisie, part-time and irregular employment patterns have become more prevalent in the lower reaches of the working class (and on the border of the underclass).

While the reduction of the income gap between black and white men has been significant, the reduction of the income gap between black and white women has been radical. Both the ratios for those with any income and those for full-time, year-round workers have manifested the virtual convergence with white median income over the 1950-79 period. While in the 1950-54 period black female income averaged only 48 percent of white female income, in the 1975-79 period it averaged 92 percent. The reduction in the female differential occurred at a steady pace over the 1950 to 1970 period, stabilizing at 0.92 in the 1970s (see Table 11.6). The ratios for the year-round, full-time employed showed the same improvement, rising from 0.58 in the 1955-59 period to 0.95 in the 1975-79 period. The lack of a difference in the patterns for all those with income and those who worked full time the year around apparently reflects the fact that black women, unlike black men, have increasingly been drawn into the labor force as paid laborers over the post-World War II period. (See Table 11.6).

When the earnings ratios for the major occupational categories are examined (see Table 11.7), it can be seen that in most cases the black to white ratios are less within any given occupation than for the total employed population. This indicates that much of the black-white differential is a result of the concentration of blacks in the lower paying occupations, rather than a result of discriminatory patterns within occupational categories. Also, it can be seen that in many cases the improvement in the position of blacks in relation to whites between 1969 and 1979 was not as great within each occupational category as was the overall improvement in black-white earnings ratios. This reflects the fact that much of the improvement in the position of blacks has come from their displacement from the low paid occupations in which they were historically concentrated (farm labor, nonfarm labor, the services) to higher paid occupations (professionals, operatives, craftsworkers, clerical workers).

Some occupations did experience a significant improvement in their black-white earnings ratios between 1969 and 1979. For example, for full-time, year-round male managers the ratio rose from 0.57 in 1969 to 0.71 in 1979. Among male service workers the ratio rose from 0.73 to 0.94 at the same time. There were also slight improvements in the position of black male craftsworkers and operatives. Among women the most significant improvements occurred for salaried professionals, where the ratio for those employed full time the year around rose from 0.95 in 1969 to 1.03 in 1979, for clerical workers it rose from 0.94 in 1969 to 1.04 in 1979, and for operatives it rose from 0.85 in 1969 to 0.92 in 1979. It should be noted that in neither 1969 nor 1979 was there a difference between black and white women employed full time the year around in nondomestic services.

TABLE 11.6: Nonwhite/White Median Annual Income Ratios, 1950–79

	All with Income		Year-Round Full-Time Workers	
	Males	Females	Males	Females
1950	0.54	0.45	—*	—
1951	0.55	0.42	—	—
1952	0.55	0.39	—	—
1953	0.55	0.59	—	—
1954	0.50	0.54	—	—
1955	0.53	0.52	0.61	0.51
1956	0.52	0.57	0.60	0.56
1957	0.53	0.58	0.61	0.58
1958	0.50	0.58	0.63	0.59
1959	0.47	0.62	0.58	0.64
1960	0.53	0.62	0.66	0.68
1961	0.52	0.67	0.63	0.66
1962	0.49	0.67	0.60	0.61
1963	0.52	0.67	0.64	0.62
1964	0.57	0.70	0.66	0.69
1965	0.54	0.73	0.63	0.68
1966	0.55	0.76	0.63	0.71
1967	0.57	0.80	0.67	0.75
1968	0.62	0.81	0.69	0.74
1969	0.59	0.85	0.68	0.82
1970	0.60	0.92	0.70	0.84
1971	0.60	0.90	0.71	0.90
1972	0.62	0.96	0.69	0.87
1973	0.63	0.93	0.70	0.87
1974	0.64	0.92	0.75	0.94
1975	0.63	0.92	0.77	0.98
1976	0.63	0.95	0.73	0.94
1977	0.61	0.88	0.72	0.95
1978	0.64	0.92	0.79	0.94
1979	0.65	0.93	0.76	0.93

*Data not available before 1955.
Source: U.S. Bureau of the Census 1981, Table 67.

Economic discrimination against black women has diminished so rapidly as to have produced a tripartite division in the labor force: white men, black (and Ladino) men, and women (black and white). Black women have been brought into the traditionally female clerical, service, and industrial occupations on more or less the same basis as white women. Patriarchal structures and sexist ideology now appear to be sufficient for capital to adequately control female workers without the need of additional racist structures and ideologies applying to women (as they were once necessary when black women were needed in the fields and as domestics). Among male workers, however, there remain strong reasons to reproduce racist structures and ideology as a way to secure low paid menial laborers. The tripartite division of labor that has emerged—minority men, majority men, and women—reflects the underlying logic of monopoly capital for *three* different types of proletarian labor—menial white collar, menial manual, and relatively skilled manual labor.

Much if not most of the declining income gap between white and black men has been effected by the migration of blacks from the rural South to urban areas, especially in the North. In fact, there was *no* significant change in the black/white male income ratio (for those with income) in the North and West from 1953 to 1974. This ratio stood at 0.74 in 1953 and 0.75 in 1974. For women, however, the ratio in the North and West rose from 0.85 to 1.13 during this same period, reflecting real changes in occupational patterns within Northern urban areas. In the South the ratio rose from 0.46 for men in 1953 to 0.54 in 1974; and for women from 0.45 to 0.74 (U.S. Bureau of the Census 1979a, p. 46). Both of these trends reflect real changes in the occupational patterns of blacks within the South.

That the declining earnings gap between blacks and whites reflects a combination of changes in entry barriers to occupations, promotional opportunities, and the concentration of blacks in jobs with relatively low pay and slight pay increments (i.e., manual labor) is reflected in the different earnings ratios of different age groups. In 1969 the ratio of black to white Anglo male earnings for 18-24 year olds was 0.83 and for 25-34 year olds 0.67. This compares to 0.56 for those aged 35-64. For women aged 18-24, the comparable ratio was 0.89 and for those aged 25-34 it was 0.87. This compares to a ratio of 0.80 for those aged 35-54 and 0.62 for those aged 55 to 64 (Perlo 1975, p. 79).

Studies done on the causes of the black-white pay differentials in the mid-1960s found that approximately 40 percent of the differential was a product of outright discrimination against blacks who have the *same* occupational background, educational experience, family background, and so on as whites; and roughly 60 percent a result of differences between white and black workers in family background, educational attainment, occupational experience, and so on (see Brown 1977, p. 168). Thus more of the black-white income gap is a product of the negative experiences of blacks before they attempt to sell their labor (less than standard education, residence, lack of oppor-

TABLE 11.7: White and Black Median Annual Earnings by Occupation, 1969 and 1979

	All Those with Earnings				Year-Round Full-Time Workers Only			
	Males		Females		Males		Females	
	1969	1979[a]	1969	1979[a]	1969	1979[a]	1969	1979[a]
Salaried professionals								
White	$10,397	$19,866	$5,305	$ 9,673	$11,536	$21,982	$7,345	$13,355
Black	7,251	15,280	6,008	11,036	8,479	16,509	6,974	13,704
	(0.70)[a]	(0.77)	(1.13)	(1.14)	(0.74)	(0.75)	(0.95)	(1.03)
Salaried managers								
White	11,383	21,817	5,349	9,971	11,944	23,342	6,210	11,749
Black	6,792	15,741	—[b]	—	6,852	16,605	—	—
	(0.60)	(0.72)			(0.57)	(0.71)		
Sales								
White	6,940	13,419	1,246	3,210	9,329	17,318	3,721	8,594
Black	4,004	7,360	1,144	3,643	—	—	—	—
	(0.58)	(0.55)	(0.92)	(1.13)				
Clerical								
White	6,910	12,080	3,630	7,100	8,032	16,100	5,172	9,723
Black	5,506	9,546	3,125	7,310	7,263	11,756	4,868	10,084
	(0.80)	(0.79)	(0.86)	(1.03)	(0.90)	(0.73)	(0.94)	(1.04)
Craftsworkers								
White	8,125	15,828	3,978	7,769	8,905	18,041	5,036	10,725
Black	5,798	11,493	—	—	6,488	14,213	—	—
	(0.71)	(0.73)			(0.73)	(0.79)		

Operatives								
White	6,480	12,513	3,119	6,511	7,525	15,375	4,385	8,755
Black	4,959	10,711	2,698	6,596	5,824	12,676	3,723	8,048
	(0.77)	(0.86)	(0.87)	(1.01)	(0.77)	(0.82)	(0.85)	(0.92)
Nonfarm laborers								
White	2,171	5,091	1,420	4,936	6,278	12,628	—	9,060
Black	3,485	6,177	—	4,264	5,328	10,933	—	—
	(1.60)	(1.21)		(0.86)	(0.85)	(0.87)		
Service laborers[c]								
White	3,828	3,865	1,390	2,978	6,671	10,374	3,637	7,450
Black	3,229	5,285	2,150	4,302	4,865	9,742	3,612	7,307
	(0.84)	(1.37)	(1.55)	(1.44)	(0.73)	(0.94)	(1.00)	(0.98)
Farm laborers								
White	807	4,161	385	1,875	3,257	9,098	—	—
Black	732	3,167	281	—	2,303	—	—	—
	(0.91)	(0.76)	(0.73)		(0.71)			
Total								
White	$7,200	$13,654	$2,683	5,983	8,737	17,427	5,078	10,244
Black	4,375	9,109	1,991	5,967	5,880	12,738	4,009	9,467
	(0.61)	(0.67)	(0.74)	(1.00)	(0.67)	(0.73)	(0.79)	(0.93)

[a]Ratio of black to white earnings in parentheses.
[b]Data not available.
[c]Nondomestic workers only.
Source: U.S. Bureau of the Census 1970, Table 50; 1981 Table 61.

449

tunity for job experience, past discriminatory practices, and so on) and less than half a result of contemporary forces being directly reproduced within capitalist enterprises (and which reflect the continued reproduction of castelike structures). It is clear, then, at least for the 1960s, that although blacks had been largely integrated into a single homogeneous industrial working class, significant remnants of the older castelike structures remain.

The role of strong unions in lessening the income gap between black and white workers should be stressed. In 1970 nonwhite males not in labor unions averaged 62 percent the income of nonunionized white men, while nonwhite men in unions averaged 83 percent that of white men. For blue-collar workers only, the comparable figures were 72 percent and 90 percent respectively (M. Reich 1981, p. 273). A study on the effect of unionization on black and white annual earnings in 1972 found that unions (even after controlling for industry characteristics) resulted in approximately a 17 percent increase of income for whites, and in approximately 40 percent increase in income for blacks (Mitchell 1980, p. 100). Where unions were strong, the black-white differential was relatively small. In the automobile industry (UAW) black male median earnings in 1969 were 0.84 of white, iron and steel (USWA) 0.83, primary nonferrous metals (USWA) 0.82, and rubber production (URWA) 0.78. This compares to industries with predominantly craft unions, weak unions, or no unions at all. For example, in furniture and fixtures the ratio was 0.69, in printing and publishing 0.68, and in professional and photographic equipment 0.67 (Perlo 1975, p. 207). It is clear that unions operate to reduce the black-white earnings differential. Unions make occupational stratification more difficult for capital to institute as well as undermine the buffer role that blacks have traditionally played (through such practices as seniority and insistence on equal pay for equal work).

It should be noted that the percentage of all employed blacks who are in trade unions is *higher* than the proportion of whites. In 1972 blacks were 12.4 percent of all trade union members, while they made up 11.6 percent of the labor force (*U.S. News and World Report*, January 22, 1973, p. 76). This is as one would expect given the disproportionate concentration of blacks in the basic industries that are organized by industrial unions.

Between 1964 and 1974 the ratio of black to white family income for those families in which *both* a husband and a wife were present rose from 0.62 to 0.75, a disappearance of one-third of the income gap in just ten years. This trend did not reflect changes in the differential probability of white and black wives working (this differential in fact decreased significantly between these years). Meanwhile, black two-parent families with a working wife had an income of 0.64 that of two-parent white families in 1964 and 0.77 in 1974 (these trends in good part reflect the considerable improvement in the earnings position of black women in relation to white women that occurred during this period; U.S. Bureau of the Census 1979a, p. 39). The black/white family income ratios vary considerably with age, reflecting a radical decline in economic discrimination. In 1974, in families where both the wife and husband had earnings and in which the husband was under age 35, the black/white earnings ratio nationally was 0.91, and in the North and West 1.01. These ratios are up from 0.71 and 0.88 respectively in 1959 (U.S. Bureau of the Census 1979a, p. 44).

In 1950 18 percent of black families did not have a husband present. This had risen to 35 percent by 1975. Meanwhile, the comparable white statistics rose from 9 percent to 11 percent. The median income of single-mother black families declined from 52 percent that of black families with a husband present in 1964, to 42 percent in 1974. In both years it was 32 percent that of median income of "male headed" white families (U.S. Bureau of the Census 1979a, pp. 30, 103). It would seem that the lack of job opportunities in the central cities combined with the ability of black women in the ghettos to subsist with the Aid to Families with Dependent Children and other welfare programs of the state has made them in good part economically independent of the often unemployed or semiemployed ghetto men. At the same time, this crystallizes their extreme poverty.

CLASS DIFFERENTIATION AMONG BLACKS

Traditionally blacks were a highly class homogeneous group, first as slaves, then as sharecroppers and domestics in the South, and then, in the first generation of migration to the North, as workers in the menial services, domestic labor, and the lowest level industrial jobs. While the majority of blacks remained part of the manual working class, in the 1960s and 1970s blacks experienced considerable class differentiation. A significant black salaried petty bourgeoisie developed that closed most of the economic gap with the equivalent category of whites, while at the same time a large and rapidly growing black underclass (composed of those who are not regularly employed) emerged in the central cities. Out of traditionally class homogeneous blacks *three* distinct and qualitatively different black social classes appear to be crystallizing: a privileged black petty bourgeoisie, a black industrial proletariat, and a black urban underclass.

The Black Petty Bourgeoisie

The consequence of the crystallization of the caste status of blacks in the last years of the nineteenth century was the formation of a small traditional petty bourgeoisie which performed services for blacks that whites considered degrading, e.g., undertakers, barbers, school teachers, journalists, ministers as well as some small retail shopkeepers. This "black bourgeoisie" came to have an interest of sorts in the maintenance of the system of segregation since it both guaranteed them a protected clientele and resulted in their becoming the leaders of "the Negro community" (see Frazier 1957).

In the 1970s there remained a handful of black-owned small family businesses and a miniscule number of black capitalists. In 1972 there were a total of 195,000 black-owned businesses in the United States (1.5 percent of all firms), of which only 1.6 percent had any paid employees at all (U.S. Bureau of the Census 1979a, p. 78). In 1969 black firms accounted for about one-fourth of one percent of both total sales and total employment of all firms in the United States. Black-owned businesses remain largely concentrated in black ghettos and are mostly in the services and the retail trades (Perlo 1975, p. 181). In 1969, 7 percent of the total receipts of black firms (compared to 39 percent of those of all firms) were in manufacturing. Sixty-three percent of the receipts of all black firms were in retail and services (compared to 28 percent of all firms). There were only 347 black-owned businesses with sales of a million or more a year, with combined sales of $877 million, about the norm for a single medium-sized U.S. corporation. Only one black-owned nonfinancial firm had more than 500 employees. There were five nonfinancial businesses with sales of $20 million or more; *MoTown Records*, the largest, grossed $46 million. The largest black-owned bank, the Independence Bank of Chicago, had assets of $56 million. The two largest black-owned companies are insurance companies, each of which had over 1,000 employees in 1969. The richest, North Carolina Mutual, had assets of $136 million (the largest white-owned insurance company had assets 157 times as large). The fiftieth largest white-owned insurance company had assets larger than *all* 41 black-owned insurance companies put together (Perlo 1975, pp. 182-83). It is clear that business ownership, both petty bourgeois and capitalist, plays an insignificant role among blacks.

With the continuing growth of supermarkets, chain stores, franchises, and so forth, most independent black businessmen, always in an extremely marginal economic position, have suffered disproportionately, being reduced to little more than a few funeral homes, restaurants, and other establishments providing still segregated services. However, in the 1960s and 1970s a new petty bourgeoisie of professional (and increasingly administrative) blacks employed by the major corporations and the state rapidly expanded, surplanting the earlier predominant traditional petty bourgeoisie as the economically privileged class among blacks (see Wilson 1978, chap. 6).

Largely in response to the riots and the civil rights movement of the 1960s, and the potential threat raised by "black power" in the U.S. military, in order to secure the support of the increasingly organized and politically active black population, a series of civil rights (voting and public accommodations) acts were passed, and a series of affirmative action programs for educational and economic institutions implemented. These largely federally initiated programs have mostly affected the emergent black new petty bourgeoisie, opening many doors into the middle levels of the corporations and the state. Although the abolition of the Jim Crow system of segregated public accommodations technically affected all blacks equally, in fact its abolition benefited those blacks with sufficient money to afford good restaurants, hotels, and so forth much more than the impoverished central-city blacks who continued using the same run down neighborhood facilities as before, and likewise with affirmative action programs. Although technically all occupations are equally affected, those blacks able to qualify for the rapidly expanding salaried white-collar positions, especially in the professions and administration, secure most of the benefit. Black industrial workers concentrated in the higher paying semiskilled and unskilled jobs that are only slowly expanding, and where consequently labor supply is greater than demand, benefit relatively little (there are relatively few new openings and very limited promotional opportunities even for those with the formal qualifications). The ghetto underclass is for the most part not affected at all by affirmative action. The poor quality of ghetto schools and the lack of decent paying job opportunities in their highly segregated areas, makes "equal access" to college, apprenticeship programs, or the professions a rather cruel joke.

The combination of the rapidly growing demand of the corporations for white-collar and middle level professional and managerial people and the state affirmative action programs has been a boon to the new black petty bourgeoisie. The corporations have since 1965 made a major effort to recruit, hire, and promote talented and educated blacks. Federal requirements that government contractors must have an affirmative action program together with the corporations' attempt to recruit ever more qualified people has made minority hiring an explicit goal of most major corporations. The reality of these radically changed hiring policies is reflected in the statistics on corporate recruiting at predominantly black college campuses. In 1960 corporate recruiters averaged just four visits a year per college; in 1965 they averaged 50 and by 1970 they averaged 297 (Wilson 1978, pp. 100-1).

Increased class differentiation among blacks since the 1960s is reflected in income distribution trends. While in 1969 the total income received by the highest income fifth of nonwhite families (roughly the black middle class plus skilled workers) was 2.72 times the total income received by the lowest 40 percent of nonwhite families with the least income, by 1978 it had risen to 3.24 times (see Table 11.8). In both years the internal differentiation among blacks was significantly greater than that among whites. In 1969 the top income fifth of white families earned only 2.16 times more than the bottom two-fifths, while in 1978, it was 2.33 times more. While the gap between the middle class and the poor is growing among both blacks and whites, it is growing more rapidly among blacks.*

The black middle class has made steady progress in closing the income gap with white families since 1947. While in 1947 the highest income fifth of black families earned only 58 percent as much as the highest income fifth of white families, by 1978 they were earning 76 percent as much.† Meanwhile, the relative progress of poorer working class families was much less. While in 1947 they earned 49 percent as much as the poorest 40 percent of white families, in 1978 they earned 59 percent as much. The economic effects of racist structures are clearly greater for the poorer segments of the blacks.

The black petty bourgeoisie has benefited enormously from the unprecedented job opportunities that have been opened to it since the 1950s. While in 1960 college-educated blacks were still largely excluded from corporate employment as professionals and administrators, these careers have been opened up since that time. The net difference in income at various educational levels in 1960 was greater for those with four or more years of college than at any other educational level (Wenger 1980, p. 64). But by 1969 black men aged 25-29 with a college degree were earning 83 percent as much as their white counterparts, while those with just a high school degree were earning 77 percent as much. In 1977 black male college graduates in this same age-group were earning 93 percent as much as whites (while high school graduates actually deteriorated to 73 percent as much as their white equivalents). Full-time, year-round employed

---

*It should be noted that since Asians (also classified as nonwhites) are heavily and increasingly middle class, the equivalent ratio for *blacks only* would not be as extreme.

†The scarcity of high incomes among middle class blacks as well as the scarcity of upper middle class and capitalist class blacks is reflected in the fact that in 1969 8 out of 1,000 white families as compared to one out of every 1,000 black families earned $50,000 or over a year (Perlo 1975, p. 18).

TABLE 11.8: Ratio of the Income Received by the Top 20 Percent of Families to Income Received by the Bottom 40 Percent

| | Ratio of Total Income Received by the Top Fifth to That of the Bottom 40 percent | | Income at Upper Limit of Selected Income Fifths | | | | Ratio of Nonwhite to White Income: Upper Limit of Income Fifths | |
| | | | Nonwhites | | Whites | | Second (Bottom 40 percent) | Fourth (Upper 20 percent) |
	Whites	Nonwhites	Second	Fourth	Second	Fourth		
1947	2.40	3.08	$1,319	$ 2,921	$ 2,692	$ 5,052	0.49	0.58
1959	2.24	3.24	2,180	5,300	$ 4,872	8,600	0.45	0.62
1964	2.26	3.00	3,100	7,000	$ 5,800	10,500	0.53	0.67
1969	2.16	2.72	5,000	10,920	$ 8,375	15,021	0.60	0.73
1974	2.24	3.03	6,548	15,868	$11,266	21,000	0.58	0.76
1978	2.33	3.24	9,081	22,195	$15,433	29,332	0.59	0.76

Sources: U.S. Bureau of the Census 1979a, pp. 34, 35; 1980c, Table 13; Wilson 1980, p. 173.

black female college graduates (of all ages) were in 1977 earning slightly *more* than their white counterparts (Wilson 1980, pp. 177-78).

Older black college graduates continue to be concentrated in those relatively lower paying occupations where pre-1960s discrimination had assigned them, e.g., teaching at predominantly black schools in social welfare agencies and the segregated services. But the younger generation of black college graduates is for the first time entering in significant numbers into high-paying fields with good possibilities for advancement, such as finance, accounting, management, engineering, and the physical sciences. This suggests that as the cohort of 1960s and 1970s black college graduates proceeds through their life cycle, the differential with white administrators and professionals will continue to diminish.

By the mid-1970s the percentage of black college students in the United States approximated the percentage of blacks in the general population. Of all college students in 1978, 10.4 percent were black. This contrasts with 6.4 percent in 1960 and 7.0 percent in 1970 (U.S. Department of Commerce 1980, p. 159). In 1965, 9.0 percent of blacks aged 20-24 were enrolled in school as compared to 20.2 percent of whites. But by 1978, 19.5 percent of blacks in this age bracket as compared to 21.7 percent of whites were in school (U.S. Department of Commerce 1980, p. 141).

The growth of the black petty bourgeoisie (as well as higher paid workers) is reflected in the growing proportion of all blacks living in the suburbs (rather than in cities or rural areas where traditionally they were overwhelmingly concentrated). In 1980, 6.5 percent of the suburban population of the United States was black (compared to 4.7 percent in 1970). In Washington, D.C., the 1980 figure was 16.7 percent, Atlanta 13.5 percent, Los Angeles 9.6 percent, Philadelphia 8.1 percent, and New York 7.6 percent—in 1970 these figures were respectively 8.3 percent, 8.4 percent, 6.2 percent, 6.7 percent, and 5.9 percent (New York *Times*, May 31, 1981, p. 16).

THE BLACK EXCLUDED POPULATION

While petty bourgeois blacks are rapidly improving their economic situation both in relationship to the black average and to the white petty bourgeoisie, the black excluded population in the central cities is losing ground in relation to both the black petty bourgeoisie and industrial working class *and* to the white average. Poverty has become endemic as a growing class of permanently unemployed blacks is created in the urban ghettos.

Labor Force Participation

In the pre-World War II period, when blacks were still concentrated in Southern agriculture, both black men and women had a higher probability of being in the labor force (either employed or actively looking for work) than whites. The contrast between black women and white women is particularly sharp. In 1910 the proportion of black women who were in the labor force was 2.75 times larger than the percentage of white women, and in 1930 it was 1.95 times as large (see Table 11.9). Black women traditionally worked outside of the home (in both the cotton fields and as domestics) while white women (once they were married) were generally full-time housewives. In the 1970s the differential between black and white women virtually disappeared as the occupational structure of these two groups converged, and on the other, the factors that excluded black people from the labor force came to balance out the greater need of (poorer) black women (both wives and single women) to work. The availability of state support (e.g., Aid to Families with Dependent Children, Food programs) after the 1930s also gave poor single and black women a subsistence alternative to domestic, menial service and field labor.

After World War II the percentage of black men in the labor force for the first time became lower than that of whites—reflecting the increasing exclusion of blacks, a significant number of whom became trapped by the displacement of unskilled service and industrial jobs from the inner cities. In 1970, 67 percent of black men over 16 were employed or actively seeking work compared to 74 percent of whites—a differential of 0.91.

TABLE 11.9: Percentage of Persons in the Civilian Labor Force

| | Whites | | Blacks | | Ratio Black/White | |
	Men	Women	Men	Women	Men	Women
1910	81	20	87	55	1.07	2.75
1930	76	20	80	39	1.05	1.95
1940	79	24	80	38	1.01	1.58
1960	75	34	70	42	0.93	1.24
1970	74	41	67	47	0.91	1.15

Note: Data for total labor force (including armed forces) for 1910 and 1930 are for persons aged 10 and over; 1940 and 1960 for persons aged 14 and over; for 1970 for persons aged 16 and over.

Sources: U.S. Bureau of the Census 1979a, p. 65.

In 1975, 91 percent of nonwhite men recorded by the U.S. Bureau of the Census in the 25-44 year-old group as compared to 96 percent of white men were in the civilian labor force. In 1960 these figures were 96 percent for nonwhites and 98 percent for whites, indicating a significant relative slippage out of the labor force for nonwhites among men in the prime of their work life. In 1960 the labor force participation rate of men aged 20-34 was about the same for nonwhite men as for white men and for those aged 35-54 it was about three percentage points lower for nonwhites. Among those aged 55-64, 77 percent of white men and 69 percent of nonwhite men were in the labor force in 1975, and among those aged 18 and 19, 73 percent of whites and only 58 percent of nonwhites were in the labor force, while among those aged 20-24, 86 percent of whites and 78 percent of nonwhites were. All of these latter differentials are much greater than they were in 1960 (U.S. Department of the Census 1979a, p. 67).

Unemployment

Before the Second World War black unemployment was actually less than white unemployment, reflecting the full utilization of blacks in semifeudal Southern agriculture, a system that was relatively immune from unemployment cycles and the necessity to have a significant reserve army of labor to keep wages down.* Political mechanisms combined with the disorganization of black sharecroppers and laborers sufficed to keep profits high in the semifeudal South. In 1930 the black/white unemployment ratio was 0.90 (Wilson 1978, p. 89). But with the forced displacement of blacks off the land and into service and industrial employment in the cities (i.e., participation in fully capitalist relations of production), they came to disproportionately serve as a reserve army of labor (putting pressure on those with jobs to keep wages down as well as a source of new recruits in times of rapid industrial growth). This was because of their newness to capitalist employment, lack of industrial skills, and economic and political disorganization (a product of their former semiserf status). In 1940 the black/white unemployment ratio was 1.2 and in the 1948-50 period about 1.7 (Wilson 1978, p. 89; Table 11.10).

---

*Large numbers of the excluded black ghetto population (who are not reported as part of the labor force) are part of the "underground economy" dealing largely in illegal services and commodities. (i.e., prostitution, gambling, drug dealing). It has been estimated, for example, that there are about 100,000 New York City blacks working in the numbers racket (Friedlander 1972, p. 180).

From the mid-1950s to the end of the 1960s the ratio of nonwhite to white unemployment stabilized at around 2.1, reflecting both the rapid migration into the lowest level urban jobs forced by expulsion from Southern agriculture and the displacement of urban unskilled jobs out of the central cities. In the 1970s, in the face of generally rising unemployment rates associated with the stagnation of American capitalism in this decade, the ratio of nonwhite/white unemployment first declined to 1.9 during the first half of the decade then rose to 2.2 during the 1976-80 period. Though significant new black migration to Northern cities ceased and blacks became increasingly better organized economically and politically because the displacement of urban menial jobs continued, black unemployment continued to be much higher than white.

The greater unemployment rates of blacks are in part a reflection of their disproportionate concentration in the less skilled jobs (service workers, nonfarm laborers, and operatives, except transport), which have the highest overall unemployment rates (for whites as well as blacks), and partly a result of past and present discrimination within broad occupations where blacks tend to be "the last hired and the first fired" (see Table 11.4). The black/white differential is considerably greater in the services and in white-collar work (professional women aside) than in blue-collar work. This reflects capital's central use of blacks in industry as well as the large number of urban blacks who have marginal positions in the services. The very high differential among professional and clerical and sales workers in good part reflects the expansion in the 1970s of black education, which has trained a large number of blacks for such work, and the resultant higher unemployment rates of new employees in these professions compared to those with seniority.

TABLE 11.10: Male Unemployment Rates for Persons Aged 16 and Over (Period Averages)

	Nonwhite	White	Nonwhite/White Ratio
1948–50	7.9%	4.7%	1.7
1951–55	6.8	3.5	1.9
1956–60	9.9	4.6	2.2
1961–65	10.4	4.9	2.1
1966–70	7.2	3.5	2.1
1971–75	10.5	5.5	1.9
1976–80	11.7	5.3	2.2

Sources: U.S. Bureau of the Census 1979a, p. 69; U.S. Department of Commerce 1981a, p. 407.

TABLE 11.11: Occupational Unemployment Rates by Race and Sex, 1977

	White		Black		Ratio of Black/White	
	Men	Women	Men	Women	Men	Women
Professional and Technical	2.1%	3.8%	6.1%	5.1%	2.9	1.3
Sales workers	3.8	6.3	9.2	19.6	2.4	3.1
Clerical workers	4.3	5.6	10.8	11.9	2.5	2.1
Craft and kindred	5.3	6.7	8.8	—*	1.7	—
Operatives (excluding transport)	7.4	10.8	11.8	16.5	1.6	1.5
Transport operatives	6.3	5.7	8.5	—	1.3	—
Nonfarm laborers	11.2	9.6	16.4	—	1.5	—
Service workers	6.3	7.6	13.7	12.6	2.2	1.7
All civilian workers	5.5	7.3	13.1	14.8	2.4	2.0
Experienced labor force	5.0	6.3	11.1	12.4	2.2	2.0

Source: U.S. Bureau of the Census 1979a, p. 214.

Among younger blacks the differential is considerably greater than the average, while among older blacks it is less. In 1978 for those aged 16-19 the nonwhite male unemployment rate (the ratio of those actively looking for work to those in the civilian labor force) was 34.4 percent (2.5 times the equivalent white rate) and for those aged 20-24 it was 20.0 percent (2.6 times the white rate). But for nonwhite men aged 55-65 it was 4.4 percent (the lowest for any age group), only 1.7 times the equivalent white rate (U.S. Department of Commerce 1980, p. 396). These extremely high official unemployment rates (which count only those actively looking for work) considerably underestimate the actual proportion of young blacks without jobs.

The difficulty of finding employment as a youth leaves an indelible impression on blacks, often resulting after a few years of unemployment in demoralization and integration into illegal and marginal "hustling" activities (with the adoption of their associated "lumpen" value system as well as a high probability of drug addiction), and thus more or less permanent inability to obtain full-time regular employment. Facing few job prospects, ghetto black youths have a very high rate of dropping out of high school (as well as little motivation to learn while in school). In 1978 New York, Chicago, Detroit, and St. Louis urban school districts all reported a black high school dropout rate of about 50 percent (the national average for all groups is about 22 percent) (New York Times, March 14, 1981, p. 10).

Studies have shown that the primary immediate reason for the exceptionally high youth unemployment among blacks in the central cities is the general lack of jobs in these areas, not direct discrimination in favor of white youths of similar characteristics (see Friedlander 1972). Because there are so few jobs for the relatively unskilled in the central cities, an elaborate system of job qualifications and protections has emerged. Black competitors for the few available new jobs are thus screened out because they lack sufficient education, experience, or skills. Youths who succeed at getting an education face barriers of apprenticeship, certification, licensing, union membership, and so on. All these barriers instituted by employers and supported by those who already have jobs, make it very difficult for the unskilled and poor (black *or* white) concentrated in central cities to secure employment.

The Black Underclass

The declining labor force participation rate of blacks as well as the constancy of the high black to white unemployment rate differential and the extremely high unemployment among black urban youths reflects the forces that are creating a rapidly growing excluded population among blacks in the United States (among whom poverty and joblessness is institutionalized).

In 1977, 29 percent of all blacks were below the poverty level, compared with 8 percent of whites. In central cities in the United States the overall household poverty rate (for all "races") was 15 percent as compared to 7 percent for metropolitan areas outside of central cities. In 1960, 51.4 percent of all blacks in the United States lived in central cities compared to 30.0 percent of whites. While this rose to 58.2 percent of all blacks in 1970, it declined to 27.9 percent for all whites (U.S. Department of Commerce 1980, pp. 23, 463).

In 1978 67 percent of all blacks interviewed by the U.S. Department of Labor who were not in the labor force (and not in school) reported that they did not want a job, while this was true for 82 percent of whites. Among blacks 11 percent of those not in the labor force reported that they were ill or disabled, compared to 7 percent of whites. Among blacks 17 percent reported that they wanted a job but were not looking (apparently because they were discouraged) as compared to only 8 percent of whites (U.S. Department of Commerce 1980a, p. 397). Blacks are disproportionately concentrated in the underclass because: they are more likely to be chronically ill and disabled; they have greater difficulty finding work; and they have given up looking for work and have disproportionately become permanently unemployable.

The typical underclass black family now consists of a mother and her children. In 1977, 71 percent of all black families below the poverty level were of this type compared to 40 percent of white families (U.S. Bureau of the Census 1979b, Table 27). Further, black single-mother families are disproportionately concentrated in the underclass, 53 percent of all single-mother black families were below the poverty level as compared to 25 percent of single mother white families, 14 percent of two-parent black families, and 5 percent of two-parent white families (U.S. Bureau of Census 1979a, p. 50). The pattern of relations between the sexes in the underclass appears to be increasingly one of living together in serial monogamy, or having more casual relationships. Since a large proportion of black men in the poor areas of the central cities where single-mother families are concentrated are unemployed, not in the labor force, or hold temporary jobs, but do not report to census takers or show up in U.S. Department of Labor surveys, it can be inferred that the *actual* proportion of *single men* below the poverty line (at least as measured by wage and salary income) roughly corresponds to the proportion of single-mother black families at this level.

In 1978 there were approximately 200,000 black men in federal and state prisons and local jails in the United States (Department of Justice 1981, Tables 6.9, 6.19). This represents roughly 2.8 percent of the age 16-65 black male population. In 1978 41 percent of the federal prison population was nonwhite (U.S. Department of Commerce 1980, p. 198). In 1978 46 percent of all the arrests in the United States by police at *all* levels for crimes of violence were of black people, as were 31 percent of all arrests for property crimes. This includes 49 percent of all arrests for murder, 59 percent of all arrests for robbery, 53 percent of arrests for prostitution, and 69 percent of arrests for gambling. On the other hand, only 27 percent of arrests for motor vehicle theft, 24 percent of arrests for embezzlement, and 33 percent of arrests for forgery and counterfeiting were of blacks (U.S. Department of Justice 1981, Table 4.7). While it is true that blacks are somewhat more likely to be arrested, convicted, and to serve time than whites at the *same economic level*, most of the black-white differential is due to the fact that blacks are much more heavily concentrated in the underclass than whites. Whether or not poor blacks actually commit more "crimes" than poor whites, being imprisoned results in making ex-prisoners less likely to live by regular employment and more likely to become integrated into a criminal subculture. The 2.8 percent rate of black incarceration (compared to the white rate of roughly 0.4 percent) means a significant percent of blacks have "spent time" at one point or another in their lives.

It is clear that in relative terms the black underclass is significantly larger than the white underclass and the black underclass is growing rapidly. This is the case at the same time as the black petty bourgeoisie is growing and quickly closing the remaining gap with the white petty bourgeoisie *and* as the majority of blacks remain manual workers concentrated in the basic industries.

Life Expectancy and Exclusion

The large black excluded population lives under conditions of duress. Their perpetual poverty is manifested in virtually all aspects of their lives, including much higher rates of mental disorder, hypertension, inadequate diet, poor housing and medical care, and extremely high crime rates. The disproportionate concentration of blacks among both the urban excluded populations and among the manual working class results in much higher death rates (and significantly lower life expectancy) among blacks than among whites. Blacks between the ages of 25 and 44 in 1975 had a probability of dying at a rate approximately 2.4 times greater than whites of the same age bracket. Blacks aged 45-64 die about 1.7 times as frequently as whites. Nonwhite infants die with twice the probability of whites. Overall, the age-adjusted death rate of blacks (the annual death rate per 100,000) was 27 percent higher in 1975 than it was for whites. This is a slight decline from 1960, when it was 30 percent higher. This means that 21 percent of all blacks who died in 1975 would not have died had they been white (23 percent in 1960, and 30 percent in 1940). In 1975, 233,000 nonwhite people died in the United States; 50,000 would not have died had they been white. (See Table 11.12.)

The differential mortality rate between whites and blacks is caused primarily by the concentration of black people in the manual working class and underclass, which have much higher mortality rates than do the middle classes. A study done of mortality rates in Chicago in 1960 showed that among males in the lowest socioeconomic districts, 65 percent of black deaths and 55 percent of white deaths would not have occurred had the same age-specific death rates applied to them as applied to suburban white males, i.e., the class differential accounts for at least 85 percent of the excess black male (aged 25-64) deaths. The equivalent figure for the poorest black women aged 25-64 was 71 percent. The comparable class effects for the next highest socioeconomic level were 66 percent for men and 56 percent for women. For the middle level socioeconomic districts 96 percent of the male differential but only 40 percent of the female differential is attributable to the class factor (see Table 11.13). It is

TABLE 11.12: Differential Death Rates by Race (deaths per 100,000 population)

Age	1940			1960			1975		
	Nonwhites	Whites	Nonwhite/White	Nonwhite	Whites	Nonwhite/White	Nonwhites	Whites	Nonwhite/White
Under one year	89.2	50.3	1.77	46.3	23.6	1.96	27.7	14.1	1.96
25–34	7.9	2.5	3.16	3.2	1.2	2.67	3.0	1.2	2.50
35–44	12.4	4.4	2.82	6.3	2.6	2.42	5.3	2.3	2.30
45–54	22.9	9.5	2.41	13.4	6.9	1.94	10.8	6.0	1.80
55–64	35.3	21.1	1.67	27.7	16.3	1.70	21.8	14.2	1.54
Overall age-adjusted death rate	19.0	13.4	1.42	12.7	9.8	1.30	10.4	8.2	1.27

Source: U.S. Bureau of the Census 1979a, pp. 123.

thus clear that especially for men, most of the effect of racism on mortality in fact manifests the class position of blacks. The residual in the Chicago study would seem to be caused by a combination of the following: first, blacks within each of the five basic socioeconomic categories are disproportionately concentrated at the lower reaches of each, thus even more of the death rate differential is attributable to class than the aggregate five-category class schema reveals; and second, even at exactly the same socioeconomic level, blacks are subjected to somewhat greater stress because of white chauvinism, discrimination in housing resulting in less safe and healthy neighborhoods, a greater probability of being put into more dangerous and less healthy jobs, and so on. But it is clear that these latter factors are secondary compared to the first in their effect on increasingly mortality, especially for men.

Causes of the Growth of the Black Underclass

Since the 1950s industry has been moving from the central cities (at the same time blacks have become increasingly concentrated there). The corporations have migrated to the suburbs, to the cities of the South and Southwest, and overseas in search of lower costs.

TABLE 11.13: **Percentage of Deaths in the Specified Group That Would Not Have Occurred as Compared with the Age-Specific Death Rate for Whites of the Same Sex in the Highest Socio-economic Districts for Ages 25-64 in Chicago, 1960**

	Males			Females		
	a	b	a/b	c	d	c/d
	Whites	nonwhites		whites	nonwhites	
SE 1	55%	65%	0.85	52%	73%	0.71
SE 2	35	53	0.66	35	63	0.56
SE 3	26	27	0.96	21	52	0.40
SE 4	14	—*	—	5	—	—
SE 5	18	—	—	2	—	—
Suburban ring	0	—	—	8	—	—

*Data not available.
Source: Kitagawa and Hauser 1973, p. 173.

In 1960, 63.0 percent of total employment in the 15 largest metropolitan areas of the United States was in the central cities. In 1970, 52.4 percent. The absolute number of jobs in these 15 central cities actually declined by 7 percent between these two years. In 1960 there were 1 million manufacturing jobs in New York City, in 1980 there were half a million. In 1980 in New York City there were only 9,000 new jobs openings in industry (and 17,000 in the services). This compares to 37,000 high school dropouts in the same year (New York Times, March 14, 1981, p. 10; Perlo 1975, p. 109).

Meanwhile, the percentage of the population of central cities of over 1 million that was black increased from 19 percent in 1960 to 28 percent in 1975 (U.S. Bureau of the Census 1979a, p. 15). The displacement of jobs from the central cities that has been occurring since the 1950s thus disproportionately and increasingly affects the crystallization of a growing black underclass. The economic and social condition of this underclass is worsening over time as the cities continue to decay, jobs are lost, and state programs to retrain and revitalize the urban economy are cut back. Blacks have suffered threefold: first, with their experience as slaves and semiserfs in the cotton plantation system of the South; second, after being expelled from this system, with a term as menial industrial and service labor in the cities; and finally, (for a large and growing minority of blacks) exclusion from the production economy as a redundant population in the decaying central cities.

What accounts for the tendency of capitalist enterprises to increasingly reject black labor in favor of newer immigrant workers (and overseas production)? A number of potential explanations can be (and have been) offered. It might, in part, be the case that the black experience of slavery and semiserfdom in the South produced certain work attitudes in the black migrants that capital found less useful than those of new workers coming from more traditional peasant relations in eastern and southern Europe (earlier) or Latin America (later). For example, it might be the case that the black response to slavery and semiserfdom was to develop the defense of resisting the development of an "internal motivation" to work, instead waiting for direct external controls (see Genovese 1967, chap. 2). This attitude, together with the lack of skills to obtain middle class status (such as many peasants from more traditional peasant relations of production brought with them), could have resulted in blacks working less hard and with less drive at other than the simple tasks that could be closely supervised. The extent that such a delayed ("present absent") slavery effect has operated within the post-World War II industrial system depends on the extent to which cultural values and work habits are resistent to transformation by the organization of capitalist enterprise (and have a life of their own). There would seem to be too much evidence of full integration of large masses of black workers into all levels of industrial employment throughout the industrial heartland of the United States (with every indication that their labor is exploited as efficiently as that of the whites who work alongside them) to give too much weight to this factor.

It might also be argued that the increasing rejection of black labor is a result of fundamental changes in the technology of contemporary industry and/or the new possibilities of mobility of industrial capital that just happened to have occurred during the period when blacks were the primary sources of menial laborers for the system. It could be the case that rapid changes in technique (automation, the virtual elimination of purely physical labor, and so on) occurred more rapidly in the post-World War II period than before, thereby leaving large masses of untrained blacks (suited for simple labor) without jobs or the realistic prospect of achieving the proper training for the new types of jobs that were opening up as machine operatives. Given the previous experience of industrial capital with training peasants to work in steel mills, automobile assembly lines, textile factories and at a whole range of "semiskilled" jobs involving running machinery, and given that the post-World War II trend has involved just as much job reorganization and creating new skills as the earlier period, it is unlikely that changes in the nature of work had much to do with the displacement of blacks. Likewise, the fact that Latin American peasants (who have considerably less industrial experience than blacks) are increasingly preferred over urban blacks for such tasks would seem to show that such an effect has not operated as an important force.

It could be argued that because of the greater availability of cheap reliable labor in Mexico, Korea, Taiwan, Texas, Southern California, Georgia (or the suburbs) or because the corporations now have an international perspective, they more readily move to where labor is cheaper and more malleable, and that again blacks just happened to be the primary source of menial laborers when this change occurred. This is unlikely. Capital has always had a tendency to move to where it could maximize its profits (the logic of profit maximization dictates that low cost producers grow while high cost producers go bankrupt). For example, the textile industry moved out of New England to the South after the Civil War. There does not appear to be anything different in the post-World War II period than before in these regards.

Explanations in terms of greater residential discrimination against blacks, inadequate public transport in the central cities, lack of information about job availability, difficulty of relocating, greater prejudice of employers, and so on all beg the question as to *why* such factors would be allowed to obstruct the profitable employment of blacks, if, in fact, capitalist enterprises could earn more or as much from exploiting their labor as that of other groups of immigrants. In the past, such factors did not obstruct the massive hiring of blacks, nor did they obstruct the hiring of the Irish, Poles, or Italians before them; nor further do they now obstruct the hiring of Mexicans and other Latins (who certainly have greater problems with transportation and information about jobs and who probably have as great a problem with prejudice and residential concentration as do blacks).

More likely explanations of the increasing redundancy of blacks in working class occupations (i.e., the rapid growth of the black underclass and the shift to the employment of first-generation Latin immigrants instead of second- and third-generation blacks in Northern cities) are: the fact that from 1914 to the 1960s blacks were continually the major source of new recruits for the most menial jobs of industrial capitalism; and since the 1930s there has been a qualitative alteration in the level of state support available to the poor, a factor that has significantly altered the incentive structure among the lowest levels of the working class (of all ethnic groups).*

---

*It should be noted that in 1972 public welfare assistance plus unemployment insurance, workmen's compensation, veterans benefits, social security, and so on accounted for 15.9 percent of total black income (compared to 8.8 percent of total white income). The ratio of income from state welfare benefits to wages and salaries was 0.20 in the case of blacks and 0.13 in the case of whites (Perlo 1975, p. 153). Although more of total black than of white income in 1972 was received in the form of transfer payments from the state, the average per capita benefits received by whites exceeded that received by nonwhites in the same year by 20 percent. Furthermore, the total received by whites exceeded that received by blacks by a factor of 9.3 times. In 1972 whites received $93.1 billion in various social welfare benefits while blacks received $10.0 billion (Perlo 1975, p. 156).

Blacks are heavily overrepresented in those income maintenance programs that are focused on aiding the underclass and poor, e.g., food stamps, Aid to Families with Dependent Children (AFDC), supplemental security income. In 1977, 43 percent of the families receiving AFDC and 27 percent of those receiving supplemental security income were black (U.S. Department of Commerce 1981a, p. 358). It should be noted that it is precisely these programs that have been decreasing in importance as a proportion of the overall state income maintenance policies (and which during the Reagan administration experienced the greatest cuts). For example, public assistance declined from 13.8 percent of all public income maintenance programs in 1970 to 6.9 percent in 1978. Meanwhile, the various federal Social Security programs (which pay out largely on the basis of previous income and, thus, benefit mostly higher income groups, rather than the underclass) increased their share of total cash benefits from all public income maintenance programs from 49.0 percent to 53.3 percent of the total (U.S. Department of Commerce 1981a, p. 335). While Social Security payments have been indexed to the rate of inflation to protect the recipients' living standard, the average monthly payment under the AFDC program declined from $353 to $271 between 1970 and 1979 (in 1979 dollars) (see U.S. Department of Commerce 1981a, p. 354).

The closure of Slavic and southern European immigration, first by World War I in 1914, then by the immigration restriction act of 1924 meant that from that time until the repeal of restrictive immigration policies in 1965 blacks were not "pushed up" out of the most menial occupations by new immigrants (except around New York City by Puerto Ricans). Blacks, thus, served as the source of menial labor for industrial capitalism longer (about 50 years, or two generations) than any other ethnic group. The Irish served for a single generation (concentrated in the 1847-54 period) after the potato famine, as did the eastern and southern Europeans (whose principal migration occurred within a 20-year period (1895-1914).

The *second generation effect*, i.e., the disinclination of the children to adopt their parent's orientation to the "old country" and the resultant willingness to work hard for little money (instead considering themselves entitled to what all other Americans receive) which is manifested by immigrants from peasant relations of production to industrial capitalism everywhere, thus produced a very different result in the case of blacks than in the case of the Irish, Slavs, or Italians. In the case of the latter groups, the second generation's expectation to be treated like any "other Americans," to have a good job, make good money, and live at an "American living standard," working at the norm for "American" labor was largely able to be realized because new ethnic groups were being recruited as the most menial laborers by the time they came of age. In the case of blacks, however, the second generation faced a brick wall. Capitalism was unwilling or unable to bring significant numbers of new menial workers into the system in the 1930s (because of the Depression), during World War II (because of the war), and for 20 years after World War II because of the restrictive immigration policies (maintained beyond their time for reasons of legitimation as well as because large numbers of Southern blacks continued to be available). Capitalism thus persisted in defining the mass of black workers as especially exploitable menial labor, even in the face of the second generation's growing resistance to this definition. The second generation experienced an increasingly painful gap between the affluent industrial America they saw about them (made all the more real by all pervasive television and advertising) and the capitalists' stubborn insistence on keeping them in the most menial low-paying jobs (which were both dignity denying and insufficient to achieve the standard of living that they now came to feel just). They increasingly began to reject their condition both by refusing to accept such jobs except when absolutely necessary, and when accepting such employment by performing inadequately.* This work attitude was in contrast to that

---

*The infusion of government money into the slums of the central cities "to combat poverty," accelerated the growth of an underground economy. High levels of

of their fathers and mothers fresh from the semifeudalism of the South. Their parents had for the most part been happy to get a job on the assembly line where the pay was considerably better than what they had been used to in the South. Thus, the employment of low-paid black menial labor in the post-World War II period became increasingly inefficient for capital. It came to make increasing economic sense to hire Ladinos fresh from the peasantry (who have the traditional work attitudes of first-generation immigrants) and to let the central cities where blacks were increasingly concentrated rot.

Changes in the importance of the legitimation function for stabilizing capitalist society occurred in the 1930s with the institution of basic welfare services (unemployment compensation, Social Security, Aid to Dependent Children, surplus food programs, and so on.) Welfare programs were expanded in the 1960s (e.g., Johnson's war on poverty). Consequently, maintaining oneself at a subsistence level without regular employment as a menial laborer became a possibility in the post-World War II period that had not existed for the second generation of earlier immigrant groups.

While the real threat of starvation would have forced the second generation of previous immigrant groups to buckle under and accept the humiliations of menial employment (or perhaps to lead a revolutionary working class movement against their conditions of labor), the existence of the new state welfare system (food stamps, aid to single mothers, and other "safety nets") assured that very few would actually starve. A growing percentage of young second (and third) generation blacks rejected "dead end," menial, humiliating, low-paid jobs, or performed very poorly in them, knowing they would not starve if they were fired. As a result, capital came to look for new groups of *first-generation* peasant workers who were motivated by the desire to work hard to save money and return to the "old country" (many of whom as "illegals" and noncitizens were not eligible for, or at least did not utilize, the wide range of state subsidies to the poor).

That it is a combination of the second-generation effect, the long-term constancy in source of menial laborers, and state welfare policies that primarily produce secondary exclusion, and not any special or unique characteristics of blacks, is born witness to by a similar phenomena now also occurring among second-generation Puerto Ricans in and around New York City (although, because large-scale

---

burglary and robbery (drug dealing, gambling rackets, prostitution, and so on) exist that provide large numbers of underclass blacks with survival incomes. Many, therefore, do not have to regularly sell their labor to industrial capital, even though they themselves are not directly receiving welfare payments.

Puerto Rican immigration did not begin until the late 1940s, the process is not as advanced as among blacks).

Once industry deserted the central cities and the black underclass subculture of the second and third generation had taken hold in the underclass, there was little incentive for capital to invest in enterprises in these areas (since much more efficient labor is available elsewhere). Further, there was no longer any incentive for capital to support state spending to maintain basic public services or the quality of life in the central cities (especially not in the growing black ghettos) since they were no longer the source of their labor force. Ghetto blacks, thus, increasingly tend to crystallize as a permanently unemployed/unemployable excluded population.

THE RELATIVE SIZE OF THE DIFFERENT CLASSES AMONG BLACKS

In Table 11.14 an attempt is made to roughly estimate both the relative sizes of the three principal classes that appear to be crystallizing among blacks and their relative growth rates over time. The percentages in this table, unlike those in earlier tables, are based on a total for the black adult male population, which includes an estimate for the size of the black underclass not counted by the U.S. Census.

In 1978 for the nation as a whole the ratio of male to female blacks under 14 recorded by the U.S. Bureau of the Census was 1.016 (1.048 for whites), for those aged 14-24, 0.961 (1.024 for whites); for those aged 25-44, 0.842 (0.988 for whites); for those aged 45-54, 0.861 (0.951 for whites); and for those aged 65 and over 0.712 (this latter figure is actually higher than the white equivalent ratio of 0.678—the only cohort where the male/female ratio is higher) (U.S. Department of Commerce 1980a, p. 29). That the black/white differential during working years is a result primary of undercount rather than higher black male differential mortality *and* that the higher ratio among blacks than among whites of retirement age is *not* the result of a minority of black men (the survivors) being more resistant to the causes of mortality that the equivalent minority of white men, but rather a result of black men of retirement age ceasing to avoid census takers as well as draft boards and police agencies (because they now have less to hide and more state welfare benefits to gain) is shown by studies of differential mortality rates. A study done in Chicago in 1960 found that the age-specific death rate for nonwhite men under 65 was 8.1 compared to 6.1 for nonwhite women, a ratio of 1.33, while that for white men was almost twice that of white women (5.0 versus 2.8 per 1,000), a ratio of 1.77 (see Table 9.3).

The estimate of the number of black men not counted by the U.S. Census is taken to be the *average* of: the difference between the number of black men the Census Bureau counts and the number there would be if there were, in fact, as many black men as black women (the Census Bureau finds 85 black men for every 100 black women for the population as a whole); and the difference between the number of black men counted and the number there would be if the sex ratio between black women and black men were, in fact, the same as between white women and white men (92 per 100 women). The first estimate assumes that the differential in the number of black men and women is wholly a result of census undercount, while the second assumes that the difference in the age structure of black men and white men (in relation to women) is totally due to census undercount. Taking the average assumes the truth lies in the middle. Using this method it is estimated that the census undercount of black men of working age in 1977 was 825,000 (and in 1960, 435,000) (see Table 11.14). These estimates are based on the assumption that either all black women are counted, since most tend to have their own apartments and unlike men in their "class" do not fear being known by government agencies; or that no white men avoid census takers. It is also assumed that all those that avoid census takers are in the underclass.

If all black men over 16 who are neither in the civilian labor force (employed or looking for work), in the military, nor in school, in institutions, or over 65 are considered to be in the underclass there were, in addition to those not counted by the U.S. Census, another 670,000 black men in the underclass in 1960 and 853,000 in 1977. If on the other hand, only the number of blacks who would be in the labor force, if the black labor force participation rate were the same as that for whites, are considered to be in the underclass (augmenting those not counted by the U.S. Census) then in 1960 there were 56,000 and in 1977 539,000 additional blacks in this "class." The higher estimate, it must be noted, includes the disabled, those who have legitimately retired early and male homemakers, many of whom should not be categorized as part of the underclass. The lower estimate assumes that there is no white underclass, an equally unrealistic assumption. Again to even out the errors due to these assumptions the average of these two estimates is used to estimate the number of those in the Black underclass who are counted by the U.S. Departments of Commerce and Labor in their official surveys. These averages are 363,000 for 1960 and 696,000 for 1977 (see Table 11.14). Adding these figures to that of the number of black prisoners and the estimates of the black undercount gives a total estimate of 923,000 for the black underclass in 1960 and 1,722,000 for 1977, an increase of 1.87 times.

TABLE 11.14: Estimates of the Size and the Rate of Growth of the Basic Classes among Blacks in the United States, 1960 and 1977 (occupational structure of males aged 16-65)

| | Urban Petty Bourgeoisie (professional and managerial) | Working Class | | | | The Underclass | | | | | | | | Traditional Occupations (Farmers, Farm Workers, and Domestics) |
| | | Urban Industrial Working Class | Service Workers (excluding domestics) | Clerical and Sales | Total Urban Working Class (including Soldiers) | Population Not in Labor Force | | | Not Counted by Census | | | | Estimated Size[a] $\frac{A+B+C+D}{2}+E$ | |
						(A) Excluding Students	(B) If Same as White Rate	$\frac{A+B}{2}$	(C) If Same as White Male Rate	(D) If Same as Black Female Rate	$\frac{C+D}{2}$	(E) Prisoners		
1960	190 (4%)[b]	2,000 (42%)	550 (12%)	220 (5%)	3190 (67%)	670	56	363 (8%)	319	550	435 (9%)	125 (3%)	923 (19%)	440 (9%)
1977	652 (9)	2,952 (42)	846 (12)	440 (6)	4500 (64)	853	539	696 (10)	666	985	825 (12)	200 (3)	1722 (24)	180 (3)
Rate of Growth 1960–1977	3.43	1.48	1.54	2.00	1.41	—[c]	—	1.92	—	—	1.90	1.60	1.87	0.41

a As a percentage of the total number of men aged 16–65 in the four aggregate categories.

b If the size of the black excluded sector in 1977 is computed as the entire population in Table 5.1, it is estimated at 1,500,000 (counting prisoners) or 22 percent of the black population (compared to 6 percent of the white population) (see U.S. Bureau of the Census 1979b, Tables 27, 28).

c Data not available.

Sources: U.S. Department of Commerce 1981a, pp. 196, 198, 374, 394, 417–18; 1966, p. 156; 1967, pp. 21, 111, 218; U.S. Bureau of the Census 1979c, p. 224; U.S. Department of Justice 1980; 1981, Tables 6.9, 6.19.

An alternative procedure can be used to estimate the size of the black underclass (see Table 3.1 to estimate the size of the entire excluded population). This method estimates the black excluded sector as all those black heads of families and female unrelated individuals below the poverty level not in the labor force, less all heads of families below the poverty level not working because they are in school, less all female unrelated individuals below the poverty level not working because they are in school, less all male heads of families not working because they are retired plus the number of male prisoners. This method assumes that the U.S. Bureau of the Census counts all family heads and single black women, that the true number of single black men is equal to the number of single black women, and that only those below the official poverty level should be counted as part of the excluded sector. This method gives the figure of 1.43 million or 22 percent of the black male population in 1977 (see Table 11.4). The slight discrepancy between the two estimates (24 percent and 22 percent) is largely accounted for by the lower estimate's exclusion of all those above the official poverty level from the excluded sector whether or not they regularly work for a living at a legal and reported occupation. It should be noted that only 40 percent of all black men who did not work at all during 1977 were reported as below the poverty level (U.S. Bureau of the Census 1979b, Table 14). Since it is quite legitimate to argue the relative merits of the various operational definitions of the excluded black population, we are probably best advised to estimate its true size as slightly under one-fourth of the total black population (up by roughly 25 percent in *relative* size, i.e., as a proportion of all blacks, between 1960 and 1977).

The only class of blacks to grow more rapidly in this period was the urban petty bourgeoisie (professional and managerials), which increased from 4 percent to 9 percent of the black male population between 1960 and 1977—a growth of 3.4 times in absolute numbers. The overwhelmingly largest group in the black population is the urban working class, which was 67 percent of the total in 1960 and 64 percent in 1977. The urban black proletariat grew by 1.4 times between 1960 and 1977. The largest segment of the black urban working class is industrial workers, which was 42 percent of all black males in both 1960 and in 1977, an increase in absolute terms of 1.5 times (see Table 11.14). It should be noted that the occupations in which blacks were traditionally heavily concentrated—farm laborers, farmers, and domestics—have become virtually insignificant, decreasing from 9 percent to 3 percent of the total between 1960 and 1977.

In summary, considerable class differentiation is occurring among blacks. Three major and distinct social classes are crystallizing, each increasingly differentiated from the others. A significant black new petty bourgeoisie is rapidly developing whose educational and economic attainments have converged with whites of the same class position (this is especially apparent looking at the relative position of younger blacks). Economic discrimination against blacks in the working class has been gradually and consistently declining. Relatively little formal discrimination remains in the basic corporate industrial sector. Most of the occupational and income gap *within* the mainstream working class occupations is a result of *past* discrimination in promotion, hiring, and education, rather than a result of present corporate or state policies. Although considerable class differentiation is occurring, it must be emphasized that blacks are essentially still socially defined as urban menial workers economically central to basic industry in the United States.

The most significant fact about the changing class position of blacks in the United States in the last generation has been the growth and crystallization of a large black excluded population in the central cities. This massive population, one-fourth of all blacks in the late 1970s (and increasing rapidly) threatens to eventually replace industrial labor as the primary class definition of blacks (and, thus, of antiblack racism) within U.S. capitalism. The parallels between the piling up of a redundant (unemployed and increasingly unemployable) black population in the central cities with the piling up of displaced Jews in central Europe in the 1920s and 1930s are ominous. Increasingly the black ghettos are being left to rot with the central cities as a whole suffering a continuing deterioration (capital has little motive to either reproduce its labor force in these areas *or* to legitimate itself among nonproletarians). At the same time the possibilities of underclass blacks (and by the logic of racialism, *all* blacks) becoming scapegoats of the system (and lightening rods for the hostilities of majority group workers and the middle class) grows (especially in the event of a crisis).

The increasing exclusion of poor blacks, like the exclusion of Jews from their traditional economic roles in eastern Europe in the preholocaust period, means that an increasing number of blacks are "redundant," dispensable, not needed for the economic functioning of capitalism. They are, in fact, increasingly a nonproductive drain on resources that could be better spent (from the viewpoint of capital) on productive investment or legitimating the system with its working class. Thus, the level of welfare support of urban blacks can be expected to continue to be cut, for the differentials in life expectancy between poor blacks and the middle class to grow, for the level of violence (individual and group) to increase, and for the black central city populations to become increasingly desperate. The visibility of their responses (e.g., antiwhite rioting) could well result in a popular viciously racist white movement that could result in "pogroms," massacres, massive forced emigration, or even systematic genocide (which although focused on the urban black underclass, would, because of racialism, affect all blacks).

LADINOS AND U.S. CAPITALISM

The northern half of Mexico was conquered by expansionist U.S. imperialism in 1848, and this region was thereby opened for intensive exploitation by U.S. capital. Within the new Southwest of the United States there were two indigenous peoples: the American Indians and the Mexicans (the latter concentrated in what was to become New Mexico and in a few settlements on the coast of upper California). Both indigenous peoples experienced the process of exclusion as their land and resources were taken over by Anglo corporations and commercial farmers. Although the 1848 treaty with Mexico (in which Mexico surrendered the northern half of its territory to the United States) stipulated that all existing land grants in the hands of Mexican nationals would be honored by the United States, by a variety of ruses, legal technicalities, frauds, violence, terror, and intimidations, about 80 percent of the land legally owned by the indigenous Mexican population was appropriated by Anglos. Thus, in the last half of the nineteenth century the position of Mexicans/ Chicanos in the United States was principally defined by the racist structure of primary exclusion (see Barrera 1979, p. 26-27).

Deprived of almost all their best land, the indigenous Mexicans were, in good part, forced either into extreme rural poverty or to provide labor for the expanding commercial agriculture and mines of U.S. capital. Mexicans (both the original settlers in Northern Mexico and the early post-1848 arrivals) who worked for Anglos were, in good part, enmeshed in relationships of debt peonage, semifeudal tenancy, and contract labor (similar to what blacks and Chinese experienced at the same time) rather than pure wage labor relationships (that were standard for white workers) (see Acuña 1981, pp. 80-85; Barrera 1979, pp. 55, 77). Well into the twentieth century in some places (on the least valuable land) a traditional Chicano ("little Mexican") independent peasantry continued to exist, largely engaging in subsistence farming supplemented by production for local markets. In other places traditional Mexican padron-peon tenancy relations (between rich and poor Chicanos) also continued to be reproduced (Barrera 1979, p. 55).

In the twentieth century the position of Mexicans/Chicanos in the United States has been defined by the racist structure of special exploitatioin/disorganization (no longer by primary exclusion). There was only a trickle of Mexican immigrants into the United States in the last half of the nineteenth century (official immigration statistics that undoubtedly grossly undercounted the actual population movement record fewer than a thousand a year for all years until 1904). But in the middle of the first decade of the twentieth century, a massive migration of Mexicans to the Southwest to work for commercial Anglo farmers began. Between 1908 and 1918 approximately 17,500 Mexicans a year were recorded as legally immigrating to the United States. In the 1920s the Mexican immigration greatly accelerated, averaging 50,000 a year throughout the decade (see U.S. Department of Commerce 1975b, p. 107).* It has been estimated that the total (legal and undocumented) immigration of Mexicans to the United States in the 1910-30 period represented approximately one-eighth of Mexico's entire population (see Acuña 1981, p. 123).

Mexicans in the post-1905 period came to replace Asians as the primary source of menial labor for Southwest (especially Californian) commercial agriculture.† They proved to be "ideal" menial laborers because unlike the Japanese and Hindus they did not attempt to leave wage labor to become small farmers. They further "hibernated" during the off season (i.e., returned to Mexico or to the Mexican/Chicano ghettos of the cities of the Southwest), thus not becoming an expense to the growers or their state. Chicano and Mexican workers were generally paid about half of what the going wage was for Anglo workers, were assigned the harder work, and (at least in the case of recent migrants from Mexico) tended to work exceptionally hard (since their intention was to save money, return home, and establish themselves as petty bourgeois or landowning peasants).

---

*It should be noted that outside of Northern New Mexico the overwhelming majority of Chicanos (people of Mexican descent born in the United States) are descended primarily from those that immigrated into the United States in the post-1905 period (in good measure from the massive 1908-29 migration to work in Southwestern agriculture).

†"Alien" status (Chinese, Japanese, Hindu, Filipino, Mexican) workers have been especially vital in California's fruit and vegetable production since its inception because this agricultural system requires a reliable, but temporary, labor force to work for only a few vital weeks in the harvest cycle of each crop. Such a labor force of necessity must be mobile. This type of agriculture is highly labor intensive and thus most sensitive to keeping labor costs down. In 1974 hired labor still represented 67 percent of the total costs of California farms. As late as 1968 only 2 percent of fruit and vegetables were harvested by machine (Pfeffer 1980, p. 27).

In the post-World War I period, Mexican labor was heavily concentrated in agriculture (in 1930, 45 percent of all employed Mexican men were in this sector) (Barrera 1979, p. 95). In 1922 Mexicans accounted for about half of all the cotton pickers in the Southwest as well as three-fourths of all fruit and vegetable labor. In 1927 they were 60 percent of sugar beet workers (Barrera 1979, p. 77). Mexican women/Chicanos were heavily concentrated as domestics (in 1930 45 percent of all those employed). In El Paso in 1920 75 percent of all domestics and 90 percent of all laundresses were Chicanos (Barrera 1979, p. 98).

Mexican labor was employed for the most part by the largest rather than the smaller commercial farms. In 1928 it was found that over 90 percent of all commercial (and labor hiring) farms of over 640 acres, in contrast to 38 percent of those under 20 acres hired Mexican or Filipino labor. Further, 83 percent of growers with over 80 acres stated that they *preferred* to hire such workers; in contrast, 59 percent of farmers of under 20 acres stated they preferred to hire white Anglo workers (Barrera 1979, p. 83).

Mexicans and Chicanos provided a large proportion of mine labor as well. It has been estimated that roughly 60 percent of Southwest unskilled mine workers in the 1900 to 1940 period were from this group (Barrera 1979, p. 83). The railway construction and maintenance workers were heavily Mexican/Chicano. In 1922 about 85 percent of railroad track workers in the Southwestern states were Chicanos/Mexicans (Barrera 1979, p. 84). In both the mines and on the railroads Chicanos/Mexicans were assigned the most menial jobs and received the lowest pay scales. For example, on the Southern Pacific railroad line in 1908, Greeks were paid $1.60 a day, Japanese $1.45, and Mexicans $1.25 (Barrera 1979, p. 85).

In the cities Mexicans/Chicanos were heavily concentrated in blue-collar occupations (in Los Angeles in 1918, 93 percent were in such occupations, compared to 53 percent of Anglos). In 1930 in the Southwest 28 percent of Mexicans/Chicano men were unskilled nonrural laborers, 9 percent semiskilled operatives, 35 percent farm labor, and 10 percent independent farmers. Within industrial sectors Mexicans/Chicanos were most concentrated in stone, clay, and glass products (in 1928, 38 percent of the total), water, light, and power (20 percent of the total), and textiles (16 percent of the total) (see Barrera 1979, pp. 88, 97).

With the onset of the Great Depression in the 1930s the mass of recent Mexican immigrant laborers in commercial agriculture in the Southwest became redundant, and as a result there were massive forced "repatriations" back to Mexico (of both "legal" and "illegal" immigrants). Official Immigration Service records report that between

1931 and 1934 300,000 Mexicans were sent back across the border. In the course of the first half of the 1930s about one-third of all Mexicans/Chicanos in the Southwest were "repatriated" (Acuña 1981, p. 138; Barrera 1979, p. 105). During the Great Depression the role the Mexicans (and before them the Asians) had played as the primary source of menial workers in Southwestern agriculture came to be performed by economically desperate whites, Anglos forced off the land (mostly from Oklahoma, Arkansas, Texas, Missouri, and adjoining areas of the Dust Bowl). By 1936 approximately 85 to 90 percent of California's migratory laborers were native-born white Americans (in contrast to less than 20 percent in the 1920s) (Barrera 1979, p. 107).*

During World War II, when prosperity was restored in the U.S. economy and a labor shortage again developed in Southwestern commercial agriculture, a massive immigration of Mexican laborers began once again. From 1943 through 1952 approximately 7,000 Mexicans legally immigrated each year to the United States, and from 1954 until 1970 approximately 45,000 (slightly less than the immigration of the 1920s). Supplementing the legal and illegal immigrant laborers an official state-sponsored program of providing Mexican contract labor to Southwestern commercial farmers was instituted. This "bracero program" was initiated in 1942.

Expanded and regularized in 1951 the bracero program provided about 250,000 laborers a year in the first half of the 1950s, about 430,000 during the last half, and once again, about 250,000 during the first half of the 1960s. The bracero program, which was designed to provide U.S. growers with cheap docile labor *when* they needed it, worked fine for the growers. But over the course of time the bracero program came under increased government regulation that made the Mexican laborers provided by this U.S. federal service more expensive. The program, further, came under increasing attack by the AFL-CIO as undermining "American labor."

In 1964 the bracero program was abolished. But by no means did this mean the end of the flow of compliant cheap Mexican labor to Southwestern agricuture. The government-regulated "braceros" were replaced by "illegals" or "undocumented" workers who came into the United States without work documents. Southwest growers (and

---

*Filipino laborers, who had a legal status in the United States that could not be revoked because the Philippines was a colony, began entering California agriculture in the 1920s and *grew* in importance during the 1930s. Like their Chinese, Japanese, Hindu, and Mexican predecessors, the Filipinos were young, single, hard-working men willing to do menial field labor for less than their predecessors or most white Anglos.

other employers throughout the United States) found undocumented workers to be an even better source of menial laborers than the braceros. While the braceros were working under contracts signed between the United States and Mexican governments that guaranteed the Mexican noncitizens certain basic rights, "illegals" (by the nature of their status in the United States) had little recourse to legal rights—and as a result could be exploited more intensely with little danger of state or union interference. By 1968 the number of estimated undocumented workers in California agriculture reached the level of the bracero program in 1964, and by 1974 grew to twice that number (Pfeffer 1980, p. 33).

The forced repatriation of Mexicans in the 1930s, as well as smaller scale repatriation campaigns in the 1950s and the deportation campaigns against "illegal aliens" since, has, in good part, been a product of the role of Mexican labor in disorganizing the working class as a whole. Workers of Mexican and Anglo background do not form a single social class. The maintenance of distinctive cultures, languages, and residences as well as the castelike assignment of work prevented the formation of a class consciousness and kept *industrial* unions among Anglo workers weak. The early *craft* unions in the Southwest largely excluded Mexicans and Chicanos from membership (for the most part attempting to exclude them from the better jobs in the mines) (see Acuña 1981, chap. 8).

Thus, instead of organizing across ethnic lines in the 1930s the thrust of poor white migrant workers was to argue for "repatriating them back to Mexico" (just as the AFL-CIO opposed the bracero program, and most of the labor movement in the 1970s and 1980s has wanted to "tighten up" on the employment of "illegal aliens" so as to reserve the better jobs for Americans). There has been and continues to be great mutual hostility on the part of menial workers (in good part undocumented Mexicans) who feel that the native-born workers are trying to monopolize special privileges, and the native-born (including many Chicanos) who feel the newest immigrants are reducing their living standards and working conditions. Because any attempt of *industrial* workers to exclude new sources of menial laborers is ineffective in the face of capital's need for such groups, the futile attempt to oppose further immigration (or deport undocumented workers) is not only ineffectual, but it greatly weakens labor's position because of the disorganizing effect it has on overall working class solidarity. The only labor strategy that can work for *industrial* workers (given that the employment of new immigrants is very profitable for capital, and thus will continue) is to organize both Anglos and undocumented Ladino workers into the same unions (in the same manner the CIO organized both blacks and whites successfully for the first time in the 1930s).

Latin America as the New Source of Specially Exploited Labor for U.S. Capitalism

By around 1970 the rural South dried up as a source of recruits for Northern industries. More blacks began returning to the South than newly migrated to the North. At the same time black industrial workers became increasingly organized, while the poor increasingly rejected their oppressive conditions. They were no longer the relatively docile cheap labor that they had been a generation before. A new source of docile menial labor for American capitalism had to be found. Just as the displaced Southern blacks had replaced the displaced Polish and Italian peasants, who had replaced the Irish before them, so too the Southern blacks are now being displaced by Ladinos.

In the 1951-60 period an average of 147,000 Southern blacks a year migrated to the North and West. In this same decade Latin Americans (including Puerto Ricans and others from the West Indies) permanently (and legally) entered the United States at the rate of 103,000 per year. In the 1961-70 period 138,000 Southern blacks a year left the South while 153,000 Latin Americans a year entered the United States (U.S. Immigration and Naturalization Service 1979, Table 13; Puerto Rico Planning Board, correspondence, and Table 11.2). When undocumented or illegal Mexican immigrants are included it is clear that by the latter half of the 1960s considerably more Ladinos were entering the United States than displaced Southern blacks entering the Northern capitalist economy. Since the early 1970s the net migration of blacks has been to the South. In the early 1970s the net immigration from Puerto Rico also slowed to a trickle. The flow of both undocumented and legal immigrants from Latin America (other than Puerto Rico) is now the overwhelming source of new menial laborers for U.S. capitalism.

In 1977, 44.4 percent of all legal and "permanent" immigrants to the United States were from Latin America and the West Indies, 32.6 percent were from Asia, and 16.0 percent were from Europe. The occupational distribution of immigrants from these three areas are very different. Of the Asian immigrants in 1978, 38 percent (of those who listed an occupation) were professional and managerial (for Chinese alone it was 53 percent, Filipinos 45 percent, and Koreans 49 percent). This compares with 34 percent of Europeans and 14 percent of Latin American immigrants who were professional or managerial. On the other hand, 62 percent of Latin American immigrants were menial laborers (operatives, unskilled labor, or service workers) as compared to 37 percent of Asians (27 percent for Chinese) and 40 percent of Europeans. Of all the *menial laborers* entering the United States as immigrants in 1978, 58 percent were from Latin America (including all of the Caribbean), 10 percent from Europe, and 30 percent from Asia. The leading Latin American and Caribbean suppliers of legal immigrants to the United States in 1975 were Mexico (15.3 percent of all legal permanent immigrants to the United States), the Dominican Republic (3.2 percent), Jamaica (3.2 percent), and Colombia (1.8 percent). Central America, it should be added, supplied 3.2 percent of all immigrants to the United States. Other leading suppliers of permanent immigrants to the United States in 1975 were the Philippines (6.2 percent), Korea (4.9 percent), China (Taiwan and Hong Kong, 4.4 percent), and India 3.4 percent (U.S. Immigration and Naturalization Service 1979, Tables 8 and 13).

It should also be noted that before the 1960s the leading source of legal and permanent Latin American immigrants to the United States was Puerto Rico, but since the 1960s it has been Mexico. In the 1951-60 period 41,000 Puerto Ricans a year migrated to the United States, compared to 30,000 Mexicans. In the 1960s, the comparable annual averages were 22,500 and 45,000. In 1970s the annual number of legal Mexican immigrants rose to about 70,000 a year, while the net migration from Puerto Rico was reduced to a dribble.

In the 1970s the flow of "documented" Mexican workers (together with those from other parts of Latin America) to the United States was dwarfed by the migration of "illegal" or undocumented workers who entered the United States without proper papers with the intention of working, saving money, and returning home (the typical motivation of virtually all immigrant groups). Estimates of the number of undocumented Mexican workers in the United States in the late 1970s varied from 1 million to 12 million. For 1980 the best estimate—very roughly—would probably be approximately 6 million (see New York *Times*, February 4, 1981, p. 27). Undocumented workers play a much more important role in some parts of the United States than others. In Los Angeles, for example, it is estimated that one out of every ten people are undocumented. In San Diego it is higher still (New York *Times*, December 28, 1980, p. 13).

The role of undocumented Mexican and other Latin American workers has become central to the profitability of the U.S. economy. They are the true equivalent of the "guest workers" of Germany and the rest of Northern Europe. As of 1982 there was no law against employers knowingly hiring undocumented workers. Twice in the 1970s proposed legislation to make it a crime to knowingly employ undocumented workers was defeated in the U.S. Senate (after it passed the House of Representatives) under pressure of business lobbyists (New York *Times*, December 28, 1980). Undocumented workers are recognized as playing such an important role in the U.S.

economy that the "regularization" of their status has been under careful consideration.

The U.S. Immigration Service regulates the supply of illegal Ladino laborers to business and agriculture (rather than making a serious effort to restrict the immigration of such workers). The Immigration Service typically winks at violations, so long as a business presses for access to menial workers and there is a labor shortage. In 1980 there were only 350 border control agents on duty at any given time on the entire U.S.-Mexican border (New York *Times*, December 5, 1980, p. 13). That the Immigration Service systematically encourages violations of U.S. immigration laws to serve business interests is testified to by its effectiveness in times of labor surplus when it is instructed to deport surplus Mexican laborers back to Mexico (Pfeffer 1978, p. 40; Barrera 1979, p. 12).

It should be noted that in 1978 59 percent of all persons of Spanish origin in the United States (recorded by the U.S. Census Bureau) were Mexican/Chicano and 15 percent Puerto Rican (U.S. Department of Commerce 1980, p. 33). Assuming approximately 6 million undocumented Mexicans in the United States not counted by the U.S. Census, approximately 70 percent of all Ladinos in the United States were Mexican/Chicano in 1978. Ladinos as a whole in 1980 represented about 8 percent of the U.S. population, compared to 12 percent for blacks.

In 1976 of all persons in the United States who spoke a language other than English as their usual language, 60 percent spoke Spanish (3.8 million). About 46 percent of these either did not speak English or had difficulty with the language. Of *all* those who reported either not being able to speak English or having difficulty with it, 66 percent were native speakers of Spanish (U.S. Department of Commerce 1980a, p. 39).

During the 1970s more undocumented Ladinos were employed in nonagricultural than in agricultural occupations. In 1978, 46 percent of apprehended "illegal" Mexican workers were employed in agriculture, while 54 percent were employed in manufacturing, construction, and the services (New York *Times*, November 10, 1980). Illegal immigrants from Latin America are preferred not only in the low-wage menial agricultural and service industries where capital finds it very difficult to find any native-born workers willing to work at the low wages offered, but also in industries that pay significantly more than the minimum wage and where undocumented Mexicans are found by employers to both work for less money and be more reliable and enthusiastic than native workers. To quote the personnel manager of a Chicago area manufacturer: "They work hard and they show up on time, they work overtime, they don't get into fights and they're relatively docile" (New York *Times*, November 10, 1980). In the San Diego and Los Angeles areas, competitive sector manufacturing and service industries as well as agriculture are heavily dependent on "illegal" workers. Undocumented workers (both Latins and Asians) have become very important in the revived "sweatshop" industries of the Northern cities. In 1980 it was estimated that there were in the New York area 3,000 "sweatshops" in the apparel trade employing about 50,000 workers (compared to about 200 in 1970) (New York *Times*, February 26, 1981:1).

The Growing Economic Role of Ladinos in the U.S. Economy

In the post-Depression period Chicano/Mexican labor in the U.S. has largely been drawn out of its traditional concentration in agriculture, mining, railroad construction, domestic services, and so on and displaced into menial industrial labor in the cities. While 28 percent of Chicano/Mexican men were employed as unskilled nonfarm labor in 1930, only 12 percent were in 1970. The figures for farm labor declined from 35 percent to 8 percent in the same period (while the figures for independent farmers declined from 10 percent to 1 percent). Meanwhile, the percentage classified as machine operatives rose from 9 percent to 25 percent, and as skilled workers from 7 percent to 21 percent (Acuña 1981, p. 281). In 1970 86 percent of the Chicano/Mexican population of the United States was urban (compared to 66 percent in 1950) (Barrera 1979, p. 139). These rather radical changes reflect the dissolution of the traditional castelike barriers that divided Anglo from Ladino workers, with the better jobs (and higher pay schedules) going to Anglo workers. Under the new system of direct competition for jobs between white Anglos, blacks, and Ladinos, the corporations ensure maximize flexibility in their labor force, minimization of wages, and maximum disorganization of the working class. Both white *and* black Anglos are increasingly resentful of Latin workers, especially illegal aliens, taking "American" jobs, while working according to Latin American standards.

Ladinos have rapidly been entering working class occupations, demonstrating a long-term tendency to displace blacks as the principal minority group in them. Between 1970 and 1977 the ratio of Ladino men to black men in menial occupations increased from 0.38 to 0.47, in industrial working class occupations from 0.43 to 0.56 and in urban labor from 0.41 to 0.52. Meanwhile, the ratio of Ladino men to black men in the professional and managerial positions decreased from 0.81 to 0.63 (see Table 11.15). The percentage of all Ladino men in the United States who were industrial workers rose from 54.9 percent to 58.6 percent between 1970 and 1977, while the percentage of all black men in these occupations declined slightly from 60.1 percent to 58.4 percent. A similar phenomenon occurred among urban manual workers. Meanwhile, the percentage of all Ladino men who were professional and managerial declined from 15.2 percent to 14.5 percent of the total, as the black percentage rose from 8.9 percent to 12.7 (see Table 11.15). It is clear that the working class is becoming increasingly Ladino, while at the same time Ladinos are becoming increasingly working class.

It should be noted that black women are considerably more likely to work outside the home than are Ladino women (especially Puerto Ricans). In 1979 the labor force participation rate of black women was 53.1 percent as compared to 48.1 percent for Mexican/Chicanas and 33.4 percent for Puerto Ricans (U.S. Department of Commerce 1981a, pp. 394, 399).

The ratio of all employed Ladino to black men in the manufacturing sector in 1970 was 0.425, slightly less than the average for all sectors—0.468. Black men (compared to Ladino men) were disproportionately concentrated in primary metals, motor vehicles, chemicals, and textiles, while Ladino men were disproportionately concentrated in fabricated metals, nonelectrical and electrical machinery, and food processing. The ratio of Ladino women to black women in manufacturing in 1970 was 0.474, considerably higher than the average for all sectors (0.299). Ladinos were especially highly concentrated in food processing and textiles (see Table 11.16).

In sum, black men tend to be concentrated more in heavy industry and Ladino men in light industry, although both groups are virtually proportionately present in the manufacturing sector. Although Chicanas are less likely to work than black women, they are proportionately much more represented in the manufacturing sector than black women.

The deteriorating position of employed Ladinos in relation to employed blacks is also reflected in the statistics on earnings. Between 1969 and 1979 the ratio of black to white male median annual earnings (for those employed full time, the year around) rose from 0.68 to 0.73, while the comparable figure for Ladino men declined from 0.80 to 0.73. Meanwhile, the ratio of black to white female median annual earnings (for those employed full time, the year around) rose from 0.79 to 0.93, while the comparable figure for Ladinas declined from 0.89 to 0.83. These figures represent a radical reversal in the position of the two groups. A reversal produced by the rapid immigration of menial laborers from Latin America, on the one

TABLE 11.15: The Relative Structural Position of Blacks and Ladinos in the United States, 1970 and 1977 Males Only

	Occupational Structure (percentage distribution)				Absolute Numbers in Each Occupation (1000s)				Ratio of Number of Ladinos to Blacks	
	1970		1977		1970		1977		1970	1977
	Blacks	Ladinos	Blacks	Ladinos	Blacks	Ladinos	Blacks	Ladinos		
Professional-managerial	8.9%	15.2%*	12.7%	14.5%*	359	289*	641	406*	0.81	0.63
Urban manual[a]	76.2	66.2	75.1	71.0	3,086	1,257	3,798	1,986	0.41	0.52
Menial labor[b]	64.9	52.0	59.6	50.4	2,628	987	3,016	1,412	0.38	0.47
Industrial workers[c]	60.1	54.9	58.4	58.6	2,436	1,042	2,952	1,640	0.43	0.56
Total	100.0	100.0	100.0	100.0	4,052	1,897	5,057	2,799	0.47	0.55

*It should be noted that a high percentage of Ladino professionals and managers are displaced middle class Cubans who fled the Cuban Revolution after 1958.

[a]Craftsworkers, foremen, operatives, nonfarm labor, nondomestic service including self-employed.

[b]Laborers (farm and nonfarm), service (including domestics), operatives.

[c]Craftsworkers, foremen, operatives, nonfarm labor including self-employed.

Source: U.S. Bureau of the Census 1970d, Tables 81, 121; 1979c, Table 53.

TABLE 11.16: Ratio of the Number of Ladinos to Blacks Employed by Industry, 1970

Lower than Average		Higher than Average		
Primary metals	0.339	Fabricated metals	0.682	
		Nonelectrtical		
Motor vehicles	0.348	machinery	0.650	
Chemicals	0.310	Electrical machinery	0.698	(0.488)*
Textiles	0.322 (0.536)*	Food processing	0.566	(0.558)*
Construction	0.440			
	All sectors	0.468	(0.299)*	
	All manufacturing	0.425	(0.474)*	

*Females
Note: Males unless otherwise noted.
Source: U.S. Bureau of the Census 1970, Table 92.

hand, and the gradual integration of most blacks into the mainstream of either the working class or the salaried petty bourgeoisie on the other (see Table 11.17).

It should be noted that the position of Ladinos is actually considerably worse than the reported figures indicated, *and* has deteriorated considerably more than the data suggest because of the large and growing number of undocumented Ladino immigrants (who for the most part are not registered by the U.S. Census). Undocumented immigrants are disproportionately located in the most menial and lowest paying jobs.

The more recent immigrant status of Ladinos is responsible for their assignment to the lowest paying, most menial occupations in the economy. As they accumulated industrial working class experience, blacks organized themselves and increasingly resisted their condition. They have been in good part integrated into the core of the working class or excluded from the labor force altogether. Ladinos are now coming into the country to take the lowest paying most menial jobs in their place. As a result, they are increasingly subject to the same racist humiliations experienced by previous waves of migrant menial workers. Similar relationships of exploitation generate similar ideologies and attitudes.

Relative Class Differentiation among Ladinos and Blacks

The overall trends in occupational composition and income primarily reflect the relative position of the working class majority among both blacks and Ladinos. The primary fact about both groups

TABLE 11.17: Median Annual Earnings of Full-Time, Year-Round U.S. Workers: Whites, Blacks, and Ladinos, 1969 and 1979

	1969		1979	
	Male	Female	Male	Female
Whites	$8,525 (1.00)*	$4,764 (1.00)	$17,427 (1.00)	$10,244 (1.00)
Blacks	5,813 (.68)	3,759 (.79)	12,738 (.73)	9,476 (.93)
Ladinos	6,840 (.80)	4,251 (.89)	12,658 (.73)	8,466 (.83)

*Numbers in parentheses are the ratios of each group to white earnings for that year.
Source: U.S. Bureau of the Census 1970d, Table 247; 1981, Table 61.

is their central role in the industrial economy. In both cases it is their working class majority that essentially defines the position of these groups in the U.S. economy.

In 1977, 75.1 percent of black men and 46.1 percent of black women were urban manual workers (nondomestic service workers, craftsworkers, operatives, foremen, and laborers). This is significantly higher than the equivalent figures for whites—53.7 percent and 31.9 percent respectively. It is of the same order, however, as the figures for Ladinos; 71.0 percent and 47.9 percent respectively. Black men are significantly more likely to be both urban manual laborers and menial laborers than Ladino men, but equally likely to be industrial workers (see Table 11.3). The difference here is accounted for by the fact that blacks are significantly more likely than Ladinos to be in service industries. While black women are more likely than Ladinas to be menial laborers (because so many more black women are in the services), Ladinas are much more likely than black women to be industrial workers (because so many are factory operatives). But black women are also considerably more likely to be professionals than Ladinas.

Class differentiation is greater among blacks than among Ladinos. The black petty bourgeoisie, on the one hand, is significantly larger than the Ladino petty bourgeoisie; on the other hand, the black underclass is significantly larger (especially its hard core of "lumpen proletarians") than the Ladino underclass.

In 1977, 12.7 percent of black men and 14.4 percent of black women were professional and managerial, in contrast to 9.8 percent of Mexican/Chicano men and 9.1 percent of Mexican/Chicano women (and 15.9 percent of Puerto Rican men and 11.8 percent of Puerto Rican women) (U.S. Bureau of the Census 1979c, pp. 8, 224). However, in the Northeast, where almost all Puerto Ricans were concentrated in 1977, 21.2 percent of black families had an income of over $20,000 compared to only 13.0 percent of Ladino families. In the West, where most Mexicans/Chicanos are concentrated, 20.8 percent of Ladino families reporting in 1977 to the U.S. Census Bureau had a family income of $20,000 or over (since this figure excludes most undocumented workers, it must be considerably discounted) (U.S. Department of Commerce 1980, p. 449). In 1977 11.6 percent of *all* Puerto Rican families in the United States had an income of over $20,000 as did 19.0 percent of all Mexicans/Chicanos, compared to 22.3 percent of all black families (and 26.9 percent of Northern black families) (U.S. Department of Commerce 1980a, p. 32; 1981, p. 452). Thus, considering the lower family income in the higher income ranges among Puerto Ricans as compared to blacks and the fact that large numbers of undocumented Mexicans who earn less than $20,000 a year do not report to the U.S. Census Bureau, it is clear that the black petty bourgeoisie is considerably larger than that of either Mexicans/Chicanos *or* Puerto Ricans. Puerto Rican professionals and managerials both appear to be concentrated in lower paying positions *and* are much less likely than black families to have a working wife (and thus not to have a middle class living standard).

The larger petty bourgeoisie among blacks than among Ladinos is reflected in the statistics on education. In 1978 19 percent of blacks had at least some college, compared to 16 percent of Ladinos (and 31 percent of whites). In this same year 74 percent of all blacks aged 25-34 in the United States had at least completed a high school education, compared to 48 percent of Mexicans/Chicanos and 48 percent of Puerto Ricans (U.S. Department of Commerce 1980, pp. 144-45).

On the other extreme, the black underclass is, in relative terms, significantly larger than the Mexican/Chicano underclass, although it is of the same order as the Puerto Rican. Since (including undocumented workers) there are roughly five times more people of Mexican/Chicano background in the United States than Puerto Ricans, it is clear that in general the Ladino underclass is much less of a significant phenomena than the black underclass.

In 1978 23.2 percent of white families were located in the central cities (of the SMSAs) as compared to 57.2 percent of black households and 51.1 percent of Ladino households. While blacks are in general more concentrated in central cities (and have a higher percentage of their population in the underclass) than Ladinos, there is a considerable difference between Puerto Ricans and Mexicans/Chicanos in this regard. While 46.3 percent of Mexican/Chicano families in 1978 were located in the central cities of the SMSAs, this was true of 79.0

percent of Puerto Rican families (U.S. Department of Commerce 1980, p. 33 and U.S. Bureau of the Census 1980c, Table 15).

In 1978 29.0 percent of nonwhite families were below the U.S. Department of Labor's officially defined poverty level, while 18.9 percent of Mexicans/Chicanos and 38.9 percent of all Puerto Ricans were (U.S. Department of Commerce 1980, pp. 33, 463). In the West in 1977 25.6 percent of blacks were below the poverty level as compared to 16.9 percent of Ladinos; in the Midwest 32.1 percent of blacks compared to 14.4 percent of Ladinos. However, in the Northeast, 27.1 percent of blacks were below the poverty level as were 34.8 percent of Ladinos (U.S. Department of Commerce 1980, p. 464).

In 1978 the black labor force participation rate for males aged 16 and over was 70.8 percent as compared to 82.7 percent for Mexicans/Chicanos and 72.6 percent for Puerto Ricans (U.S. Department of Commerce 1980, pp. 392, 397). In 1970 in the 35-44 age bracket, 88 percent of black men were in the labor force as compared to 93 percent of Mexicans/Chicanos and 88 percent of Puerto Ricans (U.S. Bureau of the Census 1970f Table 7; U.S. Bureau of the Census 1970d, U.S. Summary, Table 90). In 1977 the black unemployment rate for men aged 20-24 was 23.0 percent and that for Ladinos aged 20-24 was 12.2 percent; for men aged 35-44 it was 6.3 percent and 4.9 percent respectively (U.S. Department of Labor 1979, p. 189). In general, blacks are more likely to be below the poverty level, less likely to be in the labor force, and more likely to be unemployed than are Mexicans/Chicanos. The black underclass is clearly a considerably larger proportion of all blacks than the Mexican/Chicano underclass is a proportion of all Mexicans/Chicanos.

In 1970, 1.5 percent of the U.S. male prison and jail population was Puerto Rican and 4.0 percent Mexican/Chicano. Puerto Rican men over age 16 in 1970 were 0.6 percent and Mexican/Chicano men over age 16 were 1.9 percent of the over-16 male population (counted by the U.S. Census Bureau)—an overrepresentation factor of 2.5 and 2.1 respectively, compared to an overrepresentation factor of 4.2 for blacks (U.S. Department of Justice 1975, Table 6.38). The ratio of men to women aged 25-64 counted by the U.S. Census Bureau for people of "Spanish origin" in 1978 was 89 percent, compared to 85 percent for blacks and 97 percent for whites (U.S. Department of Commerce 1980, p. 28). The higher rate of avoiding census takers together with their considerably higher rate of incarceration suggests that the hard core underclass among blacks is significantly greater than among Ladinos (including Puerto Ricans).

Puerto Ricans (but not Mexicans/Chicanos) have shared the experience of blacks in being caught in large numbers in the central cities (especially New York) as manual industrial jobs were disappearing, and as a result have in large numbers been condemned to poverty. However, they do not appear to have suffered urban poverty and protracted unemployment long enough to have produced as large a "broken" hard core underclass as have blacks. This is reflected in the significantly lower incarceration rates for Puerto Ricans as compared to blacks, in spite of the fact that a considerably higher proportion of Puerto Ricans are below the poverty level. In summary, it is clear that in general Ladinos (including undocumented workers) are more concentrated in the working class (and are in general less class differentiated) than are blacks. This is true for both Puerto Ricans and Mexicans/Chicanos, although class differentiation is greater among Puerto Ricans, whose experience has been more like that of blacks, than among Mexicans/Chicanos—the newest major source of menial labor for U.S. capitalism.

WHO BENEFITS FROM ECONOMIC DISCRIMINATION AGAINST BLACK AND LADINO WORKERS?

Although racism hurts minority group workers more, majority group workers also suffer economically from racism directed against ethnic minorities. The ideology of racialism and the white chauvinism it generates acts to undermine working class solidarity. Instead of forming strong unions and political parties and engaging in other types of unified class action against capital, racism leads the different segments of the working class to displace their hostility onto each other, thus neutralizing their political effectiveness against capital. Majority group workers come to internalize the capitalist class ideology that sharing common "racial" characteristics gives them a common interest against fellow workers of other "races." Identifying with the wealthy of their "race" instead of with others in the same (or a slightly lower) economic position allows majority group workers to be exploited much more effectively than would be the case in the absence of racialist ideology and dominant group chauvinism.

The disorganizing effect of racism on the working class of the dominant group has been clearly illustrated historically by the contrast between the condition of the Northern and Southern white working class in the United States. Since the mid-1930s industrial workers (both white and black) in the basic Northern industries have been largely organized into effective industrial unions and have also been mobilized to pressure the state for pro-working class reforms (such as social security, unemployment insurance, recognition of unions, medicare, and so on). As a result, the condition of both black and white workers in this region is considerably better than in the

South. In the South, on the other hand, unions and other forms of effective working class political action (organized either across ethnic lines *or* on an all white basis) have been very weak. Racialism and white chauvinism have in these regions been used very effectively to undermine the development of class consciousness among white workers, workers who have largely bought the false ideology of "white supremacy" and thus hold to the illusion of having "white skin privilege." In the South the white working class has in good part been convinced that the fact that blacks earn about half of what whites earn (in 1969 median black family income in the South was 56 percent of median white family income) is more important than the fact that they are poor in relation to either the white upper class or white workers in other parts of the country (workers who have effectively organized together into unions with blacks and otherwise engage in effective class action to improve their common condition).

In the Midwest (the industrial heartland of the United States) in 1969, median black family income was 75 percent of median white family income. At the same time, median white family income in this region was 18 percent higher than in the South (U.S. Census 1970d, Table 135). In this region black and white workers, to a much greater degree than in the South, work together in classwide organizations to both effectively improve their common lot and to reduce the effect of racism. Although blacks benefit more from this association, whites clearly benefit as well (black family income in 1969 was 58 percent higher in the Midwest than in the South).

Analyses of the effect of economic discrimination against minorities on the income of majority group workers can get very complex because of the fact that many different factors other than racism influence income levels. Therefore, definitive analyses of the effect of racism must use more sophisticated statistical techniques, techniques more sophisticated than simple regional comparisons, to separate out the effect of racism from these other factors. It is necessary to employ the statistical techniques of partial correlation and/or multiple regression that statistically enable one to "hold constant" the effect of some variables, while examining the effect of the variable one is interested in on what one is trying to explain. One of the more comprehensive of such statistics is "Pearson's r," the correlation coefficient, the square of which measures the proportion of the variation in the dependent variable accounted for by the effect of the independent or explanatory variable. Table 11.18 reports the effect of racial discrimination as measured by the ratio of the black male to white male annual earnings (for those who work full time the year around) on both the level of white male earnings and the degree of economic inequality among whites in the 25 states that have at least

12 percent of their population Ladino, black, and other minorities (the groups against which racism was primarily directed in the 1960s in the United States).

The correlation between the ratio of black male to white male annual earnings and the level of white male earnings in 1969 was +0.46, i.e., the less the discrimination against blacks the higher white median income (21 percent of the entire variation in white male median income is accounted for by the variation in economic discrimination). When such factors as percentage of the population represented by ethnic minorities, percent urban, personal income per capita, percentage in manufacturing, and region (all factors that also influence the level of earnings) are controlled for (have their effect on white male earnings "taken out"), the relationship between economic discrimination against minorities on white male earnings is seen to be real (and not an artifact of these two variables' associations with the other factors that produce higher white male earnings). White workers lose economically, rather than benefit, from the effect of racial discrimination.

This conclusion is further confirmed by examining the effect of racial discrimination on the degree of equality among whites. In 1969 there was a -0.58 correlation between the ratio of black to white male median income and the white male Gini inequality index. The

TABLE 11.18: The Relationship between Black Male/White Male Earnings and Measures of White Gain, 1969

(correlation coefficients)

	Black Male/White Male Earnings Controlling For:				
	Zero Order	Percentage Minority	Percentage Urban	Personal Income per Capita	Percentage in Manu- facturing
White Male Median Earnings	+0.46	+0.33	+0.20	+0.33	+0.54
White Male Gini Inequality Index	-0.58	-0.43	-0.54	-0.64	-0.56

Notes: Data for earnings are for 1969; that for percentage minority is for 1970. Minority refers to blacks, American Indians, Asians, and people of Ladino origin. The 25 states with the greater proportion of their populations minorities (over 12 percent) are analyzed, rather than all 50 states, because it is here that there is a sufficient number of minority workers present to actually have an effect on white worker income.

Sources: U.S. Bureau of the Census 1970f, 1970j; 1970h, 1970i.

Gini inequality index measures the degree of inequality in a population, with a score of 1.00 indicating total inequality (the richest quantile has 100 percent of the income) and a score of 0.0 indicating complete income equality (each quantile has an equal share of total income). These results mean that the more discrimination against blacks the more inequality among whites (the greater the gap between the richer and poorer whites). As Table 11.19 shows, this relationship holds even when the other factors that influence income inequality are controlled for. Poorer white workers lose relatively to higher paid skilled workers, professionals, managers, owners, and so on, from economic discrimination against blacks. They are *not* pushed up into jobs with income closer to middle class income levels because of the discrimination against blacks. To the contrary, the disorganizing effect of racism aggravates their impoverished position.

There is no significant correlation between the percentage of a state's population that is of minority status and the level of white male median earnings (in 1969 the correlation coefficient between the two was -0.07, which explains one-half of one percent of the total variation in white male median earnings). (See Table 11.19.) This shows that the mere presence or absence of significant numbers of minority workers in the working class normally has no significant effect one way or another on white income levels. The presence of minority workers per se does not generally result in the disorganization and hence impoverishment of white workers. They do not necessarily lower white wages by acting as a reserve army of labor competing for jobs. And they do not necessarily increase white wages by displacing whites from low-paying positions.

TABLE 11.19: The Relationship between Percentage of Population That Is Minority and Measures of White Gain, 1969–70

	Percent Minority Controlling For:				
	Zero Order	Percentage Urban	Personal Income per Capita	Percentage in Manufacturing	Region (South/ Non-South)
White Male Median Earnings	-0.07	-0.25	-0.11	-0.06	-0.16*
White Male Gini Inequality Index	+0.50	+0.56	+0.50	+0.50	+0.45

*-0.25 when all factors are simultaneously controlled for.
Note: Data are for all 50 states.
Source: U.S. Bureau of the Census 1970f, 1970j, 1970h, 1970i.

There is, however, a significant correlation between the Gini inequality index for white males and the percentage of a state that is ethnic minority. The correlation coefficient is +0.50 (25 percent of the variation in the degree of income inequality among whites is accounted for by the proportion of the population that is minority). The higher the percentage of a state's population that is minority, the greater the *inequality* among whites, i.e., poorer whites are *not* displaced into relatively higher paying jobs by the presence of minorities. These results combined with the negative correlation between *median* white income level and the degree of economic discrimination and the lack of a relationship between percent minority and median white income means we can infer that it is *higher* income whites who gain from the presence of large numbers of minority workers, while working class whites (those around the median income level) are unaffected. Middle and capitalist class whites but *not* white workers gain from racism.

That it is in fact the effect of racism on disorganizing the working class that is responsible for lower white wages where racial discrimination is greater is demonstrated when the effect of class solidarity (as measured by the proportion of a state's nonagricultural labor force in labor unions) is controlled for. If racism is operating to disorganize the working class (weaken unions) and thus reduce white wages, the correlations between white male earnings and the black male/white male median level should either disappear (or become positive) when level of class solidarity is controlled for. Such is indeed the case. In 1969 there was a +0.01 correlation between these two factors (one ten-thousandth of the variation is accounted for). (See Table 11.20.) We can thus conclude that the more intense racial discrimination (and by implication racialism and white chauvinism) the *lower* are white working class earnings *because* of the effect of the "intermediate variable" of working class solidarity. Racism, by acting to disorganize the working class, lowers the income level of white workers.

In addition to negatively affecting the economic position of white workers through its effect on weakening labor unions, racism also negatively affects white workers through its effect on public services such as education and social welfare. Racial antagonism drives wedges between working class whites, blacks, and Ladinos and greatly reduces working class ability to build a political movement that could be effective in improving schools and other public services. Instead of working with blacks and Ladinos to raise their common living standards, racial antagonism displaces white working class concern into maintaining their minor "privileges" relative to blacks and Ladinos. Poor whites can be mobilized to prevent the busing of their children to ghetto schools so that they can stay in only slightly

TABLE 11.20: The Relationship between the Measures of Racism and White Male Earnings, 1969-70

		Controlling For:				
	Zero Order	Percentage Minority	Percentage Urban	Personal Income per Capita	Percentage in Manu- facturing	Region (South/ Non-South)
Black Male/ White Male Median Earnings	0.01	0.09	0.00	-0.00	0.02	-0.05[a]
Percentage Minority	0.14		-0.05	+0.04	0.13	+0.22

[a]-0.10 when five factors (excluding percentage minority) are controlled for.
Notes: Controlling for strength of unions. Data are for 50 states.
Sources: U.S. Bureau of the Census 1970f, 1970j, 1970h, 1970i.

better quality schools designed for poor whites, rather than insisting on the same quality education for both poor blacks *and* poor whites that is available in the wealthy suburbs (see M. Reich 1981, chap. 7).

The existence of white/Anglo chauvinsim and racialist attitudes among white/Anglo workers can not be explained in terms of their rational economic interest (which *is* antiracist). It must rather be explained as a result of the interaction of three factors: ideological manipulation by the capitalist class dominated media and educational institutions; the political and economic power of the rich that can assign jobs and petty privileges; and the need of the poor to direct the hostility generated by their oppression against something. Minorities (traditionally Jews in the European world, blacks in the United States, Armenians in the Ottoman Empire, the Chinese in Southeast Asia) are "scapegoated" and come to serve as "safety valves" of discontent in order to stabilize the capitalist system and its dominant system of property and privilege. White chauvinism and racialism transfer white workers' resentment away from the capitalist system that is its cause. It also offers pseudosatisfaction or compensations in the form of psychological benefits to poorer whites who gain a certain feeling of self-respect from knowing that as poor and oppressed as they might be at least they have the same skin color as the rich, and thus they have something to be proud of that no black can brag about. In the words of a Ku Klux Klan (KKK) slogan, "Black is beautiful, tan is grand, but white is the color of the big boss man." But it is the capitalist class, not the working class, that is the economic beneficiary of racism.

12

The Structure of Patriarchy and Class

The family has been the basic economic unit of human social organization in virtually all preclass as well as class societies. In fact, the family in most societies must be understood as fundamentally an economic structure functioning to produce and consume as a unit while at the same time reproducing a new generation of producers. Thus, the basic relationships within the family must be understood as relationships of production, consumption and reproduction, and not essentially as relationships of love, sexuality, or force.

It, therefore, follows that the fundamental relationships between males and females that have characterized all but some of the most recent of social formations (and still predominate in contemporary society) must be understood as relationships of production, consumption, and reproduction, and not manifestations of some underlying abstract or general difference in human nature between "feminine" women and "masculine" men. Relationships between the sexes structured in the family, and not any essential female and male, are the essence of the differences in treatment and behavior of men and women.

Within the family the essential relationships are those of husband/wife, mother/father, son/daughter, and brother/sister-sister/brother, and it is, thus, of these relationships of production, consumption, and reproduction that the relationships between men and women have historically been constructed. The structural position of wife characterizes an economic contribution to the husband and his kin, while the position of husband characterizes an economic contribution to the wife and her kin. The position of mother/father characterizes a contribution to the reproduction of a next generation of producers in the form of nurturing and training children. The position of sister/ brother as well as son/daughter characterizes a woman's/man's continuing (premarriage and postmarriage) economic contribution to her/his family of birth. The position of women (especially before they entered the labor market as independent wage earners) must be essentially understood within this framework.

The structural position of women both within and outside the family has varied immensely over time, among societies and among classes. This variation has been principally a product of the logic of the different modes of production and class structures within which women have existed. Although there is always a sexual division of labor, in preclass societies the relative position of the two sexes is almost always qualitatively more equalitarian than in most class societies. In class societies, the economic role, and consequently the social status of women, varies qualitatively by class. Within different parts of the world capitalist system at any given time and among different modes of production (capitalism, feudalism, slavery), the position of women in the various classes is also a qualitative variable. The role, status, and power of women is a product of structural forces based in the mode of production. There is very little of social importance that can be said about women that applies to all classes of women in all modes of production in all positions within the world system through all time.

After briefly treating the development of patriarchy through different forms of preclass and early class society, this chapter examines the specific role of women in capitalist society.* Women's

---

*During the 1970s the term "sexism" came to be used to describe a wide range of rather diverse phenomena. First, it describes the social and economic structures that differentially oppress women, most importantly the traditional housewife/mother function in the patriarchal family and low paid white-collar/service "feminine" positions in the occupational structure. Such "sexist" structures might best be labeled simply "patriarchal structures." Second, "sexism" describes theories that argue there is a biologically based difference between the sexes which produces "masculine" behavior in men and "feminine" behavior in women (i.e., which inclines women to be maternal, loving, passive, and so on and men to be aggressive, outgoing, creative, and so on), or the notion that biology is destiny. The term sexism should probably best be reserved for only such theories. This would parallel a precise use of the term "racialist," the theory that there is a biological difference between different peoples or nations that dictates different average levels of intelligence, creativity, suitability to menial labor, and so on. Third, it describes the behavior of individual men in relationships with individual women (lovers, friends, mothers, co-workers, and so on) that exhibits "macho," domineering, inconsiderate, "sexually exploitative" characteristics (that are *not* exhibited toward other males). Such behavior should probably best be

increasing centrality to labor outside of the home is focused on. An extensive discussion of the occupational distribution of women and the trends in the position of women in the economy is undertaken. In addition, the chapter examines the socialization of patriarchy, the similarities and differences between the "racial" and "sexual" divisions of labor, the question of whether or not men can be said to economically benefit from economic discrimination against women, the role and consequences of housework, the radical transformation of housework, and, consequently, the declining importance of this latter patriarchal structure. Last, the tremendous class differences among women are examined.

ORIGINS OF PATRIARCHAL STRUCTURES

The anthropological evidence that has accumulated over the last hundred years, the bulk of which has been systematically compiled in the Yale Human Area Relations' files, conclusively demonstrates that the social and political position of women in preclass societies was qualitatively more equalitarian in relation to men than it has been in class societies. However, preclass societies do exhibit a considerable range of social and political status from full equality to

---

called "male chauvinism," whether or not it occurs within patriarchal structures or is legitimated by a sexist or biological theory.

These three different phenomena, all of which have been labeled "sexism," do share an important common element—they are all differentially oppressive of women. The first is the essential structure of male dominance, the second is the theory justifying male dominance, and the third is a manifestation in interpersonal relations of male dominance. The term "sexism" is also used in other ways that do not describe the differential oppression of women. For example, there is often confusion between "the oppression of women" and "women's special oppression" or patriarchy. Most women are oppressed in many ways: by racist structures, by their position in the world capitalist system (imperialism), by their working class position in the class structure as well as by their position in patriarchal structures. The vast majority of women (those who live in the less-developed countries, ethnic minorities in the advanced capitalist countries, working class and peasant women throughout the world) in fact share with the men of their class, nation, or ethnic group a common situation, a situation that may not be experienced in exactly the same ways by men and women in every instance, but that is qualitatively the same for both sexes. Women's special oppression (above and beyond national, racial, and class oppression) is thus only one part of women's oppression for most women on the planet. In fact for the vast majority of the world's women, their special oppression vis-à-vis men is a rather secondary part of their lives, overwhelmed by the more serious oppressions of racism, nationality, and class. It is only for a rather small minority of women (generally European women in the middle classes) for whom it can truly be said that the special differential oppression of women vis-à-vis men in the same class/racial/national position is their primary form of oppression.

male dominance. The principal factors that account for the variation in the position of women are their relative economic contribution and the mode of that contribution. Further, the qualitative transformation in the extent and form of women's economic contribution is the determinant of the qualitative deterioration in the social and political position of women at the onset of class societies.

Women and men in preclass societies relate to one another essentially in four relationships: father-daughter, mother-son, sister-brother, and husband-wife. Through these four essential relationships a woman develops broader kin relations to the relatives of the father, brother, husband, and son. Production, consumption, and reproduction of the next generation occur within these relationships. In all societies there is a division of labor between daughters and fathers, sisters and brothers, husbands and wives, and mothers and sons.

A woman (at least in settled patrilocal/patrilineal societies) performs labor for her husband and his lineage and village (which generally have rights to the product of her labor). Women as wives, thus, stand in a collective relation to a husband's kin. In return, they have certain rights to the product of their husband's kin. At the same time in such societies, married women are also sisters, i.e., they maintain certain duties and rights in the lineage/village of their birth. Sisters frequently provide a part of their product to their original community as well as maintain rights in the decision-making process there. Sisters and wives are, thus, quite typically different relations of production (and consumption). And since almost every wife is also a sister, this means that a given woman may simultaneously maintain very different statuses in two different lineages (or villages or bands).

While in patrilineal/patrilocal societies the greater part of the product of the wife becomes the property of the husband's lineage, a given wife, in her role as sister in a different lineage/village, has rights to the product of the wives of her brothers, i.e., while a woman may lose control of the product of her labor to a set of brothers and sisters, she gains control over the product of another set of women (a reciprocal and symmetrical relationship that creates strong social bonds of mutual dependence). While often politically *subordinate* in the husband's lineage/village, wives tend to *share* decision-making power in the households of their brothers (see Sacks 1979, pp. 156-57, 179, 185, 191, 223).

In nonclass societies (at least in those that are patrilocal and patrilineal), motherhood normally brings with it a change in economic position and status, as a woman's relations of production in both her husband's and her own lineage/village change. In both, the earlier subordinate position of daughter/young childless wife is transformed to a more powerful position of controller of labor-power—both through a woman's influence over the affairs of her brother's children in her original lineage, and through control over her own children in her husband's lineage. An older mother's claims on her brother's children as well as on her husband's are, in good part, repayment for her earlier labor for both her brother's and husband's lineages, i.e., is a form of delayed reciprocity. Thus, what often appears in patrilocal societies as a disproportionate contribution of a young wife to her husband's household is typically balanced by both the simultaneous contribution of her brother's young wife to her (and her lineage) and the delayed contribution of her brother's and husband's children to her in her later years (Sacks 1979, pp. 119, 121, 137-38).

In most preclass societies, then, women tend to have equal access to consumption goods with men, while at the same time they tend to contribute roughly the same amount to production as do men, i.e., there is generally no systematic exploitation of women by men.

There is virtual consensus among contemporary anthropologists who have studied the question that the main determinant of the variation in the position, power, and privilege of women is the degree of their control of the productive resources and the economic surplus of their society (see for example, R. Blumberg 1978; Sacks 1975, 1979; Leacock 1972, 1981; Buenaventura-Posso and Brown 1980; Rohrlich-Leavitts, Sykes, and Weatherford 1975).

In hunting and gathering as well as in horticultural societies women bring in on the average roughly the same amount of food as do men. Of all preclass societies on which data have been compiled in the Yale Human Area Relations' files women bring in an average of 44 percent of the food supply. In only 2 percent of such societies did women contribute virtually nothing to the food supply; and in only 2 percent did they contribute more than two-thirds (R. Blumberg 1978, p. 25). Statistical studies that can evaluate the relative effects of different factors (multivariate analysis) performed on precapitalist societies for which data are available show that economic power was overwhelmingly the most important predictor of women's life options (R. Blumberg 1978, p. 31).

Reflecting the substantial economic equality of women in most preclass societies is the reality of substantially equal (nonpatriarchal) relations between the sexes. Patriarchal structures appear to be either a product of class (as well as herding) societies or an import from class societies that impact pristine preclass societies through trade, conquest, missionaries, and so on. Table 12.1 displays the results of a study of 156 societies designed to determine the correlates of substantial equality between the sexes.

TABLE 12.1: Equality between the Sexes by Societal Type

Type of Society	Substantial Equality between the Sexes	Disaggregation of Societies with Substantial Equality		Societies Where Males Have Been Described as Dominant
		Full Equality between the Sexes	Substantial Equality with Minor or Mythical Male Superiority	
Subsistence Mode				
Hunting	75%	25%	50%	25%
Gathering	77	54	23	23
Horticultural	68	30	38	32
Animal husbandry	57	21	36	43
Residence Rule				
Patrilocal	63	21	42	37
Matrilocal[a]	71	50	21	29
Neolocal/ambilocal	94	44	50	6
Descent Rule				
Patrilineal	61	19	42	39
Matrilineal	67	52	14	33
Bilateral	87	41	46	13

[a]Including avunculocal

Note: Based on a sample of 156 societies.

Source: Sanday-Reeves 1981, pp. 170, 178.

This study, which summarized existing accounts of societies, found that about three-fourths of all hunting and gathering societies and two-thirds of horticultural societies have been described by Westerners who have studied them as having substantial equality between the sexes, i.e., male dominance has been attributed to only one-fourth of hunting and gathering societies and one-third of horticultural societies. The evidence is strong, however, that the minority of preclass societies (herding societies aside) that have been depicted as patriarchal had either recently adopted patriarchal forms as a result of imperialist contact with the advanced class societies, or in some cases were falsely described as patriarchal by the male missionaries, traders, and early anthropologists who imposed patriarchal-oriented Western categories on them (see Leacock 1981; Rohrlich-Leavitt, Sykes, and Weatherford 1975; Buenaventura-Posso and Brown 1980; Sanday-Reeves 1981, chap. 7).

The variations in the degree of equality between the sexes reflects the importance of property, the importance of women's economic contribution, and the role of women in the system of inheritance and residence. The less property a society has, the more equal is the position of women. Almost all societies with bilateral descent rules (common where there is very little property to inherit) as well as virtually all societies with neolocal or ambilocal residence rules (common in simple hunting and gathering and the technologically least developed societies) have been described as having substantial equality between the sexes—87 percent and 94 percent respectively. Likewise, hunting and gathering societies have the greatest degree of substantial equality while herding societies have the least. In societies where hunting (a predominantly male activity) is most important, 25 percent of societies studied have been described as having full equality, and in societies where animal husbandry is the primary source of subsistence (again a predominantly male activity), only 21 percent. This contrasts with societies where gathering (predominantly a female activity) is the primary source of subsistence, with full equality existing in 54 percent of the cases, and where horticulture (often a female activity) is the predominant form, with 30 percent of the total.

Women's social and political status, however, is not a simple product of their economic contribution. Their status is, rather, essentially a product of their economic *power*, or their degree of control over (and indispensability for) production. When women's contribution to production is domestic rather than social, even if they are performing essential economic roles, they will have little economic power. Unless they have primary access to production, i.e., are not under the control of males in a manner analogous to workers or slaves under capitalists or masters, their potential economic power is not actually realized. Isolation in the domestic unit, while the men are engaged in cooperative economic activities, is the social condition for the subordination of women by men. The more women work autonomously from direct male supervision, the better is their economic position. Ecological conditions or economic relations that dictate a division of labor which assigns men the social and collective economic tasks while isolating women around the home can produce the relative subordination of women even when female food processing is vital to the group (Sacks 1975; R. Blumberg 1978, pp. 24-29).

Women's economic power is enhanced in the degree to which women's economic activities require a high level of expertise (and hence men can not easily be substituted for them). Women's economic power is further enhanced even when men have the appropriate skills to be able to replace them, but there is no surplus male labor to perform women's tasks, i.e., replacing them in traditionally female activity would be a difficult and costly process. It is not necessary (for women's social and political status to be undermined) that an alternative source of *all* of women's economic contribution is available, but merely that there is sufficient "substitutability at the margin." It has been estimated that a "surplus" or "reserve supply" of laborers merely 5 to 15 percent of the labor force can be sufficent to significantly undermine the economic position of a group of laborers (such as women) (R. Blumberg 1978, 28-29).

Comparative analysis of precapitalist societies confirms the multifaceted ramifications of the economic power of women on their general condition. Where women's economic power is high, there is little "wife beating" (R. Blumberg 1978, p. 24; Rohrlich-Leavitt, Sykes, and Weatherford 1975, p. 115). Women's share in political decision making is greatest where her economic control is the greatest (R. Blumberg 1978, chap. 3; Rohrlich-Leavitt, Sykes, and Weatherford 1975, p. 124). Women also tend to have control over the reproductive function when they have economic power (Rohrlich-Leavitt, Sykes, and Weatherford, 1975, p. 124). Their general "social status" or prestige in relation to men is also high under such conditions (Rohrlich-Leavitt, Sykes, and Weatherford 1975, p. 124; Buenaventura-Posso and Brown 1980; R. Blumberg 1978, chap. 3). Last, male participation in such domestic tasks as childcare and housework is greatest where women's economic power is the greatest (R. Blumberg 1978, chap. 3).

The decline in women's social and political position is a consequence of her decline in economic power. Her status is undermined when male economic activities become increasingly vital for the group and as her primary relation to production and indispensability are undermined by transformations in societies' economic processes. Such transformations can occur either as a result of the internal logic of a society (or changes in its ecology) or because of the impositions of external class societies. A study of the transformations of the traditionally equalitarian relations of the Bari Indians in Colombia showed that as the capitalist institutions of Colombian society impinged on the native Indians that men gained in relative economic power and as a consequence women's social and political position deteriorated (Buenaventura-Posso and Brown 1980).

Although women's and men's social and political status in hunting and gathering and in horticultural societies is relatively equalitarian there *is* a sharp sexual division of labor in economic tasks.* This division of labor is a product of the salience of the biological differences between the two sexes under conditions of primitive technology. Men are slightly more muscular and bigger on the average than women, and hence tend to be somewhat more effective as hunters of large animals (as well as in handling larger domesticated beasts of burden). But more important is the fact that only women give birth, and above all, that only women breast-feed. Before the nineteenth century, breast-feeding was the universal way of feeding infants. In preclass societies the average length of breast-feeding is about two years. This has traditionally put a considerable biological constraint on women's economic activities, especially given the high birth rates of such societies. Women thus are assigned (in those societies close to nature) by the logic of economic efficiency (enforced by natural selection if reason is insufficient) to those tasks most compatible with their inherent child care capacities. This generally means tasks done close to home, tasks that do not require fast or hard travel, tasks that do not present danger to small children, and tasks that can easily be picked up, interrupted, and then begun again (R. Blumberg 1978, p. 26).

A secondary factor in the assignment of different economic functions to the two sexes is the relative supply of male and female labor for the specific economic functions that must be performed. If

---

*George Murdock found that in a sample of 224 nonclass societies where men were excluded from no basic economic tasks, women were nowhere assigned primary responsibility for hunting of large animals (or for metalworking). Women in at least some societies, however, did have primary responsibility for mining, stone working, lumbering, herding, clearing land, grain grinding, and burden carrying. There are societies, however, in which women *help* men with the hunt when necessary (e.g., when a father has no sons his daughter may help him in the hunt, when a band is short of men, wives and sister may help) (see Sacks 1979, pp. 67-69; Leacock 1981, p. 37).

there should be a relative surplus or shortage of one or the other sex relative to the tasks necessary, the logic of biological compatibility is relaxed as the criterion of selection. If, for example, there are insufficient women to perform the roles in which women have the relative advantage, perhaps because of the decline of hunting of big animals and the increased importance of hunting small animals and gathering (traditionally women's work), then men will be assigned such tasks. Similarly, if male labor is insufficient for the performance of a task to which men are differentially suited, women will be assigned such tasks (R. Blumberg 1978, pp. 26-27).

The more advanced the technology employed in obtaining a living from the soil, the greater the probability that it will be men who are assigned to such tasks. In simple horticultural societies (without metallurgy), cultivation is primarily a female responsibility in 37 percent, primarily a male responsibility in 14 percent, and shared pretty much equally in 49 percent. In advanced horticultural societies (which use a metal hoe), men have primary responsibility in 23 percent and women in 50 percent. But in agrarian societies (which use the plow pulled by a large beast of burden, and where physical strength and independence from child care are important considerations), cultivation is primarily the women's responsibility in only 7 percent and primarily a male responsibility in 56 percent (Lenski and Lenski 1974, p. 191).

There are a number of aspects of agricultural production that make agriculture generally men's work. In addition to the fact that it is normally large draft animals that pull the plows (which can thus be handled easier by men), the fields are typically farther from home than are the gardens of horticultural society, and the large scale of operations means that work schedules and conditions are not easily interruptable and adjustable so as to be compatible with child-care responsibilities (unlike horticultural societies). Moreover, agriculture is considerably more productive than horticulture (i.e., is less labor intensive, per geographical unit). Fewer people can feed more people. As a result, there is more likely to be a surplus of male workers. This means that men's inherent relative compatibility for most efficiently performing agricultural tasks (given simple technology and closeness to nature) generally becomes predominant (if not through reason, then through natural selection of the most efficient economic arrangements) (R. Blumberg 1978, pp. 50-51).

Different types of agriculture are more or less labor intensive, and thus women tend to be more or less essential in different types of agricultural production. For example, wet rice agriculture requires enormous amounts of labor input and women in such systems often perform a major portion of it (unlike in the dry plow agriculture typical of Europe and America). Because women's primary economic contribution is greater under wet rice systems, their economic power, and hence social and political position is generally better in such societies (such as Southeast Asia) than those based on dry plow techniques (such as Europe). For example, in Southeast Asian countries such as Indonesia, the Philippines, and Burma, women became very important in the market trade, disposing of much of their own surplus production often on their own account independent of their husbands. This gives women an especially independent economic position, and hence an especially strong social and political role (R. Blumberg 1978, p. 51).

Within agricultural societies, the lot of peasant women is generally better in relation to the men of their class than is the case for women of the upper classes. Peasant women are essential for the *processing* of agricultural goods primarily provided by husbands and fathers: preparing food, making clothes, and so forth. Because of their central economic role, even though it is typically organized under men, their subordination in patriarchal structures although qualitatively greater than that of women in preclass society, is, nevertheless, considerably less than that of the women of higher classes (R. Blumberg 1978, p. 51).

About 10 percent of hunting and gathering societies are matrilineal (i.e., record descent and inheritance through the mother's rather than through the father's line, with men inheriting goods from their mother's brother, rather than their father). In contrast, 26 percent of horticultural societies and only 4 percent of agricultural societies are matrilineal (Lenski and Lenski 1978, p. 162). There is pressure exerted at the transition from hunting and gathering to horticulture to change the rules of descent from being male to female centered, just as there is pressure in the opposite direction at the transition to agricultural class society. There is no significant difference between the probability of being matrilineal for simple and advanced horticultural societies, i.e., the introduction of metallurgy and more intensive techniques does not affect descent rules.

The association of descent/inheritance rules with economic forms is both a direct result of the function of a given inheritance rule for different means of production, *and* a result of the strong association (but not strict correspondence) between descent and residence rules. Patrilocal societies are almost never matrilineal (4 percent are), and matrilocal societies are almost never patrilineal (2 percent are); further, patrilineal societies are almost never matrilocal (in fact 98 percent are patrilocal), and matrilineal societies rarely are patrilocal (49 percent are matrilocal while 18 percent are patrilocal) (Coult and Habenstein 1965, p. 391). There are strong reasons why locality rules are more important in economic forms than descent rules.

In hunting and gathering societies, the rules of inheritance are of little real import because there is so little property, and virtually everything of value can be easily and rather quickly made by all. In fact, 61 percent are bilineal, with the deceased's property distributed among a range of relatives and friends (Coult and Habenstein 1965, p. 528). There are no economic or social reasons why it should be any different, if only because there is no special social interest in the rather unimportant question of inheritance. The question of whether a couple lives with the parents of the husband or with the parents of the wife would seem to be determined by the importance of continuity and coordination among the small group of men in the hunting band. Fathers, sons, and brothers who grow up together and hunt together accumulate both a common knowledge of hunting grounds and learn close coordination based on blood kinship. Among these societies 62 percent are patrilocal, 16 percent matrilocal, and 17 percent neolocal (this latter the highest of any type of society) (Coult and Habenstein 1965, p. 392). For men to move to another band when they get married and for strangers to enter the band to live with sisters, does not generally make economic sense. Thus, most hunting and gathering societies are patrilocal.

In horticultural societies the question of whether husbands live in the village of their fathers or of their mother-in-law has a different logic. In only about 20 percent of horticultural societies is cultivation primarily a male responsibility. In almost half it is primarily a female responsibility (Lenski and Lenski 1974, p. 191). In horticulture, the coordination of the labor of women is more important than before. For the sake of maximizing economic productivity it is important that the association of the primary producers be reinforced by relationships being determined through the women's line. It is inefficient for the primary work group to be disrupted by the exit of sisters and the entry of strangers by marriage.

Further, productive property is more important in sedentary horticulture villages than in hunting bands. The question of inheritance is thus of greater importance than before. Since the primary tools of production are now the horticultural implements primarily used by women, it makes economic sense to inherit the means of production through the mother's line so that they stay in the *same* work group (thus encouraging care and accumulation), and for the less important tools of the hunt, used by men, to pass from a man to his sister's son. This makes greater economic sense than for the more important tools of horticulture to pass from a women to her brother's daughter (who would be part of a different work group). In general, the forces of economic efficiency operate to press societies to adopt whatever lineage pattern and location requirements that keep the means of production as well as accumulated experience within the most important work units.

The importance of coordinating horticultural labor (versus coordinating the hunt or herding), which is the determinant factor in the relative prevalence of matrilinearity and matrilocality in preclass societies, is strongly supported by the fact that 39 percent of horticultural societies where at least 85 percent of the food is obtained by horticulture are matrilineal (and 22 percent matrilocal) as compared to only 13 percent (and 6 percent) where less than 75 percent is (Lenski and Lenski 1974, p. 192). Matrilinearity is especially common among the tribes of south central Africa, which are primarily horticultural rather than pastoral or hunters and gatherers, as are most of their neighbors (e.g., the Bemba, Pende, Yao, Lele, Plateau Tonga, and many others). In these societies women traditionally have done most of the agricultural labor, while men were heavily engaged in trading as well as raiding expeditions (Harris 1979, p. 99). Where hunting and herding play a major role, the logic of horticulture, which presses toward matrilinearity and matrilocality, is neutralized by the logic of male hunting or herding (where men almost always are in charge of the large animal herds for the same reasons they are almost always the hunters of large animals).

It should be noted that of all preclass societies herding societies are the most patriarchal as well as overwhelmingly patrilineal and patrilocal (90 percent are patrilocal and 3 percent matrilocal; 65 percent patrilineal, 6 percent matrilineal) (Coult and Habenstein 1965, pp. 392, 528). In such mobile societies almost all the food as well as the supplies for clothing and keeping warm is a direct or indirect product of male activities in managing the large animals (or in trading or raiding to obtain supplements). As a consequence, women's economic power is minimal, and as a result they are generally reduced to a lower all-around status. When men are in charge of the herds, the question of the greater efficiency of keeping the animals within the same work groups, rather than transferring them to others on the death of the father, as well as the importance of maintaining the continuity of the primary working group, rather than disrupting it by the men coming and going by marriage, overrides.

It should be noted, however, that herding societies are *not* (as Engels suggested) a principal form of economic organization on the order of hunting and gathering, horticulture, or agriculture societies. They are generally marginal and are in good part, in fact, probably spin-offs of the agricultural societies to which they are typically adjacent and dependent on for supplementing their economies (through trading or raiding). It might, in fact, be the case that many nomadic herding societies were created largely by peasants who fled the increasing burdens of agricultural life in the consolidating despotic empires.

There is an additional factor that may also press horticultural societies toward matrilinearity and matrilocality (this having to do with the nature of men's labor). In horticultural societies with their greater accumulation of wealth, both trade and warfare become more important. Because of men's somewhat greater muscular strength, societies have almost universally selected (through reason or survival of the militarily strongest) men to be the soldiers. Because of men's lesser importance to horticulture, it is they who generally also become the long distance traders (to secure metal and the other things necessary in a more complex economy as well as such things that used to be gathered by a now sedentary group). The greater incidence of warfare creates the need for stronger ties among larger groups of nonrelated men. Matrilinearity, and especially matrilocality, create social bonds among nonrelated men that can be mobilized in warfare. There is, in fact, a strong empirical correlation between the frequency of external warfare and matrilocality (and matrilinearity) in preclass societies. According to Marvin Harris matrilocality "promotes the formation of male combat teams whose members are drawn from different lineages and who have learned to live together even though they do not belong to the same descent group" (Harris 1979, p. 98).

The coincidence of women's primary role as horticulturalists and the increasing importance of warfare in producing pressure to change to matrilocality is illustrated in the history of the Middle Woodlands Iroquois. When these tribes became sedentary with the introduction of maize, women came to play a more important economic role, with men absent from the village for an average of about half the time, engaging largely in raiding, warfare, and (less important than before) hunting. The Iroquois consequently changed both their locality patterns and descent rules to matrilocality and matrilinearity. Woman's economic power was enhanced not only by her increased economic role, but also by the fact that matrilocality, together with the long-term absence of husbands, meant that women organized production on their own. Further, the men were initially strangers to one another, while the women were all sisters. All things considered, the women were in a strong position to organize society's social labor. The Iroquois women played an especially strong political role (selecting the chiefs) as well as having generally high social status compared to men (Harris 1979, p. 97).

In general, it appears that there is a strong association between matrilinearity and matrilocality and the full equality of the sexes. The Sanday-Reeves study of 156 societies found that in 50 percent of matrilocal and 52 percent of matrilineal societies there was *full* equality between the sexes, in contrast to only 21 percent of patrilocal and 19 percent of patrilineal societies (see Table 12.1). The lack of any great association of "male dominance" with descent and residence rules together with the strong association of *full* equality with these factors is strong evidence in support of the thesis that the male dominance described in some preclass societies has, in fact, been mostly either a recent innovation induced by contact with class societies or a result of the Western male bias of those who studied them (see Leacock 1981; Rohrlich-Leavitt, Sykes and Weatherford 1975; Sanday-Reeves 1981, chap. 7). Imperialist impact as well as Western bias would be more or less a constant in both patrilineal/patrilocal and matrilineal/matrilocal societies. It appears that descent and residence rules do have a substantial association with the position of women in pristine preclass societies.

The role of matrilocality and matrilinearity is important in determining the relative position of women, but in itself if men have primary access to and control over production it makes little difference. Their importance in affecting the position of women occurs when women are economically central, especially in bringing in a large proportion of the food. They determine whether or not men will be in a position to organize women's labor, or whether women's strong economic role will, in fact, be transformed into economic power (and hence a strong political and social position) as it was among the Iroquois. Women's social status and political role in matrilocal and matrilineal societies is better than in patrilocal and patrilineal societies both because the former institutions are associated with a stronger economic role for women and because they directly facilitate the transformation of their strong primary economic role into greater economic power (R. Blumberg 1978, p. 28).

The more economically developed a society, the more likely the act of marriage involves an economic transaction. While 49 percent of hunting and gathering societies involve either a "bride price" (the husband's family makes a payment to the wife's family) or a dowry (the bride's family makes a payment to the husband's) the figure is 61 percent for simple horticultural and 97 percent for advanced horticultural societies. In the great majority of cases the payment is of a bride price (Lenski and Lenski 1974, p. 200). This indicates that the transfer of women to another village and lineage often requires compensation to her lineage (and village) for the loss of her economic contribution (as well as for the loss of her children and their future economic contribution). This second function of bride price is exemplified in the rule of some (especially African) societies that require in the event a wife does not give birth the bride price must be returned (or a younger sister provided).

Of all patrilocal societies 58 percent have a substantial material bride price as compared with only 7 percent of matrilocal societies. Of patrilineal societies 68 percent have a substantial bride price as compared with 31 percent of matrilineal societies. Fully 88 percent of the societies with a substantial material bride price are patrilocal and only 2 percent are matrilocal; while 67 percent of such societies are patrilineal and 10 percent matrilineal (Coult and Habenstein 1965, pp. 378, 436). The significant difference between these two comparisons indicates that locality has a greater effect than lineage in determining whether or not bride price will be paid, and thus that it is generally more a question of the woman's loss to her old work group than the loss of her children that is primarily compensated for. Bride price is most common in advanced horticultural and in herding societies (93 percent of the latter require a bride price) (Lenski and Lenski 1974, p. 269). This reflects the very important economic role women play in both types of societies—in the first as food providers and in the second as food processers of the products provided to her by the men.

Bride price and dowry are not symmetrical phenomena. The fact that dowry (or "groom price") virtually never occurs in matrilocal (or matrilineal) societies indicates that there is obviously an additional factor at work other than compensation for the loss of the labor power of an adult who moves to another village. In fact, bride price is a payment for both the loss of a woman's labor *and* the loss of her children's labor. In the case of matrilocal/matrilineal societies, while the labor of the sons/brothers is lost to another village/lineage, they do not at the same time lose any children. Only 16 percent of agricultural societies practice dowry while 63 percent have bride price (Coult and Habenstein 1965, p. 437). The relative rarity of dowry payments, even in agricultural societies where they are the most frequent, indicates that women's ability to bear children is an important social and economic asset to her new village and to her husband's lineage that is often compensated for, even when her labor may play only a secondary economic role.

"Bride price" should in no way be interpreted as implying the "purchase" of a woman or her services by the men of one lineage from another. Bride price reflects the important economic contribution performed by women and their childbearing capacity and must be understood as a compensation by one lineage to another for the loss of their economic services. It is fully compatible with total equality of the sexes, or, theoretically, even female dominance. Hypothetically one could imagine patrilocal lineages in which women were the most powerful, compensating each other for the loss of their daughters' economic contribution to other lineages upon marriage.

The only inference that can be made from the prevalence of bride pride (or dowry) is about the central economic *contribution* (not the economic *power*) of women. But since without making an economic contribution women can have no economic power, and thus are necessarily subordinate politically and socially, we can infer that as a rule where dowry exists, women are economically, politically, and socially subordinate. But we can infer nothing from the existence of bride price about the economic power or role in decision making or status of women.

The nature of bride price is revealed in many patrilineal societies where a *sister* can take a wife (for which the wife's lineage is compensated through a bride price), with the wife bearing children (by men either of her own choosing or selected by her female husband—such relationships do not usually involve homosexuality). In such marriages the sister's labor is, in good part, appropriated by the sister's lineage, while at the same time the children of the sister's wife belong to the sister's brother's lineage (which paid the bride price, exactly as would be the case if the female husband were male). Such sister-wife marriages tend to occur in families that have no sons, and thus are in danger of having neither heirs nor female labor power (but who have considerable wealth accumulated through bride wealth obtained from marrying their daughters) (Sacks 1979, pp. 77-79; Leacock 1981, p. 295).*

In many patrilineal societies there are a variety of possible husband-wife relationships only *some* of which involve a bride price. In such societies, in those marriages that do not involve a bride price, the wives do not owe labor services to the husband's kin even when they live in the husband's village. In other marriages the wife's family may transfer wealth to the husband's family (although bride price is the norm). Here, the husband goes to live in the wife's village (although patrilocality is the norm) and her kin gain rights to the husband's services (see Sacks 1979, p. 870.

The very different status of women in advanced horticultural and in herding societies does not reflect women's differential economic contribution, which is key in both, but rather the degree to which women themselves organize and control primary production. In horticultural societies where women play a central economic role, the

---

*In some classless societies, some men take on the role of wife. For example, among the Cheyenne Indians some boys who did not assume the male role as hunter/warrier became the "male wives" of hunters (performing all the economic functions of a wife for his husband—again homosexuality was not normally a part of such relationships). No special negative status was attached to the men who assumed such roles.

bride price, in fact, reflects a high degree of equality among the sexes. In contrast, the occurrence of dowry in agricultural class societies reflects the centrality of male labor and the fact that supporting a woman is sometimes an economic burden (women are not always economic assets). It should be noted that virtually all societies that practice dowry are both patrilocal and patrilineal. This implies that women have little economic power and thus that their status and power will be low. This is especially the case in the upper classes where dowry payments are the most common and the most substantial, and where women's position relative to men is also the lowest.

With the transition to agricultural class societies, the economic power of women is radically reduced, reflecting both her removal from primary access to food and other necessities *and* the loss of her autonomy in controlling her labor power. Her social status and political power are also radically reduced. Men generally handle the plow as well as all heavy domestic animals, and thus virtually monopolize the means of production, while women are reduced to the role of domestic laborers, merely processing the food and other goods provided by men in ways overseen by men. Her all-around dependency on the man then is a product of her economic dependence on him as a provider. Women's traditional job of taking care of children is reinforced by her increasing confinement to the home. Although both sexes do some craft-type work around the home, the division between "domestic labor" and "external labor" becomes qualitatively greater than it was in horticultural society. The agricultural division of labor is also reinforced by the interests of the emerging ruling class in such societies, a class which is interested in securing the largest possible economic surplus from the peasantry, and thus has an interest in men doing the agricultural labor and women doing the processing around the house, because it is this system that is the most productive and hence the one from which they can extract the greatest surplus as tax (or rent) (Sacks 1975).

The subordination of women to men that occurs concurrently with the development of class society means the all-around subordination of women. Sexual virginity becomes the norm for women at marriage. Strict penalties for extramarital sex are instituted for women. Neither becomes the case for men. Women's sexuality and ability to reproduce now come under the control of men. Women assume the status of minors, inferior in most rights to men. They are removed from having any role in political decision making. For the first time, women become subject to the general authority of their fathers and husbands.

In such societies it must be stressed that the economic power, political role, and social position of women relative to men is the greatest in the poorest classes and the least in the wealthier classes. It is in the higher classes where women have no economic role that virginity and fidelity are the most important. It is also here where the most oppressive (and often bizarre) patriarchal institutions of female seclusion develop such as veils, foot-binding, purdah (general confinement of a woman to the house), and suttee (the burning of the wife with the corpse of the husband). It is also in the higher classes of agricultural class societies where polygamy is the most common (R. Blumberg 1978, p. 52).

The transition to agricultural class societies generally requires a switch from matrilinearity and matrilocality (if they exist) to patrilinearity and patrilocality. In agricultural society it is the men who are the primary producers, and thus it is the continuity of the male laboring group that it is now most important to preserve. Disruption and loss of experience associated with men coming and going with marriage are inefficient, and further undesirable for the men's sense of solidarity (a factor that is important when they have almost total economic power—only 10 percent of agricultural societies are matrilocal). Inheritance rules that require the quite substantial means of production (beasts of burden, plows, and so on) to stay in the work group from generation to generation rather than being transferred to sister's sons who are in other work groups (as in matrilineal systems) are also more efficient in that they give the younger generation more of an incentive to take care of the tools and animals and more of an interest in their reproduction and growth than would be the case if they were continually passing out of the work group on the death of the fathers. The accumulated wealth in the means of production is considerably greater even in the peasant classes of most agricultural class societies than in advanced horticultural societies. Thus the question of inheritance is much more important. This further ensures that most agricultural class societies will not be matrilineal or matrilocal.

While much has traditionally been made (e.g., by Engels) of the male interest in guaranteeing paternity for the sake of inheritance of productive property as a primary force leading to the subordination of women, it is difficult to understand why society (or individual men) is not satisfied by the rule of the Napoleonic Code, "The husband of the mother is the father of the child." It would seem that the primary motive securing the sexual domination of women by men is rather the *status* (or ego) involved in having exclusive sexual access to women, and the pride in paternity that results. The means which makes this motive sexually asymmetrical is the almost exclusive economic power of men, which is in turn a product of men's primary access to food getting and their ability to organize the domestic labor of women.

In general, in class societies, especially in the higher classes until the period of monopoly capitalism, the position of women as qualitatively inferior to that of men was ensured by men having both the motive and the means to subordinate women. The male motive has been essentially economic (except in the wealthier classes)—the need to have domestic labor performed, but also (and especially in the upper classes) to have a servant, sexual object, soother of egos, scapegoat, object of status, source of emotional support, and so on. The male means of dominance has been their monopoly on either property in the means of production in the case of the wealthier classes, or access to the peasant plot, domesticated animals, or wage. It should be noted that in slave societies where both the men and the women worked in the fields more or less equally there was little difference in the position of the two sexes among the slaves, since male slaves did not have any more economic power than did female slaves.

WOMEN'S POSITION IN THE CAPITALIST MODE OF PRODUCTION

During the early period of capitalism, women predominantly performed the role of housewife/mother, whose contribution to the capitalist mode of production varied qualitatively by class. In the working class, even if women worked in a mill before they were married or if they were widowed or never married, almost all married women became full-time housewives, working perhaps 90-100 hours a week tending a garden, canning food, chopping wood, washing clothes, cleaning house, looking after the the children, making and mending clothes, cooking, washing up, providing emotional support to children and the working man, and so on.

Working class women came to function primarily to reproduce the labor power of their husbands, who sold their labor power directly to capital, as well as to bring up another generation of male workers (and female wife-mothers). Her labor power *was* paid for by the capitalist. It was incorporated into the value of the labor power of her husband and sons. But it was paid for in the form of a wage paid to them, and not to her. There was nothing inherently more demeaning, menial, or brutal about doing housework in comparison to working 12 hours a day in the mills or mines as a manual laborer. However, the fact that the male got the family wage, and not the wife, gave the working-class man a position of power over the woman, a position that was used to secure a degree of subordination.

Women's traditional specialization in spinning and weaving brought unmarried (mostly young) women into what was the cutting edge of capitalism in the last part of the eighteenth and first half of the nineteenth centuries, the textile industry (and later into garment making as well). Women (and children) were also preferred as the first recruits for the factory system because of their lack of protective craft traditions (which defined what workers should and should not do, and under what conditions) as well as because of their greater docility (socially conditioned in the traditional patriarchal family). These factors together meant that the labor process in textiles and garments could be relatively easily reorganized (deskilled and organized under close management supervision). The assignment of daughters to temporary industrial employment was facilitated by the undermining of the economic position of family farmers who as capitalism developed became increasingly impoverished, and consequently sent their daughters into industry to supplement the family income in an attempt to avoid bankruptcy.

But, with the exceptions of the textile and garment industries, men were the overwhelming source of the new proletarians (both skilled and unskilled). Men, who had developed and carried on the traditional artisan trades such as blacksmith or cooper, were the natural recruits for most factories. Except in the new textile and garment industries, most industrial factories at first merely transformed the organization of the traditional trades (bringing them together under one roof) rather than transformed or reorganized the actual work process.

The geographical separation of the factory from housing areas combined with the industrial discipline of the machine reduced the flexibility of the labor process to a minimum. Women's inherent capacities for giving birth and breast-feeding (for, on the average, two years) thus inhibited a mother's participation in industrial labor, as much as in hunting and gathering society it had inhibited women from engaging in the hunt of large animals. Thus, until quite recently, female wage labor was largely limited to unmarried women (mostly without child-care responsibilities.)

The greater constancy of male labor (which would not be interrupted by childbirth and periodic child-care crises) was especially important in the skilled trades, where the capitalists invested considerable training expenses in the worker and where day-to-day continuity in task performance is especially important. Constancy of employment is less of a consideration in unskilled labor, where neither frequent absences from the production process nor entering and leaving the labor force makes much difference to work performance. But in textiles, and eventually in sales and simple clerical work, a mother's traditional differential incompatibility has had such slight effect as to have eventually been overridden by other considerations.

In early capitalism, capitalist class women were qualitatively better off in material terms—they had servants and nursemaids to do the housework and child care, i.e., working class women performed these functions in the capitalist class family. These women were largely excluded from economic functions. They were restricted to performing social functions (not at all an irrelevant activity for maintaining capitalist class solidarity) such as organizing capitalist class social life and conspicuous consumption. But, such women traditionally (e.g., before women had the right to own or inherit property) were clearly subordinate to their men.

Conditions in the classical petty bourgeois family were much like those in the capitalist class family (only at a substantially lower standard of living). Such families through the end of the nineteenth century typically had a live-in servant who did the bulk of the housework and much of the child care, largely releasing the petty-bourgeois woman for social and leisure activities, or in the case of shopkeepers and farmers, to assist the husband in the small family business.

In the course of the mid- and late-nineteenth century, upper and middle class women came to acquire most of the legal rights (other than the vote) that their husbands had. Women were granted the right to own and inherit property, barriers to their admission into professional schools (such as law and medicine) came down, and so on. Even before the franchise, these two classes of women were largely granted formally equal status and equality of opportunity with the men of their class (they were allowed to more fully share in their class's privileges). But such rights as the right to inherit property or the opening of professional schools meant nothing to working class women whose relatives had no property and who had neither the educational background nor money to attend professional schools. Women of the capitalist class who were now able to own property on their own utilized these rights (realized through the inheritance of father's fortunes as well as the possibility of large alimony settlements) to in good part equalize their economic power with the men of their class, even while they continued to be excluded from most managerial positions.

As the traditional petty bourgeoisie went bankrupt, and family businesses in which the women worked were replaced by the salaried professions and administration as the primary economic basis of the middle class, petty bourgeois women found themselves without a direct relationships to the economy. At the same time the cost of servants and housing went up, most middle class women could no longer afford to hire a live-in servant to do the bulk of the house-work/child care (this was especially oppressive because of the "high" petty bourgeois standards of housework and child care), unless they themselves worked. Both the number of children going to college and the costs of higher education increased, further putting pressure on petty bourgeois women to work. A bit later both the divorce rate and the prevalence of single professional women increased. The increasing need for a second (or an independent) income in this class provided the pressure to bring down the barriers to petty bourgeois careers. Women thus increasingly entered the professions. It should be noted that petty bourgeois women's entry into salaried work followed that of working class women's entry into wage labor.

The course of the twentieth century, especially the post-1950 period, saw the radical transformation of the position of working class women. As the socially necessary labor time to reproduce the labor power of husbands and children radically decreased, married working class women for the first time became available for wage labor outside the home. At the same time the demand of the corporations for more cheap and docile white-collar and service workers greatly increased. Wives/mothers were pulled out of the home and into the offices and salesrooms.

Working Class Women's Increasing Centrality to Capitalist Production

The percentage of the U.S. labor force that is female has been constantly rising since at least 1890 (see Table 12.2). In 1978 42 percent of the labor force was female.

In the period 1950-68, while the total labor force increased by 38 million workers, the female labor force alone increased by 24 million. In this period 62 percent of the expansion in the labor force was due to the entrance of women. (Married women alone accounted for 44 percent of the *entire* increase in the labor force in the 1950 to 1974 period.) There has been no tendency for the relative female/male contribution to the expansion of the labor force to decline over the quarter century since 1950. If recent trends continue, we can expect that women will represent close to one half of the labor force around the year 2000.

While the labor force participation rate of women has been continuously rising (from 18.2 percent of all working-age women in 1890 to 49.3 percent in 1978), the labor force participation rate of

TABLE 12.2: Women Workers as a Percentage of the Civilian Labor Force

	Women in Labor Force (in millions)	Women as a Percentage of the Labor Force	Civilian Labor Force Participation Rates	
			Men	Women
1890	3.7	17.0%	84.3	18.2
1900	5.0	18.1	85.7	20.0
1920	8.2	20.4	84.6	22.7
1930	10.4	21.9	82.1	23.6
1940	13.0	24.4	82.6	25.7
1945	16.6	27.7	86.7	35.9
1950	18.4	29.6	86.8	32.8
1955	20.5	31.6	86.2	34.5
1960	23.2	33.4	82.4	37.1
1965	26.2	35.2	80.1	38.8
1970	31.5	38.1	79.2	42.8
1975	37.0	39.9	77.3	43.7
1978	41.9	41.7	77.2	49.3

Sources: U.S. Department of Commerce 1975b, pp. 127, 128; 1979, p. 392.

working-age men, at least in the post-World War II period, has been *declining*. It stood at 86.8 percent in 1950 and at 77.2 percent in 1978. In the former year the labor force participation rate of women was only 38 percent that of men, but by 1978 it had grown to 64 percent (see Table 12.2). Again, if current trends continue (and there is no tendency for them to slow down over time), the labor force participation rates of the two sexes should approach equality not too much after the year 2000.

Traditionally most women in the labor force were women without husbands. In 1890 only 14 percent of all women in the labor force were married and living with their husbands (mostly married to the disabled, the incapacitated, or to men earning only marginal incomes). As late as 1940 only 30 percent of working women were married and living with their husbands. This pattern has changed drastically over the course of the twentieth century with the freeing of women from housework and their rapid entry into the labor force. In 1978 56 percent of working women were married and living with their husbands (see Table 12.3).

It has been married women freed from the requirements of housework by the mechanization and socialization of housework and by the reduction in the socially necessary time for child care who have accounted for most of the increase in the women's labor force participation rate. Especially rapid has been the rise in the labor force participation of mothers, both those with very young children (aged 0-6) and those with youngsters (aged 6-17) (see Table 12.4). While the labor force participation rates of married women rose from 24.8 percent to 48.1 percent from 1950 to 1978, those for women with children aged 6-17 rose from 28.3 percent to 57.2 percent and those for women with children aged 0-6 increased from 11.9 percent to 41.6

TABLE 12.3: Marital Status of Women in the Labor Force

	Married Husband Present	Never Married	Widowed, Separated, or Divorced	Total
1890	13.9%	68.2%	17.9%	100%
1940	30.3	48.5	21.2	100
1950	48.0	31.6	20.4	100
1960	54.4	24.0	21.6	100
1970	58.8	22.3	18.9	100
1978	55.6	24.9	19.4	100

Sources: U.S. Department of Commerce 1975b, p. 133; U.S. Bureau of the Census 1980, p. 48.

percent. The labor force participation rate of mothers with children aged 6-17 is greater than that of women *without* children under 18, while that of women with children under 6 is now almost 90 percent that of all married women (see Table 12.4). These latter facts point to two things: first, the reduction of the socially necessary labor time required for child care, together with its gradually increasing socialization; and second, the need for women with young children to work in order to help support their families. The fact that mothers have a higher rate of labor force participation than nonmothers speaks at least in part to the motive driving women into the labor force—economic necessity.

Working class women's labor is increasingly central to the economy. Their contribution can in no way be considered either marginal or cyclical. They cannot be considered primarily a "reserve of labor," in good part entering the labor force in times of labor shortage and leaving in a time of surplus. In the 1947-74 period there was no significant correlation between the female labor force participation rate and the annual rate of economic growth. Further, in the 1947-74 period there was no significant difference in the average annual change in the female and male unemployment rates. In this period there was a -0.14 correlation (2 percent of the variance explained) between the female unemployment rate and the annual rate of economic growth, while there was a -0.28 correlation (8 percent of the variance explained) between the male unemployment rate and the annual rate of economic growth. Male unemployment varies *more*

TABLE 12.4: Civilian Labor Force Participation Rates of Women, by Marital and Child Care Status

	All Women	Never Married	All Married	Mothers with Children Aged 6-17 only*	Mothers with Children Aged 0-6*	Mothers With No Children under age 17*
1950	31.9	50.5	24.8%	28.3%	11.9%	30.3
1955	33.5	46.4	29.4	34.7	16.2	32.7
1960	34.8	44.1	31.7	39.0	18.6	34.7
1965	36.7	40.5	35.7	42.7	23.3	38.3
1970	42.6	53.0	41.4	49.2	30.3	42.2
1975	45.9	56.8	45.0	52.3	36.6	43.9
1978	49.1	60.5	48.1	57.2	41.6	44.7

*Married mothers with husband present.

Sources: U.S. Department of Commerce 1980, pp. 400-1; U.S. Bureau of the Census 1980, p. 49.

than female with the economic cycle. While there was no correlation between the percentage of women actually working in a given year and the annual rate of growth, there was a slight positive correlation for men (0.09 or 1 percent of the variation explained) (see Szymanski 1976a, pp. 40-42). There is, in fact, no tendency for women to enter the labor force in times of labor shortage and leave in times of surplus. If anything, in times of extreme crisis such as the 1930s, women are more likely to work outside of the home (in order to compensate for their husband's or father's loss of work).

Women's work, although it tends to be somewhat more seasonal than men's as well as more part time does not differ qualitatively in these respects from men's. Since 1960 about 67 percent of employed women (compared with about 87 percent of employed men) have worked full time (rather than part time) (see Table 12.5). In 1977 about 53 percent of employed women were employed the year around (50-52 weeks) as compared to 69 percent of men. The ratio of the percentage of employed women to the percentage of employed men who worked the year around has increased from 0.66 in 1950 to 0.77 in 1977, indicating the declining seasonal nature of women's work. In 1977 42.1 percent of employed women worked full time, the year around compared to 64.7 percent of employed men. The ratio of the percentage of employed women to employed men who worked the full day the year around rose from 0.56 in 1950 to 0.65 in 1977, again indicating the increased centrality of women's labor to the capitalist economy (see Table 12.5).

It should also be noted that in 1973 42.2 percent of employed married women (with husband present) worked at full-time jobs the year around as compared to 33.1 percent of the never married, and 52.1 percent of the ex-married. Further, only 31.1 percent of employed married women (with husband present) compared to 40.8 percent of never married and 23.4 percent of the ex-married had part-time jobs (U.S. Department of Labor 1975b, pp. 54).

Studies of differential labor turnover rates have shown that labor turnover is more influenced by the skill level of the job, the age of the worker, and the worker's length of service with the employer than by the sex of the worker. A 1968 study of quit rates found that women were only slightly more likely than men to quit their jobs (2.6 percent versus 2.2 percent) (U.S. Department of Labor 1969, pp. 76-77). Another study showed that men tended to change their *occupations* more frequently than did women. But the average tenure at a given job is greater for men than for women. For workers aged 25-34, women had been on the job an average of 2.2 years and men 3.2 years; for workers aged 35-44, 3.6 and 6.7 years respectively (U.S. Department of Labor 1975b, p. 61). In part this is caused by many

TABLE 12.5: Part-Time/Full-Time Work

	Percentage of Employed Working Full Time			Percentage Working Year Around			Percentage Working Full Time, Year Around		
	Male	Female	F/M Ratio	Male	Female	F/M Ratio	Male	Female	F/M Ratio
1950	90.2%	73.4%	0.81	68.5%	45.0%	0.66	65.4%	36.8%	0.56
1955	89.9	71.3	0.79	71.6	48.2	0.67	67.5	37.9	0.56
1960	86.9	67.6	0.77	68.4	46.9	0.69	63.9	36.9	0.58
1965	86.9	68.5	0.79	71.7	48.0	0.67	67.3	38.8	0.58
1970	87.6	67.8	0.77	70.5	50.7	0.72	66.1	40.7	0.62
1975	87.6	67.0	0.76	68.3	53.2	0.78	63.9	41.4	0.65
1977	87.5	67.0	0.77	68.8	53.3	0.77	64.7	42.1	0.65

Sources: U.S. Department of Labor 1975a, Table 34; U.S. Bureau of the Census 1980a, p. 55.

women dropping out of the labor force for a few years at childbirth, and in part it is a result of women having less seniority (a product of their more recent entry into the labor force). The small differential for those between aged 25 and 34, compared to that for older cohorts, suggests that the younger generation of women (including those in their prime childbearing and rearing years) are now maintaining more continuity in their employment than in the past. All the evidence points in the same direction. Women have been integrated into the wage labor force as central participants.

The majority of all married working women are from the manual-working class. In 1978 53 percent had husbands who were industrial, farm, blue-collar or service workers and 34 percent had husbands who were professionals, managers, officials, or proprietors (see Table 12.6). It can be seen that professional and managerial women are from predominantly petty-bourgeois families (as defined by husband's occupation). Approximately 69 percent of married women in manual working class jobs have husbands who are also in manual working class jobs. Husbands' and wives' occupations are relatively highly correlated, both in the manual working class and in the petty bourgeoisie. If the wife has a petty-bourgeois position the chances are very good that the husband has one too. If the wife has a manual job, the chances are very good that her husband does as well. It is legitimate to speak of homogeneous manual working class and petty bourgeois families.

TABLE 12.6: The Relation between Husband's and Wife's Occupations When Both Are Employed, 1978

Husband's Occupation	Wife's Occupation			
	Professional/ Managerial	Sales/ Clerical	Manual Working Class	1978 Total
Professional/ Managerial	55.7%(40.2%)	34.1%(36.2%)	20.7%(23.6%)	34.2%(100.0%)
Clerical/ Sales	13.2 (25.7%)	15.0 (42.9%)	10.2 (31.4%)	12.7 (100.0%)
Manual Working Class	31.0 (13.6%)	50.9 (35.3%)	69.1 (51.1%)	53.1 (100.0%)
Total	100.0	100.0	100.0	100.0

Note: Numbers in parentheses are percentaged across; numbers not in parentheses are percentaged down.

Source: U.S. Bureau of the Census, 1980a, p. 66

It should also be noted (see Table 12.6) that one-half of all married clerical and sales women have husbands who are manual workers. This suggests that the so called "white-collar revolution" is not so much a change in the U.S. class structure as it is a case of married manual working class women entering the labor force as clerical and sales workers. The transformation of working class women from homemakers to white-collar workers must not then be taken as an indicator of any decreasing social and political importance of the manual working class in the United States. Such women remain as much a part of the working class as they ever were. Lower-level clerical and sales work is surely at least as much of a source of working class consciousness as the tedium and isolation of housework.

It can also be seen from Table 12.6 that when women's occupations differ from men's, the wife's position is usually the lower status position. Of all the employed wives of professional and managerial husbands 24 percent are in manual jobs, 34 percent are in clerical and sales, and 40 percent are professional or managerial. Of all the employed wives of manual working class men 51 percent are in manual jobs and only 14 percent in professional and managerial positions, while 35 percent are in clerical and sales. This last figure once again underlines the class nature of most clerical and sales positions for women.

Women and Wage Work

The corporations have a strong motive to reproduce patriarchal relations. The sexual division of labor within industry results in enormous profits that would not otherwise be realized by capital. Women tend to be put into the more monotonous and lowest-paying jobs. The use of women allows capitalism to get these tasks done with a minimum amount of resistance, and at a lower rate of pay, than most men would easily accept.

Capital tends to prefer women for certain occupations and men for others. Women are preferred for clerical, sales, and service work, while men are favored for most industrial and managerial work (see Table 12.7). As can be seen from Table 12.7, in spite of the fact that the percentage of the labor force that is female has more than doubled since 1900, women are still only a small percentage of craftsworkers and laborers. Further, they are a smaller portion of operatives than in 1900. They are also only a little less likely than they ever were to be service workers. The most significant change over the 78-year period has been in clerical and sales work. These occupations were traditionally male. It was not until the 1940s that women came to predominate in them. By 1978, 70.6 percent of clerical and sales workers were female, up from 66.4 percent in 1970.

The proportion of all professionals who were women in 1978 was virtually the same as in 1940, although it is up somewhat from 1970 (it was 38.6 percent in 1970 and 42.7 percent in 1978). Women have increased their share of managerial jobs to almost one-fourth of the total, up from 16 percent in 1970 and 11 percent in 1940. This together with the increasing sex concentration of both clerical and sales (more female) is the most significant trend of the 1970s.

Since the 1930s the overwhelming bulk of employed women have been in either the services or in clerical and sales—58 percent in 1940, 63 percent in 1970, and 62 percent in 1978. Thus not only are women dominant in these occupations, but most women who are employed are concentrated there. In 1978 41.5 percent of employed women were in clerical and sales (up from 8.2 percent in 1900 and 28.8 percent in 1940). It is clear that corporate capitalism's rapid expansion of its clerical and sales sector has resulted in the greatest bulk of ex-housewives entering these occupations. The percentage of all employed women who are factory workers (or other operatives) has steady declined from 23.8 percent (the second largest category) in 1900 to 11.8 percent in 1978. The percentage of women who are craftsworkers is less than 2 percent, only slightly higher than in 1900. The percentage of all women who are professionals has increased slightly, but steadily, over time, from 8.1 percent in 1900 to 15.6 percent in 1978, while the percentage who are managers increased slowly from 1900 to 1940, then increased significantly during the 1970s (see Table 12.8). The only two significant trends of the 1970s have been the growth of the percentage of employed women in

TABLE 12.7: The Percentage of Each Occupation That Is Female (All employed workers)

	1900	1940	1970	1978
Professionals	35.2%	41.5%	38.6%	42.7%
Managers	4.4	11.0	15.9	23.4
Clerical and sales	20.1	43.0	66.4	70.6
Craftsworkers	2.5	2.2	3.3	5.6
Operatives	34.0	25.0	30.9	31.8
Laborers (nonfarm)	3.8	2.7	3.7	10.4
Service	71.8	61.0	66.2	62.6
Total economy	18.3	24.3	37.7	41.2

Sources: U.S. Department of Commerce 1975b, pp. 139-40; 1980, p. 415; U.S. Bureau of the Census 1980a, pp. 63-64.

professional and managerial jobs (19.0 percent in 1970 to 21.7 percent in 1978) and the decline in the percentage of employed women in factory work. The most important fact of the 1970s is the unchanged position of women in their post-World War II occupations of concentration-clerical and sales and service.

Women are heavily concentrated in just a few specific occupations. In 1978, 38 percent of all employed women were either secretaries/typists (12.0 percent of the total); food service workers (7.6 percent); primary or secondary school teachers (5.5 percent); health service workers (excluding nurses) (4.3 percent); bookkeepers (4.3 percent); or retail sales clerks (4.3 percent). The most female occupations among professionals and managerials include nurses, dietitians and therapists (where the female/male ratio in 1978 was 13.1); librarians (4.3); primary and secondary school teachers (2.5); and office managers (1.9). It is clear that women are concentrated in the lower levels of professional/managerial jobs. Most traditionally female professions became more so over the course of the 1970s (e.g., nursing, health technology, social work, primary and secondary school teaching). But during this decade women made significant inroads into a number of traditionally male professions. Among lawyers and judges the ratio rose from 0.04 to 0.10, among physicians and dentists from 0.10 to 0.12, among natural scientists from 0.11 to 0.22, among university and college professors from 0.39 to 0.51, among social scientists from 0.27 to 0.51, and among computer specialists from 0.20 to 0.30 (U.S. Bureau of the Census 1980a, pp. 63, 64). Further, the number of doctoral degrees issued to women in the health professions rose from 0.16 of those granted to men in 1970 to 0.32 in 1977. The ratio of bachelor's degrees in business and management increased

TABLE 12.8: The Female Occupational Structure (all employed workers)

	1900	1940	1970	1978
Professionals	8.1%	12.8%	14.5%	15.6%
Managers	1.4	3.2	4.5	6.1
Clerical and sales	8.2	28.8	41.5	41.5
Service	35.5	29.4	21.7	20.7
Craftsworkers	1.4	1.1	1.2	1.8
Operatives	23.8	19.5	14.5	11.8
Nonfarm Laborers	2.6	1.2	0.5	1.3
Farm Workers	19.0	4.0	1.8	1.3
Total	100.0	100.0	100.0	100.0

Sources: U.S. Department of Commerce 1975b, p. 140; 1980, p. 415.

from 0.09 to 0.23, the ratio of doctoral degrees in biological sciences from 0.14 to 0.21, in the physical sciences from 0.05 to 0.10 and the social sciences from 0.13 to 0.22 (U.S. Bureau of the Census 1980a, p. 39). It should be noted that the relative improvement of women's position in these professions is a reversal of the general post-World War II trend that lasted through the 1960s of a *declining* female/male ratio, or, at best constancy, in these occupations (Deckard 1975, pp. 318, 319).

Among the clerical and sales occupations the most female include secretaries/typists (where the female/male ratio in 1978 was 62.9); receptionists (31.7); telephone operators (15.4); teacher aides (11.7); bank tellers (10.8); bookkeepers (9.7); and cashiers (6.8). It should be noted that all these white-collar occupations became more female over the course of the 1970s, except telephone work (which became significantly more male) and reception (which showed no change).

In industrial and service work the most female occupations include packers and wrappers (where the female/male ratio in 1978 was 1.7); sewers and stitchers (18.0); textile operatives (1.5); food service workers (2.2); health service workers (8.9); and personal service workers (3.0). It should be noted that health service work, sewing, and packing and wrapping became *more* female over the course of the 1970s. At the same time, women made little or no inroads into most traditionally male, skilled manual jobs. The ratio of women to men in the construction trades stayed constant at 0.01, while that for the metal trades rose from 0.02 to 0.03 (U.S. Bureau of the Census 1980a, pp. 63-64).

The most significant trend of the 1970s is the general increase in the size of the traditionally female occupations, where the bulk of working women are concentrated to at least as great an extent as ever. A secondary trend is the entry of middle class women into professional and administrative positions that had traditionally been male. It should be noted, however, that the number of women in this latter category is very small. For example, only 1.3 percent of all employed women in 1978 were in computer programming, engineering, law, natural science, social science, or university/college teaching (all occupations in which professional women significantly improved the sex ratio in the 1970s). The great bulk of employed women continue to be concentrated in the traditional female occupations of service, clerical and sales, and a few factory occupations, such as textiles, garments and packing as well as semi-professional positions.

The ratio of female to male earnings has stayed pretty much constant from the late 1930s to the late 1970s at around 59 percent of male income (for full-time, year-round employees only) (see Table 12.9). These overall trends obscure some important countermovements in different occupational categories. Professional women experienced a slow but steady increase in their earnings level in relation to men between 1939 and 1977 (from 0.61 to 0.66 of men); while clerical women experienced a significant deterioration (from 0.69 to 0.62); operatives experienced a slight decline (from 0.63 to 0.58 that of men between 1959 and 1977). In summary, middle class women have improved their relative position in relation to working class women. Of all categories of occupations, the earnings differential between men and women is the least for professional women and the greatest for women in sales (see Table 12.9).

Most of the income differential between the two sexes is due to the fact that women are concentrated in lower paid occupations, rather than because women get paid less for comparable work. The sex typing of specific occupations as female is thus seen to be the primary reason for pay differentials between men and women. For example, in 1970 in the professions the female/male ratio for social workers was 0.81; for elementary teachers 0.81; for secondary school teachers 0.79. In clerical and sales occupations the ratio was 0.84 for bank tellers and 0.84 for cashiers. In manual occupations the ratio was 0.70 for packers and wrappers; 0.78 for textile operatives; and 0.68 for garments workers (Stellman 1977, pp. 63, 64). Undoubtedly most of the remaining differential is accounted for by men being in the higher paid more skilled positions or having more seniority than women *within* each of these occupations. Although some of the differential is attributable to unequal pay for equal work, it is clear that either women are differentially recruited into low-wage occupations or occupations that require female laborers become low paying (or both).

Among the principal factors that account for the systematic (and persistent) differential in pay between men's and women's occupa-

TABLE 12.9: The Ratio of Female to Male Median Wage or Salary Income (Year-round, full-time workers)

	1939	1959	1970	1977
Professionals	0.61	0.64	0.64	0.66
Managers	0.54	0.57	0.55	0.54
Clerical	0.69	0.68	0.64	0.62
Sales	0.51	0.42	0.43	0.42
Operatives	0.59	0.63	0.58	0.58
Service	0.60	0.56	0.56	0.61
Total	0.60	0.61	0.59	0.59

Sources: U.S. Bureau of the Census 1969, pp. 86, 88; and 1980a, p. 76

tions are: the fact that women do not receive the same quality of education and training for high-paying jobs (new middle class or manufacturing jobs in the primary sector) that men receive; and the fact that women much more than men interrupt their careers to have children, and, thus, fail to accumulate sufficient continuous job experience and on-the-job training, necessary for the higher paying occupations. These factors mean that the logic of profit maximization makes it more rational for capital to employ *men* in those primary labor market and high level internal labor market positions that require both significant investment in human capital and seniority. Those capitalists who employ women at the same rate of pay in the better jobs would lose money and suffer the consequences of the market (i.e., "sexism" of employers is *not* a matter of attitudes or consciousness). Other important factors include: the reproduction of feminine maternal and passive oriented culture that makes women less amenable to union organization and more willing to do an acceptable job for a lower rate of pay than men would; and the fact that most women *can* (and often do), again because of the reproduction of patriarchal ideology, work for less than the value of their labor power (i.e., what it takes to sustain themselves) because part of the costs of the reproduction of their labor power is normally borne either by their husbands, if married, or by their parents if they are single. (Because women's wages are generally set on this basis, unmarried working class women living alone are typically reduced to poverty.)

The traditional patriarchal ideal (reproduced within the family as well as reinforced outside of it for its own reasons by capital) maintains the notion that women will marry and withdraw for a part of their work life from the labor force. Therefore, most working class and lower middle class parents invest less in the education of their daughters than their sons (even when both get the same quantity of schooling, sons typically acquire a better quality education as well as higher aspirations) (see Brown 1977, p. 148; Lloyd and Niemi 1979, p. 140).

The fact that women, in fact, much more often interrupt their careers for the sake of their family, means both that: given limited resources it is less rational (from the point of view of maximizing family wages) for a husband-wife couple to invest in *her* job training than in his; and it is less rational (from the point of view of capital) to invest in on-the-job training for a woman than for a man (when each has identical characteristics other than their sex). Given both the lesser probability of receiving appropriate prejob or on-the-job training as well as the significantly greater probability that they will not stay continuously employed, women disproportionately enter these occupations in the "secondary" sector that require neither long-term continuous employment nor significant amounts of on-the-job training. Women tend to enter those secondary sector jobs that tend to have significantly lower rates of pay than the primary sector jobs that require continuous employment and in which on-the-job training is required (and which maximize possibilities of promotion through internal labor markets). Maximizing profits (*the* bottom line in capitalist enterprise) structurally forces capitalists (male or female, regardless of their personal attitudes) to prefer men over women at the same rates of pay for any jobs that require extensive on-the-job training (i.e., most higher paying jobs). Leaving the labor force during the years when women workers most often drop out of the labor force to have children (ages 25-35) has an especially detrimental effect on women's wages. First, capital is especially reluctant to hire a 22-year-old college graduate and give her two to three years of on-the-job training when the probability is very high that she will shortly become a mother. Second, the ages 25-35 are especially vital for establishing oneself in a successful career (e.g., professors get tenure, lawyers become partners in good law firms, managers make it into the "fast track," blue-collar workers secure the seniority they need to gain promotions and further training requisite to the better manual jobs, and so forth during these years—see Brown 1977, pp. 156-57; Lloyd and Niemi 1979, pp. 136, 156-57, 169, 184-85, 188, 228).

The fact that most women continue to interrupt their work careers for childbirth is probably the principal reason that the pay differential between women and men has been virtually constant for so long (showing no significant tendency to rise in spite of major changes in the education level and average number of years in the labor force as well as changes in women's and men's consciousness about sex roles). It continues to be as rational as ever for the profit-maximizing corporations to prefer those with a significantly greater probability of continuous employment (i.e., men), over those with a high probability of a number of major discontinuities in their work career (i.e., women), for those high paid primary sector and internal labor market positions that require extensive on-the-job training and involve a continuous accumulation of experience and continuity of performance. Although women are now in the labor force for many more years than in the last generation, the continuance of the pattern of almost certain career interruptions means that capital finds it as profitable as always to continue to employ them in the industries and occupations where on-the-job training and continuity are less important (i.e., in the lower paid secondary sector and entry positions in internal labor market).

Working class women have been rapidly drawn into wage labor in the post-World War II period because of: the corporations' radically increased need for cheap and relatively docile white-collar (clerical and sales) labor; the radical reduction in the socially necessary labor time necessary to reproduce male labor power in the home (due to the mechanization of housework, the increasing production of goods formerly produced by women in the home as commodities outside of the home, and the significant reduction in the number of years devoted to childbearing and rearing); and the increasing difficulty of meeting the socially defined minimum living standard with just one wage (in part because children, rather than bringing in supplemental income from the beginning of their teens, are increasingly a major financial burden until they complete college, or at least high school).

Women are preferred in the rapidly expanding white-collar sector (as well as in most other highly female occupations) because: their socialization in the patriarchal family tends to make them more docile workers and tends to orient them to the role of "housewife/mother" even while they are working full time (thus making them more amenable to manipulation and less likely to organize).

Women's greater docility and noncareer orientation has made them especially useful in occupations that are being "deskilled" and subject to qualitatively greater management control. In good part their introduction to office work was a result of the process of the evolution of managerial (male) and clerical work (female) occupations out of the traditional eighteenth and nineteenth century male head clerks and accountants. The mechanization and reorganization of office work was made far easier by bringing in young women than it would have been had the men who had traditionally been the highly skilled clerks been forcibly reduced to the new office proletariat. Native-born women were, of course, preferable to the new working class of European immigrants (female or male) who were flooding into manual jobs at the same time as the office proletariat was created because they were literate in English (a requisite of office labor, but not of physical labor).

Taking advantage of the artificial personality distinctions between the sexes that had been generated by earlier forms of class society, the corporations generally channeled the two sexes into types of jobs for which these *socially created* character differences were functional in maximizing worker productivity. Not only do the corporations take advantage of preexisting character differences between the sexes, but they have also reproduced and intensified them through the structures of job training programs, promotional policies, and the very nature of the work processes that they have institutionalized.*

---

*See Bardwick and Dower (1971) for an elaboration of this argument.

It is essential to distinguish between "masculine" and "feminine" as character traits that are socially conditioned, and "male" and "female" as purely biological characteristics.* Many men have feminine character traits and many women have masculine character traits. There is no socially significant innate, a priori, or biological association of masculine traits with men or feminine traits with women. The association is purely historical and socially determined. Precapitalist societies found it efficient to socialize feminine traits into women and masculine traits into men.

The feminine traits of docility, meekness, compliance, and subordination have been especially desirable in those types of jobs for which the corporations traditionally preferred women, while the masculine traits of strength, virility, risk taking, and independence are most desirable in those types of jobs for which the corporations have traditionally preferred men (Bardwick and Dower 1971).

The socially conditioned docility, compliance, and subordination of women have been especially preferred in the tasks that are the nervous system of industrial capitalism. The file clerks, typists, secretaries, and so on of the corporations traditionally have had access to the information possessed by the firms and often interact on a personal level with corporate executives and their customers. These occupations as well as most sales jobs require loyalty from employees and special subordination to management and customers.

In contrast, in a great number of manual jobs in which men specialize, strength, virility, risk taking, and independence are especially desirable traits. Such jobs include the police, construction, steel work, lumber work, and mining. It is of interest to note that males who are in jobs that require especially feminine characteristics (receptionists, secretaries, nurses, waiters, and so on) tend either to be recruited because of a tendency toward feminine traits, or to develop such traits because of the rewards and punishments inherent in such jobs. Rewards, opportunities for promotions, and salary increases will be in good part a function of how well feminine traits are demonstrated. The same is true of women in occupations that require masculine character traits. Either these occupations attract women whose character tends to be masculine, or else women come to develop such traits because of the structure of reinforcements on the job.

Because the corporations have needed a labor force that is differentiated by character traits, they have a stake in perpetuating the

---

*For one of the best analyses of character formation see W. Reich (1949).

masculine-feminine distinction, i.e., in encouraging docility and sub-ordination in women while encouraging virility in many categories of male workers. The on-the-job treatment of women clerical, sales, and service workers (as well as virtually all other types of women workers) as subordinant adjuncts to male management and customers generates and reproduces patriarchal structures.

The value of feminine traits in women workers and masculine traits in men workers was more characteristic of earlier than of contemporary capitalism. When physical strength and risk are more important, masculinity is more profitable among workers assigned to such tasks. When relationships with secretaries and servants are close and personal, femininity is more valued (and profitable). But as automation progresses, as physical strength and risk become less central to manual labor, and as serving, smiling, and other forms of docility become less important in office work, selling, and the services (with the socialization, automation, division of labor, and deperson-alization that is occurring in these occupations) masculinity and feminity are of less importance. The nature of most jobs is being "desexed" as well as "deskilled" as automation, socialization, and the division of labor proceed. Thus, while as important in many job categories as ever (e.g., police, structural iron workers, lumberjacks as well as receptionists, personal secretaries, and waitresses), sex typing of occupations is of less inherent value than before in most basic factory and general office work positions. As the nature of both types of work converges to essentially tending machines requiring little physical exertion or creative abilities, it now makes little differ-ence whether masculine, feminine, or neuter personalities are employ-ed in most occupations.

Nevertheless, there are still considerable advantages to keeping some categories of jobs defined as "women's work" and others as "men's work." When men (at least ethnic majority men) and women are mixed more or less indiscriminately in a given specific occupation (as rather rarely occurs in the working class), there is considerable pressure for the average wage to be higher than if the occupation were subdivided into two suboccupations, one female and the other male, this because men would press for the traditional family wage, and it would be difficult to pay men and not women doing exactly identical work a significantly higher wage. It is much easier to pay women less for work that can be defined as essentially different than men's with the men's work defined as superior or more skilled.

It might perhaps also be the case that the need for capitalism to reproduce sexist ideology in order to legitimate both the countinuance of the patriarchal family and patriarchal job structures (as well as because of its military and consumption functions) leads the corporations to follow hiring policies that are not always economically rational in every specific case. Just as the slave lords of the antebellum South did not always act to maximize their profits because of the logic of the master-slave relationship and the paternalistic and aristocratic ideology it generated, it might well be the case that the imperatives of the maintenance of sexist ideology result in not hiring women for certain categories of jobs where their employment in competition with men would result in the general lowering of wages and consequently in an increased rate of profit (but where, as a result, the credibility of sexist ideology would be undermined). There might well be a parallel here with the reluctance of slave lords to use slaves in industry, especially in skilled positions. The use of slaves for such labor, while economically profitable, tended to undermine the racist myths about the inherent stupidity and laziness of blacks, myths on which the vitally important master-slave relationship depended.

THE PARALLEL BETWEEN RACISM AND SEXISM

Unlike white chauvinism, male chauvinism does not appear to function to disorganize the working class. Male workers do not, as a result, loose economically from discrimination against women, as they *do* lose from discrimination against ethnic minorities (see Chapter 11).

There was no association between earnings discrimination against women and male median earnings for the 50 states of the United States in 1969. When urban areas only are examined, the basic correlation coefficient is –0.02 (less than 1 percent of the variation explained) and when whites are examined, the correlation coefficient is –0.08 (see Table 12.10). Earnings discrimination against women has no appreciable impact on the level of male earnings, one way or the other.

When the relationship between earnings discrimination against women and the degree of earnings inequality among men is examined a positive relationship is found, i.e., the greater the discrimination against women, the more *equal* is the male earnings distribution. When urban areas only are examined a +0.68 correlation coefficient is found, (46 percent of the variation explained), and when whites only are examined, the correlation coefficient is +0.56 (31 percent of the variation explained) (see Table 12.10). When the effects of percentage urban, percentage in manufacturing, region, and percentage ethnic minority are controlled for, the basic correlation holds. This indicates that earnings discrimination against women *does* concentrate men in

TABLE 12.10: Economic Discrimination against Women and Male Gain, 1969

		Controlling for					
	Zero Order	Percent Urban	Personal Income per Capita	Percentage in Manufacturing	Region	Percent Ethnic Minority	All Factors Controlled for Simultaneously
Correlation between White Female/White Male Median Earnings and White Male Gain							
White male median earnings	-0.08	-0.10	—*	-0.08	+0.10	-0.05	+0.10*
White male inequality index	+0.56	+0.57	+0.57	+0.63	+0.52	+0.35	+0.28
Correlation between Urban Female/Urban Male Median Earnings and White Male Gain							
Urban male median earnings	-0.02	-0.12	—*	-0.02	+0.11	-0.10	+0.08*
Urban male inequality index	+0.68	+0.74	+0.81	+0.69	+0.70	+0.56	+0.68

*Personal income per capita is not used as a control here because of its close conceptual relation to male median earnings.
Note: Pearsonian correlation coefficients.
Source: U.S. Bureau of the Census 1970; U.S. Department of Commerce 1973.

the better paying jobs in each state. Although men *as a whole do not* gain by earning more because of economic discrimination against women, *poorer* paid male workers do gain some from having women displace them from the lower paid jobs, and thus, logically, the better paid workers, professionals, and managers must lose a bit from this discrimination (since overall men do not gain). It should also be noted that although men are everywhere concentrated in the better paying jobs because of economic discrimination against women, the median pay for these relatively better paying jobs must be *less* in those states where discrimination against women is the greatest (since the median pay of males does not vary with the level of earnings discrimination against women).

When the relationship between the two measures of earnings discrimination and measure of the strength of the working class—the percentage of the nonagricultural labor force in unions—is examined, it is found that there is no relationship between the two factors. When urban areas only are examined the correlation coefficient is 0.00, and when whites only are examined it is -0.18 (see Table 12.11). When the effects of percentage urban, personal income per capita, percentage in manufacturing, region, and percentage ethnic minority are controlled for there is no substantial difference in these correlations. Thus, male chauvinism can not be operating as a divisive force undermining the solidarity of the working class (as manifested in the relative proportion of the labor force in unions).

Racism and sexism then are not analogous in their effect on white and male earnings and earnings distributions. Racism is significantly more important than sexism as an instrument of a divide and rule strategy by capital. Racism and sexism do however tend to be functional substitutes for one another as alternative sources of menial laborers. White women are often used in place of minority men and women in a range of menial and low-paying jobs. The correlation coefficient between black male/white male median earnings (a measure of racial discrimination) and urban female/urban male median earnings (a measure of sexual discrimination) in 1969 was for the 50 states of the United States -0.44 (19 percent of the variation explained). The correlation between the percentage of a state's population that is minority and urban female/urban male median earnings was +0.49.

When the indicator of sexual discrimination in the labor market is the ratio of white female to white male median earnings, the relationships observed are even stronger. In this case the correlation with black male/white male median earnings is -0.50, and the correlation with percentage ethnic minority is +0.67.

TABLE 12.11: The Effect of Economic Discrimination against Women and the Strength of the Working Class as Measured by the Percentage of the Nonagricultural Labor Force in Unions, ca. 1969

| | Zero Order | Controlling for | | | | | |
		Percent Urban	Personal Income per Capita	Percentage in Manufacturing	Region	Percent Ethnic Minority	All Five Factors Controlled for Simultaneously
Urban Female/ Male earnings	0.00	−0.04	−0.24	+0.01	+0.11	+0.15	−0.06
White Female/ Male Earnings	−0.18	−0.19	−0.30	−0.18	+0.01	−0.02	−0.12

Note: Pearsonian correlation coefficients. Data are for 50 states.
Source: U.S. Department of Labor 1969; U.S. Bureau of the Census 1970; U.S. Department of Commerce 1973.

TABLE 12.12: The Relation between Racial and Sexual Economic Discrimination, 1969, 1970

		Controlling for				
	Zero Order	Percent Ethnic Minority	Percentage Urban	Personal Income per Capita	Percent in Manufacturing	Region (South/Non-South)
Correlations between Urban Female/Urban Male Median Earnings and the Indicators of Racial Discrimination						
Black male/white male median earnings	−0.44	−0.24	−0.47	−0.57	−0.45	−0.41
Percentage ethnic minority	+0.49	—	+0.48	+0.53	+0.49	+0.46
Correlations between White Female/White Male Median Earnings and the Indicators of Racial Discrimination						
Black male/white male median earnings	−0.50	−0.21	−0.50	−0.54	−0.52	−0.40
Percentage ethnic minority	+0.67	—	+0.68	+0.67	+0.67	+0.60

Note: Earnings are for 1969, other data are for 1970. Data are for the 50 states.
Sources: U.S. Bureau of the Census 1970d, 1970e, 1970f, 1970g.

These relationships do not lose strength when personal income per capita, percentage of the labor force in manufacturing, region of the country, and percentage of the population that is urban are held constant (see Szymanski 1976b). These correlations indicate that where there are insufficient numbers of blacks and Ladinos, or where economic discrimination against these groups is mitigated, white women are pressed into service to perform many of the same types of jobs that these people otherwise would perform.

Although women and ethnic minorities do not compete with one another for the *entire* range of low-paying menial jobs, they do compete for a wide range of them—many categories of service work, for example, are equally accessible to minority men and to white women as well as, of course, to minority women. The same is true of semiskilled and domestic labor. It has been estimated that substitutability in merely 5 to 15 percent of positions is sufficient to have such an effect (R. Blumberg 1978; p. 27).

The major occupation from which women are pretty much excluded is nonfarm labor, while the major occupations from which minority men are largely excluded are clerical and sales work. It seems, with these major exceptions, that when minority people are available for the menial jobs they are used for them, but when they are not, or when discrimination against them is mitigated, white women come to fill many of these same occupations.

HOMEMAKING

The early capitalist system perpetuated and further developed the division of labor in which the working class man worked outside the home, while the wife took care of virtually all other tasks necessary to keep him in reasonable shape to keep going to the factory, while at the same time bringing up another generation of workers (and wives of workers). Before the development of socialized and mechanized housework (sewing machines, washing machines, vacuum cleaners, dishwashers, prepared foods, store-bought clothes, refrigerators, and especially central heating and hot and cold running water), and the development of scientific birth control and modern medicine (which have resulted in smaller numbers of children to take care of), the labor equivalent of one industrial worker was required for every two workers to keep the working class family functioning.

Women's continued specialization in these tasks was not so much due to men's greater compatibility with factory work, as (similar to previous societies) with the continued greater compatibility of women with child care related tasks. Only women bore children, and it was necessary that they bear large numbers of them because so many died before reaching adulthood. Moreover, modern birth control techniques were not available, and modern formula feeding and other technical aids to infant and child care had not yet been developed. All this, but above all the requirements of breast-feeding, meant that women, and not men, would continue to specialize in homemaking.

Working class women are much more likely than middle class women both to identify with the homemaker role and to assert that they like housework. Ann Oakley found that 60 percent of the working class women in her study in contrast to only 20 percent of the middle class women stated they liked homemaking. She also found that 75 percent of working class women tended to define themselves primarily as homemakers as compared with only 25 percent of middle class women (Oakley 1974, pp. 66, 72, 123). Although she found a high level of dissatisfaction with homemaking in all classes, there was an especially high level of dissatisfaction among women in higher class positions. She found that 62 percent of the women she studied with low status waged jobs and 100 percent of those women with high status jobs felt dissatisfied with homemaking. Another study found that about the same proportion of full-time homemakers in the middle and working class aspired to have a "career" and were satisfied with homemaking—about 30 to 35 percent (Ferree-Marx 1980, p. 106). It appears that when a working class woman is asked whether or not she "likes housework" she is probably comparing it with her paid job (and evaluates it positively), but when asked whether or not she is "dissatisfied," answers in absolute, rather than relative terms, reflecting the inherent failure of homemaking to be rewarding.

If homemaking is more oppressive than wage labor for the *working class* it is not because it requires more hours (it does not), it is inherently more menial or degrading (it is not), it is less creative or more boring (it is not), or because women do not identify with the homemaking role (they do). It is rather because full-time homemaking makes women economically dependent on their husbands, who thus tend to become dominant because of the women's lack of economic power, and because of its isolating nonsocialized nature, which cuts women off from other adults through most of the day (unlike wage labor, which puts people in relationships of solidarity and cooperation with others).

The relative role of husband and wife in decision making in the family is in good part a function of the relative economic power of each partner. When the woman works full time outside of the home her political role is significantly enhanced. When she brings home an income of more or less the same size as the man's her position is enhanced further. When she brings home all or most of the income, she is normally dominant in decision making (see Kreps 1976, pp. 107-8). Direct relationship to the means of production provides the basis for economic independence for women. It is the key resource in the decision-making process.

The classical studies of the effects of which spouse brings home the wage on the relative position of husband and wife were done on families where the husband became chronically unemployed and consequently became reliant on his wife for economic support. These studies show a sharp deterioration in the power position of the man and a strong tendency for the wife to become the dominant partner (see, for example, Bakke 1940, sect. 2; Komarovsky 1940, chap. 2). Blood and Wolfe in their classic study of Detroit families found that in families where the wife worked the husband's power was less than in those families where she did not. They further found that the less the husband worked the more power was exercised by the wife, and that the more years the wife had worked since marriage, the greater her power relative to her husband (1960, pp. 40-41).

The effect of the proletarianization of women on their role in the family (largely effected through her independent source of income) is greatly inhibited by the fact that working wives typically make much less than their husband, thus perpetuating the wife's economic dependency. Even though the ratio of earnings of women who work full time the year around stayed pretty much constant at around 0.59 from the 1950s through the end of the 1970s, because an ever increasing percentage of women worked, the ratio of *total* female to male income rose from 0.19 in 1950 to 0.25 in 1970 and 0.28 in 1977 (U.S. Department of Commerce 1980, p. 460). More important for the amount of potential economic power possessed by women, however, are: her earning potential if she were to work full time (here the 0.59 figure is central), and the actual proportion of family income working wives bring to the household. In 1970 working wives accounted for 26.7 percent of family income, and in 1977 26.1 percent. Wives who worked full time the year around brought in 38.6 percent of total family income in 1970 and 38.2 percent in 1977 (U.S. Bureau of the Census 1980a, p. 79).

In the 1967 to 1975 period a divorced woman who did not remarry experienced an average decline in real income of 29 percent, while men who did not remarry experienced an average 19 percent decline. Because women traditionally provide the bulk of support for children after separation, the ratio of income to need declined 7 percent for women but increased by 30 percent for men (Vanek 1980, p. 286). The potential of dissolution of marriage (a very real possibility in late monopoly capitalism) exerts considerable force in favor of the contin-uation of male dominance within the family. Thus although women are growing in economic power as they enter the labor force, the clear predominance of the man in bringing home the family income (combined with the probability that she would bear the greater burden of child care in the event of a breakup) leaves most wives in an economically dependent position. It is of interest to note that except in the very poorest and very richest families, the *working* wife's proportional contribution to family income is more or less a constant (women contribute somewhat more in the poorest families, men in the very richest).

It is not necessary for a given wife to be actually working for the general proletarianization of women to have an effect on her. Many wives have worked for considerable lengths of time and are planning to go back to work again. These women, having had the experience of wage labor, and knowing that it is readily available again when they need it, can well have a relationship to their husbands more like that of working women. Further, the socially acceptable standards of what is proper in husband-and-wife relationships (who should make decisions, how much housework each should do, and so on) are in good measure established, with a cultural lag to be sure, by the *typical* experience of the families in a class. Thus the experience of working women is coming increasingly to influence the relationships between all men and women especially in the working class.

The husband's relative role in decision making varies by class. Petty-bourgeois husbands as a rule have greater decision making power in the family than do working class men (see Blood and Wolfe 1960, p. 31; Vanfossen 1979, p. 309). This is primarily a result of the fact that in the petty-bourgeoisie women are much less likely to work than in the working class (but also in its upper reaches, the fact that if she does work she tends to bring in a smaller portion of the family income). In sum, the relative economic power of nonprofessional petty-bourgeois wives is less than for most working-class wives. The rather small minority of petty-bourgeois families in which the wife works full time at a professional job and brings home an income comparable to that of her husband are an exception to the general middle class pattern. It is in these families, perhaps above all others, that there is most likely fairly equal participation in decision making.

The relatively greater power of middle class husbands compared to working class husbands is transmitted to the household division of labor. Although different studies have found different results about the distribution of household chores between the working class and the middle class, the bulk of evidence suggests that professional and managerial men do the least housework. Blood and Wolfe found that in their sample of Detroit families that the higher the husband's income, the greater the proportion of household tasks performed by women (1960, p. 60). Ann Oakley found that high income middle class men "tend to be low on help with housework." Oakley also found working class men to rank low, and low income middle class men to rank high on contribution to housework (1974, pp. 137, 141). Studies on male contribution to child care tend to show that there is a slight tendency for middle class men to help out more than working class men in this area (Reid 1977, p. 154; Oakley 1974, p. 137). The low general participation of high-income middle-class men in housework would seem to reflect both their greater economic power relative to their wives and the lesser probability of their wives' working full time (and hence the greater time the wives have for household tasks). The petty-bourgeois husbands' relatively greater participation in child care responsibilities might well indicate that some involvement with children is considered to be more a positive form of recreational activity in this class than among poorer families. The tendency of lower income men to participate more in general household tasks would seem to reflect both their lesser economic power in relation to their wives and the greater need for help around the house, coming from the greater probability of their wives working full time outside of the home. It could very well be that working class males' lesser involvement with child care reflects the greater demands of tiring menial labor on working class men, and thus their greater need for rest and relaxation after work. It could also be in good part a residual of the patriarchal values of traditional peasant life where child care was, above all else, clearly the women's responsibility (it should be remembered that most working class families are still only about two generations away from rural life most often in the U.S. South or central or southern Europe).

The Effect of Homemaking on Women's Consciousness

Women have traditionally been more politically conservative than men (see Duverger 1955; Szymanski 1978, chap. 5). Women voted for the German right in the 1920s and 1930s in greater numbers than did men, even though the right's program for women was "kitchen, church, and children." The women's vote prevented the Communist Party and its allies from taking over the Italian government in the elections of 1948 and kept Allende from being elected president of Chile in 1958. Wherever there have been Socialist and Communist parties competing with religious and nationalist parties for the loyalties of the masses of people, the evidence indicates that women historically have disproportionately supported the religious and nationalist rather than the leftist parties (even though these latter parties typically have programs far more supportive of women's rights than do the former).

It is the parochializing and isolating effect of specialization in domestic labor rather than in socialized production outside of the home that is the cause of women's traditionally greater conservatism. Homemaking promotes mysticism and religiosity as well as a tendency to see problems as individual or personal rather than structural. Most of a homemaker's time is spent with children, being exposed to the mass media, or performing trivial tasks as an individual. Homemaking insulates a woman from the collective experience of working life (encouraging her to see her problems as unique) and thus hinders the development of a progressive political consciousness. In contrast, the effect of wage labor, especially in the working class, is to provide the woman worker with the structural opportunity for greater intraclass communication. Socialized labor facilitates talking about common problems and focusing on collective solutions, provides the space necessary to develop collective responses, clarifies the structural nature of collective problems, and creates the feeling that individual hopes for personal solutions are not viable (see Lipset 1959, 1960, chap. 7; Szymanski 1978 chap. 3; Kerr and Siegel 1964).

An examination of political attitudes taken from the 1975 and 1976 National Opinion Research Center's annual General Social Survey shows that the political differences between the sexes is in fact a result of women being disproportionately engaged in homemaking. Table 12.13 shows that there is a clear and systematic difference between employed women and homemakers, with employed women being significantly more progressive on five of the ten questions and homemakers being significantly more progressive on none. It should be noted that 4 percent more employed women defined themselves as liberals and 3 percent more supported McGovern (see Table 12.13). The difference between the two groups is particularly strong on civil rights, civil liberties, feminism, and antimilitarism, in all cases, of course, with employed women being more progressive. It should be noted that when men are compared to employed women, employed women are significantly more progressive on six questions, while men are more progressive on only one; however, when homemakers are compared to men, men are significantly more progressive on five questions, with homemakers more progressive on none. It is clear that homemaking is a conservatizing force.

Looking at the middle class separately it can be seen that on nine of the ten questions at least 2 percent more employed women than homemakers were progressive (see Table 12.14). We also see that while there is at least a two percentage point difference in favor of men on eight of the ten questions when comparing homemakers to men, this is the case with only one question when comparing men to

TABLE 12.13: Political Attitudes by Sex and Women's Employment Status, 1975-76

Percentage of Those With Opinions Who:	Men	Employed Women	Female Homemakers
Define themselves as liberals	50.9%	50.4%	46.4%
Supported McGovern in 1972	40.4	44.0	41.2
Support greater welfare spending	18.9	18.4	20.9
Support reduced military spending	32.2	35.4	25.1
Think that communism might be all right at least for some	25.6	19.3	16.5
Are favorably inclined toward the People's Republic of China	44.0	44.0	43.3
Support the right of Communists to speak	60.0	67.6	45.7
Think that it is right for blacks to push even where they are not wanted	24.6	34.3	25.4
Think that interracial marriage should be legal	66.8	73.2	57.4
Do not think that women's place is in the home	65.0	70.3	58.4

Sources: National Opinion Research Center General Social Surveys, 1975 and 1976.

employed women. Within the middle class homemaking is very clearly a conservatizing force. In the working class, however, at least during the mid-1970s there was little or no tendency for employed women to be more progressive than homemakers (both were more conservative than men).

The tendency for homemaking to operate as a conservatizing force operates the most strongly among younger women. Middle class employed women under 40 are more progressive than homemakers on all ten questions (see Table 12.15). On nine of the ten questions these women were also at least two percentage points more progressive than middle class men under age 40, even while on seven of the questions men were at least two percentage points more progressive

TABLE 12.14: Political Attitudes of Middle Class and Working Class by Sex and Women's Employment Status, 1975–76

Percentage of Those With Opinions Who:	Middle Class[a]			Working Class[b]		
	Men	Employed Women	Female Homemakers	Men	Employed Women	Female Homemakers
Define themselves as liberals	44.0%	48.6%	37.7%	54.7%	49.2%	40.3%
Supported McGovern in 1972	31.5	38.8	32.7	46.9	47.7	44.7
Support greater welfare spending	14.6	14.5	15.0	21.6	23.4	20.8
Support reduced military spending	41.1	40.2	35.1	26.9	25.9	20.9
Think that Communism might be all right for at least some countries	27.0	26.2	20.7	21.5	15.8	14.1

Are favorably inclined toward the People's Republic of China	47.5	52.5	41.2	43.5	43.8	43.1
Support the right of Communists to speak	69.2	69.5	63.1	51.1	38.7	43.8
Think that it is right for blacks to push even where they are not wanted	35.7	47.3	32.6	16.3	22.3	22.7
Think that interracial marriage should be legal	78.4	79.7	69.1	57.3	47.6	52.1
Do not think that women's place is in the home	76.8	74.5	71.4	57.3	50.7	58.8

aThis category consists of all persons in the U.S. Census categories of professional, technical, and kindred, managers and administrators, and farmers and farm managers. Employed women are defined by their own occupations, homemakers by that of their husbands.

bThis category consists of craftsworkers and kindred, operatives, laborers, and service workers.

Source: National Opinion Research Center Social Surveys 1975 and 1976.

TABLE 12.15: Political Attitudes by Sex and Women's Employment Status for Person's Less Than 40 Years Old, 1975–76

Percentage of Those With Opinions Who:	Middle Class			Working Class		
	Men	Employed Women	Female Homemakers	Men	Employed Women	Female Homemakers
Define themselves as liberals	57.1%	60.0%	49.0%	65.8%	62.1%	50.7%
Supported McGovern in 1972	42.5	48.6	33.3	48.2	53.2	51.3
Support greater welfare spending	14.8	21.7	16.5	23.4	28.4	27.1
Support reduced military spending	49.1	52.1	40.3	22.8	33.3	25.5
Think that Communism might be all right for at least some countries	25.0	33.9	22.7	28.2	10.7	15.3

Are favorably inclined toward the People's Republic of China	49.4	53.3	39.0	46.4	40.0	37.3
Support the right of Communists to speak	79.3	83.6	77.4	59.2	58.3	52.8
Think that it is right for blacks to push even where they are not wanted	48.8	63.9	42.0	22.3	30.9	30.4
Think that interracial marriage should be legal	92.0	91.8	81.3	72.9	68.8	61.0
Do not think that women's place is in the home	87.2	91.5	89.7	61.7	67.5	67.1

Sources: National Opinion Research Center Social Surveys, 1975 and 1976.

than homemakers. It is in this subgroup—young middle class women—that the conservatizing effect of housework is the strongest.

The tendency for employed women to be more progressive than homemakers *is* observable among working class women under age 40. On five of the ten questions there was at least a two percentage point difference in the 1975-76 period in the direction of greater progressivism among the employed. The conservatizing effect of homemaking, however, is not as strong here as in the middle class.

Among middle class women aged 40 and over the general tendency observable among all middle class women operates (although with not quite the same strength as among younger middle class women). There is at least a two percentage point difference in favor of employed women over homemakers on six of the ten questions. Among working class women aged 40 and older no effect of homemaking can be detected.

In summary, homemakers are clearly more conservative than employed women. Employed women in the United States are generally as progressive, if not more progressive, than men, thus indicating that at least most of the tendency for women to be more conservative than men is attributable to differential participation in the wage labor force. These results indicate that homemaking is a parochializing force that hinders the development of progressive structural understandings, while wage labor (for men or women) under socialized conditions promotes structural understandings of a progressive kind.

The conservatizing effect of homemaking operates more strongly in the middle class and more strongly among the young. These effects appear to be additive, i.e., it is among younger middle class women that the conservatizing effect of housework is the greatest, while among older working class women there appears to be no relationship at all (at least in the mid-1970s) between homemaking and conservatism. This would seem to reflect a rather homogeneous female political culture in the working class (especially among older working class women) that incorporates both employed women and homemakers, perhaps due to relatively frequent changes in status (dropping in and out of the labor force at different points in the female life cycle). This appears to be in sharp contrast to the formation of political consciousness among middle class women where there was a considerable difference between homemakers and employed women (who are in good part professionals as well as mostly college educated), especially among younger women, with employed women considerably more progressive than homemakers.

The Transformation of Homemaking and the Socialization of Women's Labor

Revolutionary changes have occurred in the technology of home-making for the working class family since the end of the nineteenth century. Traditionally women grew and canned much of the basic foodstuffs of the working class family, made most of the clothes and many households items, cleaned and washed entirely by hand, and had large numbers of children and breast-fed for lengthy periods.

Indoor plumbing and modern energy were, for the working class, just technological possibilities at the turn of the century. It was not until the 1920s that gas, electricity, and indoor plumbing became nearly universal in urban areas. It was not until the end of the nineteenth century that canned foods become common. Virtually all goods except bread were normally prepared from scratch by the working class homemakers until the early years of the twentieth century (Strasser 1980).

Domestic work became less and less important for capitalism as housework became increasingly mechanized and socialized, and as child care came to take less time and became increasingly socialized. With modern prepared foods, refrigerators, slow cookers, and micro-wave ovens the job of feeding the family has come to require only a fraction of what it formerly required of women's time. The introduc-tion of washing machines, wash and wear clothes, vacuum cleaners, and dishwashers likewise shrunk the necessary time for cleaning, washing, and ironing. Modern medicine, which has greatly reduced infant mortality, and the modern norm of having just two or three children (a corollary of increased affluence and urbanization) together with formula feeding, disposable diapers, and the rapid growth of day care services, kindergartens, and universal primary schools have all reduced the time and energy necessary for childbearing and child care.

Women who work outside of the home spend less than half of the number of hours doing housework as women who do not work outside of the home. Working women in the early 1970s were shown to have averaged 26 hours a week doing housework compared to 55 hours a week for nonworking women. While employed women aver-aged 3.5 hours a day doing housework during the week and 5 hours a day on weekends, nonemployed women averaged 8.5 hours on week-days and 6 hours on weekends (Vanek 1974). Thus even on weekends nonworking women labor more on housework than do working women (see also Hedges and Barnett 1972). The difference was shown not to be a result of the number of children, the age of children, or the amount of help in household tasks but rather to be a result of "lower" housekeeping standards, greater efficiency in performing tasks, and greater reliance on foods and services purchased in the market.

These strongly contrasting figures suggest that working women are performing housework in the *socially necessary labor time*, while nonworking women are engaging in "make-work" designed to fill their day and to fulfill their self-image as performers of an important social function. The number of hours devoted by nonworking women to housework has not changed since the mid-1920s, in spite of the great advances in the productivity and socialization of housework (Vanek 1974). This supports the conclusion that the greater part of such labor today is above and beyond the *socially necessary labor time* required to perform these tasks adequately.

Little empirical support can be found for the idea that women perform two jobs while men perform only one. A Department of Labor study found that in 1965-66 married working women averaged 71.4 hours a week on paid work, commuting to work, housework, and family tasks while married working men averaged 66.5 hours (Hedges and Barnett 1972, p. 11). Vanek found that employed wives spent an average of 71 hours a week (on wage work, household work, and commuting to work) compared to 63 hours a week for employed husbands (8 hours less than working wives). She also found that working husbands spend about 8 hours *more* than nonemployed housewives on these three tasks (Vanek 1980, p. 277). The sex differentials in total time given to family-related tasks does not vary greatly between the sexes.

Vanek found that in the United States in the 1960s married men on the average spent only one-third as much time as women in doing household chores (1980, p. 277). Studies on Finland, France, and Japan done about the same time showed that men in these countries spend from between 30 percent and 50 percent as much time at household chores than did women. A study of families in Syracuse, New York, in 1971 showed that in childless families where the wife was aged 25-39 and did not work men did 20 percent as much housework as the wife, and when the wife did work outside the home 39 percent as much. In families with two children (the younger being between 2 and 5) men also did 20 percent of the housework when the wife was not employed, but 27 percent when the wife did work outside of the home. Regardless of the age of children or the number of children the greatest change resulting from women working was not in the increase in time spent on housework by men, but in the *reduction* in time spent by working women. For example, in childless families, with the wife aged 25-39, working reduced her household chore time from an average of 5.9 hours a day to 3.6 hours (while the husband's contribution in absolute terms did not change appreciably). For families with two children (the youngest between the age of 2 and 5), working outside of the house reduced her time at household chores from 8.2 to 6.2 hours, while the absolute amount of time spent by the husband was unchanged (U.S. Department of Labor 1975, Table 75). Blood and Wolfe also found that the *proportion* of time men spend on housework increases significantly, and further that men assume a number of traditionally female tasks when the wife works outside of the home. They found in corroboration other studies, that when women worked outside of the home and the husband did not there was a radical increase in the proportion of household tasks performed by men as well as a radical reduction in the number of traditionally female tasks, and an increase in the number of household-related traditionally male tasks performed by the working wife (Blood and Wolfe 1960, p. 62).

In summary, the great increase in productivity and the socialization of homemaking is freeing women from full-time household duties for participation in the labor force outside of the home. It no longer takes a team of two workers to support a household, one to sell *his* labor power and the other to look after both. While during the early period of capitalism the necessity for women to perform domestic work for most of the population was undoubtedly the most important material basis of patriarchy, such can not be considered the case in advanced capitalism.

CONCLUSION: WOMEN AND CLASS IN MONOPOLY CAPITALISM

Both the special oppression of women—patriarchy—and their class oppression vary considerably by class within capitalist society. The condition of women varies qualitatively from the working class to the petty bourgeoisie to the capitalist class. In good part this variation is a result of the differential labor force participation of the various classes and of the types of jobs the different classes of women pursue. This variation is also in part a product of the differential motives and means possessed by the men of the different classes for enforcing patriarchy on their nonworking wives.

Women with working class husbands are more likely to work outside of the home than are wives of the petty bourgeoisie or the capitalist class. They are also more likely to work than wives of marginal workers or men in the excluded sector. In 1969 about 46 percent of all wives whose husbands earned between $4,000 and

$8,000 a year worked. They correspond to the heart of the manual working class (the median annual income of male machine operatives in manufacturing in 1968 was $6,200). The higher the income of husbands (above the very low earnings range), the lower the percentage of wives who work (see Table 12.16). In 1969 only 18 percent of women whose husbands made over $25,000 worked outside of the home—this is only 38 percent as many as in families where the husband brought home from $5,000 to $7,000. These data strongly suggest that it is economic necessity—not pursuit of creative careers, desire for "pin money," desire to escape the home, and so on—that drive women to work, since the greater the husband's income the less likely they are to leave the home.

The fact that working class wives are more likely to work than are petty-bourgeois wives suggests that the effect of having an independent income is greater in the working class than in the petty bourgeoisie. On the one hand this means that the condition of working class women stems more from their on-the-job exploitation as wage workers, and less from their at-home experience as homemakers, than is the case for petty-bourgeois women. Petty-bourgeois women typically remain at home as homemakers (spending 55 or so hours a week in housework). Most of this time is above and beyond the socially necessary labor time required to perform these tasks adequately, but it is apparently required in order to preserve a petty-bourgeois life-style as well as to give the wife a feeling that her role is important. The distinctive oppression of housework is more central

TABLE 12.16: Labor Force Participation of Wives in March 1969, by Earnings of Husbands in 1968

Earnings of Husbands	Percentage of All Wives in Labor Force
$ 0– 999	33
1,000– 1,999	38
2,000– 2,999	42
3,000– 3,999	44
4,000– 4,999	45
5,000– 5,999	47
6,000– 6,999	47
7,000– 7,999	45
8,000– 9,999	41
10,000–14,999	35
15,000–24,999	26
25,000 and over	18

Source: Kreps 1971, p. 23.

in this class than in the working class, while the burden of doing both house *and* wage work is heaviest in the working class.

The fact that most petty-bourgeois women who *do* work outside of the home have "careers" rather than "jobs," typically as professionals, means that their working conditions are significantly better than those of working class women. Petty-bourgeois women have considerably greater autonomy and creativity in their work. Their jobs are considerably more rewarding than those of working class women—who are under the constant direct supervision of their bosses, whose work tasks typically have no inherent meaning for the worker and who earn far less than professional women.

Middle class women with professional or managerial careers benefited considerably from the affirmative action programs of the 1970s. It appears that the bulk of the remaining discrimination here is a result of past practices as well as the decisions of many women to take time off from their careers to have children, rather than a result of contemporary discrimination in either admissions to schools, hiring, or promotion policies of the state or private corporations. Women in the professions now have for the most part both very good and rather well paying jobs, as well as promotional opportunities pretty much the equivalent of men. While they have not yet achieved full equality with the men of their class, they would seem to be significantly less oppressed than middle class housewives and qualitatively less oppressed than either working class housewives or working class wage-working women.

Quite different from either petty-bourgeois or working class women are the women of the capitalist class. The situation of these women can hardly be called oppressive. Neither the special oppression of women nor general class oppression is of much consequence in this class, although a considerable division of labor along sex lines *is* maintained. Rather few of the women of this class work either for a salary or as managers of enterprises (but when they do it is in relatively high positions). Most involve themselves primarily in various volunteer "civic work" projects, organizing charitable functions, and running the other social activities of the capitalist class (activities that play a key role in the social cohesiveness of this class). Others amuse themselves as international "jet-setters" (Domhoff 1971, chap. 2). These women in good measure set the social and cultural standards for the rest of the population. They are presented as models to admire and emulate. In all their activities they are "on top," surrounded by servants, employees, and sycophants.

These women, unlike working class and petty bourgeois women, are freed from all the drudgery of housework and child care by the wealth of their families. They have maids and cooks and live-in child care to relieve them of these responsibilities. Moreover, capitalist class men have largely lost the means to enforce patriarchy on their wives. On the one hand the generally highly educated women of this class can find well paid employment relatively easily if necessary (if only because of family and personal connections with other members of the propertied class). On the other hand, the lucrative possibilities of alimony and inheritance give capitalist class women a security unknown to women of the working class or the petty bourgeoisie. In sum, even though there is a sexual division of labor in the contemporary capitalist class, patriarchy can little more be said to exist here than in most hunting and gathering or horticultural societies, where there was also a sexual division of labor based on essential equality. The women of the capitalist class have nothing of consequence in common with their working class "sisters." They are already liberated— liberated from the special oppression of women and liberated from the class oppression of working people.

Wives are often brutalized by their husbands, much more often in subtle ways than through actual physical "battering," as a scape-goat for the oppressive existence of the husband (either as a manual laborer or as a small businessmen). The aggression built up on the job, which can not be directly taken out on the boss, or on customers, suppliers and competitors, can relatively safely (i.e., without retribu-tion) be taken out against an economically dependent wife. It would seem that such manifestations of male chauvinism are most char-acteristic of traditional petty-bourgeois and working class families, rather than of new petty-bourgeois families with working wives or of capitalist class families. Capitalist class men, for example, have many subordinates (both men and women) on which to take out their aggressions. Further, their work is inherently more enjoyable than that of other classes of men, and their wives are more often than not economically independent of them, thus they have less aggression to displace onto wives, and the wives are less likely to put up with it. Working class women (in the office or factory), rather than the wives of men of the capitalist class, are more likely to bear the brunt of their male chauvinism. It must be emphasized that the cause of all forms of male chauvinism is ultimately to be located within the logic of capitalism; either in its generation of patriarchal structures, in the internalization of its sexist ideology, or as a compensation for the daily oppressions of working class or petty-bourgeois life.

Patriarchal structures are both the essential way women are specially oppressed *and* the cause of the other manifestations of women's special oppression—male chauvinism and sexist ideology. While women of the capitalist class are not oppressed in any significant sense by patriarchal structures, and while there are qualitative differences between the petty bourgeoisie and the working class, and between women who are primarily housewives and women who primarily work outside of the home, male chauvinism and sexist ideology would seem to be pretty much constant (although, of course, there is considerable individual variation in male chauvinist behavior— e.g., rape, wife battering—as well as in the way it is expressed and what class of women it primarily affects).

Although all women may be equally caricatured by sexist ideology, not all women suffer equally from its effects. The women most oppressed by it are those who internalize the ideal of being a "good mother" and "good wife," and who thus desire to provide their families with all the conveniences and support the ideal family requires. For a working class or lower petty-bourgeois woman to accomplish this ideal two factors are necessary: first, that she work more or less full time outside of the house to secure enough money to buy the appliances, goods, services, and education that the ideal dictates; and second, that she strive also to be the full-time mother and wife the ideal requires. The impossibility of doing both well puts incredible pressure on women of these classes, a pressure that can well lead to hypertension, emotional breakdowns, alcoholism, and so on as well as be the energy that can be mobilized by the women's liberation movement.

The largest as well as the most oppressed section of women appears to be working class women. But it would seem to be the case that petty-bourgeois homemakers (and perhaps unmarried white-collar women) suffer more from the patriarchal structures of the family (or from the lack of security the family provides). Now that the socially necessary labor time for the drudgery of housework has been so greatly reduced, and the typical woman is coming to spend most of her laboring time in wage labor, the primary form of her oppression is becoming that of a wage worker—a position shared with her brothers and husbands. The lot of working class women is becoming more like that of working class men, with the major difference increasingly becoming the subordination to patriarchal structures on the job experienced by working women. Patriarchy is in good measure being socialized.

It is women in those occupations that structurally put women in touch with one another who are most likely to become politically conscious. It is young and single white-collar workers for the largest firms in the larger cities, students in the larger colleges and universities who live close together, and professional women in situations where there are numbers of women who are in a similar position, and hence who are more in touch with one another, who have the strongest tendency to become Feminist (Dixon 1971). It is house-wives, together with private domestic workers, service and white-collar workers for small firms in smaller cities, and women with a minimum of work experience outside of the home who tend to be the least Feminist (as well as the least class conscious). This is the case because such women are more isolated from one another, and more closely tied to children and husbands than are women in the former categories—not because they are any less subjected to patriarchy. Working class women (including those married women in white-collar jobs whose husbands are manual workers) who work outside of the home are the most likely to develop class consciousness because the socialized conditions of their labor make more transparent the causes of their condition, leading them to see their collective strength and facilitating communication among equals. At the same time their direct experience is reinforced by their interacting closely with their men (who are in a similar class situation).

Women who are released from the home by the socialization and mechanization of housework and are pulled into the wage economy are thereby largely released from the parochializing effect of house-work and exposed directly to class relations. These women are placed in conditions of close contact with large numbers of other workers or professionals who face a similar condition. There they are able to see more clearly the causes of their problems, to feel their collective power, to talk to one another about their common situation, to develop a common realization that their condition is not unique or personal, but rather a product of the institutions of class society, and then to do something about it. Women's consciousness (whether Feminist or class) thus develops among women primarily *outside* of the home.

In summary, the very process that is socializing women's struc-tural relations (because it is profitable for advanced capitalism) is also ripening the conditions not only for the overturning of women's special oppression but also for the building of class solidarity among men and women.

13

Conclusion: Alternatives to Class Society

As long as there have been classes there has been hostility and resistance. The dominated classes have not passively accepted their lot. In this concluding chapter the growth of the socialist movement and its attempt to abolish classes is examined. The origins of anti-class ideas within European feudal society, the formulation of socialist ideas as minor currents within the classical English and French Revolutions, the development of utopian socialism in the early nineteenth century, the growth of working class and especially Marxist socialism over the course of the last third of the nineteenth century, the consolidation of working class socialism around 1900, and the first actual attempts to construct socialist societies in the post-1917 period are all treated.

EARLY HISTORY OF ANTICLASS MOVEMENTS

There were a number of anarcho-communist millenial groups that drew their support from among the peasantry and especially oppressed artisans and proletarians during the late Middle Ages when traditional feudal relationships were being disrupted by the growth of market forces.* During the English peasant revolt of 1381, John Ball preached opposition to lords and kings and the equality of all. Ball celebrated the popular proverb "When Adam delved and Eve

---

*The discussion in this section relies heavily on Cohn 1961; Laidler 1968, pt. 1; MacKenzie 1966, chap. 2.

span, who was then a gentleman?" Ball, arguing within the Christian tradition, maintained that evil men had introduced serfdom and other inequities against the will of God. Ball advocated that the great lords, judges, and lawyers had to be deposed so that all men could enjoy equal freedom, rank, and power, as God had intended (Cohn 1961, p. 211; MacKenzie 1966, p. 22).

In the fifteenth century in Bohemia the Taborites, largely building on the urban poor, developed a communist ideology and maintained themselves for a generation in their own towns. Taborite communities were intended to be completely equalitarian without private property and held together by love (Cohn 1961: 228-230). The Taborites believed the Millenium was to be characterized by the abolition of taxes, dues, rents and all forms of private property, as well as the extermination of all nobles and lords. "All shall live together as brothers, none shall be subject to another." After the capture of the last Taborite stronghold in 1452 the Taborite communist tradition survived only in a sect called the Bohemian or Moravian Brethren which, in order to survive at all, gave up the idea of spreading its system by military conquest, and instead became pacifist and apolitical (Cohn 1961, p. 237).

Anticlass communist currents also emerged during the Protestant Reformation in Germany in the Peasant War of the 1520s and 1530s, especially among the radical Anabaptists in the city of Munster. Thomas Müntzer, the leading figure of the German Peasant's revolt believed (at least at the end of his life) that all things should be common to all, all should receive according to their needs, and there should be neither kings nor lords (Cohn 1961, pp. 258-59). The center of activitist Anabaptism became the city of Munster, which saw a powerful movement supported by the mass of the unemployed and insecure proletarians, many of whom streamed into the city, inspired by the teaching of Thomas Müntzer and his disciple Hans Hut. Steps were taken to establish communal ownership of virtually all material goods including foodstuffs and private houses. Money was effectively abolished. In fact, the surrender of money was made the test of true Christianity (Cohn 1961, pp. 251-95). Like the Taborites a hundred years before in Bohemia, the Munster Anabaptists were crushed by military force. But Anabaptism has survived to the present day in such North American communities as the Mennonites and the Hutterian Brethren (the latter of which continues to practice full Christian communism) (Cohn 1961, p. 306).

Communist currents emerged in the English Revolution of the mid-seventeenth century. The Levellers, who had considerable support among the rank and file of Cromwell's New Model Army, drew the democratic ideas of the revolution to their logical conclusion by attacking all class privilege. They saw the Golden Age of England as the time before the Norman conquest (which they saw as having placed a privileged hierarchy in power after destroying the original communal form of English property). The extreme formulation of Leveller ideology was expressed by Gerald Winstanley, the leader of a small group known as the Diggers, who were explicit in their demand for the restoration of communism. In 1649 the Diggers actually attempted to take over and farm some land according to communist principles. They were, however, dispersed by the Army (MacKenzie 1966, p. 23). Winstanley maintained that, "there shall be no buying and selling of the earth, nor the fruits thereof . . . If any of a family want other provisions, they may go to the storehouse and fetch without money. . . . As everyone works to advance the common stock, so every one shall have the use of any commodity in the storehouse for his pleasure and comfort and livelihood, without buying or selling or restraint from anybody" (Laidler 1968, p. 40).

The greatest appeal of anticlass and communist ideas during the late Middle Ages came from the poor, who were most affected by the growth of commercial relations: marginal workers, new proletarians, and the unemployed, both in rural and urban areas. The uprooted poor were shaken by economic deprivation as well as by the undermining of traditional authority (both of which were caused by economic dislocations encumbent on commercialization). It was these uprooted poor who formed the basis for the first socialist movements in European history (Cohn 1961, pp. 314-15).

During the French Revolution a militant communist current emerged under the leadership of Babeuf. It was said that 17,000 men were prepared in April 1796 to follow his lead in a general insurrection against all inequality. He believed that all private property should be abolished and placed in the hands of the nation and that the distribution of society's resources should occur on the basis of need. Leaders would receive the same remuneration as ordinary workers and would rotate in office to prevent entrenchment in power (Laidler 1968, pp. 46-47). Babeuf however, was arrested before he could call for the insurrection and was executed. Babeuf had an enduring influence on modern socialism, however, largely through his follower Buonarrotti, who had considerable success in spreading Babeuf's ideas among those who were to play a leading role in the foundation of modern working class socialist parties in France, Great Britain, Germany, and Belgium. Babeuf, unlike the earlier socialists, was not inspired by millenial religion. Rather, he gave careful attention to questions of organization, strategy, and tactics, developing an elaborate propaganda machine and secret cells. He was the first socialist to argue that working class power had to be won by an armed and carefully prepared revolution against the wealthy and powerful (MacKenzie 1966, pp. 24-25; Lichtheim 1969, pp. 20-23).

After the defeat of the French Revolution and the reversal of the progressive hopes it inspired, hopes which for a generation had been formulated in terms of political and insurrectionary action, the primary expression of anticlass and equalitarian ideas became utopian socialism.

UTOPIAN SOCIALISM

The followers of Saint-Simon in France advocated a system in which productive property would belong to the state, inheritance would be abolished, and the most intelligent would gravitate to the top decision-making positions, with everyone working according to their ability and receiving a reward according to services rendered (Laidler 1968, p. 53).* Another French Utopian Socialist, Cabet, wrote an influential novel that advocated an equalitarian socialist society in which the state owned most of the means of production and divided the product of industry equally among workers. There were a number of attempts to put Cabet's ideas into practice (some in the United States) (Laidler 1968, p. 48).

The most influential of the French Utopian Socialists was Charles Fourier. Fourier, however, was less thoroughgoing in his socialism than most other Utopians. He advocated the division of the product of industry according to labor, capital, and talent, not just according to work or need. While the Saint-Simonists envisioned a large-scale industrial state technocratic socialism, the Fourierists envisioned small-scale communities. The communities, established according to Fourierist principles were the most successful of all non-religious communities. The most famous of these was the Brooks Farm Phalanx in Massachusetts and the North American Phalanx in New York (Laidler 1968, pp. 56-60, 106-7; Lichtheim 1969, p. 34).

---

*The discussion in this section relies heavily on Bestor 1950; Holloway 1951; Laidler 1968, pt. 1; Lichtheim 1969, pt. 1; and Noyes 1870. For other discussions of various utopian socialist communities see Andrews 1953; Bennett 1967; Burton 1939; Carden 1971; Fried 1970, chaps. 1, 2; Harrison 1969; Kantor 1973; Spiro 1956; and Peters 1967.

Together with Fourier the most influential figure in the secular Utopian Socialist movement was Robert Owen, a wealthy British capitalist. Owen's ideas were thoroughly communist and left no room for private property. He advocated, and in fact attempted to set up, communities in which both labor and distribution of the products of labor were equal for all. In 1824 in Indiana he set up a colony according to his pure communist principles. However, after three years and the expenditure of most of his fortune, the colony failed. Owen, who recruited through newspaper adds, found that his colony had more people willing to share equally in distribution than share equally in work (Laidler 1968, pp. 94-95). The Utopian socialist colonies, unlike earlier Christian communism, did *not* base themselves primarily on the poorest and most oppressed sections of the rural and urban populations. They instead recruited mainly from intellectuals and artisans. This reflects the fact that they were not so much a manifestation of the resistance against class, which stems from the immediate pressures of class oppression, as an attempt to live a more rational life on the part of people who were intellectually convinced of the virtue of more equalitarianism.

The most successful attempts to live according to the communist principle "from each according to one's ability and to each according to one's needs" were achieved by those inspired by Christianity, such as the descendants of the German Anabaptists (e.g., the Hutterites) as well as other Christians who like them took the Biblical injunction "And Ye Shall Have all Things in Common" literally. The successful Christian communist groups recruited from working people and peasant farmers. The Shakers, a Christian sect who saw their founder Mother Ann as the second Savior (God came to earth the first time as a man, Jesus; the second time as a woman, Mother Ann), established full communism in the 1780s and thrived for 150 years under these principles. Numerous other Christian groups including George Rapp's Harmony Society, the Amana Colonies in Iowa, and John Humphrey Noyes' fascinating Onieda commune in upstate New York prospered for many years according to full communist principles (see Fried 1970, chap. 2). The success of both secular and religious communism in the early nineteenth century in the United States reflects both the dislocations caused by the spread of commercial relationships in this period and the general wave of political reaction (and the discrediting of revolutionary aspirations) in the post-French Revolution generation.*

---

*Karl Marx maintained that Utopian Socialists, especially those inspired by Robert Owen, played a progressive role in proving the viability of equalitarian and communal ways of production and distribution:

With the exception of a few viable Christian groups, most of the early nineteenth century communist communities in the United States withered away by the last years of the century, largely falling victim to the ever more intense commercialization and individualization of the broader society. It should be noted, however, that a few survived, most prominently the Shakers and the Hutterities. The Hutterities have continued to thrive and grow in the last years of the twentieth century on the upper Great Plains of the United States and Canada (in spite of what has at times been considerable political, economic, and social pressure from the outside).

THE SOCIALIST WORKING CLASS MOVEMENT

As both the secular and religious utopian socialist movements declined the modern socialist movement based in the industrial working class grew. This new working class socialism was oriented to transforming existing capitalist relations through political struggle and eventual social revolution (rather than through setting up ideal communities that would prove by example the superiority of socialism to *all classes* of the population). The old utopian strategy was to eventually win over everyone, rich and poor alike, to living according to socialist principles by demonstrating in practice the superiority of socialism as a way of life. The new strategy, like that of Babeuf, understood that socialism has a class basis, with some people favoring it because they would benefit; while others, namely the rich and powerful opposing it, because they would loose. The new socialism was based on class struggle, and in the case of its Marxist and anarchist variants, on the understanding that the ruling class would give up its privileges only when confronted with superior military force.

We speak of the co-operative movement, especially the co-operative factories raised by the unassisted efforts of a few bold "hands." The value of these great social experiments cannot be over-rated. By deed, instead of by argument, they have shown that production on a large scale, and in accord with the behests of modern science, may be carried on without the existence of a class of masters employing a class of hands; that to bear fruit, the means of labour need not be monopolised as a means of dominion over, and of extortion against, the labouring man himself; and that, like slave labour, like serf labour, hired labour is but a transitory and inferior form, destined to disappear before associated labour plying its toil with a willing hand, a ready mind, and a joyous heart. In England, the seeds of the co-operative system were sown by Robert Owen; the working men's experiments, tried on the Continent, were, in fact, the practical upshot of the theories, not invented, but loudly proclaimed, in 1848 (Marx 1864, p. 383).

The Marxist socialism that came to dominate much of the working class movement argued (contrary to utopian socialism) that an equalitarian social order based on the communist principle of from each according to one's ability, to each according to one's needs, would be possible only when all of society was transformed through a political seizure of state power by the organized working class, which would then use its state to reinforce spontaneous tendencies toward communalism rather than to undermine them. A workers' state would teach all children the moral superiority of communism over individualism, give economic incentives, including loans, to cooperative enterprises, and, *crucially*, give political support to workers' organizations as well as repress both capitalist enterprises and the capitalist class's attempts to resume state power.

Marxist socialism differed from anarchism (and syndicalism, with which it was in competition in the working class movement through World War I) on the question of the process of creating full communist relations. The anarchists argued that more or less immediately after the seizure of state power by the working class the entire repressive state apparatus would be dismantled, and that people would then immediately begin to live according to the principle of from each according to their ability, to each according to their needs. The Marxists, on the other hand, did not share the extreme optimism of their opponents (even while agreeing with their ultimate vision). They put forth a rather more realist ("scientific") view of the problems and contradictions of socialist construction. Marxists have always argued that a period of a "dictatorship of the proletariat" would be necessary in which the working class would have to repress the old propertied class and their manifestations in antisocialist movements and ideologies.*

Marxists believed that the individualist propensities of people, so deeply rooted in the old society, would take a generation or more to be wiped out and replaced with an appropriately high level of consciousness that would make the communist idea of distribution according to need (rather than by work) actually viable:

---

*To Quote Marx:
This socialism is the *declaration of the permanence of the revolution*, the *class dictatorship* of the proletariat as the necessary transit point to the *abolition of class distinctions generally*, to the abolition of all the relations of production on which they rest, to the abolition of all the social relations that correspond to these relations of production, to the revolutionizing of all the ideas that result from these social relations (Marx 1850, p. 223).

> Both for the production on a mass scale of this communist conscious-
> ness, and for the success of the cause itself, the alteration of men on
> a mass scale is necessary, an alteration which can only take place in
> a practical movement, a revolution; this revolution is necessary,
> therefore, not only because the ruling class cannot be overthrown in
> any other way, but also because the class overthrowing it can only
> in a revolution succeed in ridding itself of all the muck of ages and
> become fitted to found society anew (Marx and Engels 1845, p. 69).

In the revolutions that swept Europe in 1848 socialism played a
subsidiary role. This was especially true in France, where the ideas
of Louis Blanc had considerable influence in the French working
class. Working class secular socialism (leaving aside the Babeuf conspiracy during the first French Revolution) came, for the first time,
to be a force. Karl Marx and Friedrich Engels themselves became
socialists in the period just before the outbreak of these revolutions,
played a role in them in the German Rhineland, and, in fact, wrote
the *Communist Manifesto* in 1848 as a contribution to a socialist
program and an analysis for the working class movement of this
period. However, the revolutionary movements of 1848, especially
their socialist wings, were thoroughly crushed, with many of their
leading figures including Karl Marx forced into exile. The next
decade and a half was a period of general reaction (something like the
period after the Congress of Vienna in 1815) that saw very little
working class socialist activity anywhere. It was not until the mid-
1860s that the young working class socialist movement recovered
from its defeats of 1848-49.

In 1864 the International Workingmen's Association (IWMA) was
founded (the First International) on the initiative of French and
British trade union leaders who saw the desirability of organized
contacts among European workers for the purpose of rendering assistance to each other (e.g., to prevent international migration of cheap
labor being used to drive down wage rates). The IWMA was based on
individual membership and at its peak in 1870 had 800,000 members.
It became a major force in Belgium and Switzerland, and achieved
some success in France, Italy, Spain, and Germany. A number of
varieties of socialism were represented in the International. At its
founding there was considerable debate among such currents as the
Lassallians in Germany (who exclusively advocated political and reformist actions, i.e., no strikes or revolutions); the Proudhonist anarchists in France (who advocated establishing a federation of self-
autonomous communes); and the Marxists. Later the primary struggle
in the International became that between Marx and the extreme
anarchism represented by Bakunin. In 1872, after the peak of the

influence of the organization had passed, Marx achieved hegemony when the anarchists were expelled (Caute 1966, p. 53; MacKenzie 1966, pp. 58-77).

The revival of working class socialism suffered a severe blow with the repression that followed the violent suppression of the Paris Commune in 1871. This first working class led revolution (which held power in Paris for almost two months in the wake of France's defeat in the 1870-71 Franco-Prussian War) was brutally put down with thousands executed. Throughout Europe working class organizations were repressed out of fear of repeat occurrences. The International Workingmen's Association suffered mortally from this repression and was finally disbanded in 1876. Nevertheless, it left a considerable legacy of Marxist socialist ideas that soon came to have a considerable influence throughout Europe.

Anarchist ideas gained considerable currency, especially in southern Europe, where peasant individualism was still a strong force in the proletariat in the 1870s. In 1873 there were risings under anarchist leadership in Barcelona, Seville, Cadiz, and Cartegena in Spain. However, in the 1880s and 1890s Marxist ideals became predominant in the European working class movement with the rapid proliferation and growth of socialist parties. In 1889 the new socialist parties came together and formed another International (the Second International), now constituted on the basis of an affiliation of rather strong working class socialist parties (Caute 1966, pp. 54-55; MacKenzie 1966, p. 76).

Great Britain

Following the failure of Robert Owen's attempt to establish communist communities in the United States in the 1820s, he turned his efforts to building the trade union and cooperativist movements in Great Britain and infusing them with a socialist consciousness.* Owenite ideas had considerable currency in both the trade unions and the producer's and consumer's cooperatives that were springing up in Great Britain in the early 1830s. Owen was the leading figure in the Grand National Consolidated Trades Union, which at its height claimed over half a million members. This union struggled with employers to improve conditions and attempted to set up worker-owned cooperatives to drive the capitalists out of business as

---

*The discussion in this section relies heavily on Caute 1966; Cole 1948; Laidler 1968, chaps. 10, 17, 18, 31; and MacKenzie 1966.

well as rejected political action in favor of the idea of an eventual general strike of all workers that would bring the capitalist system down. However, in the face of state repression the Owenite union movement collapsed in the mid-1830s.

In the latter part of the 1830s the Chartist Movement became a major force in Great Britain. The working class demand for a People's Charter that would give the working class the vote and democratize Parliament became the central issue in the British working class. It was pressed by giant demonstrations, petitions, and riots. With the collapse of the Chartist movement in 1848, the primary thrust of British working class activity was redirected into trade unionism of a less agressive and politically more moderate kind than had been the case since the early 1830s.

However, in the 1860s a socialist left reemerged within the British Trade Union movement (as manifested in the British Unionist's initiation of the First International). In the 1880s the British labor movement became an important independent force in British politics. The Social-Democratic Federation (which came to have Marxian politics) was founded in the 1880s, although it never attained a large membership. The Independent Labor Party (ILP), a non-Marxist socialist group founded in the early 1890s, became a greater force. The ILP advocated the collective ownership and control of the means of production (to be achieved through parliamentary reforms). In the mid-1900s the Labour Party (which was based on the trade unions) became a significant group in Parliament. In 1918 the Labour Party adopted a program of immediate nationalization of land, railways, mines, electricity, insurance, harbors, and so on. By the mid-1920s this party, with its now clearly (reformist) socialist program, had become the equal of the other major parties in voting strength, having firmly established itself and its moderate socialism in the British working class (Caute 1966, pp. 57-58; MacKenzie 1966, pp. 83-89; Laidler 1968, pp. 316-19).

In 1945 the Labour Party won control of the British government in a landslide election and instituted a number of important pro-working class reforms (national health insurance, nationalization of some basic industries, greatly expanded social security programs, public housing, and so on). However, in spite of the fact that it has never repealed the clause in its constitution pledging to turn over *all* basic industry to the working class, it has stopped far short of this traditional socialist goal. All subsequent Labour governments foresook any significant reforms (as well as advocacy of socialism), although the party maintains a vaguely socialist image. It remains the party of the British working class.

Germany

Germany was the first country to produce a massive socialist (and Marxist) working class party.* In 1863 the German Working-men's Association under the leadership of Ferdinand Lassalle was founded. Lassalle, the principal opponent of Marx and his supporters in the German working class movement, emphasized the centrality of gaining universal suffrage and through it reforms (rather than industrial action or cooperatives) (Laidler 1968, pp. 224-28; Caute 1966, p. 59). By 1864 Lassalle's party had about 5,000 members. Another German working class socialist grouping was founded a few years after Lassalle's in which Wilhelm Liebknecht and August Bebel, followers of Karl Marx, became the leaders (Laidler 1968, p. 230). In the elections of 1871 the two socialist groupings together polled about 100,000 votes, and in 1874, 350,000. In 1875 the two groups united into the German Socialist Party (SPD) under the Gotha Program (which represented a compromise between the ideas of Lassalle and the ideas of Marx). In 1877 the new Unified Party won 500,000 votes and sent nine representatives to the German Reichstat. In 1878, the German state responded to the rapidly growing German working class socialist movement by enacting repressive legislation that made it illegal for the socialists to hold meetings or to publish or distribute newspapers or other literature. However, they continued to be allowed to run candidates for Parliament. By 1890 (in spite of the restrictive legislation) they had become the single largest party in Germany securing almost a million and a half votes. In 1890 the antisocialist laws were abandoned. During the period of illegal activity the Marxist tendency in the Party became predominant. This development was ratified at the Party's congress at Erfurt in 1891, where for the first time a fully Marxist program was adopted (MacKenzie 1966, pp. 100-3; Laidler 1969, p. 232). After 1891 the Social Democratic Party continued to grow in influence in the German working class; emerging as the leading force in the world socialist movement because of its size, organization, and intellectual caliber.

With the collapse of the German army in early November 1918, the socialist movement became *the* leading political force in Germany. Workers' councils were organized to run factories throughout Germany. Socialism was in the air. The old propertied classes were

---

*The discussion in this section relies heavily on Berlau 1949; Caute 1966; Hunt 1964; Kolko 1968; Kolko and Kolko 1972; Laidler 1968, chaps. 19, 20, 21, 32; Lidtke 1966; Lutz 1922; Morgan 1965; and Schorske 1955.

demoralized and in disarray. A general strike was called by the Workers' and Soldiers' Councils. Workers marched through the streets proclaiming revolution. But the Social Democratic Party (SPD) leaders, who formed the first post-Kaiser government, did not implement the program of the SPD. Instead they merely called for the universal franchise on the basis of proportional representation and the guarantee of civil liberties. The failure of the right-wing Social Democrats who controlled the government in this decisive period of upheaval to implement a socialist program caused the left-wing Socialists to split from the government and call for authentically socialist policies. The most left of these groups, the Spartacans, under the leadership of Rosa Luxemburg and Karl Liebknecht called for working class insurrection. With the collusion of the right-wing Social Democratic government the leaders of this organization were killed by right-wing gangs and the revolutionary movement was crushed.

The elections for the National Assembly in 1919 gave the Social Democrats 39 percent of the vote and the independent Socialists (who were to their left) about 8 percent. The revolutionary Spartacans boycotted the election (Laidler 1968, pp. 506-7; MacKenzie 1966, p. 141). The new Communist Party formed in good part from the remnants of the Spartacans led a number of attempted insurrections in the early 1920s (the most prominent were focused in Bavaria and Hamburg) that were quickly crushed by the state. The German Communist Party (KPD), however, consolidated itself, becoming the largest Communist Party in the world outside of the Soviet Union. In 1928 it won 11 percent of the vote and in 1932, 17 percent. (By this latter year it had grown to almost the size of the Social Democrats, whose share of the vote shrank from 30 percent to 20 percent between these same years.) While the middle class was streaming into the Nazi Party during the early Depression years, the German working class was moving toward revolutionary politics as represented by the KPD.

One of Hitler's first acts was to ban both the Social Democratic and the Communist Parties (as well as unions and strikes). In short order the concentration camps were set up for working class militants (especially Communist leaders). Communists activists as well as other revolutionaries were either jailed (and mostly eventually exterminated) or driven into exile by the Nazi government. Nevertheless, as the Allied armies swept the Nazis from power in 1945, there was a spontaneous rebirth of traditional German working class socialism. Workers attempted to seize control of factories and once again revolutionary socialism was in the air. In the eastern part of Germany, the Soviet army at first allowed this spontaneous movement to take its course (virtually all the former owners and managers fled with Hitler's armies, most attempting to surrender to the Americans). The Soviets, however, soon took direct control out of the workers' hands, in favor of a broad front of tendencies and only partial nationalization. Within a few years Soviet policy once again changed with the institution of full nationalization and highly centralized planning. The German Democratic Republic (GDR) was declared in 1949 under the leadership of the Socialist Unity Party (a merger of the large East German section of the Social Democratic Party with the smaller, but powerful, Communist Party). Although instituted under the guidance of the Soviet Union (and pretty much a mirror image of the Soviet model of socialism), the GDR proceeded to institute a wide range of radical economic and social measures that greatly benefited the German working class (see Kolko 1968, chap. 20; Kolko and Kolko 1972, chap. 5).

Meanwhile, in the western zones of occupied Germany the Allied armies, worried about the rebirth of the strong German working class revolutionary movement, immediately took power away from the spontaneous workers' councils, banned all strikes, and prohibited the formation of anything other than union locals. In many places the local Nazi authorities were temporarily kept in office and the old Nazi Army was kept mobilized for months to ensure "law and order" (i.e., prevent social revolution). The Social Democrats in the West emerged from the war significantly stronger than the Communists (who had been almost totally decimated by 12 years of Nazi terror and intense anticommunist propaganda). In the first postwar West German elections in 1947, the Communist Party received 9.5 percent of the vote as compared to 35.0 percent by the Social Democrats. It should be noted that immediately after the war the majority tendency of the Social Democrats favored thorough nationalization of German industry and a more or less complete socialist transformation of German society. However, ten years of repression then prosperity under watchful U.S. guidance once again took the revolutionary edge off the West German socialism. The Communist Party was banned and the mainstream of the SPD returned to its 1920s policies of moderate reform. The SPD remains the party of the West German working class, receiving 43 percent of the vote in 1980.

France

The French Revolution of 1830 saw considerable agitation in the working class for improvement in its economic and political condition.* In the period after this revolution, the socialist ideas of the rebellious workers fused with the armed traditions of revolutionary democrats in working class uprisings in Lyon in 1831 and 1834, and in Paris in 1832 and 1834. Blanqui, a follower of Babeuf, become the leading figure of this movement (Lichtheim 1969, p. 63). In the 1840s Louis Blanc became the most influential French Socialist, supplanting both the insurrectionist tradition of Blanqui and the utopian traditions associated with Fourier and Saint-Simon. Blanc, calling himself a "scientific socialist," integrated socialist ideas with an economic analysis. Blanc, unlike the utopian socialists, addressed his appeal to the French working class, calling for the establishment of state-owned "social workshops" under workers' control that would provide employment to all. Blanc's vision was one of communism. It was Blanc who coined the formula later adopted by Marxists of "From each according to his ability, to each according to his needs" (Laidler 1968, pp. 60-64). During the revolutions of 1848, Blanc came to have a considerable following in the French working class. A watered down version of his "social workshops" was set up in early 1848 but it was soon sabotaged by the government. In the summer of 1848 a working class insurrection in Paris was bloodily crushed by the government.

Repressed and demoralized as a result of the reaction following 1848, the French Left (similar to the rest of the early working class socialist movement in Europe) did not revitalize until the late 1860s, when groups in the Blanqui tradition as well as others associated with the cooperativist and mutualist ideas of Proudhon became a force in the working class. In 1871, after the humiliating defeat of France by Prussia, the Parisian working class again rose up in revolt, establishing a working class run commune. For almost two months the working class held power in Paris (the first time in history that a secular socialist working class movement had ever held state power). The Paris Commune abolished both the professional army and the professional police, arming the masses of the working class. The Commune made all public officials subject to election (and deposition at any time), paying all at a wage no higher than that of skilled workers (MacKenzie 1966, p. 74). The Commune was violently suppressed with thousands shot in the streets as they were captured. Many times more were imprisoned and exiled. Socialist and union activity was banned in France for years.

---

*The discussion in this section relies heavily on the following: Hobsbawm 1962; Kolko 1968, chap. 4; Kolko and Kolko 1972, pp. 151-60; Laidler 1968, chaps 8, 22; Lissagaray 1967; Lorwin 1914; Mason 1930; MacKenzie 1966, chaps 4, 11; Wohl 1966.

Working class radicalism, however, reemerged in the late 1870s. In 1882 two major socialist parties were formed, the orthodox Marxists (who emphasized revolution) under the leadership of Jules Guesde, and the Possibilists, who emphasized reforms (Laidler 1968, pp. 281-85).

France also saw a major split between the syndicalists, who rejected political action (including voting) in favor of the general strike and economic action as the way to bring about socialism, and the Marxists and Possibilists, who endorsed political action as part of the strategy for change. The syndicalists came to dominate the union movement. In 1892 the national trade union federation adopted the idea of the general strike as the primary strategy to bring about socialism against the advice of the Marxists (who then withdrew from the federation). In 1895 the General Confederation of Labor (CGT) was formed according to revolutionary syndicalist principles. In the 1890s the syndicalists discarded their earlier rejection of revolutionary violence and endorsed industrial sabotage, maintaining that the success of a general strike in bringing about the downfall of capitalism and its replacement by a combined economic-political leadership of a trade union federation depended on militant leadership. The syndicalists won over a number of socialists who became disillusioned with the reformist activities of the socialist parties. While the syndicalists became the dominant force in French unions, the socialist parties became a major force in Parliament, gaining (in spite of syndicalist's abstentionism) more than 50 seats in 1893. Syndicalism rather than Marxism continued to be the dominant political current in the French working class movement until just before World War I (Laidler 1968, chap. 22; MacKenzie 1966, p. 114).

The two main socialist parties merged in 1905 on a program that accepted both the eventual need for a revolution *and* the necessity of pursuing short-run reforms. In 1906 the new unified Socialist Party polled almost 900,000 votes and in 1914 it raised its total to 1.4 million, sending over 100 representatives to the French Parliament. Throughout this period the syndicalist-dominated trade union movement, itself divided between revolutionary and reformist oriented wings, insisted on keeping its independence from the working class Socialist Party (Laidler 1968, p. 304; MacKenzie 1966, p. 118). In France, as in Germany, anticlass ideas gained hegemony in the working class.

Although in the wake of the general European working class upheaval of 1918-19 the Communist Party became an important force in the French working class, the Socialist Party remained larger through France's defeat by Germany in 1940. In 1936 a Popular Front led by Socialist Leon Blum with the support of the Communist

Party (the Party voted with Blum but declined any ministeries) assumed the reigns of government and proceeded to institute a series of important working class reforms (e.g., the 40-hour week, improved social security, legalized collective bargaining, and nationalization of the munitions industries). However, widespread working class enthusiasm was crushed (as were strikes) when it became clear that the Blum government was not about to initiate a thorough socialist transformation of French society. In the wake of disillusionment, the reactivated right replaced the Blum government in 1938 and, in good part, collaborated with the Nazi invaders, establishing the violently antisocialist profascist Vichy regime in that part of France not occupied by Hitler's armies.

The Communist Party grew into a major force by leading the active French resistance to the Nazis. Its resultant immediate postwar prestige spread way beyond the working class of the leftist Socialists. It emerged from the war much stronger than the old Socialist Party. In the face of the Allied military occupation of France, the French Communists, in spite of their considerable strength, choose to join a coalition government led by Charles de Gaulle, rather than attempt to lead a revolutionary process (as the local Communist Parties did in Greece and Yugoslavia). The Communist Party continued to be the principal working class party throughout the post-World War II period. The election of Francois Mitterrand and the landslide victory of his reborn Socialist Party in 1980 (with a moderate program of reform) represented the first time since the 1930s that this party successfully challenged the Communists for predominance within the French working class. In the 1980 legislative elections the Socialist Party received 37.5 percent, the Communist Party 16.2 percent, and independent Socialists 2.0 percent of the total vote cast. The vast majority of French workers continue to identify themselves as socialists (of one or another variety).

THE SOCIALIST MOVEMENT IN THE UNITED STATES

The working class socialist movement in the United States originated from the migration of revolutionary refugees (mostly workers) from Germany after the crushing of the revolutions of 1848.* In 1853 these immigrants organized the American Workingmen's Alliance,

---

*The discussion in this section relies heavily on: Boyer and Morais 1965; Caute 1978; Draper 1957; Dubofsky 1969; Fine 1928; Forster 1952; Fried 1970; Galenson 1960; Glazer 1961; Hicks 1961; Kipnis 1952; Laslett 1970; Lipset and Laslett 1974; Pollack 1962; Shannon 1955; and Weinstein 1967.

whose purpose was to build an independent labor party in the United States. However, the energy of the émigres of 1848 was soon absorbed in the antislavery movement and working class socialism withered until the late 1860s. The rapid expansion of capitalism in this period, the intensification of immigration, the rapid growth of industrial urban slums, and the disillusionment of the immigrants about their life in the United States (there were many myths about the streets being "paved in gold") combined to give birth to both leftist working class parties and militant unionism. The National Labor Union had over 200,000 members in 1869, many of its leading members were also members of the International Workingmen's Association (Laidler 1968, p. 577; Fried 1970, p. 182). In 1870 a provisional central committee of the International Workingmen's Association in the United States was set up that had over 30 sections based in different immigrant groups. The International's world headquarters was moved to the United States in 1872 in the face of repression in Europe. In 1869 a group of German immigrants organized a Lassallean group, the Universal German Workingmen's Association, which in 1877 became the Socialist Labor Party (SLP). In the wake of a national wave of strikes and urban riots in the summer of 1877 the Socialists did quite well in local elections. They polled 7,000 votes in Chicago, 9,000 in Cincinnati, 6,000 in Buffalo, and actually elected a number of city officials in Milwaukee. Socialist influence had spread out of the German immigrant communities. By 1877 there were 8 socialist newspapers in English (and 14 in German) (Fried 1970, p. 185). In spite of its Lassallean origins the SLP adopted Marxist noninsurrectionist politics, and after a nadir in the mid-1880s (following the hysteria and repression after the Haymarket incident of 1886 in which a number of police were killed at a strike rally) grew over the course of the 1890s (Laidler 1968, pp. 578-79; Fried 1870, p. 190).

In the 1870s and 1880s the major trade union movement in the United States was the Knights of Labor. The Knights called for the abolition of the wage system and for public and cooperative ownership of industry. Feeling that strikes were futile, the Knights called for political action as well as for workers to establish producer and consumer cooperatives as the way to replace capitalism with socialism. The Knights had over 1 million members (it was not necessary to be a worker to be a member). Although the Knights' leadership officially repudiated the use of strikes, members would occasionally be driven to take strike action out of desperation. In fact, a rare successful strike against railroad baron Jay Gould gave considerable impetus to the organization.

In the course of the winter of 1885-86 a more or less spontaneous movement grew up within the Knights of Labor calling for a general strike in the spring of 1886 for the eight-hour day. The traditional beginning of spring, May 1, was set for the strike to begin, the idea being that all the working people of the United States should refuse to work until the capitalists granted the eight-hour day. Only in Chicago, the center of working class radicalism and militant unionism, was the strike successful. After a number of workers were killed on a picket line by the police, a rally was called in downtown Chicago in protest (at the Haymarket Square). At the end of the rally someone (whose identify has never been determined) threw a dynamite bomb into the ranks of the police, killing a number. The first national Red Scare, which included widespread repression against all working class radical organizations as well as the Knights of Labor, ensued. The Knights as well as the rest of the socialist and working class movement suffered greviously (the Knights, in fact, never recovered).

It is of interest to note that the 1886 events in Chicago became the historical origin of May Day (International Workers' Day), which is celebrated throughout most of the world on May 1. In support of the American movement, as well as in support of their own movement for the eight-hour day, the European Socialist Parties called a 24-hour general strike for May 1, 1890. The idea caught on and the Second International made May 1 an international day of workers' solidarity. The International called for an annual one-day strike that would: express the support of workers in every land for the struggle of workers everywhere; commemorate the martyrs who had suffered and those who had been killed in the struggle for workers' liberation; and express the immediate demands of the working class in each country for the eight-hour day (as well as raise other issues) (see Boyer and Morais 1965, chap. 3).

In the late 1880s and 1890s an anticapitalist movement grew up in the United States that achieved considerable support, especially among small family farmers and sharecroppers of the South and Midwest—The People's Party. Many unions including the remnants of the Knights of Labor and the United Mine Workers supported the People's Party (also known as the Populists). The People's Party advocated the nationalization and public ownership of all the railways, banks, and grain elevator companies, as well as the break up of the monopolies. It favored small-scale economic units (of which the family farm was the ideal) and cooperatives as the way society should be organized economically. In the presidential elections of 1892 it won 9 percent of the vote. It also won the governorship of four states, two U.S. Senate seats and 11 seats in the House of Representatives. For a few years, the People's Party was a major force in both the Midwest and the South. In 1896 the People's Party split, with its center and right wing fusing with the Democratic Party behind the candidacy of William Jennings Bryan (who had a reputation as a moderate Populist because of his rhetoric against big financial interests). The left wing of the party, which was based mostly among the poor dirt farmers of the southern Midwest, largely joined the new Socialist Party in the first years of the twentieth century (see Hicks 1961; Pollack 1962).

The Socialist Labor Party became fractured in the late 1890s between those who advocated "revolution pure and simple" (i.e., that the party should not fight for any reforms within capitalism such as increased wages or ending racial discrimination because the advocacy of such demands was "nonsense and untrue"), and those who insisted that the Socialists must fight for short run improvements in workers' lives. In 1899 the former tendency, articulated by Daniel DeLeon, gained control and the other left the party. In 1901 this latter faction together with left-wing ex-Populists and other independent Socialists including Eugene Debs (who was a prominent militant labor leader, recently converted to socialism) and Victor Berger, a prominent Milwaukee Socialist, formed the Socialist Party. The majority of the membership of the new Socialist Party, unlike that of the old Socialist Labor Party (which was based mostly on immigrant workers) was native born. In 1912 approximately 80 percent of its membership had been born in the United States (Laidler 1968, pp. 582-83; Weinstein 1967, p. 328).

The new Socialist Party grew rapidly, winning 900,000 votes for president in 1912 (approximately 6 percent of the total vote) and considerably more actual support (many workers did not vote for Socialist candidates because they were afraid of "wasting their vote"; many Socialist votes were not counted in areas where no Socialist was a poll watcher). In 1912 the party had over 1,000 members holding public office, including 79 mayors, 300 aldermen, and 20 state legislators. The first socialist U.S. Congressman was elected in 1910. In 1912 there were a total of 323 different socialist newspapers and journals. The largest of these, the *Appeal to Reason*, had a circulation of three-fourths of a million. Others such as the *Jewish Daily Forward* and *National Ripsaw* had circulations of over 100,000. Other than in a few industrial concentrations such as Milwaukee (where there was a Socialist mayor most of the time between 1910 and 1940), Bridgeport, Connecticut (where there was a Socialist Mayor until the 1950s), Reading, and New York City, the largest concentrations of Socialist support were in areas with large numbers of poor farmers or miners such as Oklahoma, Texas, Arkansas, Missouri, Nevada, and Idaho (Fried 1970, pp. 382-83).

Socialist ideas had considerable influence in many unions, among them the brewers, the carpenters, the shoemakers, and the coal miners. It was common for the constitutions of the early unions to have preambles that declared support for public ownership of the means of production. However, after the demise of the Knights of Labor, unions were pretty much limited to organizing craftsworkers. The now dominant American Federation of Labor came to focus its activities on the day-to-day issues of better working conditions, shorter hours, and better pay ("more, more, more") rather than on transforming the capitalist system.

In 1905 a number of left-wing Socialists and leftist unionists came together because of a call by the radical Western Federation of Miners (which had been leading a series of militant and violently suppressed strikes in Colorado and Idaho) to form a new revolutionary union movement—the Industrial Workers of the World (IWW). Within a few years the IWW came to adopt syndicalist politics similar to those of the dominant union tendency in France. They felt that participation in elections or working for political reforms was a mistake that only fostered illusions and that capitalism would have to be gotten rid of through a general strike of all working people. Unlike the American Federation of Labor affiliated unions, IWW unions refused to sign labor contracts that pledged not to strike. It organized mostly the unskilled, focused on campaigning against the capitalist system, and led a number of very militant strikes. The IWW soon came to have an exclusively working class membership (it was hostile to intellectuals as a matter of principle). The "Wobblies" came to have considerable influence (at least for a time) among Western metal miners, lumber workers of the Northwest, agricultural laborers in California and the upper Midwest, and textile workers in the Northeast (especially around Lawrence, Massachusetts, and Paterson, New Jersey). It had perhaps 100,000 members at its peak just before World War I. During the war it was systematically repressed by the U.S. government for refusing to support the U.S. side in the war, and never recovered (Fried 1970, pp. 448-49; Dubofsky 1969; Boyer and Morais 1965, chap. 6).

The Socialist Party, which like the IWW refused to support World War I, also suffered from repression by the U.S. government. Its leaders, like those of the IWW, were arrested and imprisoned, its periodicals were excluded from the mails, and its members suffered considerable intimidation. However, at the end of the war the Socialist Party emerged with approximately the same membership as before (about 100,000), but its social basis had changed. It lost much of its support among small farmers in the Midwest and picked up considerable support among the new immigrant workers in industrial areas such as New York City. In 1919 53 percent of the party was foreign born (Weinstein 1967, p. 328).

Although Eugene Debs received over a million votes for president from his cell in the federal penitentiary in Atlanta (where he had been sentenced for a speech against U.S. participation in World War I), the party soon faded away as a significant force in the U.S. working class. In 1919 the Socialist Party split on the issue of the Russian Revolution, with the party's Left leaving the organization to found the new Communist Party. The Communist Party, composed of about 90% foreign-born immigrant workers through the 1920s, became a minor force in the working class, leading a number of major strikes. In the 1930s the Communists expanded rapidly (especially after 1934), growing to about 100,000 members in the mid-1940s. It played a major role in organizing and leading a number of important unions, such as the United Automobile Workers, the United Steel Workers, the United Electrical Workers, the Mine Mill and Smelter Workers (the successor of the old Western Federation of Miners), the International Longshoremen and Warehousemen's Union, the National Maritime Union, and the International Woodworkers of America. Communists and Communist supporters were elected to public office in New York City, including a congressman, Mark Antonio, and New York City councilman, Benjamin Davis (who had heavy support in Harlem). The party was effectively repressed in the early 1950s (see Caute 1978).

In conclusion, we see that socialist ideas through the 1940s played an important role in the U.S. working class. However, socialist ideas never established firm roots (as socialism did in *all* the other industrial capitalist countries). Numerous explanations have been offered as to why no massive working class socialism consolidated in the United States (see Lipset and Laslett 1974). Some of the explanations offered do not appear to carry too much weight since they are not factors which, in fact, differentiate between Europe and the United States. It has been said that the state repression of the Left, especially in the 1917-23 and 1947-56 periods was responsible, but the European socialist movement experienced equivalent if not worse repression. It has been said that there was greater upward mobility in the United States that channeled discontent into the individual pursuit of the good life (rather than forcing workers to take class action, as would be the case if individual mobility was blocked). However, the rate of upward mobility in the United States was not significantly different than in the industrial areas of Europe. The two-party system induced by the plurality take-all system of voting and various constitutional and religious traditions in the United States have also been suggested as causes. Yet, in Europe single district plurality take-all systems were common before the rise of the socialist working class parties, and conservative traditions were also prevalent in many countries where socialist movements later gained hegemony in the working class.

It would seem that the two principal factors that were systematically different in Europe and the United States and thus appear to be factors in accounting for the lack of a massive socialist working class tradition in the United States are: the ethnic diversity and consequent mutual antagonism and ethnic identifications of the U.S. working class; and the exceptional standard of living that American workers maintained from the beginnings of industrialization through the 1960s. As has been seen, unlike as in Europe the new industrial working class in the United States was made of up immigrants from many different foreign countries, each speaking their own language, each with their own customs and religions, each living in their own ethnic communities, and each (except for the Jews) considering their life here as that of temporary migrant laborers. The first generation of workers identified as Polish, Italian, Jewish, Irish, and so forth and not as workers. The oppressions of life in America were, in good part, attributed to ethnic prejudice or bad luck, and, in any event, were often considered the cost of accumulating money to go home. The immigrants did not feel trapped by the system. Nor did they feel that they had that much in common with other ethnic groups, some of which were in a slightly better position (and towards whom they felt jealous), and others of whom they had slight advantages over (and towards whom they felt protective of their petty privilege). Ethnic differences and antagonisms were often manipulated by the capitalists to keep the various groups in the working class from uniting with each other against the interests of the owners of industry. Hostility between the older Irish immigrants and the new southern and eastern Europeans was used just as later was the antagonism between the southern and eastern Europeans and the new immigrant workers from the South (especially blacks).

The other major factor that seems to have operated to undermine socialism in the U.S. working class was the immediate comparison that immigrant workers and their children could make to living standards in the old country (or the South) with their condition in the industrial areas of the U.S. However exploitative and oppressive conditions were, workers clearly had a higher standard of living in the United States than in Europe. This was confirmed also by the fact that the majority of immigrant workers eventually decided to stay in the United States. The U.S. capitalist system claimed credit for the high living standards of American workers, and in the absence of an effective alternative explanation offered by a leftist party, succeeded in receiving it. It should be noted, however, that in the 1970s the living standards of the working class in western and northern Europe (e.g., Germany, Switzerland, the Low Countries, and Scandinavia) caught up to, and in most cases surpassed, that of U.S. workers (although the disparity between U.S. wages and those in areas where the new migrants were coming from, mostly Latin America, remained the same). It should also be noted that the degree of ethnic diversity in the U.S. working class no longer differs substantially from that of Europe. In both areas there is now a majority of ethnically homogeneous workers speaking the same language and sharing common traditions and customs, and a significant minority of immigrant workers concentrated in the lowest paid and most menial jobs, and who consequently suffer all-around discrimination and humiliation. Thus, the two factors that seem to have played the principal role in hindering the development of socialist consciousness among U.S. workers, while facilitating it among European workers, are operative no longer. The U.S. working class is no longer an exception. In the future, then, one would expect that a revival of socialist ideas in the Western working class should have a similar appeal in both Europe and the United States (but not, necessarily equal to that of socialism in the less-developed countries).

A third factor that would seem to have played a role in the hindering of a socialist consciousness among U.S. workers is the fact that until the Vietnam War the United States never clearly lost a war. U.S. society was, thus, spared the confidence-shaking delegimitizing effects that are the consequent of such events. Americanism and the American economic system (capitalism) were, thus, never discredited the way they were in most of Europe, especially Russia, Germany, and Italy after World War I, or in Italy, France, Greece, and most of eastern Europe after World War II (or in France in 1871 and Russia in 1905). The patriotism incumbent on the Spanish American War, and especially the victories of the First and Second World Wars, caught the U.S. working class up in the "great American celebration," consolidating patriotic sentiments that had been carefully fostered in the compulsory educational system (e.g., the Pledge of Allegiance, the Star Spangled Banner, required civics, American history courses, and so on). The second generation of immigrants was particularly susceptible to American patriotism (and the acceptance of capitalism that it was made to imply) by the inferiorization of those who identified with the old country's ways. Thus, to be an American became very important for the self-respect of the immigrants' children. And being an American was justified and reinforced not only by higher living standards compared to the old country, but also by the great military victories in which working class youth participated as soldiers.

THE USSR

Except for two months of the Paris Commune of 1871, the first time a working class movement with a secular ideology ever took state power was in the Russian Revolution of 1917.* It was in Russia for the first time that a working class revolution was able to overthrow capitalist institutions and attempt to implement the socialist ideal of the abolition of exploitative class relations.

Although Russia was predominantly a rural and peasant country there were some major industrial concentrations (the most important of which was in Petrograd, where the means of production were campatible to those in Western Europe). In 1912, 43 percent of all workers worked in factories employing over 1,000. There were 3 million workers in 1900, half of whom had fathers who had also been workers, with most of the rest being migrants (often seasonal) from peasant areas—and who, thus, had close contacts with the peasantry. The Russian working class lived in incredibly poor conditions of overcrowding, malnutrition, and lack of sanitation as well as worked under especially dignity denying and exploitative conditions. The industrial working class and its organizations became major forces in the industrial areas.

The first Marxist group in Russia, the Emancipation of Labor, was founded by young intellectuals in 1883. In 1895 V.I. Lenin helped organize the Militant Union for the Emancipation of Labor, the first group with significant support from factory workers. In 1898 the Marxist Russian Social Democratic Labor Party was formed. Although they were illegal, the Russian Social Democrats soon gained considerable support among Russian workers. In 1912 there was a formal split between the reformists (Mensheviks) and the revolutionaries (Bolsheviks) within the Russian Party (with Lenin becoming the principal figure among the Bolsheviks). In January 1917 the Bolshevik organization had about 23,000 members (mostly factory workers and soldiers). In February 1917 there was a spontaneous revolution set off by a strike of women workers in Petrograd, a strike that proved contagious in the intolerable conditions of the winter of 1917, when the Russian army was falling apart in the face of a German offensive (after three years of bloody war), food was scarce, and the peasantry was seething with resentment against their land-

---

*This section relies heavily on: Bornstein 1974; Caute 1966; Gregory and Stuart 1974; Laidler 1968, pt. 4; Lane 1971; Lane 1977; Liebman 1970; Nettl 1967; Osborn 1970; Parkin 1971; Trotsky 1967; Wolf 1969; Yanowitch and Fisher 1973; Yanowitch 1977.

lords and the czar (their sons were dying in the war by the hundreds of thousands). Grass-root councils both among factory workers and soldiers in the army were set up throughout Russia. These "Soviets" together with a new provisional government assumed political power, displacing the czarist state. Over the course of 1917 discontent and tension grew, manifesting itself in a series of spontaneous and militant demonstrations in the summer against a government that was becoming increasingly unpopular because it brought neither peace, land, nor bread. The Provisional Government met these demonstrations with repression of the Left (e.g., Lenin had to go into hiding).

The Bolshevik membership and support nevertheless continued to grow astronomically. From a membership of 23,000 in January, it grew to about 250,000 in October (Schapiro 1960, p. 171). The Bolsheviks won the majority of the vote in the Soviets of the major industrial areas and in September began calling for All Power to the Workers' Councils and Peace, Land, Bread. At the All-Russian Congress of Workers' Councils held in late October 45 percent of the elected delegates were Bolsheviks and 25 percent Social Revolutionaries (the majority of which supported the Bolsheviks). The Bolsheviks had won the leadership of the Russian working class. Conditions had reached the boiling point in the fall and the Bolsheviks organized an insurrection that overthrew the Provisional Government and established the system of workers' councils as the sole political power in the country (see Liebman 1970 and Wolf 1969).

The new government of workers' councils with Bolshevik leadership nationalized the land, turning it over to the peasants, took over the major industries, granted independence to Poland and Finland, radically liberalized family legislation, greatly strengthened the unions, reduced the wages of state officials to that of workers, and implemented wide-ranging equalitarian and socialist programs.

The new society organized by Russian socialists experienced considerable hardships in its first generation. First, there was a long and bitter civil war in which the old propertied class, armed and aided by troops from over a dozen capitalist countries (including the United States), tried to overthrow the new workers' government. Then there was a bitter conflict with the peasantry, first about supplying the urban workers with enough food, and later around replacing individual farming with more efficient and socialized collective farms. The new socialist state was also faced with a trade boycott by the Western powers (the United States did not recognize the new regime until 1933), the need to rapidly industrialize to improve living standards and defend against a threatened second invasion by the major capitalist countries, the Nazi invasion of 1941 (which cost the lives of approximately 20 million Soviets), and the costly reconstruction of the devastated most developed western part of the country from 1945 to 1950. From the mid-1930s the Soviets also had to bear the incredible costs of trying to maintain military parity first with Germany and Japan and then with the United States (which emerged from World War II as the overwhelmingly dominant force in the world). All three of these powers were the self-declared enemy of socialism in general and the Soviet Union in particular. In the face of these grievous problems the Soviet Union experienced many sharp internal conflicts (some of which became rather bloody) as well as a great concentration of decision-making power. Nevertheless, as the first country in the world in which the working class actually seized political power (and held it for more than a few months), and where a protracted attempt was made to institute the socialist idea of abolishing exploitative classes, it is very important for us to examine the extent of class inequality and social differentiation that came to exist in the USSR.

The average wages of various sectors of the Soviet labor force in 1965 and 1973 are shown in Table 13.1. The highest paid are industrial engineering and technical personnel, who in 1973 earned an average of 1.27 times the wages of industrial workers. In 1973 it was only this group that earned more than industrial workers. The

TABLE 13.1: Changes in Average Wages in the USSR, 1965–73

Category of Wage Earners	1965 (in rubles)	1973 (in rubles)	Increase (%)	Ratio of Wages to Industrial Worker Wages (1973)
Employees of the state apparatus	106	126	19	0.86
Industrial engineering and technical personnel	148	185	25	1.27
Education and culture employees	94	121	29	0.83
Trade and service employees	75	102	36	0.70
Industrial white-collar workers	86	119	38	0.82
Industrial workers	102	146	43	1.00
State Farm workers	72	116	61	0.79
Collective farmers	49	87	78	0.60
All workers and employees (excluding collective farmers)	97	135	39	0.92

Source: Hough, 1976.

spread between the highest and lowest paid groups was 2.1 times, while in 1965 it had been 3.0 times. The eight-year trend from 1965 to 1973 shows a clear tendency for the highest paid occupations in 1965 to have the slowest rate of growth in wages while the lowest paid occupations had the highest rates of growth. The major exception to this trend would appear to be industrial workers, who were rather well paid in 1965 but who nevertheless received the highest increase in wages of any nonagricultural group.

Perhaps a better idea of the wage spread in the Soviet Union can be gotten from data on occupations within the same industry. In 1965 the average wages of machine-building personnel in Leningrad (a key industry in a major manufacturing city) showed that the highest paid category of workers, the executives of labor collectives and of public and state organizations, earned 1.7 times the wages of skilled operatives (Shkaraton 1973, p. 81). In the construction industry in 1969 the highest paid managers and specialists earned about 1.4 times as much as time-rate workers in the highest pay grade (Osborn 1970, p. 176).

It should be noted that the average earnings of production workers in certain segments of Soviet industries exceed those of engineering and technical personnel in many industries. For example, in 1969, steel workers averaged 145 rubles a month, lumber workers 143, and coal miners (the highest paid) 210. This compared with monthly earnings of 138 rubles for engineering and technical personnel in light industry and the same group's average monthly salary of 172 rubles in Soviet industry as a whole (Yanowitch 1977, p. 32). There appears to be a strong tendency towards egalitarianism in wages and also a tendency to favor industrial workers. The trend toward wage equalization has been continuous since the 1940s (D. Lane 1971, p. 73).

The highest paid people in the Soviet Union are prominent artists, writers, leading university administrators, professors, and scientists. In the mid-1960s the president of the Soviet Academy of Sciences made 1,500 rubles a month and leading university presidents 1,200. A few famous artists and performers have incomes in the same range. In the 1960s and 1970s leading government officials earned about 600 rubles a month, about four times the mid-1970s wages of industrial workers, and leading enterprise directors from 190 to 400 rubles a month (exclusive of bonuses), which was about 1.3 to 2.7 times worker wages (Matthews 1972, pp. 91-93).

In 1956 the ratio of the wage exceeded by the top 10 percent of Soviet employees and workers (excluding only collective farmers) to the wage exceeded by 90 percent was 4.4, in 1964, 3.7, in 1970, 3.2, and in 1975 (if the intentions of the plan were fulfilled) 2.9 (Hough

1976, p. 12). Again, the rather strong egalitarian trend in the Soviet Union can be seen. In the United States in 1974, the similar spread (in family income) was roughly 6.2 times (U.S. Department of Commerce, 1975, p. 373). In 1956 the ratio of the average wages of the 10 percent highest paid to the 10 percent lowest paid was 8 to 1; in 1975 it was only 4 to 1. In the United States in 1974, the similar ratio was roughly 12 to 1 (Yanowitch 1977, p. 25). Even those whose conceptualization of income distribution is designed to make Soviet income distribution look as nonegalitarian as possible have been forced to conclude that it is about twice as egalitarian as the American (Wiles 1974, p. 48).

When, as such critical authors do, the ratio of the lower limits of the upper decile are compared to the upper limits of the lower decile the Soviet income differentiation looks somewhat less egalitarian than it really is because the absence of very high incomes in the Soviet Union is not taken into account. The very highest incomes in the Soviet Union (of which there are very few) are roughly ten times more than the average industrial wage, while the wages of the highest level state ministers and enterprise managers are about 2.7 to 4.0 times the average industrial wage. The ratios of the very highest to the average industrial wage must be compared to the equivalent income distribution in the United States. In the United States in 1973, there were about 1,000 individuals who had an income of at least a million dollars a year, while the annual wage in manufacturing was $8,500 (U.S. Department of Commerce 1975, pp. 233, 366). Assuming (very conservatively) a million dollars a year as the highest income level in the United States, this is a ratio of roughly 115 times compared to the Soviet ratio of approximately ten times. In the United States the pay of top managers (including income from stock options) in the leading corporations in the mid-1970s was around a million dollars a year. For example, in 1970 the president of ITT earned $1,242,000, the president of Xerox $1,032,000, and the president of Atlantic Richfield $972,000 (Tuckman 1973, pp. 44-45). Again, comparing such incomes to the income of U.S. production workers, we have a ratio of roughly 115:1 as compared to the equivalent Soviet ratio of about 2.7:1 between the best paid managers and the average industrial wage, and a ratio of about 4:1 between the heads of ministries and the average industrial wage. Thus, when we compare the highest incomes with the average income, we see that the Soviet Union is far more egalitarian than the United States.

Furthermore, while there has been no appreciable decrease in income inequality in the last generation in the United States, in the 20 years between the mid-1950s and the mid-1970s the Soviets have eliminated about half of the inequality in their income distribution (reducing the ratio of the highest decile to the lowest decile average wages from 8 to 1 to 4 to 1)—a radical reduction in inequality in a very short time (U.S. Department of Commerce 1975a, p. 392).

In the United States in 1973, male self-employed professionals earned on average $20,500 a year while salaried physicians and surgeons earned $25,000 (U.S. Department of Commerce 1975a, pp. 366, 370). The ratio of these earnings to the average industrial wage in the United States in 1973 was 2.4:1 and 2.9:1 respectively. This is approximately the same as the ratio in the Soviet Union of the highest managerial incomes to the industrial wage, and considerably more than the average managerial wage to the average industrial wage. Thus, the spread between top management and production workers in the Soviet Union is more or less the same as that between petty bourgeois professionals and industrial workers in the United States. This suggests that the leading stratum in the Soviet Union is, at least in income terms, similar to the U.S. professional petty bourgeoisie rather than to the U.S. capitalist class (of either top corporate managers or the multimillionaire wealthy).

Soviet data on wages are complicated by two factors. On the one hand, they underestimate the income of managers and directors by leaving out bonuses earned over and above wages (bonuses average about 25 to 30 percent of managerial wages) as well as their privileged access to fringe benefits such as automobiles, summer houses, and so on (Gregory and Stuart 1974, pp. 189-90, 399). On the other hand, the state provides a wide range of free and heavily subsidized goods and services that disproportionately favor the low income groups.

State pricing policy sets the price of basic necessities such as basic foodstuffs below their value and luxury goods above their value. This means that a wage spread of 3:1 is actually considerably less than this when measured against the actual value of the goods and services purchased by the high and low wage earners. Most of the lowest wage earners' income goes to purchase goods and services obtainable below their value (or cost of production) while a good share, if not most, of the income of the highest wage earners purchases goods at a cost considerably above their value (e.g., automobiles and personal luxury goods) (Bornstein 1974).

Besides the equalizing effect of the pricing policy on necessities and luxuries, another major equalizing effect comes from social welfare services (often referred to as the "social wage"). Such benefits available to all include free medical care, free education at all levels including college, heavily subsidized housing (rents are set at below the level required to maintain housing), heavily subsidized child care, generous pensions, paid maternity leave, and so on, all of which considerably increase family income for manual workers in particular (Osborn 1970, p. 50). The relative proportion of the social wage in total worker compensation has risen over the last generation. As a percentage of individual earnings it rose from 23 percent in 1940 and 29 percent in 1950, to 35 percent through the 1960s (Osborn 1970, p. 32). Because the social wage adds about the same absolute amount to each household, it has a considerable equalizing effect on total family income. In 1966 it has been estimated that free goods and services averaged about 60 percent of the income of the lowest paid workers families but only 20 percent of the income of the highest paid. In heavy industry the spread of about 2 to 1 in take-home wages is reduced to about 1.5 to 1 because of the egalitarian effect of services provided on the basis of need (Osborn 1970, pp. 48-50). In addition to trends toward reducing wage differentials and increasing free goods and services, in recent years the minimum wage and pensions have been greatly increased, and also the income tax used increasingly to promote equality (Parkin 1971, p. 144).

While it could be that higher paid strata in the Soviet Union have far easier access to scarce goods, such as cars and housing (thus manifesting far greater inequality in possession of material goods than is suggested by the income distribution), this does not appear to be the case. The relative egalitarianism of income *is* reflected in the distribution of housing. A study done in the mid-1960s showed that the quality of housing for higher professionals was, on average, about 1.7 times better than that of simiskilled workers. Another study found that sociooccupational status only correlated about 0.1 with the amount of housing space per family (D. Lane 1971, p. 78). There is no consistent pattern of neighborhoods differentiated by income level. There are, for example, a few fairly exclusive neighborhoods in Moscow where leading officials of the Communist Party and its employees live, but there are also many cases (for example) of janitors and full professors at leading universities living in the same apartment building. It is normal for government and enterprise officials to live in the same apartments as production workers (see Osborn 1970, chap. 6).

Similar, but not quite as egalitarian, results have been found for automobile ownership. Studies show that enterprise directors and leading professional people have about a 2.5 times higher probability of owning an automobile than do manual workers (Shkaraton 1973b, p. 95; Yanowitch 1977, p. 45). Thus, the chances of owning a car are roughly proportional to the income differential between the highest paid managers and production workers, and do not reflect any special access to automobiles by the intelligentsia beyond that accounted for by their higher incomes.

In summary, although it certainly is true that managers receive bonuses averaging 25 to 30 percent of their income (workers receive bonuses as well) and have access to special privileges such as the automobiles belonging to the enterprise, the weight of the evidence leads us to conclude that such effects, when set against the generous subsidies to the lower paid strata, do not make the distribution of material goods more unequal. In fact, the evidence suggests that the distribution of material goods is even *more* egalitarian than the income statistics indicate. In conclusion, it would appear that the differences in material living standards between managers and government ministers in the USSR and industrial workers come close to the difference between professionals and industrial workers in the Western capitalist countries. Nothing like the gap between millionaires and workers that exists in the United States can be found in the USSR. It would seem that socialism has been a success, at least in radically reducing economic inequality, eliminating a wealthy propertied class, and in guaranteeing a wide range of free and heavily subsidized goods and services to the working class (goods that are provided on the basis of need).

Numerous studies of social class formation, i.e., access to education, mobility, intergenerational linkage of privileged positions, social backgrounds of the Soviet power elite, intermarriage and friendship patterns, consciousness, and life-style confirm the inferences drawn from the statistics of income distribution (see Szymanski 1979a, chap. 4 for a summary of these studies). The evidence on income distribution reported here together with that on social class formation shows that: first, there is no wealthy class that has an income remotely comparable to that of the economic elite in the capitalist countries; second, no privileged elite social stratum exists with its own highly distinctive life-style, exclusive intermarriage patterns, and virtual certainty of passing on its top positions to its children (as is the case in the capitalist countries); third, there is an income differential in the Soviet Union between the higher level managers and the scientific and technical intelligentsia on the one hand and the manual working class on the other roughly similar to that between higher level professionals and manual workers in the United States; fourth, there are distinctive life-style and intermarriage patterns as well as intergenerational linkages among the scientific and technical intelligentsia that tend to make them a social stratum distinct from both the working class *and* from the "power elite" of managers and officials; fifth, tendencies for either the scientific-technical or the managerial-political intelligentsia to crystallize into a social class are significantly weaker than the class division that exists in the capitalist countries between the economic elite and manual workers (the gap between the professional stratum and the working class in the USSR is roughly equivalent to that existing between professionals and manual workers in the United States); and sixth, the incumbents of decision-making positions in the economy and state apparatus are not integrated into the technical intelligentsia. Rather, the managerial stratum appears to be significantly closer to the manual working class than is the scientific-technical intelligentsia.

In conclusion, while the Soviet social structure may not match the Communist or socialist ideal, it is both qualitatively different from, and more equalitarian than, that of the Western capitalist countries. Socialism has made a radical difference in favor of the working class.*

CHINESE SOCIALISM

After the Russian Revolution, the most significant attempt to establish a socialist society has been that of the Chinese.† In 1949 the Communist Party of China came into power in a country containing 25 percent of the world's people. It commenced to construct a socialist society that since 1958 has defined itself as qualitatively different (more equalitarian and democratic) than that of the Soviet Union.

Although China was even more of a peasant society than was prerevolutionary Russia, the Chinese working class played a key role in the Chinese Revolution in giving birth to the Communist Party as a major political force. A group of Chinese students and intellectuals who were attracted by the Russian Revolution of 1917 founded the Chinese Communist Party in 1921. But very soon this new party had a base in the Chinese working class (in 1919 there were 1.5 million workers in China heavily concentrated in a few coastal centers). By 1923 the party had become the leading political force in the urban working class, organizing many unions and strikes. The party had also played a key role in organizing railway workers and miners in many areas of China, including the province of Hunan. This combined with the influence of Marxist ideas on the peasantry induced through the seasonal migration of laborers from the coastal cities (where they were politicized) to the interior towns gave the Communists a con-

---

*For a full discussion of Soviet society see Szymanski 1979a and forthcoming.

†This discussion in this section relies heavily on: Andors 1977; Bettleheim 1974; Hoffman 1974; Howe 1973, 1978; Schram 1973; Sidel 1974; Wheelwright and McFarlane 1970; Wolf 1969, chap. 3.

siderable base to influence and lead events when a peasant insurrection broke out in Hunan Province in 1926 (see Wolf 1969, chap. 3).

The Communists were violently repressed by the Kuomintang (under Chiang Kai-shek) in 1927 (after he used them to get himself into power). Because of this violent repression, in which many thousands of Communists and militant unionists were killed, the Communists found it very difficult to work in the cities. They came to concentrate their energy on working among the peasants (where they had considerable success). Building up large peasant armies the Communists were able in the 1946-49 period to win a civil war against the U.S.-supported KMT and seize power.

Although the Chinese did not consider that they began to implement distinctively *socialist* measures until 1955, the Chinese Revolution immediately undertook the institutionalization of tremendous equalitarian changes in Chinese society. The land was expropriated from the landlords and turned over to the peasantry. Massive welfare and educational programs were undertaken. The commanding peaks of the economy were nationalized and run so as to maximize economic growth. In 1955 the factories that had been left in the hands of the capitalists were nationalized, with full compensation paid to the owners in bonds. At the same time landownership was collectivized (with peasants working it in cooperative groups rather than by individual families). Beginning in 1958 the Chinese grew increasingly critical of Soviet socialism, which they attacked for being bureaucratic, giving too much stress to economic incentives, instituting privileges, and making little attempt to break down the division of labor between the managerial and technical strata and the laborers. During the period of the Great Proletarian Cultural Revolution, a number of rather drastic changes were made in the direction of decreasing inequality, minimizing the role of economic incentives, debureaucratication, and undermining the division of labor. However, since the death of Mao Tse-tung, with whom these changes had been associated, many of these reforms have been reversed and a system very much like that of the Soviets restored. Let us examine the Chinese variant of socialism as it appeared in the 1967-77 period (the period during which it differed the most from the Soviet model).

Mao Tse-tung's theory of building socialism, which emphasized popular mobilization and voluntarism more than did the Soviet model, was first implemented in the 1958-59 period (during the Great Leap Forward) and reversed in the early 1960s in the face of serious economic difficulties. It was once again implemented during the Cultural Revolution after 1966. Mao Tse-tung argued that classes continue to exist and be regenerated in socialist society, and specifically that the regeneration of the ruling class tends to occur out of party, state, and enterprise officials (because of the continuation of a division of labor between them and ordinary workers, and because of the privileges and power the former group accrues to themselves). Mao argued that the only way to prevent the reemergence of such a state capitalist class or "state bourgeoisie" was to ensure the thorough integration of the elite with the working people and to move to breakdown the division of labor between mental and menial labor as well as to radically decrease privileges and prerogatives. This implied that all administrative and technical personnel had to participate in physical labor, and that all workers should participate in decision making and technical innovation. It implied that income and life-style differentials had to be decreased. Mao also argued that social consciousness should progressively displace individual material incentives (such as bonuses, piecework, and wage differentials) in motivating workers, so that a communist consciousness of social responsibility could be created. Mao emphasized the role of human will over technological constraints. For example, Mao argued: "The people and the people alone make history"; and "the spirit can be transformed into a material force" (Wheelwright and McFarlane 1970, p. 126). Mao tended to argue that very rapid progress in both industrialization and the achievement of cooperative consciousness and institutions could be achieved by collective enthusiasm and leadership, independent of the backwardness of technological conditions (Wheelwright and McFarlane 1970, chaps 4, 5, 6).

From 1960 until 1966 Mao and his allies were a minority in the Chinese Communist Party leadership. Teng Hsiao-ping and Liu Shao-chi, who essentially had the same ideas about socialist construction as did the Soviets, were predominant. However in 1966 a massive student upheaval in support of Mao's ideas broke out. In 1967 this upheaval, the Cultural Revolution, engulfed China in turmoil so thorough as to wipe out the Communist Party as an effective organization through much of China, while radically criticizing and displacing both individual leaders and leadership structures. Once Mao gave his public approval to the student movement (a few months after it began) it grew like wildfire, sweeping aside even the majority of the Party politburo and putting Mao back into the leadership of China. Within a few months something like 15 to 20 million students had organized themselves into Red Guards. They traveled all over China (being provided with free transport, food, and accommodation) carrying criticism of leading party, state, and enterprise officials everywhere they went. They attempted to destroy traditional ideas, customs, and habits and in their place substitute new socialist and communist ones (Wheelwright and McFarlane 1970, chaps. 5, 6).

The mass movement soon spread to the working class, especially to the younger and less secure (the temporary and contract workers who lacked job tenure, trade union protections, and the many welfare benefits guaranteed to the permanent enterprise workers). However, large numbers of permanent and older workers, many of whom had been critics of the often heavy-handed way enterprises were run, supported the movement as well. Workers in January 1967 began to seize control of factories, displacing the old administrative party committees and appointing factory directors with new Revolutionary Committees elected by workers. The enthusiasm of large groups of workers for the Cultural Revolution came to equal that of the students. However, while the students tended to be motivated primarily by idealism, the workers were more involved in issues of bonuses, material incentives, management methods, the role of trade unions, the routine of daily work, the role of administrators, and so on.

The disproportionate involvement of the temporary and less privileged workers in the Cultural Revolution was given testimony to by attempts to abolish the distinction between temporary and permanent workers, and by the abolition of the trade unions. The unions were considered to be the defenders of the special privileges of the permanent workers against the interests of the temporary workers (Andors 1977, pp. 165-67; Schram 1973, pp. 244, 315).

Large numbers of government, party, and enterprise officials were "sent down" to May 7 cadre schools, where they had to re-educate themselves about socialism through a combination of physical labor and the study of Mao's writings. Eighty percent of all administrators and officials in Peking were sent to such schools (Sidel 1974, p. 34). All enterprise, technical, and administrative personnel were required to share in physical labor. Older workers were brought into the schools to teach manual labor skills and to recount stories about life in the old prerevolutionary society. Students were sent to workplaces to do physical labor as part of their education. Students also had to do two years of physical labor in the countryside before they could attend college (Schram 1973, p. 312).

Although many of the institutional changes and practices of the Cultural Revolution were reversed during the course of the 1970s, with China, in good part, reverting to the practices of the 1960-66 period, there were lasting effects of the Cultural Revolution. The participation of workers in the Cultural Revolution reaffirmed their political status, enhanced their influence in running factories, and expanded their influence in social life (see Schram 1973, p. 317).

Top income in China (leaving aside income from state bonds accruing to former capitalists that were guaranteed ongoing income from their property in exchange for support of the revolution) after the Cultural Revolution ranged between 200 and 400 Yuan a month. These top salaries are received by the top senior ministers, a few of the top managers in the largest and most important enterprises, top level officials, leading academics, and a few prominent artists. Managers of large enterprises typically have incomes in the 150-200 neighborhood (Howe 1978, p. 177; Hoffman 1974, pp. 102-3, 156). This compares with the average production worker's salary of about 60 Yuan a month (Howe 1978, p. 180).

One study found that in a sample of eight factories there was a ratio of 1.6 between the maximum administrators' salaries and the maximum production workers' salaries, while another found a ratio of roughly 4:1 between top administrative salaries and the lowest enterprise salaries (Andors 1977, p. 221; Goldwasser and Dowty 1975, p. 199). The ratio between the very highest salaries and the average income is about 6.5, while the ratio between the salaries of top managers and the average is about 3 to 1. These figures are approximately the same as comparable figures for the USSR and reflect considerably more equalitarianism than exists in the West.

Since 1958 there has been a steady tendency for the income spread to decrease. There have been a series of upgradings of the lowest paid workers. In 1963 lower paid workers were raised one wage grade (on the eight point grade system). In 1971 the bottom three of the eight grades of industrial workers were upgraded (as were the bottom six of the 30 grades in the state administration). In October, 1977 the lowest 40 percent of workers received raises (Howe 1978, p. 176).

The spread in Chinese incomes (just as is the case in the USSR) is reduced by two factors: first, the Chinese subsidize or sell at cost most of the basic necessities of life such as medical care, education, grains, and housing, while charging very high prices for luxury goods such as radios, watches, and televisions (thus the higher wages of administrators can actually buy much less in relation to workers' salaries than can the lower wages of production workers). For example, the retail price of cereals is essentially the price paid the peasant, i.e., the state assumes the costs of transporting and marketing grains (Bettleheim 1974, p. 64). The welfare system also flattens the distribution of real income for permanent urban workers. The "social wage," which roughly represents the same absolute amount for most permanent urban workers includes heavily subsidized medicine and health care, 56 paid maternity days' leave, day care services, recreational facilities, and poverty assistance. It seems that enterprises set aside about 25 percent of their total wage bill for their welfare funds. The proportion of the wage fund going to welfare expenditures has risen significantly from 1958 to the mid-1970s. Rents are set at between 2 and 5 percent of workers' income (Hoffman 1974, p. 157; Howe 1978, pp. 184-85; Schram 1973, p. 252).

In the early 1950s the Chinese adopted the traditional Soviet system of bonuses and piecework. At its maximum application in 1957, 42 percent of industrial workers were on the piecework system (compared to a peak of 72 percent in the USSR) (Howe 1973, p. 119). After 1958 piecework was phased out. Bonuses or premiums for fulfilling or overfulling work quotas became general in the 1950s, but also declined in importance after 1957. But, unlike piece rates, they *were* revived in 1961 and 1962. Rates of bonus payment in the mid-1960s were from 20 to about 40 percent of the wage bill (Hoffman 1974, p. 107; Howe 1973, p. 122). Bonuses were again abolished in the 1966-68 period along with all remnants of piece work (and in the late 1970s again reinstituted).

The basic philosophy of the Cultural Revolution was equalitarian. It not only called for reduction in salary differentials, but also for restrictions on the use of wages as a material incentive to motivate workers to produce. In place of the material incentives of piece work, bonuses, and highly differentiated wage scales, the Maoists emphasized "moral incentives"—both of socialist consciousness and nonmaterial competition, i.e., the motive to surpass other collectives or individuals in output. Group competition among work units, factories, and individual competition, with the most productive getting awards, their pictures posted, red banners on their machines, and so on became common (Hoffman 1974, pp. 112-14). Group meetings that included self-criticism sessions where slacking workers were criticized and the most productive praised by other workers also became important institutions. Mass campaigns were organized to inspire revolutionary zeal in workers. Mass meetings were held regularly. Attempts were made to make workers aware of all aspects of the production process and to get them to understand that the success of the mass campaigns depended on their efforts (Hoffman 1974, pp. 118, 119).

The privileges of administrative and technical personnel were reduced during the Cultural Revolution. Access to special housing, better food, and clothing and education for their children were curtailed (Schram 1973, p. 313). There continues to be little difference in life-styles among most administrative and professional people and the average urban workers. Administrators and professionals dress little different from workers and they mostly live in the same apartment buildings (Hoffman 1974, p. 157).

The Cultural Revolution resulted in a considerable influx of workers into governmental positions. While before the Cultural Revolution workers represented 23 percent of the total number of those in governmental positions, after the Cultural Revolution they were 48 percent (Andors 1977, p. 212).

In summary, Chinese socialism, in spite of a number of rather radical shifts in policy, has greatly improved the life of the average working person in China, while radically reducing traditional inequality. Like Soviet socialism, it has eliminated the wealthy propertied classes and instituted guarantees of a decent standard of living (given prerevolutionary Chinese conditions this latter represents a most substantial improvement in the life of the average person, even while minimal by Western or Soviet standards).

The movement toward the creation of classless society, which came to power in both the largest and in the most populous countries on earth in 1917 and 1949 respectively, while not abolishing classes altogether, clearly has made qualitative changes in that direction. Whatever other problems the existing socialist countries might have (and however major the differences among them) the viability of the socialist project has been demonstrated. It would seem that their relatively low living standards (compared to much of Western Europe and the United States) as well as highly centralized decision making and the restrictions on organized opposition to their forms of socialism are results of the very serious problems these first socialist societies have encountered from the legacy of the extreme poverty of their recent pasts as well as from foreign hostility and invasion. The rapid progress that these first socialist societies have been making in economic growth, raising living standards, expanding the "social wage," and increasing popular participation gives substantial evidence that the eventual socialist project of abolishing classes can not only be realized in the existing socialist countries, but in the presently capitalist countries as well.

CONCLUSION: FUTURE PROSPECTS

Although fluctuating in strength from decade to decade the movement against organizing society by classes has been gaining momentum since the late Middle Ages. It accelerated over the course of the nineteenth century until it bore fruit in the prevalence of socialist consciousness among the working classes of most capitalist countries by the end of the century. The anticlass movement became a major force throughout Europe and its extensions. Temporarily slowed down by pre-World War I prosperity, equalitarian movements received great impetus by the catastrophic suffering of World War I (the first successful revolution led by working class people occurred, and the Marxist Left was stimulated throughout the world). Again, as a result of the havoc caused by World War II (and the tremendous prestige gained by the Soviet Union because of its defeat of Nazi Germany) Marxist socialism received another major infusion of strength around the world. In the immediate post-World War II period Marxism became a major force through much of the less-developed world. The second most important socialist revolution of the twentieth century occurred in China. In the 1945-48 period it looked like there was a very good chance that most of the world was about to go socialist.

After a wave of international reaction reinforced by the restoration of economic prosperity, class relations were largely stabilized throughout the world under the watchful guidance of the most powerful class society the world has ever seen (the United States). During the 1950-80 generation the revolutionary energy of the anticlass movement in the advanced capitalist countries waned under the temptations of the most sustained period of increase in living standards and advances in social welfare ever experienced by the working class (with a good dose of repression thrown in in some countries such as the United States, Germany, Portugal, Spain, and Greece). In the less-developed capitalist countries, however, the struggle against class inequality continued. Socialism triumphed in Cuba in 1960 and in Vietnam (after a protracted and bloody struggle) in 1975. The last years of the 1970s once again saw the energization of the equalitarian wave with revolutions in Iran, Nicaragua, Ethiopia, Zimbabwe, El Salvador, Angola, and Mozambique.

The radical decline in inequality and the improvement in living conditions of the formerly dominated classes in the USSR, Eastern Europe, China, and the other socialist countries has given the working people of these countries the expectation of (and security to insist on) continued rapid progress toward full equalitarianism, participatory democracy, and affluence. To the extent that progress toward any of these goals is blocked, significant disillusionment with leadership and/or mass movements to continue progress can be expected. Thus, phenomena such as the Chinese Cultural Revolution (essentially a mass movement for greater equality and participation and equalitarianism, as well as affluence) can be expected to develop in the socialist world.

In the advanced capitalist countries of Western Europe and North America the long-term period of prosperity ended in the 1970s. This part of the world capitalist system slowly sank into economic stagnation, with rising unemployment and decline in working class living standards. The virtual elimination of the agricultural populations of these countries in the post-World War II generation meant that most migrations of new menial workers into capitalist enterprises have to occur from the less-developed countries (e.g., Latin America, the Arab world, Turkey, Korea, and so on). To the extent that such immigration is blocked, economic stagnation leads to increasing social class crystallization, with parents of the upper and middle classes effectively being able to reserve most positions in their class to their children, and the children of workers increasingly condemned to live out their lives as workers. Such a tendency for a caste-like crystallization of the class structure of industrial capitalist society, long used to both increasing living standards and significant upward mobility into the middle class, could well prove to be explosive. The curtailment in the expansion of the growth of new middle class positions and the continued decline of independent small businesses combined with economic stagnation in a fully urban capitalist society could well generate massive hostility toward the class system. On the other hand, economic stagnation combined with *increased* immigration of increasingly desperate displaced peasants from the less-developed countries could well result in an increase in virulent racism (against the specially exploited) within the working class. Further, the scarcity of petty bourgeois positions is likely to produce a revitalization of anti-Semitism and anti-Asian sentiments in the petty bourgeoisie.

The long term trend (since the mid-nineteenth century) of the working and living conditions of the working class to improve, which allowed the incorporation of the working class in the advanced capitalist countries into the formal electoral process (which has not generally been the case in the poorer capitalist countries) may well be in serious danger. The experience of the last hundred years has produced the expectation in the working class that their conditions will continually improve, and feelings of injustice when living and working conditions decline. Anger and frustration can be expected to mount, as the gap between expectations and reality grows. A slowdown in productivity and a decline in the rate of profit is likely to induce capital to press for a take back of the significant Social Security gains made by the working class, an increase in economic incentives (including a decrease in job security) as well as an accelerated decrease in real wages. It is unlikely that this process could proceed very far within the framework of parliamentary elections before a popular party (or leaders) who opposed such measures was elected. The difficulties of pursuing austerity measures in a stagnate economy with parliamentary forms was demonstrated in the 1920s and 1930s, when most of the parliamentary regimes of the world collapsed in favor of rightist dictatorships. Similar conditions are likely to produce similar results.

The continued high level of socialization of the labor process, the ready availability in most countries (the United States being the outstanding exception) of socialist ideas, the gap between expectations and reality and the roll back of social reforms and restrictions on the democratic process are very likely to reinvigorate the working class socialist movement everywhere. If capitalism with its qualitative class divisions, is unable to meet most people's essential needs, revolutionary socialism will once again be put on the historical agenda in the West. The question of the justice of the existence of classes will once again become problematic as the probabilities that the class orders of the advanced capitalist countries might collapse become real.

The movement against the maintenance of inequality is irrepressible (even while it experiences long waves of enthusiasm, repression, and demoralization). In the less-developed capitalist countries, the socialist countries and the advanced capitalist countries the forces of equalitarianism are strengthening. The days of class society and qualitative social inequality are numbered. Barring the destruction of the human race in a mass collective nuclear suicide, the restoration of the classless societies in which most human beings ever born have lived could everywhere well become a reality in the next century.

Appendix: A Critique of Alternative Conceptualizations of Class

In this appendix the major alternative conceptualizations of class in terms of ideas/subjectivity, power, market relations, and the technical division of labor as well as some alternative conceptualizations in terms of relations of production are outlined and critiqued. Further, the functionalist, force and organizational/ideological theories of the origin and reproduction of class inequality are examined and criticized. Special emphasis is given to various Marxian attempts to redefine traditional Marxist class categories in ways essentially similar (at least in part) to other modes of class concepualization. Thus, the definitions of E.P. Thompson, Stanley Aronowitz, and Adam Przeworski are treated with the conservative subjectivist class categorizations such as those of Talcott Parsons; Dahrendorf is treated with such theorists as Stanislaw Andreski and Vilfredo Pareto; Wallerstein (as well as Paul Sweezy and Andre Gunder Frank) are treated with Max Weber; and Nicos Poulantzas (and the Ehrenreichs) are treated along with Seymour Martin Lipset, Richard Hamilton, and Daniel Bell.

CLASS AS A COMMON POSITION IN THE DISTRIBUTION OF POWER

There are a number of influential theorists, especially in the tradition of conservative European thought, who define class in terms of the distribution of power in society. These include Ralph Dahrendorf, Stanislaw Andreski, Vilfredo Pareto, Roberto Michels, and Gaetano Mosca.

Ralph Dahrendorf defines classes as "social conflict groups the determinant . . . of which can be found in the participation in or exclusion from the exercise of authority within any imperatively coordinated association" (1959, p. 138). Dahrendorf explicitly rejects the idea that classes can be defined in, or are reducible to economic categories. He argues that classes within economic organizations are merely special cases of a more general phenomenon of class: "Classes are neither primarily nor at all economic groupings" (1959, p. 139).

Dahrendorf has an essentially two class model of society: those with authority and those who are dominated. He argues that the dominated in any authority structure tend to struggle (in their class interest) as a group against those in authority. Unlike the functionalists, but like both the Marxists and Marxian subjectivists, Dahrendorf sees classes as active units in society and social development.

Vilfredo Pareto, Roberto Michels, and Gaetano Mosca all develop very similar theories of both class and the causes of social inequality. They all tend to see society divided into two groups: the "elite" and the "nonelite." Pareto argues that there are ". . . two strata in a population: (1) a lower stratum, the nonelite, . . . then: (2) a higher stratum, the elite, which is divided into two: (a) a governing elite, and (b) a nongoverning elite" (1935, paragraph 2034).

The Force Theory of the Basis of Class

There are two principal tacks typically taken by those who maintain that power is the basis of class: first, physical or military force is both the original source of class inequality *and* the continuing basis of its reproduction (Stanislaw Andreski is perhaps the most influential contemporary proponent of this position); and second, control of organization and ideology is the original and continuing source of class inequality. Roberto Michels has probably presented the most developed argument in this tradition.

Stanislaw Andreski probably makes the strongest contemporary case for the primacy of force in determining class structure. Andreski (1968) argues that the degree of inequality in societies is normally considerably greater than what would be functionally necessary for the smooth working of that society, i.e., that the functionalist explanation of class inequality explains only a relatively small part of the inequality in society. He argues that it is relatively easy for those in positions of authority to use their position to extend privileges once the habit of obedience becomes established. Great differentials in wealth, he argues, can only be maintained by coercion. Economic power is derivative from military power. Those who wield military power consequently achieve supreme station in society. In disagreements violence is the argument of last resort.

Andreski argues that the variations in the amount of inequality in society stem largely from variations in the military participation ratio (MPR), i.e., the proportion of the adult population of a society that is mobilized militarily. The greater the proportion of the people who bear arms, the more democratic the society; the fewer people with military training and equipment, the more stratified the society (1968, chap. 2). According to Andreski's argument, a number of other factors influence the MPR and through it the degree of stratification in society: first, the difficulty of acquiring military skills, i.e., the more time and endurance required, the more stratified the society; second, the cost of equipment, i.e., the more expensive military equipment, the fewer people who will be effectively armed, and hence the less democratic the society; and third, whether or not military technology is primarily individually or collectively operated, i.e., the smaller the group that can fight effectively, the more democratic is the society. Another factor, which according to Andreski, plays an important role in determining the degree of class inequality in society is the "facility of suppression," or the ease by which the military rulers can defeat opposition. A number of factors operate on the facility of suppression such as: first, the availability of sheltered terrain, the more mountainous or otherwise difficult the terrain, and hence the greater probability of guerrilla resistence being effective, the more democratic will be the society; second, the efficiency of the secret police; and third, the relative differential in the quality of armaments available to the military establishment and the people. Andreski further maintains that the greater the ferocity (the more total) is war, the more the people must be mobilized, and hence, the more democratic the society (see 1968, chaps. 2 and 4).

Andreski summarizes the history of the interrelations between warfare and the degree of stratification in society in support of his theory. He argues that the extreme hierarchy of feudalism was destroyed by the introduction of both improved infantry tactics and firearms. These innovations were able to beat mounted and armored knights and destroy the aristocracies' heavily fortified castles with techniques that were far cheaper, and hence more available to the people, than were the traditional means of feudal warfare. The remainder of the feudal vestiges of extreme inequality were destroyed with the introduction of conscript armies and total war during the French Revolution and the Napoleonic Wars. For the first time in the modern period average peasants and common citizens were armed and mobilized for war by the French. This required all other European countries to do the same in order to resist the massive French armies. But to secure the loyalty and motivate the peasant soldiers who were now being trained for the first time in socially very dangerous arts, considerable democratization of society was necessary. This meant the universal franchise and land reform, first in France, then elsewhere, the expansion of state-run welfare programs, compulsory education, and so on. The new massive conscript armies, furthermore, were not as effective as the older mercenary or knightly armies in suppressing popular resistence. This was an additional factor in the democratization of society. In general, wherever there is universal conscription, rather than a small professional army, there tends to be less class stratification.

The Organizational/Ideological Theory of Class Inequality

Roberto Michels, like Pareto, argues that a society can not exist without a dominant class, and that the state can not be anything other than the organ of a minority which always imposes an exploitative order of domination over the majority. But according to Michels, it is not, as Andreski argues, control over military force, but rather organizational control over the channels of communication, ideology, and knowledge that leadership in large organizations gives that is the basis of power, and, hence, of class. It is the logic of organization which (together with the psychological potentials of individuals) that leads to domination. The very nature of organization inplies domination:

> . . . oligarchy depends upon what we may term the psychology of organization itself, that is to say, upon the tactical and technical necessities which result from the consolidation of every disciplined political aggregate. Reduced to its most concise expression, the fundamental sociological law of political parties . . . may be formulated in the following terms: It is organization which gives birth to the domination of the elected over the electors, of the mandataries over the mandators, of the delegates over the delegators. Who says organization, says oligarchy (Michels 1913, p. 365).

In order to live people must organize. But once organization comes into existence, it comes to dominate the people who establish it. Michels argues that there must be a division of labor within large organizations. It would simply be impossible for all members of a large organization to concern themselves with every detail that arises. The larger the organization, the more things that it has to concern itself with, the more unlikely it becomes that any one individual can participate in the full range of activities. Both size and technical considerations dictate that some people must come to specialize in leadership so that the organization can become effective.

It is not only the drive for dominance or power over others that motivates leaders to consolidate and advance their position. Especially in organizations of the oppressed there is both great prestige and financial reward associated with leadership positions. Once those who have never before experienced such rewards become accustomed to them, they hang on tenaciously.

Leaders of organizations are in a position to realize their drives and interests in maintaining power. They control the channels of communication within their organizations. It is they who run the press, and it is they who plan and run meetings as well as dominate them through their superior oratorical ability. Michels argues that the drive of the leaders to consolidate their power is inevitably realized because of the inherent needs of the masses of people. According to Michels, people are inherently apathetic and crave domination, i.e., people strive to be ruled.

The heart of Michels' argument is psychological. The organizational exigencies provide only the occasion for the realization of oligarchy. It is "human nature" that includes an innate dual propensity to dominate and strive after power and privilege on the one hand, and to subordinate oneself on the other that is in the last analysis the cause of oligarchy and bureaucratization (see Michels 1913).

A Critique of the Force Theory of Stratification

The force theory incorporates some important insights into the nature of inequality. According to Mao Tse-tung's famous proverb: "Political power grows out of a barrel of a gun." Without the ability to mobilize or control superior military force no group or class can secure or maintain privileges. All of history teaches this. When there are disputes among groups or classes about controlling valued goods, in the last resort those with superior force take what they want.

However, the real issue is not whether force is the *arbiter* of last resort, and thus whether or not force is behind the preservation of privilege (which it clearly is), but rather how do those with superior force acquire that force; and second, can the exercise of pure force either create *or* reproduce inequality either in degree or in quality. The evidence from history would appear to answer no on both counts.

Force is no mere act of will. It requires instruments and organization to be effective. The triumph of arms is based on economic power and organization stemming from relations of production of a society. Force is not an elemental social factor. It is rather derivative from economic factors in two ways. First, superior military force in good measure is a product of superior technological abilities and the quantity of military goods that can be produced. That society, or class, which can produce more and better cannons, more and better airplanes, more and better tanks, and so on, tends to be the society or class with superior military power. Thus, the military superiority of the rising bourgeoisie over the feudal landlords was in good part a product of the former's intimate relation to the means of production of military goods. The triumph of the towns over the feudal countryside was based on the economic power of the towns, and firearms were a weapon of the towns.

Superior military force does not only depend on superior technology and productivity to produce superior weaponry (as the U.S. learned in Vietnam). It depends just as much on organization, tactics, and morale (of both the actual fighters and the civilians backing them up). But organization and morale, too, are products of the relations of production in a society. For example, the extensive use of skirmishing tactics and guerrilla warfare by the Americans against the British in the American Revolution was a product of the fact that the Americans were in good part a hunting people living in a relatively decentralized and equalitarian society. Likewise, the success of the guerrilla movement in Vietnam was a product of the superior organization and morale of the Vietnamese, factors derivative from the social structure of Vietnam.

Force acts as a "midwife" of a new social formation. Revolutions commonly result in the overthrow of one class by another. But force is not effective against the development of economic forces. When superior military forces conquer a more advanced economic form (e.g., when Mongolian tribemen conquered China) the old social structure is typically maintained with new individuals in the top class positions. Force can not produce a class structure. It can not significantly determine the degree or quality of inequality. At best it can change the individuals in power. When a social structure or class system is deteriorating the mere use of force can not hold it together. The development of a class system is in the last instance a product of the logic of the prevailing mode of production. This does not mean that force can not be used effectively as a means of repression, but rather that when the logic of the mode of production generates massive support for a new class structure it will emerge, regardless of how repressive the old ruling class attempts to be:

> In the first place all political power is originally based on an economic, social function, and increases in proportion as the members of society, through the dissolution of the primitive community, become transformed into private producers, and thus become more and more divorced from the administrators of the common functions of society. Secondly, after the political force has made itself independent in relation to society, and has transformed itself from its servant into its master, it can work in two different directions. Either it works in the sense and in the direction of the natural economic development, in which case no conflict arises between them, the economic development being accelerated. Or it works against economic development, in which case, as a rule, with but few exceptions, force succumbs to it. These few exceptions are isolated cases of conquest, in which the more barbarian conquerors exterminated or drove out

the population of a country and laid waste or allowed to go to ruin productive forces which they did not know how to use (Engels 1894, p. 252).

Property (contrary to what Proudhon argues) is not based on theft. Wealth is not created, and economic inequalities are neither created nor reproduced, because of the forcible expropriation of some by others. Rather economic inequality occurs because of the inherent working of economic systems. Under capitalism the fact that some must sell their labor power to others in order to live, i.e., that surplus value accrues to the propertied class, means that the owing class accumulates more and more wealth, while the working class is unable to do so. This process does not occur through force. The role of force is solely to prevent theft, trespass, sabotage, or rebellion, in the event that the mechanisms of ideological control, habit, and aspirations of upward mobility are insufficient to get the working class to play by the rules of capitalism (e.g., the freedom of contract).

A wealthy class is able to continue in its position only so long as it is making a positive contribution to society. Once such a class comes to serve only its narrow self-interest against the general interest of society its days are numbered. No amount of force can sustain its position for long when it loses its social function in providing for the needs of at least a very considerable sector of society. The sustained and successful use of force requires a relatively loyal sector of the population from which soldiers and police are recruited. More fundamentally, a population ruled only through physical force tends to resist subtly and explicitly in a thousand different ways, and in the event of a major social crisis, is raw material for massive disruption and revolution.

As long as a wealthy ruling class provides jobs, a reasonable standard of living, protects the population from excessive violence and disruption of their lives, provides basic welfare, and otherwise provides for the satisfaction of people's (often increasing) needs and demands, it will maintain the support of the people. But once its rule becomes more negative than positive, once the primary aspect of its domination becomes growing poverty, unemployment, decline in the standard of living, decline in social services, growing domestic violence, loss of wars, environmental destruction, and so on its legitimacy is undermined, and its domination destabilized; and the situation soon ensues where it can maintain its rule only by force. As the Shah's rule in Iran, Somoza's in Nicaragua, the colonial rule of the Portuguese in Angola and Mozambique, the pro-American regime in Vietnam, and numerous other situations in the twentieth century have shown, once the situation gets to this point, no amount of superior military force can indefinitely preserve the social order. The use of force in such conditions tends to alienate the masses of people even more, polarizing things and driving the formerly neutral against the government. Tyranny is overthrown.

The position of wealthy ruling classes from the beginning of history has been based not in superior military force, but in their performing positive functions for the whole (or at least a considerable section) of society. In Engels' words:

> Here we are only concerned with establishing the fact that the exercise of a social function was everywhere the basis of political supremacy; and further that political supremacy has existed for any length of time only when it discharged its social functions. However great the number of despotisms which rose and fell in Persia and India, each was fully aware that above all it was the entrepreneur responsible for the collective maintenance of irrigation throughout the river valleys, without which no agriculture was possible there. It was reserved for the enlightened English to lose sight of this in India; they let the irrigation canals and sluices fall into decay, and are now at last discovering, through the regularly recurring famines, that they have neglected the one activity which might have made their rule in India at least as legitimate as that of their predecessors (Engels 1894, p. 248).

A Critique of Michels

A major weakness in Michels' argument lies in his untenable recourse to explanation in terms of a universal ahistorical and unchangeable "human nature." He roots the striving for power and privilege as well as the "craving for submission" to leaders in the biologically given. If as the evidence of both social psychology and anthropology suggests "human nature" is in good part a social product, then under different social conditions that generate nonauthoritarian character structure, leaders and led would behave quite differently. It *is* true, as Michels argues, that leadership is necessary and that direct participatory democracy cannot work in large-scale organizations, but this should not be taken to mean that there must be a permanent division of labor between *groups* of individuals on all questions (the leading *class* and the led). All this necessarily implies is that there must be a division of roles (which can perhaps be filled by different people at different times and by different people on different questions—e.g., the Athenians selected leaders by lot.)

Michels presents his argument about the need for leadership in static terms as if it were equally compelling at all times in all large groups. This is a mistake. Depending on the problems faced, the need for coordination and strong leadership varies immensely. For example, primitive tribes had war chiefs who generally were active only during war situations (and they were held closely accountable to the warriors). Ancient Rome appointed dictators in times of war. In general, in times of crisis in any type of society (classless, capitalist, socialist), leadership and discipline become stronger than otherwise.

There is no doubt that in a complex technological society no one is able to concern him or herself with every detail of decision making, and further that some people are simply more capable or willing than others of assuming specific responsibilities. Therefore, some people must specialize in some things that others know (or want to know) little about, and no person can concern himself with every detail of group decision making. These are purely technical truisms. But there is no inherent reason that *basic* policy decisions can not normally be made either by the people concerned or with their authentic involvement (with specialists providing the necessary technical information for intelligent decisions). Only if we assume a drive in human nature for power and privilege and for domination and submission can we assume that specialists will normally use their position to gain power and privilege with the masses of people acquiescing.

Michels' most fundamental failing is his lack of understanding that the structural forces which produce the degree of centralized leadership in a society (or organization) account for the decisions made by a "power elite" as well as the effectiveness of those decisions. A group of leaders are not able to assume power as a matter of will. Only when a society requires strong leadership does strong leadership exist. Michels fails to grasp that the decisions and effectiveness of leaders is a product of the logic of the mode of production within which they operate. For example, in the case of union leaders, all the forces of the corporations with which they deal and the state within which unions operate put pressures on and provide many incentives for union leaders to be "responsible"; on the other hand, there are considerable penalties for class conscious militance. High salaries are necessary to keep union leaders from "defecting" only because of the temptations provided by the corporations. An upper middle class life-style and consciousness of union leaders is created by the environment of capitalist society. The threat of imprisonment, fines, and other punishments is a product of the capitalist state. The possibilities of being appointed to government commissions, of securing a good job if and when one leaves the union are products of class society. If the social forces within which union leaders were immersed reinforced democratic, equalitarian, and militant behavior, rather than the opposite, union leaders would behave very differently. If, for example, there were no temptations of high salaries or high status outside the union movement, but the only source of increased income or prestige lay in increasing the living standards of workers (e.g., if union leaders were paid at 125 percent of the average member's salary), if they had no fear of physical or economic retribution by the state or corporations, but instead feared only being deposed by discontented workers, their behavior would be quite different. Quite different because the structure in which they operated would be qualitatively different. Structural forces, not innate power hunger, must be understood as the basis of inequality.

This argument applies equally to the top political leaders (the "power elite") and to the wealthiest people in a society. If top politicians were to make decisions which (within the capitalist economic framework) resulted in lowering corporate profits, to which business responded by not investing (since they had little incentive in the form of anticipated profit to do so), rapidly growing unemployment and a declining standard of living would provoke growing popular opposition to the politicians. The greater the economic crisis provoked by business' not investing, the greater the probability of anticapitalist politicians' losing the next election. If, on the other hand, politicians cooperate with capital (in the absence of a massive socialist movement and a crisis induced by the logic of the capitalist system such as the Great Depression of the 1930s and economic conditions remain reasonably stable) reelection is likely. Structural mechanisms of this kind can operate totally independently of other more direct mechanisms as: the probability of getting a good job with a corporation after a period of government service (if the government administrator or legislator performs well for capital while in office), the possibilities of obtaining election funding from the wealthy, the fact that many government leaders own corporate stock or have inherited wealth and have intimate ties (friendship and kin) with the capitalist class, and so on. All of these latter factors also predispose politicians to adopt a business point of view.

Likewise with the corporate wealthy themselves, if they did not act to maximize their profits (and hence to reproduce the class structure) by minimizing labor costs and maximizing net income, they would go under in the competitive struggle (i.e., they would cease to be capitalists); while others, more efficient maximizers than themselves, would assume their position. Any capitalist that tries to pay his or her workers more, while charging consumers less, will on the average (assuming productivity and marketing costs constant) reduce profits, and thus funds for reinvestment in more efficient machinery and expanded production. Hence, he or she would lose the competitive advantage with those who are making a higher profit (and who are thus able to modernize and expand). Because of the transparency of these processes to capitalists, and because of the conditioning that goes into making for success in business, few capitalists ever even think about consciously reducing profits for the sake of workers and consumers. But it is the logic of the capitalist economic system, not an inherent drive to wealth or power, that drives the capitalists and hence is the source of class inequality under capitalism.

Thus within a given institution, such as a union (or a university), within the state or within the corporate economy, the behavior of decision makers is ultimately determined by the structural logic of the capitalist system, not by a psychological striving for power. The origins and reproduction of class inequality thus must be understood as a product of the logic of the prevailing mode of production. The degree and quality of class inequality, both of which vary considerably through history, are accounted for by structural forces, not by a universal psychological drive for power (or wealth or prestige).

CLASS AS A RELATIONSHIP OF DISTRIBUTION OR COMMON MARKET POSITION

Much of mainstream American sociology defines class in terms of the income a group receives (or its position in relation to the means of distribution), which in turn is reflected in one's general style of life and "life chances." This mode of defining class is in the tradition of Max Weber. Weber formulated two different conceptions of class. In the early drafts of his magnum opus, *Economy and Society*, he made determination by markets a necessary component of "class situation." For example, in the section of this work which Weber did not have a chance to revise before his death in 1920 he defined classes as follows:

> In our terminology, "classes" are not communities; they merely represent possible, and frequent, bases for communal action. We may speak of a "class" when (1) a number of people have in common a specific causal component of their life chances, in so far as (2) this component is represented exclusively by economic interests in the possession of goods and opportunities for income, and (3) is represented under the conditions of the commodity or labor markets (Weber 1922, p. 927).

However, in that part of *Economy and Society* devoted to definitions (part 1), which he did carefully rework again and again (see Guenther Roth's introduction, p. xciv), Weber dropped the criterion of market determination from his definition. In Weber's most mature work class is defined in terms of position in the "economic order" (independently of whether or not such a position is a product of markets):

> 'Class situation' means the typical probability of (1) producing goods, (2) gaining a position in life and, (3) finding inner satisfactions, a probability which derives from the relative control over goods and skills and from their income-producing uses within a given economic order.
>
> 'Class' means all persons in the same class situation: (a) A *'property'* class is primarily determined by property differences, (b) a *'commercial'* class by the marketability of goods and services, (c) a *'social'* class makes up the totality of those class situations within which individual and generational mobility is easy and typical (Weber 1922, p. 302).

In his latter definition Weber appears to use "commercial class" in the sense in which he formerly used "class." He, thus, expanded his concept of class to include both "property classes" and "social classes," neither of which are determined by either market position or a broader position in relations of distribution. In fact, in his final definition Weber, by stressing "producing goods" as the first aspect of his definition and property class as his first example of a class, seems to be suggesting that class is primarily a relation of production (similar to Marx). Weber's earlier definition of class (unlike Marx's) excludes as a matter of definition slaves, serfs, feudal lords, and so on because the position of these groups was not determined by markets. His latter definition (like Marx's) includes these groups (as social and property classes).*

Anthony Giddens, an influential "neo-Weberian" British sociologist, has expanded on Weber's early definition of class in terms of "common market situation." Giddens, defining "market capacity" as

---

*Considerable popular misrepresentation of the Weberian concept of class in terms of "market determination" resulted from the widespread currency of the Hans Gerth and C.W. Mills' translation of Chapter 9 of *Economy and Society*, entitled "Class, Status and Party," which appeared in their *From Max Weber* (1946). This essay was a translation from the unrevised earlier sections of *Economy and Society*. The influence of this translation has been so great that in the general literature the term "Weberian conception of class" includes "market determination." In spite of its inaccuracy, I will not deviate from this general usage.

"all forms of relevant attributes which individuals may bring to the bargaining encounter" (1973 p. 103), goes on to argue:

> There are three sorts of market capacity which can be said to be normally of importance . . . "ownership of property in the means of production; possession of educational or technical qualifications; and possession of manual labor power. In so far as it is the case that these tend to be tied to closed patterns of inter- and intra-generational mobility, this yields the foundation of a basic three-class system in capitalist society: an "upper," "middle" and "lower" or "working class" (1973, p. 107).

The Weberian tradition of defining classes by economically determined life chances (rooted in relations of distribution) is strongly manifested in contemporary American sociology, which commonly defines classes in terms of income or wealth. Even when Socioeconomic Status (SES, a composite of income, prestige of job, and years of education) is used, income is generally understood to be the primary determinant, or at least a good indicator, of the other factors. For example, Kurt Mayer and Walter Buckley argue: "In a class system, the social hierarchy is based primarily on differences in monetary wealth and income" (1970, p. 15).

Another influential, contemporary "Weberian" definition of class, which also builds on Weber's early definition of class, is that of Immanuel Wallerstein's world systems theory. This school defines class in terms of common position in relation to the *world* market:

> The division of a world-economy involves a hierarchy of occupational tasks, in which tasks requiring higher levels of skill and greater capitalization are reserved for higher ranking areas. Since a capitalist world economy essentially rewards accumulated capital, including human capital, at a higher rate than "raw" labor power, the geographical maldistribution of these occupational skills involves a strong trend towards self-maintenance. The forces of the marketplace reinforce them rather than undermine them (Wallerstein 1974, p. 350).

According to Wallerstein, ". . . the emergence, consolidation, and political roles of classes and status groups must be appreciated as elements of this world system" (1974, p. 351).

Like the early Weber, Wallerstein argues that classes as real social units only occasionally exist: "Classes do not have some permanent reality. Rather, they are formed, they consolidate themselves, they disintegrate, or disaggregate, and they are re-formed" (Wallerstein 1979, p. 224). The issue according to Wallerstein is under what conditions do potential classes come to "operate as a group in the politico-economic arenas and even to some extent as a cultural entity" (Wallerstein 1974, p. 351).

Wallerstein considers slaves in the U.S. South prior to 1867, serfs and semiserfs in Latin America and Russia in the nineteenth century, and contemporary industrial workers in Western Europe as all essentially in the *same* class—the working class of the world capitalist system. At the same time wealthy merchants in the sixteenth century, twentieth-century industrial capitalists, and eighteenth-century slaveowning plantation lords in the Caribbean are considered to be part of the same class—the capitalist class of the world capitalist system. Those that produce wealth for sale within the world market are part of the working class. Those that control such wealth are capitalists. Differences among slaves, serfs and industrial workers are considered to be merely differences in the "mode of labor control" (a factor considered to be of secondary importance).

Paralleling his definition of classes in terms of market relations, Wallerstein defines capitalism as "production for sale in a market in which the object is to realize a maximum profit" (Wallerstein 1979, pp. 15, 16, 159, 285). Unlike the traditional Marxist school Wallerstein defines classes essentially in a *quantitative* rather than a *qualitative* way. As long as production is for markets (commodity production), for Wallerstein all groups that exploit labor are capitalists, while all that are exploited are workers, regardless of the form (or quality) of the relationship between the market-oriented exploiters and exploited.

Wallerstein defines the bourgeois as "those who receive part of the surplus value they do not themselves create and use some of it to accumulate capital" (1979, p. 285). The proletariat, according to Wallerstein, are "those who yield part of the value they have created to others" (1979, p. 288). Wallerstein goes on to explicitly delineate himself from the traditional Marxist approach:

> Let us be quite clear what this approach to the concept of proletarian does. It eliminates as a defining characteristic of the proletarian the payment of wages to the producer (1979, p. 288).

A Critique of Class as a Market Relation

Definitions must be accepted or rejected on the basis of their practical usefulness, i.e., the analytical power of conceptualizing reality in different ways. Thus whether classes should be defined as relations of production *or* market relations (and whether or not capitalism should be defined as commodity production or as exploitation by wage labor) is *solely* a question of the historical and contemporary analytical power of the two alternative conceptions.

The definition of capitalism as commodity production employed by Andre Gunder Frank (1967), Paul Sweezy (1976), and Immanuel Wallerstein (1974, 1979) implies that all predominantly commercial societies regardless of their dominant labor-owner relations are capitalist (the propertied classes in each are capitalists and the producing classes in each proletarians), and thus each share common essentials that distinguish them from essentially different societies (with qualitatively different propertied and producing classes) in which production for sale in markets prevails. We would thus expect that such societies and classes tend to have more in common with each other than with other types of societies and classes, *and* that what they have in common is specific and concrete enough to shed considerable light on the entire social structure. If we find that the set of primarily commodity-producing societies have very little in common with each other, and thus that this criterion does not clearly differentiate this set of societies from societies in which commodity production does not prevail, the conceptualization in terms of market relations must be considered deficient.

Societies in which production for sale predominated have included the early Roman Empire, the ancient Greek city-states, Babylon in the first milleneum B.C., Byzantium, Europe in the sixteenth to eighteenth centuries, the Arab Empires from around 900 to 1200, Europe and the United States today, Japan in the late Tokugawa period (1750-1868), Peru in the sixteenth century, and Brazil in the seventeenth century. The question is, are societies such as these *essentially* the same and do they as a set differ fundamentally from societies where production was for use, such as the ancient Egyptian Empire, precolonial India, the empire of the Mongols, and so on. The answer to both of these questions would seem to be *no*. The ancient empires in which commodity production prevailed and those in which production for use (with tribute in kind) predominated would seem to have more in common with each other than the ancient empires with commodity production have in common with the contemporary societies of Western Europe and North America.

Further, defining capitalism as commodity production defines away many key problems. Rather than asking why capitalism as the predominant mode of production developed first in northwestern Europe, we must ask why it developed first in ancient Mesopotamia. We must address questions like what accounted for the decline and collapse of capitalism in ancient Greece and Rome. Questions like why did Japan become capitalist after the Meiji restoration disappear, since by definition Japan was capitalist *before* the Meiji restoration. In fact the definition of capitalism as commodity production raises many false questions while leading us away from key problems. It classifies such a wide array of highly diverse societies as "capitalist" as to deprive the term of historical and analytical usefulness.

By defining most of the world from the sixteenth century as part of the capitalist system, Frank (1967), Sweezy (1976), and Wallerstein (1974, 1979) confuse the very basic differences within the world from that time, while at the same time obscuring the very fundamental changes that occurred in the world economy since the sixteenth century. By using the term "capitalism" so broadly as to include virtually everything since the sixteenth century in its net, they have watered the term down to be worse than useless—worse than useless because it hides rather than highlights the fundamental differences and transformations in social structure in both Europe and the world since the sixteenth century.

Wallerstein in his treatment of slavery (and other noncapitalist relations of production that occur within the capitalist world system) confuses the difference between the *hegemonic* or *predominant* relations of production within a world system with the various component systems of relations of production. Each social formation, whether a nation-state or an interrelated world system, normally has a predominant mode of production whose logic structures and conditions all social, economic, and political processes that go on within that formation, including secondary relations of production. The predominant mode of production need not be that which incorporates the most people, or even that which produces the largest material output, merely that which organizes or structures the rest. Thus, for example, the United States and the European world system were *capitalist* social formations in the 1850s because their economies were essentially structured by the logic of *capitalist* production (exploitation through wage labor), e.g., the need for imports and exports of industrial capitalism in England, the North of the United States, and other Western European countries. Capitalist logic predominated, even though most producers in the United States as well as the rest of the capitalist world system were slaves, serfs, peasants, or independent petty-bourgeois producers (e.g., family farmers, artisans, and so on).

The growing importance of slavery after the late eighteenth century in the United States was a product of the rapid growth of capitalist relations of production in England and the North of the United States (relations that produced rapid industrialization and a rapid growth in the demand for cheap cotton). But the fact that slavery in the nineteenth century was essentially determined by the capitalist logic of the world system did not mean that the social, political, and economic institutions of the United States South (or other regions of the capitalist world system) were distinctively capitalist. Even though the logic of world capitalism caused the slave system to prosper and predominate in the South, the logic of the master-slave relation nevertheless prevailed in that region (a logic qualitatively different than the logic of wage-labor capital). The *cause* of the hegemony of master-slave or capital-wage labor relations in a region must not be confused with the question of whether or not master-slave or capitalist-worker logic prevails there.

The insistence by Wallerstein as well as Paul Sweezy and Andre Gunder Frank on treating all forms of relations of production within a capitalist world system as essentially the same (i.e., variations on wage labor and capital) must be judged on the basis of the analytical power of this approach compared to that of the more traditional Marxist approach that sees qualitatively different relations of production within a capitalist world economy. The advantage of treating slavery as "coerced wage labor" as does Wallerstein is that it emphasizes the fact that the U.S. South's social and economic structure was a product of the developing capitalism in Great Britain and not an autonomous development. The disadvantage of this treatment is that it obscures the systematic qualitative differences in the social structures of the different parts of the capitalist world system. Thus in questions having to do with the historical *causes* of slavery in the South, Wallerstein's approach is adequate, but in questions having to do with Southern politics, the efficiency of slavery, the relations among poor and rich whites, Southern family forms, the causes of the attempted Southern secession, and so on, it is not helpful, since it leads us to look for the essential similarities between the South *and* the North and England, not the qualitative differences that studies such as those of Eugene Genovese show were, in fact, the causes of these phenomena (see Genovese 1967, 1968, 1969, 1974).

Approaches such as those of Frank, Sweezy, and Wallerstein can result in seriously faulty analyses by directing investigators away from focusing on the *contradictions* among the various systems of relationships of production prevailing within a single world system, contradictions such as those that gave rise to the American Civil War. Such approaches have difficulty in systematically accounting for such events because they can not comprehend that the two *qualitatively different* logics of production in the United States in the 1850s placed *contradictory* demands on the U.S. state. The logic of capitalism in the North required high tariffs, aid for railways and canals, facilitation of immigration, free land to farmers, aid to higher education to produce engineers, and so on; while that of slavery required low tariffs, inhibitions on Western settlement by small farmers, discouragement of immigration, low state spending, and so on. Because of the far greater productive potentialities of capitalism that were being realized in the rapid growth of the North, the state was in danger of being turned into the instrument of capital. Thus the slaves lords had no choice but to attempt to establish their own national state if they were to have a chance of preserving their distinctive economic and social system. It is difficult to see how a framework that treated Northern and Southern relations of production as essentially the same could satisfactorily account for occurrences such as the U.S. Civil War.

The advantage of the traditional Marxist conceptualization is to highlight the qualitative *differences* between the South and the North, thus sensitizing us to the causes of the Civil War, the uniqueness of Southern family life, and so on. At the same time, there need be no real disadvantage caused by forgetting that the qualitatively different Southern civilization was a product of capitalist development in other parts of the world capitalist system. Traditional Marxist analysis (e.g., Maurice Dobb's *Studies in the Development of Capitalism*, 1963) have been quite adept at explaining developments in one part of the capitalist system by events in other parts. Thus a traditional Marxist focus on relations of production can easily include Wallerstein's central concern by emphasizing that the South *was* a product of the logic of the world capitalist system without sacrificing the ability to explain the qualitative differences in the social structure of different parts of that system.

Traditional Marxism's problematic is one of classes and class contradictions. For Marxists, for example, it is the inherent logic of the master-slave or lord-serf relationship that generates the basic institutions and culture of slave or classical feudal society. It is, further, the inherent contradictions of these relationships that are the cause of their decline and the rise of new classes and new class relationships. The contradictions of preexisting class relations must be looked to as the source of historical change (including the development of world systems). Failure to do this leads to the type of eclectic historical analysis engaged in by both Weber and Wallerstein, which in the last analysis is no analysis at all, but merely an historical description.

CLASS AS A COMMON POSITION
WITHIN THE TECHNICAL DIVISION OF LABOR

Some theorists define class in good part in terms of the nature of the occupations or jobs of people, their special skills or particular tasks, or the nature of their product. One common mode of defining class in terms of the technical division of labor is dividing the class structure according to skill levels (e.g., "unskilled," "semi-skilled," and "skilled" *manual* workers are defined as working class, nonmanual employees as middle class, and so on).

Richard Hamilton, following a common practice within the political sociology tradition (whose most influential spokesperson has been Seymor Martin Lipset), categorizes class according to the manual-nonmanual distinction. Hamilton argues, "that the terms 'working class,' 'blue-collar' and manual" can be used interchangeably, while the terms "middle class," "white collar" and "nonmanual" can as well (Hamilton 1972, p. 152). In defense of the manual-nonmanual boundary as primary he argues:

> The manual jobs, in a very general way, are those involving relatively greater contributions of physical labor that is expended in the production of goods or the performance of onerous services. The manual jobs, for the most part, are paid less than the nonmanual; they involve less on-the-job autonomy, carry less prestige, and are performed in less attractive surroundings.
>
> The use of the term 'middle class' as the equivalent of nonmanual is obviously imprecise since the latter does include a small upper class or elite. The nonmanual jobs, in the majority of cases, have better pay, more prestige, and cleaner, more pleasant, and less noisy surroundings. The holders of white collar jobs either make the major decisions in occupational life or they execute, transmit and carry out the order of others. Their basic function is the specification and transmission of those orders to the manual ranks together with the collection of performance records (Hamilton 1972, p. 152).

Another mode of defining class in such terms is exemplified in the theories of Daniel Bell and other theorists of "post-industrial society" who argue that the technical experts (engineers, scientists, professional managers, and so on) are becoming the new dominant class. Bell argues (in a somewhat exaggerated manner): "In the Scientific City of the future, there are already foreshadowed three classes: the creative elite of scientists and the top professional administrators . . . ; the middle class of engineers and the professionate; and the proletariat of technicians, junior faculty and teaching assistants" (Bell 1973, pp. 213-14).

Many who define class in terms of position in the technical division of labor have a tendency to be technological determinists, i.e., to see classes as arising and reproducing as a result of the logic of increasing efficiency or the industrialization process.* Thus, it is the imperatives of modern industry (not capitalist relations of production or the functional requisites of *all* societies) that generates a class of economic decision makers who have essential control over the economy. This is true regardless of whether or not they are private capitalists with legal ownership rights in corporations, or state administrators with only de facto control. Most of these theorists would argue, using such a conception of class, that there is a convergence in the class structures of the Soviet Union and China *and* the advanced capitalist countries such as the United States. Such technological determinists argue that the imperatives of modern industrial technology necessarily produce a professional stratum of scientists and engineers, a lower class of "continuous process" workers to look after the increasingly automated machinery, as well as a (growing) class of personal service workers and lower level white-collar workers to staff the growing offices and administrative centers.

Nicos Poulantzas

There are a number of theorists close to the Marxist tradition who define class in large part in terms of the technical division of labor, rather than, as does traditional Marxism, purely in terms of the relations of production. Undoubtedly the most influential of these is Nicos Poulantzas.† Poulantzas defines class in terms of three dimensions. The first dimension is "economic": whether or not one's labor is productive or nonproductive. By productive labor, Poulantzas means labor that both directly produces material wealth *and* is exploited (or produces surplus value), i.e., the difference between what the laborer produces and what the worker is paid goes to the

---

*There are some theorists who share the technological determinist view of the reproduction of classes, but who do not define classes in terms of positions within the technical division of labor. For example, Gerhard Lenski, who defines classes primarily in terms of relationships of force or institutionalized power, argues that "variations in technology will be the most important single determinant of variations in distribution" (1966, p. 90).

†Poulantzas' work on class should be understood as an attempt to *defend* the traditional Marxist idea that the leading revolutionary agent in society is the industrial proletariat against such theorists as Andre Gorz and Serge Mallet on the one hand who argue that it is now the more educated and highly skilled; and on the other hand, those theorists such as Frantz Fanon and Herbert Marcuse, who argue that it is now the excluded sector, the "lumpen proletariat" or the more oppressed and poorest segments of society.

one who purchases the worker's labor power. The second dimension is "Ideological": whether or not one's labor is mental or manual, i.e., whether or not one has knowledge of the production process or merely executes processes controlled and understood by others. The third dimension is "Political": whether or not one supervises or controls labor power in the production process. The political criterion is very close to what Marxists traditionally have meant by "relations of production," but the first two (the economic and the ideological) in fact describe different positions within the technical division of labor; namely the character of one's output (material or not), and one's level of knowledge of the production process (mental or manual labor). It should be noted that what Poulantzas labels as the economic has components of both the technical division of labor (what is produced) and the relations of production (whether or not one is exploited) (see Poulantzas 1974, pt. 3).

Poulantzas includes in the capitalist class: those positions that have legal economic ownership rights in production; those positions that have "real" economic ownership (de facto power to assign the means of production to given uses and to dispose of the product obtained) although they do not have legal title; and those that have only *possession* of the means of production (the capacity to put the means of production into operation, or actual control over the physical operation of production), even when they do not exercise real economic ownership (i.e., de facto control).

Poulantzas considers corporate managers to be part of the capitalist class, not because they fundamentally control the means of production, but rather because of the social *functions* they perform (Poulantzas 1974, p. 180). He goes on to define the heads of the state apparatus as also part of the bourgeoisie since they too perform capitalist class *functions* (Poulantzas 1974, p. 187).

Poulantzas categorizes the working class as those positions which: produce surplus value in the process of material production, do *not* have authority over the production process, and do *not* have general technical knowledge of the production process. Any position that does not fulfill *all three* of these criteria is considered part of the "new petty bourgeoisie." That is, positions that do not produce surplus value in producing material goods; or have authority over production; *or* have generalized technical knowledge are in the new petty bourgeoisie, *not* the working class. In good part, then, the category new petty bourgeoisie is a residual category for Poulantzas. It includes all employees who do *not* fit into either the capitalist class (the lower level managers) or the working class (such as clerical and sales workers, service workers, technicians, and foremen). Service, commercial, sales, and clerical workers are considered to be part of the new petty bourgeoisie since even while they are exploited, lack control over the production process, and engage in menial rather than mental labor, they do not perform "productive labor," i.e., they perform a different function in the technical division of labor than do true workers.*

A Critique of Class Categorization
by the Technical Division of Labor

Class conceptualizations in terms of the technical division of labor, such as those of the political sociology tradition (e.g., Hamilton), Poulantzas, and the Ehrenreichs must in the last analysis be evaluated in terms of how useful they are in allowing us to predict the behavior of various groups. To define groups as in the *same* class suggests that such groups generally have more in common than groups located in different class positions. The validity of the manual/nonmanual distinction (used by Hamilton and Poulantzas), whether or not material goods are produced (a criterion used by Poulantzas), and whether or not a group functions to reproduce class relations (a criterion used by the Ehrenreichs) must be judged by whether or not such criteria result in the specification of analytically useful class categories.

If clerical, sales, and commerical workers (all nonmanual and nonproducers of material goods) generally share the social characteristics of and tend to behave politically more like professionals and managers (also nonmanual, nonproducers) more than industrial workers, then it is valid to make a manual/nonmanual (and a productive/nonproductive) dichotomy. If this is not true, such a categorization obscures rather than assists class analysis. In fact, a prima facie case can easily be made that, at least in the latter years of the twentieth century, most office and sales workers, and certainly most service workers, share both the conditions of labor *and* the

---

*Another contemporary influential Marxian categorization of class structure is that of Barbara and John Ehrenreich, who argue: "The relations which define class arise from the place occupied by groups in the broad social division of labor, and from the basic patterns of control over access to the means of production and of appropriation of the social surplus" (1979, p. 11). They go on to define the professional-managerial class as "consisting of salaried mental workers who do not own the means of production and whose major function in the social division of labor may be described broadly as the reproduction of capitalist culture and capitalist class relations" (1979, p. 12). Thus, like Poulantzas, the Ehrenreichs incorporate *both* elements of relations of production and elements of the technical division of labor into their class definitions (see Szymanski, 1979b for a critique of the Ehrenreichs' argument).

social and political characteristics of industrial workers more than they share the conditions of labor, social characteristics, and political tendencies of professionals and managers. Most types of nonsupervisory/nonprofessional employees have generally similar relations of production, therefore fundamental categorizations in terms of manual/ nonmanual such as those of Hamilton and Poulantzas are not useful. It is likewise with Poulantzas' distinction of production of material goods. There is little reason to believe that the act of producing material things rather than services has fundamental effects on social characteristics or political tendencies, *or* that (again in the latter part of the twentieth century) such labor is in fact usually performed under qualitatively different conditions than most industrial labor. Both productive and nonproductive laborers have generally similar relations of production and this can be expected to develop broadly similar consciousness. It is the same with the Ehrenreichs' dichotomization around reproduction of capitalist relationships. If it is valid to define a class in terms of whether or not their *function* is to reproduce class relations, then it is valid to define workers in munitions industries out of the working class because their labor allows the capitalists to maintain a world empire, i.e., because their economic function is to *reproduce capitalist class* relations, just as surely as it is that of the professionals who propagate ideology.

SUBJECTIVIST CONCEPTUALIZATIONS OF CLASS

Talcott Parsons, the most influential idealist sociologist in post-World War II American sociology, defines a class as a plurality of kinship units that have approximately the same status or, alternatively, an aggregate of such units, individual and/or collective, that in their own estimation and those of others in the society occupy positions of approximately equal status (Parsons 1940, 1949). The units of a class are families, families which evaluate themselves as more or less equal in relation to other sets of families (i.e., classes) which they regard as either socially or morally inferior or superior to themselves (i.e., have equal "status").

Robin Williams, another influential post-World War II American sociologist, defines class as follows: "The distribution of privileges . . . begins to take on full sociological meaning only when it is related to *prestige rankings, social-interaction groupings* and *beliefs and values held in common.* We shall use the term 'social class' to refer to an aggregate of individuals who occupy a broadly similar position in the scale of privilege" (Williams 1960, p. 98).

For Parsons and Williams it is the collective feelings a set of people have about themselves and other sets of people, i.e., their subjective consciousness and identifications, that define class. This mode of defining and identifying class is a popular one in contemporary American sociology and has been "operationalized" by both those (the purely subjective idealists) who try to establish the class of individuals through asking people themselves what class they are a part of, and by others who use a "reputational method" of asking acquaintances and members of a community what class they think certain other individuals are in.

The subjectivist-functionalist tradition of Parsons and Williams as well as the self-definitional and reputation approaches to establishing class to which they are tied frame class evaluation in terms of "higher," "middle," and "lower." They assume an essential continuum of class position from the "lowest" to the "highest" with no natural cut off points as well as that classes are not organic or active social units. Each researcher normally draws their own boundaries among what are considered as either statistical aggregates or passive groupings.

Marxian Subjectivist Categorizations of Class

There are other traditions that share with Parsonian idealism a subjective definition of class (in terms of people's self-sonsciousness). This is true of both the school that is sometimes referred to as "Hegelian Marxism" as well as some highly empiricist Marxians such as E. P. Thompson (both of which define class essentially in terms of class consciousness).*

---

*While Georg Luckas (1967) is often cited as Hegelian Marxist, he actually defines class, even in his early and most influential writings, in terms of social relations of production (even while he emphasized the role of class consciousness in understanding the behavior of classes):

Bourgeoisie and proletariat are the only pure classes in bourgeoisie society. They are the only classes whose existence and development are entirely dependent on the course taken by the modern evolution of production. . . (p. 59).
. . .[the proletariat] appears in the first instance as the pure object of societal events. In every aspect of daily life in which the individual worker imagines himself to be the subject of his own life he finds this to be an illusion that is destroyed by the immediacy of his existence, (pp. 165-66).

And like the rest of the Marxist tradition, Luckas makes the distinction between a class objectively defined (a class *an sich*) and a class conscious class *für sich* that is an active historical force:

Only, when the consciousness of the proletariat is able to point out the road along which the dialectics of history is objectively impelled, but which it cannot travel unaided, will the consciousness of the proletariat awaken to a consciousness of the process, and only then will the proletariat become the identical subject-object of history whose praxis will change reality (1967, p. 197).

Luckas, in fact, presents one of the stronger materialist statements of the meaning of class consiousness within the orthodox Marxist tradition. He insists on defining class consciousness not in terms of either individuals' or class's actual consciousness, but rather in terms of its rationally "imputed" consciousness, which he argues actually determines its behavior:

By relating consciousness to the whole of society it becomes possible to infer the thoughts and feelings which men would have in a particular situation if they were able to assess both it and the interests arising from it in their impact on immediate action and on the whole structure of society. . . . Now class consciousness consists in fact of the appropriate and rational reactions "imputed" to a particular typical position in the process of production. This consciousness is, therefore, neither the sum nor the average of what is thought or felt by the single individuals who make up the class. And yet the historically significant actions of the class as a whole are determined in the last resort by this consciousness and not by the thought of the individual. . . (1967, p. 51).

Antonio Gramsci, sometimes cited as having a subjectivist conception of class, also defined class in terms of relations of production. Gramsci, drawing the traditional Marxist distinction between an active class, conscious class and a class that is a mere object of historical forces, discusses the process of developing class consciousness. He specifies social classes as based in their role in economic production:

Every social class, coming into existence on the original basis of an essential function in the world of economic production, creates within itself, organically, one or more groups of intellectuals who give it homogeneity and consciousness of its function not only in the economic field but in the social and political field as well. . . (1959, p. 118).

In speaking about the potentials of the proletariat as a ruling class Gramsci argues that it must develop a class consciousness of itself, *without* suggesting that such a consciousness is a part of the definition of the proletariat:

The proletariat, in order to be able to rule as a class, must rid itself of all corporative hangovers, of all syndicalist prejudices and incrustations. . . . The metalworkers, the joiners, the builders, etc., must not only think as proletarians and no longer as metalworkers, joiners or builders, but they must take a step forward: they must think as members of a class which aims at leading the peasants and the intellectuals, of a class which can conquer and build socialism only if aided and followed by the great majority of these social strata. If it does not do this, the proletariat does not become a leading class. . . (1959, p. 36).

Thompson (1963) is probably the most influential contemporary Marxian taking such an approach. In his work *The Making of the English Working Class*, he argues:

> ... By class I understand an historical phenomenon, unifying a number of disparate and seemingly unconnected events, both in the raw material of experience and in consciousness. I emphasize that it is an *historical* phenomenon. I do not see class as a "structure" nor even as a "category," but as something which in fact happens . . . in human relationships. . . .
>
> And class happens when some men, as a result of common experiences (inherited or shared), feel and articulate the identity of their interests as between themselves, and as against other men whose interests are different from (and usually opposed to) theirs. The class experience is largely determined by the productive relations into which men are born—or enter involuntarily. Class consciousness is the way in which these experiences are handled in cultural terms: embodied in traditions, value-systems, ideas and institutional forms. If the experience appears as determined, class consciousness does not. We can see a *logic* in the responses of similar occupational groups undergoing similar experiences, but we cannot predicate any *law*. Consciousness of class arises in the same way in different times and places, but never in just the same way (pp. 9, 10).
>
> Class is defined by men as they live their own history, and in the end, this is the only definition (p. 11).

Stanley Aronowitz offers a similar subjectivist definition of class. He argues that a set of people form a class only when they are class conscious and politically active:

> The formation of a group of people within the social structure must be one that involves the following characteristics if they are to constitute a class: (1) They must enter into "manifold relations" as a consequence of the development of (a) means of communication, (b) division of labor, and (c) a certain level of material culture that allows social intercourse; (2) they must have a *separate* mode of life interests and cultural formation that brings them into conflict with other classes; and (3) they must represent themselves politically, that is, speak in their own name (Aronowitz 1979, p. 217).

Adam Przeworski offers one of the most extreme subjectivist definitions of class, defining class solely in terms of collective identification and organization. He argues that classes do not exist unless they have a common ideology and are politically active, and thus that consciousness or ideology is prior to class formation: "The ideological class struggle is a struggle about class before it is a struggle among classes" (1976 p. 28). He goes on to argue:

> ... it is necessary to emphasize that classes are not prior to their organization: the concept of class organization does not mean that classes are given as such and *only* then organized, but, to the contrary, that classes appear as historical subjects only when they are organized, only when carriers of relations of production form social relations characterized by shared collective identification and organization. . . (Przeworski 1976, p. 32).

Although they offer essentially subjective definitions of class, authors such as Thompson, Aronowitz, and Przeworski reflect the influence of the Marxist tradition in situating their definitions within a framework where relations of production still play a role. But all those in the Marxian subjectivist tradition see classes (even though conditioned by economic factors) as essentially primary formations. Classes are seen as in good part uncaused by antecedent social forces. Class consciousness is then in essence the result of historical accident, individual intervention, will, unique combinations of events, spontaneity, or political strategy.

Those who define class in terms of class consciousness, *unlike* those in the subjectivist tradition within mainstream sociology (such as Talcott Parsons) see classes as organic units of societies, *not* as continuums. Further, they see these organic units of society, perhaps more than any other perspective, as the primary social actors in society and in the making of history. Last, the Marxian subjectivist mode of class definition sees classes existing only at certain periods and places. If workers or peasants identify themselves primarily in terms of their religion or nation, rather than as classes with class interests, they are not considered to be classes (and consequently society can not be considered to be class stratified).

A Critique of the Subjectivist Conceptualizations of Class

Both the mainstream sociological and Marxian subjectivist conceptualizations of class suffer from the inability to understand where class consciousness, shared class beliefs and identifications, or prestige comes from. By taking classes as more or less given by their ideas and behavior, such approaches mystify the processes of class formation and transformation, thereby obscuring rather than clarifying the social forces at work in generating class structure (as well as the future transformation of classes). This problem is most serious for those schemata that consider people to be in whatever class they think they are in as well as (to a somewhat lesser extent) for those that use the "reputational method" (allowing one's acquaintances to define one's class). At least theorists like Parsons have an explanation, however inadequate, of why there are different levels of prestige and why there are common identifications (which they then use to account for the existence of classes). While some useful information can be gleaned from what someone's reputation is, or even from what people's self-conceptions are, the basic question of what people really are, and further why and how they are that way, are not considered within the framework of most subjectivists. The fact that some factory workers think of themselves (or have others think of them) as middle class and others as lower or working class is considered to be more fundamental than the fact that they have identical relations of production—a claim that can not be empirically supported.

To maintain that a group of workers or peasants are a religious or national group instead of essentially a class just because they conceive of themselves and their activities primarily in terms of Christianity, Protestantism, Islam, Judaism, black nationalism, being white, and so on is to miss the essence of most struggles that have occurred since the origin of class society. The superficial acceptance of historical actors' self-definitions would lead an analysis of the struggle in northern Ireland between the poorer and more marginal working class and the propertied and the skilled working class to conclude that it was the Protestants fighting the Catholics about religion; an analysis of the Lebanonese civil war between the poorer workers and peasants and the propertied and middle classes to conclude that it was essentially a religious war over the principles of Islam and Maronite Christianity; and an analysis of "racial" conflicts in the United States to the conclusion that they were really about whites' not liking blacks.

To abandon the analytical power of Marxist objective class analysis for subjectivist conceptions of class is to give up the ability to analyze history. In understanding how class structure or the economy operates, the potential for political consciousness developing, "religious," "racial," and "national" struggles, the general motion of a society, and so on, one would be foolish to rely on people's images (or self-images) rather than on reality.

Those in the Marxian tradition who share the subjectivist view of class tend to criticize the mainstream Marxist tradition for "determinism" (by which they seem to really mean fatalism, or the feeling that since things are lawfully determined one can not influence the historical process). They often seem to think they are laying the basis for revolutionary transformation by "freeing" the working classes from such determination through their conceptualizations. Revolution or continued oppression then, in their eyes, is not a matter of objective conditions, but rather a matter of will and organization. By logical extension the poor are to be blamed for their poverty since they lack the will to change their condition. Lack of success is a result of bad strategy, failure to seize the moment, or lack of will, not historical processes.

Marxian subjectivism fails to grasp the distinction between fatalism and the lawfulness of human behavior. Marxism has always argued that people revolt (and are successful at revolution) because of a conjuncture of historical forces (including degree of oppression, delegitimation crises, a leading class with the ability and vision to carry through the revolutionary process, and so on), i.e., that revolution is *completely* lawful, while at the same time, an active *intervention* in history. Marxism sees no contradiction between historical materialism (determinism) and active intervention. Intervention by classes and parties is not random or willful, but rather a product of historical forces, forces that behave in an understandable and predictable (not arbitrary, random, or mystical) fashion.

The failure to grasp the importance of objective historical forces in generating class consciousness and political behavior has generally been associated with two kinds of political mistakes. The first is what has been called "adventurism" or "ultraleftism." If the success or failure of a political intervention or revolution is a product of will, organization, discipline, and so on (rather than objective conditions), stronger will, discipline, and so on should be able to change society at any time (or at least in a much wider variety of circumstances than has generally been thought possible). The second mistake is demoralization. If the working class does not actively intervene to change history, if it is not acting as a progressive force, then the working class itself is to blame. In fact, historically subjectivism has been associated with both the ultra-left (e.g., Weathermen, Baader-Meinhof, the Red Brigade, and so on), and academic nonactivist leftism (much of the Western intellectual Left of the 1970s).

The Functionalist Theory of Class

Talcott Parsons is a functionalist who feels that inequality in status is necessary in order for society to function effectively. He argues that: first, moral evaluation in terms of inferior and superior is a crucial aspect of people's social behavior; second, different individual evaluations must agree if social order is to be possible, and hence if society is to operate in all of our interests, rather then there being a Hobbsian war of all against all; third, this evaluation of individuals and tasks in terms of inferiority and superiority is socially necessary to motivate people to perform the most important tasks (and hence if society is to function in satisfying our needs); and fourth, these socially necessary normative rankings *are* social stratification (or the class system). Parsons then sees differential ranking as *necessary* for social stability and the adequate functioning of social institutions (see Parsons 1940).

Parsons sees a necessity of a hierarchy of status (as well as of power and wealth) in order to motivate people to train for and skillfully perform the most difficult and important jobs in the society. He sees a considerable differentiation in both the skills required, the relative social contribution of positions and competence (some abilities are rare, some positions require long and difficult training), and thus that society must channel the most able into the most important jobs so that all of society benefits. Stratification and class are seen as the positive consequences of such social allocation. Those in top status positions are there because they benefit all of society. Their top status (and high income and authority) is both the reward for their disproportionate contribution to the welfare of society, *and* is a functional necessity to get the job done, i.e., it is necessary to get their subordinates or social inferiors to perform the more menial and less important tasks.

The functionalist argument about the universal necessity of social stratification or class inequality has been most sharply presented by Kingsley Davis and Wilber Moore (1945). Similarly to Parsons, Davis and Moore argue that stratification and class are a necessary outcome of any viable society's requirement of placing, recruiting, training, and motivating individuals in the social structure. They argue: first, some positions in society are inherently more agreeable than others, and hence, if rewards of income, status, and power were equal, most people would gravitate to such positions independent of how important they were for society, leaving other, perhaps more important positions, unfilled; second, some positions require special talents or training (e.g., doctors require approximately eight years of college acquired at considerable expense and sacrifice to themselves and their families), thus inequalities in income, status, and power are necessary to motivate capable people to make the sacrifices necessary to acquire socially necessary training and skills; third, some positions are socially more important than others (e.g., doctors, scientists, top managers), and hence society must be sure to recruit the most capable people (e.g., there are a limited number of people with the natural ability to be good nuclear physicists or brain surgeons) to these jobs by disproportionately rewarding them; fourth, everyone must be motivated to perform their job to the best of their ability, again, by rewarding better performance (and hence greater social contribution) with more money, status, and power. (It benefits all patients to have highly paid, and hence highly motivated, doctors treating them—even the very poor.) Stratification (or class structure) then is the differential reward structure socially necessary as an inducement to obtain properly qualified individuals correctly distributed in the occupational structure and to motivate them to perform well once there.

The essential determinants of relative ranks of different social positions are then: first, the relative importance positions have for society, and second, the amount of talent the positions require. Davis and Moore discuss the actual income, status, and power rankings in society in terms of these two functional necessities. They argue that top religious leaders (popes, bishops, ministers, and so on) have very high status (and often considerable power and income as well), because of the great importance for society of religion (and hence good religious leadership) as a social cement or means of generating solidarity to keep society together (and people committed enough to their social institutions to make them work well). They argue that top political leaders (kings, presidents, members of Congress, Supreme Court justices, and so on) have especially large amounts of power (and typically high incomes and prestige as well) because of the tremendous importance of the state (and hence political leadership) in maintaining law and authority in the overall planning and direction of society. They argue that political action implies authority, i.e., that officials can only command effectively because they have respect, and that citizens obey (rightly) because they defer to those in authority, and hence law and order are maintained and society coordinated in the interests of all (i.e., stratification is inherent in the nature of political relationships). Top economic leaders or businessmen have especially high incomes (and status and power) both because coordinating the production of wealth and introducing innovations is very important for society and because there is such a scarcity of really good economic organizers (entrepreneurs). Finally, they argue, scientists, engineers, and the like (who have command of technical skills and scientific knowledge) are functionally more important for society than the average worker, but are not as important as religious, political, or economic leaders, since information and skills are never as important for society's welfare as the "integration of goals" or general leadership and coordination. Hence, scientists, teachers, engineers, and so on, while having higher salaries and prestige than the average worker, receive less than society's and economy's top leadership receives.

A Critique of Functionalist Theories of Class

A number of fundamental criticisms can be raised against the functionalist argument about the causes of class inequality. The functionalist argument that some positions are more important to society than others, and especially their classification as the most important positions of top businessmen, religious leaders, kings, and politicians are especially open to attack. While it might or might not be true that society could operate without priests, politicians, kings, or capitalists, it certainly *is* true that society could not operate without agricultural workers, carpenters, textile workers, construction workers, transportation workers, and so on. In what sense can it be said that priests are more important to society than those who grow food? A society without working people would immediately collapse, while a society without priests, capitalists, and political rulers *might* find itself with leadership problems, but whether or not it could be organized efficiently without such people is certainly an open question. Thus, any realistic appraisal of the relative importance of positions in a society must rank such basic economic roles as food, clothing, and housing producers as the most important.

Further, it should be noted that in such important activities as health care in large urban areas relatively low-paid garbage collectors, street sweepers, and exterminators actually play a more important role in keeping a city healthy than do highly paid medical specialists. A similar thing could be said about many other functionally important activities. We could imagine a society functioning without corporate lawyers, bankers, landlords, advertising executives, and brain surgeons, yet such people in capitalist society have the highest prestige, income, and power. In general it appears that those whose functional contribution to society is the most indispensable more often than not are the *lowest* paid, have the lowest status, and have the least power—quite the contrary of what the functionalist theory predicts.

The functionalist assumption about a scarcity of talent is questionable. In fact, most jobs in society can be performed reasonably well by almost anyone if people are given the educational opportunities to learn the appropriate skills. It is a considerable exaggeration to argue that only a few people are born with the ability to be successful businessmen, bishops, kings, or presidents. In fact, people learn leadership skills as well as technical knowledge. The educational and class system encourages such learned abilities in upper and upper middle class children, while discouraging them in working class children. Further, the amount of special skill or knowledge necessary in most jobs is grossly exaggerated by professional ideology. Each profession spends considerable effort legitimating its privileges by appeals to arguments about the "difficulty" and "importance" of its contribution. For example, both the legal and medical professions are highly mystified. Every effort is made to claim a monopoly of special expertise in contrast to the alleged utter ignorance of the lay person. In fact, most practical medical skills can be learned by almost anyone within six months to a year, as has been demonstrated by training programs for medical paraprofessionals both in the U.S. military and by Chinese paramedics ("barefoot doctors").

The functionalist argument about the need to motivate people to undergo the "sacrifices" of extensive training is on especially weak ground. It is difficult to argue that students who attend four years of college and another four years of graduate or professional school at the expense of their parents or are on a state scholarship are sacrificing something compared to those who start menial work in a factory or office after graduating from high school. The flexibility and psychic rewards, the freedom from responsibility, and the opportunity for social and intellectual activity that student life provides all indicate that the problem for society is not how to motivate youth to go to college and professional school but rather how to keep them out.

The functionalists are right that some jobs in society are inherently more agreeable than others, and thus, other things equal, there is in fact a tendency for people to go into more agreeable positions and avoid the least agreeable. However, the most agreeable positions are, for the most part, exactly those that also have the *most* (and not as the functionalist theories should predict the *least*) prestige, income, and power. A consistent application of the functionalist logic would lead one to expect that the inherently most menial and boring jobs, such as dishwasher, garbage collector, agricultural stoop laborer, coal miner, assembly-line worker, and so on would be precisely the highest paid and highest status jobs in the society. This is because the individuals with such positions must be compensated for undertaking the inherently least rewarding jobs. Positions such as political leaders, college teachers, research scientists, economic decision makers, and so on that have the highest level of job satisfaction and in which many people would happily remain employed at a considerable reduction in income rather than undertake menial physical labor should be the lowest paid and lowest in prestige. That the functionalist theory predicts the opposite of what is in fact the case is a major challenge to its validity in explaining contemporary class society.

The strongest point of the functionalist argument would seem to be its discussion of inequality as a reward for performance *within* a given position, i.e., to motivate people to perform to their utmost.

Indeed, socialist societies such as the USSR in the late 1920s and 1930s, Cuba after 1968, and China after the Cultural Revolution introduced greater income inequality (or at least increased use of incentives) after periods of experimenting with radical income equality (in response to problems of insufficient productivity or motivation of workers).

However, the amount of inequality, especially in income, that exists in contemporary class societies (or indeed in any traditional class society) seems to be far more than would be necessary to merely motivate effective performance. One would think that a range of income of three or four times from the lowest paid to the highest paid within industrial sectors (such as exists in countries like China and the Soviet Union) would be sufficient to motivate even the most money-conscious individuals to perform to their maximum under pain of loss of income, and with hope of promotion (and increase of income). It is difficult to imagine someone who was money conscious shirking because he or she was earning only $10,000 a year, since by working harder he or she could "only" earn $25,000. The fact that the income spread between top business people with incomes over $1 million a year and the lowest paid workers in the United States with incomes of less than $7,000 is on the order of 150 to 1 suggests that most income (and prestige) inequality is not a result of any functional necessity to motivate people. The annual rate of increase in productivity and the overall rate of economic growth in the Soviet Union has consistently been at least double that of the United States, even though the spread between the top and bottom income tenths in the USSR is approximately four times, while that in the United States is approximately twelve times.

Further, it is a mistake for the functionalists to think that it is only competitive or scarce goods such as income, power, or even status (higher or lower than someone else's) that can or does motivate people to do a good job. People are motivated as well by inherent joy in work, by the inherent pride of doing a good job, by a sense of social duty in performing for others, by the fear of informal social sanctions such as ridicule if one shirks or produces a shoddy product, by the promise of approval and praise if one does well. Indeed, preclass society did quite well, without significant differences in wealth, power, or even status, in motivating people to perform their economic functions.

But this said there *is* considerable validity in this part of the functionalist argument. The development of classes out of primitive equalitarian society resulted in a considerable expansion of the productivity of society. This wealth resulted in a leisure class that produced the first science, written literature, and formal art. In fact, the drive of the early slaveowners to increase their wealth had the consequence of producing Greek culture. The striving to increase profit and expand their individual wealth motivated the early capitalists to build factories and industrialize Europe, thus laying the material basis for a considerable increase in general material living standards, an improvement in life expectancy, the growth of science, and so on, which has occurred in the period of industrial capitalism. Likewise, the spectacular economic growth of the European socialist countries in the twentieth century has been in part based on maintaining income differentials to motivate workers.

But the functionalist interpretation of these events is ahistorical. It argues both that human nature is unchanging in its desire to maximize scarce goods, such as income or wealth, and that what is functional for society at point a is also functional at point b. But what motivates people is very much a social and an historical product, and the effect of a given process, such as the maximization of the income and wealth of a class of private capitalists on society can at one point be most beneficial for most people, while at another future time become most detrimental, i.e., contradictions can develop in a process that transform it from being functional to "dysfunctional." Thus, it can be argued that the pursuit of private profit in the nineteenth and early twentieth centuries was essentially functional since it increased living standards, advanced science, and so on, but since that time that it has become a dysfunctional force for most of society by generating war, environmental destruction, depression and unemployment, poverty, technologically unnecessary boring work, and so on, i.e., that capitalism now undermines, rather than facilitates, the satisfaction of society's basic economic and cultural needs. Yet the amount of inequality in society has not decreased in correspondence to the increasingly dysfunctional operation of profit maximization.

Critiques of the functionalist argument often emphasize the ways that inequality hinders the operation of an effective economy. They maintain that class inequality means that the children of the higher classes tend to acquire the necessary skills and resources and thus tend to monopolize society's top positions. They have the best education. They inherit their parents' fortunes. They have intellectual and other stimulation in the home that gives them the motivation to succeed. On the other hand, children of the poor, no matter how "innately intelligent" are discriminated against in education, beaten down when they show initiative and creativity, and are pressured to start work early to support themselves. Thus, stratification, rather than facilitating the discovery of and the channeling of the most talented people into the most important positions tends to make the best paying and most powerful positions in large part hereditary. Consequently, to society's detriment, less qualified people are put in such positions than would be the case if there was true competition among the children of all (see Tumin, 1953).

Class inequality is also dysfunctional for society in that in order to make the working classes reasonably compliant and satisfied in their positions (a requisite of social stability), workers develop a low self-image of themselves while their initiative and creativity are blocked. Often they just follow orders while soldiering (doing the least work that can be gotten away with), rather than committing themselves totally to their work as they would if they controlled their labor and its product.

Class inequality also tends to generate class hostility of the poor against the rich, manifested in strikes, riots, rebellions, and other forms of resistance on the one hand, and in conservative and fascist ideologies on the other (to defend the existing distribution of power and wealth). The economic disruption caused by the resistance of the oppressed as well as the repression and obstacles to progress that are the consequence of the latter ideologies would appear to be clear negative aspects of the inequality of class society, in terms of maximizing its product.

SOME CONTEMPORARY MARXIST VARIATIONS

There have been a number of attempts to modify traditional Marxist class analysis within the framework of class as a relationship of production. These modifications attempt to take into account developments in class structure that have occurred since the turn of the century. Two of the more influential of these have been those of new working class/expanded working class theory and of Erik Wright.

Expanded Working Class/New Working Class Theory

Expanded working class/new working class theorists define the working class solely by the wage relation, and thus argue that all—no matter how well paid, no matter how much technical knowledge, no matter whether or not they produce surplus value, no matter how much authority in production (short of fundamental control)—are part of the working class *because* they are employed by capital and thus lack real economic ownership. This tradition thus includes not only industrial, service, clerical, and sales workers, but also technicians, engineers, scientists, university professors, employed doctors and lawyers, government officials, and lower and middle level corporate management in the working class.

This analysis first achieved popularity in France in the early 1960s largely through the works of Serge Mallet (1975) and Andre Gorz (1967). It then achieved considerable currency in the student movement in both Europe and the United States during the late 1960s. This notion of an "expanded working class" (the "old" plus the "new" working class) became the class analysis of such American leftist organizations as the New American Movement and the journal *Socialist Review* (formerly *Socialist Revolution*). Perhaps the best statement of the position that it is the wage relation which defines class is that of Francesca Freedman: ". . . the wage-relationship, the instrument of the production of surplus value, becomes the worker's economic relation to society" (1975, p. 49). Freedman argues that virtually everyone in contemporary capitalist society is in one of the two great classes:

> With the generalization and development of capitalist production society is, as Marx predicted, more and more divided into two great classes, bourgeoisie and proletariat. . . . The other social classes under capitalism, the farmers and the petite bourgeoisie, have been more and more pressured out of existence by the power of capital. (1975, p. 51).

Expanded working class theorists generally go so far as to include lower and middle level management in the working class as its highest "vertical sector" or faction and engineers and employed scientists and university professors as its most educated and skilled "horizontal sector" (see Freedman 1975, pp. 63-65).

Although the theorists of the new working class/expanded working class argue that the common bond of receiving a wage or salary means that all those who do share a common class position vis-á-vis those who do not in the most fundamental sense have more in common with each other than with the capitalist class, they generally go on to argue that there are significant differences or factions within the expanded working class that are generated by the logic of the capital accumulation process (see Freedman 1975, p. 51).

Among expanded or new working class theorists there are differences about which sector of the proletariat is potentially the most active in its opposition to the capitalist class. There seem to be essentially three positions: first, those (such as Serge Mallet and Andre Gorz) who argue that it is the technical and most highly educated employees; second, those (such as Freedman) who suggest that it is clerical, sales, and service workers; and third, those (such as the *Socialist Review* and the New American Movement) that argue that one can expect no sector of the expanded working class to necessarily be the most actively anticapitalist.

Although for expanded working class theory the mode of conceptualizing class structure is similar to that of Karl Marx, it is inadequate as an analytical tool to describe and predict the behavior of classes. As became apparent to the mainstream Marxist tradition over the course of the twentieth century, to include managers and employed professionals with industrial and clerical workers as part of the working class implies that managers and employed professionals are essentially similar in life style, consciousness, and so on, and have essentially similar interests with industrial workers and thus should be expected to behave socially and politically in essentially the same manner. Historical experience came to show that such groups are in fact socially more closely integrated with the traditional petty bourgeoisie (and at least the higher level managerial stratum, closely oriented politically to the capitalist class).

At the same time, again and again, whether in the advanced capitalist countries (France in 1968 and 1981), or in the less-developed capitalist countries (El Salvador in the 1980s) the traditional working class continues to show that it is the most leftist of all classes, while people in managerial and most professional positions normally tend to rally behind the capitalist class. Throughout the world wherever a significant Left exists, it tends to be disproportionately supported by the industrial working class (even when that Left has ceased to be revolutionary, e.g., in most of Western Europe in the 1960s and 1970s).

Thus the conceptualization of classes in terms of *de facto* relations of production (i.e., exploitation and control over labor power) rather than whether or not one has *formal* ownership rights in an enterprise (and thus technically receives a wage/salary or profits/rents) is the more useful analytical mode of class categorization. Such a conceptualization in fact gives us a picture of social structure that best allows us to distinguish essential similarities and differences in ways that allow us to understand social and political behavior.

Erik Wright and Contradictory Class Locations

Another influential contemporary attempt to modify traditional Marxist class categorization that attempts to incorporate elements of the analysis of the theorists of the expanded working class/new working class on the one side and the analysis of Nicos Poulantzas

on the other is the schema of class categorization offered by Erik
Wright.

Wright sees three central processes underlying the capital-labor
relationship that should thus serve as the basis for categorizing class
structure:

> . . . control over the physical means of production; control over
> labour power; control over investments and resource allocation . . . .
> it must be stressed that these three processes are the real stuff of
> class relations in capitalist society . . . .
>
> The fundamental class antagonism between workers and cap-
> italists can be viewed as a polarization on each of these three
> underlying processes or dimensions: capitalists control the accumu-
> lation process, decide how the physical means of production are to
> be used, and control the authority structure within the labor
> process. Workers, in contrast, are excluded from the control over
> authority relations, the physical means of production, and the
> investment process. These two combinations of the three processes
> of class relations constitute the two basic antagonistic class loca-
> tions within the capitalist mode of production (1978, p. 73).

Wright's principal idea is to define "contradictory class locations" as positions in the class structure that, unlike proletarian and
capitalist positions, are *inconsistent* on the basis of the three class-
producing processes defined above (see Wright 1978, p. 74).

Wright sees three contradictory class locations intermediate
between the capitalist class, the traditional petty bourgeoisie, and the
proletariat. Between the bourgeoisie and the proletariat he sees a
managerial position occupied by top managers, middle managers,
technocrats, bottom managers, foreman, and line supervisors. All of
these positions according to Wright are intermediate in the amount
of control they have over the means of production and/or the labor
power of others (middle managers, technocrats, and foremen), *or*
which do exercise control over the physical means of production and
labor power but do *not* have fundamental control over investments
and resources (top managers).

Between the traditional petty bourgeoisie and the proletariat
Wright sees "semiautonomous employees" who lack control over the
labor power of others, but who do have minimal control over the
physical means of production and resource allocation. Included
among semiautonomous employees are positions such as those of
university professors and engineers:

> In their immediate work environment, they maintain the work
> process of the independent artisan while still being employed by

capital as wage labourers. They control *how* they do their work, and have at least some control over *what* they produce. A good example of this is a researcher in a laboratory or a professor in an elite university. Such positions may not really involve control over other people's labour power, yet have considerable immediate control over conditions of work (i.e., research). More generally, many white collar technical employees and certain highly skilled craftsmen have at least a limited form of this autonomy in their immediate work processes. Such minimal control over the physical means of production by employees outside of the authority hierarchy constitutes the basic contradictory location between the petty bourgeoisie and the proletariat (Wright 1978, p. 81).

The positions of small employers intermediate between the bourgeoisie and the petty bourgeoisie form the third contradictory class location Wright specifies. These are small employers whose family produces a significant proportion of their income through their involvement in production, but whose employees also produce a significant proportion (Wright 1978, p. 80). Wright estimates that this group includes those employers who have less than 10 to 50 employees (1976, p. 90).

Wright sees the proletariat and the capitalist classes as the ideologically and most politically consistent classes because of their consistency in the three class-forming processes. The occupants of the three contradictory locations on the other hand, because they are in contradictory positions are potentially mobilizable by either of the classes they are between (Wright 1978, pp. 105-9).

Wright argues in the mainstream Marxist tradition that it is proletarians, those who lack control over labor power and the means of production regardless of their position in the technical division of labor—whether they produce surplus value, are skilled, do manual work, and so on—who are potentially the leading anticapitalist force in all capitalist societies. Thus, although Wright's categorization of class is original, its central political prediction is identical to that of classical Marxism (unlike that of either the new working class theorists or Poulantzas).

A number of critiques can be raised of Wright's schema. Two of Wright's class-producing processes would seem to reduce to the same thing (what Poulantzas labels "possession" of the means of production), namely: first, control over the physical means of production; and second, control over labor power. It is difficult to see how one could control equipment without setting into motion (i.e., controlling) labor power. Moreover, controlling labor power is integrally and necessarily wrapped up with controlling equipment. (How many jobs can be done without tools?) Reflecting on this problem, there is an inconsistency in Wright's conceptualization. Wright (1978) changes (without comment) his textual definition of the two categories of possession, substituting "control over the labor power *of others*" for simply "control over labor." What control over the physical means of production in practice comes to mean is either control over the labor power of others *or* control over your own labor power. Wright's reconceptualization on this point fails. There are *two*, not three, social processes comprising class relations: first, control over investment resources, or *what* is produced (economic ownership); and second, operational control over labor power (in the limiting case, only your own), or *how* production occurs. When we employ a single dimension of the degree of control over labor power much of Wright's claim for "contradictory" status for small employers and semiautonomous employees evaporates, leaving small employers clearly in the lower rungs of the capitalist class and semiautonomous employees in a position very similar to that of the traditional petty bourgeoisie.

Wright's conceptualization has the problem of inconsistently using the term "contradictory locations." Sometimes it is used in the sense of a position having one or two characteristics in common with the proletariat and one or two in common with the capitalist class; in other places it is used to mean a status consistently *intermediate* between two of the three basic classes of his class-defining variables. He categorizes small employers as in a contradictory location in good part because they are intermediate in control over the labor power of others. Middle managers are considered to be in contradictory locations because they are *intermediate* in economic ownership and possession. Other locations are placed in contradictory locations because they are *inconsistent* on the dimensions of class, e.g., foremen and semiautonomous employees. It seems that Wright's notion is more powerful when used in the latter sense (i.e., the way in which he actually defines the concept).

In the last analysis, as Wright himself argues when he talks about those in working class positions ultimately sharing an interest in socialism, the specification of class boundaries can only be resolved on the basis of how useful different definitions are in allowing us to understand and predict social phenomena (especially political struggles). There is no a priori reason why classes should be defined in terms of relations of production rather than in terms of income, SES, consciousness, or anything else, nor is there any a priori reason why there cannot be five, ten, or any number of classes (as well as intermediate positions). Questions of definition can only be resolved on the basis of usefulness in allowing us to both understand and change the world. Just as Wright applies this criterion to criticize Poulantzas, so it too must be used to evaluate his notion of contradictory locations.

The notion of contradictory locations suggests a coherence of sets of locations outside of the three basic classes, while the more traditional attempt to put virtually everyone into the three basic classes (plus the excluded sector or "lumpen proletariat," a category Wright rejects) assumes a continuum *within* each of the three classes and rather distinct boundaries between them (with only a relatively small number of positions or individuals truly ambiguous). The validity of the two modes of class definition must be decided in terms of how well they correspond to the actual distribution of relations of production as well as on the basis of how well they allow us to understand social class formation and class struggle. It does not appear that the coherence and distinctiveness suggested by Wright in fact exists among semiautonomous employees, managers, or small employers. Neither does it appear that the case for a variety of qualitatively unique relations of production for each of these groups can stand.

The traditional petty bourgeoisie is in a contradictory location par excellence. It is in a contradictory or inconsistent position in relation to the two basic classes because it has economic ownership and control over its own physical means of production, but does not have significant control over the labor power of others. If then the traditional petty bourgeoisie is considered to be in a contradictory location between the bourgeoisie and the proletariat, there would seem to be little to distinguish it from the semiautonomous employees who have at least minimal control over investment resources and control over their physical means of production without controlling the labor of others, and middle level managers and technocrats who are intermediate in the three dimensions.* While "independent" small businessmen have legal ownership of their property, they are typically so hemmed in by the banks to which they are in debt, their suppliers, and the laws of capitalist markets that they in fact have only limited real economic ownership and control over their physical means of production, thus making them more or less equivalent to middle level managers or semiautonomous employees in this regard. More often than not, employed middle managers and technocrats tend to have *diluted* or partial control over a large mass of invest-

---

*The traditional petty bourgeoisie is *not*, as Wright suggests, part of a precapitalist mode of production (although it had its historical origins in such a mode). It is today fully integrated into and virtually completely a part of the capitalist mode. Independent farmers buy virtually all of their supplies from corporations and sell most of their produce directly or indirectly to other corporations. Independent shopkeepers likewise serve as outlets for the produce of the corporations. In no sense do such producers and distributors today form an autonomous economic system.

ments, physical means of production, and the labor power of others. While independent small businessmen have a higher degree of control over their employees and assets, they control many fewer workers and much less in assets. The typical traditional petty bourgeois *does* have control over the labor-power of others even while most of their earnings come from their own labor power (i.e., wife, children, part-time help, and seasonal help are virtually essential aspects of working a family farm or small shop). In summary, Wright's contention that middle managers, technocrats, and semiautonomous employees are in qualitatively separate locations from the traditional petty bourgeoisie is not sustainable in Wright's own terms. All of these groups must be considered a part of an expanded petty bourgeoisie with new or salaried and old, traditional, or independent components.

It would seem that although there are some differences along the lines Wright points out between the rugged individualism of the traditional petty bourgeoisie and the careerism and noneconomic liberalism of the new petty bourgeoisie, a distinctive petty-bourgeois consciousness, life-style, intermarriage patterns, and politics *does* exist that in large part encompasses both of these groups, i.e., there is a distinctive class formation or social class based on these groups, rather than two or more distinctive ones each with its own distinctive consciousness, life-style, intermarriage patterns, customs, and politics. Middle managers, employed professionals, independent professionals, and most independent businessmen tend to feel socially comfortable with each other, relatively freely intermarry, live in similar neighborhoods, maintain basically similar life-styles, and so on, i.e., they tend to form into a single social class.

CONCLUSION

The major alternatives to orthodox Marxist class categorization and its theory of reproduction of classes have been examined. Class categorizations in terms of generalized power, market position, the technical division of labor, and subjective factors as well as alternative conceptualizations in terms of relations of production have been examined and criticized. Also critiqued were theories of the origin and reproduction of class in terms of superior military force, superior organizational/ideological resources, and the necessity to realize the universal functional requisites of society. In each case, a tentative and summary critique was presented that maintained that the alternative categorizations and theorists are not as analytically adequate as the Marxist alternative. Special emphasis was given to critiquing the attempts to synthesize Marxism with the various other methods of class categorization, e.g., Dahrendorf, Wallerstein, Poulantzas, Thompson, and Aronowitz. Again it must be stressed that the critiques do not claim to be definitive.

A resolution of the question of whether or not Marxist or essentially non-Marxist methods of class analysis are superior, and whether or not the traditional Marxist approach or the various attempts to synthesize Marxism with other approaches are better can *only* be made through a comprehensive *empirical* examination of the analytical power of each of the various alternatives. Definitive evaluations of the power of different modes of class categorization and political analysis can *only* be based on careful empirical evidence of the results of different modes of categorization and analysis in heightening, rather than obscuring, our understanding of social structures and political processes. The bulk of this book was an attempt to offer substantive support for the superiority of the Marxist claim in both of these regards.

References

Abrahamson, Mark, and Ephraim Mizruchi. 1976. *Stratification and Mobility*. New York: Macmillan.

Acuña, Rodolfo. 1981. *Occupied America*. New York: Harper & Row.

Althusser, Louis. 1969. "Ideology and Ideological State Apparatuses." In *Lenin and Philosophy*. London: New Left Books, 1971.

American Jewish Committee. 1973. *American Jewish Yearbook*. Vol. 74. New York.

Anderson, Perry. 1974a. *Passages from Antiquity to Feudalism*. London: New Left Review.

———. 1974b. *Lineages of the Absolutist State*. London: Monthly Review Press.

Andors, Stephen. 1977. *China's Industrial Revolution*. New York: Pantheon.

Andreski, Stanislav. 1968. *Military Organization and Society*. Berkeley: University of California Press.

Andrews, Edward. 1953. *The People Called Shakers*. New York: Oxford University Press.

Aronowitz, Stanley. 1973. *False Promises: The Shaping of American Working Class Consciousness*. New York: McGraw-Hill.

———. 1979. "The Professional-Managerial Class or Middle Strata." In *Between Labor and Capital*, edited by Pat Walker. Boston: South End Press.

Bakke, Edward W. 1940. *Citizens Without Work*. New Haven: Yale University Press.

Balibar, Etienne. 1968. "The Basic Concepts of Historical Materialism." In *Reading Capital*, edited by Louis Althusser and Etienne Balibar. London: New Left Books, 1970.

Baltzell, E. Digby. 1958. *Philadelphia Gentlemen: The Making of a National Upper Class*. New York: The Free Press.

———. 1964. *The Protestant Establishment, Aristocracy and Caste in America*. New York: Vintage.

Baran, Paul, and Paul Sweezy. 1966. *Monopoly Capital*. New York: Monthly Review Press.

Bardwick, Judith, and Elizabeth Dower. 1971. "Ambivalence: The Socialization of Women." In *Woman in Sexist Society*, edited by Vivian Gornick and Barbara Moron. New York: Basic Books.

Barrera, Mario. 1979. *Race and Class in the Southwest*. Notre Dame, Ind.: University of Notre Dame Press.

Beeghley, Leonard. 1978. *Social Stratification in America: A Critical Analysis of Theory and Research*. Santa Monica, Calif.: Goodyear.

Bell, Daniel. 1973. *The Coming of Post-Industrial Society*. New York: Basic Books.

Bendix, Reinhard, and Seymour Martin Lipset, eds. 1953. *Class, Status and Power*. New York: The Free Press.

———. 1966. *Class, Status and Power*. 2d ed. New York: The Free Press.

Bennett, John. 1967. *Hutterian Brethren*. Stanford, Calif.: Stanford University Press.

Berger, Bennet. 1960. *Working Class Suburbs*. Berkeley: University of California Press.

Berlau, A. Joseph. 1949. *The German Social Democratic Party, 1914-1924.*. New York: Columbia University Press.

Berman, Daniel. 1978. *Death on the Job*. New York: Monthly Review Press.

Bernstein, Basil. 1975. *Class and Pedagogies*. Washington, D.C.: Organization for Economic Cooperation and Development.

Bestor, Anthur. 1950. *Backwoods Utopias*. Philadelphia: University of Pennsylvania Press.

Bettleheim, Charles. 1974. *Cultural Revolution and Industrial Organization in China*. New York: Monthly Review Press.

Blau, Peter, and Otis Duncan. 1967. *The American Occupational Structure*. New York: Wiley.

Blauner, Robert. 1964. *Alienation and Freedom: The Factory Worker and His Industry*. Chicago: The University of Chicago Press.

Bloch, Marc. 1961. *Feudal Society*. Chicago: University of Chicago Press.

Blood, Robert, and Donald Wolfe. 1960. *Husbands and Wives: The Dynamics of Married Living*. Glencoe, Ill.: The Free Press.

Blumberg, Paul. 1972. *The Impact of Social Class*. New York: Thomas Y. Crowell.

———. 1960. *Inequality of an Age of Decline*. New York: Oxford University Press.

Blumberg, Rae. 1978. *Stratification: Socioeconomic and Sexual Inequality*. Dubuque, Iowa: Wm. C. Brown.

Bonacich, Edna. 1973. "A Theory of Middleman Minorities." *American Sociological Review* 38 (October): 583-94.

———. 1980. "Class Approaches to Ethnicity and Race." *The Insurgent Sociologist* (Fall) 10, no. 2.

Bonacich, Edna, and John Modell. 1981. *The Economic Basis of Ethnic Solidarity*. Berkeley, Calif.: University of California Press.

Bornstein, Morris. 1974. "Soviet Price Theory and Policy." In *The Soviet Economy: A Book of Readings*, edited by Morris Bornstein and Daniel Fusfeld. 4th ed. Homewood, Ill.: Richard Irwin.

Bowles, Samuel, and Herbert Gintis. 1976. *Education in Corporate America*. New York: Basic Books.

Boyer, Richard, and Herbert Morais. 1965. *Labor's Untold Story*. New York: United Electrical, Radio and Machine Workers of America.

Braverman, Harry. 1974. *Labor and Monopoly Capital: The Degradation of Work in the Twentieth Century*. New York: Monthly Review Press.

Bronfenbrenner, Urie. 1970. "Socialization and Social Class Through Time and Space." In *Readings on Social Stratification*, edited by Melvin Tumin. Englewood Cliffs, N.J.: Prentice-Hall.

Brown, Henry P. 1977. *The Inequality of Pay*. Berkeley: University of California Press.

Buenaventura-Posso, Elisa, and Susan Brown. 1980. "Forced Transition from Egalitarianism to Male Dominance: The Bari of Colombia." In *Women and Colonization*, edited by Mona Etienne and Eleanor Leacock. New York: Praeger.

Burawoy, Michael. 1979. *Manufacturing Consent*. Chicago: University of Chicago Press.

Burbach, Roger, and Patricia Flynn. 1980. *Agribusiness in the Americas*. New York: Monthly Review Press.

Burnbaum, Linda, and Bob Wing. 1981. "Toward a Communist Analysis of Black Oppression and Basic Liberation." Pt. 2. *Line of March* 8 (September-October).

Burton, Katherine. 1939. *Paradise Planters: The Story of Brook Farm*. New York: Longmans, Green.

Carchedi, Guglielmo. 1977. *On the Economic Identification of Social Classes*. London: Routledge and Kegan Paul.

Carden, Maren L. 1971. *Oneida: Utopian Community to Modern Corporation*. New York: Harper & Row.

Castells, Manuel. 1980. *The Economic Crises and American Society*. Princeton: Princeton University Press.

Castles, Stephen, and Godula Kosack. 1973. *Immigrant Workers and Class Structure in Western Europe*. New York: Oxford University Press.

Caute, David. 1966. *The Left in Europe Since 1789*. New York: McGraw-Hill.

———. 1978. *The Great Fear*. New York: Simon and Schuster.

Cheyney, Edward. 1936. *The Dawn of a New Era 1250-1453*. New York: Harper & Row.

Childe, V. Gordon. 1951. *Social Evolution*. Cleveland: Meridian Books.

———. 1954. *What Happened in History*. Baltimore: Penguin.

Chinoy, Eli. 1955. *Automobile Workers and the American Dream*. Boston: Beacon.

Chiswick, Barry. 1980. "Immigrant Earnings Patterns by Sex, Race and the Ethnic Groupings." *Monthly Labor Review* (October).

Claessen, Henri J. M., and Peter Skalnik. 1978. *The Early State*. The Hague: Monton.

Clinard, Marshall, and Robert Meier. 1979. *Sociology of Deviant Behavior*. New York: Holt, Rinehart and Winston.

Clinard, Marshall, and Peter Yeager. 1980. *Corporate Crime*. New York: The Free Press.

Cohn, Norman. 1961. *The Pursuit of the Millennium*. New York: Harper & Row.

Cohen, Robin; Peter Gutkind; and Phyllis Brazier. 1979. *Peasants and Proletarians: the Struggle of Third World Workers*. New York: Monthly Review Press.

Cole, G.D.H. 1948. *Short History of the British Working Class Movement 1789-1947*. London: G. Allen and Unwin.

Coleman, Richard, and Lee Rainwater. 1978. *Social Standing in America: New Dimensions of Class*. New York: Basic Books.

Conrad, Peter, and Rochelle Kern, eds. 1981. *The Sociology of Health and Illness*. New York: St. Martin's Press.

Corey, Lewis. 1935. *The Crisis of the Middle Class*. New York: Little.

Coult, Allan, and Robert Habenstein. 1965. *Cross Tabulations of Murdock's World Ethnographic Sample*. Columbia, Mo.: University of Missouri Press.

Coxon, Anthony, and Charles Jones, eds. 1975. *Social Mobility*. Baltimore: Penguin.

Critchley, John. 1978. *Feudalism*. London: George Allen and Unwin.

Crozier, Michel. 1971. *The World of the Office Worker*. New York: Schocken Books.

Dahrendorf, Ralph. 1959. *Class and Class Conflict in Industrial Society*. Stanford, Calif.: Stanford University Press.

Davidson, Basil. 1961. *The African Slave Trade*. Boston: Little, Brown.

Davis, Brion D. 1971. "The Continuing Contradiction of Slavery." In *The Debate Over Slavery*, edited by Ann J. Lane. Urbana, Ill.: University of Illinois.

Davis, Kingsley, and Wilber Moore. 1945. "Some Principles of Stratification." *American Sociological Review* 10:242-49.

Davis, Mike. 1981. "Why the U.S. Working Class is Different." *New Left Review*, no. 123 (September-October).

Deckard, Barbara Sinclair. 1975. *The Women's Movement*. New York: Harper & Row.

Dimitrov, Georgi. 1935. *For the Unity of the Working Class Against Fascism*. Sofia: Sofia Press, 1969.

Dixon, Marlene. 1971. "Public Ideology and the Class Composition of the Women's Movement." *Berkeley Journal of Sociology* 16.

Dobb, Maurice. 1963. *Studies in the Development of Capitalism*. New York: International.

Domhoff, G. William. 1967. *Who Rules America?* Englewood Cliffs, N.J.: Prentice-Hall.

———. 1970. *The Higher Circles*. New York: Vintage.

———. 1974. *Bohemia Grove and Other Retreats*. New York: Harper & Row.

Draper, Theodore. 1957. *The Roots of American Communism*. New York: Viking Press.

Duberman, Lucile. 1976. *Social Inequality*. New York: Harper & Row.

Dubofsky, David. 1969. *We Shall Be All*. Chicago: Quadrangle.

Duverger, Maurice. 1955. *The Politics of Women*. Paris: UNESCO.

Dye, Thomas. 1976. *Who's Running America?* Englewood Cliffs, N.J.: Prentice-Hall.

Edwards, Richard. 1979. *Contested Terrain*. New York: Basic Books.

Edwards, Richard; Michael Reich; and David Gordan. 1975. *Labor Market Segmentation*. New York: D.C. Heath.

Edwards, Richard; Michael Reich; and Thomas Weisskopf, eds. 1972. *The Capitalist System*. 1st ed. Englewood Cliffs, N.J: Prentice-Hall.

———. 1978. *The Capitalist System*. 2d ed. Englewood Cliffs, N.J: Prentice-Hall.

Enrenreich, Barbara, and John Ehrenreich. 1979. "The Professional-Managerial Class." In *Between Labor and Capital*, edited by Pat Walker. Boston: South End Press.

Eitzen, Stanley. 1968. "Two Minorities: The Jews of Poland and the Chinese of the Philippines." *The Jewish Journal of Sociology*, 10, no. 2 (December).

Elkins, Stanley. 1959. *Slavery: A Problem in American Institutional and Intellectual Life.* Chicago: The University of Chicago Press.

Ellis, Robert, and W. Clayton Lane. 1968. "Social Mobility and Social Isolation." In *Permanence and Change in Social Class*, edited by W. Clayton Lane. Cambridge, Mass.: Schenkman.

Engels, Friedrich. 1894. *Anti-Dühring.* Moscow: Foreign Languages Publishing House, 1962.

Ermann, M. David, and Richard Lundman. 1978. *Corporate and Governmental Deviance.* New York: Oxford University Press.

Fain, T. Scott. 1980. "Self-Employed Americans: Their Number Have Increased." *Monthly Labor Review* (November).

Fanon, Frantz, 1963. *The Wretched of the Earth.* New York: Grove Press.

Farb, Peter. 1968. *Man's Rise to Civilization.* New York: Avon.

Feldstein, Stanley, and Lawrence Costello, eds. 1974. *The Ordeal of Assimilation: A Documentary History of the U.S. Working Class.* Garden City, N.Y.: Doubleday.

Fenstermaker-Berk, Sarah, ed. 1980. *Women and Household Labor.* Beverly Hills: Sage.

Ferman, Louis; Joyce Kornbluh; and Alan Haber. 1971. *Poverty in America.* Ann Arbor: University of Michigan Press.

Ferree-Marx, Myrd. 1980. "Satisfaction with Housework: The Social Context." In *Women and Household Labor*, edited by Sarah Fenstermaker-Berk. Beverly Hills: Sage.

Fine, Nathan. 1928. *Labor and Farmer Parties in the U.S.* New York: Rand School of Social Science.

Fitch, Robert, and Mary Oppenheimer. 1970. "Who Rules the Corporations?" *Socialist Revolution*, nos. 4, 5, 6 (July-December).

Fogel, Robert W., and Stanley Engerman. 1974. *Time on the Cross: The Economics of American Negro Slavery.* Boston: Little, Brown.

Forster, William. 1952. *History of the CPUSA.* New York: International.

Frank, Andre G. 1967. *Capitalism and Underdevelopment in Latin America.* New York: Monthly Review Press.

Frazier, E. Franklin. 1957. *The Black Bourgeoisie.* New York: Macmillan.

Freedman, Francesca. 1975. "The Internal Structure of the American Proletariat." *Socialist Revolution*, no. 26 (October-December).

Fried, Albert, ed. 1970. *Socialism in America.* Garden City, N.Y.: Doubleday.

Friedlander, Stanley. 1972. *Unemployment in the Urban Core.* New York: Praeger.

Friedman, Andrew. 1977. *Industry and Labour.* London: Macmillan.

Galenson, Walter. 1960. *The CIO Challenge to the AFL.* Cambridge, Mass.: Harvard University Press.

Gallup Poll. 1980. *The Gallup Poll: Public Opinion 1979.* Wilmington, Del.: Scholarly Resources.

Gans, Herbert. 1962. *The Urban Villages.* New York: The Free Press.

———. 1967. *The Levittowners.* New York: Vintage.

Genovese, Eugene. 1967. *The Political Economy of Slavery.* New York: Vintage.

———. 1968. *In Red and Black*. New York: Vintage.

———. 1969. *The World the Slaveholders Made*. New York: Vintage.

———. 1971a. "Rebelliousness and Docility in the Negro Slave." In *The Debate Over Slavery*, edited by Ann J. Lane. Urbana: University of Illinois Press.

———. 1971b. "American Slaves and Their History." In *The Debate Over Slavery*, edited by Ann J. Lane. Urbana: University of Illinois Press.

———, ed. 1973. *Slave Economies*. New York: John Wiley.

———. 1974. *Roll Jordon Roll*. New York: Vintage.

Geschwender, James. 1978. *Racial Stratification in America*. Dubuque, Iowa: Wm. C. Brown.

Giddens, Anthony. 1973. *The Class Structure of the Advanced Societies*. New York: Barnes & Noble.

Glazer, Nathan. 1961. *The Social Basis of American Communism*. New York: Harcourt, Brace.

Goldthorpe, John; David Lockwood; Frank Bechhofer; and Jennifer Platt. 1968a. *The Affluent Worker*. Vol. I: Industrial Attitudes and Behavior. Cambridge: Cambridge University Press.

———. 1968b. *The Affluent Worker*. Vol. II: Political Attitudes and Behavior. Cambridge: Cambridge University Press.

———. 1969. *The Affluent Worker*. Vol. III: The Affluent Worker in the Class Structure. Cambridge: Cambridge University Press.

Goldwasser, Janet, and Stuart Dowty. 1975. *Huan-Ying: Workers' China*. New York: Monthly Review Press.

Gordon, David. 1972. *Theories of Poverty and Underemployment*. Lexington, Mass.: Lexington Books.

Gorz, Andre. 1967. *Strategy for Labor*. Boston: Beacon.

Gossett, Thomas. 1963. *Race: The History of an Idea in America*. Dallas: Southern Methodist University Press.

Gough, Aberle; Kathleen Schneider; and David Schneider, eds. 1961. *Matrilineal Kinship*. Berkeley: University of California Press.

Gramsci, Antonio. 1959. *The Modern Prince and Other Essays*. New York: International.

Greenberg, Stanley. 1980. *Race and State in Capitalist Development*. New Haven: Yale University Press.

Gregory, Paul, and Robert Stuart. 1974. *Soviet Economic Structure and Performance*. New York: Harper & Row.

Grey, Alan. 1969. *Class and Personality in Society*. New York: Atherton Press.

Guerin, Daniel. 1973. *Fascism and Big Business*. New York: Monad Press.

Guralnick, Lillian. 1962. "Mortality by Occupation and Industry Among Men 20 to 64 Years of Age, U.S., 1950." *Vital Statistics, Special Reports*. Washington, D.C.: U.S. Bureau of the Census.

Gutkind, Peter, and Peter Waterman. 1977. *African Social Studies*. New York: Monthly Review Press.

Gutman, Herbert. 1976. *Work, Culture and Society*. New York: Vintage.

Hacker, Louis. 1940. *The Triumph of American Capitalism*. New York: Simon and Schuster.

Hamilton, Richard. 1967. *Affluence and the French Worker in the Fourth Republic*. Princeton, N.J.: Princeton University Press.

———. 1972. *Class and Politics in the United States*. New York: John Wiley.

———. 1975. *Restraining Myths: Critical Studies of U.S. Social Structure and Politics*. New York: John Wiley.

Harris, Marvin. 1964. *Patterns of Race in the Americas*. New York: Walker.

———. 1971. *Culture, Man and Nature*. New York: Thomas Y. Crowell.

———. 1974. *Cows, Pigs, Wars and Witches*. New York: Vintage.

———. 1977. *Cannibals and Kings: The Origins of Cultures*. New York: Vintage.

———. 1979. *Cultural Materialism*. New York: Random House.

Harrison, John. 1969. *Quest for the New Moral World: Robert Owen and the Owenites in Britain and America*. New York: Scribner.

Hedges, Janice, and Jeanne Barnett. 1972. "Working Women and the Division of Household Tasks." *Monthly Labor Review* (April).

Heller, Celia, ed. 1969. *Structured Social Inequality*. New York: Macmillan.

Hicks, John. 1961. *The Populist Revolt*. Lincoln: University of Nebrasks Press.

Hill, Judah, 1975. *Class Analysis: The United States in the 1970s*. Emeryville, Calif.: Class Analysis.

Hilton, Rodney, ed. 1976. *The Transition from Feudalism to Capitalism*. London: New Left Review.

Hobsbawm, Eric. 1959. *Primitive Rebels*. Manchester, England: University of Manchester.

———. 1962. *The Age of Revolution*. Cleveland: World.

———. 1964. *Labouring Men*. Garden City, N.Y.: Doubleday.

———. 1965. *Introduction to Karl Marx: Pre-Capitalist Economic Formations*. New York: International.

Hodges, Harold. 1964. *Social Stratification: Class in America*. Cambridge, Mass.: Schenkman.

Hoffman, Charles. 1974. *The Chinese Worker*. Albany: State University of New York Press.

Hollingshead, August, and Frederick Redlich. 1958. *Social Class and Mental Illness*. New York: John Wiley.

Holloway, Mark. 1951. *Heavens on Earth: Utopian Communities in America*. New York: Library Publisher.

Hough, Jerry. 1976. "The Brezhnev Era: The Man and the System." *Problems of Communism* (March-April).

Howard, Bob, and John Logue. 1978. *American Class Society*. Kent, Ohio: Kent Popular Press.

Howe, Christopher. 1973. *Wage Patterns and Wage Policy in Modern China*. Cambridge, England: Cambridge University Press.

———. 1978. *China's Economy*. New York: Basic Books.

Hunt, Richard. 1964. *German Social Democracy 1918-1933*. New Haven: Yale University Press.

Jeffries, Vincent, and H. Edward Ransford. 1980. *Social Stratification: A Multiple Hierarchy Approach*. Boston: Allyn & Bacon.

Jiryis, Sabri. 1968. *The Arabs in Israel*. New York: Monthly Review Press.

Johnson, Stephen. 1976. "How the West Was Won." *Insurgent Sociologist* 6 (Winter).

Kahl, Joseph. 1957. *The American Class Structure*. New York: Rinehard.

Kanter, Rosa Beth. 1972. *Commitment and Community: Communes and Utopias in Sociological Perspective*. Cambridge, Mass.: Harvard University Press.

Kerr, Clark, and Abram Siegel. 1964. "The Inter-Industry Propensity to Strike." In *Labor and Management in Industrial Society*, edited by Clark Kerr. Garden City, N.Y.: Doubleday.

Kinsey, Alfred; Wardell Pomeroy, and Clyde Martin. 1953. "Social Level and Sexual Outlet." In *Class, Status and Power*, edited by Seymour Lipset and Reinhard Bendix. Glencoe, Ill.: The Free Press.

Kipnis, Ira. 1952. *The American Socialist Movement 1897-1912*. New York: Columbia University Press.

Kitagawa, Evelyn, and Philip Hauser. 1973. *Differential Mortality in the United States*. Cambridge, Mass.: Harvard University Press.

Kohn, Melvin. 1968. "Social Class and Parental Values." In *Permanence and Change in Social Class*, edited by W. Clayton Lane. Cambridge, Mass.: Schenkman.

Kolko, Gabriel. 1962. *Wealth and Power in America*. New York: Praeger.

———. 1968. *The Politics of War*. New York: Random House.

———. 1976. *Main Currents in Modern American History*. New York: Harper & Row.

Kolko, Gabriel, and Joyce Kolko. 1972. *The Limits of Power*. New York: Harper & Row.

Komarovsky, Mirra. 1940. *The Unemployed Man and His Family*. New York: Dryden Press.

Koos, Earl L. 1960. "Illness in Regionville." In *Sociological Studies in Health and Sickness*, edited by Dorrian Apple. New York: McGraw-Hill.

Kornblum, William. 1974. *Blue Collar Community*. Chicago: University of Chicago Press.

Kornhauser, Arthur. 1965. *Mental Health of the Industrial Worker*. New York: John Wiley.

Kotz, David. 1978. *Bank Control of Large Corporations in the United States*. Berkeley: University of California Press.

Kreps, Juanita. 1971. *Sex in the Marketplace: American Women at Work*. Baltimore: Johns Hopkins Press.

———, ed. 1976. *Women and the American Economy: A Look to the 1980's*. Englewood Cliffs, N.J.: Prentice-Hall.

Kuczynski, Jürgen. 1967. *The Rise of the Working Class*. New York: World University Library.

Kudat, Ayse, and Sabuncuoglu, Mine. 1980. "The Changing Composition of Europe's Guestworker Population." *Monthly Labor Review* (October).

Laidler, Harry. 1968. *History of Socialism*. New York: Thomas Y. Crowell.

Lane, Ann J., ed. 1971. *The Debate Over Slavery: Stanley Elkins and His Critics*. Urbana: University of Illinois Press.

Lane, David. 1971. *The End of Inequality*. Baltimore: Penguin.

———. 1976. *The Socialist Industrial State*. Boulder, Colo.: Westview Press.

Lane, David, and Felicity O'Dell. 1978. *The Soviet Industrial Worker*. New York: St. Martin's Press.

Lane, W. Clayton, ed. 1968. *Permanence and Change in Social Class*. Cambridge, Mass.: Schenkman.

Laslett, John. 1970. *Labor and the Left*. New York: Basic Books.

Lauman, Edward O. 1969. "The Social Structure of Religious and Ethnoreligious Groups in the Metropolitan Community." *American Sociological Review* 34 (April).

Leacock, Eleanor Burke. 1981. *Myths of Male Dominance*. New York: Monthly Review Press.

————. 1972. "Introduction." In Friedrich Engels, *The Origin of the Family, Private Property and the State*. New York: International.

Lejeune, Robert, ed. 1972. *Class and Conflict in American Society*. Chicago: Markham.

Lenski, Gerhard. 1966. *Power and Privilege*. New York: McGraw-Hill.

Lenski, Gerhard, and Jean. 1974. *Human Societies*. 2d ed. New York: McGraw-Hill.

————. 1978. *Human Societies*. 3d ed. New York: McGraw-Hill.

Leon, Abram. 1950. *The Jewish Question: A Marxist Interpretation*. New York: Pathfinder Press, 1970.

Lewellen, Wilbur. 1971. *The Ownership Income of Management*. New York: National Bureau of Economic Research.

Lichtheim, George. 1969. *The Origins of Socialism*. New York: Praeger.

Lidtke, Vernon. 1966. *The Outlawed Party: Social Democracy in Germany 1878-1890*. Princeton, N.J.: Princeton University Press.

Liebman, Marcel. 1970. *The Russian Revolution*. New York: Vintage.

Light, Ivan H. 1972. *Ethnic Enterprise in America*. Berkeley: University of California Press.

Lipset, Seymour M. 1960. *Political Man*. Garden City, N.Y.: Doubleday.

Lipset, Seymour M., and Reinhard Bendix. 1959. *Social Mobility in Industrial Society*. Berkeley: University of California Press.

Lipset, Seymour M., and John Laslett. 1974. *Failure of a Dream*. Garden City, N.Y.: Doubleday.

Lissagaray, Prosper. 1967. *History of the Commune of 1871*. New York: Monthly Review Press.

Lloyd, Cynthia B., and Beth T. Niemi. 1979. *The Economies of Sex Differentials*. New York: Columbia University Press.

Lockwood, David. 1958. *The Blackcoated Worker*. London: Allen and Unwin.

Longino, Charles, and David Bromley. 1973. *White Racism and Black Americans*. Cambridge, Mass.: Schenkman.

Loren, Charles. 1977. *Classes in the United States*. Davis, Calif.: Cardinal.

Lorwin, Lewis. 1914. *Syndicalism in France*. New York: Columbia University Press.

Luckas, Georg. 1967. *History and Class Consciousness*. Cambridge, Mass.: M.I.T. Press.

Lundberg, Ferdinard. 1968. *The Rich and the Super-Rich*. New York: Stuart.

Lustick, Ian. 1980. *Arabs in the Jewish State*. Austin: University of Texas Press.

Lutz, Ralph. 1922. *The German Revolution 1918-1919*. Stanford, Calif.: Stanford University Press.

MacKenize, Norman. 1966. *Socialism: A Short History*. New York: Harper & Row.

McWilliams, Carey. 1935. *Factories in the Field*. Santa Barbara, Calif.: Peregrine, 1971.

Magubane, Bernard M. 1979. *The Political Economy of Race and Class in South Africa*. New York: Monthly Review Press.

Mahler, Raphael. 1946. "Antisemitism In Poland." In *Essays on Antisemitism*, edited by Koppel Pinson. New York: Conference on Jewish Relations.

Mallet, Serge. 1975. *Essays on the New Working Class*. St. Louis: Telos

Mandell, Betty Reid, ed. 1975. *Welfare in America: Controlling the "Dangerous Classes."* Englewood Cliffs, N.J.: Prentice-Hall.

Marcuse, Herbert. 1964. *One-Dimensional Man*. Boston: Beacon.

Marx, Karl. 1846. "Letter to P. V. Annenkov, December 28, 1846." In Karl Marx and Frederick Engels, *Selected Works*. vol. 2. Moscow: Foreign Languages Publishing House, 1958.

———. 1847. *The Poverty of Philosophy*. New York: International, 1963.

———. 1850. "The Class Struggles in France." In Karl Marx and Frederick Engels, *Selected Works*. Vol. 1. Moscow: Foreign Languages Publishing House, 1958.

———. 1859. "Preface to a Contribution to the Critique of Political Economy." In Karl Marx and Frederick Engels, *Selected Works*. Vol. 1. Moscow: Foreign Languages Publishing House, 1958.

———. 1864. "Inaugural Address of the Working Men's International Association." In Karl Marx and Frederick Engels, *Selected Works*. Vol. 1. Moscow: Foreign Languages Publishing House, 1958.

———. 1867. *Capital*. Moscow: Foreign Languages Publishing House.

Marx, Karl, and Friedrich Engels. 1845. *The German Ideology*. New York: International, 1947.

———. 1849. "Manifesto of the Communist Party." In Karl Marx and Frederick Engels, *Selected Works*. Vol. 1. Moscow: Foreign Languages Publishing House, 1958.

Mason, Edward. 1930. *The Paris Commune*. New York: Macmillan.

Matthews, Mervyn. 1972. *Class and Society in Soviet Russia*. New York: Walker.

Mayer, Kurt, and Walter Buckley. 1970. *Class and Society*. New York: Random House.

Mayo, Elton. 1933. *The Human Problems of an Industrial Civilization*. New York: Viking Press, 1960.

Meshikov, S. 1969. *Millionaires and Managers*. Moscow: Progress.

Michels, Roberto. 1913. *Political Parties*. New York: Collier Books, 1962.

Miller, S. M. 1969. "Comparative Social Mobility." In *Structured Social Inequality*, edited by Celia Heller. New York: Macmillan.

Mills, Charles Wright. 1953. *White Collar*. New York: Oxford University Press.

Mitchell, Daniel. 1980. *Unions, Wages and Inflation*. Washington, D.C.: Brookings Institution.

Montagu, M. F. Ashley, 1953. *Man's Most Dangerous Myth: The Fallacy of Race*. New York: Harper & Brother.

Moore, Barrington. 1966. *Social Origins of Dictatorship and Democracy.* Boston: Beacon.

Morgan, Roger P. 1965. *The German Social Democrats 1864-1872.* Cambridge, England: Cambridge University Press.

Mosca, Gaetano. 1939. *The Ruling Class.* New York: McGraw-Hill.

National Opinion Research Center. 1978. *Code Book for General Social Surveys 1972-1978.* Williamstown, Mass.: Williams College.

National Safety Council. 1979. *Accident Facts.* 1979 ed. Chicago.

Nettl, J. P. 1967. *The Soviet Achievement.* New York: Harcourt, Brace and World.

Noyes, John H. 1870. *History of American Socialisms.* New York: Hillary House, 1961.

Oakley, Ann. 1974. *The Sociology of Housework.* New York: Pantheon.

Osborn, Robert. 1970. *Soviet Social Policies.* Homewood, Ill.: The Dorsey Press.

Paige, Jeffery. 1975. *Agrarian Revolution: Social Movements and Export Agriculture in the Underdeveloped World.* New York: The Free Press.

Pareto, Vilfredo. 1935. *The Mind and Society: A Treatise on General Sociology* New York: Dover Publications.

Parkin, Frank. 1971. *Class Inequality and Political Order.* New York: Praeger.

Parsons, Talcott. 1940. "An Analytical Approach to the Theory of Social Stratification." In *Essays in Sociological Theory.* New York: The Free Press.

———. 1949. "Social Classes and Class Conflict in the Light of Recent Sociological Theory." In *Essays in Sociological Theory.* New York: The Free Press.

———. 1971. *The Systems of Modern Societies.* Englewood Cliffs, N.J.: Prentice-Hall.

Peres, Yechanan. 1971. "Ethnic Relations in Israel." *American Journal of Sociology* 76 (May):1021-47.

Perlo, Victor. 1975. *Economics of Racism USA: Roots of Black Inequality.* New York: International.

Peters, Victor. 1967. *All Things Common.* Minneapolis: University of Minnesota Press.

Pfeffer, Max. 1980. "The Labor Process and Corporate Agriculture: Mexican Workers in California." *Insurgent Sociologist* (Fall).

Pinson, Koppel, ed. 1946. *Essays on Antisemitism.* New York: Conference on Jewish Relations.

Piore, Michael J., ed. 1979. *Unemployment and Inflation.* White Plains, N.Y.: M.E. Shape.

Pirenne, Henri. 1937. *Economic and Social History of Medieval Europe.* New York: Harcourt, Brace.

Piven, Frances, and Richard Cloward. 1971. *Regulating the Poor.* New York: Vintage.

The Playboy Report on American Men. 1979. New York: Playboy Magazine.

Polanyi, Karl. 1944. *The Great Transformation.* New York: Rinehart.

———. 1957. *Trade and Market in the Early Empires.* New York: The Free Press.

Pollack, Norman. 1962. *The Populist Response to Industrial America*. Cambridge, Mass.: Harvard University Press.

Poulantzas, Nicos. 1974. *Classes in Contemporary Capitalism*. London: New Left Books.

Przeworski, Adam. 1976. "The Process of Class Formation." Mimeographed. Chicago: Department of Political Science, University of Chicago (cited in Wright 1976).

Rainwater, Lee; Richard Coleman; and Handel Gerald. 1959. *Working Man's Wife*. New York: Oceana Publications.

Reich, Michael. 1981. *Racial Inequality*. Princeton, N.J.: Princeton University Press.

Reich, Wilhelm. 1949. *Character Analysis*. New York: Farrar, Straus and Giroux.

Reid, Ivan. 1977. *Social Class Difference in Britain*. London: Open Books.

Reiman, Jeffrey. 1979. *The Rich Get Richer and the Poor Get Prison*. New York: John Wiley & Sons.

Roach, Jack; Llewellyn Gross; and Orville Gursslin. 1969. *Social Stratification in the United States*. Englewood Cliffs, N.J.: Prentice-Hall.

Rodman, Hyman. 1968. "The Lower-Class Value Stretch." In *Race, Class and Power*, edited by Raymond Mach. New York: Van Nostrand.

Rohrlich-Leavitt, Ruby; Barbara Sykes; and Elizabeth Weatherford. 1975. "Aboriginal Woman: Male and Female Anthropological Perspectives." In *Towards an Anthropology of Women*, edited by Rayna R. Reiter. New York: Monthly Review Press.

Rosenblum, Gerald. 1973. *Immigrant Workers: Their Impact on American Labor Radicalism*. New York: Basic Books.

Rossidies, Daniel. 1976. *The American Class System*. Boston: Houghton Mifflin.

Rothman, Robert. 1978. *Inequality and Stratification in the United States*. Englewood Cliffs, N.J.: Prentice-Hall.

Sacks, Karen. 1975. "Engels Revisited: Women, the Organization of Production, and Private Property. In *Towards an Anthropology of Women*, edited by Rayna R. Reiter. New York: Monthly Review Press.

———. 1979. *Sisters and Wives*. Westport, Conn.: Greenwood Press.

Sahlins, Marshall. 1972. *Stone Age Economics*. Chicago: Aldine.

———. 1968. *Tribesmen*. Englewood Cliffs, N.J.: Prentice-Hall.

Sanday-Reeves, Peggy. 1981. *Female Power and Male Dominance*. New York: Cambridge University Press.

Sawyer, Malcolm. 1976. "Income Distribution in OECD Countries." In *OECD Economic Outlook, Occasional Studies*. Paris: Organization for Economic Cooperation and Development.

Schapiro, Leonard. 1960. *The Communist Party of the Soviet Union*. New York: Random House.

Schneider, Herbert. 1952. *Religion in 20th Century America*. Cambridge, Mass.: Harvard University Press.

Schorske, Carl. 1955. *German Social Democracy 1905-1917*. Cambridge, Mass.: Harvard University Press.

Schram, Stuart, ed. 1973. *Authority, Participation and Cultural Change in China*. New York: Cambridge University Press.

Schroeder, Gertrude. 1974. "Consumption in the USSR." In *The Soviet Economy: A Book of Readings*, edited by Morris Bornstein and Daniel Fusfield. 4th ed. Homewood, Ill.: Richard Irwin.

Schweitzer, Arthur. 1964. *Big Business and the Third Reich*. Bloomington, Ind.: Indiana University Press.

Scott, John. 1979. *Corporations, Classes and Capitalism*. New York: St. Martin's Press.

Sehgal, Ellen, and Joyce Vialet. 1980. "Documenting the Undocumented." *Monthly Labor Review* (October).

Sennett, Richard, and Jonathan Cobb. 1972. *The Hidden Injuries of Class*. New York: Vintage.

Service, Elman. 1975. *Origins of the State and Civilization*. New York: W. W. Norton.

Shanin, Teodor, Ed. 1971. *Peasants and Peasant Societies*. Baltimore: Penguin.

Shannon, David. 1955. *The Socialist Party of America*. New York: Macmillan.

Sherman, Howard. 1969. *The Soviet Economy*. Boston: Little, Brown.

Shkaraton, O. J. 1973a. "Sources of Social Differentiation of the Working Class in Soviet Society." In *Social Stratification and Mobility in the USSR*, edited by Murray Yanowitch and Wesley Fisher. White Plains, N.Y.: International Arts and Science Press.

———. 1973b. "Social Groups in the Working Class of a Developed Socialist Society." In *Social Stratification and Mobility in the USSR*, edited by Murray Yanowitch and Wesley Fisher. White Plains, N.Y.: International Arts and Sciences Press.

Shostak, Arthur. 1969. *Blue Collar Life*. New York: Random House.

Shostak, Arthur, and William Gomberg, eds. 1964. *Blue Collar World*. Englewood Cliffs, N.J.: Prentice-Hall.

Sidel, Ruth. 1974. *Families of Fengsheng*. Baltimore: Penguin.

Simoniya, N.A. 1961. *Overseas Chinese in Southeast Asia*. Data Paper no. 45. Ithaca, New York: Southeast Asia Program, Department of Far Eastern Studies, Cornell University.

Singh, Vijai. 1976. *Caste, Class and Democracy*. Cambridge, Mass.: Schenkman.

Sklare, Marshall. 1971. *America's Jews*. New York: Random House.

Smith, James, and Stephen Franklin. 1974. "The Concentration of Personal Wealth 1922-1969." *The American Economic Review* 64, no. 2 (May).

Snyder, Louis. 1939. *Race: A History of Modern Ethnic Theories*. New York: Longmans, Green.

Spiro, Melford. 1970. *Kibbutz: Venture in Utopia*. New York: Schocken.

Srole, Leo S., and Anita Fisher, eds. 1975. *Mental Health and the Metropolis: The Midtown Manhattan Study*. New York: Harper & Row.

Starobin, Robert. 1970. *Industrial Slavery in the Old South*. New York: Oxford University Press.

Stavenhagen, Rodolfo. 1975. *Social Classes in Agrarian Societies*. Garden City, N.Y.: Anchor Books.

Stellman, Jeanne Magen. 1977. *Women's Work, Women's Health*. New York: Pantheon.

Stern, Phillip. 1973. *Rape of the Taxpayer*. New York: Random House.

Stinchcombe, Arthur. 1966. "Agriculture, Enterprise and Rural Class Relations." In *Class, Status and Power*, 2d ed., edited by Reinhard Bendix and Seymour Martin Lipset. New York: Free Press.

Stone, Katherine. 1975. "The Origins of Job Structures in the Steel Industry." In Richard Edwards; Michael Reich; and David Gordon, *Labor Market Segmentation*. New York: D.C. Heath.

Strasser, Susan. 1980. "An Enlarged Human Existence? Technology and Household Work in Nineteenth Century America." In *Women and Household labor*, edited by Sarah Fenstermaker-Berk. Beverly Hills: Sage.

Stromberg, Ann, and Shirley Harkess. 1978. *Women Working: Theories and Facts in Perspective*. Palo Alto, Calif.: Mayfield.

Stryker, Sheldon. 1959. "Social Structure and Prejudice." *Social Problems* 6, no. 4 (Spring).

Sweezy, Paul. 1976. "The Transition from Feudalism to Capitalism." In *The Transition from Feudalism to Capitalism*, edited by Rodney Hilton. London: New Left Review.

Szymanski, Albert. 1976a. "The Socialization of Women's Oppression." *Insurgent Sociologist* 6, no. 2 (Winter).

———. 1976b. "Racism and Sexism as Functional Substitutes in the Labor Market." *Sociological Quarterly* 17, no. 1 (Winter).

———. 1976c. "Racial Discrimination and White Gain." *American Sociological Review* 41, no. 3 (Winter).

———. 1977. "Male Gain from Sexual Discrimination." *Social Forces* 56, no. 2 (December).

———. 1978. *The Capitalist State and the Politics of Class*. Boston: Winthrop.

———. 1979a. *Is the Red Flag Flying? The Political Economy of the Soviet Union*. London: Zed Press.

———. 1979b. "A Critique and Extension of the PMC." In *Between Labor and Capital*, edited by Pat Walker. Boston: South End Press.

———. 1981. *The Logic of Imperialism*. New York: Praeger.

———. Forthcoming. *The Political Economy of Human Rights*. London: Zed Press.

Tasca, Angelo. 1966. *The Rise of Italian Fascism*. New York: Fertig.

Thernstrom, Stephen. 1969. *Poverty and Progress*. New York: Antheneum.

Thielbar, Gerald W., and Saul D. Feldman. 1972. *Issues in Social Inequality*. Boston: Little, Brown.

Thompson, E. P. 1963. *The Making of the English Working Class*. New York: Vintage.

Trotsky, Leon. 1957. *History of the Russian Revolution*. Ann Arbor: University of Michigan Press.

———. 1971. *The Struggle Against Fascism in Germany*. New York: Pathfinder.

Trow, Martin. 1958. "Small Businessmen and Support for McCarthy." *The American Journal of Sociology* 64, no. 3 (November):270-81.

Tuckman, Howard. 1973. *The Economics of the Rich*. New York: Random House.

Tully, J. C.; E. F. Jackson; and R. F. Curtis. 1975. "Trends in Occupational Mobility in Indianapolis." In *Social Mobility*, edited by Anthony Coxon and Charles Jones. Baltimore: Penguin.

Tumin, Melvin, ed. 1970. *Readings on Social Stratification*. Englewood Cliffs, N.J.: Prentice-Hall.

————. 1953. "Some Principles of Stratification: A Critical Analysis." *American Sociological Review* 18 (August);387-94.

Turner, Jonathan, and Charles Starness. 1976. *Inequality in America*. Pacific Palisades, Calif.: Goodyear.

U.S. Bureau of the Census. 1940. *Census of the Population. Summary*. Washington, D.C.: Government Printing Office.

————. 1950a. *Census of the Population. Summary*. Washington, D.C.: Government Printing Office.

————. 1950b. *Census of the Population. Subject Reports: Occupational Characteristics*. Washington, D.C.: Government Printing Office.

————. 1969. *Current Population Reports. Income Growth Rates 1939-1968 for Persons by Occupation and Industry for the U.S.* P-60, no. 69. Washington, D.C.: Government Printing Office.

————. 1970a. *U.S. Census, Special Reports: American Indians*. Washington, D.C.: Government Printing Office.

————. 1970b. *U.S. Census, Special Reports: The Chinese and Japanese Population in the US.* Washington, D.C.: Government Printing Office.

————. 1970c. *U.S. Census, Special Reports: Occupational Characteristics*. Washington, D.C.: Government Printing Office.

————. 1970d. *Census of the Population. General Social and Economic Characteristics: U.S. Summary*. Washington, D.C.: Government Printing Office.

————. 1970e. *Current Population Reports. Characteristics of the Population below the Poverty Level: 1969.* Series P-60, no. 75. Washington, D.C.: Government Printing Office.

————. 1970f. *U.S. Census of the Population. Special Reports: Persons of Spanish Origin*. Washington, D.C.: Government Printing Office.

————. 1970g. *Census of the Population. Special Reports: Industrial Characteristics*. Washington, D.C.: Government Printing Office.

————. 1970h. *Census of the Population. General Population Characteristics*. Washington, D.C.: Government Printing Office.

————. 1970i. *Census of the Population. Detailed Characteristics: U.S. Summary*. Washington, D.C.: Government Printing Office.

————. 1970j. *Census of the Population. Detailed Characteristics* (for each of the 50 states). Washington, D.C.: Government Printing Office.

————. 1972. *Census of Manufacturing*. Washington, D.C.: Government Printing Office.

————. 1979a. *Current Population Reports: The Social and Economic Status of the Black Population in the United States*. Series P-23, no. 80. Washington, D.C.: Government Printing Office.

————. 1979b. *Current Population Reports: Characteristics of the Population Below the Poverty Level: 1977.* Series P-60, no. 119. Washington, D.C.: Government Printing Office.

————. 1979c. *Current Population Reports: Money Income of Families and Persons: 1977.* Series P-60, no. 118. Washington, D.C.: Government Printing Office.

———. 1980a. *Current Population Reports: A Statistical Portrait of Women in the United States 1978.* Series P-23, no. 100. Washington, D.C.: Government Printing Office.

———. 1980b. *Current Population Reports: Money Income of Families and Persons: 1979.* Series P-60, no. 123. Washington, D.C.: Government Printing Office.

———. 1981. *Current Population Reports: Money Income of Families and Persons: 1979.* Series P-60, no. 129. Washington, D.C.: Government Printing Office.

U.S. Congress. Joint Economic Committee. 1976. *Estimating the Social Costs of National Economic Policy.* 94th Cong., 2d sess.

U.S. Department of Commerce. 1966. *Statistical Abstract of the U.S. for 1965.* Washington, D.C.: Government Printing Office.

———. 1967. *Statistical Abstract of the U.S. for 1966.* Washington, D.C.: Government Printing Office.

———. 1973. *Statistical Abstract of the U.S. for 1972.* Washington, D.C.: Government Printing Office.

———. 1975a. *Statistical Abstract of the U.S. for 1974.* Washington, D.C.: Government Printing Office.

———. 1975b. *Historical Statistics of the U.S.* Washington, D.C.: Government Printing Office.

———. 1977. *Statistical Abstract for 1976.* Washington, D.C.: Government Printing Office.

———. 1979. *Statistical Abstract of the U.S. for 1978.* Washington, D.C.: Government Printing Office.

———. 1980. *Statistical Abstract for 1979.* Washington, D.C.: Government Printing Office.

———. 1981. *Statistical Abstract of the U.S. for 1980.* Washington, D.C.: Government Printing Office.

U.S. Department of Health, Education and Welfare. National Center for Health Statistics. 1972. *Infant Mortality Rates: Socioeconomic Factors.* Series 22, no. 4. Washington, D.C.: Government Printing Office.

———. 1977. *Health: United States 1975.* Washington, D.C.: Government Printing Office.

U.S. Department of Health and Human Services. 1978. *Facts of Life and Death.* Washington, D.C.: Government Printing Office.

———. 1980. *Vital and Health Statistics. Basic Data on Depressive Symptomatology: U.S. 1974-75.* Washington, D.C.: Government Printing Office.

U.S. Department of Health and Human Services. National Center for Health Statistics. Vital and Health Statistics. 1979a. *Use Habits Among Adults of Cigarettes, Coffee, Aspirin and Sleeping Pills—United States.* 1976. Series 10, no. 131. Washington, D.C.: Government Printing Office.

———. 1979b. *Food Consumption Profiles of White and Black Persons Aged 1-74 Years: U.S. 1971-1974.* Series 11, no. 210. Washington, D.C.: Government Printing Office.

———. 1980. *Selected Health Characteristics by Occupation: United States 1975-1976.* Series 10, no. 133. Washington, D.C.: Government Printing Office.

U.S. Department of Justice, Law Enforcement Assistance Administration. 1975. *Sourcebook of Criminal Justice Statistics 1974.* Washington, D.C.: Government Printing Office.

———. 1979. *Criminal Victimization in the United States 1977.* Washington, D.C.: Government Printing Office.

———. 1980. *Sourcebook of Criminal Justice Statistics 1979.* Washington, D.C.: Government Printing Office.

———. 1981. *Sourcebook of Criminal Justice Statistics 1980.* Washington, D.C.: Government Printing Office.

U.S. Department of Labor. 1969a. *Handbook of Women Workers.* Washington, D.C.: Government Printing Office.

———. 1969b. *Directory of National and International Labor Unions in the U.S.* Washington, D.C.: Government Printing Office.

———. 1971. *Handbook of Labor Statistics for 1970.* Washington, D.C.: Government Printing Office.

———. 1975a. *Handbook of Labor Statistics for 1974.* Washington, D.C.: Government Printing Office.

———. 1975b. *Handbook of Women Workers.* Washington, D.C.: Government Printing Office.

———. 1978. *Handbook of Labor Statistics for 1978.* Washington, D.C.: Government Printing Office.

U.S. Immigration and Naturalization Service 1979. *Annual Report for 1979.* Washington, D.C.: Government Printing Office.

Vanek. JoAnn. 1974. "Time Spent in Housework." *Scientific American* 231, no. 5 (November).

———. 1980. "Household Work, Wage Work, and Sexual Equality." In *Women and Household Labor*, edited by Sarah Fenstermaker-Berk. Beverly Hills: Sage.

Vanfossen, Beth E. 1979. *The Structure of Social Inequality.* Boston: Little, Brown.

Van Woodward, C. 1974. *The Strange Career of Jim Crow.* New York: Oxford University Press.

Veblen, Thorstein. 1921. *Engineers and the Price System.* New York: Viking Press.

Vishniak, Mark. 1946. "Antisemitism in Tsarist Russia." In *Essays on Antisemitism*, edited by Koppel Pinson. New York: Conference on Jewish Relations.

Wallerstein, Immanuel. 1974. *The Modern World System.* New York: Academic Press.

———. 1979. *The Capitalist World Economy.* New York: Cambridge University Press.

Weber, Max. 1922. *Economy and Society.* Edited by Guenther Roth and Claus Wittich. 3 vol. New York: Bedminister Press, 1968.

———. 1946. *From Max Weber.* Edited by Hans H. Gerth and C. Wright Mills. New York: Oxford University Press.

Weinberg, Martin, and Colin Williams. 1980. "Sexual Embourgeoisment? Social Class and Sexual Activity: 1938-1970." *American Sociological Review* 45 (February).

Weinryb, Bernard. 1946. "The Economic and Social Background of Modern Antisemitism." In *Essays on Antisemitism*, edited by Koppel Pinson. New York: Conference on Jewish Relations.

Weinstein, James. 1967. *The Decline of Socialism in America*. New York: Monthly Review Press.

Wenger, Morton. 1980. "State Response to Afro-American Rebellion." *Insurgent Sociologist* 10, no. 2 (Fall).

Wheelwright, Edward, and Bruce McFarlane. 1970. *The Chinese Road to Socialism*. New York: Monthly Review Press.

Wilczynski, Jozef. 1970. *The Economics of Socialism*. London: Allen and Unwin.

Wiles, Peter. 1974. *Distribution of Income: East and West*. New York: American Elsevier.

William, Robin. 1960. *American Society*. 2d ed. New York: Knopf.

Willie, Charles Vert. 1979. *The Caste and Class Controversy*. Bayride, N.Y.: General Hall.

Wilson, William J. 1978. *The Declining Significance of Race*. Chicago: University of Chicago Press.

———. 1980. *The Declining Significance of Race*. 2d ed. Chicago: University of Chicago Press.

Wittfogel, Karl. 1957. *Oriental Despotism*. New Haven: Yale University Press.

Wohl, Robert. 1966. *French Communism in the Making 1914-1924*. Stanford, Calif.: Stanford University Press.

Wolf, Eric R. 1966. *Peasants*. Englewood Cliffs, N.J.: Prentice-Hall.

———. 1969. *Peasant Wars of the Twentieth Century*. New York: Harper & Row.

Wright, Erik. 1973. *The Politics of Punishment*. New York: Harper & Row.

———. 1976. *Class Structure and Income Inequality*. Ph.D. dissertation, University of California, Berkeley.

———. 1978. *Class, Crisis and the State*. London: New Left Press.

Yanowitch, Murray. 1977. *Social and Economic Inequality in the Soviet Union*. White Plains, N.Y.: M. E. Sharpe.

Yanowitch, Murray, and Wesley Fisher, eds. 1973. *Social Stratification and Mobility in th USSR*. White Plains, N.Y.: International Arts and Science Press.

Zeitlin, Maurice, ed. 1977. *American Society, Inc.* 2d ed. Chicago: Markum.

Index

Aborigines, Australian, 373
abortion, attitudes toward, 346
accidents, job related, 307
advanced capitalist countries, class structure, 110-13, 115
advanced capitalist countries, income distribution, 113-16
advertising, 168, 179, 243, 247, 259
affirmative action, 430, 441, 453-54, 557
Africa, 33
agricultural societies, 514, 515
agricultural workers, 238, 246
agriculture, origins of, 18, 23, 28, 50
agriculture, U.S., 167, 172-76, 246
Aid to Families with Dependent Children, 105-06
alcohol use, 333
Algerians (in France), 407, 409
Alien Land Act, 395
Althusser, Louis, 365
American Federation of Labor, 202, 227, 440, 580
American socialism, failure of, 581-83
"Americanism", 228, 266
Amerindians (*see also* Indios), 33, 359, 365, 373-76, 476
Anabaptists, 562-63
anarchism, 567, 568-69
Andreski, Stanislaw, 602-04
anti-immigrant feeling, 227
Antonio, Mark, 581
apartheid, 419-23, 426, 428
aristocracy of labor, 200, 202
Aristotle, 357
Armenians (as middlemen minorities), 379, 380
armies, origins of, 26, 604
Aronowitz, Stanley, 627, 628
arrests, 336-38
artisans, 163, 196

Aryan race, 360-61, 368
Asian Americans, 366, 397, 432, 477, 479, 481
Asiatic mode of production, 50-53, 65
aspirin, 307
assimilation, 371, 390
authoritarian personality, 347
auto ownership, 97

Babeuf, Francois, 563
Ball, John, 561-62
Banfield, Edward, 56-57
banks, 123, 126, 131, 132, 134-37, 144, 167, 175
banks, control of, 136
battering (wife beating), 504, 558
Bell, Daniel, 620
Berger, Victor, 579
biological differences between women and men, 505, 506, 517
black capitalism, 452, 453
black excluded sector, 453, 456-71, 476, 490, 491
black excluded sector, size of, 435-74
black families, 462
black income trends, 443-50, 454-56
black labor force participation, 456-58, 461, 490
black life expectancy, 463
black migration to north, 435-38, 441, 447, 481
black petty bourgeoisie, 451-56, 474
black prisoners, 462, 490
black racism, 417
black underclass (growth of), 466-70
black unemployment, 458-61
black workers, 441-51, 453, 469-70, 474
blacks (U.S.), 110, 221, 251, 362, 364, 370, 376, 404, 410, 412, 413, 419, 429, 430, 431, 432, 433-97

blacks, attitudes toward, 349, 351, 352, 353, 438

blacks, class differentiation in, 451-76, 487-91

blacks and social welfare, 468-69, 470, 471

Blanc, Louis, 562, 574

Blangui, Louis, 574

Blum, Leon, 576

boarding schools (upper class), 148-49

Bohemia Grove, 152

Bolshevik Party, 584-85

bonds, 95, 97

book reading, 334

Bracero Program, 479-80

bourgeoisie, comprador, 128

bourgeoisie, internal, 128-29

bourgeoisie, national, 64, 128

Brazil, 35-36, 412-13

breast feeding, 323-24

bride price, 511-14

British Labor Party, 570

Bryant, William Jennings, 578

Buonarrotti, 563

Burawoy, Michael, 214

bureaucratic control (of labor process), 208-09, 213-15

Burgess, John, 363

Cabet, Etienne, 564

California, agriculture, 394-95, 477

capital gains, 101

capital punishment, attitude towards, 338

capitalism, 7, 58, 59, 74-75, 84, 85, 92, 94, 97, 106, 109, 115-17, 177

capitalism (origins of), 58-65

capitalist class life style, 146-47

capitalist class, nonmonopoly middle sector, 125-26

capitalist class, origins, 120-23

capitalist class position, 115-17, 120-56, (df*123), (df129), 282, 286

capitalists (as a social class), 144-55

capitalists, heredity, 138, 155, 281, 286-87

capitalists, small, 125-27, 155

Carribbean, 30, 31, 32

castes, 80, 81, 368, 399, 418-22

Chaing Kai-Shek, 593

Chamberlain, Houston Steward, 361

Chartist Movement, 570

Cherokee Nation, 374

Chicanos, 476-81, 484-91

chiefdoms and rank societies, origins of, 15-21

childcare, 504, 505, 515-17, 519, 521, 532, 553-54

childrearing, 319, 323-25

China, 51, 61, 592-98

China: income inequalities, 596-97

Chinese (as cheap labor), 394, 512

Chinese (as middlemen minorities), 379, 380, 391-98

Chinese Communist Party, 592

Chinese Exclusion Act, 394

Chinese Revolution, 592

Christian communism, 561-62, 565-66

church attendance, 329

church officials, 90

cities, 66, 75

cities, class differentiation of, 225-26, 270

civil liberties, attitudes toward, 190

class (definitions of), 3-6, 76-78, 602, 611-15, 619-24, 637-45

class consciousness (class for itself), 81-83, 118-19

class consciousness (working class), 203, 224, 225, 228, 236, 239, 240, 241, 245, 256-57, 261, 262-63, 265-69, 270, 279, 425-26

class identification, 117-18

class interest (definition of), 81-82

class lines, hardening of, 285, 600

class origins, 21-28

class solidarity/disorganization, 492-96

class structure, views of, 262

*definition

class struggle, 83
clerical workers, 84, 111, 113, 241–43, 244–45, 247, 255, 259, 266, 517, 519 526–29, 530, 533, 534
collective bargaining, 257, 275–76
common market position (as criteria of class), 612–19
communism, 267, 561–68, 572–74, 576, 581, 584–98
Communist Party (U.S.), 582
communist threat, 349–51
community colleges, 295
Congress of Industrial Organizations, 228, 440, 481, 581
consciousness of kind (group solidarity), 366–67, 373, 378
conservatism, 188–91, 264, 271
consumption patterns and class, 330–31
contradictory class locations, 640–43
cooperatives, farm, 176
coordination of labor power, 124
corporate agriculture, 175–76
corporate crime, 341–42
corporate directors, 138–39, 139–40
corporations, 97, 129, 133
corporations, control of, 137–39
corporations, family control, 137–38, 144
corporations, formation of, 121–22
cottage industry (putting-out system), 121, 195
country clubs, 151
courts, 339–41
craftsworkers, 196, 197, 200–03, 208–09, 210, 235, 237, 238, 259
credit, 179, 243, 247
crime, (df 334–35), 342
crime, victims of, 338
criminals, 90–91, 109, 167, 198
Cromwell, Oliver, 563
crops, effect on land tenure, 69, 71–73
Cuba, 36
culture of poverty, 271

Dahrendorf, Ralf, 602
daVinci, Leonardo, 358

Davis, Benjamin, 581
Davis, Kingsley and Moore, Wilber, 631–37
Debs, Eugene, 579, 580
debt, farm, 175
debt instruments, 96
debutante balls, 149, 153
De Cobineau, Arthur, 361
DeGaulle, Charles, 576
DeLeon, Daniel, 579
democracy (in primitive societies), 12, 24
Democratic Party, support of, 268
dental care, 314
depression, 316
descent rules, 503, 507–13
diet, 311
Diggers, 563
dignity (of workers), 263–64
discrimination against blacks, trends in, 441–56, 474
discrimination against minorities, effect on majority group workers, 491–99
discrimination against women, effect on male earnings, 536–45
discrimination, nature of, 447
diseases, incidence of, 312
division of labor, 9, 15
divorce, 319, 321
Dobb, Maurice, 619
domestic labor, 240
domestication of animals, 17
dowry, 511–14
drug use, 333
dual labor market, 441
DuPont, 125, 129

Eastern European emigrants, 223
economic cycles, 110, 600
economic surplus, 23, 51
education, 63, 148–49, 178, 183, 255, 264, 265, 270, 281, 289–96
Egypt (ancient), 28
Ehrenreich, John and Barbara, 623–24
embourgeoisment (of working class), 270–71

employment, sectional distribution of (working class), 246-56
engineers, 182-83
English peasant revolt of 1381, 561-66
English revolution of 1640s, 563
enrichment of jobs, 208-09, 216
entrepreneur, 123
Episcopalianism, 148
equalitarianism, causes of, 11, 12
ethnic communities, 226
ethnic identity, 225, 227-28, 271
ethic of manhood, 263
excluded sector, 85, 86-87, 91, 92, 105-06, 108-10, 118-19
exclusion, relationships of, 373-76, 404, 432
expanded working class theory, 637-39
exploitation, 7, 77-78, 85, 94, 124, 125

Factories, early, 121, 194, 195, 198-99, 217, 219
factories, size of, 196
factory laborers (early), 517
factory workers, origins, 197-99, 202, 203, 205, 213, 217
false consciousness, 82, 83
families, decision-making in, 542-43, 545
family farmers, 110, 113, 118, 162-64, 167, 172-76
family farming, decline of, 172-76
family patterns, 326, 347, 497, 500-16, 542-45, 556
family size, 320-21
Fanon, Frantz, 621
feminine psychology, 531, 533-35
Fascism, 192, 347
feudalism (classical), 49-51, 59, 383
fiefs, 49, 50
Filipinos, 479
finance capitalists, 122-23, 127, 132, 134-38, 142
Finnish emigrants, 224
food consumption and class, 331

force theory (of class inequality), 3, 603-04, 606-09
Ford, Henry, 125, 131, 390
Fordism, 194, 216
foremen, 88-89, 90, 117, 203, 205, 210
Fourier, Charles, 564-65
franchises, 168-70, 176
Frank, Andre Gunder, 616, 617, 618
Freedman, Francesca, 638-39
French Communist Party, 576
French Revolution, 563-64
friendship networks, upper class, 146, 149, 150, 319, 325
functionalism, 3, 631-37

Gambling, 331
genocide, 374-76, 378, 432
German emigration, 220, 224
Giddens, Anthony, 613
God, belief in, 329
Gorz, Andre, 638
Gramsci, Antonio, 626
Grant, Madison, 361
Great Leap Forward, 593
Great Proletarian Cultural Revolution (China), 593-95, 597-98, 599
Greece (ancient), 29-30
Guesde, Jules, 575
"guest workers", 401, 407-08, 409

Hamilton, Richard, 348, 351, 620, 623
happiness, 315
heading societies, 509
health, 298, 311
health care employment, 255
Hegelian Marxism (Marxian subjectivism), 625-30
Hill, Judah, 87
home ownership (meaning of), 97, 265
homestead steal strike of 1892, 202, 226
horticultural societies, 10-15, 17, 19, 20, 28, 503, 512
household division of labor, 545, 554-55

housewives, 249
housework, 504, 515, 516, 519, 522, 526, 533, 535-46, 560
housework, transformation of, 553-54, 560
Hughes, Howard, 132
human capital, 532
hunting and gathering society, 9-15, 17, 501-12, 517
Hutterites, 562, 566
hypertension, 306

Idealism, 3, 625-30
ideology, 365
immigrants, children of, 228, 400
immigrants from Latin America, 481-84
immigrants in U.S. working class, 219-22, 228
immigrants, radicalization of, 224, 436, 577-80
immigrants, reverse flow of, 223
immigration from Europe to U.S., 219-27, 388, 405-06, 435, 436
immigration, motivation for, 223-24, 388, 405
immigration policy (U.S.), 483
immigration restrictions, 258, 259, 362-64, 406, 436, 469
imperialism (economic role of), 63
income, distribution of, 100-04, 107-08, 113-16
indentured servitude, 32
independent commodity production, 78-79, 164
Indians (Asian), 380
Indios, 410-12, 413
individualism, 188, 265, 268, 347
industrial agriculture, 74, 84
industrial concentration, 133
industrial unionism, 424-25, 426
industrial workers, 233, 238, 251, 255
Industrial Workers of the World (IWW), 227, 228, 580
industrial workers class, origins of, 194-204
infant mortality, 303

inferiority of producers, ideology of, 67
insurance companies, 137
intensification (of economic life), 15, 17, 18
intermediate strata, 92, 93, 116, 122, 184
internal labor markets, 212, 531-32
International Workingmen's Association, 568-69, 577
I.Q., 363
Irish emigrants, 218, 220
iron law of oligarchy, 604-06, 609, 612
Iroquois, 510
Israeli racism, 415-17
Italian emigration, 220

Japan, 114
Japanese (as middlemen minorities), 379, 394-98
Japanese feudalism, 51
Japanese racism, 414
Jefferson, Thomas, 359
Jews (and anti-Semitism), 24, 82, 145, 151, 154-55, 223, 224, 227, 358, 364, 370-71, 375, 377-378, 379, 380, 381-90, 397-98, 415-17, 427, 432, 600
Jim Crow system, 438, 441, 453
job satisfaction, 314-15
Junior League, 153
juvenile delinquency, 248

Kingdoms, origins of, 25, 51
kinship (social role of), 26
Knights of Labor, 577-78
Kolko, Gabriel, 100
Ku Klux Klan, 227, 389

Labor contracting, 200-22
labor/land ratio, 65-69, 70
labor migration (peasants to cities), 220, 370
the labor process, 178, 179, 194-217
Ladino workers, 484-88

Ladino workers in U.S. economy (growth of), 484–88

Ladinos, 251, 270, 279, 370, 410–12, 430, 468, 469, 476–91

Ladinos (class differentiation in), 487–91

land tenure, transformation of, 55–56, 58, 59, 68, 70–71, 75

Lassalle, Ferdinard, 571

Latin American race relations, 410–14

Laughlin, H. H., 363

leadership (in primitive societies), 13–15

Lebanon, 382

legal professionals, 170

legitimation, 25

legitimation problem, 178, 183

Leibniz, 358

leisure, 331, 333

Lenin, V. I., 584

Lenski, Gerhard, 621

Levelers, 563

life expectancy, 298–310

Lincoln, Abraham, 438

Luckas, Georg, 625

lumpen proletariat, 85, 87, 91, 118

Lundberg, George, 131

Machinery, introduction of, 196, 197, 204, 217–18

magazine readership, 334

Mallet, Serge, 638

managerial control of corporations, 139, 141, 142

managerial salaries, 142, 177, 259

managers, 85–86, 88, 123, 124, 138–44, 155, 287

manual labor, stigma of, 262

manual workers (blue collar), 233, 234–38

manufacture, 196

manufacturing sector, 249

Mao Tse-tung, 593–94, 606

Marcuse, Herbert, 621

market power, 67, 611–619

markets, role of, 68, 611–619

marriage patterns, 319, 321, 511–13, 526

marriage, upper class, 146, 148–49, 152, 154

Marx, Karl, 5–7, 81, 571

Marxist socialism, 566–98

mass media, 333, 582

master-slave relationship (paternalism), 37–41, 204, 205

Mather, Cotton, 376

May Day (International Workers' Day), origins of, 578

Mayo, Elton (Industrial Relations School), 213, 216

medical care, quality of, 308–10, 312

medical insurance, 308–09

medical professionals, 170

Mellon family, 125, 131, 138

men's clubs, upper class, 150–51, 155

mental health, 314–18

merchants (merchant capital), 24, 28, 50, 58, 60, 121, 127, 195, 383

mergers, corporate, 133, 139

metallurgy, 24

Mexican immigration to U.S., 476–84

Michels, Robert, 602, 604–06, 609–11

middle class (petty bourgeoisie), 86–87, 92, 97, 113, 116–17, 118, 157–93 (df 157–59), 281–82, 372, 380

middle class identification, 180

middle class, income, 186–87

middle class politics, 189–93

middle class, salaried (new), 158, 159–62, 177–93, 373, 378, 380, 397

middle class values, 187–88, 190–91, 378, 379

middleman minorities, 81, 376–98, 411, 427, 429

migrant labor, 73–74, 423

militarization, 178

military, attitude towards, 353

military participation ratio, 603

military spending, 179, 182

millenial communist movements, 561–63

millionaires, 122, 129, 131

minimum wage, 105–06, 109

mining workers, 246
minorities (class differences within), 429-32
Mitterand, Francois, 576
mode of production, 84
monopolization (concentration of capital), 132, 166-67, 168
monopoly capital, 190
monopoly (versus competitive) sector, 250
monopoly sector of capitalist class, 125-27, 156
Morgan, J. P., 122-23, 131
Mosca, Gaetano, 602-03
mulattos, 412-13
multiple class positions, 91-92
Muntzer, Thomas, 562

Nation, (df 355)
National Labor Union, 577
nationalism (of minorities), 424, 430
nationalism and class, 430-31
nationalization, 191
neurosis, 318
New Deal, 103
new investment capital, 137
new working class theory, 637-39
newspaper readership, 334
Nordic race, 361-63, 389, 414
nuclear power, attitude toward, 343-44

Occupational illness, 308
occupational structure of U.S., 229-34, 244
office work, transformation of, 242-44
office workers, 177
Oklahoma, 374-75
old petty bourgeoisie, decline of, 163-77
Onieda Commune, 565
operational control (possession), 76-77, 86, 123
operatives (machine) (semi-skilled workers), 197, 203, 236, 237-38, 259

organization, ideological theory of class, 3, 602-05, 609-12
organizational membership, 327
Osage Indians, 375
overpopulation, 69
Owen, Robert, 565, 569

Pakistanis (in the U.K.), 407-08, 409
Palestine, 382
Palestineans, 380-416
Pareto, Vilfredo, 602
Paris Commune, 574
Parsons Talcott, 624-25, 627, 629, 631
patriarchal ideology, 531, 533, 536, 559
patriarchy, origins of, 499, 516
peasant families, 56
peasant handicraft production, 55
peasant mentality, 56-57
peasant solidarity, 57
peasants (peasant mode of production), 48, 51, (df 52), 53-58, 59-60, 69, 71
peasants, economic rationality of, 54, 57
peasants, politics of, 57
pension funds, 134
people, a, (df 355)
people of color, (df 361)
People's Party (Populists), 578-79
petty bourgeoisie, old (independent), 110, 158, 164-76, 177, 184-93
piecework, 202, 211-12
plantations, 73
Plato, 357
pogroms, 387, 388, 394
police, 66, 180-81, 255, 339
political attitudes, 342-54
political decentralization (economic consequences of), 60-61
political repression, effect of, 271
political units, size of, 64
poor, the, 104-10
population control, 17-18
"post-industrial" society, 620
Poulantzas, Nicos, 87, 128, 621-24

poverty level, 104–05, 109
powered machinery, introduction, 205–07
prebendal domain, 53
primitive accumulation, 63
primitive equalitarian societies, 8–26
prisoners, 91, 340–41, 490
private ownership of the means of production, 125–26
private property, 10–11, 27, 51
production workers, 113, 233, 238–39, 266
productive capitalists, 127
productive (versus unproductive) workers, 624
productivity, 107–08, 124, 199, 215, 219, 246, 257–59
professionals, 110–11, 115, 158, 160–62, 170, 177, 185–92, 261, 526–30
profits, 107, 109, 144, 205–06
prostitutes, 90–91
Przeworski, Adam, 627–28
psychiatric treatment, 318
psychosis, 318
public relations, 183
Puerto Ricans, 471, 481–82, 483, 488–91

Quotas, admission, 389

Race, (df 356), (df 365–68)
race riots, 437, 452
racialism (race theories), 356–67, 370, 402
racism, 34, (df 368), 369, 538–41
racism against blacks (history), 438–41
racism and commercial farmers, 417, 420, 422, 425, 427, 428
racism and mining, 421, 423, 425
racism, causes of, 495–96
racism and industrial capitalists, 418, 420, 422–23, 425, 439
racist structures, (fn 368)
ranches, 73
rape, 337

real economic ownership, 76–77, 85, 124, 126, 137–39, 141, 142
realization problem, 178–79
reciprocity (redistribution in primitive society), 13–14, 19–20, 24, 26, 27, 28
reconstruction, 433
redundant populations, 376
relations of production, rural, 65–75
religion, 116, 327
religion, upper class, 148
research and development, 179, 182
residence rules, 503, 507–16
retail stores, 168–70
revolutions of 1848, 568, 574
riots, 119
Rockefeller family, 122–23, 126, 136, 138
Roman Catholic Church and racism, 357
Rome (ancient), 29–30, 48
Roosevelt, Theodore, 362
Russian Revolution, 584–85

Sacrifice, ideology of, 264
Saint-Simon, Henri, 564, 576
sales sector, petty bourgeoisie, 179
sales workers, 246, 259, 266
sargents, 90
scalp bounties, 374
schools, upper class, 145, 147–50, 152, 155
science, 182, 190
scientific research, 162
second generation (immigrants), effect of, 400, 469–70
the "second serfdom", 68, 384, 418
self-employed, 110–11, 113, 116, 118, 158, 162, 164–66
semi-feudalism (see also peasants/peasant mode of production), 52
semi-professionals, 88–89, 117, 178
serfdom, 47–51, 59, 66, 67–69, 383
serfdom, productivity of, 50–51, 59
serfs, emancipation, 50, 59
service business, 170, 172

service workers, 113, 239-40, 241, 246, 247, 250, 251, 254, 259, 266, 526-29

sexism, 498-99

sexual division of labor, 498, 500, 506, 516-36, 544, 555, 557

sexuality, 319, 321, 322-23, 325, 515

Shakers, 565-66

sharecropping, 54-55, 60, 69-71, 430, 435

slave families, 516

slave personality, 38-40

slave revolts, 40

slave drivers, 41

slavery, 29-47, 65-66, 67-69, 73, 78, 357, 359, 364, 365

slavery (ancient), 29-30

slavery, contradictions of, 43-47

slavery, development of modern, 26-37, 359

slavery, incentives in, 44-45

slavery, profitability of, 43-45

slaves, cost of, 45-46

slaves, house, 41, 42

slaves, industrial, 46, 47-48

slaves, occupations, 41-43

slaves, rights of, 34-36

slaves, standard of living, 36-37

sleeping pills, 306-07

small businessmen, 158-59, 162, 166, 166-72, 177, 185-86, 187, 190

small holding (commercial family farming), 71

smoking, 306

social class, (df 79-81), 83, 87, 92, 94, 116

social class formation, 81, 83, 86, 87, 116-19

social differentiation among peasants, 70-71, 73

social mobility, 280, 289

social mobility, causes of, 280-81, 288-89

Social Register, 139, 145, 146, 149-50, 151, 159

social security (welfare), 105-06, 190, 198

social work, origins of, 154

social workers, 190

socialism, British (history of), 569-70

socialism, French (history of), 573-76

socialism, future of, 598-601

socialism, German (history of), 571-73

socialism, history of, 560

socialism, U.S. (history of), 576-83

Socialist Labor Party, 577, 579

socialist movements, 183, 227, 267-68, 561-601

Socialist Party (U.S.), 578-81

socialization of the labor process (effect of), 265-68

Solidarity (Polish), 599

South, U.S., 110, 433, 435-37

Southwest of U.S. (Atzlan), 476, 479

special exploitation, relationships of, 398-408, 432

Spencer, Herbert, 360

state, the, origins of, 21-28

state, the, role in class structure, 82, 219, 246-47

state administration, 183

state capitalists, 124

state, employment, 254-55

state officials, 89-90

state peasantry (see also Asiatic mode of production), 60

status, 115, 116, 187, 189, 264

stock ownership, 95, 96, 97, 101, 103, 122, 124, 134, 137, 139, 142, 212

stress, 305-07, 315-16

strike breakers, 119

strikes, effect of, 277

Strong, Josiah, 362

students, 90

subjectivist conceptualization of class, 624-30

subsidies, 179

success, symbols of, 265

succession of racial groups, 403-04

suicide, 303-05

surplus value (see also exploitation), 115

Sweden, 216

Sweezy, Paul, 616, 617, 618
symptoms of disease, recognition of, 310
syndicalism (French), 575

Taborites, 562
tax, origins of, 20, 21
taxes, 20, 21, 103-04, 114, 127
Taylorism, 194, 204, 211, 212, 216
technical division of labor (as basis of class), 619-24
technological development, 62
technological innovation, 178
television, 334
temporary wage labor (of peasants), 56
tenancy, 70
textile industry, 121, 196, 197-98
Thompson, E. P., 625, 627, 628
toilet training, 324
tolerance, 349, 409
trade (early), 28
trade unions, attituded toward, 344-45
trust funds, 95, 136
Tschopik, Harry, 56
Turner, Frederick Jackson, 364

U.S. Civil War, 47, 218
U.S. working class, formation of, 217-28
U.S.S.R. (Union of Socialist Soviet Republics), 584-92
U.S.S.R.: income inequality, 585-91
U.S.S.R.: social class formation, 591
undocumented workers (illegal aliens), 480-81, 482-84
unemployed (reserve army of labor), 90, 106-07, 108-09, 305
unemployment, 261
union leaders, 276
unionization, 191, 208-09, 214, 225, 227-28, 255, 257, 268, 272-78, 419, 424, 444
unions and minorities, 440, 450, 480, 492, 495
unions, bureaucratization of, 276-77

unions, effect of, 273-76, 277, 440, 492-96
unions, membership of, 273
unions, militance of, 277
universities, 183, 190, 294-95
universities, upper class, 149-50, 152-53
unskilled workers (laborers), 237, 238
upper class resorts, 149, 152, 155
upper class women, 152-53
upward mobility, 155, 600
urban political machines, 226
usury, 383
utopian socialism, 564-67

Vanderbilt family, 123
virginity, 515
Voltaire, Francois, 359

Wage and salary income, 101, 116, 126-27
wage differentials, 259-60
wage labor, 84-85
wage labor, rural, 72, 74
wages, equalization among advanced capitalist countries, 258-59
wages (level of), 60, 106, 108, 199-200, 215, 222, 256-59, 269, 274
Walker, General Francis C., 375
Wallerstein, Immanuel, 614-19
war casualities, 303, 354
warfare, effect of, 510
water control (hydraulic societies), 22, 23, 51, 52, 61
wealth distribution, 94-99
Weber, Max, 611, 614, 615-19
welfare, 105-06, 109-10, 114, 178, 179, 183
West Indians (in the U.K.), 407-08, 409
wet rice agriculture, 506
wheel, the, 18
white collar workers, 117, 177, 233, 241-46, 271
white race, the, 361
white skin privilege, 417, 425
William the Conqueror, 25-26

Williams, Robin, 624–25

Winstanley, Gerald, 563

women, 79, 92–93, 94, 152, 153, 197, 198, 217, 251–54, 343, 497–560

women and early capitalism, 516–17

women, capitalist class, 517–18, 557–58

women, equality with men, 503, 508, 512, 514–18, 542–45

women, legal equality with men, 518

women, petty bourgeois, 518, 542, 544, 546, 552, 556, 557–60

women, politics of, 545, 552, 560

women, trends in economic role of, 519–29

women, trends in wages, 529–30

women's clubs, upper class, 153

women's labor, 500–06, 516–36

women's labor force participation, 520–26, 556

women's unemployment, 522–23

women's working class, 542, 543, 544, 546, 552, 556, 557–60

worker dissatisfaction, 233, 263

working class, 85, 92, 97, 113, 115–16, 117, 118, 194–217, 230, 233, 282, 283

working class education, 263, 290–96

working class family patterns, 268, 270

working class friendship patterns, 269, 270

working class leisure, 264

working class mobility aspirations, 283

working class politics, 204, 223, 224, 228, 264, 278–85, 342–54 (see also socialist movements)

working class psychology, 259–89

working class racism, 351–53, 402–03, 409, 418–19, 422, 424–26, 428, 439, 480

working class, size of, 230–34

worker participation, 208–09, 216

Wright, Erik, 86, 89, 640–44

About the Author

ALBERT J. SZYMANSKI is an associate professor of sociology at the University of Oregon, where he has been teaching since 1970. He has been active in the progressive movement within sociology since 1968. He is a founding member of the Union of Radical Sociologists, and has been on the editorial board of the *Insurgent Sociologist* since 1971.

Dr. Szymanski has also published the following books: *The Capitalist State and the Politics of Class* (1978); *Is the Red Flag Flying: The Political Economy of the USSR Today* (1980); and *The Logic of Imperialism* (1982). Another book *The Political Economy of Human Rights: The USSR and the USA* is currently in press. He is now doing research and writing on the causes of the economic stagnation and crisis of world capitalism. Dr. Szymanski has also published in many professional sociology journals, including the *American Journal of Sociology*, *Social Forces*, and the *American Sociological Review*, as well as in a number of left journals, for example, *Monthly Review*, *The New Left Review*, the *Review of Radical Political Economics*, and *Socialist Review*.

Dr. Szymanski received his Ph.D. from Columbia University in 1971 and his B.A. from the University of Rhode Island in 1964.